Laws and Legislation

nova science publishers

www.novapublishers.com

Laws and Legislation

An Overview of Corporate Securities Law in Four English-Language Jurisdictions
Graeme Baber (Author)
2023. ISBN: 979-8-88697-753-0 (Hardcover)
2023. ISBN: 979-8-88697-862-9 (eBook)

The British Judges of the International Court of Justice: An Explication? The Later Jurists
Graeme Baber (Author)
2022. ISBN: 978-1-68507-735-8 (Hardcover)
2022. ISBN: 978-1-68507-899-7 (eBook)

The British Judges of the International Court of Justice: An Explication? Overview, McNair and Lauterpacht
Graeme Baber (Author)
2021. ISBN: 978-1-68507-226-1 (Hardcover)
2021. ISBN: 978-1-68507-419-7 (eBook)

Collected Papers: Financial Regulation in Estonia, Poland and Latvia within the Context of European Union Membership
Graeme Baber (Author)
2021. ISBN: 978-1-53619-467-8 (Hardcover)
2021. ISBN: 978-1-53619-559-0 (eBook)

Gravity of Wisdom in International Criminal Law
Farhad Malekian (Author)
2021. ISBN: 978-1-68507-171-4 (Hardcover)
2021. ISBN: 978-1-68507-330-5 (eBook)

More information about this series can be found at https://novapublishers.com/product-category/series/laws-and-legislation-series/

Graeme Baber

An Overview of Banking Law in Four English-Language Jurisdictions

nova
science publishers
www.novapublishers.com

https://doi.org/10.52305/TIOX7680

Library of Congress Cataloging-in-Publication Data

ISBN: 979-8-88697-793-6

Published by Nova Science Publishers, Inc. † New York

To my Mum, the memory of my Dad (1945-2021),
and all others who helped me to publish my monographs

Contents

List of Tables

Preface

In October 2021, with the exciting project of my two monographs on the British judges of the International Court of Justice well on the way to completion – the first, i.e., '*The British Judges of the International Court of Justice: An Explication? Overview, McNair and Lauterpacht*', had been published, and the second, i.e., '*The British Judges of the International Court of Justice: An Explication? The Later Jurists*' was in its middle phase of writing, it occurred that two further books might be possible – but, this time, in financial, rather than international, law. When I joined BPP Law School as an LLM Lecturer in 2010, the Director of LLM Programmes, Barry Rider, asked me to write and teach four modules – two of which were titled 'United Kingdom (UK) and International Banking Law' and 'UK Corporate Securities Law'. In these areas, international standards and guidelines and European Union legislation were beginning to roll off the Press at an almost alarmingly rapid rate, as a co-ordinated response to the events of the Global Financial Crisis. This was excellent news for a financial law lecturer, especially one who had a good grasp of the workings of financial instruments. Although writing these courses, and publishing articles, comments, briefings and updates – especially in Thomson Reuters' journal '*The Company Lawyer*' with the co-operation of the House Editor the late Scott McHugh who, in particular, showed a lot of enthusiasm for the publication therein of my trilogy of articles on 'Basel III implementation and the European Union' in 2012 – these were written at a time when the Capital Requirements Regulation and the fourth Capital Requirements Directive were in their formative stages, required much energy and quite a lot of time, it gave me an eagerness for, and grasp of, these developing fields. Readers of my monograph titled '*The European Union and the Global Financial Crisis: A View from 2016*' will be able to see how busy the European Union was in drafting and publishing financial legislation in the wake of the Global Financial Crisis. It was fortunate that I was able to harness this activity and put it comprehensively into writing on the cusp of the UK's Brexit vote.

These two books, as proposed in October 2021, were entitled '*An Overview of Banking Law in Six English-Language Jurisdictions*' and '*An Overview of Corporate Securities Law in Six English-Language Jurisdictions*', and the jurisdictions to be covered were Australia, Canada, New Zealand, Singapore, South Africa and the United States of America. They were to have a common introduction in each of the six country-specific chapters, which introduced the law of the place to which the relevant chapter was dedicated. This would be followed by law specific to the country and to the field. In the event, six jurisdictions proved to be a mammoth effort of research and writing – and would have led to monographs that were of lengths with which the publisher would not have been happy. Thus, reluctantly, they were revised to four jurisdictions, and became '*An Overview of Corporate Securities Law in Four English-Language Jurisdictions*' – i.e., the monograph which you are currently reading, and '*An Overview of Corporate Securities Law in Four English-Language Jurisdictions*' – its sister publication which I would also like you to acquire and assimilate.

Both books have a considerable coverage of the law in each of the four jurisdictions, although more has been omitted than has been included therein – which confirms the title 'An Overview'. If my selection of material has been reasonable, then it will provide the reader with a good idea as to the scope and content of the law of banking or – in the accompanying monograph – the law of securities' transactions, within the four jurisdictions addressed in each book. Wishing you all the best with your reading.

Graeme Baber
December 2022

List of Abbreviations

ADI	Authorised deposit-taking institution (Australia)
APRA	Australian Prudential Regulation Authority
ASIC	Australian Securities and Investments Commission
AUD	Australian Dollar(s)
BIS	Bank for International Settlements
CAD	Canadian Dollar(s)
FDIC	Federal Deposit Insurance Corporation (USA)
IBRD	International Bank for Reconstruction and Development
IMF	International Monetary Fund
NOHC	Non-operating holding company (Australia)
NZD	New Zealand Dollar(s)
OCC	Office of the Comptroller of the Currency (USA)
RBA	Reserve Bank of Australia
RBNZ	Reserve Bank of New Zealand
SEC	Securities and Exchange Commission (USA)
UK	United Kingdom of Great Britain and Northern Ireland
USA	United States of America
USD	United States Dollar(s)
WTO	World Trade Organization

Acknowledgments

The author and publishers wish to thank the following, who have provided information on request:

Messrs. Nicolas Marion, Senior Director, Payments Policy, and Jan Wollenberg, Advisor/Economist, Financial Services Division, Financial Sector Policy Branch, Department of Finance, Government of Canada.

Chapter 1

Australia

Abstract

The political and legal systems of Australia are based on a federal model that was founded in 1901. Sources of Australian law comprise statute law, common law and equity. The High Court of Australia is at the apex of both the federal court structure and the state court organisation in that jurisdiction. The regulatory framework for Australian banks includes the Reserve Bank of Australia (RBA), the Australian Securities and Investment Commission (ASIC) and the Australian Prudential Regulation Authority (APRA). The APRA is the principal supervisor of the business of banking in Australia, which is carried out by authorised deposit-taking institutions (ADIs). The Banking Act 1959 provides for the APRA to prudentially supervise ADIs. The leading aims of the Act are to protect the interests of depositors in ADIs and to promote stability in Australia's financial system. The Act contains provisions that one would expect to find there – such as the authorisation framework for ADIs, and also more surprising rules – such as that giving the Act precedence over any conflicting items within the Corporations Act 2001.

Keywords: ADI, APRA, banking, court, depositors, liabilities, NOHC, offence

Introduction

The Australian legal system is introduced. Then, the regulatory framework for banks in Australia is outlined. The main section of this chapter surveys the Banking Act 1959, concentrating especially on banking business and ADIs. The last section concludes.

An Introduction to the Legal System of Australia

Essentials

The Australian political and legal systems work on a federal model that was founded in 1901[1] [1]. The Australian legal system functions on a two-tiered basis, i.e., at federal and state levels [1].

The two main sources of Australian law are statute law and common law (i.e., case law) [1]. Another such source is the law of equity [2]. The English Judicature Acts of the 1870s

---

1 It is submitted that the reference to the year 1901 is to the date of entry into force of the Act to Constitute the Commonwealth of Australia, which is 1st January 1901 (Government of Australia (2022), "Infosheet 13 – The Constitution," accessed February 2, 2022, <https://www.aph.gov.au/About_Parliament/House_of_Representatives/Powers_practice_and_procedure/00_-_Infosheets/Infosheet_13_-_The_Constitution>). The subsection entitled 'Commonwealth of Australia Constitution Act 1900', below in the current section, covers the Act to Constitute the Commonwealth of Australia.

combined the separate courts of common law (such as the Court of King's/Queen's Bench) and equity (such as the Court of Chancery), so that all courts have both common law and equitable powers – which has been applied in all states and territories of Australia except for New South Wales, whose Supreme Court includes a Common Law Division and Equity Division[2] that are each run by a Chief Judge [2].

The Parliamentary Legislative Process

Each of the nine Parliaments in Australia comprises: (i) a lower house – the House of Representatives in the federal parliament and the Legislative Assembly in the parliaments of the states and territories, (ii) an upper house – the Senate in the federal parliament and the Legislative Council in the parliaments of the states and territories, and (iii) Her Majesty the Queen or her representative (now His Majesty King Charles III or his representative) – the Governor-General at federal level, the Governor (states), or the Administrator (territories) [3]. The procedure for law-making in Australia is as follows: (i) a proposal is made for making or amending a law, (ii) parliamentary draftsmen draft the bill, and the relevant minister introduces the bill in parliament[3], (iii) the bill undergoes three readings during which it is extensively discussed and debated, (iv) if both houses of parliament pass the bill with a majority vote, then it is sent to the Governor-General/Governor for royal assent, (v) the bill becomes an Act of Parliament [4].

Subordinate Legislation

In cases in which the subject matter of legislation is technical or likely to change often, the parliament is empowered to 'delegate' the formulation of the detailed regulations to a subordinate body[4] [5]. As delegated legislation is made under the enabling Act of Parliament's authority, the rules therein must be made in the way that the enabling Act specifies [5].

The Doctrine of Precedent

A lower court in a given judicial hierarchy is bound by a decision on a point of law by a higher court on that same ladder [6]. For example, a single Supreme Court justice in New South Wales

---

[2] In addition to these two Divisions – which administer the trial jurisdiction of the Supreme Court of New South Wales, that Court also has a supervisory jurisdiction over other courts and tribunals of New South Wales – which is operated by its Court of Appeal and Court of Criminal Appeal (The Supreme Court of New South Wales (2022), "About the Supreme Court," accessed January 31, 2022, <https://www.supremecourt.justice.nsw.gov.au/Pages/sco2_aboutus/sco2_aboutus.aspx>).

[3] A bill may be initiated in either house of parliament, although some bills must begin in the lower house (Harris, J., and Croese, C. (2015), *Contract Law in Context* (Melbourne: Oxford University Press Australia), 7).

[4] The subordinate body is usually the Governor-General/Governor, a minister of the government department that is responsible for implementing the Act of Parliament, a local council, a statutory government agency or a professional body (Ciro, T., Goldwasser, V., and Verma, R. (2019), *Law and Business*, 5th Edition (Melbourne: Oxford University Press), 39).

is obliged to apply the rule from a decision of the Court of Appeal in New South Wales if the two cases involve similar facts [7].

Equitable Remedies

Equitable remedies are discretionary, and exist to preclude unethical conduct, i.e., behaviour that is not founded on justice, fairness and good conscience [8]. The doctrines of estoppel and unconscionable bargains comprise examples of equitable intervention [8]. Equitable remedies include an injunction – in which a court directs the defendant to cease from effectuating acts that could damage the plaintiff's interest, and an order for specific performance – which instructs the defendant to perform its contractual obligations as the parties originally agreed [9].

The Relationship between Statute Law and Common Law

If statute law and common law are at variance, then statute law prevails [10]. Statute law can alter the common law – including the principles of equity, if the relevant statute is adequately explicit in stating its intention to do this [11].

Courts

Courts fashion the law by the manner in which they interpret provisions of statutes [7]. In applying statutory rules in a variety of factual circumstances, the court my need to consider the policy underpinning the pertinent statute and the stated purpose of that statute in order to determine whether the relevant provision within it applies to a particular situation [7].

There exists a federal court system, in which there may be an appeal from federal circuit courts to the Full Court of the Federal Court of Australia[5], and from the latter to the High Court of Australia [12, 13]. There is also a state court system, in which there may be an appeal from local courts to the appropriate District Court, and from the latter to the Supreme Court of the particular state [12]. In the Supreme Court, a case is normally commenced before a sole judge, whose decision may be appealed to a three-member Court of Appeal of that Supreme Court or to the Full Court of the Federal Court of Australia [13, 14]. Whilst determinations of the Court of Appeal or the Full Court may be appealed to the High Court of Australia, the High Court must first accord special leave to appeal [15]. There is no further appeal from a judgment of the High Court of Australia [15].

[5] The Federal Court of Australia resolves disputes on federal law, such as immigration, intellectual property and taxation (Harris, J., and Croese, C. (2015), *Contract Law in Context*, 9).

Tribunals

Whilst tribunals provide a cheaper and less formal means to settle disputes than courts, unlike the latter they are not determinative of legal rights – but settle disputes concerning the application of particular provisions [16]. Tribunals may be restricted in scope – such as the Migration Review Tribunal, or general[6] – for instance the Administrative Appeals Tribunal [16]. There may be an appeal on a point of law from an administrative tribunal to the Supreme Court of the relevant state or to the Federal Court of Australia, and thenceforth to the High Court of Australia [16].

Commonwealth of Australia Constitution Act 1900

The Act to constitute the Commonwealth of Australia – whose short title is the Commonwealth of Australia Constitution Act [17] – established the Commonwealth of Australia [18]. The Federal Parliament of the Commonwealth comprises the Queen (now King Charles III), a Senate and a House of Representatives [19]. The Queen's (King's) appointment of a Governor-General is Her (His) Majesty's representative in the Commonwealth of Australia [20]. Legislative powers of the Federal Parliament include those with regard to legal tender[7] [21], banking except for state banking[8] [22], insurance bar state insurance[9] [23], promissory notes and bills of exchange [24], and bankruptcy and insolvency [25]. If the law of a state is incompatible with a law of the Commonwealth of Australia, then the latter prevails – and the former is invalid "to the extent of the inconsistency" [26].

Australia Act 1986

The Australia Act 1986 terminates the power of the Parliament of the UK to legislate for Australia or any of its states or territories [27]. It empowers the parliament of each state of Australia to legislate with extra-territorial application [28].

---

[6] Some states have general tribunals that resolve administrative law challenges to decisions of the government and some private disputes – such as small claims at civil law and disagreements as to residential tenancy; these include the Victorian Civil and Administrative Tribunal and the New South Wales Civil and Administrative Tribunal (Harris, J., and Croese, C. (2015), *Contract Law in Context*, 11).

[7] The Commonwealth of Australia Constitution Act refers to "Currency, coinage, and legal tender:" (Government of Australia (2021), "Commonwealth of Australia Constitution Act 1900," adopted on July 9, 1900, entered into force on January 1, 1901, Compilation No. 6 of July 29, 1977, registered on November 18, 2021, Part V, Paragraph 51(xii)).

[8] Legislative powers of the Federal Parliament include those in respect of "Banking other than State banking; also State banking extending beyond the limits of the State concerned, the incorporation of banks, and the issue of paper money:" (Government of Australia (2021), "Commonwealth of Australia Constitution Act 1900," adopted on July 9, 1900, entered into force on January 1, 1901, Compilation No. 6 of July 29, 1977, registered on November 18, 2021, Part V, Paragraph 51(xiii)).

[9] Legislative powers of the Federal Parliament include those relating to "Insurance, other than State insurance; also State insurance extending beyond the limits of the State concerned:" (Government of Australia (2021), "Commonwealth of Australia Constitution Act 1900," adopted on July 9, 1900, entered into force on January 1, 1901, Compilation No. 6 of July 29, 1977, registered on November 18, 2021, Part V, Paragraph 51(xiv)).

Comment

Australia is gradually emerging as a federal, common law system from its position in the English legal structure in the time of its status as a British colony. Australian law and practice tends to be based on that of England and Wales. Since the implementation of the Australia Act 1986, the influence of the UK Parliament over the Australian legislature has substantially declined. In the event of a clash between Australian federal law and Australian state law, the former prevails over the latter to the extent of the contradiction.

The Regulatory Framework for Australian Banks

Reserve Bank of Australia

The Commonwealth Bank of Australia was founded in 1911 [29]. It was renamed the Reserve Bank of Australia (RBA) in 1959 [30]. The general powers of the RBA are as follows[10].

> The Bank has such powers as are necessary for the purposes of this Act [(i.e., the Reserve Bank Act 1959)] and any other Act conferring functions on the Bank and, in particular, and in addition to any other powers conferred on it by this Act and such other Acts, has power: (a) to receive money on deposit; (b) to borrow money; (c) to lend money; (d) to buy, sell, discount and re-discount bills of exchange, promissory notes and treasury bills; (e) to buy and sell securities issued by the Commonwealth [of Australia] and other securities; (f) to buy, sell and otherwise deal in foreign currency, specie, gold and other precious metals; (g) to establish credits and give guarantees; (h) to issue bills and drafts[,] and effect transfers of money; (i) to underwrite loans; and (j) to do anything incidental to any of its powers [31].

The Australian Securities and Investments Commission

The ASIC is an independent agency of the Government of Australia [32]. In carrying out its functions and exercising its powers, the ASIC – under the Australian Securities and Investment Act 2001 – must try to: "maintain, facilitate and improve the performance of the financial system and the entities within that system" [33], "promote the confident and informed participation of investors and consumers in the financial system" [34], "administer the laws that confer functions and powers on it effectively and with a minimum of procedural requirements" [35], "receive, process and store, efficiently and quickly, the information given to ASIC under

[10] The RBA's website notes: "The Reserve Bank of Australia (RBA) is Australia's central bank[,] and derives its functions and powers from the *Reserve Bank Act 1959*. Its duty is to contribute to the stability of the currency, full employment, and the economic prosperity and welfare of the Australian people. It does this by conducting monetary policy to meet an agreed medium-term inflation target, working to maintain a strong financial system and efficient payments system, and issuing the nation's banknotes. The RBA provides certain banking services[,] as required[,] to the Australian Government and its agencies, and to a number of overseas central banks and official institutions. Additionally, it manages Australia's gold and foreign exchange reserves." (Government of Australia (2022), "Reserve Bank of Australia: About the RBA," accessed February 16, 2022, <https://www.rba.gov.au/about-rba/>; emphasis original).

the laws that confer functions and powers on it" [36], "ensure that information is available as soon as practictable for access by the public" [37], and "take whatever action it can take, and is necessary, in order to enforce and give effect to the laws of the Commonwealth [of Australia] that confer functions and powers on it"[11] [38], whilst taking into consideration the impact of the performance of its functions and the exercise of its powers will have on competition within the financial field [39].

The Australian Prudential Regulation Authority

The Australian Prudential Regulation Authority Act 1998 established the APRA [40]. The main purposes for founding the APRA are to regulate entities in the financial sector in agreement with other laws of the Commonwealth of Australia that cater for prudential regulation or "retirement income standards" [41], administer the schemes for financial claims for which the Banking Act 1959 and Insurance Act 1973 provide [42], and develop the necessary administrative procedures and practice to perform this regulation and administration [43]. In discharging its functions and exercising its powers, the APRA is to balance the following objectives: competition, competitive neutrality, contestiblility, efficiency and financial safety – and, in so balancing, is to advance the stability of the financial system in Australia [44]. The Banking Act 1959 provides for the APRA to prudentially supervise ADIs[12] [45]. It is to this federal statute that the next section turns.

Banking Act 1959

Main Objects of the Banking Act 1959

The main objects of the Banking Act 1959 are to safeguard the interests of depositors in ADIs in ways that are compatible with the ongoing development of a workable, competitive and groundbreaking banking industry [46], and to further stability in Australia's financial system [47].

Banking Business and ADIs

Authority to Carry on Banking Business

An person commits an indictable offence if (s)he or it engages in banking business[13] in Australia, and is either a body corporate that is neither the Reserve Bank of Australia nor an

[11] In the present consolidated version of the Australian Securities and Investments Commission Act 2001 – from which these quoted clauses are drawn, paragraph 1(2)(c) is omitted, i.e., the six quoted clauses originate from paragraphs 1(2)(a), 1(2)(b), 1(2)(d), 1(2)(e), 1(2)(f) and 1(2)(g) of the Australian Securities and Investments Commission Act 2001, respectively.

[12] 'ADI' is an abbreviation for 'authorised deposit-taking institution' ((Government of Australia (2021), "Banking Act 1959," adopted on April 23, 1959, entered into force on January 14, 1960, Compilation No. 60 of December 8, 2021, registered on December 16, 2021, s.5(1)).

[13] 'Banking business' is "a business that consists of banking within the meaning of paragraph 51(xiii) of the [Commonwealth of Australia] Constitution [Act 1900]" or "a business that is carried on by a corporation to

ADI, or not a body corporate[14] [48]. A body corporate that wishes to acquire authority to conduct banking business in Australia must apply for this in writing to the APRA[15] [49], which may set criteria for this authority to be granted[16] [50]. If APRA grants the authority, then it must provide the applicant with written notice of the according of this permission – and the authority is to be in writing [51]. APRA may reject the application if the applicant is a subsidiary of another body corporate that does not possess a NOHC[17] authority[18] [52]; it may

which paragraph 51(xx) of the Constitution applies and that consists, to any extent, of: (i) both taking money on deposit (otherwise than as part-payment for identified goods or services) and making advances of money; or (ii) other financial activities prescribed by the regulations for the purposes of this definition" (Government of Australia (2021), "Banking Act 1959," adopted on April 23, 1959, entered into force on January 14, 1960, Compilation No. 60 of December 8, 2021, registered on December 16, 2021, s.5(1)). Fn 8 states Paragraph 51(xiii) of the Commonwealth of Australia Constitution Act 1900. Paragraph 51(xx) of the Commonwealth of Australia Constitution Act 1900 includes powers to make laws regarding "[f]oreign corporations, and trading or financial corporations formed within the limits of the Commonwealth [of Australia]" amongst legislative powers of the Federal Parliament (Government of Australia (2021), "Commonwealth of Australia Constitution Act 1900," adopted on July 9, 1900, entered into force on January 1, 1901, Compilation No. 6 of July 29, 1977, registered on November 18, 2021, Part V, Paragraph 51(xx)).

[14] This offence is not committed if there is a determination in force that disapplies to the person the relevant subsection of the Banking Act 1959 – which is s.8(1) for a body corporate and s.7(1) otherwise (Government of Australia (2021), "Banking Act 1959," adopted on April 23, 1959, entered into force on January 14, 1960, Compilation No. 60 of December 8, 2021, registered on December 16, 2021, ss.7(1)(c) and 8(1)(d)). APRA may give written notice and determination that "any or all of the following provisions of this Act [(i.e., the Banking Act 1959)] do not apply to a person while the determination is in force: (a) a provision of Division 1, 1AA or 1A of Part II (other than section 11A, 11B or 11C); (b) section 66; (c) section 66A; (d) section 67; (e) section 69" (Government of Australia (2021), "Banking Act 1959," adopted on April 23, 1959, entered into force on January 14, 1960, Compilation No. 60 of December 8, 2021, registered on December 16, 2021, s.11(1)).

[15] The application must be "accompanied by a copy of the Act, charter, deed of settlement, memorandum of association and articles of association of the body corporate, or other document by which the body corporate is constituted" (Government of Australia (2021), "Banking Act 1959," adopted on April 23, 1959, entered into force on January 14, 1960, Compilation No. 60 of December 8, 2021, registered on December 16, 2021, s.10(1)).

[16] Information that the APRA provides includes the following: "... APRA has two pathways available to become an ADI: the direct and the restricted pathway. The **direct pathway** is suitable for applicants that have existing resources and capabilities with which to establish an ADI. It allows the applicant to conduct its intended banking business from the granting of its licence. The applicant must demonstrate [that] it meets the full prudential framework and is ready to commence banking business prior to being granted an ADI licence. The **restricted pathway** is suitable for applicants that do not have the resources and capabilities to establish an ADI and need time to develop these. This pathway allows applicants to conduct limited banking business as a Restricted ADI before being required to meet the full prudential framework. It can assist applicants in seeking the investment required to operationalise their business, test their operational model, progress their compliance with the prudential framework and their application for an ADI licence. ... Common characteristics of a suitable direct applicant include: • Substantial capital resources at the point of application and/or a very clear avenue for access to such capital; • A significant existing banking-related business ([such as] lending); • An existing governance structure at the point of application that wholly or substantially mirrors the requirements of APRA's governance prudential standard and any other relevant prudential standards ([such as] an independent Chair, majority independent directors on the board, board audit committee etc.); • A good breadth of suitably-experienced staff in key roles at the point of application; •A demonstrated operational track record of building or running a banking-related business. Prospective applicants will need to agree the most suitable pathway with APRA, as part of the pre-application process. Eligibility for either pathway is ultimately at APRA's discretion." (Australian Prudential Regulation Authority (2021), APRA: Guidelines – Licensing: locally-incorporated ADIs – August 2021 (Sydney: Australian Prudential Regulation Authority), 9-10; emphasis original).

[17] '*NOHC*' is an abbreviation for 'non-operating holding company' (Government of Australia (2021), "Banking Act 1959," adopted on April 23, 1959, entered into force on January 14, 1960, Compilation No. 60 of December 8, 2021, registered on December 16, 2021, s.5(1)).

[18] A '*NOHC authority*' is "an authority under subsection 11AA(2) [of the Banking Act 1959]" (Government of Australia (2021), "Banking Act 1959," adopted on April 23, 1959, entered into force on January 14, 1960, Compilation No. 60 of December 8, 2021, registered on December 16, 2021, s.5(1)). That provision states: "APRA may grant the authority [to be a NOHC] if it considers it appropriate to do so." (Government of Australia (2021), "Banking Act 1959," adopted on April 23, 1959, entered into force on January 14, 1960, Compilation No. 60 of December 8, 2021, registered on December 16, 2021, s.11AA(2)). A body corporate must apply in

make the authority conditional upon the parent body corporate being an authorised NOHC[19] [53]. The APRA may impose conditions – or additional prerequisities – on the body corporate's authority to undertake banking business in Australia (as an ADI) [54], or may vary or revoke such qualifications [55]. The Banking Act 1959 provides for situations in which the APRA

writing to the APRA for the latter to be empowered to grant to the former the authority to be a NOHC; "[t]he authority operates as an authority in relation to the body corporate and any ADIs that are subsidiaries of the body corporate from time to time" (Government of Australia (2021), "Banking Act 1959," adopted on April 23, 1959, entered into force on January 14, 1960, Compilation No. 60 of December 8, 2021, registered on December 16, 2021, s.11AA(1)).

[19] An '*authorised NOHC*' is "a body corporate: (a) in relation to which an authority under subsection 11AA(2) [of the Banking Act 1959] is in force; and (b) that is a NOHC of an ADI or ADIs" (Government of Australia (2021), "Banking Act 1959," adopted on April 23, 1959, entered into force on January 14, 1960, Compilation No. 60 of December 8, 2021, registered on December 16, 2021, s.5(1)). The second sentence of fn 18 sets out subsection 11AA(2) of the Banking Act 1959.

may[20], and must[21], revoke that authority. It also sets rules for a body corporate to carry on banking business in Australia (as an ADI) for a limited time[22].

Prudential Supervision and Monitoring of ADIs and Authorised NOHCs

The APRA, in writing, may determine standards concerning prudential issues with which all ADIs, all authorised NOHCs, the subsidiaries or ADIs or authorised NOHCs, a specified class of any of the aforementioned, or one or more of the aforementioned that are expressly identified, must comply[23] [56]. It may – in writing – vary or revoke a prudential standard [57].

---

[20] The APRA *may* revoke a body corporate's authority to perform banking business in Australia as an ADI, "if APRA is satisfied that: (a) the body corporate has … provided, in connection with its application for the authority, information that was false or misleading in a material particular; or (b) the body corporate has failed to comply with any of the following: (i) a requirement of this Act [(i.e., the Banking Act 1959)]; (ii) a requirement of the *Financial Sector (Collection of Data) Act 2001*; (iii) a requirement of the regulations or any other instrument made under this Act; (iv) a requirement of a provision of another law of the Commonwealth [of Australia], if the provision is specified in the regulations, (v) a direction under this Act; (vi) a condition of its section 9 authority [(to carry out banking business in Australia as an ADI)]; or (c) it would be contrary to the national interest for the authority to remain in force; or (d) it would be contrary to financial system stability in Australia for the authority to remain in force; or (e) it would be contrary to the interests of depositors of the body corporate for the authority to remain in force; or (f) the body corporate has failed to pay: (i) an amount of levy or late penalty to which the *Financial Institutions Supervisory Levies Collection Act 1998* applies; or (ii) an amount charged under section 51 of the *Australian Prudential Regulation Authority Act 1998*; or (g) the body corporate is insolvent and is unlikely to return to solvency within a reasonable period of time; or (h) the body corporate has ceased to carry on banking business in Australia; or (j) the body corporate is a foreign corporation within the meaning of paragraph 51(xx) of the [Commonwealth of Australia] Constitution [Act 1900], and: (i) the body corporate is unlikely to be able to meet its liabilities in Australia[,] and is unlikely to be able to do so within a reasonable period of time; or (ii) an authority (however described) for the body corporate to carry on banking business in a foreign country has been revoked or otherwise withdrawn in that foreign country; (k) if the section 9 authority is to cease to have effect on a day specified in the authority – [then] it is unlikely to be appropriate, at or before that day, to grant the body corporate a section 9 authority that is not subject to a time limit" (Government of Australia (2021), "Banking Act 1959," adopted on April 23, 1959, entered into force on January 14, 1960, Compilation No. 60 of December 8, 2021, registered on December 16, 2021, s.9A(2); emphasis original). The last sentence of fn 13 lays down Paragraph 51(xx) of the Commonwealth of Australia Constitution Act 1900. Section 51 of the Australian Prudential Regulation Authority Act 1998 states: "(1) APRA may, by legislative instrument, fix charges to be paid to APRA by a person[,] in respect of: (a) services and facilities [that] APRA provides [to] the person; or (b) applications or requests (however described) [which are] made to APRA under any law of the Commonwealth [of Australia]. … (2) A charge fixed under subsection (1) must be reasonably related to the costs and expenses incurred[,] or to be incurred[,] by APRA in relation to the matters to which the charge relates[,] and must not be such as to amount to taxation." (Government of Australia (2021), "Australian Prudential Regulation Authority Act 1998," adopted on June 29, 1998. entered into force on July 1, 1998, Compilation No. 46 of July 1, 2021, registered on July 30, 2021, s.51). Unless the APRA determines that abiding by the following procedures could engender a delay in revocation of the authority to effect banking business in Australia as an ADI which would be against both the national interest and the interest of depositors with the relevant body corporate, it must not revoke this authority under subsection 9A(2) of the Banking Act 1959, unless: (a) it has given this body corporate written notice which advises the latter: (i) that it is considering revoking the authority for reasons specified therein, (ii) that the body corporate may make submissions to it about the possible revocation, and (iii) of the date by which these submission must be made, and (b) it has considered these submissions by the date by which it had specified that it would do so (Government of Australia (2021), "Banking Act 1959," adopted on April 23, 1959, entered into force on January 14, 1960, Compilation No. 60 of December 8, 2021, registered on December 16, 2021, ss.9A(3) and 9A(4)).

[21] The APRA *must* revoke a body corporate's authority to discharge banking business in Australia as an ADI, "if: (a) the body corporate, by notice in writing to APRA, requests the revocation of the authority; and (b) APRA is satisfied that the revocation of the authority: (i) would not be contrary to the national interest; and (ii) would not be contrary to the interests of depositors of the body corporate" (Government of Australia (2021), "Banking Act 1959," adopted on April 23, 1959, entered into force on January 14, 1960, Compilation No. 60 of December 8, 2021, registered on December 16, 2021, s.9A(1)).

[22] Sections 9D, 9E and 9F of the Banking Act 1959 set out these provisions.

[23] The Banking Act 1959 provides for the APRA to particularise its standards regarding prudential matters, thus: "A standard may impose different requirements to be complied with: (a) in different situations; or (b) in respect of

Every ADI, authorised NOHC, or a subsidiary of an ADI or authorised NOHC, must comply with each prudential standard that applies to it [58]. The APRA's is responsible for collecting and analysing information about prudential matters regarding ADIs and authorised NOHCs [59], encouraging and promoting the effectuation of sound practices by ADIs and authorised NOHCs relating to prudential issues [60], and evaluating the discharge and effectiveness of these practices [61]. The provisions within the Banking Act 1959 that concern protection of depositors – in large part, amongst others, do not apply to foreign ADIs[24].

Protection of Depositors

The APRA is obliged to exercise its functions and powers under Division 2 of Part II of the Banking Act 1959 – i.e., Provisions relating to the carrying on of banking business: Protection of depositors[25], for the safeguarding of the depositors of the sundry ADIs and for the furtherance of stability of the financial system in Australia [62]. By giving the latter notice in

---

different activities; including requirements to be complied with by different classes of ADIs, authorised NOHCs or subsidiaries of ADIs or authorised NOHCs." (Government of Australia (2021), "Banking Act 1959," adopted on April 23, 1959, entered into force on January 14, 1960, Compilation No. 60 of December 8, 2021, registered on December 16, 2021, s.11AF(1A)); "Without limiting the prudential matters in relation to which APRA may determine a standard, a standard may require: (a) each ADI or authorised NOHC; or (b) each ADI or authorised NOHC included in a specific class of ADIs or authorised NOHCs; or (ba) each subsidiary of an ADI or of an authorised NOHC; or (bb) each subsidiary of an ADI or of an authorised NOHC, included in a specified class of subsidiaries; or (c) a specified ADI or authorised NOHC; or (d) each of 2 or more specified ADIs or authorised NOHCs; or (e) a specified subsidiary of an ADI or of an authorised NOHC; or (f) each of 2 or more specified subsidiaries of ADIs or of authorised NOHCs; to ensure that its subsidiaries (or particular subsidiaries), or it and its subsidiaries (or particular subsidiaries), collectively satisfy particular requirements in relation to prudential matters." (Government of Australia (2021), "Banking Act 1959," adopted on April 23, 1959, entered into force on January 14, 1960, Compilation No. 60 of December 8, 2021, registered on December 16, 2021, s.11AF(1AA)); "A standard may provide for APRA to exercise powers and discretions under the standard, including (but not limited to) discretions to approve, impose, adjust or exclude specific prudential requirements in relation to one or more specified ADIs or authorised NOHCs, or one or more specified subsidiaries of ADIs or authorised NOHCs." (Government of Australia (2021), "Banking Act 1959," adopted on April 23, 1959, entered into force on January 14, 1960, Compilation No. 60 of December 8, 2021, registered on December 16, 2021, s.11AF(2)).

[24] The first three subsections of section 11E of the Banking Act 1959 read: "(1) The provisions listed in subsection (1A) do not apply in relation to: (a) business of a foreign ADI (other than Australian business assets and liabilities); or (b) the management of a foreign ADI, to the extent that the management relates to such business of the foreign ADI. (1A) The provisions are as follows: (a) sections 12, 13BA and 13C [of the Banking Act 1959], and Subdivision B of Division 2 (statutory management); (b) subsections 13A(1) to (2), to the extent that those subsections relate to statutory management; (c) sections 62B, 62C, 62D and 62E. (1B) The following provisions do not apply in relation to a foreign ADI: (a) Division 2 (apart from the provisions in that Division listed in subsection (1A)); (b) Division 2AA." (Government of Australia (2021), "Banking Act 1959," adopted on April 23, 1959, entered into force on January 14, 1960, Compilation No. 60 of December 8, 2021, registered on December 16, 2021, s.11E(1)-(1B)). A '*foreign ADI*' is "a body corporate that: (a) is a foreign corporation within the meaning of paragraph 51(xx) of the [Commonwealth of Australia] Constitution [Act 1900]; and (b) is authorised to carry on banking business in a foreign country; and (c) has been granted an authority under section 9 [of the Banking Act 1959] to carry on banking business in Australia" (Government of Australia (2021), "Banking Act 1959," adopted on April 23, 1959, entered into force on January 14, 1960, Compilation No. 60 of December 8, 2021, registered on December 16, 2021, s.5(1)). The 'Australian business assets and liabilities' of a foreign ADI, to which paragraph 11E(1)(a) of the Banking Act 1959 refers, are: "(a) the assets and liabilities of the foreign ADI in Australia, (b) any other assets and liabilities of the foreign ADI that: (i) are related to its operations in Australia; and (ii) if regulations are made for the purposes of this subparagraph – are of a kind specified in those regulations." (Government of Australia (2021), "Banking Act 1959," adopted on April 23, 1959, entered into force on January 14, 1960, Compilation No. 60 of December 8, 2021, registered on December 16, 2021, s.11E(3)). The final sentence of fn 13 sets out Paragraph 51(xx) of the Commonwealth of Australia Constitution Act 1900. The text to fns 15 and 16, the sentence immediately-following that text, and the text to fns 17 and 18, together comprise subsections (2), (2A), (3) and (3A) of section 9 of the Banking Act 1959.

[25] Division 2 of Part II of the Banking Act 1959 comprises sections 12-16AAA of the Act.

writing, the APRA may require an ADI to furnish it – within the time that the notice specifies – with such information, which it stipulates therein, that relates to the financial stability of the ADI[26] [63]. An ADI commits an indictable offence if it deems it to be likely that it will be unable to satisfy its obligations or considers that it is close to suspending payment, and (in either case) does not inform the APRA of the situation right away [64]. The APRA could "investigate the affairs of an ADI, appoint a person to investigate the affairs of an ADI, take control of the ADI's business or appoint an administrator to take control of the ADI's business" [65], if the ADI informs the APRA that the former deems it likely to become unable to fulfil its obligations or considers that is near to suspending payment [66], the APRA considers that the ADI – without assistance – may become unable to realise its obligations or suspend payment, or it is probable that the ADI will not be able to engage in banking business in Australia in accordance with the interests of its depositors or the stability of the financial system in that country [67], the ADI becomes unable to satisfy its obligations or suspends payment [68], an external administrator has been installed at a holding company of the ADI, and the APRA considers this appointment to present a significant threat to the stability of Australia's financial system, the ADI's functioning or soundness, or the interest of the last-mentioned's depositors [69], or – if the ADI is a foreign ADI[27] – an application for the appointment of an external administrator of that ADI has been submitted in an overseas state, or such an appointment has been made [70]. The APRA may take control of the 'target' body corporate's business or appoint an administrator to take this control [71], if that body corporate is an authorised NOHC of an ADI, a subsidiary of an authorised NOHC of an ADI, or a subsidiary of an ADI [72], the condition in subsection 13A(1D) of the Banking Act 1959[28], that in subsection 13A(1E) of the Banking Act 1959[29] or that in subsection 13A(1F) of the Banking

---

[26] This stipulation "may include a requirement to supply books, accounts or documents" (Government of Australia (2021), "Banking Act 1959," adopted on April 23, 1959, entered into force on January 14, 1960, Compilation No. 60 of December 8, 2021, registered on December 16, 2021, s.13(1)). If an ADI does not observe "a requirement to provide information, books, accounts or documents under this section" (– i.e., section 13 of the Banking Act 1959 – which is entitled 'ADI to supply information to APRA'), then the APRA could "investigate the affairs of" that ADI "or appoint a person to do so" (Government of Australia (2021), "Banking Act 1959," adopted on April 23, 1959, entered into force on January 14, 1960, Compilation No. 60 of December 8, 2021, registered on December 16, 2021, s.13(4)).

[27] Fn 24 defines the term '*foreign ADI*'.

[28] This subsection of the Banking Act 1959 states: "The condition in this subsection is satisfied[,] if: (a) either: (i) a Banking Act statutory manager has taken control of the relevant ADI; or (ii) the conditions in any[,] or all[,] of paragraphs (1)(a), (b), (c), (d) or (e) are satisfied in relation to the relevant ADI, and APRA intends that a Banking Act statutory manager will take control of the relevant ADI; and (b) APRA considers that the target body corporate provides services that are, or conducts business that is, essential to the capacity of the relevant ADI to maintain its operations." (Government of Australia (2021), "Banking Act 1959," adopted on April 23, 1959, entered into force on January 14, 1960, Compilation No. 60 of December 8, 2021, registered on December 16, 2021, s.13A(1D)). 'Paragraphs (1)(a), (b), (c), (d) or (e)' refers to paragraphs 13A(1)(a), 13A(1)(b), 13A(1)(c), 13A(1)(d) and 13A(1)(e) of the Banking Act 1959, respectively, which are set out in the sentence containing fn 27.

[29] This subsection of the Banking Act 1959 specifies: "The condition in this subsection is satisfied[,] if: (a) either: (i) a Banking Act statutory manager has taken control of the relevant ADI; or (ii) the conditions in any[,] or all[,] of paragraphs (1)(a), (b), (c), (d) or (e) are satisfied in relation to the relevant ADI, and APRA intends that a Banking Act statutory manager will take control of the relevant ADI; and (b) APRA considers that it is necessary for a Banking Act statutory manager to take control of the target body corporate, in order to facilitate the resolution of any of the following: (i) the relevant ADI; (ii) an authorised NOHC of the relevant ADI; (iii) a relevant group of bodies corporate of which the relevant ADI is a member; (iv) a particular member[,] or particular members[,] of such a group." (Government of Australia (2021), "Banking Act 1959," adopted on April 23, 1959, entered into force on January 14, 1960, Compilation No. 60 of December 8, 2021, registered on December 16, 2021, s.13A(1E)). 'Paragraphs (1)(a), (b), (c), (d) or (e)' refers to paragraphs 13A(1)(a),

Act 1959[30] is met [73], the 'target' body corporate is incorporated in Australia [74], and that entity "is not a body corporate of a kind specified in regulations (if any) made for the purpose of this paragraph" [75]. If an ADI becomes unable to fulfil its obligations or suspends payment, then those of its assets[31] that are in Australia are to be at hand to satisfy its liabilities, in the following order[32]: (1) the ADI's liabilities, if any, to the APRA due to the rights that the latter has against the former under section 16AI of the Banking Act 1959[33] or section 16AIC of the Banking Act 1959[34] [76], (2) the ADI's debts, if any, to the APRA under section 16AO of the

---

13A(1)(b), 13A(1)(c), 13A(1)(d) and 13A(1)(e) of the Banking Act 1959, respectively, which are laid down in the sentence containing fn 27.

[30] This subsection of the Banking Act 1959 declares: "The condition in this subsection is satisfied[,] if: (a) there is an external administrator of the target body corporate, or APRA considers that, in the absence of external support: (i) the target body corporate may become unable to meet its obligations; or (ii) the target body corporate may suspend payment; and (b) APRA considers that it is necessary to take an action mentioned in subsection (1C) [of section 13A of the Banking Act 1959, i.e., take control of the 'target' body corporate's business or appoint an administrator to take this control,] in respect of the target body corporate[,] in order to enable the relevant ADI to maintain its operations, or in order to facilitate the resolution of any of the following: (i) the relevant ADI; (ii) an authorised NOHC of the relevant ADI; (iii) a relevant group of bodies corporate of which the relevant ADI is a member; (iv) a particular member[,] or particular members[,] of such a group." (Government of Australia (2021), "Banking Act 1959," adopted on April 23, 1959, entered into force on January 14, 1960, Compilation No. 60 of December 8, 2021, registered on December 16, 2021, s.13A(1F)).

[31] These assets exclude "any interest in an asset (or a part of an asset) in a cover pool for which the ADI is the issuing ADI" ((Government of Australia (2021), "Banking Act 1959," adopted on April 23, 1959, entered into force on January 14, 1960, Compilation No. 60 of December 8, 2021, registered on December 16, 2021, s.13A(3A)).

[32] The present subsection, i.e., subsection 13A(3) of the Banking Act 1959, "does not constrain: (a) the exercise of powers or the performance of functions[,] under this Act[,] of a Banking Act statutory manager of an ADI; or (b) an entity acting at the direction or request of a Banking Act statutory manager of an ADI exercising powers or performing functions under this Act" (Government of Australia (2021), "Banking Act 1959," adopted on April 23, 1959, entered into force on January 14, 1960, Compilation No. 60 of December 8, 2021, registered on December 16, 2021, s.13A(3AA)). Subdivision B of Division 2 of Part II of the Banking Act 1959, is titled 'Provisions dealing with control of a body corporate's business by a Banking Act statutory manager', and comprises sections 14A-16AA of the Act.

[33] This section of the Banking Act 1959 is entitled 'Substitution of APRA for account-holder as ADI's creditor', and states: "(1) When an ADI becomes a declared ADI, then, by force of this subsection, the right of an account-holder who has a protected account with the ADI to be paid an amount by the ADI in connection with the account: (a) is reduced to the extent of the account-holder's entitlement under this Subdivision [(i.e., Subdivision C of Division 2AA of Part II of the Banking Act 1959, which comprises sections 16AF-16AIC of the Act,) that is] connected with the account; and (b) to the extent of the reduction, becomes a right of APRA. (2) APRA may exercise or assign a right [which] it has under paragraph (1)(b)." (Government of Australia (2021), "Banking Act 1959," adopted on April 23, 1959, entered into force on January 14, 1960, Compilation No. 60 of December 8, 2021, registered on December 16, 2021, s.16AI). An ADI becomes a 'declared ADI' "as a result of the Minister having made a declaration under section 16AD" of the Banking Act 1959 (Government of Australia (2021), "Banking Act 1959," adopted on April 23, 1959, entered into force on January 14, 1960, Compilation No. 60 of December 8, 2021, registered on December 16, 2021, s.16AIA(1)(a)). Section 16AD is titled 'Declaration that Subdivision C applies in relation to ADI'; its first subsection reads: "The Minister may declare that Subdivision C [(which is entitled 'Payment of account-holders with declared ADI') of Division 2AA (which is titled 'Financial claims scheme for account-holders with insolvent ADIs') of Part II (which is entitled 'Provisions relating to the carrying on of banking business') of the Banking Act 1959] applies in relation to a specified ADI[,] if any of the following requirements are satisfied: (a) APRA has applied under section 16AAA [of the Banking Act 1959] for the ADI to be wound up; (b) a Banking Act statutory manager is in control of the ADI's business." (Government of Australia (2021), "Banking Act 1959," adopted on April 23, 1959, entered into force on January 14, 1960, Compilation No. 60 of December 8, 2021, registered on December 16, 2021, s.16AD(1)).

[34] This section of the Banking Act 1959 is titled 'Consequences of transferred liabilities determination once certificate of transfer issued', and – with italicized subtitles – declares: "*Application of section* (1) This section applies[,] if: (a) APRA has made a transferred liabilities determination; and (b) APRA has issued a certificate of transfer under section 33 of the *Financial Sector (Transfer and Restructure) Act 1999*[,] stating that the transfer is to take effect. *Receiving body entitled to total payment amount* (2) The receiving body is entitled to be paid by APRA an amount equal to the total payment amount specified in the determination. *Reduction of rights and*

Banking Act 1959[35] [77], (3) the ADI's liabilities, if any, in Australia in association with protected accounts which account-holders maintain with the ADI [78], (4) the ADI's debts, if any, to the RBA [79], (5) the ADI's liabilities, if any, under an industry support contract that is attested under section 11CB of the Banking Act 1959[36] [80], and (6) the ADI's other liabilities, if any, in the order of their priority aside from the current subsection (i.e., subsection 13A(3) of the Banking Act 1959) [81]. An ADI commits an indictable offence, if the assets[37] which it holds in Australia are of a value that is less than the total of its deposit liabilities there, and the APRA has not authorised the ADI to hold assets of a lower monetary worth than that of its deposit liabilities [82]. If the APRA appoints someone to investigate the affairs of an ADI under subsections 13(4)[38] or 13A(1)[39] of the Banking Act 1959, then this investigator is entitled to access the ADI's books, accounts and documents and to require the ADI to give him or her information or facilities to carry out the investigation [83]. The ADI commits an offence, if it refuses this access to the investigator or does not provide him or her with this information or

---

entitlements of account-holder (3) An account-holder's entitlement under this Subdivision [(i.e., Subdivision C of Division 2AA of Part II of the Banking Act 1959, which consists of sections 16AF-16AIC of the Act,)] to be paid an amount in respect of a protected account kept with the declared ADI[,] is reduced to nil. *Declared ADI liable to APRA for total payment amount* (4) The declared ADI is liable to pay to APRA an amount equal to the sum of the total payment amount specified in the determination. (5) That liability is due and payable to APRA[,] when the certificate of transfer comes into force. (6) Despite paragraph 16AI(1)(b) [of the Banking Act 1959], APRA does not have the right mentioned in that paragraph." (Government of Australia (2021), "Banking Act 1959," adopted on April 23, 1959, entered into force on January 14, 1960, Compilation No. 60 of December 8, 2021, registered on December 16, 2021, s.16AIC; emphasis original). Point (b) in the first sentence of fn 33 comprises paragraph 16AI(1)(b) of the Banking Act 1959.

[35] This section of the Banking Act 1959 is titled 'APRA's costs of administration', and specifies: "(1) The costs incurred by APRA in relation to the exercise of its powers and the performance of its functions under this Division [(i.e., Division 2AA of Part II of the Banking Act 1959, which consists of sections 16AB-16AU of the Act,)] relating to a declared ADI[,] are a debt due by the declared ADI to APRA. (2) The debt is admissible to proof against the declared ADI in the winding up of the ADI. (3) Subsection (1) does not apply to the amounts of entitlements under Subdivision C [(which is entitled 'Payment of account-holders with declared ADI' and which comprises sections 16AF-16AIC of the Act) of Division 2AA (which is titled 'Financial claims scheme for account-holders with insolvent ADIs') of Part II (which is entitled 'Provisions relating to the carrying on of banking business') of the Banking Act 1959]." (Government of Australia (2021), "Banking Act 1959," adopted on April 23, 1959, entered into force on January 14, 1960, Compilation No. 60 of December 8, 2021, registered on December 16, 2021, s.16AO).

[36] This section of the Banking Act 1959 is titled 'APRA may certify an industry support contract', and reads: "(1) APRA may certify an industry support contract[,] if all of the parties to the contract make a written request to APRA that the contract be certified and APRA considers it appropriate to certify the contract. The certification must be by notice in writing to the parties to the contract. (2) Part VI [of the Banking Act 1959] applies to a refusal under this section to certify an industry support contract." (Government of Australia (2021), "Banking Act 1959," adopted on April 23, 1959, entered into force on January 14, 1960, Compilation No. 60 of December 8, 2021, registered on December 16, 2021, s.11CB). Part VI of the Banking Act 1959 is entitled 'Reconsideration and Review of decisions', and consists of sections 51A-51D of the Act.

[37] The term 'assets' in this paragraph (i.e., paragraph 13A(4)(a) of the Banking Act 1959) excludes "goodwill and any assets or other amount excluded by the prudential standards for the purposes of this subsection" (i.e., subsection 13A(4) of the Banking Act 1959) (Government of Australia (2021), "Banking Act 1959," adopted on April 23, 1959, entered into force on January 14, 1960, Compilation No. 60 of December 8, 2021, registered on December 16, 2021, s.13A(4)(a)). Moreover, "[f]or the purposes of subsection (4) [(i.e., subsection 13A(4) of the Banking Act 1959)]: (a) the ADI's deposit liabilities are taken not to include an amount equal to the total of the face values of all the covered bonds issued by the ADI; and (b) the assets of the ADI are taken not to include: (i) any interest in an asset (or part of an asset) in a cover pool for which the ADI is the issuing ADI; or (ii) any loan to a covered bond special purpose vehicle that relates to an asset (or a part of an asset) in a cover pool for which the ADI is the issuing ADI" (Government of Australia (2021), "Banking Act 1959," adopted on April 23, 1959, entered into force on January 14, 1960, Compilation No. 60 of December 8, 2021, registered on December 16, 2021, s.13A(4A)).

[38] The last sentence of fn 26 lays down subsection 13(4) of the Banking Act 1959.

[39] The sentence in the text that contains fn 27, sets out subsection 13A(1) of the Banking Act 1959.

these facilities [84]. After a decision is taken that a Banking Act statutory manager will assume control of a body corporate's business, the APRA must give that entity written notice of this acquisition of control[40] [85]. If the APRA takes control of a body corporate's business or appoints an administrator of this business, then it must make sure that either it or the administrator has control of the business until it: (i) deems it no longer necessary for it or the administrator to remain in control of the business [86], or (ii) has applied for the body corporate to be liquidated [87]. The APRA may apply to the Federal Court of Australia for an order that an ADI be dissolved, if it considers that the ADI is unable to pay its debts and could not be restored to solvency within a reasonable time[41] [88]; it must promptly inform the Minister of this application [89].

Financial Claims Scheme for Account-Holders with Insolvent ADIs

The primary purpose of Division 2AA of Part II of the Banking Act 1959[42] is to provide for a financial claims scheme for account-holders of ADIs that: (i) permits the Minister to make a declaration about an ADI, if either the APRA has applied for the ADI to be dissolved[43] or a Banking Act statutory manager is in control of the business of the ADI[44] [90], (ii) entitles account-holders who have particular protected accounts with a declared ADI to be paid

---

[40] Subdivision B of Division 2 of Part II of the Banking Act 1959, which is entitled 'Provisions dealing with control of a body corporate's business by a Banking Act statutory manager' and which comprises sections 14A-16AA of the Act, contains rules relating to the Banking Act statutory manager's operation of the relevant entity's business.

[41] The APRA's application for an ADI to be wound up must be made under section 459P of the Corporations Act 2001, and the liquidation is to be carried out in compliance with that Act (Government of Australia (2021), "Banking Act 1959," adopted on April 23, 1959, entered into force on January 14, 1960, Compilation No. 60 of December 8, 2021, registered on December 16, 2021, s.16AAA(3)-(4)). Section 459P of the Corporations Act 2001 is titled 'Who may apply for order under section 459A', and states: "(1) Any one or more of the following may apply to the Court for a company to be wound up in insolvency: (a) the company; (b) a creditor (even if the creditor is a secured creditor or is only a contingent or prospective creditor); (c) a contributory; (d) a director, (e) a liquidator or provisional liquidator of the company; (f) ASIC; (g) a prescribed agency. (2) An application by any of the following, or by persons including any of the following, may only be made with the leave of the Court: (a) a person who is a creditor only because of a contingent or prospective debt; (b) a contributory; (c) a director; (d) ASIC. (3) The Court may give leave[,] if satisfied that there is a *prima facie* case that the company is insolvent, but not otherwise. (4) The Court may give leave subject to conditions. (5) Except as permitted by this section, a person cannot apply for a company to be wound up in insolvency." (Government of Australia (2022), "Corporations Act 2001," adopted on June 28, 2001, entered into force on July 15, 2001, Compilation No. 113 of January 1, 2022, registered on January 25, 2022, s.459P; emphasis added). Section 459A of the Corporations Act 2001 is entitled 'Order that insolvent company be wound up in insolvency', and declares: "On an application under section 459P [of the Corporations Act 2001], the Court may order that an insolvent company be wound up in insolvency" (Government of Australia (2022), "Corporations Act 2001," adopted on June 28, 2001, entered into force on July 15, 2001, Compilation No. 113 of January 1, 2022, registered on January 25, 2022, s.459A). The term '*Court*' means "any of the following courts: (a) the Federal Court [of Australia]; (b) the Supreme Court of a State or Territory; (c) the Federal Circuit and Family Court of Australia (Division 1); (d) a court to which section 41 of the *Family Law Act 1975* applies because of a Proclamation made under subsection 41(2) of that Act (Government of Australia (2022), "Corporations Act 2001," adopted on June 28, 2001, entered into force on July 15, 2001, Compilation No. 113 of January 1, 2022, registered on January 25, 2022, s.58AA(1); emphasis original).

[42] Division 2AA of Part II of the Banking Act 1959 is titled 'Financial claims scheme for account-holders with insolvent ADIs', and comprises sections 16AB-16AU of the Act. Fn 33 sets out section 16AI, paragraph 16AIA(1)(a) and subsection 16AD(1) of the Banking Act 1959. Fn 34 lays down section 16AIC of the Banking Act 1959. Fn 35 comprises section 16AO of the Banking Act 1959. Part II of the Banking Act 1959 is entitled 'Provisions relating to the carrying on of banking business'.

[43] Fn 41 and its accompanying text introduce the application for an ADI to be wound up.

[44] Subdivision B of Division 2 of Part II of the Banking Act 1959, which is titled 'Provisions dealing with control of a body corporate's business by a Banking Act statutory manager' and which consists of sections 14A-16AA of the Act, contains rules pertaining to the Banking Act statutory manager's operation of the relevant entity's business.

specified sums to maintain the liquidity of the account-holders, before they would receive payment in a liquidation of the ADI [91], (iii) substitutes the APRA for these account-holders as a creditor of the declared ADI, to the extent of those entitlements [92], and allows the APRA to smooth a transfer of business from the declared ADI to a receiving entity under the Financial Sector (Transfer and Restructure) Act 1999, by entitling that entity to amounts as regards the protected accounts [93]. 'Declared ADI' refers to the declaration that the Minister may make concerning an identified ADI under section 16AD of the Banking Act 1959 – as long as one of the two requirements listed in subsection 16AD(1) of the Banking Act 1959 is fulfilled[45] [94].

---

[45] The final sentence of fn 33 specifies subsection 16AD(1) of the Banking Act 1959. The other subsections of section 16AD of the Banking Act 1959 read – with italicized subtitles – as follows: "*Declaration to specify amount for meeting entitlements* (2) The declaration must also specify the amount (if any) that is to be credited to the Financial Claims Scheme Special Account in connection with the application of Subdivision C [(which is entitled 'Payment of account-holders with declared ADI' and which comprises sections 16AF-16AIC of the Act) of Division 2AA of Part II of the Banking Act 1959,)] in relation to the declared ADI. If APRA's application under section 16AAA [of the Banking Act 1959] was made on or after 12 October 2011, [then] the amount must not be more than [AUD] 20,000,000,000. *Declaration to specify amount for administration* (3) The declaration must also specify the amount (if any) that is to be credited to the APRA Special Account in connection with the administration of this Division [(i.e., Division 2AA of Part II of the Banking Act 1959, which comprises sections 16AB-16AU of the Act,)] in relation to the declared ADI. The amount must not be more than [AUD] 100,000,000. *Amendment of specification of amounts* (4) The Minister may amend a declaration made under subsection (1) [(last sentence of fn 33)], but only to change the specification of an amount under subsection (2) or (3), within the limit set in that subsection. *Declaration cannot be revoked* (5) The Minister cannot revoke a declaration made under subsection (1). *Declaration or amendment not disallowable* (6) A declaration made under subsection (1), or an amendment of the declaration, is a legislative instrument, but section 42 (disallowance) of the *Legislation Act 2003* does not apply to the declaration or amendment. *Effect of declaration or amendment* (7) The declaration or amendment: (a) commences from the time [that] it is made, despite subsection 12(1) of the *Legislation Act 2003*; and (b) has effect according to its terms. (7A) Subsection 12(2) (retrospective application of legislative instruments) of the *Legislation Act 2003* does not apply to the declaration or amendment. *Declaration not to specify ADI by reference to class* (8) Subsection 13(3) of the *Legislation Act 2003* does not apply to a declaration under subsection (1) [of the Banking Act 1959 (final sentence of fn 33)] specifying an ADI." (Government of Australia (2021), "Banking Act 1959," adopted on April 23, 1959, entered into force on January 14, 1960, Compilation No. 60 of December 8, 2021, registered on December 16, 2021, s.16AD(2)-(8); emphasis original). The text to fn 41 states subsections (1) and (5) of section 16AAA of the Banking Act 1959, which is titled 'APRA's powers to apply for ADI to be wound up'. Section 42 of the Legislation Act 2003 is entitled 'Disallowance of legislative instruments', and states: "(1) If: (a) notice of a motion to disallow a legislative instrument[,] or a provision of a legislative instrument[,] is given in a House of the Parliament within 15 sitting days of that House[,] beginning on the first sitting day after a copy of the instrument was laid before that House; and (b) within 15 sitting days of that House[,] beginning on the first sitting day after the giving of that notice, the House passes a resolution, in pursuance of the motion, disallowing the instrument or provision; [then] the instrument or provision so disallowed is repealed immediately after the passing of that resolution. (2) If: (a) notice of a motion to disallow a legislative instrument[,] or a provision of a legislative instrument[,] is given in a House of the Parliament within 15 sitting days of that House[,] beginning on the first sitting day after a copy of the instrument was laid before that House; and (b) at the end of 15 sitting days of that House[,] beginning on the first sitting day after the giving of that notice of motion: (i) the notice has not been withdrawn and the motion has not been called on; or (ii) the motion has been called on, moved and (where relevant) seconded[,] and has not been withdrawn or otherwise disposed of; [then] the instrument or provision specified in the motion is then taken to have been disallowed[,] and is repealed at that time. (3) If: (a) notice of a motion to disallow a legislative instrument[,] or a provision of a legislative instrument[,] is given in a House of the Parliament within 15 sitting days of that House[,] beginning on the first sitting day after a copy of the instrument was laid before that House; and (b) before the end of 15 sitting days of that House[,] beginning on the first sitting day after the giving of that notice of motion, the House of Representatives is dissolved or expires, or the Parliament is prorogued; and (c) at the time of the dissolution, expiry or prorogation, as the case may be: (i) the notice has not been withdrawn and the motion has not been called on; or (ii) the motion has been called on, moved and (where relevant) seconded[,] and has not been withdrawn or otherwise disposed of; [then] the legislative instrument is taken, for the purposes of subsections (1) and (2), to have been laid before the first-mentioned House on the first sitting day of that first-mentioned House after the dissolution, expiry or prorogation, as the case may be." (Government of Australia (2019). "Legislation Act 2003," Adopted (as Legislative Instruments Act 2003) on December 17, 2003, Entered into force (as Legislative Instruments Act

Governance

A person commits an offence, if (s)he is a disqualified person[46] [95] who is, or acts as, a director or senior manager of an ADI [96], a senior manager of the Australian workings of a foreign ADI[47] [97], a director or senior manager of an authorised NOHC[48] [98], or an auditor of an ADI or an authorised NOHC [99], and – for a person who is a disqualified person solely because (s)he was disqualified under section 21 of the Banking Act 1959[49] – (s)he is disqualified from

---

2003) on January 1 2005, Compilation No. 39 of February 24, 2019, Registered on February 25, 2019, s.42). Subsection 12(1) of the Legislation Act 2003 is subtitled 'When do legislative instruments and notifiable instruments commence?', and declares: "A legislative instrument or a notifiable instrument commences: (a) at the start of the day after the day [that] the instrument is registered; or (b) so far as the instrument provides otherwise – in accordance with such provision." (Government of Australia (2019). "Legislation Act 2003," Adopted (as Legislative Instruments Act 2003) on December 17, 2003, Entered into force (as Legislative Instruments Act 2003) on January 1 2005, Compilation No. 39 of February 24, 2019, Registered on February 25, 2019, s.12(1)). Subsection 12(2) of the Legislation Act 2003 is subtitled 'Retrospective application', and specifies: "[I]f a legislative instrument or notifiable instrument, or a provision of such an instrument, commences before the instrument is registered, [then] the instrument or provision does not apply in relation to a person (other than the Commonwealth [of Australia] or an authority of the Commonwealth) to the extent that[,] as a result of that commencement: (a) the person's rights[,] as at the time [at which] the instrument is registered[,] would be affected so as to disadvantage the person; or (b) liabilities would be imposed on the person in respect of anything done or omitted to be done before the instrument is registered." (Government of Australia (2019). "Legislation Act 2003," Adopted (as Legislative Instruments Act 2003) on December 17, 2003, Entered into force (as Legislative Instruments Act 2003) on January 1 2005, Compilation No. 39 of February 24, 2019, Registered on February 25, 2019, s.12(2)). Subsection 13(3) of the Legislation Act 2003 reads: "If enabling legislation confers on a person the power to make a legislative instrument or notifiable instrument: (a) specifying, declaring or prescribing a matter; or (b) doing anything in relation to a matter; then, in exercising the power, the person may identify the matter by referring to a class or classes of matters." (Government of Australia (2019). "Legislation Act 2003," Adopted (as Legislative Instruments Act 2003) on December 17, 2003, Entered into force (as Legislative Instruments Act 2003) on January 1 2005, Compilation No. 39 of February 24, 2019, Registered on February 25, 2019, s.13(3)). "For the purposes of subsection 3," i.e., subsection 13(3) of the Legislation Act 2003, the term '*matter*' "includes thing, person and animal" (Government of Australia (2019). "Legislation Act 2003," Adopted (as Legislative Instruments Act 2003) on December 17, 2003, Entered into force (as Legislative Instruments Act 2003) on January 1 2005, Compilation No. 39 of February 24, 2019, Registered on February 25, 2019, s.13(4)).

[46] A person is a '*disqualified person*' if, at any juncture, "(a) the person has been convicted of an offence against or arising out of: (i) this Act [(i.e., the Banking Act 1959)]; or (ii) the *Financial Sector (Collection of Data) Act 2001*; or (iii) the *Corporations Act 2001*, the Corporations Law that was previously in force, or any law of a foreign country that corresponds to that Act or to that Corporations Law; or (b) the person has been convicted of an offence against or arising out of a law in force in Australia, or the law of a foreign country, where the offence related or relates to dishonest conduct, or to conduct relating to a company that carries on business in the financial sector; or (c) the person has been or becomes bankrupt; or (d) the person has applied to take the benefit of a law for the relief of bankrupt or insolvent debtors; or (e) the person has compounded with his or her creditors; or (f) the Federal Court of Australia has disqualified the person under section 21 [of the Banking Act 1959]; or (g) the person has been disqualified under the law of a foreign country from managing, or taking part in the management of, an entity that carries on the business of banking or insurance or otherwise deals in financial matters." (Government of Australia (2021), "Banking Act 1959," adopted on April 23, 1959, entered into force on January 14, 1960, Compilation No. 60 of December 8, 2021, registered on December 16, 2021, s.20(1); emphasis original). Subsection 20(2) of the Banking Act 1959 extends the reference to 'the person has been convicted of an offence' in paragraph 20(1)(b) of the Banking Act 1959, thus: "A reference in subsection (1) to a person who has been convicted of an offence includes a reference to a person in respect of whom an order has been made relating to the offence under: (a) section 19B of the *Crimes Act 1914*; or (b) a corresponding provision of a law of a State, a Territory or a foreign country." (Government of Australia (2021), "Banking Act 1959," adopted on April 23, 1959, entered into force on January 14, 1960, Compilation No. 60 of December 8, 2021, registered on December 16, 2021, s.20(2); emphasis original).

[47] Fn 24 defines the term '*foreign ADI*'.

[48] The first sentence of fn 19 defines the term '*authorised NOHC*'.

[49] Section 21 of the Banking Act 1959 is titled 'Court power of disqualification', and states: "(1) On application by APRA, the Federal Court of Australia may, by order, disqualify a person from being or acting as a person referred to in subsection (2), for a period that the Court considers [to be] appropriate, if the Court is satisfied

being, or acting as, that director, senior manager or auditor [100]. A body corporate commits an offence, if a disqualified person[50] [101] is, or acts as, a director or senior manager of the body corporate if the last-mentioned is an ADI [102], a senior manager of the Australian functionings of the body corporate if the latter is a foreign ADI[51] [103], a director or senior manager of the body corporate if the last-mentioned is an authorised NOHC[52] [104], or an auditor of the body corporate if the latter is an ADI or an authorised NOHC [105], and for a person who is a disqualified person entirely because (s)he was disqualified under section 21 of the Banking Act 1959[53] – (s)he is disqualified from being, or acting as, that director, senior manager or auditor [106], and (for any disqualified person) the body corporate permits the person to be, or act as, a director, senior manager or auditor [107]. The APRA may make a written declaration that the ADI or authorised NOHC remove a director or senior manager of an ADI, a senior manager of the Australian runnings of a foreign ADI, or a director or senior manager of an authorised NOHC [108], if the APRA is satisfied that the person does not fulfil at least one of the criteria for fitness and propriety which the prudential standards set out [109], or – either, for a person who is a disqualified person wholly because (s)he was disqualified under section 21 of the Banking Act 1959 – (s)he is disqualified from being, or acting as, that director, senior manager or auditor [110], or – otherwise – is a disqualified person[54] [111].

---

that: (a) the person is not a fit and proper person to be or act as such a person; and (b) the disqualification is justified. (2) For the purposes of subsection (1), the Court may disqualify a person from being or acting as one or more of the following: (a) a director or senior manager of: (i) a particular ADI; or (ii) a class of ADIs; or (iii) any ADI; (other than a particular foreign ADI, a class of foreign ADIs or any foreign ADI), (b) a senior manager of the Australian operations of: (i) a particular foreign ADI; or (ii) a class of foreign ADIs; or (iii) any foreign ADI; (c) a director or senior manager of: (i) a particular authorised NOHC; or (ii) a class of authorised NOHCs; or (iii) any authorised NOHC; (d) an auditor of: (i) a particular ADI or a particular authorised NOHC; or (ii) a class of ADIs or a class of authorised NOHCs; or (iii) any ADI or any authorised NOHC. (3) In deciding whether it is satisfied as mentioned in paragraph (1)(a) [(i.e., that 'the person is not a fit and proper person to be or act as' a director, senior manager or auditor)] the Court may take into account: (a) any matters [that are] specified in the regulations for the purposes of this paragraph; and (b) any criteria for fitness and propriety [which are] set out in the prudential standards; and (c) any other matters [that] the Court considers [to be] relevant. (4) In deciding whether the disqualification is justified as mentioned in paragraph (1)(b), the Court may have regard to: (a) if the application is for the person to be disqualified from being or acting as a director or senior manager – the person's conduct in relation to the management, business or property of any corporation; and (b) if the application is for the person to be disqualified from being or acting as an auditor – the person's conduct in relation to the functions or duties of the person as required under this Act and the prudential standards; and (c) in any case – any other matters [that] the Court considers [to be] relevant. (5) As soon as practicable after the Court disqualifies a person under this section, APRA must cause particulars of the disqualification (a) to be given: (i) if the person is, or is acting as, a person referred to in subparagraph (2)(a)(i) – to the ADI concerned; or (ii) if the person is, or is acting as, a person referred to in subparagraph (2)(b)(i) – to the foreign ADI concerned; or (iii) if the person is, or is acting as, a person referred to in subparagraph (2)(c)(i) – to the authorised NOHC concerned; or (iv) if the person is, or is acting as, a person referred to in subparagraph (2)(d)(i) – to the ADI or authorised NOHC concerned; and (b) to be published in the *Gazette*." (Government of Australia (2021), "Banking Act 1959," adopted on April 23, 1959, entered into force on January 14, 1960, Compilation No. 60 of December 8, 2021, registered on December 16, 2021, s.21; emphasis original). It is opined that the '*Gazette*' refers to the *Commonwealth of Australia Gazette*, which includes the *Government Notices Gazette*, a *Special Gazette* that usually accommodates a single notice, and a *Periodic Gazette* which may contain many notices relating to a specific topic (Government of Australia (2022), "National Library of Australia – Government Gazettes: Commonwealth," accessed August 24, 2022, <https://www.nla.gov.au/research-guides/finding-government-gazettes/finding-government-gazettes-commonwealth>).

[50] Fn 46 defines the term '*disqualified person*'.

[51] Fn 24 defines the term '*foreign ADI*'.

[52] The first sentence of fn 19 defines the term '*authorised NOHC*'.

[53] Fn 49 lays down section 21 of the Banking Act 1959.

[54] Subsections 23(3)-(5) of the Banking Act 1959 provide: "Before directing an ADI or authorised NOHC to remove a person, APRA must give written notice to: (a) the person; and (b) the ADI or NOHC; giving each of them a reasonable opportunity to make submissions on the matter. (4) If a submission is made to APRA in response to

Covered Bonds

Covered bonds are debentures that an ADI issues[55], liabilities to the holders of which (or their representatives) are both recoverable from the ADI and secured by assets that a covered bond special purpose vehicle[56] holds[57] [112]. The cover pool for the covered bonds comprises the assets which the covered bond special purpose vehicle beneficially owns, to the extent that these secure the liabilities to the holders or their representatives equally, or in precedence to, any other liabilities[58] [113]. An ADI must not issue a covered bond, if the total value of assets in cover pools that secure covered bonds which the ADI has issued would exceed 8% – or such other percentage as the regulations stipulate – of the value of the assets of the ADI in Australia[59] [114]. By way of a written notice to the ADI, the APRA may direct an ADI not to issue a covered bond – if the APRA has reason to hold that the ADI has infracted a provision of the Banking Act 1959, a regulation concerning prudential requirements or a prudential standard which relates to covered bonds, or has presented a direction to the ADI under section 11CA of the Banking Act 1959[60] [115]. There must be a monitor for each cover pool [116], which is

---

the notice, [then] APRA must have regard to the submission and may discuss any matter contained in the submission with such persons as it considers [to be] appropriate for the purpose of assessing the truth of the matter. (5) A notice given under subsection (3) to a person, an ADI or an authorised NOHC must state that any submissions made in response to the notice may be discussed by APRA with other persons[,] as mentioned in subsection (4)." (Government of Australia (2021), "Banking Act 1959," adopted on April 23, 1959, entered into force on January 14, 1960, Compilation No. 60 of December 8, 2021, registered on December 16, 2021, s.23(3)-(5)).

[55] This Division, i.e., Division 3A of Part II of the Banking Act 1959, which is entitled 'Covered bonds' and which comprises sections 24-31F of the Act, "does not apply in relation to: (a) a foreign ADI; or (b) a bond, note or other debenture, liabilities in relation to which are secured wholly by assets that are not in Australia" (Government of Australia (2021), "Banking Act 1959," adopted on April 23, 1959, entered into force on January 14, 1960, Compilation No. 60 of December 8, 2021, registered on December 16, 2021, s.25).

[56] The covered bond special purpose vehicle's purpose "must relate only to the covered bonds" (Government of Australia (2021), "Banking Act 1959," adopted on April 23, 1959, entered into force on January 14, 1960, Compilation No. 60 of December 8, 2021, registered on December 16, 2021, s.26(2)).

[57] Section 24 of the Banking Act 1959, which is titled 'Guide to this Division', i.e., Division 3A of Part II of the Banking Act 1959', declares: "This Division provides for the issue of covered bonds by ADIs. An ADI issuing covered bonds must provide assets to secure the covered bonds and related liabilities. These assets are held by a covered bond special purpose vehicle. Some of the assets [that are] held by the covered bond special purpose vehicle form the cover pool for the covered bonds. The ADI must not issue covered bonds[,] if the combined value of assets in cover pools securing covered bonds [which are] issued by the ADI would exceed 8%, or other such percentage as is prescribed by the regulations, of the value of the ADI's assets in Australia." (Government of Australia (2021), "Banking Act 1959," adopted on April 23, 1959, entered into force on January 14, 1960, Compilation No. 60 of December 8, 2021, registered on December 16, 2021, s.24).

[58] The Banking Act 1959 describes the term 'covered bond liabilities of the ADI' thus: "The liabilities to the holders or representatives, and any other liabilities [that are] secured by assets [which are] beneficially owned by the covered bond special purpose vehicle, are ***covered bond liabilities*** of the ADI. [A] liability to the ADI, other than a liability in relation to a derivative or the provision of services, secured in priority to any liability to the holders or representatives is not a ***covered bond liability*** of the ADI." (Government of Australia (2021), "Banking Act 1959," adopted on April 23, 1959, entered into force on January 14, 1960, Compilation No. 60 of December 8, 2021, registered on December 16, 2021, s.26(4)-(5); emphasis original).

[59] In addition to the current section of the Banking Act 1959, i.e., section 28 of that Act – which is titled 'Restrictions on issuing covered bonds – 8% rule', the final sentence of section 24 of the Banking Act 1959 comprises a statement which is essentially the same as that in the text to the present footnote (fn 59). Fn 57 lays down section 24 of the Banking Act 1959.

[60] Section 11CA of the Banking Act 1959 is entitled 'APRA may give directions in certain circumstances'. Subsections (1), (1AA), (1AB), (1AC), (2), (2AA) and (2A) of this section of the Act are as follows: "(1) APRA may give a body corporate that is an ADI or an authorised NOHC a direction of a kind specified in subsection (2)[,] if APRA has reason to believe that: (a) the body corporate has contravened a provision of: (i) this Act; or (ii) the *Financial Sector (Collection of Data) Act 2001*; or (b) the body corporate has contravened a prudential requirement regulation or a prudential standard; or (c) the body corporate is likely to contravene this Act, a prudential requirement regulation, a prudential standard or the *Financial Sector (Collection of Data) Act 2001*,

and the direction is reasonably necessary for one or more prudential matters relating to the body corporate; or (d) the body corporate has contravened a condition or direction under this Act or the *Financial Sector (Collection of Data) Act 2001*; or (e) the direction is necessary in the interests of: (i) if the body corporate is an ADI – depositors of the ADI; or (ii) if the body corporate is an authorised NOHC – depositors of any ADI that is a subsidiary of the NOHC; or (f) the body corporate is, or is about to become, unable to meet its liabilities; or (g) there is, or there might be, a material risk to the security of the body corporate's assets; or (h) there has been, or there might be, a material deterioration in the body corporate's financial condition; or (i) the body corporate is conducting its affairs in an improper or financially unsound way; or (j) the failure to issue a direction would materially prejudice the interests of: (i) if the body corporate is an ADI – depositors of the ADI; or (ii) if the body corporate is an authorised NOHC – depositors of any ADI that is a subsidiary of the NOHC; or (k) the body corporate is conducting its affairs in a way that may cause or promote instability in the Australian financial system. (1AA) APRA may give a body corporate that is an ADI or is an authorised NOHC a direction of a kind specified in subsection (2)[,] if APRA has reason to believe that: (a) a subsidiary of the body corporate has contravened a provision of: (i) this Act; or (ii) the *Financial Sector (Collection of Data) Act 2001*; or (b) a subsidiary of the body corporate has contravened a prudential requirement regulation or a prudential standard; or (c) a subsidiary of the body corporate is likely to continue to contravene this Act, a prudential requirement regulation, a prudential standard or the *Financial Sector (Collection of Data) Act 2001*; or (d) the direction is in respect of a subsidiary of the body corporate and is necessary in the interests of: (i) if the body corporate is an ADI – depositors of the ADI; or (ii) if the body corporate is an authorised NOHC – depositors of any ADI that is a subsidiary of the NOHC; or (e) a subsidiary of the body corporate is, or is about to become, unable to meet the subsidiary's liabilities; or (f) there is, or there might be, a material risk to the security of the assets of a subsidiary of the body corporate; or (g) there has been, or there might be, a material deterioration in the financial condition of a subsidiary of the body corporate; or (h) a subsidiary of the body corporate is conducting the subsidiary's affairs in an improper or financially unsound way; or (j) a subsidiary of the body corporate is conducting the subsidiary's affairs in a way that may cause or promote instability in the Australian financial system; or (k) a subsidiary of the body corporate is conducting the subsidiary's affairs in a way that may cause it to be unable to continue to supply services to: (i) if the body corporate is an ADI – the ADI; or (ii) if the body corporate is an authorised NOHC – any ADI that is a subsidiary of the NOHC; or (l) the direction is in respect of a subsidiary of the body corporate and the failure to issue a direction would materially prejudice the interests of: (i) if the body corporate is an ADI – depositors of the ADI; or (ii) if the body corporate is an authorised NOHC – depositors of any ADI that is a subsidiary of the NOHC. (1AB) However, APRA can only make a direction as a result of a ground referred to in paragraph (1AA)(a), (b), (c), (e), (f), (g), (h) or (k)[,] if APRA considers that the direction is reasonably necessary for one or more prudential matters relating to the body corporate. (1AC) APRA may give a body corporate that is a subsidiary of an ADI or of an authorised NOHC a direction of a kind specified in subsection (2)[,] if: (a) APRA has given the ADI or authorised NOHC a direction under subsection (1AA) because one or more of the grounds referred to in that subsection have been satisfied in respect of the subsidiary; or (b) APRA may give the ADI or authorised NOHC a direction under subsection (1AA) because one or more of the grounds referred to in that subsection have been satisfied in respect of the subsidiary. ... (2) The kinds of direction that the body corporate may be given are directions to do, or to cause a body corporate that is its subsidiary to do, any one or more of the following: (aa) to comply with the whole[,] or a part[,] of: (i) this Act; or (ii) the *Financial Sector (Collection of Data) Act 2001*; (ab) to comply with the whole[,] or a part[,] of a condition or direction referred to in paragraph (1)(d); (a) to comply with the whole[,] or a part[,] of a prudential requirement regulation or a prudential standard; (b) to order an audit of the affairs of the body corporate, at the expense of the body corporate, by an auditor chosen by APRA; (c) to remove a director or senior manager of the body corporate from office; (d) to ensure [that] a director or senior manager of the body corporate does not take part in the management or conduct of the business of the body corporate[,] except as permitted by APRA; (e) to appoint a person or persons as a director or senior manager of the body corporate for such term as APRA directs; (f) to remove any auditor of the body corporate from office and appoint another auditor to hold office for such term as APRA directs; (g) not to give any financial accommodation to any person; (h) not to accept the deposit of any amount; (i) not to borrow any amount; (j) not to accept any payment on account of share capital, except payments in respect of calls that fell due before the direction was given; (k) not to repay any amount paid on shares; (l) not to pay a dividend on shares; (m) not to repay any money on deposit or advance; (n) not to pay or transfer any amount or asset to any person, or create an obligation (contingent or otherwise) to do so; (o) not to undertake any financial obligation (contingent or otherwise) on behalf of any other person; (p) to make changes to the body corporate's systems, business practices or operations; (q) to reconstruct, amalgamate or otherwise alter all[,] or part[,] of any of the following: (i) the business, structure or organisation of the body corporate; (ii) the business, structure or organisation of the group constituted by the body corporate and its subsidiaries; (r) to do, or to refrain from doing, anything else in relation to the affairs of the body corporate. A direction under paragraph (n) not to pay or transfer any amount or asset[,] does not apply to the payment or transfer of money pursuant to an order of a court or a process of execution. (2AA) However, APRA must not direct, or give a direction that would cause or require, a covered bond special purpose vehicle to: (a)

neither the issuing ADI for the cover pool [117] nor an associated entity of that ADI[61] [118]. The APRA may, by written notice passed to a covered bond special purpose vehicle, direct that entity to return to its issuing ADI an asset to the extent that, at the moment which the direction is given, this asset does not secure covered bond liabilities of that ADI [119] – but only if the APRA may give a direction under section 11CA of the Banking Act 1959[62] to the issuing ADI [120].

deal, or not deal, with an asset to the extent that the asset secures covered bond liabilities of an ADI; or (b) make a payment, or not make a payment, in relation to a covered bond liability of an ADI. (2A) Without limiting the generality of subsection (2) a direction referred to in a paragraph of that subsection may: (a) deal with some only of the matters referred to in that paragraph; or (b) deal with a particular class or particular classes of those matters; or (c) make different provision with respect to different matters or different classes of matters." (Government of Australia (2021), "Banking Act 1959," adopted on April 23, 1959, entered into force on January 14, 1960, Compilation No. 60 of December 8, 2021, registered on December 16, 2021, ss.11CA(1)-(1AC) and 11CA(2)-(2A); emphasis original).

[61] The cover pool monitor's functions are: "(a) to assess the keeping, by the issuing ADI or covered bond special purpose vehicle concerned, of an accurate register of the assets in the cover pool; (b) to assess compliance by the issuing ADI with sections 31 and 31A [of the Banking Act 1959]; (c) to make reports relating to the matters in paragraphs (a) and (b) available to the issuing ADI (or any substituted entity) for distribution to the holders of covered bonds or their representatives; (d) to provide reports relating to the cover pool to APRA[,] on written request by APRA; (e) such functions (if any) as are prescribed by the regulations." (Government of Australia (2021), "Banking Act 1959," adopted on April 23, 1959, entered into force on January 14, 1960, Compilation No. 60 of December 8, 2021, registered on December 16, 2021, s.30(4)). Section 31 of the Banking Act 1959 is titled 'Assets that may be in cover pools'; its first subsection specifies: "An asset in a cover pool must be one of the following: (a) an at call deposit held with an ADI and convertible into cash within 2 business days; (b) a bank accepted bill or certificate of deposit that: (i) matures within 100 days; and (ii) is eligible for repurchase transactions with the Reserve Bank [of Australia]; and (iii) was not issued by the ADI that issued the covered bonds [which are] secured by the assets in the cover pool; (c) a bond, note, debenture or other instrument issued or guaranteed by the Commonwealth [of Australia], a State or a Territory; (d) a loan [that is] secured by a mortgage, charge or other security interest over residential property in Australia; (e) a loan [which is] secured by a mortgage, charge or other security interest over commercial property in Australia; (f) a mortgage insurance policy or other asset [that is] related to a loan covered by paragraph (d) or (e); (g) a contractual right relating to the holding or management of another asset in the cover pool; (h) a derivative [that is] held for one or more of the following purposes: (i) to protect the value of another asset in the cover pool; (ii) to hedge risks in relation to another asset in the cover pool; (iii) to hedge risks in relation to liabilities secured by the assets in the cover pool; (i) an asset of a kind prescribed by the regulations for the purposes of this paragraph." (Government of Australia (2021), "Banking Act 1959," adopted on April 23, 1959, entered into force on January 14, 1960, Compilation No. 60 of December 8, 2021, registered on December 16, 2021, s.31(1)). Section 31A of the Banking Act 1959 is entitled 'Maintenance of cover pools'; its first two subsections read: "(1) The value of assets in a cover pool must be at least 103%, or such other percentage as is prescribed by the regulations, of the face value of the covered bonds secured by the assets. (2) The value of assets covered by paragraph 31(1)(b) (bank accepted bills or certificates of deposit) in a cover pool must not exceed 15% of the face value of the covered bonds secured by the assets." (Government of Australia (2021), "Banking Act 1959," adopted on April 23, 1959, entered into force on January 14, 1960, Compilation No. 60 of December 8, 2021, registered on December 16, 2021, s.31A(1)-(2)).

[62] Fn 60 comprises subsections (1), (1AA), (1AB), (1AC), (2), (2AA) and (2A) of section 11CA of the Banking Act 1959.

The Banking Executives Accountability Regime

An ADI must fulfil its accountability, personnel, deferred remuneration and notification obligations [121], unless the Minister has exempted it[63] or a class of which it is a member[64] – or unless it is a foreign ADI[65] [122].

Accountability Obligations

An ADI's accountability objections are to take reasonable steps[66] to undertake its business with honesty, integrity, due skill, care and diligence [123], relate to the APRA in an open, constructive and co-operative manner, [124], preclude issues from arising in the operation of its business that would adversely influence the ADI's prudential reputation or standing [125], ensure that each of its accountable persons[67] satisfies his or her accountability obligations under

---

[63] The relevant subsection of the Banking Act 1959 states: "The Minister may, by written notice given to an ADI, exempt the ADI from compliance with this Part." (Government of Australia (2021), "Banking Act 1959," adopted on April 23, 1959, entered into force on January 14, 1960, Compilation No. 60 of December 8, 2021, registered on December 16, 2021, s.37A(1)). 'This Part' is Part IIAA of the Banking Act 1959, which is titled 'The Banking Executive Accountability Regime' and which comprises sections 37-37KC of the Act.

[64] The pertinent subsection of the Banking Act 1959 declares: "The Minister may, by legislative instrument, exempt a class of ADIs from compliance with this Part." (Government of Australia (2021), "Banking Act 1959," adopted on April 23, 1959, entered into force on January 14, 1960, Compilation No. 60 of December 8, 2021, registered on December 16, 2021, s.37A(2)). 'This Part' is Part IIAA of the Banking Act 1959 (last sentence of fn 63).

[65] Fn 24 defines the term '*foreign ADI*'.

[66] Section 37CB of the Banking Act 1959 is entitled 'Taking reasonable steps', and reads: "Without limiting what constitutes the taking of reasonable steps in relation to a matter for the purposes of this Division, the taking of reasonable steps in relation to that matter includes having: (a) appropriate governance, control and risk management in relation to that matter; and (b) safeguards against inappropriate delegations of responsibility in relation to that matter; and (c) appropriate procedures for identifying and remediating problems that arise[,] or may arise[,] in relation to that matter." (Government of Australia (2021), "Banking Act 1959," adopted on April 23, 1959, entered into force on January 14, 1960, Compilation No. 60 of December 8, 2021, registered on December 16, 2021, s.37CB). 'This Division' is Division 2 of Part IIAA of the Banking Act 1959 (final sentence of fn 63), which is titled 'Accountability obligations' and which consists of sections 37C, 37CA and 37CB of the Act.

[67] An individual is an '*accountable person*' of either an ADI or a subsidiary of an ADI, if (s)he: "(a) either: (i) in the case of the ADI – holds a position in the ADI or in another body corporate of which the ADI is a subsidiary; or (ii) in the case of a subsidiary of the ADI – holds a position in the subsidiary; and (b) because of that position, has actual or effective senior executive responsibility: (i) for management or control of the ADI; or (ii) for management or control of a significant or substantial part or aspect of the operations of the ADI or the relevant group of bodies corporate that is constituted by the ADI and its subsidiaries" (Government of Australia (2021), "Banking Act 1959," adopted on April 23, 1959, entered into force on January 14, 1960, Compilation No. 60 of December 8, 2021, registered on December 16, 2021, s.37BA(1)). An individual is also an '*accountable person*' if (s)he: "(a) holds a position in, or relating to, the ADI; and (b) because of that position, has a responsibility, relating to the ADI: (i) of a kind [that is] set out in subsection (3) [(i.e., subsection 37BA(3) of the Banking Act 1959 – which is reproduced in the next sentence of the present footnote (fn 67))]; or (ii) of a kind [that is] determined under subsection (4) [(i.e., subsection 37BA(4) of the Banking Act 1959) – which is replicated in the last sentence of the current footnote (fn 67))]" (Government of Australia (2021), "Banking Act 1959," adopted on April 23, 1959, entered into force on January 14, 1960, Compilation No. 60 of December 8, 2021, registered on December 16, 2021, s.37BA(2)). For the purposes of subparagraph 37BA(2)(b)(i) of the Banking Act 1959 – which the immediately-preceding sentence of the present footnote (i.e., fn 67) contains, "the following are the responsibilities: (a) responsibility for oversight of the ADI as a member of the Board of the ADI; (b) senior executive responsibility for carrying out the management of all the business activities of the ADI and its subsidiaries, including: (i) allocating to accountable persons responsibility for all parts or aspects of the relevant group of bodies corporate that is constituted by the ADI and its subsidiaries; and (ii) reporting directly to the Board of the ADI; (c) senior executive responsibility for management of the ADI's financial resources; (d) senior executive responsibility for overall risk controls and/or overall risk management arrangements of the ADI; (e) senior executive responsibility for management of the ADI's operations; (f) senior executive responsibility for information management, including information technology systems, for the ADI;

section 37CA of the Banking Act 1959[68] [126], and make sure that each of its subsidiaries which is not an ADI acts in accordance with all these obligations as if the subsidiary were an ADI [127].

Key Personnel Obligations

An ADI's key personnel obligations are to ensure that the responsibilities of its accountable persons and its subsidiaries – subject to subsections 37D(2)[69] and 37D(3)[70] of the Banking Act 1959 – include all elements of the functioning of the pertinent group of bodies corporate that

---

(g) senior executive responsibility for management of the ADI's internal audit function; (h) senior executive responsibility for management of the ADI's compliance function; (i) senior executive responsibility for management of the ADI's human resources function; (j) senior executive responsibility for management of the ADI's anti-money laundering function" (Government of Australia (2021), "Banking Act 1959," adopted on April 23, 1959, entered into force on January 14, 1960, Compilation No. 60 of December 8, 2021, registered on December 16, 2021, s.37BA(3)). The "APRA may, by legislative instrument, determine a responsibility for the purposes of subparagraph (2)(b)(ii) [(i.e., subparagraph 37BA(2)(b)(ii) of the Banking Act 1959 – which the sentence immediately preceding the immediately-preceding sentence of the current footnote (fn 67) includes)] (other than a responsibility set out in subsection (3) [(i.e., subsection 37BA(3) of the Banking Act 1959 – which is reproduced in the immediately-preceding sentence of the present footnote (fn 67)])." (Government of Australia (2021), "Banking Act 1959," adopted on April 23, 1959, entered into force on January 14, 1960, Compilation No. 60 of December 8, 2021, registered on December 16, 2021, s.37BA(4)).

[68] This section of the Banking Act is entitled 'The accountability obligations of an accountable person'; its first subsection specifies: "(1) The accountability obligations of an accountable person of an ADI, or of a subsidiary of an ADI, are to conduct the responsibilities of his or her position as an accountable person: (a) by acting with honesty and integrity, and with due skill, care and diligence; and (b) by dealing with APRA in an open, constructive and cooperative way; and (c) by taking reasonable steps in conducting those responsibilities to prevent matters from arising that would adversely affect the prudential standing or prudential reputation of the ADI."(Government of Australia (2021), "Banking Act 1959," adopted on April 23, 1959, entered into force on January 14, 1960, Compilation No. 60 of December 8, 2021, registered on December 16, 2021, s.37CA(1)).

[69] This subsection of the Banking Act states: "Paragraph (1)(a) [of section 37D of the Banking Act 1959 (text to fns 69-71)] does not apply in relation to a responsibility [that is] excluded by APRA under subsection 37BB(2) or (3) [of the Banking Act 1959]." (Government of Australia (2021), "Banking Act 1959," adopted on April 23, 1959, entered into force on January 14, 1960, Compilation No. 60 of December 8, 2021, registered on December 16, 2021, s.37D(2)). Subsection 37BB(2) of the Banking Act 1959 reads: "APRA may, by written notice given to an ADI or a subsidiary of an ADI, exclude specified responsibilities that would, apart from this section [(i.e., section 37BB of the Banking Act 1959, which is titled 'Exception for responsibilities excluded by APRA',)] cause any person who holds a position in, or relating to, the ADI or subsidiary to be an accountable person." (Government of Australia (2021), "Banking Act 1959," adopted on April 23, 1959, entered into force on January 14, 1960, Compilation No. 60 of December 8, 2021, registered on December 16, 2021, s.37BB(2)). Subsection 37BB(3) of the Banking Act 1959 specifies: "APRA may, by legislative instrument, exclude specified responsibilities that would, apart from this section [(i.e., section 37BB of the Banking Act 1959, which is entitled 'Exception for responsibilities excluded by APRA')], cause any person who holds a position in, or relating to: (a) an ADI [that is] included in a class of ADIs [which is] specified in the instrument; or (b) a subsidiary of an ADI [that is] included in a class of such subsidiaries [which is] specified in the instrument; to be an accountable person." (Government of Australia (2021), "Banking Act 1959," adopted on April 23, 1959, entered into force on January 14, 1960, Compilation No. 60 of December 8, 2021, registered on December 16, 2021, s.37BB(3)).

[70] This subsection of the Banking Act declares: "If the ADI is a foreign ADI, [then] the ADI's obligation under paragraph (1)(a) [of section 37D of the Banking Act 1959 (text to fns 69-71)] is taken to be an obligation to ensure that the responsibilities of the ADI's accountable persons cover: (a) all parts or aspects of the operations of each Australian branch of the ADI; and (b) for each Australian branch of the ADI, the responsibility to which subsection 37BA(6) [of the Banking Act 1959] applies." (Government of Australia (2021), "Banking Act 1959," adopted on April 23, 1959, entered into force on January 14, 1960, Compilation No. 60 of December 8, 2021, registered on December 16, 2021, s.37D(3)). Subsection 37BA(6) of the Banking Act 1959 is captioned 'Head of an Australian branch of a foreign ADI', and states: "Without limiting subsection (1) [(i.e., subsection 37BA(1) of the Banking Act 1959 (first sentence of fn 67)], an individual is also an ***accountable person***, of an ADI that is a foreign ADI, if he or she has senior executive responsibility for the conduct of all the activities of an Australian branch of the foreign ADI." (Government of Australia (2021), "Banking Act 1959," adopted on April 23, 1959, entered into force on January 14, 1960, Compilation No. 60 of December 8, 2021, registered on December 16, 2021, s.37BA(6); emphasis original). Fn 24 defines the term '*foreign ADI*'.

constitute the ADI and its subsidiaries [128] and each of the responsibilities to which subsection 37BA(2) of the Banking Act 1959[71] applies [129], ensure that none of the ADI's accountable persons are prohibited from being such by section 37DA of the Banking Act 1959[72] [130], observe any directions that the APRA issues to the ADI under section 37DB of the Banking Act 1959[73] [131], and take reasonable steps to make sure that each of the ADI's subsidiaries which is not an ADI complies with paragraphs 37D(1)(b) and 37(1)(c) of the Banking Act 1959[74] as if the subsidiary were an ADI [132].

Deferred Remuneration Obligations

An ADI's deferred remuneration objectives are to: (a) ensure that, regarding the variable remuneration[75] obligations of an accountable person of the ADI, (i) the payment of a part of those earnings is deferred for a period, (ii) the amount of that part is at least the sum which

---

[71] The second sentence of fn 67 sets out subsection 37BA(2) of the Banking Act 1959.

[72] This section of the Banking Act 1959 is titled 'People prohibited from being an accountable person'; its first subsection reads: "A person is prohibited from being an accountable person[,] if the person: (a) is not registered under Subdivision B of Division 6 [of Part IIAA of the Banking Act 1959, which is entitled 'Registration of accountable persons' and which comprises sections 37H and 37HA of the Act]; or (b) is disqualified under section 37J [of the Banking Act 1959]." (Government of Australia (2021), "Banking Act 1959," adopted on April 23, 1959, entered into force on January 14, 1960, Compilation No. 60 of December 8, 2021, registered on December 16, 2021, s.37DA(1)). Section 37J of the Banking Act 1959 is entitled 'APRA may disqualify an accountable person'; its first two subsections are headed 'Disqualification by APRA', and specify: "(1) APRA may disqualify a person from being or acting as an accountable person, for a period that APRA considers appropriate, if APRA is satisfied that: (a) the person has not complied with his or her accountability obligations under section 37CA [of the Banking Act 1959]; and (b) having regard to the seriousness of the non-compliance, the disqualification is justified. (2) For the purposes of subsection (1), APRA may disqualify a person from being or acting as an accountable person of one or more of the following: (a) a particular ADI; (b) a particular subsidiary of an ADI; (c) a class of ADIs; (d) a class of subsidiaries of ADIs; (e) any ADI; (f) any subsidiary of an ADI." (Government of Australia (2021), "Banking Act 1959," adopted on April 23, 1959, entered into force on January 14, 1960, Compilation No. 60 of December 8, 2021, registered on December 16, 2021, s.37J(1)-(2)). Fn 68 lays down the first subsection of section 37CA of the Banking Act 1959.

[73] Section 37DB of the Banking Act 1959 is titled 'APRA may direct an ADI to reallocate responsibilities'; its first subsection states: "APRA may give an ADI a written declaration to reallocate responsibility to which paragraph 37D(1)(a) [of the Banking Act 1959] applies[,] if APRA has reason to believe that the current allocation of the responsibility is likely to give rise to a prudential risk." (Government of Australia (2021), "Banking Act 1959," adopted on April 23, 1959, entered into force on January 14, 1960, Compilation No. 60 of December 8, 2021, registered on December 16, 2021, s.37DB(1)). The text to fns 69-71 sets out subparagraph 37D(1)(a) of the Banking Act 1959.

[74] The text to fn 72 sets out subparagraph 37D(1)(b) of the Banking Act 1959. The text to fn 73 lays down subparagraph 37D(1)(c) of the Banking Act 1959.

[75] Section 37EA of the Banking Act 1959 is entitled 'Meaning of variable remuneration', and defines this term thus: "(1) The ***variable remuneration*** of an accountable person of an ADI, or a subsidiary of an ADI: (a) means so much of the accountable person's total remuneration as is conditional on the achievement of objectives; and (b) includes so much of the accountable person's total remuneration as is remuneration of a kind determined under paragraph (3)(a) or (4)(a). (2) [R]emuneration of a kind determined under paragraph (3)(b) or (4)(b) is not ***variable remuneration*** of an accountable person of an ADI, or a subsidiary of an ADI. (3) APRA may, by written notice given to an ADI, or a subsidiary of an ADI, determine that: (a) remuneration of a particular kind, of one or more accountable persons of the ADI or subsidiary, is variable remuneration; or (b) remuneration of a particular kind, of one or more accountable persons of the ADI or subsidiary, is not variable remuneration. A determination under this subsection may apply to all accountable persons of the ADI or subsidiary, or be limited to a particular accountable person or class of accountable persons of the ADI or subsidiary. (4) APRA may, by legislative instrument, determine that: (a) remuneration of a particular kind is variable remuneration; or (b) remuneration of a particular kind is not variable remuneration." (Government of Australia (2021), "Banking Act 1959," adopted on April 23, 1959, entered into force on January 14, 1960, Compilation No. 60 of December 8, 2021, registered on December 16, 2021, s.37EA; emphasis original).

section 37EB of the Banking Act 1959[76] specifies, and (iii) this period is at least the time that section 37EC of the Banking Act 1959[77] requires [133], (b) have a remuneration policy in operation which requires that, if the person has not complied with his or her accountability obligations that section 37CA of the Banking Act 1959[78] specifies, then the person's variable remuneration is to be lowered by an amount which correlates with the failure [134], (c) make sure that, if the remuneration policy requires the variable remuneration to be lowered because of that failure, the amount of this reduction is not paid to the individual concerned [135], and (d) take reasonable steps to ensure that, if variable remuneration may become due to an accountable person of one of the ADI's subsidiaries that is not itself an ADI, then the subsidiary observes points (a), (b) and (c) as if it were an ADI [136].

Notification Obligations

An ADI's notification obligations are to: (a) give to the APRA a document which complies with section 37FA of the Banking Act 1959[79] – an accountability statement – for each of its accountable persons, and make sure that the APRA is informed of any change to the accountability statement within the 'period'[80] [137], (b) provide the APRA with a document which conforms to section 37FB of the Banking Act 1959[81] – an accountability map, and ensure

[76] Subsection 37EB(1) of the Banking Act 1959 includes a table which determines, for four specified categories of 'accountable person', the percentage of his or her variable remuneration that is required to be deferred in accordance with subsections 37EB(2), 37EB(3) and 37EB(4) of the Banking Act 1959.

[77] This section of the Banking Act 1959 is titled 'Minimum period of deferral'; its first two subsections read: "(1) The required period under subparagraph 37E(1)(a)(iii) [of the Banking Act 1959 (text to the current footnote (i.e., fn 77))] in relation to variable remuneration of an accountable person of an ADI, or a subsidiary of an ADI, is: (a) 4 years; or (b) a shorter period approved by APRA under subsection (4) in relation to the variable remuneration; starting on the day after the day on which the decision was made granting the accountable person the variable remuneration. (2) However, if, at the end of the period under subsection (1), the ADI or subsidiary considers that the accountable person is likely to have failed to comply with his or her accountability obligations under section 37CA [of the Banking Act 1959 (fn 68 comprises subsection 37CA(1) of the Banking Act 2009)], that period is extended until the day [on which] the ADI or subsidiary determines whether he or she has failed to comply." (Government of Australia (2021), "Banking Act 1959," adopted on April 23, 1959, entered into force on January 14, 1960, Compilation No. 60 of December 8, 2021, registered on December 16, 2021, s.37EC(1)-(2)).

[78] Fn 68 sets out the first subsection of section 37CA of the Banking Act 1959.

[79] This section of the Banking Act 1959 is entitled 'Accountability statements', and states: "(1) For the purposes of paragraph 37F(1)(a) [of the Banking Act 1959 (text to fns 79-80)], an accountability statement of an ADI, or of a subsidiary of an ADI, for an accountable person of the ADI or subsidiary[,] must contain a comprehensive statement of: (a) the part or aspect of the ADI's or subsidiary's operations of which the accountable person has actual or effective responsibility for management or control; and (b) the responsibilities of the accountable person, including any responsibilities to which paragraph 37D(1)(a) [of the Banking Act 1959] applies or subsection 37D(3) [of the Banking Act 1959] applies, as the case requires; and (c) the matters determined by APRA under subsection (2). (2) APRA may, by legislative instrument, determine matters for the purposes of paragraph (1)(c)." (Government of Australia (2021), "Banking Act 1959," adopted on April 23, 1959, entered into force on January 14, 1960, Compilation No. 60 of December 8, 2021, registered on December 16, 2021, s.37FA).The text to fns 69-71 lays down paragraph 37D(1)(a) of the Banking Act 1959. The first sentence of fn 70 specifies subsection 37D(3) of the Banking Act 1959.

[80] The 'period' is either 14 days or such time as the APRA determines by legislative instrument (Government of Australia (2021), "Banking Act 1959," adopted on April 23, 1959, entered into force on January 14, 1960, Compilation No. 60 of December 8, 2021, registered on December 16, 2021, s.37F(2)-(3)).

[81] This section of the Banking Act 1959 is titled 'Accountability map', and declares: "(1) For the purposes of paragraph 37F(1)(b) [of the Banking Act 1959 (text to fns 81-82)], an accountability map of an ADI must contain the following information: (a) the names of all of the accountable persons of the ADI and its subsidiaries; (b) details of the reporting lines and lines of responsibility of those accountable persons; (c) sufficient information to identify an accountable person for each of the responsibilities to which paragraph 37(D)(1)(a) [of the Banking Act 1959] applies or subsection 37D(3) [of the Banking Act 1959] applies, as the case requires; (d) information of a kind determined by APRA under subsection (2). (2) APRA may, by legislative instrument, determine kinds

that the APRA is notified of any alteration to the accountability map within the 'period'[82] [138], (c) inform the APRA of an event within the 'period'[83] which section 37FC of the Banking Act 1959[84] lists [139], and (d) take reasonable steps to make certain that each of its subsidiaries which is not an ADI acts in accordance with points (a) and (c) as if the subsidiary were an ADI [140].

Foreign Exchange and Foreign Investment

The Governor-General may make regulations that are compatible with the Banking Act 1959 for purposes which concern foreign exchange or Australia's foreign exchange resources [141], the protection of the AUD or of Australian revenue or public credit [142], or foreign investment in Australia or contrariwise, or overseas control or ownership of property[85] in Australia or of Australian property abroad or conversely [143]. These regulations must make provision for, or relate to, either exchange rates [144] or at least one of seventeen other items[86]. Apart from a

---

of information for the purposes of paragraph (1)(d)." (Government of Australia (2021), "Banking Act 1959," adopted on April 23, 1959, entered into force on January 14, 1960, Compilation No. 60 of December 8, 2021, registered on December 16, 2021, s.37FB). The text to fns 69-71 sets out paragraph 37D(1)(a) of the Banking Act 1959. The first sentence of fn 70 comprises subsection 37D(3) of the Banking Act 1959.

[82] Fn 80 states the value of the 'period'.

[83] Fn 80 specifies the value of the 'period'.

[84] This section of the Banking Act 1959 is entitled 'Events for which APRA must be notified', and states: "For the purposes of paragraph 37F(1)(c) [of the Banking Act 1959 (text to fns 83-84)], the following events must be notified to APRA by an ADI: (a) a person ceasing to be an accountable person of the ADI or of a subsidiary of the ADI; (b) the dismissal or suspension of an accountable person by the ADI, or subsidiary of the ADI, because the person has failed to comply with his or her accountability obligations under [section] 37CA [of the Banking Act 1959]; (c) the reduction of the variable remuneration of a person by the ADI, or subsidiary of the ADI, because the person has failed to comply with his or her accountability obligations under section 37CA [of the Banking Act 1959]; (d) the ADI becoming aware of: (i) a breach by the ADI of its accountability obligations under section 37C [of the Banking Act 1959]; or (ii) a breach by an accountable person of the ADI, or of a subsidiary of the ADI, of his or her accountability obligations under section 37CA [of the Banking Act 1959]." (Government of Australia (2021), "Banking Act 1959," adopted on April 23, 1959, entered into force on January 14, 1960, Compilation No. 60 of December 8, 2021, registered on December 16, 2021, s.37FC). The text to fns 66-68 sets out section 37C of the Banking Act 1959. Fn 68 lays down the first subsection of section 37CA of the Banking Act 1959.

[85] The antepenultimate sentence of fn 86 defines the term '*property*' in section 39 of the Banking Act 1959.

[86] These items are: "the control or prohibition of the buying, borrowing, selling, lending or exchanging in Australia of, or other dealings in Australia with, foreign currency by or on behalf of any person, and of the buying, borrowing, selling, lending or exchanging outside Australia of, or other dealing outside Australia with, foreign currency by or on behalf of a person who is a resident; ... the control or prohibition of any transaction that has the effect of or involves a purchase, borrowing, sale, loan or exchange of, or that otherwise relates to, foreign currency, being a transaction that takes place[,] in whole or in part[,] in Australia or to which a person who is a resident is a party; ... the control or prohibition of the buying, borrowing, selling, lending or exchanging outside Australia of, or other dealing outside Australia with, Australian currency by or on behalf of any person, and of the buying, borrowing, selling, lending or exchanging in Australia, or other dealing in Australia with, Australian currency by or on behalf of a person who is not a resident; ... the control or prohibition of any transaction that has the effect of or involves a purchase, borrowing, sale, loan or exchange of, or that otherwise relates to, Australian currency, being a transaction that takes place[,] in whole or in part[,] outside Australia or to which a person who is not a resident is a party; ... the control or prohibition of the taking or sending out of Australia, and of the bringing or sending into Australia, of Australian currency or foreign currency; ... requiring any person who is a resident and who has power to sell, or to procure the sale of, any foreign currency, or any person (whether a resident or not) who has power to sell in Australia, or to procure the sale in Australia of, any foreign currency, to sell, or to procure the sale of, that currency as prescribed; ... requiring any person who is not a resident and who has power to sell, or to procure the sale of, any Australian currency, or any person (whether a resident or not) who has power to sell outside Australia, or to procure the sale outside Australia of, any Australian

situation in which the opposite intention arises, the regulations apply both within and outside Australia [145].

Gold

Part IV of the Banking Act 1959, which regulates transactions in gold in Australia, is only in operation either wholly or partially – and then ceases to be in force – on a proclamation of the Governor-General [146]. Under Part IV of the Act, gold can only be taken or sent out of Australia with the written consent of the RBA [147].

Part IV of the Banking Act 1959 determines that a person who possesses gold coins, the total value of the gold content of which exceeds the decreed amount, must deliver the excess

currency, to sell, or to procure the sale of, that currency as prescribed; … the control or prohibition of the taking, sending or transfer of any securities to a place outside Australia (including the transfer of securities from a register in Australia to a register outside Australia), and of the bringing, sending or transfer of any securities to Australia from a place outside Australia (including the transfer of securities from a register outside Australia to a register in Australia); … the control or prohibition of the buying, borrowing, selling, lending or exchanging of, or other dealing with, property that is in Australia, or of Australian securities that are outside Australia, by or on behalf of a person who is not a resident; … the control or prohibition of any transaction that has the effect of or involves a purchase, borrowing, sale, loan or exchange of, or that otherwise relates to, property that is in Australia, or of Australian securities that are outside Australia, being a transaction to which a person who is not a resident is a party; … the control or prohibition of the buying, borrowing, selling, lending or exchanging of, or other dealing with, property that is outside Australia, or of foreign securities that are in Australia, by or on behalf of a person who is a resident; … the control or prohibition of any transaction that has the effect of or involves a purchase, borrowing, sale, loan or exchange of, or that otherwise relates to, property that is outside Australia, or of foreign securities that are in Australia, being a transaction to which a person who is a resident is a party; … requiring any person who is a resident[,] and by whom moneys are payable to a person who is not a resident[,] to pay those moneys within such time as is fixed by[,] or under[,] the regulations; … the control or prohibition of the importation or exportation of goods; … the obtaining by the Reserve Bank [of Australia] (or by a person authorized by the Bank for the purpose) of information, and the examination by the Bank (or by a person authorized by the Bank for the purpose) of accounts, books, documents or other papers, for purposes related to the exercise of the Bank's powers or the performance of the Bank's functions under the regulations; … prescribing penalties not exceeding a fine of 1,000 penalty units, or imprisonment for a period not exceeding 5 years, for offences against the regulations made under this section; and … empowering a court to order the forfeiture, or the disposal in accordance with the directions of the Reserve Bank, of Australian currency, foreign currency, goods or other property in respect of which an offence against the regulations made under this section has been committed" (Government of Australia (2021), "Banking Act 1959," adopted on April 23, 1959, entered into force on January 14, 1960, Compilation No. 60 of December 8, 2021, registered on December 16, 2021, s.39(2)(b)-(r)). In section 39 of the Banking Act 1959, which is titled 'Power to make regulations' and in Part III of the Act – which is entitled 'Foreign exchange, foreign investment etc.', the following terms apply: "[The phrase '*Australian currency*'] includes notes, coins, postal notes, money orders, bills of exchange, promissory notes, drafts, letters of credit and travellers' cheques [that are] payable or expressed in Australian money, and also includes rights, and instruments of title, to Australian money. [The expression '*Australian securities*'] means securities or other property included in a class of securities or property [which is] specified in the regulations as Australian securities. [The phrase '*foreign currency*'] includes notes, coins, postal notes, money orders, bills of exchange, promissory notes, drafts, letters of credit and travellers' cheques [that are] payable or expressed otherwise than in Australian money, and also includes rights and instruments of title, to money other than Australian money. [The expression '*foreign securities*'] means securities or other property included in a class of securities or property [that is] specified in the regulations as foreign securities. [The word '*property*'] includes securities and rights under securities. [The word '*resident*'] means (a) a person, not being a body corporate, who is ordinarily resident in Australia; and (b) a body corporate which is incorporated in Australia. [The word '*securities*'] includes shares, stock, bonds, debentures, debenture-stock, treasury bills and notes, and units or sub-units of a unit trust, and also includes deposit receipts in respect of the deposit of securities and documents of title to securities." (Government of Australia (2021), "Banking Act 1959," adopted on April 23, 1959, entered into force on January 14, 1960, Compilation No. 60 of December 8, 2021, registered on December 16, 2021, s.39(8)).

gold to the RBA[87] – unless this excess is lawfully in that person's possession for the purpose of being worked for his or her profession or trade [148]. Subject to this Part (i.e., Part IV) of the Act, a person shall neither dispose of gold to a person other than the RBA or a person that the RBA has authorised in writing to buy gold, nor acquire gold from any person other than the RBA or a person so authorised[88] [149]. A person may neither work, nor use in manufacture, any gold which is not lawfully in that person's possession for the purpose of being worked or used in association with his or her profession or trade [150].

Part IV of the Banking Act 1959 does not apply to wrought gold[89] [151]. The RBA may, either totally or to the extent specified in its written instrument, exempt a person from the application of all, or any of the provisions, of this Part of the Act [152].

Control of Interest Rates

The RBA is empowered – with the approval of the Treasurer – to publish regulations that provide for, or relate to, the control of rates of interest payable to, or by, persons in the course of their banking business [153], and the control of rates of discount that are chargeable by those persons [154]. Such regulations may state that interest will not be payable with regard to a sum deposited in the course of banking business, which is repayable either on demand or beyond the end of a period that those regulations specify [155].

Powers of the APRA

Investigation and Examination

The APRA may appoint[90] a person to investigate, and report on, prudential issues concerning a body corporate that is an ADI, an authorised NOHC, or a subsidiary of either an ADI or an authorised NOHC[91] [156]. The body corporate must grant the investigator access to its

[87] The amount to be paid for this excess gold is "an amount determined in accordance with such price as is fixed and published by the Reserve Bank [of Australia] or, at the option of the person delivering the gold, such amount as is determined in an action for compensation against the Reserve Bank" (Government of Australia (2021), "Banking Act 1959," adopted on April 23, 1959, entered into force on January 14, 1960, Compilation No. 60 of December 8, 2021, registered on December 16, 2021, s.44).

[88] A person may purchase gold from the RBA or from a person that the RBA has authorised in writing to sell gold, and the RBA or a person so authorised may vend gold to a person, "for the purpose of its being worked or used by the purchaser in connexion with the person's profession or trade" (Government of Australia (2021), "Banking Act 1959," adopted on April 23, 1959, entered into force on January 14, 1960, Compilation No. 60 of December 8, 2021, registered on December 16, 2021, s.45(2)).

[89] '*Wrought gold*' is "gold and gold alloys which[,] on view[,] have apparently been worked or manufactured for professional or trade purposes ..." (Government of Australia (2021), "Banking Act 1959," adopted on April 23, 1959, entered into force on January 14, 1960, Compilation No. 60 of December 8, 2021, registered on December 16, 2021, s.47(2)).

[90] This appointment is to be in writing, and must particularise "the prudential matters that are to be the subject of the investigation and report" (Government of Australia (2021), "Banking Act 1959," adopted on April 23, 1959, entered into force on January 14, 1960, Compilation No. 60 of December 8, 2021, registered on December 16, 2021, s.61(1)).

[91] The APRA may appoint an investigator to inquire into, and report on, prudential issues "in relation to: (a) [text to the present footnote (i.e., fn 91)]; or (b) if a body corporate that is an ADI is a subsidiary of a foreign corporation (whether or not the ADI is itself a foreign ADI): (i) another subsidiary of the foreign corporation (other than a body mentioned in paragraph (a)[)], being a subsidiary that is incorporated in Australia; or (ii) the Australian

documents, books and accounts, and must give him or her such information and facilities as (s)he requires to carry out the investigation and construct the report[92] [157]. If an investigator reasonably believes that a person has control or custody of any documents, books or accounts which are pertinent to his or her investigation, then (s)he may give written notice to that person, requiring production of any or all of the documents, books or accounts to the investigator[93] [158]. If an investigator reasonably believes or suspects that a person – the examinee – is able to provide information that is relevant to the investigation, then (s)he may give written notice to the examinee requiring the latter to give him or her all reasonable assistance concerning the investigation [159], and to appear before him or her for examination [160]. The investigator may question the examinee on oath or affirmation that the statements which the latter will make will be true [161], require the examinee to answer a question that is put to him or her at the examination and which is pertinent to an issue that the former is either investigating or to investigate [162], and make a sound, or audiovisual, recording of all, or any part, of the examination [163]. The investigator must effectuate a written record – including a transcript of a recording, which is to comprise statements that are made at the examination [164], and must a give a free copy of this record to the examinee – subject to any conditions that the former imposes [165]. The examinee, and any other person who has control, possession or custody of that copy – or a copy of it – must observe these conditions[94] [166].

Requisition of Information

The APRA may require an ADI, an authorised NOHC, or a subsidiary of an ADI or of an authorised NOHC, to give information to it regarding either the instructee or a member of a pertinent group of bodies corporate of which that ADI, authorised NOHC or subsidiary is a member[95] [167]. Furthermore, the APRA may require any other person who conducts any

---

operations of another subsidiary of the foreign corporation (other than a body mentioned in paragraph (a)[)], being a subsidiary that is not incorporated in Australia and [which] carries on business in Australia; if it is satisfied that such a report is necessary" (Government of Australia (2021), "Banking Act 1959," adopted on April 23, 1959, entered into force on January 14, 1960, Compilation No. 60 of December 8, 2021, registered on December 16, 2021, s.61(1)(b)).

[92] If the body corporate fails to do either of these things, then it commits an offence (Government of Australia (2021), "Banking Act 1959," adopted on April 23, 1959, entered into force on January 14, 1960, Compilation No. 60 of December 8, 2021, registered on December 16, 2021, s.61(3)).

[93] If the person does not produce to the investigator the documents, books or accounts that the latter requires, then the former commits an offence (Government of Australia (2021), "Banking Act 1959," adopted on April 23, 1959, entered into force on January 14, 1960, Compilation No. 60 of December 8, 2021, registered on December 16, 2021, s.61A(2)). A person also commits an offence, "if: (a) the person knows that an investigator is investigating, or is about to investigate, a matter; and (b) the person: (i) conceals, destroys, mutilates or alters a book, account or document relating to the matter; or (ii) if a book, account or document relating to the matter is in a particular State or Territory – takes or sends the book, account or document out of that State or Territory[,] or out of Australia; and (c) the person intended that the investigation or proposed investigation would be delayed or obstructed as a result of that conduct" (Government of Australia (2021), "Banking Act 1959," adopted on April 23, 1959, entered into force on January 14, 1960, Compilation No. 60 of December 8, 2021, registered on December 16, 2021, s.61B).

[94] If a person does not act in accordance with any requirement concerning the investigator's examination, then (s)he commits an offence (Government of Australia (2021), "Banking Act 1959," adopted on April 23, 1959, entered into force on January 14, 1960, Compilation No. 60 of December 8, 2021, registered on December 16, 2021, s.61G).

[95] The APRA may also require information to be furnished thus: "(a) … ; (b) … ; (c) … ; (ca) if an ADI is a subsidiary of a foreign corporation (whether or not the ADI is itself a foreign ADI): (i) another subsidiary of the foreign corporation (other than a body mentioned in paragraph (a), (b) or (c) [text to the current footnote (i.e., fn 95))] that is incorporated in Australia may be required to give APRA information in respect of the subsidiary; or (ii) another subsidiary of the foreign corporation (other than a body mentioned in paragraph (a), (b) or (c) [text to

banking business in Australia to supply it with information relating to this banking business [168]. The requirement to provide information to the APRA may include an instruction to produce documents, books or accounts[96] [169], but must not call for information, documents, books or accounts to be furnished in respect of the affairs of any individual customer of the ADI – unless these concern prudential matters which are connected with either the ADI or any member of a relevant group of bodies corporate of which that ADI is a member [170].

Other Provisions of the Banking Act 1959

Powers of the Federal Court of Australia

1. To direct regulated persons to comply with the Banking Act 1959. If an ADI, an authorised NOHC, or a subsidiary of an ADI or of an authorised NOHC, is convicted of an offence against the Banking Act 1959 or the regulations, then the Full Court of the Federal Court of Australia[97] may, upon application of the Attorney-General, direct the ADI, authorised NOHC or subsidiary to observe the provisions of the Act or regulations with which the ADI, authorised NOHC or subsidiary has not complied [171]. In default of this observance within the specified period, the Federal Court of Australia may authorise the APRA to take control of, and to continue, the business of the ADI, authorised NOHC or subsidiary [172]. If the APRA has assumed control of this business, then it is to remain in control of, and will continue, the business, until such time as the Federal Court of Australia is satisfied that the APRA need not remain in control and permits it to cease [173]. *2. Injunctions and damages.* In specified circumstances of legal or regulatory breach[98], the Federal Court of Australia may grant an injunction that restrains the person from participating in the conduct – and which may require that person to perform a specified act[99] [174]. If a person has refused or omitted, is refusing or omitting, or is proposing to refuse or omit, to carry out an act that (s)he is required to do by a provision of the Banking Act 1959, the regulations, the prudential standards or the non-ADI lender rules, a condition

---

the present footnote (i.e., fn 95)]) that is not incorporated in Australia and [which] carries on business in Australia may be required to give APRA information in respect of its Australian operations" (Government of Australia (2021), "Banking Act 1959," adopted on April 23, 1959, entered into force on January 14, 1960, Compilation No. 60 of December 8, 2021, registered on December 16, 2021, s.62(1)(ca)).

[96] If the APRA requires a person to provide information, documents, books or accounts and the latter does not observe this requirement, then the person commits an indictable offence (Government of Australia (2021), "Banking Act 1959," adopted on April 23, 1959, entered into force on January 14, 1960, Compilation No. 60 of December 8, 2021, registered on December 16, 2021, s.62(1A)-(1B)).

[97] The subsection titled 'Courts', which is in the section above entitled 'An Introduction to the Legal System of Australia', includes information about the Full Court of the Federal Court of Australia.

[98] These circumstances comprise a situation in which "a person has engaged, is engaging or is proposing to engage, in conduct that constituted, constitutes or would constitute: (a) a contravention of: (i) a provision of this Act [(i.e., the Banking Act 1959)], the regulations, the prudential standards or the non-ADI lender rules; or (ii) a condition imposed or specified under this Act; or (iii) a direction by APRA under this Act; or (b) attempting to contravene the provision, condition or direction; or (c) aiding, abetting, counselling or procuring a person to contravene the provision, condition or direction; or (d) inducing or attempting to induce ... a person to contravene the provision, condition or direction; or (e) being in any way, directly or indirectly, knowingly concerned in, or party to, the contravention by a person of the provision, condition or direction; or (f) conspiring with others to contravene the provision, condition or direction" (Government of Australia (2021), "Banking Act 1959," adopted on April 23, 1959, entered into force on January 14, 1960, Compilation No. 60 of December 8, 2021, registered on December 16, 2021, s.65A(1)).

[99] The Court may grant an interim injunction, pending determination of this application (Government of Australia (2021), "Banking Act 1959," adopted on April 23, 1959, entered into force on January 14, 1960, Compilation No. 60 of December 8, 2021, registered on December 16, 2021, s.65A(8)).

specified or imposed under the Act, or a direction that the APRA has given in accordance with the Act, then the Court may grant an injunction which requires this person to perform that Act [175]. If an application for an injunction under either of the above provisions has been made, then the Court may grant an injunction by consent of all the parties to the proceedings – even if it is not satisfied that the relevant rule applies [176]. The Court may vary or discharge an injunction that it has granted in accordance with the above provisions [177]. If the Court has power to grant an injunction restraining a person from participating in certain conduct or requiring a person to perform a particular act, then the Court may – either in addition to, or instead of, the grant of the injunction, order this person to pay damages to any other person [178].

Restriction of on Establishment or Maintenance of Representative Offices of Foreign Banks

A person, apart from an ADI, commits an offence, if the person conducts banking business in an overseas jurisdiction but does not do so in Australia and founds or maintains in Australia a representative office totally or partly in association with the continuation of that business in the foreign country, the APRA did not provide its written consent to the establishment or maintenance of this representative office, and there is no determination in effect under section 11 of the Banking Act 1959[100] that the current provision does not apply to the person [179].

Conduct of Directors, Employees and Agents

In situations in which it is necessary to establish, for the purposes of the Banking Act 1959 or the regulations, the state of mind of a person aside from a body corporate in connection with particular conduct, it is enough to show that the behaviour was engaged in by an employee or agent of that person within the bounds of his or her actual or apparent authority, and that the employee possessed the state of mind [180]. Any conduct that is engaged in on behalf of a person other than a body corporate by an employee or agent of that person within the purview of his or her actual or apparent authority shall be considered, for the purposes of the Banking Act 1959 and the regulations, to have also been participated in by the first-mentioned person – unless that person establishes that (s)he took reasonable precautions and exercised due diligence in order to eschew the conduct [181].

Protection from Liability

A person is not liable to any person regarding anything done or not done in good faith and without negligence, in the performance or exercise – or apparent performance or exercise – of functions, duties or powers under the Banking Act 1959 [182].

---

[100] Section 11 of the Banking Act 1959 is titled 'APRA may determine that provisions of this Act do not apply'; its first two subsections state: "(1) APRA may, in writing, determine that any or all of the following provisions of this Act do not apply to a person[,] while the determination is in force: (a) a provision of Division 1, 1AA or 1A of Part II (other than section 11A, 11B or 11C); (b) section 66; (c) section 66A; (d) section 67; (e) section 69. (2) The determination: (a) may be expressed to apply to a particular person or to a class of persons; and (b) may specify the period during which the determination is in force; and (c) may be subject to specified conditions." (Government of Australia (2021), "Banking Act 1959," adopted on April 23, 1959, entered into force on January 14, 1960, Compilation No. 60 of December 8, 2021, registered on December 16, 2021, s.11(1)-(2)). The present provision (i.e., the text to the current footnote (fn 100)) is subsection 67(1) of the Banking Act 1959, which falls within section 11(1)(d) of the Act.

Precedence over Any Conflicting Provisions of the Corporations Act 2001
Notwithstanding any provision of the Corporations Act 2001, the Banking Act 1959 has effect [183].

Comment

The Banking Act 1959 contains items that one would expect to find there, such as the authorisation framework for ADIs and the powers of investigation and examination of the APRA. It also includes more surprising provisions, such as that giving the Banking Act 1959 precedence over any conflicting provisions of the Corporations Act 2001 – as ordinarily one would expect there to be no significant issues of legislative conflict between provisions currently in force within a jurisdiction. The rules relating to the powers of the Federal Court of Australia are particularly welcome, as they explain to users of the Act what the legal framework for the business of banking is beyond the supervision of the APRA – and describing the remedies of the Court (i.e., injunctions and damages) and the circumstances under which the APRA may refer an alleged infraction in order to attempt to secure one of these means of legal redress shows legislative clarity and frankness.

Conclusion

This chapter introduces the legal system of Australia, outlines the regulatory framework for banks in Australia, and sets out provisions from the Banking Act 1959, concentrating in particular on banking business and ADIs. The next chapter explores the law of banking in Canada.

Chapter 2

Canada

Abstract

Although Canada was a founding Member State of the United Nations, it did not become wholly independent from the United Kingdom (UK) until 1982; from thenceforth, no Act of the UK Parliament would apply in Canada. The Canadian constitution empowers both its parliament and the provincial and territorial legislatures to enact laws. The civil law governs matters of private law in the Province of Quebec, whilst the common law applies in the other Canadian provinces. The Canadian constitution is the highest source of law; it lists areas of the law that are within the exclusive legislative authority of the federal parliament, and those which are assigned solely to the provincial and territorial legislatures. The law of banking is within the purview of the federal legislature. In spheres in which statute has not defined the law, the common law applies in all provincial and territorial jurisdictions bar Quebec – which operates its own civil code that is based upon its constitutional jurisdiction over civil and property rights. The Supreme Court of Canada may accept appeals from the Federal Court of Appeal and the provincial and territorial Courts of Appeal; its judgments are final. Part I of the Constitution Act 1982 consists solely of the Canadian Charter of Rights and Freedoms, which sets out fundamental freedoms, democratic rights, mobility rights, legal rights, official languages of Canada, and minority language educational rights; the Charter includes a rule that empowers the Parliament of Canada or a provincial legislature to temporarily disapply the fundamental freedoms and legal rights within the Charter from an Act that it has passed or from a provision of it. The Bank of Canada Act precisely states the powers that Canada's central bank is entitled to exercise. The legislation for the financial institutions of Canada is reviewed every five years, or less. A bank may only carry out business, once the Superintendent of Financial Institutions has, by order, approved the commencement and undertaking of business by the bank. Subject to the Bank Act, a bank may neither engage in, nor conduct, any business, other than that of banking and business which normally pertains to it. On application by a foreign bank, the Minister of Finance may make an order that permits it to establish a branch in Canada to conduct business there. On application by an authorized foreign bank, the Superintendent of Financial Institutions may make an order that approves the initiation of, and engagement in, business in Canada by this bank. Every person who, without reasonable cause, infracts any provision of the Bank Act or the regulations, has committed an offence. Whilst different elements of the Bank Act fit together well, it contains idiosyncrasies. The Canada Deposit Insurance Corporation Act specifies clearly how deposit insurance works for depositors of funds in Canadian banks. The Canadian Payments Act is a clear, straightforward legislative instrument. The Retail Payment Activities Act does not apply to a payment service provider that performs retail payment activities, if it is a bank or an authorized foreign bank.

Keywords: bank, court, deposit, federal, foreign, Minister, rights, Superintendent

Introduction

The legal system of Canada is introduced. The law of banking falls within the ambit of the federal legislative process[101]. Thus, the Bank of Canada Act is visited, followed by the Bank Act – which contains the preponderance of Canada's primary banking legislation. Subsequent sections scan the Canada Deposit Insurance Corporation Act, the Canadian Payments Act and the Retail Payment Activities Act, respectively. Finally, there are comments and a conclusion.

An Introduction to the Legal System of Canada

Essentials

In 1867, the Parliament of the UK passed the British North America Act, which separated the Provinces of Upper Canada and Lower Canada within the Province of Canada – renaming these the Provinces of Ontario and Quebec, respectively [184], and united the Provinces of Canada, New Brunswick and Nova Scotia into one Dominion of Canada – comprising New Brunswick, Nova Scotia, Ontario and Quebec [185]. Although Canada was a founding Member State of the United Nations – signing its Charter on 26th June 1945 and depositing its instrument of ratification with the Government of the USA on 9th November 1945 [186, 187], it did not become fully independent from the UK until 1982 – when the Canada Act 1982 passed by the Parliament of the UK set out in its Schedule B the Constitution Act 1982 of Canada [188] and stated the following.

> No Act of the Parliament of the United Kingdom passed after the *Constitution Act, 1982*[102] comes into force[103] shall extend to Canada as part of its law [189].

Canada operates a federal system – the Canadian constitution empowers both its parliament and the provincial and territorial legislatures to enact laws [190]. Canada is a bijural state – issues of private law in its Province of Quebec are governed by the civil law, whilst the common law applies in the other Canadian provinces [191].

The Parliamentary Legislative Process

This procedure is similar to its equivalent in Australia[104]. The following passage describes it.

---

[101] Section 91 of the Constitution Act 1875 places the law of banking within the sole legislative authority of the Parliament of Canada (sentence immediately-following the text to fn 105).

[102] Emphasis original.

[103] On 17th April 1982, Her Majesty Queen Elizabeth II signed the Proclamation of the Constitution Act, which brought into effect the Constitution Act 1982 (Government of Canada (2022), "Library and Archives Canada: Proclamation of the Constitution Act, 1982," accessed May 17, 2022, <https://www.bac-lac.gc.ca/eng/discover/politics-government/proclamation-constitution-act-1982/Pages/proclamation-constitution-act-1982.aspx>).

[104] The section entitled 'The Parliamentary Legislative Process', in Chapter 1, describes how a legislative proposal becomes an Act of Parliament in Australia – which is similar at federal and state/territorial levels.

The federal and provincial legislatures enact laws in the form of statutes. The executive can also enact laws in the form of regulations without resort to the legislative process, provided [that] the authority to make regulations has been granted by statute. Statutes are proposed in the legislatures as "bills." ... The initial proposal of a bill to the legislative chamber is known as the first reading. ... After the first reading, the legislative chamber debates and scrutinises the bill in a process called the second reading. Following debate, the chamber votes on the bill. If the bill carries, the chamber then refers the bill to a committee of legislative members for further scrutiny and possible revision. After the committee has completed its review, the chamber votes on whether the bill can proceed to the third reading, in which the chamber considers the bill in its final form. At the federal level, if a bill passes the third reading in one chamber (usually the House of Commons), then it must also be introduced in the other chamber (usually the Senate), where the bill must again receive, first, second and third readings before it can proceed to enactment. ... A federal bill can proceed to enactment[,] once it has passed the third reading in both chambers. A provincial bill can proceed to enactment immediately after the initial third reading, as each province has only one legislative chamber. ... A bill that has passed the third reading becomes enacted as a statute once it receives Royal Assent by the Governor General (for federal legislation) or the Lieutenant Governor (for provincial legislation). In keeping with their ceremonial roles, the Governor General and Lieutenant Governors will abide by the will of the legislature in granting Royal Assent to legislation [192].

Sources of Law

Whilst the Canadian constitution is the highest source of law, this constitution defines the other sources of law in accordance with subject matter and jurisdiction [192]. Thus, section 91 of the Constitution Act 1867[105] lists areas of the law that are within "the exclusive legislative Authority of the Parliament of Canada" [193]. These include, amongst other things: the regulation of commerce and trade [194], the raising of money by any system or mode of taxation [195], the borrowing of money upon the public credit [196], currency and coinage [197], the incorporation of banks, banking, and the issuance of paper money [198], savings banks [199], promissory notes and bills of exchange [200], interest [201], legal tender [202], insolvency and bankruptcy [203], the criminal law – including criminal procedure but excluding the constitution of courts of criminal jurisdiction [204], and "Such Classes of Subjects as are expressly excepted in the Enumeration of the Classes of Subjects by this Act assigned exclusively to the Legislatures of the Provinces" [205]. Section 92 of the Constitution Act 1867 states that, "[i]n each Province[,] the Legislature may exclusively make Laws in relation to Matters coming within the Classes of Subjects next hereinafter enumerated" [206], which include – amongst other things: "Direct Taxation within the Province in order to [secure]

[105] In 1982, Canada renamed the British North America Act the 'Constitution Act 1867' (Encyclopedia Britannica (2022), "British North America Act: United Kingdom [1867]," accessed May 18, 2022, <https://www.britannica.com/event/British-North-America-Act>). Item 1(1) of the Schedule to the Constitution Act 1982 states: "Section 1 [of the British North America Act 1867] is repealed and the following substituted therefor: "1 This Act may be cited as the *Constitution Act, 1867*." (Government of the United Kingdom of Great Britain and Northern Ireland/Government of Canada (2021), "Constitution Act 1982," adopted on March 29th, 1982, entered into force on April 17th, 1982, consolidated to January 1st, 2021, Schedule, Item 1(1); emphasis original). The first sentence of the subsection entitled 'Essentials', above in the current section – which is titled 'An Introduction to the Legal System of Canada', presents the British North America Act.

the raising of a Revenue for Provincial Purposes" [207], "The borrowing of Money on the sole Credit of the Province" [208], "... Licenses in order to [secure] the raising of a Revenue for Provincial, Local, or Municipal Purposes" [209], "The Incorporation of Companies with Provincial Objects" [210], "The Administration of Justice in the Province, including the Constitution, Maintenance and Organization of Provincial Courts, both of Civil and of Criminal Jurisdiction, and including Procedure in Civil Matters in those Courts" [211], and "Generally all Matters of a merely local or private nature in the Province" [212]. In fields in which statute has not defined the law, the common law applies in all provincial and territorial jurisdictions save Quebec – which operates its own civil code that is grounded in its constitutional jurisdiction over civil and property rights [192].

Courts

The federal court system includes Federal Courts and the Tax Court of Canada, from which an appeal may lie to the Federal Court of Appeal [192, 213]. Spheres of law in which the Federal Courts specialize include civil cases that concern terrorism, federal-provincial disputes, intellectual property and maritime law; the Tax Court of Canada hears appeals from assessments for taxation [214].

The provincial and territorial court system includes Courts, Superior Courts, and specialist courts – such as family courts, small claims courts and youth courts[106] [215]. Superior Courts hear the most serious civil and criminal cases[107], and are empowered to review the decisions of the (lower) Courts [216]. Superior Courts are divided into trial-level and appeal-level courts – or Courts of Appeal – which hear appeals from the trial-level courts [216].

The Supreme Court of Canada may accept[108] appeals from the Federal Court of Appeal and the provincial and territorial Courts of Appeal [214]. Judgments of the Supreme Court of Canada are final [214]. This court also determines significant issues regarding the Constitution of Canada, as well as complex parts of public or private law [214]. The Government of Canada may ask the Supreme Court of Canada for its opinion on major issues of law [214].

Tribunals

Although administrative tribunals are outside the court system, they play a crucial role in settling disputes in Canadian society [216]. Decisions of these tribunals may be reviewed in court, in order to make certain that they are acting fairly and in accordance with the law [216].

[106] All provinces and territories have two levels of trial court, bar Nunavut – which has one (Government of Canada (2015), Department of Justice: Canada's System of Justice, Cat. No J2-32/2015E-PDF. Ottawa: Her Majesty the Queen in Right of Canada, 22).

[107] Superior Courts may have specialized divisions – for instance, the Ontario Superior Court of Justice has branches for bankruptcy, commercial law, estates and family law issues (Somerville, C., and Sun, W. (2021), "Legal systems in Canada: overview," published July 1, 2021, accessed May 19, 2022, <https://uk.practicallaw.thomsonreuters.com/w-013-0460?transitionType=Default&contextData=(sc.Default)&firstPage=true>).

[108] The Supreme Court of Canada tends not to agree to hear appeals, unless it considers these to be of national significance (Somerville, C., and Sun, W. (2021), "Legal systems in Canada: overview," published July 1, 2021, accessed May 19, 2022, <https://uk.practicallaw.thomsonreuters.com/w-013-0460?transitionType=Default&contextData=(sc.Default)&firstPage=true>).

The Constitution of Canada

The Constitution of Canada comprises the Canada Act 1982 – including the Constitution Act 1982 [217], the Acts[109] and Orders[110] to which the Schedule to the Constitution Act 1982 refers [218], and amendments to any of these Acts and orders [219]. The Constitution Act 1982 is clear about the legal status of this Constitution.

> The Constitution of Canada is the supreme law of Canada, and any law that is inconsistent with the provisions of the Constitution is, to the extent of the inconsistency, of no force or effect [220].

The Canadian Charter of Rights and Freedoms

Part I of the Constitution Act 1982 consists solely of the Canadian Charter of Rights and Freedoms – and may be cited as such [221]. The Charter "guarantees the rights and freedoms set out in it[,] subject only to such reasonable limits prescribed by law as can be demonstrably justified in a free and democratic society"[111] [222].

The Canadian Charter of Rights and Freedoms only applies to decisions, act and omissions of the Parliament and Government of Canada, and of the legislature and government of each province.

> This Charter applies **(a)** to the Parliament and government of Canada in respect of all matters within the authority of Parliament[,] including all matters relating to the Yukon Territory and Northwest Territories; and **(b)** to the legislature and government of each province in respect of all matters within the authority of the legislature of each province[112] [223].

The Parliament of Canada may proclaim in an Act of Parliament – or the legislature of a province may declare in an Act of this legislature – that the Act, or a provision thereof, will

[109] These Acts are the Constitution Act 1867 (fn 105), the Manitoba Act 1870, the Constitution Act 1871, the Parliament of Canada Act 1875, the Constitution Act 1886, the Canada (Ontario Boundary) Act 1889, the Alberta Act, the Saskatchewan Act, the Constitution Act 1907, the Constitution Act 1915, the Constitution Act 1930, the Statute of Westminster 1931, the Constitution Act 1940, the Newfoundland Act, the Constitution Act 1960, the Constitution Act 1964, the Constitution Act 1965, the Constitution Act 1974, the Constitution Act (No. 1) 1975, and the Constitution Act (No. 2) 1975 (Government of the United Kingdom of Great Britain and Northern Ireland/Government of Canada (2021), "Constitution Act 1982," adopted on March 29th, 1982, entered into force on April 17th, 1982, consolidated to January 1st, 2021, Schedule, Items 1(1), 2(1), 5, 7, 9-10, 12-18, 21 and 25-30).

[110] These Orders are the Rupert's Land and North-Western Territory Order, the British Columbia Terms of Union, the Prince Edward Island Terms of Union, and the Adjacent Territories Order (Government of the United Kingdom of Great Britain and Northern Ireland/Government of Canada (2021), "Constitution Act 1982," adopted on March 29th, 1982, entered into force on April 17th, 1982, consolidated to January 1st, 2021, Schedule, Items 3-4, 6 and 8).

[111] Section 7 of the Constitution Act 1982 provides an example of these limits: "Everyone has the right to life, liberty and security of the person[,] and the right not to be deprived thereof *except in accordance with the principles of fundamental justice*." (Government of the United Kingdom of Great Britain and Northern Ireland/Government of Canada (2021), "Constitution Act 1982," adopted on March 29th, 1982, entered into force on April 17th, 1982, consolidated to January 1st, 2021, s.7; emphasis added).

[112] The bold emphasis for the letters '(a)' and (b)' is present in the original text.

operate despite a rule which sections 2[113], 7[114], 8[115], 9[116], 10[117], 11[118], 12[119], 13[120], 14[121] or 15[122] of the Canadian Charter of Rights and Freedoms contains[123] [224]. This proclamation becomes

---

113 Section 2 of the Canadian Charter of Rights and Freedoms – which is also section 2 of the Constitution Act 1982 – is entitled 'Fundamental freedoms', and states: "Everyone has the following fundamental freedoms: **(a)** freedom of conscience and religion; **(b)** freedom of thought, belief, opinion and expression, including freedom of the press and other media of communication; **(c)** freedom of peaceful assembly; and **(d)** freedom of association." (Government of the United Kingdom of Great Britain and Northern Ireland/Government of Canada (2021), "Constitution Act 1982," adopted on March 29th, 1982, entered into force on April 17th, 1982, consolidated to January 1st, 2021, s.2; emphasis original).

114 Fn 111 sets out section 7 of the Canadian Charter of Rights and Freedoms – which is also section 7 of the Constitution Act 1982, and which is titled 'Life, liberty and security of person'.

115 Section 8 of the Canadian Charter of Rights and Freedoms – which is also section 8 of the Constitution Act 1982 – is entitled 'Search or seizure', and specifies: "Everyone has the right to be secure against unreasonable search or seizure." (Government of the United Kingdom of Great Britain and Northern Ireland/Government of Canada (2021), "Constitution Act 1982," adopted on March 29th, 1982, entered into force on April 17th, 1982, consolidated to January 1st, 2021, s.8).

116 Section 9 of the Canadian Charter of Rights and Freedoms – which is also section 9 of the Constitution Act 1982 – is titled 'Detention or imprisonment', and reads: "Everyone has the right not to be arbitrarily detained or imprisoned." (Government of the United Kingdom of Great Britain and Northern Ireland/Government of Canada (2021), "Constitution Act 1982," adopted on March 29th, 1982, entered into force on April 17th, 1982, consolidated to January 1st, 2021, s.9).

117 Section 10 of the Canadian Charter of Rights and Freedoms – which is also section 10 of the Constitution Act 1982 – is entitled 'Arrest or detention', and states: "Everyone has a right on arrest or detention **(a)** to be informed promptly of the reasons therefor; **(b)** to retain and instruct counsel without delay and to be informed of that right; and **(c)** to have the validity of the detention determined by way of *habeas corpus* and to be released if the detention is not lawful." (Government of the United Kingdom of Great Britain and Northern Ireland/Government of Canada (2021), "Constitution Act 1982," adopted on March 29th, 1982, entered into force on April 17th, 1982, consolidated to January 1st, 2021, s.10; emphasis original).

118 Section 11 of the Canadian Charter of Rights and Freedoms – which is also section 11 of the Constitution Act 1982 – is titled 'Proceedings in criminal and penal matters', and specifies: "Any person charged with an offence has the right **(a)** to be informed without unreasonable delay of the specific offence; **(b)** to be tried within a reasonable time; **(c)** not to be compelled to be a witness in proceedings against that person in respect of the offence; **(d)** to be presumed innocent until proven guilty according to law in a fair and public hearing by an independent and impartial tribunal; **(e)** not to be denied reasonable bail without just cause; **(f)** … to the benefit of trial by jury [subject to one exception,] where the maximum punishment for the offence is imprisonment for five years or a more severe punishment; **(g)** not to be found guilty on account of any act or omission[,] unless, at the time of the act or omission, it constituted an offence under Canadian or international law or was criminal according to the general principles of law recognized by the community of nations; **(h)** if finally acquitted of the offence, not to be tried for it again[,] and, if finally found guilty and punished for the offence, not to be tried or punished for it again; and **(i)** if found guilty of the offence[,] and if the punishment for the offence has been varied between the time of commission and the time of sentencing, to the benefit of the lesser punishment." (Government of the United Kingdom of Great Britain and Northern Ireland/Government of Canada (2021), "Constitution Act 1982," adopted on March 29th, 1982, entered into force on April 17th, 1982, consolidated to January 1st, 2021, s.11; emphasis original).

119 Section 12 of the Canadian Charter of Rights and Freedoms – which is also section 12 of the Constitution Act 1982 – is entitled 'Treatment or punishment', and reads: "Everyone has the right not to be subjected to any cruel and unusual treatment or punishment." (Government of the United Kingdom of Great Britain and Northern Ireland/Government of Canada (2021), "Constitution Act 1982," adopted on March 29th, 1982, entered into force on April 17th, 1982, consolidated to January 1st, 2021, s.12).

120 Section 13 of the Canadian Charter of Rights and Freedoms – which is also section 13 of the Constitution Act 1982 – is titled 'Self-crimination', and states: "A witness who testifies in any proceedings has the right not to have any incriminating evidence so given used to incriminate that witness in any other proceedings, except in a prosecution for perjury or for the giving of contradictory evidence." (Government of the United Kingdom of Great Britain and Northern Ireland/Government of Canada (2021), "Constitution Act 1982," adopted on March 29th, 1982, entered into force on April 17th, 1982, consolidated to January 1st, 2021, s.13).

121 Section 14 of the Canadian Charter of Rights and Freedoms – which is also section 14 of the Constitution Act 1982 – is entitled 'Interpreter', and specifies: "A party or witness in any proceedings who does not understand or speak the language in which the proceedings are conducted[,] or who is deaf[,] has the right to the assistance of an interpreter." (Government of the United Kingdom of Great Britain and Northern Ireland/Government of

obsolete five years after it comes into effect – or such earlier date as the declaration prescribes [225]. The Parliament of Canada, or the legislature of a province, may re-enact the proclamation [226]. The five-year limit of the declaration's effectiveness applies to this re-enactment [227]. The Charter sets out the following categories of rights and freedoms: fundamental freedoms[124], democratic rights[125], mobility rights[126], legal rights[127], official languages of Canada[128], and minority language educational rights[129].

Comment

Whilst the Dominion of Canada was set up in 1867 "with a Constitution similar in Principle to that of the United Kingdom" [228], the independent state of Canada has – out of necessity – moved away from the UK constitutional model except in fundamental elements such as the British monarch as Head of State, a bicameral Parliament of Canada and a legal system predominated by the common law. There are significant differences between the Canadian constitutional and legal system and that of the UK. These include Canada being a federation and the UK being an unconventional model with various degrees of devolution to the parliaments and courts of Northern Ireland, Scotland and Wales based on historical factors as well as contemporary preferences (for instance Scots law having developed separately from

---

Canada (2021), "Constitution Act 1982," adopted on March 29th, 1982, entered into force on April 17th, 1982, consolidated to January 1st, 2021, s.14).

[122] Section 15 of the Canadian Charter of Rights and Freedoms – which is also section 15 of the Constitution Act 1982 – comprises two subsections, the first of which is titled 'Equality before and under law and equal protection and benefit of law', and the second of which is entitled 'Affirmative action programs'; these read: "**(1)** Every individual is equal before and under the law[,] and has the right to the equal protection and equal benefit of the law without discrimination and, in particular, without discrimination based on race, national or ethnic origin, colour, religion, sex, age[,] or mental or physical disability. ... **(2)** Subsection (1) does not preclude any law, program or activity that has its object the amelioration of conditions of disadvantaged individuals or groups[,] including those that are disadvantaged because of race, national or ethnic origin, colour, religion, sex, age[,] or mental or physical disability." (Government of the United Kingdom of Great Britain and Northern Ireland/Government of Canada (2021), "Constitution Act 1982," adopted on March 29th, 1982, entered into force on April 17th, 1982, consolidated to January 1st, 2021, s.15; emphasis original).

[123] The Constitution Act 1982 declares the following in respect of the operation of this exception: "An Act or a provision of an Act in respect of which a declaration made under this section [(i.e., section 33 of the Constitution Act 1982)] is in effect[,] shall have such operation as it would have but for the provision of this Charter referred to in the declaration." (Government of the United Kingdom of Great Britain and Northern Ireland/Government of Canada (2021), "Constitution Act 1982," adopted on March 29th, 1982, entered into force on April 17th, 1982, consolidated to January 1st, 2021, s.33(2)).

[124] Section 2 of the Canadian Charter of Rights and Freedoms sets down its fundamental freedoms. Fn 113 specifies section 2 of the Charter.

[125] Sections 3-5 of the Canadian Charter of Rights and Freedoms comprise its democratic rights.

[126] Section 6 of the Canadian Charter of Rights and Freedoms lays down its mobility rights.

[127] Sections 7-15 of the Canadian Charter of Rights and Freedoms contain its legal rights. Fns 111 states section 7 of the Charter. Fns 115-122 set out sections 8-15 of the Charter, respectively.

[128] Subsection 16(1) of the Canadian Charter of Rights and Freedoms – which is also subsection 16(1) of the Constitution Act 1982 – is titled 'Official languages of Canada, and states: "English and French are the official languages of Canada[,] and have equality of status and equal rights and privileges as to their use in all institutions of the Parliament and government of Canada." (Government of the United Kingdom of Great Britain and Northern Ireland/Government of Canada (2021), "Constitution Act 1982," adopted on March 29th, 1982, entered into force on April 17th, 1982, consolidated to January 1st, 2021, s.16(1)). Sections 16(2)-(3), 16.1 and 17-22 of the Canadian Charter of Rights and Freedoms contain details as to the rights that the Charter grants concerning these languages.

[129] Section 23 of the Canadian Charter of Rights and Freedoms consists of its minority language educational rights.

English and Welsh law), Canada having a written constitution and the UK possessing no such comprehensive document, and the Constitution of Canada including a charter of rights – which is presently impossible in the case of the UK's Human Rights Act 1998 regarding the 'Constitution of the UK' unless there is universal agreement within the UK's legislature that the Human Rights Act 1998 is to be a superior source of law to other Acts of Parliament – in which case there would also need to be a specified special mechanism to repeal or modify this Act.

It is noteworthy that the Canadian Charter of Rights and Freedoms includes a rule that empowers the Parliament of Canada or a provincial legislature – as appropriate – to temporarily disapply the fundamental freedoms and the legal rights within the Charter from an Act that it has passed or from a provision of it[130]. Whilst it may be argued that such a facility enables lawmakers to sidestep the effect of the Charter as a superior source of law to that of legislation, it might be conversely contended that the Parliament of Canada has not as yet made use of this provision [229].

Regarding its journey from British colony to independent state, Australia followed the path of Canada. The British North America Act 1867 founded the Dominion of Canada[131]; the Act to Constitute the Commonwealth of Australia 1900 established the Commonwealth of Australia[132]. The Canada Act 1982 provides for the cessation of the power of the Parliament of the UK to legislate for Canada[133]; the Australia Act 1986 terminates the power of that Parliament to legislate for Australia or any of its states or territories[134].

Bank of Canada Act

Establishment of the Bank of Canada

The Bank of Canada Act establishes the Bank of Canada [230], as a body corporate [231]. Its head office is in Ottawa [232].

The Powers of the Bank of Canada

The Bank of Canada[135] may purchase and sell coin and gold and silver bullion [233], buy and sell foreign currencies and maintain deposit accounts with domestic or foreign banks to facilitate these operations [234], purchase and sell securities that the Government of Canada or

[130] The last paragraph of the subsection entitled 'The Canadian Charter of Rights and Freedoms', above in the present section – which is titled 'An Introduction to the Legal System of Canada', lays down this rule, which section 33 of the Constitution Act 1982 contains.

[131] The first sentence of the subsection entitled 'Essentials', above in the current section – which is titled 'An Introduction to the Legal System of Canada', conveys this information.

[132] The first sentence of the subsection entitled 'Commonwealth of Australia Constitution Act 1900', in the section titled 'An Introduction to the Legal System of Australia' in Chapter 1, imparts this information.

[133] The text to fns 102 and 103 sets out this information.

[134] The first sentence of the subsection entitled 'Australia Act 1986', in the section titled 'An Introduction to the Legal System of Australia' in Chapter 1, specifies this information.

[135] The word '*Bank*' in the Bank of Canada Act means "the Bank of Canada" (Government of Canada (2022), "Bank of Canada Act, S.C., 1934 (24 & 25 Geo V), c. 43; R.S.C., 1985, c. B-2," adopted on July 3, 1934, entered into force on March 11, 1935, last amended on January 31, 2020, consolidated to May 2, 2022, s.2).

of any Canadian province issues or guarantees [235], buy and sell securities which the Government of the USA, Japan, the UK or a Member State of the European Union issues or guarantees [236], purchase and sell special drawing rights that the IMF issues [237], for the purposes of advancing the stability of the Canadian financial system or conducting monetary policy – buy and sell from any person financial instruments which comply with the policy that the Governor of the Bank of Canada[136] has established or to the degree that the Governor determines to be necessary in order to address grave and abnormal stress on the financial system or a financial market [238], make loans or advances for periods of six months or less to any member of the Canadian Payments Association[137] which takes either security in any property, or an assignment or transfer of its title, right or interest in any property located in Canada [239], make loans or advances for periods of no more than six months to the Government of Canada or of any Canadian province – on taking security in readily-marketable securities that such a government issues or guarantees [240], make loans to the Government of Canada or of any Canadian province – subject to specified conditions[138] [241], accept deposits from the Government of Canada, and pay interest on these deposits [242], accept deposits from a member of the Canadian Payments Association[139] [243] – and pay interest on those deposits if the money deposited is to be used to make loans or advances for periods of not more than six months to any member of the Canadian Payments Association[140] [244], accept deposits from any provincial government or from any agency or corporation of the Government of Canada [245], open accounts in the BIS or a central bank of any foreign state, accept deposits from these and from the IMF, the IBRD and any other official international financial organisation,

---

[136] The word '*Governor*' in the Bank of Canada Act means "the Governor of the Bank [of Canada] or the person acting for the Governor pursuant to this Act" (Government of Canada (2022), "Bank of Canada Act, S.C., 1934 (24 & 25 Geo V), c. 43; R.S.C., 1985, c. B-2," adopted on July 3, 1934, entered into force on March 11, 1935, last amended on January 31, 2020, consolidated to May 2, 2022, s.2).

[137] The Canadian Payments Act establishes the Canadian Payments Association, whose members comprise the Bank of Canada, every bank and authorized foreign bank, every co-operative credit association, loan company or trust company that the Canada Deposit Insurance Corporation Act designates as a 'bridge institution', and any other person who is entitled to be a member of the Canadian Payment Association under Part 1 of the Canadian Payments Act (which is titled 'Canadian Payments Association Establishment and Membership', and which contains sections 3, 4 and 4.1 of that Act,) and who establishes this entitlement on application to the Canadian Payments Association for membership therein (Government of Canada (2022), "Canadian Payments Act, R.S.C., 1985, c. C-21," adopted on November 26, 1980, as "An Act to revise the Bank Act, to amend the Quebec Savings Bank Act and the Bank of Canada Act, to establish the Canadian Payments Association and to amend other Acts in consequence thereof: Part IV – An Act to establish the Canadian Payments Association," entered into force on December 1, 1980, last amended on April 2, 2021, consolidated to May 2, 2022, s.4(1)). The section below titled 'Canadian Payments Act', provides information concerning the Canadian Payments Act. The section below entitled Canada Deposit Insurance Corporation Act, supplies information regarding the Canada Deposit Insurance Corporation Act. The first sentence of fn 141 defines the term '*bank*'. The first sentence of fn 142 defines the term '*authorized foreign bank*'.

[138] These stipulations are: "such loans outstanding at any one time shall not, in the case of the Government of Canada, exceed one-third of the estimated revenue of the Government of Canada for its fiscal year[,] and shall not, in the case of a provincial government, exceed one-fourth of that government's estimated revenue for its fiscal year, and such loans shall be repaid before the end of the first quarter after the end of the fiscal year of the government that has contracted the loan" (Government of Canada (2022), "Bank of Canada Act, S.C., 1934 (24 & 25 Geo V), c. 43; R.S.C., 1985, c. B-2," adopted on July 3, 1934, entered into force on March 11, 1935, last amended on January 31, 2020, consolidated to May 2, 2022, s.18(j)).

[139] This does not include an authorized foreign bank that is subject to the requirements and restrictions of subsection 524(2) of the Bank Act (Government of Canada (2022), "Bank of Canada Act, S.C., 1934 (24 & 25 Geo V), c. 43; R.S.C., 1985, c. B-2," adopted on July 3, 1934, entered into force on March 11, 1935, last amended on January 31, 2020, consolidated to May 2, 2022, s.18(1.1)). The text to fns 249 and 250 comprises subsection 524(2) of the Bank Act.

[140] The text to fn 137 refers to these loans and advances.

act as mandatory, agent, correspondent or depository for any of these organisations or banks, and pay interest on any of the deposits [246], act as a custodian of the financial assets of the Canada Mortgage and Housing Corporation and the Canada Deposit Insurance Corporation [247], obtain, hold, lease or dispose of immovables or real property [248], accept deposits of money that an Act of Parliament requires or authorizes to be transferred to the Bank of Canada, and, in conformity with that Act, pay interest on money thus deposited and pay out money to any person who is entitled to it thereunder [249], and engage in any business activity which is ancillary to, or consequential on, something that the Bank of Canada Act permits or requires the Bank of Canada to do [250].

Acquisition of Collateral Securities

The Bank of Canada may acquire from any bank[141], or from any authorized foreign bank[142] which is not subject to the requirements and restrictions of subsection 524(2) of the Bank

[141] A '*bank*' is a bank that is listed in Schedule I or II to the Bank Act (Government of Canada (2022), "Bank of Canada Act, S.C., 1934 (24 & 25 Geo V), c. 43; R.S.C., 1985, c. B-2," adopted on July 3, 1934, entered into force on March 11, 1935, last amended on January 31, 2020, consolidated to May 2, 2022, s.2; Government of Canada (2022), "Bank Act, S.C. 1991, c. 46," adopted on December 13, 1991, entered into force on June 1, 1992, last amended on February 26, 2022, consolidated to May 2, 2022, s.2). As at 31st December, 2021, Schedule I of the Bank Act lists the following banks: B2B Bank, Bank of Montreal, Bridgewater Bank, Caisse populaire acadienne ltée, Canadian Imperial Bank of Commerce, Canadian Tire Bank, Canadian Western Bank, Coast Capital Savings Federal Credit Union, Concentra Bank, CS Alterna Bank, Digital Commerce Bank, Equitable Bank, Exchange Bank of Canada, Fairstone Bank of Canada, First Nations Bank of Canada, General Bank of Canada, Haventree Bank, Home Bank, HomeEquity Bank, Laurentian Bank of Canada, Manulife Bank of Canada, Motus Bank, National Bank of Canada, Peoples Bank of Canada, President's Choice Bank, RFA Bank of Canada, Rodgers Bank, Royal Bank of Canada, Tangerine Bank, The Bank of Nova Scotia, The Toronto-Dominion Bank, Vancity Community Investment Bank, VersaBank, and Wealth One Bank of Canada (Government of Canada (2023), "Bank Act, S.C. 1991, c. 46," adopted on December 13, 1991, entered into force on June 1, 1992, last amended on March 4, 2023, consolidated to March 20, 2023, Schedule I). Schedule II of the Bank Act catalogues the following banks: Amex Bank of Canada, Bank of China (Canada), Cidel Bank Canada, Citco Bank Canada, Citibank Canada, CTBC Bank Corp. (Canada), Habib Canadian Bank, HSBC Bank Canada, ICICI Bank Canada, Industrial and Commercial Bank of China (Canada), J.P. Morgan Bank Canada, KEB Hana Bank Canada, SBI Canada Bank, Shinhan Bank Canada, and UBS Bank (Canada) (Government of Canada (2023), "Bank Act, S.C. 1991, c. 46," adopted on December 13, 1991, entered into force on June 1, 1992, last amended on March 4, 2023, consolidated to March 20, 2023, Schedule II).

[142] An '*authorized foreign bank*' is a foreign bank that is subject to an order under subsection 524(1) of the Bank Act (Government of Canada (2022), "Bank of Canada Act, S.C., 1934 (24 & 25 Geo V), c. 43; R.S.C., 1985, c. B-2," adopted on July 3, 1934, entered into force on March 11, 1935, last amended on January 31, 2020, consolidated to May 2, 2022, s.2; Government of Canada (2022), "Bank Act, S.C. 1991, c. 46," adopted on December 13, 1991, entered into force on June 1, 1992, last amended on February 26, 2022, consolidated to May 2, 2022, s.2). Subject to section 12 of the Bank Act(, the first subsection of which the next sentence in the present footnote (i.e., fn 142) reproduces), a '*foreign bank*' is "an entity incorporated or formed by[,] or under the laws of[,] a country other than Canada[,] that **(a)** is a bank according to the laws of any foreign country where it carries on business; **(b)** carries on business in any foreign country that, if carried on in Canada, would be, wholly or to a significant extent, the business of banking, **(c)** engages, directly or indirectly, in the business of providing financial services[,] and employs, to identify or describe its business, a name that includes the word "bank," "banque," "banking" or "bancaire," either alone or in combination with other words, or any word or words in any language other than English or French corresponding generally thereto, **(d)** engages in the business of lending money and accepting deposit liabilities [that are] transferable by cheque or other instrument, **(e)** engages, directly or indirectly, in the business of providing financial services and is affiliated with another foreign bank, **(f)** controls another foreign bank, or **(g)** is a foreign institution, other than a foreign bank within the meaning of any of paragraphs (a) to (f), that controls a bank [which is] incorporated or formed under this Act [(i.e., the Bank Act)], but does not include a subsidiary of a bank named in Schedule I [of the Bank Act] as that Schedule read immediately before the day [that] section 184 of the *Financial Consumer Agency of Canada*

Act[143], and hold, any property that the bank or authorized foreign bank holds as security under Part VIII of the Bank Act[144] [251], and exercise every remedy and right as regards any security so acquired which the bank or authorized foreign bank could have exercised [252].

Comment

The Bank of Canada Act states with precision the powers that Canada's central bank is entitled to exercise. This Act grants the Bank of Canada considerable scope as to the parties from which it may acquire collateral securities.

Bank Act

Status and Powers of a Bank[145]

Subject to the terms of the Bank Act, a bank has the powers, privileges and rights of a natural person [253]. It has the legal capacity of a natural person [253].

Sunset Provision

The legislation for Canada's financial institutions is reviewed every five years, or less [254]. The Federal Budget of 2021 extended the next review of the Bank Act from 2023 to 2025 [255].

Act comes into force, unless the Minister has specified that subsection 378(1) [of the Bank Act] no longer applies to the bank" (Government of Canada (2022), "Bank Act, S.C. 1991, c. 46," adopted on December 13, 1991, entered into force on June 1, 1992, last amended on February 26, 2022, consolidated to May 2, 2022, s.2; emphasis original). The first subsection of section 12 of the Bank Act states: "The Minister may, by order, and subject to such terms and conditions as the Minister considers appropriate, exempt for the purposes of any provision of this Act any entity from being a foreign bank that, but for that order, would be a foreign bank." (Government of Canada (2022), "Bank Act, S.C. 1991, c. 46," adopted on December 13, 1991, entered into force on June 1, 1992, last amended on February 26, 2022, consolidated to May 2, 2022, s.12(1)). The word '*Minister*' is a reference to "the Minister of Finance" (Government of Canada (2022), "Bank of Canada Act, S.C., 1934 (24 & 25 Geo V), c. 43; R.S.C., 1985, c. B-2," adopted on July 3, 1934, entered into force on March 11, 1935, last amended on January 31, 2020, consolidated to May 2, 2022, s.2; Government of Canada (2022), "Bank Act, S.C. 1991, c. 46," adopted on December 13, 1991, entered into force on June 1, 1992, last amended on February 26, 2022, consolidated to May 2, 2022, s.2). The text to fns 247 and 248 sets out subsection 524(1) of the Bank Act.

[143] The text to fns 249 and 250 lays down subsection 524(2) of the Bank Act.

[144] Part VIII of the Bank Act is titled 'Business and Powers', and comprises sections 409-463 of that Act.

[145] The first sentence of fn 141 defines the term '*bank*'.

Subject to two exceptions[146], banks – and authorized foreign banks[147] – are not to conduct business in Canada after 30th June 2025 [256].

Incorporation of a Bank

On the application of at least one person[148] that is made in accordance with the Bank Act, the Minister[149] may issue letters patent[150] to incorporate a bank[151] [257]. The Minister only

146 These exceptions are: "The Governor in Council may, by order, extend [only once] by up to six months the time during which banks may continue to carry on business[,] and authorized foreign banks may continue to carry on business in Canada." (Government of Canada (2022), "Bank Act, S.C. 1991, c. 46," adopted on December 13, 1991, entered into force on June 1, 1992, last amended on February 26, 2022, consolidated to May 2, 2022, s.21(2)), and "If Parliament dissolves on the day set out in subsection (1) [(i.e., subsection 21(1) of the Bank Act) – which is 30th June 2025 (text to fns 146 and 147),] or on any day within the six-month period before that day or on any day within an extension ordered under subsection (2) [(i.e., subsection 21(2) of the Bank Act)], banks may continue to carry on business, and authorized foreign banks may continue to carry on business in Canada, until the end of the 180th day after the first day of the session of the next Parliament." (Government of Canada (2022), "Bank Act, S.C. 1991, c. 46," adopted on December 13, 1991, entered into force on June 1, 1992, last amended on February 26, 2022, consolidated to May 2, 2022, s.21(4)). A bank may engage in business in every part of Canada, and, subject to the Bank Act, to the degree to which – and in the way in which – the laws of any foreign jurisdiction allow (Government of Canada (2022), "Bank Act, S.C. 1991, c. 46," adopted on December 13, 1991, entered into force on June 1, 1992, last amended on February 26, 2022, consolidated to May 2, 2022, ss.15(2) and 15(4)).

147 The first sentence of fn 142 defines the term '*authorized foreign bank*'.

148 A '*person*' is "a natural person, an entity or a personal representative" (Government of Canada (2022), "Bank Act, S.C. 1991, c. 46," adopted on December 13, 1991, entered into force on June 1, 1992, last amended on February 26, 2022, consolidated to May 2, 2022, s.2). An '*entity*' is "a body corporate, trust, partnership, fund, an unincorporated association or organization, Her Majesty in right of Canada or of a province, an agency of Her Majesty in either of such rights[,] and the government of a foreign country of any political subdivision thereof and any agency thereof" (Government of Canada (2022), "Bank Act, S.C. 1991, c. 46," adopted on December 13, 1991, entered into force on June 1, 1992, last amended on February 26, 2022, consolidated to May 2, 2022, s.2). The last sentence of fn 154 defines the term '*body corporate*'. A '*personal representative*' is "a person who stands in place of[,] and represents[,] another person[,] and, without limiting the generality of the foregoing, includes, as the circumstances require, a trustee, an executor, an administrator, a committee, a guardian, a tutor, a curator, an assignee, a receiver, an agent or an attorney of any person, but does not include a delegate" (Government of Canada (2022), "Bank Act, S.C. 1991, c. 46," adopted on December 13, 1991, entered into force on June 1, 1992, last amended on February 26, 2022, consolidated to May 2, 2022, s.2).

149 The term '*Minister*' means the Minister of Finance (penultimate sentence of fn 142).

150 The phrase '*letters patent*', "in respect of an instrument authorized to be issued under this Act, means letters patent in a form [that is] approved by the Superintendent" (Government of Canada (2022), "Bank Act, S.C. 1991, c. 46," adopted on December 13, 1991, entered into force on June 1, 1992, last amended on February 26, 2022, consolidated to May 2, 2022, s.2). Fn 155 defines the term '*Superintendent*'.

151 The Minister may only do this "subject to this Part" of the Bank Act (Government of Canada (2022), "Bank Act, S.C. 1991, c. 46," adopted on December 13, 1991, entered into force on June 1, 1992, last amended on February 26, 2022, consolidated to May 2, 2022, s.22(1)). 'This Part' is Part III of the Bank Act, which is entitled 'Incorporation and Continuance', and which comprises sections 22-44 of this Act. Subsection 22(1) of the Bank Act does not govern the incorporation of a federal credit union (Government of Canada (2022), "Bank Act, S.C. 1991, c. 46," adopted on December 13, 1991, entered into force on June 1, 1992, last amended on February 26, 2022, consolidated to May 2, 2022, s.22(1)). A '*federal credit union*' is "a bank that, within the meaning of section 12.1 [of the Bank Act], is organized and carries on business on a cooperative basis" (Government of Canada (2022), "Bank Act, S.C. 1991, c. 46," adopted on December 13, 1991, entered into force on June 1, 1992, last amended on February 26, 2022, consolidated to May 2, 2022, s.2). Section 12.1 of the Bank Act states: "**(1)** For the purposes of this Act, a federal credit union is organized and carries on business on a cooperative basis[,] if **(a)** a majority of its members are natural persons; **(b)** it provides financial services primarily to its members; **(c)** membership in the federal credit union is wholly or primarily open, in a non-discriminatory manner, to persons who can use the services of the federal credit union and who are willing and able to accept the responsibilities of membership; **(d)** each member has only one vote; **(e)** a delegate has only one vote[,] even though the delegate is a member or represents more than one member; **(f)** dividends on any membership share

provides such letters regarding the subsidiary of a foreign bank[152] if (s)he is satisfied that satisfactory conditions exist for this bank's operation in its home jurisdiction[153] [258]. An application for letters patent to incorporate a bank must specify the names of its first directors[154], and be filed with the Superintendent[155] – together with other material, information and evidence as (s)he may require [259].

---

are limited to the maximum percentage [that is] fixed in the federal credit union's letters patent or by-laws; and **(g)** surplus funds arising from the federal credit union's operations are used **(i)** to provide for the financial stability of the federal credit union, **(ii)** to develop its business, **(iii)** to provide or improve common services to members, **(iv)** to provide for reserves or dividends on membership shares[,] and shares, **(v)** for community welfare or the propagation of cooperative enterprises, or **(vi)** as a distribution to its members as a patronage allocation. ... **(2)** Paragraph (1)(c) is subject to any restrictions in the by-laws of the federal credit union on the class of persons to which membership may be available, as long as the restrictions are consistent with applicable laws with respect to human rights." (Government of Canada (2022), "Bank Act, S.C. 1991, c. 46," adopted on December 13, 1991, entered into force on June 1, 1992, last amended on February 26, 2022, consolidated to May 2, 2022, s.12.1; emphasis original).

[152] The second sentence of fn 153 defines the term '*subsidiary*'. The second sentence of fn 142 defines the term '*foreign bank*'.

[153] Section 24 of the Bank Act reads: "If a proposed bank would be a subsidiary of a foreign bank, within the meaning of paragraphs (a) to (f) of the definition ***foreign bank*** in section 2 [of the Bank Act], and the application for letters patent to incorporate the bank is made by a non-WTO Member foreign bank, [then] letters patent to incorporate the bank may not be issued[,] unless the Minister is satisfied that treatment as favourable for banks to which this Act applies exists or will be provided in the jurisdiction in which the foreign bank principally carries on business, either directly or through a subsidiary." (Government of Canada (2022), "Bank Act, S.C. 1991, c. 46," adopted on December 13, 1991, entered into force on June 1, 1992, last amended on February 26, 2022, consolidated to May 2, 2022, s.24; emphasis original). A '*subsidiary*' is an entity that is controlled by another entity (Government of Canada (2022), "Bank Act, S.C. 1991, c. 46," adopted on December 13, 1991, entered into force on June 1, 1992, last amended on February 26, 2022, consolidated to May 2, 2022, s.5). The second sentence of fn 142 defines the term '*foreign bank*'. The second sentence of fn 148 defines the term '*entity*'. The preantepenultimate sentence of fn 157 defines the term '*control*'.

[154] A '*director*' is "a natural person occupying the position of director, by whatever name called, of a body corporate"; the phrase '*board of directors*' – or '*directors*' – "refers to the directors of a body corporate as a body" (Government of Canada (2022), "Bank Act, S.C. 1991, c. 46," adopted on December 13, 1991, entered into force on June 1, 1992, last amended on February 26, 2022, consolidated to May 2, 2022, s.2). A '*body corporate*' is "an incorporated body[,] wherever or however incorporated" (Government of Canada (2022), "Bank Act, S.C. 1991, c. 46," adopted on December 13, 1991, entered into force on June 1, 1992, last amended on February 26, 2022, consolidated to May 2, 2022, s.2).

[155] The word '*Superintendent*' refers to "the Superintendent of Financial Institutions appointed pursuant to the *Office of the Superintendent of Financial Institutions Act*" (Government of Canada (2022), "Bank Act, S.C. 1991, c. 46," adopted on December 13, 1991, entered into force on June 1, 1992, last amended on February 26, 2022, consolidated to May 2, 2022, s.2; emphasis original). Subsection 4(1) of the Office of the Superintendent of Financial Institutions Act declares: "There is hereby established an office of the Government of Canada called the Office of the Superintendent of Financial Institutions over which the Minister shall preside[,] and for which the Minister shall be responsible." (Government of Canada (2022), "Office of the Superintendent of Financial Institutions Act, R. S. C. 1985, c. 18 (3rd Supp.), Part I," entered into force on July 2, 1987, last amended on December 13, 2018, consolidated to May 16, 2022, s.4(1)). Subsection 5(1) of the Office of the Superintendent of Financial Institutions states: "The Governor in Council shall appoint an officer called the Superintendent of Financial Institutions to be the deputy head of the Office." (Government of Canada (2022), "Office of the Superintendent of Financial Institutions Act, R. S. C. 1985, c. 18 (3rd Supp.), Part I," entered into force on July 2, 1987, last amended on December 13, 2018, consolidated to May 16, 2022, s.5(1)). The objects of the Office of the Superintendent of Financial Institutions *as regards financial institutions* – those concerning pension plans are separately stated in subsection 4(2.1) of the Office of the Superintendent of Financial Institutions Act – are as follows "**(a)** to supervise financial institutions in order to determine whether they are in sound financial condition and are complying with their governing statute law and supervisory requirements under that law; **(b)** to promptly advise the management and board of directors of a financial institution in the event [that] the institution is not in sound financial condition or is not complying with its governing statute law or supervisory requirements under that law and, in such a case, to take, or require the management or board to take, the necessary corrective measures or series of measures to deal with the situation in an expeditious manner; **(c)** to promote the adoption[,] by management and boards of directors of financial institutions[,] of policies and procedures [which are] designed to control and manage risk; and **(d)** to monitor and evaluate system-wide or

Before issuing letters patent to incorporate a bank, the Minister must take into consideration all issues that (s)he considers to be pertinent to the application [260]. These matters are to include the nature and sufficiency of the applicant's or applicants' financial resources as a source of ongoing financial support for the bank [261], the feasibility and soundness of the applicant's or applicants' plans for the future development and conduct of the bank's business [262], the business experience and record of the applicant(s) [263], the applicant's or applicants' integrity and character, or, if an applicant is a body corporate[156], its reputation for being run in a way that is compatible with the standards of integrity and good character [264], whether the bank will be managed responsibly with the competence and experience which is appropriate for involvment in the workings of a financial institution [265], the impact of any integration of the operations and businesses of the applicant(s) with those of the bank on the conduct of those operations and businesses [266], the opinion of the Superintendent concerning the degree to which the proposed corporate structure of the applicant(s) and its or their affiliates[157] may affect the regulation and supervision of the bank, in view of the nature and scope of the proposed financial services activities to be undertaken by the bank and its affiliates – and the nature and extent of regulation and supervision that apply to the proposed financial services activities to be conducted by these affiliates [267], that a bank which will be a federal credit union will be organized and engage in business on a co-operative basis in compliance with section 12.1 of the Bank Act[158] [268], and the best interests Canada's financial system [269]. The letters patent incorporating a bank are to specify[159] the name of the

---

sectoral events or issues that may have a negative impact on the financial condition of financial institutions." (Government of Canada (2022), "Office of the Superintendent of Financial Institutions Act, R. S. C. 1985, c. 18 (3rd Supp.), Part I," entered into force on July 2, 1987, last amended on December 13, 2018, consolidated to May 16, 2022, s.4(2)).

[156] The final sentence of fn 154 defines the term '*body corporate*'.

[157] An '*affiliate*' is "an entity that is affiliated with another entity within the meaning of section 6 [of the Bank Act]" (Government of Canada (2022), "Bank Act, S.C. 1991, c. 46," adopted on December 13, 1991, entered into force on June 1, 1992, last amended on February 26, 2022, consolidated to May 2, 2022, s.2). The second sentence of fn 148 defines the term '*entity*'. Section 6 of the Bank Act states: "**(1)** One entity is affiliated with another entity[,] if one of them is controlled by the other or both are controlled by the same person. ... **(2)** Despite subsection (1), for the purposes of subsection 265(1) and 283(1) [of the Bank Act], one entity is affiliated with another entity[,] if one of them is controlled, determined without regard to paragraph 3(1)(d) [of the Bank Act], by the other[,] or both are controlled, determined without regard to paragraph 3(1)(d), by the same person." (Government of Canada (2022), "Bank Act, S.C. 1991, c. 46," adopted on December 13, 1991, entered into force on June 1, 1992, last amended on February 26, 2022, consolidated to May 2, 2022, s.6; emphasis original). The first sentence of fn 148 defines the term '*person*'. For the purposes of the Bank Act, "**(a)** a person controls a body corporate[,] if securities of the body corporate to which are attached more than 50 per cent of the votes that may be cast to elect directors of the body corporate are beneficially owned by the person[,] and the votes attached to those securities are sufficient, if exercised, to elect a majority of the directors of the body corporate; **(a.1)** a person controls a federal credit union[,] if the person and all of the entities controlled by the person have the right to exercise more than 50 per cent of the votes that may be cast at an annual meeting or to elect the majority of the directors of the federal credit union; **(b)** a person controls an unincorporated entity, other than a limited partnership, if more than 50 per cent of the ownership interests, however designated, into which the entity is divided are beneficially owned by that person and the person is able to direct the business and affairs of the entity; **(c)** the general partner of a limited partnership controls the limited partnership; and **(d)** a person controls an entity[,] if the person has any direct or indirect influence that, if exercised, would result in control in fact of the entity." (Government of Canada (2022), "Bank Act, S.C. 1991, c. 46," adopted on December 13, 1991, entered into force on June 1, 1992, last amended on February 26, 2022, consolidated to May 2, 2022, s.3(1); emphasis original). The first sentence of fn 154 defines the terms '*director*' and '*directors*'. The last sentence of fn 154 defines the term '*body corporate*'. Fn 151 defines the term '*federal credit union*'.

[158] Fn 151 includes section 12.1 of the Bank Act.

[159] In the letters patent that incorporate a bank, the Minister may set out any provision – which does not contravene the Bank Act – that (s)he deems to be advisable, in order to take into consideration the distinctive circumstances of the proposed bank (Government of Canada (2022), "Bank Act, S.C. 1991, c. 46," adopted on December 13,

bank, only if applicable– that the bank is a federal credit union, the province in which the bank's head office is to be located, and the date upon which the bank was, or is to be, established [270]. The Minister may impose terms and conditions regarding the issuance of letters of patent incorporating a bank, as (s)he considers necessary or suitable [271].

Commencement and Conduct of Business

A bank may only engage in business, once the Superintendent[160] has, by order, approved the commencement and undertaking of business by the bank[161] [272].

Capital Structure of a Bank

Subject to the Bank Act and a bank's by-laws, the bank's shares may be issued to such persons[162], at such times and for such consideration as its directors[163] may determine [273]. Shares of a bank must be in registered form[164], and without par or nominal value [274].

A bank which is not a federal credit union[165] must possess one class of shares – to be classified as 'common shares' – that are non-redeemable, and in which the rights of the shareholders are equal in every respect[166] [275]. These rights must include the right to vote at all shareholders' meetings, bar a situation in which only holders of a specified category of shares are entitled to vote [276], the right to receive dividends that are declared on these shares [277], and the right to receive the remaining property of the bank upon its dissolution [278]. The by-laws of a bank which is not a federal credit union may make provision for more than

---

1991, entered into force on June 1, 1992, last amended on February 26, 2022, consolidated to May 2, 2022, s.28(2)).

160 Fn 155 defines the term '*Superintendent*'.

161 The first sentence of fn 141 defines the term '*bank*'.

162 The first sentence of fn 148 defines the term '*person*'.

163 The first sentence of fn 154 defines the terms '*director*' and '*directors*'.

164 The phrase '*registered form*', "in respect of a security, means a security in registered form as determined in accordance with subsection 83(4) [of the Bank Act]" (Government of Canada (2022), "Bank Act, S.C. 1991, c. 46," adopted on December 13, 1991, entered into force on June 1, 1992, last amended on February 26, 2022, consolidated to May 2, 2022, s.2). A '*security*' is "**(a)** in relation to a body corporate, a share of any class of shares of the body corporate or a debt obligation of the body corporate, and includes a warrant of the body corporate, but does not include a deposit with a financial institution or any instrument evidencing such a deposit or, for greater certainty, a membership share, and **(b)** in relation to any other entity, any ownership interest in[,] or debt obligation of[,] the entity" (Government of Canada (2022), "Bank Act, S.C. 1991, c. 46," adopted on December 13, 1991, entered into force on June 1, 1992, last amended on February 26, 2022, consolidated to May 2, 2022, s.2; emphasis original). A security is in *registered form,* "if **(a)** it specifies a person [who or which is] entitled to the security or to the rights [that] it evidences, and its transfer is capable of being recorded in a securities register; or **(b)** it bears a statement that it is in registered form" (Government of Canada (2022), "Bank Act, S.C. 1991, c. 46," adopted on December 13, 1991, entered into force on June 1, 1992, last amended on February 26, 2022, consolidated to May 2, 2022, s.83(1); emphasis original).

165 A federal credit union may only issue shares, "if its by-laws set out the following: "**(a)** whether the shares may be issued to persons who are not members; **(b)** the maximum number, if any, of shares of any class that the federal credit union is authorized to issue; **(c)** the number of classes of shares; and **(d)** the rights, privileges, restrictions and conditions attaching to the shares of each class" (Government of Canada (2022), "Bank Act, S.C. 1991, c. 46," adopted on December 13, 1991, entered into force on June 1, 1992, last amended on February 26, 2022, consolidated to May 2, 2022, s.60.1(1); emphasis original). Fn 151 defines the term '*federal credit union*'.

166 However, "[n]o bank shall designate more than one class of its shares as "common shares" or any variation of that term" (Government of Canada (2022), "Bank Act, S.C. 1991, c. 46," adopted on December 13, 1991, entered into force on June 1, 1992, last amended on February 26, 2022, consolidated to May 2, 2022, s.60(2)).

one class of shares; if so, these rules must specify the conditions, restrictions, rights and privileges that attach to each category of shares [279], and the maximum number of shares of any class, if any, which the bank is authorized to issue [280].

Bank Governance

Every director[167], employee and officer[168] of a bank must comply with the Bank Act, the regulations, the instrument that incorporates the bank[169], and the bank's by-laws [281]. In exercising any of the powers, and fulfilling any of the duties, of a director or an officer, every director and officer is to act in good faith and honestly – taking into consideration the bank's best interests [282], and exercise the diligence, skill and care that a reasonably prudent person would do in comparable circumstances [283].

A bank must have at least seven directors[170] [284]. One half or more of the directors of a bank which is a subsidiary of a foreign bank, and a majority of the directors of any other bank, are to be resident Canadians at the moment of each director's election or appointment [285]. A director of a bank need not hold its shares[171] [286].

The shareholders of a bank which is not a federal credit union[172] may remove any director – or all the directors – from office, by resolution at a special shareholders' meeting[173] [287]. Unless the Bank Act provides otherwise, the directors of a bank which is not a federal credit

[167] The first sentence of fn 154 defines the term '*director*'.

[168] An '*officer*' is "**(a)** in relation to a body corporate, a chief executive officer, president, vice-president, secretary, controller, treasurer and any other natural person [who is] designated as an officer of the body corporate by by-law or by resolution of the directors of the body corporate, and **(b)** in relation to any other entity, any natural person [who is] designated as an officer of the entity by by-law, by resolution of the members thereof or otherwise" (Government of Canada (2022), "Bank Act, S.C. 1991, c. 46," adopted on December 13, 1991, entered into force on June 1, 1992, last amended on February 26, 2022, consolidated to May 2, 2022, s.2; emphasis original). The final sentence of fn 154 defines the term '*body corporate*'. The second sentence of fn 148 defines the term '*entity*'.

[169] The first sentence of fn 141 defines the term '*bank*'.

[170] The first sentence of fn 154 defines the terms '*director*' and '*directors*'.

[171] At least two thirds of the directors of a federal credit union, or any higher proportion for which its by-laws provide, must be members – or representatives of members – of the federal credit union (Government of Canada (2022), "Bank Act, S.C. 1991, c. 46," adopted on December 13, 1991, entered into force on June 1, 1992, last amended on February 26, 2022, consolidated to May 2, 2022, s.159.1).

[172] Any director of a federal credit union may be removed from office, by resolution at a special meeting of the persons who are entitled to vote in this director's election (Government of Canada (2022), "Bank Act, S.C. 1991, c. 46," adopted on December 13, 1991, entered into force on June 1, 1992, last amended on February 26, 2022, consolidated to May 2, 2022, s.173(1.1). Fn 151 defines the term '*federal credit union*'.

[173] If "the holders of any class or series of shares of a bank have the exclusive right to elect one or more directors, [then] a director so elected may be removed only by a resolution at a meeting of the shareholders of that class or series (Government of Canada (2022), "Bank Act, S.C. 1991, c. 46," adopted on December 13, 1991, entered into force on June 1, 1992, last amended on February 26, 2022, consolidated to May 2, 2022, s.173(2)). Similarly, "[i]f members of a federal credit union have the exclusive right to elect one or more directors, [then] a director so elected may be removed only by a resolution of the members having that right" (Government of Canada (2022), "Bank Act, S.C. 1991, c. 46," adopted on December 13, 1991, entered into force on June 1, 1992, last amended on February 26, 2022, consolidated to May 2, 2022, s.173(2.1)). Moreover, in instances in which the Bank Act or a bank's by-laws make provision for cumulative voting, "a director may be removed from office[,] only if the number of votes [that are] cast in favour of a motion to remove the director is greater than the product of the number of directors required by the by-laws and the number of votes [which are] cast against the motion" (Government of Canada (2023), "Bank Act, S.C. 1991, c. 46," adopted on December 13, 1991, entered into force on June 1, 1992, last amended on March 4, 2023, consolidated to March 20, 2023, s.168(1)(g); point (g) in fn 177 also sets out paragraph 168(1)(g) of the Bank Act).

union may – by resolution – pass, amend or repeal any by-law that regulates the bank's affairs or business [288]. The directors must submit this by-law, amendment or repeal, to the shareholders at their next meeting, and the latter may pass a resolution which confirms or modifies the by-law, amendment or repeal[174] [289]. A shareholder who is entitled to vote at an annual general meeting of shareholders, may make a proposal to draft, amend or repeal a by-law [290].

On the application of a bank that is authorized to do this by special resolution, the Minister[175] may approve a proposal to add, amend or remove any provision that the Bank Act allows to be placed in the bank's incorporating instrument [291]. On receiving this application, the Minister may issue letters patent to fulfil this proposal [292].

The directors of a bank which is not a federal credit union, may pass, amend or repeal any by-laws to alter the maximum number – if there is one – of shares of any class that the bank is permitted to issue [293], found new classes of shares [294], change the designation of all or any of the bank's shares, and add, modify or remove any conditions, restrictions, rights and privileges in respect of all or any of the bank's shares [295], alter the shares of any class or series into a different number of shares of the same class or series, or into an identical or a dissimilar number of shares of other classes or series [296], divide a class of shares into series, and set the maximum number of shares – if there is to be one – in each series and the conditions, restrictions, rights and privileges attached thereto [297], sanction the directors to perform the actions in the immediately-preceding clause [298], authorize the directors to modify the conditions, restrictions, rights and privileges that are attached to unissued shares of any series [299], revoke, lessen or enlarge any authority that is conferred under the two immediately-preceding clauses [300], raise or lower the number of directors, or the minimum or maximum number of directors – subject to subsection 159(1) of the Bank Act[176] and section 168 of this Act[177] [301], alter the name of the bank [302], or change the province in which the bank's head

---

[174] Nonetheless, "[i]f a by-law, or an amendment to or a repeal of a by-law, is rejected by the shareholders, or is not submitted to the shareholders by the directors as required under subsection (2) [(i.e., subsection 188(2) of the Bank Act – which the text to the current footnote (fn 174) states)], [then] the by-law, amendment or repeal ceases to be effective from the date of its rejection or the date of the next meeting of shareholders, as the case may be, and no subsequent resolution of the directors to make, amend or repeal a by-law having substantially the same purpose or effect is effective until it is confirmed, or confirmed as amended, by the shareholders" (Government of Canada (2022), "Bank Act, S.C. 1991, c. 46," adopted on December 13, 1991, entered into force on June 1, 1992, last amended on February 26, 2022, consolidated to May 2, 2022, s.188(4)).

[175] The term '*Minister*' means the Minister of Finance (penultimate sentence of fn 142).

[176] The text to fn 170 sets out subsection 159(1) of the Bank Act.

[177] Section 168 of the Bank Act is titled 'Cumulative voting'; its first subsection reads: "Where this Act or the by-laws provide for cumulative voting, **(a)** there shall be a stated number of directors fixed by by-law[,] and not a minimum and maximum of directors; **(b)** each shareholder entitled to vote at an election of directors has the right to cast a number of votes [that is] equal to the number of votes attached to the shares [which are] held by the shareholder multiplied by the number of directors to be elected, and the shareholder may cast all such votes in favour of one candidate or distribute them among the candidates in any manner; **(c)** a separate vote of shareholders shall be taken with respect to each candidate nominated for director[,] unless a resolution is passed unanimously permitting two or more persons to be elected by a single vote; **(d)** if a shareholder has voted for more than one candidate without specifying the distribution of the votes among the candidates, [then] the shareholder is deemed to have distributed the votes equally among the candidates for whom the shareholder voted; **(e)** if the number of candidates nominated for director exceeds the number of positions to be filled, [then] the candidates who receive the least number of votes shall be eliminated until the number of candidates remaining equals the number of positions to be filled; **(f)** each director ceases to hold office at the close of the next annual meeting of shareholders following the director's election; **(g)** a director may be removed from office[,] only if the number of votes [that are] cast in favour of a motion to remove the director is greater than the product of the number of directors required by the by-laws and the number of votes [which are] cast against the motion [(last sentence of fn 173)]; and **(h)** the number of directors required by the by-laws may be

office is located [303]. The directors must submit a by-law, or an amendment to or a repeal of a by-law, that is made under subsection 217(1) of the Bank Act[178] to the shareholders, who may, by special resolution, confirm, amend or reject it [304].

No insider[179] may knowingly sell, either directly or indirectly, a security[180] of a distributing bank or of any of that bank's affiliates[181], if (s)he neither owns nor has fully paid for this security [305]. Notwithstanding subsection 270(2) of the Bank Act[182], an insider may sell a security that (s)he does not own, if (s)he owns another security which is convertible into the security that (s)he sold, or if (s)he owns a right or option to acquire the security which (s)he sold, and if – within ten days from the date of this sale – (s)he exercises the conversion right, option or privilege and delivers the security so obtained to its purchaser, or transfers the convertible security, right or option to the buyer [306]. No insider may knowingly, either directly or indirectly, purchase or sell a call option or put option that relates to a security of a bank or of any of its affiliates [307]. The Bank Act also provides for civil remedies for insider trading and tipping – for which it uses an extended definition of the terms '*insider*' and '*security*'[183].

Business and Powers of a Bank

Subject to the Bank Act, a bank may neither engage in, nor conduct, any business, other than that of banking, and business which normally pertains to banking [308]. The business of banking includes supplying financial services [309], acting as a financial agent [310], furnishing portfolio management and investment counselling services [311], and issuing charge, credit or payment cards – and, in collaboration with others, employing a charge, credit or payment card plan [312]. The Bank Act specifies other activities that a bank may

decreased[,] only if the number of votes [that are] cast in favour of a motion to decrease the number of directors is greater than the product of the number of directors required by the by-laws and the number of votes [which are] cast against the motion" (Government of Canada (2022), "Bank Act, S.C. 1991, c. 46," adopted on December 13, 1991, entered into force on June 1, 1992, last amended on February 26, 2022, consolidated to May 2, 2022, s.168(1); emphasis original).

178 The immediately-preceding sentence in the text, i.e., that containing fns 176 and 177, sets out subsection 217(1) of the Bank Act.

179 As regards a distributing bank, an '*insider*' is "**(a)** a director or officer of the bank; **(b)** a director or officer of a subsidiary of the bank; **(c)** a director or officer of a body corporate that enters into a business combination with the bank; or **(d)** a person employed or retained by the bank" (Government of Canada (2022), "Bank Act, S.C. 1991, c. 46," adopted on December 13, 1991, entered into force on June 1, 1992, last amended on February 26, 2022, consolidated to May 2, 2022, s.270(1); emphasis original). The second sentence of fn 153 defines the term '*subsidiary*'.

180 The second sentence of fn 164 defines the term '*security*'.

181 The first sentence of fn 157 defines the term '*affiliate*'.

182 The immediately-preceding sentence in the text, i.e., that containing fns 179-181, lays down subsection 270(2) of the Bank Act.

183 Sections 271, 271.1 and 272 of the Bank Act set out these provisions. Fn 179 contains the non-extended definition of the term '*insider*'. The second sentence of fn 164 comprises the non-extended definition of the term '*security*'.

undertake[184], as well as restrictions on trade[185], fiduciary activities[186], deposit-taking[187], guarantees[188], dealing in securities[189], insurance business[190], insurance mediation[191], leasing[192],

---

[184] A "bank may **(a)** hold, manage and otherwise deal with[,] real property; **(b)** provide prescribed bank-related data processing services; **(c)** outside Canada or, with the prior written approval of the Minister, in Canada, engage in any of the following activities, namely, **(i)** collecting, manipulating and transmitting **(A)** information that is primarily financial or economic in nature, **(B)** information that relates to the business of a permitted entity, as defined in subsection 464(1) [of the Bank Act], or **(C)** any other information that the Minister may, by order, specify, **(ii)** providing advisory or other services in the design, development or implementation of information management systems, **(iii)** designing, developing or marketing computer software, and **(iv)** designing, developing, manufacturing or selling, as an ancillary activity to any activity referred to in any of subparagraphs (i) to (iii) that the bank is engaging in, computer equipment [that is] integral to the business of financial institutions or to the provision of financial services; **(c.1)** with the prior written approval of the Minister, develop, design, hold, manage, manufacture, sell or otherwise deal with[,] data transmission systems, information sites, communication devices or information platforms or portals that are used **(i)** to provide information that is primarily financial or economic in nature, **(ii)** to provide information that relates to the business of a permitted entity, as defined in subsection 464(1), or **(iii)** for a prescribed purpose or in prescribed circumstances; **(c.2)** engage, under prescribed terms and conditions, if any are prescribed, in specialized business management or advisory services; **(d)** promote merchandise and services to the holders of any payment, credit or charge card issued by the bank; **(e)** engage in the sale of **(i)** tickets, including lottery tickets, on a non-profit public service basis in connection with special, temporary and infrequent non-commercial celebrations or projects that are of local, municipal, provincial or national interest, **(ii)** urban transit tickets, and **(iii)** tickets in respect of a lottery [that is] sponsored by the federal government or a provincial or municipal government or an agency of any such government or governments; **(f)** act as a custodian of property; **(g)** act as receiver, liquidator or sequestrator; and **(h)** provide identification, authentication or verification services." (Government of Canada (2022), "Bank Act, S.C. 1991, c. 46," adopted on December 13, 1991, entered into force on June 1, 1992, last amended on February 26, 2022, consolidated to May 2, 2022, s.410(1); emphasis original). The term '*Minister*' means the Minister of Finance (penultimate sentence of fn 142). Subsection 464(1) of the Bank Act defines the phrase '*permitted entity*' as: "an entity in which a bank is permitted to acquire a substantial investment under section 468 [of the Bank Act]" (Government of Canada (2022), "Bank Act, S.C. 1991, c. 46," adopted on December 13, 1991, entered into force on June 1, 1992, last amended on February 26, 2022, consolidated to May 2, 2022, s.464(1)). The first two subsections of section 468 of the Bank Act list permitted equity investments of a bank, and subsections (3)-(12) of section 468 of the Bank Act qualify the circumstances under which a bank may acquire control of, or acquire or increase a substantial investment in, the entities specified in subsections (1) and (2) of that section. A '*financial institution*' is "**(a)** a bank or an authorized foreign bank, **(b)** a body corporate to which the *Trust and Loan Companies Act* applies, **(c)** an association to which the *Cooperative Credit Associations Act* applies, **(d)** an insurance company or a fraternal benefit society incorporated or formed under the *Insurance Companies Act*, **(e)** a trust, loan or insurance corporation incorporated by[,] or under[,] an Act of the legislature of a province, **(f)** a cooperative credit society incorporated and regulated by[,] or under[,] an Act of the legislature of a province, **(g)** an entity that is incorporated or formed by[,] or under[,] an Act of Parliament or of the legislature of a province[,] and that is primarily engaged in dealing in securities, including portfolio management and investment counselling, and **(h)** a foreign institution." (Government of Canada (2022), "Bank Act, S.C. 1991, c. 46," adopted on December 13, 1991, entered into force on June 1, 1992, last amended on February 26, 2022, consolidated to May 2, 2022, s.2; emphasis original). The first sentence of fn 141 defines the term '*bank*'. The first sentence of fn 142 defines the terms '*authorized foreign bank*'. The final sentence of fn 154 defines the term '*body corporate*'. The second sentence of fn 148 defines the term '*entity*'. A '*foreign institution*' is "an entity that is **(a)** engaged in the business of banking, the trust, loan or insurance business, the business of a cooperative credit society or the business of dealing in securities[,] or is otherwise engaged primarily in the business of providing financial services, and **(b)** incorporated or formed otherwise than by[,] or under[,] an Act of Parliament or of the legislature of a province" (Government of Canada (2022), "Bank Act, S.C. 1991, c. 46," adopted on December 13, 1991, entered into force on June 1, 1992, last amended on February 26, 2022, consolidated to May 2, 2022, s.2; emphasis original). The first subsection of section 10 of the Bank Act defines the phrase '*substantial investment in a body corporate*', and the second and third subsections of section 10 of the Bank Act define the term '*increases substantial investment in a body corporate*'; these read: "**(1)** A person has a substantial investment in a body corporate[,] where **(a)** the voting rights attached to the aggregate of any voting shares of the body corporate [that are] beneficially owned by the person and by any entities controlled by the person[,] exceed 10 per cent of the voting rights attached to all of the outstanding voting shares of the body corporate; **(b)** the aggregate of any shares of the body corporate [which are] beneficially owned by the person and by any entities controlled by that person represents ownership of greater than 25 per cent of the shareholders' equity of the body corporate; or **(c)** in the case of a body corporate that is a federal credit union, **(i)** the voting rights of the person and of entities controlled by the person exceed 10 per cent of the aggregate of the voting

rights that may be exercised by members and shareholders; or **(ii)** the aggregate of any shares and membership shares of the federal credit union [which are] beneficially owned by the person and by any entities controlled by the person[,] represents ownership of greater than 25 per cent of the members' and shareholders' equity of the federal credit union. … **(2)** A person who has a substantial investment in a body corporate pursuant to paragraph (1)(a) increases that substantial investment[,] when the person or any entity controlled by the person **(a)** acquires beneficial ownership of additional voting shares of the body corporate in such number as to increase the percentage of voting rights attached to the aggregate of the voting shares of the body corporate [which are] beneficially owned by the person and by any entities controlled by the person; or **(b)** acquires control of any entity that beneficially owns any voting shares of the body corporate in such number as to increase the percentage of voting rights attached to the aggregate of the voting shares of the body corporate [which are] beneficially owned by the person and by any entities controlled by the person. … **(3)** A person who has a substantial investment in a body corporate pursuant to paragraph (1)(b) increases that substantial investment[,] when the person or any entity controlled by the person **(a)** acquires beneficial ownership of additional shares of the body corporate in such number as to increase the percentage of the shareholders' equity of the body corporate [which is] represented by the aggregate of the shares of the body corporate [that are] beneficially owned by the person and by any entities controlled by the person; or **(b)** acquires control of any entity that beneficially owns any shares of the body corporate in such number as to increase the percentage of the shareholders' equity of the body corporate [which is] represented by the aggregate of the shares of the body corporate [that are] beneficially owned by the person and by any entities controlled by the person." (Government of Canada (2022), "Bank Act, S.C. 1991, c. 46," adopted on December 13, 1991, entered into force on June 1, 1992, last amended on February 26, 2022, consolidated to May 2, 2022, s.10(1)-(3); emphasis original). The first sentence of fn 148 defines the term '*person*'. The preantepenultimate sentence of fn 157 defines the term '*control*'. Fn 151 defines the term '*federal credit union*'.

[185] Except as it is authorized so to do by, or under, the Bank Act, a bank must neither transact in goods, merchandise or wares, nor carry on any trade or other business (Government of Canada (2022), "Bank Act, S.C. 1991, c. 46," adopted on December 13, 1991, entered into force on June 1, 1992, last amended on February 26, 2022, consolidated to May 2, 2022, s.410(2)).

[186] In Canada, "[n]o bank shall act … as **(a)** an executor, administrator or official guardian[,] or a guardian, tutor, curator, judicial adviser or committee of a mentally incompetent person; or **(b)** a trustee for a trust" (Government of Canada (2022), "Bank Act, S.C. 1991, c. 46," adopted on December 13, 1991, entered into force on June 1, 1992, last amended on February 26, 2022, consolidated to May 2, 2022, s.412; emphasis original).

[187] In Canada, "[a] bank shall not accept deposits … unless **(a)** it is a member institution, as defined in section 2 of the *Canada Deposit Insurance Corporation Act*; **(b)** it has been authorized under subsection 26.03(1) of that Act to accept deposits without being a member institution, as defined in section 2 of that Act; or **(c)** the order approving the commencement and carrying on of business by the bank authorizes it to accept deposits solely in accordance with subsection (3) [(i.e., subsection 413(3) of the Bank Act)]" (Government of Canada (2022), "Bank Act, S.C. 1991, c. 46," adopted on December 13, 1991, entered into force on June 1, 1992, last amended on February 26, 2022, consolidated to May 2, 2022, s.413(1); emphasis original). Section 2 of the Canada Deposit Insurance Corporation Act defines a '*member institution*' as "a corporation that has deposit insurance under this Act" (Government of Canada (2022), "Canada Deposit Insurance Corporation Act, R.S.C. 1985, c. C-3," adopted on February 17, 1984, entered into force on February 17, 1984, last amended on April 30, 2022, consolidated to May 2, 2022, s.2). Section 26.02 of the Canada Deposit Insurance Corporation Act states: "If a federal member institution intends to accept deposits payable in Canada while no longer being a member institution, [then] it must apply to the [Canada Deposit Insurance] Corporation for an authorization to do so. The application must be in a form that is acceptable to the Corporation[,] and must contain the information that the Corporation may require." (Government of Canada (2022), "Canada Deposit Insurance Corporation Act, R.S.C. 1985, c. C-3," adopted on February 17, 1984, entered into force on February 17, 1984, last amended on April 30, 2022, consolidated to May 2, 2022, s.26.02). A '*federal member institution*' is "a federal institution that is a member institution" (Government of Canada (2022), "Canada Deposit Insurance Corporation Act, R.S.C. 1985, c. C-3," adopted on February 17, 1984, entered into force on February 17, 1984, last amended on April 30, 2022, consolidated to May 2, 2022, s.2). A '*federal institution*' is "a bank, company or association referred to in section 8 [of the Canada Deposit Insurance Corporation Act]" (Government of Canada (2022), "Canada Deposit Insurance Corporation Act, R.S.C. 1985, c. C-3," adopted on February 17, 1984, entered into force on February 17, 1984, last amended on April 30, 2022, consolidated to May 2, 2022, s.2). Section 8 of the Canada Deposit Insurance Corporation Act reads: "For the purposes of this Act, the following are federal institutions: **(a)** a bank; **(b)** a company to which the *Trust and Loan Companies Act* applies; and **(c)** a retail association within the meaning of regulations made under the *Cooperative Credit Association Act*." (Government of Canada (2022), "Canada Deposit Insurance Corporation Act, R.S.C. 1985, c. C-3," adopted on February 17, 1984, entered into force on February 17, 1984, last amended on April 30, 2022, consolidated to May 2, 2022, s.8; emphasis original). The first subsection of section 26.03 of the Canada Deposit Insurance Corporation Act declares: "Subject to section 26.04 [of the Canada Deposit Insurance Corporation Act], the [Canada Deposit Insurance]

Corporation may give that authorization [(i.e., the authorization that section 26.02 of the Canada Deposit Insurance Corporation Act – which the third sentence of the present footnote (i.e., fn 187) sets out – introduces),] if **(a)** [Repealed … ;] **(b)** the sum of all the deposits held by the federal member institution that are less than $150,000 [(i.e., CAD 150,000)] and payable in Canada is less than one per cent of the sum of all the deposits held by the institution that are payable in Canada; **(c)** the institution has informed all its depositors, in accordance with any rules that may be prescribed by the by-laws, **(i)** that the institution has applied to become authorized to accept deposits while no longer being a member institution, **(ii)** that[,] after the institution receives that authorization, no deposit with the institution will be insured[,] in whole or in part[,] by the Corporation, and **(iii)** that the institution's obligation to repay the deposit to the depositor will be assumed by a member institution if an option referred to in subparagraph (d)(i) or (ii) is not exercised; **(d)** in respect of each deposit that is held by the institution, the institution has **(i)** obtained from the depositor an acknowledgement in writing that the deposit will no longer be insured[,] in whole or in part[,] by the Corporation after the institution receives authorization to accept deposits without being a member institution, **(ii)** at the request in writing of the depositor, paid to the depositor the principal amount of the deposit and interest determined in accordance with rules prescribed by the by-laws[,] and has not charged any fee or penalty in connection with the payment, or **(iii)** obtained from a member institution an agreement in writing to assume the institution's liability in relation to the deposit on the same terms and conditions; and **(e)** the institution has paid to the Corporation a fee determined in accordance with rules prescribed by the by-laws." (Government of Canada (2022), "Canada Deposit Insurance Corporation Act, R.S.C. 1985, c. C-3," adopted on February 17, 1984, entered into force on February 17, 1984, last amended on April 30, 2022, consolidated to May 2, 2022, s.26.03(1)). Subsection 413(3) of the Bank Act specifies: "A bank referred to in paragraph (1)(b) or (c) [(i.e., paragraphs 413(1)(b) and 413(1)(c) of the Bank Act – which are clauses (b) and (c), respectively, in the first sentence of the current footnote (i.e., fn 187),] shall ensure that, on each day that is at least 30 days after the bank receives the authorization referred to in that paragraph, **A/B ≤ 0.01**[,] where **A** is the sum of all amounts each of which is the sum of all the deposits [that are] held by the bank at the end of a day in the preceding 30 days each of which deposits is less than $150,000 [(i.e., CAD 150,000)] and payable in Canada; and **B** is the sum of all amounts each of which is the sum of all deposits [that are] held by the bank at the end of a day in those preceding 30 days and payable in Canada." (Government of Canada (2022), "Bank Act, S.C. 1991, c. 46," adopted on December 13, 1991, entered into force on June 1, 1992, last amended on February 26, 2022, consolidated to May 2, 2022, s.413(3); emphasis original).

[188] The first two subsections of section 414 of the Bank Act state: "**(1)** A bank shall not guarantee on behalf of any person the payment or repayment of any sum of money[,] unless **(a)** the sum of money is a fixed sum of money with or without interest thereon; and **(b)** the person on whose behalf the bank has undertaken to guarantee the payment or repayment has an unqualified obligation to reimburse the bank for the full amount of the payment or repayment to be guaranteed. … **(2)** Paragraph (1)(a) does not apply where the person on whose behalf the bank had undertaken to guarantee the payment or repayment is a subsidiary of the bank." (Government of Canada (2022), "Bank Act, S.C. 1991, c. 46," adopted on December 13, 1991, entered into force on June 1, 1992, last amended on February 26, 2022, consolidated to May 2, 2022, s.414(1)-(2); emphasis original). The second sentence of fn 153 defines the term '*subsidiary*'.

[189] In Canada, "[a] bank shall not deal … in securities to the extent prohibited or restricted by such regulations as the Governor in Council may make for the purposes of this section [(i.e., section 415 of the Bank Act)]" (Government of Canada (2022), "Bank Act, S.C. 1991, c. 46," adopted on December 13, 1991, entered into force on June 1, 1992, last amended on February 26, 2022, consolidated to May 2, 2022, s.415).

[190] A bank is not permitted to "undertake the business of insurance[,] except to the extent permitted by this Act [(i.e., the Bank Act)] or the regulations" (Government of Canada (2022), "Bank Act, S.C. 1991, c. 46," adopted on December 13, 1991, entered into force on June 1, 1992, last amended on February 26, 2022, consolidated to May 2, 2022, s.416(1)). The phrase '*business of insurance*' means "**(a)** the issuance of any annuity[,] if the liability in respect of the annuity is contingent on the death of a person; and **(b)** the insurance of any debt obligation, any of whose terms and conditions are established on the basis of mortality considerations, under which the issuer is obliged to make periodic payments" (Government of Canada (2022), "Bank Act, S.C. 1991, c. 46," adopted on December 13, 1991, entered into force on June 1, 1992, last amended on February 26, 2022, consolidated to May 2, 2022, s.416(6); emphasis original).

[191] A bank is allowed to neither "act in Canada as agent for any person in the placing of insurance," nor "lease or provide space in any branch in Canada of the bank to any person [who or which is] engaged in the placing of insurance" (Government of Canada (2022), "Bank Act, S.C. 1991, c. 46," adopted on December 13, 1991, entered into force on June 1, 1992, last amended on February 26, 2022, consolidated to May 2, 2022, s.416(2)). The first sentence of fn 148 defines the term '*person*'.

[192] In Canada, "[a] bank shall not engage … in any personal property leasing activity in which a financial leasing entity, as defined in subsection 464(1) [of the Bank Act], is not permitted to engage" (Government of Canada (2022), "Bank Act, S.C. 1991, c. 46," adopted on December 13, 1991, entered into force on June 1, 1992, last amended on February 26, 2022, consolidated to May 2, 2022, s.417). Subsection 464(1) of the Bank Act defines the phrase '*financial leasing entity*' as: "an entity **(a)** the activities of which are limited to the financial leasing

making loans on the security of residential property[193], the appointment of receivers[194], partnership[195], and – if the bank is a subsidiary of a foreign bank and is not controlled by a "WTO Member resident"[196] [313] – the opening of branches in Canada[197]. The Bank Act provides for the Governor Council to make regulations concerning the activities of bank in

of personal property and such related activities as are prescribed[,] and whose activities conform to such restrictions and limitations thereon as are prescribed; and **(b)** that, in conducting the activities referred to in paragraph (a) in Canada, does not **(i)** direct its customers or potential customers to particular dealers in the leased property or the property to be leased, **(ii)** enter into lease agreements with persons in respect of any motor vehicle having a gross vehicle weight, as that expression is defined by the regulations, of less than twenty-one tonnes, or **(iii)** enter into lease agreements with natural persons in respect of personal household property, as that expression is defined by the regulations" (Government of Canada (2022), "Bank Act, S.C. 1991, c. 46," adopted on December 13, 1991, entered into force on June 1, 1992, last amended on February 26, 2022, consolidated to May 2, 2022, s.464(1); emphasis original).

[193] A bank is not permitted to "make a loan in Canada on the security of residential property in Canada for the purpose of purchasing, renovating or improving that property, or refinance such a loan, if the amount of the loan, together with the amount then outstanding of any mortgage having an equal or prior claim against the property, would exceed 80 per cent of the value of the property at the time of the loan" (Government of Canada (2022), "Bank Act, S.C. 1991, c. 46," adopted on December 13, 1991, entered into force on June 1, 1992, last amended on February 26, 2022, consolidated to May 2, 2022, s.418(1)). That subsection (i.e., subsection 418(1) of the Bank Act) "does not apply in respect of **(a)** a loan [that is] made or guaranteed under the *National Housing Act*[,] or any other Act of Parliament by[,] or pursuant to[,] which a different limit on the value of property[,] on the security of which the bank may make a loan[,] is established; **(b)** a loan[,] if repayment of the amount of the loan that exceeds the maximum amount set out in subsection (1) [(i.e., subsection 418(1) of the Bank Act),] is guaranteed or insured by a government agency or a private insurer approved by the Superintendent; **(c)** the acquisition by the bank[,] from an entity[,] of securities issued or guaranteed by the entity that are secured on any residential property, whether in favour of a trustee or otherwise, or the making of a loan by the bank to the entity against the issue of such securities; or **(d)** a loan [that is] secured by a mortgage[,] where **(i)** the mortgage is taken back by the bank on a property disposed of by the bank, including where the disposition is by way of a realization of a security interest, and **(ii)** the mortgage secures payment of an amount payable to the bank for the property." (Government of Canada (2022), "Bank Act, S.C. 1991, c. 46," adopted on December 13, 1991, entered into force on June 1, 1992, last amended on February 26, 2022, consolidated to May 2, 2022, s.418(2); emphasis original). Fn 155 defines the term '*Superintendent*'. The second sentence of fn 148 defines the term '*entity*'. Subsection 418.1(1) of the Bank Act limits the amount that a bank can charge a borrower in respect of "insurance or a guarantee against default on a loan made in Canada on the security of residential property," subject to regulations made under subsection 418.1(2) of the Bank Act (Government of Canada (2022), "Bank Act, S.C. 1991, c. 46," adopted on December 13, 1991, entered into force on June 1, 1992, last amended on February 26, 2022, consolidated to May 2, 2022, s.418.1(1)).

[194] A bank is not allowed to "grant to a person the right to appoint a receiver[,] or a receiver and manager[,] of the property or business of a bank" (Government of Canada (2022), "Bank Act, S.C. 1991, c. 46," adopted on December 13, 1991, entered into force on June 1, 1992, last amended on February 26, 2022, consolidated to May 2, 2022, s.420). The first sentence of fn 148 defines the term '*person*'.

[195] A bank may only "be a general partner in a limited partnership or a partner in a general partnership … with the approval of the Superintendent" (Government of Canada (2022), "Bank Act, S.C. 1991, c. 46," adopted on December 13, 1991, entered into force on June 1, 1992, last amended on February 26, 2022, consolidated to May 2, 2022, s.421(1)). Fn 155 defines the term '*Superintendent*'. A '*general partnership*' is "any partnership other than a limited partnership" (Government of Canada (2022), "Bank Act, S.C. 1991, c. 46," adopted on December 13, 1991, entered into force on June 1, 1992, last amended on February 26, 2022, consolidated to May 2, 2022, s.421(2)).

[196] The Bank Act designates such a bank as a '*non-WTO Member Bank subsidiary*' (Government of Canada (2022), "Bank Act, S.C. 1991, c. 46," adopted on December 13, 1991, entered into force on June 1, 1992, last amended on February 26, 2022, consolidated to May 2, 2022, s.422.1).

[197] A 'non-WTO Member Bank subsidiary' (fn 196 and accompanying text) may not open any branch in Canada – except for its head office and a single branch, without the Minister's approval (Government of Canada (2022), "Bank Act, S.C. 1991, c. 46," adopted on December 13, 1991, entered into force on June 1, 1992, last amended on February 26, 2022, consolidated to May 2, 2022, s.422.2). The term '*Minister*' means the Minister of Finance (penultimate sentence of fn 142).

connection with benchmarks[198] [314], eligible financial contracts[199] and derivatives[200] [315]. It contains a prohibition for a bank to issue specified debt obligations[201] [316].

Investments

A bank's directors[202] are to establish, and the bank[203] shall observe, standards, policies and procedures for investment that a reasonable, prudent person would apply concerning a portfolio of investments and loans – in order to avoid excessive risk of loss and attain a respectable return [317]. The total value of all ownership interests in the business growth fund – and the entities which this fund controls[204] – that a bank and its subsidiaries hold, must be no more than CAD 200 million[205] [318]. No bank may acquire control of, or hold, obtain or increase a substantial investment[206] in, any entity bar a permitted entity[207], subject to exceptions concerning indirect

---

[198] A '*benchmark*' is "a price, estimate, rate, index or value that is **(a)** determined from time to time by reference to an assessment of one or more underlying interests; **(b)** made available to the public, either free of charge or on payment; and **(c)** used for reference for any purpose, including **(i)** determining the interest payable, or other sums that are due, under loan agreements or other financial contracts or instruments, **(ii)** determining the value of financial instruments or the price at which they may be bought or sold, and **(iii)** measuring the performance of financial instruments" (Government of Canada (2022), "Bank Act, S.C. 1991, c. 46," adopted on December 13, 1991, entered into force on June 1, 1992, last amended on February 26, 2022, consolidated to May 2, 2022, s.415.3(2); emphasis original).

[199] An '*eligible financial contract*' is "an agreement of a prescribed kind" (Government of Canada (2022), "Bank Act, S.C. 1991, c. 46," adopted on December 13, 1991, entered into force on June 1, 1992, last amended on February 26, 2022, consolidated to May 2, 2022, s.415.2(3); Government of Canada (2022), "Canada Deposit Insurance Corporation Act, R.S.C. 1985, c. C-3," adopted on February 17, 1984, entered into force on February 17, 1984, last amended on April 30, 2022, Consolidated to May 2, 2022, s.39.15(9)).

[200] A '*derivative*' is "an option, swap, futures contract, forward contract or other financial or commodity contract or instrument whose market price, value, delivery obligations, payment obligations or settlement obligations are derived from, referenced to or based on an underlying interest, including a price, rate, index, value, variable, event, probability or thing" (Government of Canada (2022), "Bank Act, S.C. 1991, c. 46," adopted on December 13, 1991, entered into force on June 1, 1992, last amended on February 26, 2022, consolidated to May 2, 2022, s.415.2(2)).

[201] Section 415.1 of the Bank Act states: "**(1)** It is prohibited for a bank to issue a debt obligation in relation to which the amounts of principal and interest owing are guaranteed to be paid from loans or other assets held by an entity that is created and organized for the principal purpose of holding those loans or other assets[,] and with the intention of legally isolating those loans or other assets from the bank, unless **(a)** the debt obligation is a covered bond as defined in section 21.5 of the *National Housing Act*; **(b)** the bank is a registered issuer as defined in section 21.5 of that Act[,] other than one whose right to issue covered bonds has been suspended; and **(c)** the debt obligation is issued under a registered program as defined in section 21.5 of that Act." … **(2)** The Governor in Council may make regulations exempting any type of debt obligation from the application of subsection (1)." (Government of Canada (2022), "Bank Act, S.C. 1991, c. 46," adopted on December 13, 1991, entered into force on June 1, 1992, last amended on February 26, 2022, consolidated to May 2, 2022, s.415.1; emphasis original). A '*debt obligation*' is "a bond, debenture, note or other evidence of indebtedness of an entity, whether secured or unsecured" (Government of Canada (2022), "Bank Act, S.C. 1991, c. 46," adopted on December 13, 1991, entered into force on June 1, 1992, last amended on February 26, 2022, consolidated to May 2, 2022, s.2).

[202] The first sentence of fn 154 defines the terms '*director*' and '*directors*'.

[203] The first sentence of fn 141 defines the term '*bank*'.

[204] The preantepenultimate sentence of fn 157 defines the term '*control*'.

[205] The sum paid for an ownership interest at the time of its issuance determines its value (Government of Canada (2022), "Bank Act, S.C. 1991, c. 46," adopted on December 13, 1991, entered into force on June 1, 1992, last amended on February 26, 2022, consolidated to May 2, 2022, s.465.1(2)).

[206] Fn 184 defines the terms '*substantial investment in a body corporate*' and '*increases substantial investment in a body corporate*'.

[207] The second sentence of fn 148 defines the term '*entity*'. The third sentence of fn 184 defines the term '*permitted entity*'.

investments[208], temporary investments, acquisitions of ownership interests and realizations of securities[209], investment in accordance with specialized financing regulations[210] and the business growth fund and any entity that this fund controls[211] [319].

---

[208] Subsection 466(2) of the Bank Act states: "A bank may, subject to Part XI [of the Bank Act, which is titled 'Self-dealing', and which comprises sections 485.1-506 of this Act], acquire control of, or acquire or increase a substantial investment in, an entity[,] other than a permitted entity[,] by way of **(a)** an acquisition of control of an entity referred to in any of paragraphs 468(1)(a) to (j) [of the Bank Act (text to fns 212-217)], or of a prescribed entity, that controls[,] or has a substantial interest in[,] the entity; or **(b)** an acquisition of shares or ownership interests in the entity[,] by **(i)** an entity referred to in any of the paragraphs 468(1)(a) to (j), or a prescribed entity, that is controlled by the bank, or **(ii)** an entity controlled by an entity referred to in any of paragraphs 468(1)(a) to (j), or a prescribed entity, that is controlled by the bank." (Government of Canada (2022), "Bank Act, S.C. 1991, c. 46," adopted on December 13, 1991, entered into force on June 1, 1992, last amended on February 26, 2022, consolidated to May 2, 2022, s.466(2); emphasis original). The first sentence of fn 141 defines the term '*bank*'. The preantepenultimate sentence of fn 157 defines the term '*control*'. Fn 184 defines the terms '*substantial investment in a body corporate*' and '*increases substantial investment in a body corporate*'. The second sentence of fn 148 defines the term '*entity*'. The third sentence of fn 184 defines the term '*permitted entity*'.

[209] Subsection 466(3) of the Bank Act declares: "A bank may, subject to Part XI [of the Bank Act, which is entitled 'Self-dealing', and which contains sections 485.1-506 of this Act], acquire control of, or acquire or increase a substantial investment in, an entity[,] by way of **(a)** a temporary investment permitted by section 471 [of the Bank Act]; **(b)** an acquisition of shares of a body corporate or of ownership interests in an unincorporated entity permitted by section 472 [of the Bank Act]; or **(c)** a realization of security permitted by section 473 [of the Bank Act]." (Government of Canada (2022), "Bank Act, S.C. 1991, c. 46," adopted on December 13, 1991, entered into force on June 1, 1992, last amended on February 26, 2022, consolidated to May 2, 2022, s.466(2); emphasis original). The first sentence of fn 141 defines the term '*bank*'. The preantepenultimate sentence of fn 157 defines the term '*control*'. Fn 184 defines the terms '*substantial investment in a body corporate*' and '*increases substantial investment in a body corporate*'. The second sentence of fn 148 defines the term '*entity*'. Subsections (1) and (4) of section 471 of the Bank Act read: "**(1)** Subject to subsection (4), a bank may, by way of a temporary investment, acquire control of, or acquire or increase a substantial investment in, an entity[,] but, within two years, or any other period that may be specified or approved by the Superintendent, after acquiring control or after acquiring or increasing the substantial investment, as the case may be, it shall do all things necessary to ensure that it no longer controls the entity or has a substantial investment in the entity ... . **(4)** If a bank, by way of temporary investment, acquires control of, or acquires or increases a substantial investment in, an entity for which the approval of the Minister would have been required under subsection 468(5) [of the Bank Act] if the bank had acquired the control, or acquired or increased the substantial investment, under section 468 [of the Bank Act, then] the bank must, within 90 days after acquiring control or after acquiring or increasing the substantial investment, **(a)** apply to the Minister for approval to retain control of the entity or to continue to hold the substantial investment in the entity[,] for a period specified by the Minister or for an indeterminate period on any terms and conditions that the Minister considers appropriate; or **(b)** do all things necessary to ensure that, on the expiry of the 90 days, it no longer controls the entity or does not have a substantial investment in the entity." (Government of Canada (2022), "Bank Act, S.C. 1991, c. 46," adopted on December 13, 1991, entered into force on June 1, 1992, last amended on February 26, 2022, consolidated to May 2, 2022, ss.471(1) and 471(4); emphasis original). Fn 155 defines the term '*Superintendent*'. The term '*Minister*' means the Minister of Finance (penultimate sentence of fn 142). The first two subsections of section 472 of the Bank Act specify: "**(1)** Despite anything in this Part [(i.e., Part IX of the Bank Act, which is titled 'Investments', and which comprises sections 464-484 of this Act)], if a bank or any of its subsidiaries has made a loan to an entity[,] and, under the terms of the agreement between the bank, or any of its subsidiaries, and the entity with respect to the loan and any other documents governing the terms of the loan, a default has occurred, [then] the bank may acquire **(a)** if the entity is a body corporate, all or any of the shares of the body corporate, **(b)** if the entity is an unincorporated entity, all or any of the ownership interests in the entity; **(c)** all or any of the shares[,] or all or any of the ownership interests[,] in any entity that is an affiliate of the entity; **(d)** all or any of the shares of a body corporate that is primarily engaged in holding shares of, ownership interests in[,] or assets acquired from[,] the entity or any of its affiliates; or **(e)** all or any of the ownership interests in any entity that is primarily engaged in holding shares of, ownership interests in[,] or assets acquired from[,] the entity or any of its affiliates. ... **(2)** If a bank acquires shares or ownership interests in an entity under subsection (1), [then] the bank shall, within five years after acquiring them, do all things necessary to ensure that the bank does not control the entity or have a substantial investment in the entity." (Government of Canada (2022), "Bank Act, S.C. 1991, c. 46," adopted on December 13, 1991, entered into force on June 1, 1992, last amended on February 26, 2022, consolidated to May 2, 2022, s.472(1)-(2); emphasis original). The first sentence of fn 157 defines the term '*affiliate*'. The first two subsections of section 473 of the Bank Act state: "**(1)** Despite anything in this Act, a bank may acquire **(a)**

an investment in a body corporate, **(b)** an interest in an unincorporated entity, or **(c)** an interest in real property[,] if the investment or interest is acquired through the realization of a security interest held by the bank or any of its subsidiaries. ... **(2)** Subject to subsection 73(2) [of the Bank Act], if a bank acquires control of, or acquires a substantial investment in, an entity by way of the realization of a security interest held by the bank or any of its subsidiaries, [then] the bank shall, within five years after the day on which control or the substantial investment is acquired, do all things necessary, or cause its subsidiary to do all things necessary, as the case may be, to ensure that the bank no longer controls the entity or has a substantial investment in the entity." (Government of Canada (2022), "Bank Act, S.C. 1991, c. 46," adopted on December 13, 1991, entered into force on June 1, 1992, last amended on February 26, 2022, consolidated to May 2, 2022, s.473(1)-(2); emphasis original). The second sentence of fn 153 defines the term '*subsidiary*'. Subsection 73(2) of the Bank Act declares: "Where a bank or any of its subsidiaries, through the realization of security, acquires any shares of the bank or of any body corporate that controls the bank or any ownership interests in an unincorporated entity that controls the bank, the bank shall, or shall cause its subsidiaries to, as the case may be, within six months after the day of the realization, sell[,] or otherwise dispose of[,] the shares or ownership interests." (Government of Canada (2022), "Bank Act, S.C. 1991, c. 46," adopted on December 13, 1991, entered into force on June 1, 1992, last amended on February 26, 2022, consolidated to May 2, 2022, s.73(2)).

[210] Subsection 466(4) of the Bank Act states: "A bank may, subject to Part XI [of the Bank Act, which is titled 'Self-dealing', and which consist of sections 485.1-506 of this Act], acquire control of, or hold, acquire or increase a substantial investment in, an entity other than a permitted entity[,] if it does so in accordance with regulations made under paragraph 467(d) [of the Bank Act] concerning specialized financing." (Government of Canada (2022), "Bank Act, S.C. 1991, c. 46," adopted on December 13, 1991, entered into force on June 1, 1992, last amended on February 26, 2022, consolidated to May 2, 2022, s.466(4)). The first sentence of fn 141 defines the term '*bank*'. The preantepenultimate sentence of fn 157 defines the term '*control*'. Fn 184 defines the terms '*substantial investment in a body corporate*' and '*increases substantial investment in a body corporate*'. The second sentence of fn 148 defines the term '*entity*'. The third sentence of fn 184 defines the term '*permitted entity*'. Paragraph 467(d) of the Bank Act reads: "The Governor in Council may make regulations ... concerning specialized financing for the purposes of subsection 466(4) [of the Bank Act]" (Government of Canada (2022), "Bank Act, S.C. 1991, c. 46," adopted on December 13, 1991, entered into force on June 1, 1992, last amended on February 26, 2022, consolidated to May 2, 2022, s.467(d)).

[211] Subsection 466(4.1) of the Bank Act declares: "Subject to section 465.1 [of the Bank Act], subsections [466](4.2) to [466](4.4) and Part XI [of the Bank Act, which is titled 'Self-dealing', and which consist of sections 485.1-506 of this Act], a bank may hold, acquire or increase a substantial investment in the business growth fund or any entity that the business growth fund controls." (Government of Canada (2022), "Bank Act, S.C. 1991, c. 46," adopted on December 13, 1991, entered into force on June 1, 1992, last amended on February 26, 2022, consolidated to May 2, 2022, s.466(4.1)). The text to fns 204 and 205 states the first subsection of section 465.1 of the Bank Act. Fn 205 sets out the second subsection of section 465.1 of the Bank Act. Subsections 466(4.2)-(4.4) read: "**(4.2)** For greater certainty, a bank is prohibited from acquiring control of the business growth fund or any entity that the business growth fund controls. ... **(4.3)** A bank is prohibited from holding or acquiring a substantial investment in the business growth fund or any entity that the business growth fund controls[,] if the business growth fund or any entity that the growth fund controls[,] holds or acquires shares of, or other ownership interests in, any of the following entities, or in any entity that controls any of the following entities: **(a)** an entity referred to in any of paragraphs 468(1)(a) to (j) [of the Bank Act (text to fns 212-217)]; **(b)** an entity that is primarily engaged in the leasing of motor vehicles in Canada[,] for the purpose of extending credit to a customer or financing a customer's acquisition of a motor vehicle; **(c)** an entity that is primarily engaged in providing temporary possession of personal property, including motor vehicles, to customers in Canada[,] for a purpose other than to finance the customer's acquisition of the property; **(d)** an entity that acts as an insurance broker or agent in Canada; or **(e)** an entity that is engaged in any prescribed activity. ... **(4.4)** A bank is prohibited from holding or acquiring a substantial investment in the business growth fund or any entity that the business growth fund controls[,] if the business growth fund or any entity that the business growth fund controls holds shares of, or other ownership interests in, an entity[,] or holds a loan made to an entity and, in respect of that entity and its affiliates, the aggregate value of the following exceeds $100,000,000 [(i.e., CAD 100 million)]: **(a)** all ownership interests that are held by the bank, the bank's subsidiaries, the business growth fund or the entities that the business growth fund controls, the value of those ownership interests as determined by the amount paid for them at the time [that] each was first acquired by any of those entities; and **(b)** the outstanding principal of all loans held by the business growth fund or the entities that the business growth fund controls." (Government of Canada (2022), "Bank Act, S.C. 1991, c. 46," adopted on December 13, 1991, entered into force on June 1, 1992, last amended on February 26, 2022, consolidated to May 2, 2022, s.466(4.2)-(4.4); emphasis original). The first sentence of fn 141 defines the term '*bank*'. Fn 184 defines the terms '*substantial investment in a body corporate*' and '*increases substantial investment in a body corporate*'. The second sentence of fn 148 defines the term '*entity*'. The preantepenultimate sentence of fn 157 defines the term '*control*'.

Subject to subsections 468(4) to 468(6) and Part XI of the Bank Act,[212] a bank may acquire or increase a substantial investment in, or gain control of, a bank[213] [320], a bank holding company[214] [321], a body corporate[215] to which the Trust and Loan Companies Act applies [322], an association to which the Cooperative Credit Associations Act applies [323], an insurance company – or a fraternal benefit society – that is established or incorporated by, or under, the Insurance Companies Act [324], an insurance holding company [325], a loan, insurance or trust corporation which is founded or incorporated by, or under, an Act of a provincial legislature [326], a co-operative credit society that is created or incorporated by, or under, an Act of a provincial legislature [327], an entity[216] which is formed or incorporated by, or under, an Act of Parliament or of a provincial legislature, and that is mainly involved in dealing in securities [328], or an entity which is set up or incorporated, and regulated, by means other than by, or under, an Act of Parliament or of a provincial legislature, and that is predominantly engaged outside Canada in a business which, if conducted in Canada, would be the business of banking, insurance, dealing in securities or supplying fiduciary services, or that of a co-operative credit society[217] [329]. A bank may acquire an investment in a body corporate,

---

[212] Part XI of the Bank Act is entitled 'Self-dealing', and comprises sections 485.1-506 of this Act.

[213] The first sentence of fn 141 defines the term '*bank*'. The preantepenultimate sentence of fn 157 defines the term '*control*'.

[214] A '*bank holding company*' is "a body corporate that is incorporated or formed under Part XV [of the Bank Act, which is titled 'Bank Holding Companies' and which consists of sections 662-964 of this Act] (Government of Canada (2022), "Bank Act, S.C. 1991, c. 46," adopted on December 13, 1991, entered into force on June 1, 1992, last amended on February 26, 2022, consolidated to May 2, 2022, s.2).

[215] The last sentence of fn 154 defines the term '*body corporate*'. Fn 184 defines the terms '*substantial investment in a body corporate*' and '*increases substantial investment in a body corporate*'.

[216] The second sentence of fn 148 defines the term '*entity*'.

[217] Subject to subsections 468(3)-468(6) and Part XI of the Bank Act – which is entitled 'Self-dealing', and which consists of sections 485.1-506 of this Act, "a bank may acquire control of, or acquire or increase a substantial investment in, an entity, other than an entity referred to in any of paragraphs (1)(a) to (j) [i.e., paragraphs 468(1)(a) to 468(1)(j) of the Bank Act (text to fns 212-217)], whose business is limited to one or more of the following: **(a)** engaging in any financial service activity that a bank is permitted to engage in under any of paragraphs 409(2)(a) to (d) [of the Bank Act (sentence immediately preceding the text to fn 184)],) or any other activity that a bank is permitted to engage in under section 410 or 411 [of the Bank Act]; **(b)** acquiring or holding shares of, or ownership interests in, entities in which a bank is permitted under this Part to hold or acquire; **(c)** engaging in the provision of any services exclusively to any or all of the following, so long as the entity is providing those services to the bank or any member of the bank's group, namely, **(i)** the bank, **(ii)** any member of the bank's group, **(iii)** any entity that is primarily engaged in the business of providing financial services, **(iv)** any permitted entity in which an entity referred to in subparagraph (iii) has a substantial investment, or **(v)** any prescribed person, if it is doing so under prescribed terms and conditions, if any are prescribed; **(d)** engaging in any activity that a bank is permitted to engage in, other than an activity referred to in paragraph (a) or (e), that relates to **(i)** the promotion, sale, delivery or distribution of a financial product or financial service that is provided by the bank or any member of the bank's group, or **(ii)** if a significant portion of the business of the entity involves an activity referred to in subparagraph (i), the promotion, sale, delivery or distribution of a financial product or financial service that is provided by any other entity that is primarily engaged in the business of providing financial services; **(e)** engaging in the activities referred to in the definition *closed-end fund, mutual fund distribution entity, mutual fund entity* or *real property brokerage entity* in subsection 464(1) [of the Bank Act]; and **(f)** engaging in prescribed activities, under prescribed terms and conditions, if any are prescribed." (Government of Canada (2022), "Bank Act, S.C. 1991, c. 46," adopted on December 13, 1991, entered into force on June 1, 1992, last amended on February 26, 2022, consolidated to May 2, 2022, s.468(2); emphasis original). 'This Part' is Part IX of the Bank Act, which is titled 'Investments', and which comprises sections 464-484 of this Act. The first sentence of fn 184 lays down subsection 410(1) of the Bank Act. Fn 185 states subsection 410(2) of the Bank Act. Section 411 of the Bank Act reads: "**(1)** Subject to section 416 [of the Bank Act], a bank may **(a)** act as agent for any person in respect of the provision of any service that is provided by a financial institution, a permitted entity as defined in subsection 464(1) [of the Bank Act (third sentence of fn 184),] or a prescribed entity[,] and may enter into an arrangement with any person in respect of the provision of that service; or **(b)** refer any person to any such financial institution or entity. … **(2)** The Governor in Council may make

or an interest in an unincorporated entity or in real property[218], if the investment or interest is obtained through the realization of a security interest that the bank or any of its subsidiaries[219] holds[220] [330].

Neither a bank nor its prescribed subsidiaries[221] may acquire an interest in real property or improve such real property in which any of these has an interest, if the total value of all interests of the bank in real property after this acquisition or improvement exceeds the prescribed percentage of the bank's regulatory capital [331]. The Bank Act contains a corresponding provision regarding equity acquisitions[222].

Without the Superintendent's[223] approval, neither a bank nor its subsidiaries may acquire assets from, or transfer assets to, a person, if A + B > C, where A is the value of these assets, B is the total value of all assets that the bank and its subsidiaries obtained from, or conveyed

---

regulations respecting the disclosure of **(a)** the name of the principal for whom a bank is acting as agent pursuant to subsection (1); and **(b)** whether any commission is being earned by a bank when acting as agent pursuant to subsection (1)." (Government of Canada (2022), "Bank Act, S.C. 1991, c. 46," adopted on December 13, 1991, entered into force on June 1, 1992, last amended on February 26, 2022, consolidated to May 2, 2022, s.411; emphasis original). Fn 190 contains subsections 416(1) and 416(6) of the Bank Act. Fn 191 sets out subsection 416(2) of the Bank Act. The first sentence of fn 141 defines the term '*bank*'. The preantepenultimate sentence of fn 157 defines the term '*control*'. Fn 184 defines the terms '*substantial investment in a body corporate*' and '*increases substantial investment in a body corporate*'. The second sentence of fn 148 defines the term '*entity*'. The word '*prescribed*' means 'prescribed by regulation' (Government of Canada (2022), "Bank Act, S.C. 1991, c. 46," adopted on December 13, 1991, entered into force on June 1, 1992, last amended on February 26, 2022, consolidated to May 2, 2022, s.2). The fifth sentence of fn 184 defines the term '*financial institution*'.

218 The phrase '*real property*' "includes a leasehold interest in real property" (Government of Canada (2022), "Bank Act, S.C. 1991, c. 46," adopted on December 13, 1991, entered into force on June 1, 1992, last amended on February 26, 2022, consolidated to May 2, 2022, s.2).

219 The second sentence of fn 153 defines the term '*subsidiary*'.

220 Contingent on subsection 73(2) of Bank Act, "if a bank acquires control of, or acquires a substantial interest in, an entity[,] by way of the realization of a security interest held by the bank or any of its subsidiaries, [then] the bank shall, within five years after the day on which control or the substantial investment is acquired, do all things necessary, or cause its subsidiary to do all things necessary, as the case may be, to ensure that the bank no longer controls the entity or has a substantial investment in the entity" (Government of Canada (2022), "Bank Act, S.C. 1991, c. 46," adopted on December 13, 1991, entered into force on June 1, 1992, last amended on February 26, 2022, consolidated to May 2, 2022, s.473(2)). The final sentence of fn 209 sets out subsection 73(2) of the Bank Act. The first sentence of fn 141 defines the term '*bank*'. The preantepenultimate sentence of fn 157 defines the term '*control*'. Fn 184 defines the term '*substantial investment in a body corporate*'. The second sentence of fn 148 defines the term '*entity*'. The second sentence of fn 153 defines the term '*subsidiary*'.

221 A '*prescribed subsidiary*' is "a subsidiary that is one of a prescribed class of subsidiaries" (Government of Canada (2022), "Bank Act, S.C. 1991, c. 46," adopted on December 13, 1991, entered into force on June 1, 1992, last amended on February 26, 2022, consolidated to May 2, 2022, s.464(1)). The second sentence of fn 153 defines the term '*subsidiary*'. The penultimate sentence of fn 217 defines the term '*prescribed*'.

222 Section 477 of the Bank Act is entitled 'Limits on equity acquisitions', and states: "A bank shall not, and shall not permit its prescribed subsidiaries to, **(a)** purchase or otherwise acquire any participating shares of any body corporate or any ownership interests in any unincorporated entity, other than those of a permitted entity in which the bank has, or by virtue of the acquisition would have, a substantial investment, or **(b)** acquire control of an entity that holds shares or ownership interests referred to in paragraph (a), if the aggregate value of **(c)** all participating shares, excluding participating shares of permitted entities in which the bank has a substantial investment, and **(d)** all ownership interests in unincorporated entities, other than ownership interests in permitted entities in which the bank has a substantial investment, beneficially owned by the bank and its prescribed subsidiaries, exceeds, or the purchase or acquisition would cause that aggregate value to exceed, the prescribed percentage of the regulatory capital of the bank." (Government of Canada (2022), "Bank Act, S.C. 1991, c. 46," adopted on December 13, 1991, entered into force on June 1, 1992, last amended on February 26, 2022, consolidated to May 2, 2022, s.477; emphasis original). The first sentence of fn 141 defines the term '*bank*'. The first sentence of fn 221 defines the term '*prescribed subsidiary*'. The third sentence of fn 184 defines the term '*permitted entity*'. The preantepenultimate sentence of fn 157 defines the term '*control*'. Fn 184 defines the term '*substantial investment in a body corporate*'.

223 Fn 155 defines the term '*Superintendent*'.

to, that person, in the year ending immediately prior to the acquisition or transfer, and C is 10% of the total value of the bank's assets – as shown in the bank's annual statement immediately preceding the transfer [332]. The Bank Act specifies several instances of non-application of this asset transfer rule, such as assets that are debt obligations of an entity that the bank controls [333].

Bank Capital and Liquidity

By order, the Superintendent[224] may designate a bank[225] as a domestic systemically important bank, unless the Minister[226] advisers the Superintendent that (s)he considers it not to be in the public interest to do this[227] [334]. In a similar way, the Superintendent may revoke such a designation [335]. In making or rescinding this designation, the Superintendent must take into account all factors that (s)he deems to be relevant – which include whether the distress or failure of the bank could significantly impact Canada's financial system [336].

In respect of its operations, a bank must maintain sufficient capital, and suitable, adequate types of liquidity, and shall observe any regulations concerning these matters[228] [337]. If the bank is a Domestically Systemically Important Bank[229], then it must maintain the minimum capacity to absorb losses for which subsection 485(1.2) of the Bank Act provides[230], and adhere to regulations in respect of this requirement [338]. The Bank Act empowers the Governor in Council to make regulations for, and the Superintendent to provide guidelines and

---

224 Fn 155 defines the term '*Superintendent*'.

225 The first sentence of fn 141 defines the term '*bank*'.

226 The term '*Minister*' means the Minister of Finance (penultimate sentence of fn 142).

227 The following financial institutions of Canada are Domestic Systemically Important Banks: Bank of Montreal, Canadian Imperial Bank of Commerce, National Bank of Canada, Royal Bank of Canada, The Bank of Nova Scotia, and The Toronto-Dominion Bank (Office of the Superintendent of Financial Institutions – Canada (2021), "Industry Letter: June 17, 2021 – OSFI sets the Domestic Stability Buffer level to 2.50% effective October 31, 2021," accessed June 10, 2022, <https://www.osfi-bsif.gc.ca/Eng/fi-if/in-ai/Pages/dsb20210617-let.aspx>). Two financial institutions of Canada are Global Systemically Important Banks – Royal Bank of Canada and The Toronto-Dominion Bank (Financial Stability Board (2021), 2021 List of Global Systemically Important Banks (G-SIBs): 23 November 2021 (Basel: Financial Stability Board), 3).

228 This includes all the guidelines that the Office of the Superintendent of Financial Institutions has provided concerning the implementation in Canada of the capital and liquidity standards for banks that the Basel Committee on Banking Supervision has issued – which can be accessed from the Office's website at https://www.osfi-bsif.gc.ca/Eng/fi-if/rg-ro/gdn-ort/gl-ld/Pages/default.aspx#cpt.

229 The first sentence of fn 227 lists Canada's Domestic Systemically Important Banks.

230 Subsections 485(1.2), 485(1.21) and 485(1.3) of the Bank Act state: "**(1.2)** For each domestic systemically important bank, the Superintendent shall, by order made after consulting with the other members of the committee established under subsection 18(1) of the *Office of the Superintendent of Financial Institutions Act*, provide for the amount that constitutes the bank's minimum capacity to absorb losses. … **(1.21)** The amount set under subsection (1.2) consists of capital, prescribed shares and prescribed liabilities, which have the value determined in accordance with any criteria [that] the Superintendent considers appropriate. … **(1.3)** Despite subsection (1.2), if[,] before the order is made, the Minister advises the Superintendent that the Minister is of the opinion that the amount provided for by the Superintendent is not in the public interest, [then] the Superintendent shall provide for another amount in accordance with that subsection." (Government of Canada (2022), "Bank Act, S.C. 1991, c. 46," adopted on December 13, 1991, entered into force on June 1, 1992, last amended on February 26, 2022, consolidated to May 2, 2022, s.485(1.2)-(1.3); emphasis original). Subsection 18(1) of the Office of the Superintendent of Financial Institutions Act specifies: "There is hereby established a committee consisting of **(a)** the Superintendent; **(a.1)** the Commissioner of the Financial Consumer Agency of Canada; **(b)** the Governor of the Bank of Canada; **(c)** the Chief Executive Officer of the Canada Deposit Insurance Corporation; and **(d)** the Deputy Minister of Finance." (Government of Canada (2022), "Office of the Superintendent of Financial Institutions Act, R. S. C. 1985, c. 18 (3rd Supp.), Part I," entered into force on July 2, 1987, last amended on December 13, 2018, consolidated to May 16, 2022, s.18(1); emphasis original).

orders to, a Domestic Systemically Important Bank in Canada [339] – with which it is required to comply[231] [340].

[231] Subsections 485(2), 485(3), 485(3.1), 485(3.2) and 485(4) of the Bank Act declare: "**(2)** The Governor in Council may make regulations[,] and the Superintendent may make guidelines[,] respecting the maintenance by banks of adequate capital and adequate and appropriate forms of liquidity[,] and the maintenance by domestic systemically important banks of the minimum capacity to absorb losses. … **(3)** Notwithstanding that a bank is complying with regulations or guidelines made under subsection (2), the Superintendent may, by order, direct the bank **(a)** to increase its capital; or **(b)** to provide additional liquidity in such forms and amounts as the Superintendent may require. … **(3.1)** If the Superintendent becomes aware that a domestic systemically important bank is not maintaining its minimum capacity to absorb losses, [then] the Superintendent shall notify the other members of the committee established under subsection 18(1) of the *Office of the Superintendent of Financial Institutions Act* and may, by order, take any measures that he or she considers appropriate, including **(a)** limiting the growth of the bank's total assets; **(b)** limiting or prohibiting acquisitions of assets by the bank; **(c)** limiting or prohibiting discretionary payments in respect of the bank's shares or subordinated indebtedness; **(d)** limiting or prohibiting purchases by the bank, or redemptions, of the bank's shares, subordinated indebtedness or prescribed liabilities; **(e)** limiting or prohibiting reductions of the bank's stated capital; and **(f)** limiting or prohibiting the opening of new branches by the bank. … **(3.2)** Before making an order under subsection (3.1) or varying or revoking such an order, the Superintendent shall consult with the other members of the committee established under subsection 18(1) of the *Office of the Superintendent of Financial Institutions Act*. … **(4)** A bank shall comply with an order made under subsection (3) or (3.1) within the time that is specified in the order." (Government of Canada (2022), "Bank Act, S.C. 1991, c. 46," adopted on December 13, 1991, entered into force on June 1, 1992, last amended on February 26, 2022, consolidated to May 2, 2022, s.485(2)-(4); emphasis original). The final sentence of fn 230 sets out Subsection 18(1) of the Office of the Superintendent of Financial Institutions Act.

Self-Dealing

A bank[232] may, neither directly nor indirectly, enter into any transaction[233] with a related party[234], save as Part XI of the Bank Act[235] provides [341]. The Bank Act sets out a few exceptions from this rule, which include, for instance, the following provisions.

---

[232] The first sentence of fn 141 defines the term '*bank*'.

[233] For the purposes of Part XI of the Bank Act (fn 235), "entering a transaction with a related party of a bank includes **(a)** making a guarantee on behalf of the related party; **(b)** making an investment in any securities of the related party; **(c)** taking an assignment of[,] or otherwise acquiring[,] a loan made by a third party to the related party; and **(d)** taking a security interest in the securities of a related party" (Government of Canada (2022), "Bank Act, S.C. 1991, c. 46," adopted on December 13, 1991, entered into force on June 1, 1992, last amended on February 26, 2022, consolidated to May 2, 2022, s.488(1)); emphasis original). The first sentence of fn 234 defines the term '*related party of a bank*'.

[234] For the purposes of Part XI of the Bank Act (fn 235), "a person is a related party of the bank[,] where the person **(a)** is a person who has a significant interest in a class of shares or in membership shares of the bank; **(b)** is a director or senior officer of the bank or of a body corporate that controls the bank[,] or is acting in a similar capacity in respect of an unincorporated entity that controls the bank; **(c)** is the spouse or common-law partner, or child who is less than eighteen years of age, of a person described in paragraph (a) or (b); **(d)** is an entity that is controlled by a person referred to in any of paragraphs (a) to (c); **(e)** is an entity in which a person who controls the bank has a substantial investment; **(f)** is an entity in which the spouse or common-law partner, or a child who is less than eighteen years of age, of a person who controls the bank[,] has a substantial investment; or **(g)** is a person, or forms part of a class of persons, designated under subsection (3) or (4) as, or deemed under subsection (5) to be, a related party of the bank ..." (Government of Canada (2022), "Bank Act, S.C. 1991, c. 46," adopted on December 13, 1991, entered into force on June 1, 1992, last amended on February 26, 2022, consolidated to May 2, 2022, s.486(1); emphasis original). The first sentence of fn 148 defines the term '*person*'. The first sentence of fn 141 defines the term '*bank*'. The first sentence of fn 154 defines the term '*director*'. The final sentence of fn 154 defines the term '*body corporate*'. Fn 184 defines the term '*substantial investment in a body corporate*'. The preantepenultimate sentence of fn 157 defines the term '*control*'; this definition is modified for subsection 486(1) of the Bank Act (above in the present footnote (i.e., fn 234)), as follows "**(7)** For the purposes of determining whether an entity or a person has a substantial investment for the purposes of paragraph (1)(e) or (f) [(i.e., s.486(1)(e) or s.486(1)(f) of the Bank Act)], the reference to "control" and "controlled" in section 10 [of the Bank Act] shall be construed as references to "control, within the meaning of section 3 [of the Bank Act], determined without regard to paragraph 3(1)(d) [of the Bank Act]" and "controlled, within the meaning of section 3, determined without regard to paragraph 3(1)(d)," respectively. ... **(8)** For the purposes of paragraph (1)(d) [(i.e., s.486(1)(d) of the Bank Act)], ***controlled*** means "controlled, within the meaning of section 3 [of the Bank Act], determined without regard to paragraph 3(1)(d) [of the Bank Act]." (Government of Canada (2022), "Bank Act, S.C. 1991, c. 46," adopted on December 13, 1991, entered into force on June 1, 1992, last amended on February 26, 2022, consolidated to May 2, 2022, s.486(7)-(8); emphasis original). The second sentence of fn 148 defines the term '*entity*'. Fn 184 defines the term '*substantial investment in a body corporate*', and includes the first three subsections of section 10 of the Bank Act – the first of which sets out the definition of this phrase. Subsections 486(3), 486(4) and 486(5) of the Bank Act read: "**(3)** For the purposes of this Part [(i.e., Part XI of the Bank Act (fn 235))], the Superintendent may, with respect to a particular bank, designate as a related party of the bank **(a)** any person or class of persons whose direct or indirect interest in[,] or relationship with[,] the bank or a related party of the bank[,] might reasonably be expected to affect the exercise of the best judgment of the bank in respect of a transaction; or **(b)** any person who is a party to any agreement, commitment or understanding referred to in section 9 [of the Bank Act,] if the bank referred to in that section is the particular bank. ... **(4)** Where a person is designated as a related party of a bank pursuant to subsection (3), the Superintendent may also designate any entity in which the person has a substantial investment and any entity controlled by such an entity[,] to be a related party of the bank. ... **(5)** Where, in contemplation of a person becoming a related party of a bank, the bank enters into a transaction with the person, the person is deemed for the purposes of this Part [(i.e., Part XI of the Bank Act,)] to be a related party of the bank in respect of that transaction." (Government of Canada (2022), "Bank Act, S.C. 1991, c. 46," adopted on December 13, 1991, entered into force on June 1, 1992, last amended on February 26, 2022, consolidated to May 2, 2022, s.486(3)-(5); emphasis original). Fn 155 defines the term '*Superintendent*'. The first subsection of section 9 of the Bank Act states: "For the purposes of Part VII and Division 7 of Part XV [of the Bank Act], if two or more persons have agreed, under any agreement, commitment or understanding, whether formal or informal, verbal or written, to act jointly or in concert in respect of **(a)** shares of a bank or of a bank holding company that they beneficially own, **(b)** shares or ownership interests that they beneficially own of any entity that controls any entity that beneficially owns shares of a bank or of a bank holding company, **(c)** shares or ownership interests that they beneficially own of any entity that controls any entity that beneficially owns shares of a bank or bank holding company, [then] those persons are deemed to be a single person who is acquiring beneficial ownership of the aggregate number of shares of the bank or bank holding company[,] or shares or ownership interests of the entity

A bank may enter into a transaction with a related party of the bank[,] if the transaction consists of a deposit by the bank with a financial institution[236] that is a direct clearer or a member of a clearing group under the by-laws of the Canadian Payments Association[237] and the deposit is made for clearing purposes [342].

A bank may borrow money from, take deposits from, or issue debt obligations to, a related party of the bank [343].

Foreign Banks

Regarding its business in Canada, a foreign bank[238] may neither carry out the business of accepting deposit liabilities [344], nor act as an agent for the acceptance of deposit liabilities for either a foreign bank or an entity which is associated with a foreign bank [345], nor represent to the public that any instrument which it issues is a deposit or that any liability which it incurs is a deposit [346] – unless it is an authorized foreign bank[239] [347] or a foreign co-operative credit society that the Minister[240] has authorized to conduct the business of a

company, [then] those persons are deemed to be a single person who is acquiring beneficial ownership of the aggregate number of shares of the bank or bank holding company[,] or shares or ownership interests of the entity that are beneficially owned by them." (Government of Canada (2022), "Bank Act, S.C. 1991, c. 46," adopted on December 13, 1991, entered into force on June 1, 1992, last amended on February 26, 2022, consolidated to May 2, 2022, s.9(1); emphasis original). Fn 214 defines the term '*bank holding company*'. Subsection 486(2) of the Bank Act provides the following exception to the scope of the definition in subsection 486(1) of the Bank Act of '*related party of a bank*': "Where an entity in which a bank has a substantial investment would, but for this subsection, be a related party of the bank only because a person who controls the bank controls the entity or has a substantial investment in the entity, and the person does not control the entity or have a substantial investment in the entity otherwise than through the person's controlling interest in the bank, the entity is not a related party of the bank." (Government of Canada (2022), "Bank Act, S.C. 1991, c. 46," adopted on December 13, 1991, entered into force on June 1, 1992, last amended on February 26, 2022, consolidated to May 2, 2022, s.486(2)).

[235] Part XI of the Bank Act is titled 'Self-dealing', and comprises sections 485.1-506 of this Act.

[236] The fifth sentence of fn 184 defines the term '*financial institution*'.

[237] The first sentence of fn 137 supplies information concerning the Canadian Payments Association.

[238] The second sentence of fn 142 defines the term '*foreign bank*'.

[239] The first sentence of fn 142 defines the term '*authorized foreign bank*'.

[240] The term '*Minister*' means the Minister of Finance (penultimate sentence of fn 142).

co-operative credit society [348]. A foreign bank may only borrow money in Canada as part of its business there, if it maintains a Canadian branch as section 522.05 of the Bank Act[241] or section 522.19 of the Bank Act[242] allows or it conducts business in Canada as that section

[241] This section of the Bank Act states: "A foreign bank, or an entity that is incorporated or formed otherwise than by or under an Act of Parliament or of the legislature of a province and that is associated with a foreign bank, that does not have a financial establishment in Canada[,] may maintain a branch in Canada[,] or engage in or carry on business in Canada[,] so long as less than **(a)** the prescribed portion – or[,] if no portion is prescribed, 10 per cent – of its business in Canada, determined in the prescribed manner, consists of one or more of the activities referred to in any of paragraphs (a) to (g) of the definition of ***financial services entity*** in subsection 507(1) [of the Bank Act]; and **(b)** the prescribed portion – or[,] if no portion is prescribed, 10 per cent – of its business outside Canada, determined in the prescribed manner, consists of one or more of the activities referred to in any of **(i)** paragraphs (a) to (g) of the definition of ***financial services entity*** in subsection 507(1), and **(ii)** paragraph (h) of that definition, except under prescribed circumstances." (Government of Canada (2022), "Bank Act, S.C. 1991, c. 46," adopted on December 13, 1991, entered into force on June 1, 1992, last amended on February 26, 2022, consolidated to May 2, 2022, s.522.05; emphasis original). The second sentence of fn 142 defines the term '*foreign bank*'. The second sentence of fn 148 defines the term '*entity*'. The penultimate sentence of fn 217 defines the term '*prescribed*'. Subsection 507(1) of the Bank Act defines the phrase '*financial services entity*' as: "an entity, other than an entity referred to in any of paragraphs 468(1)(a) to (i) [of the Bank Act] or a leasing entity, that engages in activities at least the prescribed portion – or if no portion is prescribed, 10 per cent – of which, determined in the prescribed manner, consists of one or more of the following activities: **(a)** providing any financial service; **(b)** acting as a financial agent; **(c)** providing investment counselling and portfolio management services; **(d)** issuing payment, credit or charge cards[,] and, in cooperation with others, including other financial institutions, operating a payment, credit or charge card plan; **(e)** engaging in the activities referred to in the definition *closed-end fund, mutual fund distribution entity* or *mutual fund entity* in subsection 464(1) [of the Bank Act]; **(f)** engaging in prescribed activities, under prescribed terms and conditions, if any are prescribed; **(g)** engaging in any activity referred to in paragraph [507(1)](a) to (f) [(of the Bank Act, i.e., points (a) to (f) in the current footnote (fn 241),)] as an agent for another entity referred to in any of those paragraphs or in any paragraphs 468(1)(a) to (j) [of the Bank Act]; or **(h)** acquiring or holding control of, or becoming a major owner of, an entity referred to in any of paragraphs [507(1)](a) to (g) [(of the Bank Act, i.e., points (a) to (g) in the present footnote (fn 241),)] or any of paragraphs 468(1)(a) to (j) [of the Bank Act]." (Government of Canada (2022), "Bank Act, S.C. 1991, c. 46," adopted on December 13, 1991, entered into force on June 1, 1992, last amended on February 26, 2022, consolidated to May 2, 2022, s.507(1); emphasis original). The text to fns 212-217 sets out paragraphs (a)-(j) of subsection 468(1) of the Bank Act. The clause that corresponds to the text to fn 217 comprises paragraph (j) of subsection 468(1) of the Bank Act; the preceding clauses within this sentence set out paragraphs (a)-(i) of subsection 468(1) of the Bank Act.

[242] This section of the Bank Act reads: "**(1)** Subject to the requirements relating to approval set out in Division 5 [of Part XII (entitled 'Foreign Banks') of the Bank Act, which is titled 'Approvals' and which contains sections 522.2, 522.21, 522.211 and 522.22 of this Act], and subject to subsection (2), a foreign bank, or an entity that is incorporated or formed otherwise than by or under an Act of Parliament or of the legislature of a province and that is associated with a foreign bank, that has a financial establishment in Canada[,] may maintain a branch in Canada or engage in or carry on business in Canada, so long as **(a)** less than the prescribed portion – or if no portion is prescribed, 10 per cent – of its business in Canada, determined in the prescribed manner, consists of one or more of the activities referred to in any of **(i)** paragraphs 522.08(1)(a) to (f) [of the Bank Act (i.e., points (a) to (f) in the sixth sentence of the current footnote (fn 242))], and **(ii)** paragraphs (a) to (g) of the definition ***financial services entit***y in subsection 507(1) [of the Bank Act (i.e., points (a) to (g) in the fifth sentence of fn 241)]; **(b)** less than the prescribed portion – or if no portion is prescribed, 10 per cent – of its business outside Canada, determined in the prescribed manner, consists of one or more of the activities referred to in any of **(i)** paragraphs 522.08(1)(a) to (f) [of the Bank Act (i.e., points (a) to (f) in the sixth sentence of the present footnote (fn 242))], **(ii)** paragraphs (a) to (g) of the definition ***financial services entity*** in subsection 507(1) [of the Bank Act (i.e., points (a) to (g) in fifth sentence of fn 241)], and **(iii)** paragraph (h) of that definition [Act (i.e., point (h) in fifth sentence of fn 241)], except under prescribed circumstances; and **(c)** in the opinion of the Minister, the business in Canada is the same as, or similar, related or incidental to, the business outside Canada of the foreign bank or the entity associated with a foreign bank. **(2)** A foreign bank – or an entity associated with a foreign bank – that maintains a branch[,] or engages in or carries on any business under subsection (1)[,] may not in Canada engage in any leasing activities." (Government of Canada (2022), "Bank Act, S.C. 1991, c. 46," adopted on December 13, 1991, entered into force on June 1, 1992, last amended on February 26, 2022, consolidated to May 2, 2022, s.522.19; emphasis original). The second sentence of fn 142 defines the term '*foreign bank*'. The second sentence of fn 148 defines the term '*entity*'. The penultimate sentence of fn 217 defines the term '*prescribed*'. The term '*Minister*' means the Minister of Finance (penultimate sentence of fn 142). Paragraphs (a) to (f) of subsection 522.08(1) of the Bank Act declare: "Subject to subsection (2) and the

permits [349], and it discloses that it is neither regulated as a financial institution[243] in Canada nor a member institution of the Canada Deposit Insurance Corporation and that the liability which it incurs through this borrowing is not a deposit[244] [350] – unless it is an authorized foreign bank [351] or a foreign co-operative credit society that the Minister has approved to undertake the business of a co-operative credit society [352]. A foreign bank, or an entity that is connected to a foreign bank, which lacks a financial establishment in Canada, may acquire,

---

requirements relating to approval set out in Division 5 [of Part XII (titled 'Foreign Banks') of the Bank Act, which is entitled 'Approvals' and which comprises sections 522.2, 522.21, 522.211 and 522.22 of this Act], a foreign bank[,] or an entity associated with a foreign bank[,] may acquire or hold control of, or a substantial investment in, a Canadian entity, other than an entity referred to in any of paragraphs 468(1)(a) to (i) [of the Bank Act (final two sentences of fn 241)], whose business is limited to one or more of the following: **(a)** engaging in **(i)** any financial service activity that a bank is permitted to engage in under any of paragraphs 409(2)(a) to (d) [of the Bank Act], or **(ii)** any other activity that a bank is permitted to engage in under section 410 or 411 [of the Bank Act]; **(b)** acquiring or holding shares of, or ownership interests in, entities that a foreign bank[,] or an entity associated with a foreign bank[,] is permitted to acquire or hold under this Division [(i.e., Division 4 of Part XII of the Bank Act, which is titled 'Financial Establishment in Canada' and which consists of sections 522.07-522.19 of this Act)] or Division 8 [(of Part XII of the Bank Act, which is entitled 'Transitional' and which consists of sections 522.29, 522.3, 522.31, 522.32 and 522.33 of this Act)] – other than limited commercial entities, except in prescribed circumstances; **(b.1)** acquiring or holding shares of, or ownership interests in, entities incorporated or formed otherwise than by or under an Act of Parliament or of the legislature of a province; **(c)** engaging in the provision of any services exclusively to any or all of the following, so long as the Canadian entity is also providing those services to the foreign bank or to any member of the foreign bank's group, namely, **(i)** the foreign bank, **(ii)** any member of the foreign bank's group, **(iii)** any entity that is primarily engaged in the business of providing financial services, **(iv)** any entity in which an entity referred to in subparagraph (iii) has a substantial investment[,] and that is **(A)** an entity in which a bank is permitted to acquire a substantial investment under section 468 [of the Bank Act (text to fns 212-217 (subsection 468(1) of the Bank Act), and the first sentence of fn 217 (subsection 468(2) of the Bank Act))], **(B)** an entity in which a foreign bank[,] or an entity associated with a foreign bank[,] is permitted to acquire a substantial investment under this section [(i.e., section 522.08 of the Bank Act)] and section 522.07 [of the Bank Act (last sentence of the current footnote (i.e., fn 242))], or **(C)** a prescribed entity, or **(v)** any prescribed person, if it is doing so under prescribed terms and conditions, if any are prescribed; **(d)** engaging in any activity that a bank is permitted to engage in – or in any other prescribed activity –, other than an activity referred to in paragraph (a) or (e), that relates to **(i)** the promotion, sale, delivery or distribution of a financial product or financial service that is provided by the foreign bank or by any member of the foreign bank's group, or **(ii)** if a significant portion of the business of the Canadian entity involves an activity referred to in subparagraph (i), the promotion, sale, delivery or distribution of a financial product or financial service that is provided by any other entity that is primarily engaged in the business of providing financial services; **(e)** engaging in the activities referred to in the definition ***closed-end fund***, ***mutual fund distribution entity***, ***mutual fund entity*** or ***real property brokerage entity*** in subsection 464(1) [of the Bank Act]; and **(f)** engaging in prescribed activities, under prescribed terms and conditions, if any are prescribed." (Government of Canada (2022), "Bank Act, S.C. 1991, c. 46," adopted on December 13, 1991, entered into force on June 1, 1992, last amended on February 26, 2022, consolidated to May 2, 2022, s.522.08(1); emphasis original). The preantepenultimate sentence of fn 157 defines the term '*control*'. Fn 184 defines the term '*substantial investment in a body corporate*'. Section 522.07 of the Bank Act states: "Subject to the requirements relating to approval set out in Division 5 [of Part XII of the Bank Act, which is titled 'Approvals' and which comprises sections 522.2, 522.21, 522.211 and 522.22 of this Act], a foreign bank[,] or an entity associated with a foreign bank[,] may acquire or hold control of, or a substantial investment in, a Canadian entity, other than an entity referred to in any of paragraphs 468(1)(a) to (i) [of the Bank Act (last two sentences of fn 241)]." (Government of Canada (2022), "Bank Act, S.C. 1991, c. 46," adopted on December 13, 1991, entered into force on June 1, 1992, last amended on February 26, 2022, consolidated to May 2, 2022, s.522.07).

[243] The fifth sentence of fn 184 defines the term '*financial institution*'.

[244] The Bank Act provides an exception from this disclosure, as follows: "The disclosure is not required in respect of **(a)** a borrowing of a prescribed class or type[,] or a borrowing in prescribed circumstances or in a prescribed manner; or **(b)** except as may be provided in any regulations, a borrowing **(i)** from a person in an amount of $150,000 [(i.e., CAD 150,000)] or more, or **(ii)** through the issue of instruments in denominations of $150,000 [(i.e., CAD 150,000)] or more." (Government of Canada (2022), "Bank Act, S.C. 1991, c. 46," adopted on December 13, 1991, entered into force on June 1, 1992, last amended on February 26, 2022, consolidated to May 2, 2022, s.520.1(3); emphasis original). The penultimate sentence of fn 217 defines the term '*prescribed*'. The first sentence of fn 148 defines the term '*person*'.

possess control of, or hold a substantial investment in, a Canadian entity, provided that, as a result of the acquisition, neither the foreign bank, nor this entity, nor any entity that is associated with the foreign bank, either controls or becomes a major owner of a Canadian entity to which any of paragraphs (a) to (i) of subsection 461(1) of the Bank Act[245] apply, or of a Canadian financial services entity [353].

Authorized Foreign Banks[246]

On application by a foreign bank[247], the Minister[248] may make an order that allows it to found a branch in Canada to conduct business there [354]. (S)he may make the order subject to the restrictions to which subsection 540(1) of the Bank Act refers[249] and to the requirements that section 627.74 of the Bank Act specifies[250] [355]. The foreign bank must file an application with the Superintendent[251], together with any other documentation that the latter may require[252]

[245] The clause that corresponds to the text to fn 217 comprises paragraph (j) of subsection 468(1) of the Bank Act; the preceding clauses within this sentence lay down paragraphs (a)-(i) of subsection 468(1) of the Bank Act.

[246] The first sentence of fn 142 defines the term '*authorized foreign bank*'.

[247] The second sentence of fn 142 defines the term '*foreign bank*'.

[248] The term '*Minister*' means the Minister of Finance (penultimate sentence of fn 142).

[249] This subsection of the Bank Act states: "Where subsection 524(2) [of the Bank Act (text to fns 249 and 250)] applies, the authorized foreign bank shall not, in respect of its business in Canada, **(a)** except as permitted by subsection (4) [(i.e., subsection 540(4) of the Bank Act (second sentence of the present footnote (fn 249)))], engage in the business of accepting deposit liabilities, or otherwise borrow money; **(b)** subject to the regulations, act as an agent for any person in the taking of deposit liabilities; or **(c)** guarantee any securities[,] or accept any bills of exchange or depository bills[,] that are **(i)** issued by any person, and **(ii)** intended by the issuer or any party to be sold or traded." (Government of Canada (2022), "Bank Act, S.C. 1991, c. 46," adopted on December 13, 1991, entered into force on June 1, 1992, last amended on February 26, 2022, consolidated to May 2, 2022, s.540(1); emphasis original). Subsection 540(4) of the Bank Act is headed 'Authorized borrowing', and specifies: "For the purposes of paragraph (1)(a) [(i.e., paragraph (a) of subsection 540(1) of the Bank Act (point (a) in the first sentence of the current footnote (fn 249)))], an authorized foreign bank may **(a)** accept deposit liabilities or otherwise borrow money from **(i)** a financial institution other than a foreign bank, or **(ii)** a foreign bank described in any of subparagraphs 508(1)(a)(i) to (iii) [of the Bank Act], by means of financial instruments that cannot be subsequently sold or traded; or **(b)** accept deposit liabilities or otherwise borrow money, from prescribed classes of entities referred to in subparagraphs (a)(i) or (ii), by means of financial instruments that can be sold to[,] or traded with[,] those classes of entities, in accordance with regulations made pursuant to subsection (6)." (Government of Canada (2022), "Bank Act, S.C. 1991, c. 46," adopted on December 13, 1991, entered into force on June 1, 1992, last amended on February 26, 2022, consolidated to May 2, 2022, s.540(4); emphasis original). The first sentence of fn 142 defines the term '*authorized foreign bank*'. The fifth sentence of fn 184 defines the term '*financial institution*'. The second sentence of fn 142 defines the term '*foreign bank*'.

[250] This section of the Bank Act is titled 'Authorized foreign banks – customers and the public', and reads: "An authorized foreign bank that is subject to this section under an order referred to in subsection 524(2) [of the Bank Act (text to fns 249 and 250),] shall disclose to its customers and to the public that it does not accept deposits in Canada and that it is not a member institution of the Canada Deposit Insurance Corporation." (Government of Canada (2023), "Bank Act, S.C. 1991, c. 46," adopted on December 13, 1991, entered into force on June 1, 1992, last amended on March 4, 2023, consolidated to March 20, 2023, s.627.74). The first sentence of fn 142 defines the term '*authorized foreign bank*'.

[251] Fn 155 defines the term '*Superintendent*'.

[252] The procedure for this application is as follows: "**(2)** Before filing an application, a foreign bank applicant shall, at least once a week for a period of four consecutive weeks, publish, in a form [that is] satisfactory to the Superintendent, a notice of intention to make the application in the *Canada Gazette* and in a newspaper in general circulation at or near the place where its principal office is to be situated. … **(3)** A person who objects to the proposed order may, within thirty days after the date of the last publication under subsection (2), submit the objection in writing to the Superintendent. … **(4)** On receipt of an objection, the Superintendent shall inform the Minister of it. … **(5)** On receipt of an objection, and if the application for the order has been received, the Superintendent shall, if satisfied that it is necessary and in the public interest to do so, hold[,] or cause to be held[,] a public inquiry into the objection as it relates to the application[,] and, on completion of the inquiry, the

[356]. The Minister makes the order, taking into consideration all issues that (s)he consider to be pertinent to the application[253] [357]. The order specifies the name of the authorized foreign bank – and, if applicable, the name under which it is allowed to conduct business in Canada [358], the province in which the authorized foreign bank's main office is to be located [359], whether the authorized foreign bank is subject to any restrictions and requirements to which subsection 524(2) of the Bank Act[254] refers [360], and the date upon which the order comes into force[255] [361].

On application by an authorized foreign bank, the Superintendent may make an order that approves the initiation of, and engagement in, business in Canada by this bank[256] [362]. The Superintendent may make this order only if (s)he is satisfied that the authorized foreign bank has submitted a power of attorney in compliance with subsection 536(2) of the Bank Act[257] [363], deposited in Canada unencumbered assets of a type that (s)he approves, the total value of which – determined in accordance with Generally Accepted Accounting Principles [364] –

Superintendent shall report the findings of the inquiry to the Minister. ... **(6)** Within thirty days after receiving the report, the Minister shall make it available to the public." (Government of Canada (2022), "Bank Act, S.C. 1991, c. 46," adopted on December 13, 1991, entered into force on June 1, 1992, last amended on February 26, 2022, consolidated to May 2, 2022, s.525(2)-(6); emphasis original). The second sentence of fn 142 defines the term '*foreign bank*'. Fn 155 defines the term '*Superintendent*'. The term '*Minister*' means the Minister of Finance (penultimate sentence of fn 142).

[253] These matters are to include: "**(a)** the nature and sufficiency of the financial resources of the foreign bank as a source of continuing financial support for the carrying on of its business in Canada; **(b)** the soundness and feasibility of plans for the foreign bank for the future conduct and development of its business in Canada; **(c)** the business record and past performance of the foreign bank; **(d)** the reputation of the foreign bank for being operated in a manner that is consistent with the standards of good character and integrity; **(e)** whether the proposed authorized foreign bank will be operated responsibly by persons with the competence and experience [that are] suitable for involvement in the operation of a financial institution; **(f)** the impact of any integration of the business and operations in Canada of the authorized foreign bank with those of its affiliates in Canada[,] on the conduct of those businesses and operations; and **(g)** the best interests of the financial system in Canada." (Government of Canada (2022), "Bank Act, S.C. 1991, c. 46," adopted on December 13, 1991, entered into force on June 1, 1992, last amended on February 26, 2022, consolidated to May 2, 2022, s.526(a)-(g); emphasis original). The second sentence of fn 142 defines the term '*foreign bank*'. The first sentence of fn 148 defines the term '*person*'. The fifth sentence of fn 184 defines the term '*financial institution*'. The first sentence of fn 157 defines the term '*affiliate*'.

[254] The text to fns 249 and 250 comprises subsection 524(2) of the Bank Act.

[255] The Minister of Finance "may set out in the order any provision not contrary to this Act [(i.e., the Bank Act)] that the Minister considers advisable in order to take into account the particular circumstances of the proposed authorized foreign bank with respect to the carrying on of business in Canada" (Government of Canada (2022), "Bank Act, S.C. 1991, c. 46," adopted on December 13, 1991, entered into force on June 1, 1992, last amended on February 26, 2022, consolidated to May 2, 2022, s.527(2)), and "may impose any terms and conditions in respect of the order that the Minister considers appropriate" (Government of Canada (2022), "Bank Act, S.C. 1991, c. 46," adopted on December 13, 1991, entered into force on June 1, 1992, last amended on February 26, 2022, consolidated to May 2, 2022, s.527(3)). The Superintendent must ensure that a notice is published in the *Canada Gazette*, of the making of the order (Government of Canada (2022), "Bank Act, S.C. 1991, c. 46," adopted on December 13, 1991, entered into force on June 1, 1992, last amended on February 26, 2022, consolidated to May 2, 2022, s.527(4)). The first sentence of fn 142 defines the term '*authorized foreign bank*'. Fn 155 defines the term '*Superintendent*'.

[256] The bank may not start to carry on business in Canada until this order authorizes it to do so (Government of Canada (2022), "Bank Act, S.C. 1991, c. 46," adopted on December 13, 1991, entered into force on June 1, 1992, last amended on February 26, 2022, consolidated to May 2, 2022, s.534(2)).

[257] This subsection of the Bank Act states: "The authorized foreign bank shall provide the principal officer with a power of attorney expressly authorizing the principal officer to receive all notices under the laws of Canada from the Minister or Superintendent[,] and shall[,] without delay[,] submit a copy of the power of attorney to the Superintendent." (Government of Canada (2022), "Bank Act, S.C. 1991, c. 46," adopted on December 13, 1991, entered into force on June 1, 1992, last amended on February 26, 2022, consolidated to May 2, 2022, s.536(2)). The first sentence of fn 142 defines the term '*authorized foreign bank*'. The term '*Minister*' means the Minister of Finance (penultimate sentence of fn 142). Fn 155 defines the term '*Superintendent*'.

is to be CAD 100,000 for an authorized foreign bank that is subject to the restrictions and requirements to which subsection 524(2) of the Bank Act refers[258], and CAD 5 million or any larger amount that the Superintendent stipulates for any other authorized foreign bank [365], and observed all other pertinent requirements of the Bank Act [366].

Subject to the Bank Act, an authorized foreign bank may only engage in the business of banking and any business that appertains to banking business [367]. The business of banking includes supplying financial services [368], acting as a financial agent [369], furnishing portfolio management and investment counselling services [370], and issuing payment, credit or charge cards and, in collaboration with others, employing a charge, credit or payment card plan [371]. An authorized foreign bank may carry out other specified activities[259], but may neither deal in goods, merchandise or wares nor undertake any trade or other business – except as authorized by, or under, the Bank Act [372].

Subject to the regulations, an authorized foreign bank which is not subject to the restrictions and regulations to which subsection 524(2) of the Bank Act[260] refers, may not – regarding its business in Canada – act as agent for any person[261] in the taking of a deposit[262] of less than

[258] The text to fns 249 and 250 lays down subsection 524(2) of the Bank Act.

[259] The "authorized foreign bank may, in Canada, **(a)** hold, manage and otherwise deal with real property; **(b)** provide prescribed bank-related data processing services; **(b.1)** with the prior written approval of the Minister, engage in any of the following activities, namely, **(i)** collecting, manipulating and transmitting **(A)** information that is primarily financial or economic in nature, **(B)** information that relates to the business of an entity in which a bank is permitted to acquire a substantial investment under section 468 [of the Bank Act (text to fns 212-217 (subsection 468(1) of the Bank Act), and the first sentence of fn 217 (subsection 468(2) of the Bank Act)),] or to the business of a Canadian entity acquired or held under section 522.08 [of the Bank Act (fn 242 includes subsection 522.08(1) of the Bank Act)], and **(C)** any other information that the Minister may, by order, specify, **(ii)** providing advisory or other services in the design, development or implementation of information management systems; **(iii)** designing, developing or marketing computer software, and **(iv)** designing, developing, manufacturing or selling, as an ancillary activity to any activity referred to in subparagraphs (i) to (iii) that the authorized foreign bank is engaging in, computer equipment integral to the provision of information services related to the business of financial institutions or to the provision of financial services; **(b.2)** with the prior written approval of the Minister, develop, design, hold, manage, manufacture, sell or otherwise deal with data transmission systems, information sites, communication devices[,] or information platforms or portals[,] that are used **(i)** to provide information that is primarily financial or economic in nature, **(ii)** to provide information that relates to the business of an entity in which a bank is permitted to acquire a substantial investment under section 468 [of the Bank Act] or to the business of a Canadian entity acquired or held under section 522.08 [of the Bank Act], or **(iii)** for a prescribed purpose or in prescribed circumstances; **(b.3)** engage, under prescribed terms and conditions, if any are prescribed, in specialized business management or advisory services; **(c)** promote merchandise and services to the holders of any payment, credit or charge card issued by the authorized foreign bank; **(d)** engage in the sale of **(i)** tickets, including lottery tickets, on a non-profit public service basis in connection with special, temporary and infrequent non-commercial celebrations[,] or projects that are of local, municipal, provincial or national interest, **(ii)** urban transit tickets, and **(iii)** tickets in respect of a lottery [that is] sponsored by the federal government[,] or a provincial or municipal government[,] or an agency of any of those governments; **(e)** act as a custodian of property; **(f)** act as receiver, liquidator or sequestrator; and **(g)** provide identification, authentication or verification services." (Government of Canada (2022), "Bank Act, S.C. 1991, c. 46," adopted on December 13, 1991, entered into force on June 1, 1992, last amended on February 26, 2022, consolidated to May 2, 2022, s.539(1); emphasis original). The first sentence of fn 142 defines the term '*authorized foreign bank*'. The term '*Minister*' means the Minister of Finance (penultimate sentence of fn 142). The second sentence of fn 148 defines the term '*entity*'. The first sentence of fn 141 defines the term '*bank*'. The fifth sentence of fn 184 defines the term '*financial institution*'. Fn 184 defines the term '*substantial investment in a body corporate*'.

[260] The text to fns 249 and 250 sets out subsection 524(2) of the Bank Act.

[261] The first sentence of fn 148 defines the term '*person*'.

[262] In this section of the Bank Act, i.e., section 546 of the Bank Act, 'deposit' has the meaning that subsection 545(3) of the Bank Act gives to it (Government of Canada (2022), "Bank Act, S.C. 1991, c. 46," adopted on December 13, 1991, entered into force on June 1, 1992, last amended on February 26, 2022, consolidated to May 2, 2022, s.546(2)). Subsection 545(3) of the Bank Act states that the word '*deposit*' has the meaning that the Schedule to

CAD 150,000 and payable in Canada [373]. An authorized foreign bank must not deal in securities within Canada, to the degree forbidden or limited by any regulations that the Governor in Council may make for the purposes of this section (i.e., section 548) of the Bank Act [374].

An authorized foreign bank may not engage in the business of insurance[263] in Canada, except to the extent which the Bank Act or the regulations allow [375]. It must neither act as an insurance intermediary, nor supply or lease space in any of its branches in Canada to any person that carries out the placing of insurance [376].

An authorized foreign bank may not conduct any personal property leasing activity in Canada, in which a financial leasing entity[264] is not allowed to engage [377]. Subject to four exceptions[265], it is permitted neither to make a loan in Canada on the security of Canadian

---

the Canada Deposit Insurance Corporation Act would give to it for the purposes of deposit insurance, if that Schedule were to be read without reference to subsections 2(2), (5) and (6) of that Schedule, but excludes 'prescribed deposits' (Government of Canada (2022), "Bank Act, S.C. 1991, c. 46," adopted on December 13, 1991, entered into force on June 1, 1992, last amended on February 26, 2022, consolidated to May 2, 2022, s.545(3)). Section 2 of the Schedule to the Canada Deposit Insurance Corporation Act – excluding subsections 2(2), 2(5) and 2(6) of that Schedule (fn 293) and also subsections 2(2.1), 2(2.2) and 2(4) (which have been repealed) – reads: "**2(1)** Subject to subsection (2), for the purposes of this Act and the by-laws of the Canada Deposit Insurance Corporation, ***deposit*** means the unpaid balance of the aggregate of moneys received or held by a federal institution, provincial institution or local cooperative credit society, from[,] or on behalf of[,] a person in the usual course of the deposit-taking business of the institution, for which the institution **(a)** has given[,] or is obligated to give[,] credit to that person's account[,] or has issued[,] or is obligated to issue[,] a receipt, certificate, debenture (other than a debenture issued by a bank to which the *Bank Act* applies), transferable instrument, draft, certified draft or cheque, prepaid letter of credit, money order or other instrument in respect of which the institution is primarily liable, and **(b)** is obligated to repay the moneys on a fixed day, on demand by that person or within a specified period of time following demand by that person, including any interest accrued or payable to that person. ... **(1.1)** For greater certainty, an unpaid balance of moneys received or held by an institution from[,] or on behalf of[,] a mortgagor in respect of realty taxes on mortgaged property[,] is a deposit. The moneys are considered to be repayable on the earlier of the due date of the taxes or the date [that] the mortgage is discharged. ... **(1.2)** For greater certainty, moneys are considered to be a deposit[,] or part of a deposit[,] if they are paid in respect of a deposit that is held in a registered education savings plan or registered disability savings plan under[,] or because of[,] **(a)** the *Canada Education Savings Act* or a *designated provincial program* as defined in subsection 146.1(1) of the *Income Tax Act*; **(b)** any other program that has a similar purpose to a designated provincial program referred to in paragraph (a) and that is funded, directly or indirectly, by a province; **(c)** the *Canada Disability Savings Act* or a *designated provincial program* as defined in subsection 146.1(1) of the *Income Tax Act*; or **(d)** any other program that has a similar purpose to a designated provincial program referred to in paragraph (c) and that is funded, directly or indirectly, by a province. ... **(3)** For the purposes of subsection (1), if a trust company has deposited moneys in its own guaranteed trust fund on behalf of itself as trustee, [then] it shall be deemed to be obligated to repay the moneys to the same extent as it would have been obligated to repay the moneys had the moneys be deposited by a trustee other than itself. ... **(7)** A patronage allocation does not constitute a deposit." (Government of Canada (2022), "Canada Deposit Insurance Corporation Act, R.S.C. 1985, c. C-3," adopted on February 17, 1984, entered into force on February 17, 1984, last amended on April 30, 2022, consolidated to May 2, 2022, Schedule, ss.2(1), 2(1.1), 2(1.2), 2(3) and 2(7); emphasis original).

[263] In this section (i.e., section 549) of the Bank Act, the phrase '*business of insurance*' "includes **(a)** the issuance of any annuity[,] if the liability in respect of the annuity is contingent on the death of a person; and **(b)** the issuance of any debt obligation, any of whose terms and conditions are established on the basis of mortality considerations, under which the issuer is obliged to make periodic payments." (Government of Canada (2022), "Bank Act, S.C. 1991, c. 46," adopted on December 13, 1991, entered into force on June 1, 1992, last amended on February 26, 2022, consolidated to May 2, 2022, s.549(5); emphasis original). The first sentence of fn 148 defines the term '*person*'.

[264] The second sentence of fn 192 defines the term '*financial leasing entity*'.

[265] The restriction in subsection 551(1) of the Bank Act does not apply to "**(a)** a loan made or guaranteed under the *National Housing Act*[,] or any other Act of Parliament by or under which a different limit on the value of property on the security of which the authorized foreign bank may make a loan is established' **(b)** a loan[,] if repayment of the amount of the loan that exceeds the maximum amount in subsection (1) [(text to current footnote (i.e., fn 265))] is guaranteed or insured by a government agency or [by] a private insurer approved by

residential property for the purpose of buying, renovating or improving this property, nor to refinance a loan for this purpose, if the amount of the loan – together with sum outstanding of any mortgage having a prior or equal claim against the property – would exceed 80% of the property's value at the time of the loan [378].

Other than with the Superintendent's approval, an authorized foreign bank may be neither a partner in a general partnership[266] nor a general partner in a limited partnership [379]. No 'non-WTO Member authorized foreign bank'[267] may open a branch in Canada, except for its principal office and one branch, without the Minister's approval [380]. Subject to one exception[268] and to the current Part of the Bank Act (i.e., Part XII.1, which is entitled 'Authorized foreign banks' and which comprises sections 523 to 627 of this Act), an authorized foreign bank may – without the interposition of any other person: (a) accept a deposit from any person, and (b) pay all, or part of, the principal of this deposit, and all, or part of, the interest on it, to the order of that person [381].

An authorized foreign bank must maintain on deposit in Canada with a Canadian financial institution which the Superintendent has mandated, unencumbered assets of a type that (s)he has approved, the total value of which – determined in accordance with Generally Accepted Accounting Principles [364] – shall equal CAD 100,000 for an authorized foreign bank that is subject to the restrictions and requirements to which subsection 524(2) of the Bank Act refers[269] [382], and the higher of CAD 5 million and 5% of the authorized foreign bank's liabilities regarding its business in Canada for any other authorized foreign bank [383]. These assets are to be kept with this financial institution, pursuant to a deposit agreement that is entered into with the Superintendent's prior approval [384].

---

the Superintendent; **(c)** the acquisition[,] by the authorized foreign bank[,] from an entity of securities issued or guaranteed by the entity that are secured on any residential property, whether in favour of a trustee or otherwise, or the making of a loan by the authorized foreign bank to the entity against the issue of those securities; or **(d)** a loan [that is] secured by a mortgage[,] where **(i)** the mortgage is taken back by the authorized foreign bank on a property disposed of by it, including where the disposition is by way of a realization of a security interest, and **(ii)** the mortgage secures payment of an amount payable to the authorized foreign bank for the property." (Government of Canada (2022), "Bank Act, S.C. 1991, c. 46," adopted on December 13, 1991, entered into force on June 1, 1992, last amended on February 26, 2022, consolidated to May 2, 2022, s.551(2); emphasis original). The first sentence of fn 142 defines the term '*authorized foreign bank*'. Fn 155 defines the term '*Superintendent*'. The second sentence of fn 148 defines the term '*entity*'.

[266] A '*general partnership*' in subsection 553.1(1) of the Bank Act (text to the present footnote (i.e., fn 266)) is "any partnership other than a limited partnership" (Government of Canada (2022), "Bank Act, S.C. 1991, c. 46," adopted on December 13, 1991, entered into force on June 1, 1992, last amended on February 26, 2022, consolidated to May 2, 2022, s.553.1(2)).

[267] A '*non-WTO Member authorized foreign bank*' in section 554 of the Bank Act (i.e., the current footnote (i.e., fn 267) and accompanying text) is "an authorized foreign bank that is not controlled by a WTO Member resident" (Government of Canada (2022), "Bank Act, S.C. 1991, c. 46," adopted on December 13, 1991, entered into force on June 1, 1992, last amended on February 26, 2022, consolidated to May 2, 2022, s.554(1)).

[268] This exception reads: "**(2)** Paragraph (1)(b) [(i.e., paragraph 556(1)(b) of the Bank Act, which is point (b) in the text to the present footnote (i.e., fn 268),)] does not apply[,] if, before payment, the money deposited in the authorized foreign bank pursuant to paragraph (1)(a) [(i.e., paragraph 556(1)(b) of the Bank Act, which is point (a) in the text to the current footnote (i.e., fn 268),)] is claimed by some other person **(a)** in any action or proceeding to which the authorized foreign bank is a party[,] and in respect of which service of a writ or other process originating that action or proceeding has been made on the authorized foreign bank, or **(b)** in any other action or proceeding pursuant to which an injunction or order made by the court requiring the authorized foreign bank not to make payment of that money[,] or make payment of it to some person other than the depositor[,] has been served on the authorized foreign bank, and, if a claim is made, the deposited money may be paid to the depositor with the consent of the claimant, or to the claimant with the consent of the depositor." (Government of Canada (2022), "Bank Act, S.C. 1991, c. 46," adopted on December 13, 1991, entered into force on June 1, 1992, last amended on February 26, 2022, consolidated to May 2, 2022, s.556(2); emphasis original).

[269] The text to fns 249 and 250 sets out subsection 524(2) of the Bank Act.

The Regulation of Banks by the Superintendent

A bank[270] shall furnish the Superintendent[271] with the information, at the times and in the form, that (s)he may require [385]. Within thirty days of each of the bank's annual meetings, it must supply a return to the Superintendent, which shows the name, citizenship and residence of each director[272] who holds office immediately after the meeting [386], the mailing address of each of these directors [387], the bodies corporate[273] of which each of these directors is a director or officer, and the firms of which (s)he is a member [388], the affiliation – within the meaning that section 162 of the Bank Act[274] provides – with the bank of each of these directors [389], the name and role of each of these directors who are officers or employees of the bank or of any of its affiliates[275] [390], the name of each of the bank's committees on which each of these directors serves [391], the expiry date of the term of each of these directors [392], and the date of appointment, name and address of the bank's auditor(s) [393].

If, in the Superintendent's view, a bank – or a person[276] in respect of a bank – is committing or about to commit an act that is an unsound or unsafe practice in carrying out the business of the bank, or is pursuing or about to pursue any course of behaviour that is an aforementioned practice in undertaking the bank's business, then the Superintendent may direct this bank or person to stop, or refrain from, committing the act or pursuing the course of behaviour, and to effect such acts as – in the Superintendent's opinion – are necessary to put the situation right [394]. Other than the possibility of the Superintendent making a temporary direction[277], (s)he may issue no direction to a bank or a person with respect to a bank, unless that bank or person is given a reasonable opportunity to make representations concerning the matter [395].

The Superintendent may, by order, remove a person from office as a senior officer or director of a bank, if (s)he opines that this person is unsuitable to hold such office on the basis of his or her business record, character, competence, conduct or experience [396], or because the person has infracted, or, through action or negligence, has contributed to the breach of the Bank Act or the regulations that are made under it, a direction made under section 645 of the Bank Act[278], an order made under subsection 485(3) of the Bank Act[279] a condition or restriction with regard to the order approving the inception and continuation of the bank's

---

[270] The first sentence of fn 141 defines the term '*bank*'.

[271] Fn 155 defines the term '*Superintendent*'.

[272] The first sentence of fn 154 defines the terms '*director*' and '*directors*'.

[273] The last sentence of fn 154 defines the term '*body corporate*'.

[274] This section of the Bank Act states: "The Governor in Council may make regulations specifying the circumstances under which a natural person is affiliated with a bank for the purposes of this Act." (Government of Canada (2022), "Bank Act, S.C. 1991, c. 46," adopted on December 13, 1991, entered into force on June 1, 1992, last amended on February 26, 2022, consolidated to May 2, 2022, s.162). The first sentence of fn 141 defines the term '*bank*'.

[275] The first sentence of fn 157 defines the term '*affiliate*'.

[276] The first sentence of fn 148 defines the term '*person*'.

[277] The Superintendent may make a temporary direction regarding an unsound or unsafe practice by a bank, if, in his or her opinion, "the length of time required for representations to be made … might be prejudicial to the public interest" (Government of Canada (2022), "Bank Act, S.C. 1991, c. 46," adopted on December 13, 1991, entered into force on June 1, 1992, last amended on February 26, 2022, consolidated to May 2, 2022, s.645(3)). Fn 155 defines the term '*Superintendent*'. The first sentence of fn 141 defines the term '*bank*'.

[278] The text to fn 276 sets out subsection 645(1) of the Bank Act. The text to fn 277 lays down subsection 645(2) of the Bank Act. Fn 277 abridges subsection 645(3) of the Bank Act.

[279] The second sentence of fn 231 specifies subsection 485(3) of the Bank Act.

business, or a prudential agreement made under section 644.1 of the Bank Act[280] or an undertaking that the bank gives to the Superintendent [397]. In forming his or her opinion, the Superintendent must consider whether the interests of the bank's creditors and depositors have been, or are likely to be, prejudiced by the person holding office as a senior officer or director [398]. The Superintendent must notify the bank, and the person concerned, of any removal order that (s)he intends to make, and must grant them a period of at least fifteen days from the date of the notice to make relevant representations to him or her[281] [399]. The senior officer or director ceases to hold that office as of the date upon which the removal order is made – or any later date which this order specifies [400]. Within thirty days of receipt of notice of the removal order, or within any longer period that the Court[282] allows, the senior officer or director, or the bank, may appeal[283] the issue to the Federal Court [401], which may set aside the removal order or dismiss the appeal [402].

Subject to the Bank Act, where any of the circumstances that subsection 648(1.1) of this Act[284] describes exist with regard to a bank, the Superintendent may take control of the bank's

---

280 This section of the Bank Act states: "The Superintendent may enter into an agreement, called a "prudential agreement," with a bank[,] for the purposes of implementing any measure [that is] designed to maintain or improve its safety and soundness." (Government of Canada (2022), "Bank Act, S.C. 1991, c. 46," adopted on December 13, 1991, entered into force on June 1, 1992, last amended on February 26, 2022, consolidated to May 2, 2022, s.644.1). Fn 155 defines the term '*Superintendent*'. The first sentence of fn 141 defines the term '*bank*'.

281 If the Superintendent opines "that the public interest may be prejudiced by the director or senior officer continuing to exercise the powers[,] or carry out the duties and functions[,] of that office during the period for making representations, [then] the Superintendent may make an order suspending the director or senior officer. The suspension may not extend beyond 10 days after the expiration of that period." (Government of Canada (2022), "Bank Act, S.C. 1991, c. 46," adopted on December 13, 1991, entered into force on June 1, 1992, last amended on February 26, 2022, consolidated to May 2, 2022, s.647.1(4)). The Superintendent must promptly "notify the director or senior officer, as the case may be, and the bank[,] of a removal order or suspension order" (Government of Canada (2022), "Bank Act, S.C. 1991, c. 46," adopted on December 13, 1991, entered into force on June 1, 1992, last amended on February 26, 2022, consolidated to May 2, 2022, s.647.1(5)). Fn 155 defines the term '*Superintendent*'. The first sentence of fn 154 defines the term '*director*'. The first sentence of fn 141 defines the term '*bank*'.

282 The Bank Act defines the term '*court*' (rather than the word '*Court*' – which is used in the text to the present footnote (i.e., fn 282)) as "**(a)** in the Province of Ontario, the Superior Court of Justice, **(b)** in the Province of Quebec, the Superior Court of the Province, **(c)** in the Provinces of Nova Scotia, British Columbia and Prince Edward Island, the Supreme Court of the Province, **(d)** in the Provinces of New Brunswick, Manitoba, Saskatchewan and Alberta, the Court of Queen's Bench for the Province, **(e)** in the Province of Newfoundland and Labrador, the Trial Division of the Supreme Court of the Province, and **(f)** the Supreme Court of Yukon, the Supreme Court of Northwest Territories and the Nunavut Court of Justice" (Government of Canada (2022), "Bank Act, S.C. 1991, c. 46," adopted on December 13, 1991, entered into force on June 1, 1992, last amended on February 26, 2022, consolidated to May 2, 2022, s.2; emphasis original).

283 An appeal does not stay a removal order (Government of Canada (2022), "Bank Act, S.C. 1991, c. 46," adopted on December 13, 1991, entered into force on June 1, 1992, last amended on February 26, 2022, consolidated to May 2, 2022, s.647.1(9)).

284 This subsection of the Bank Act is headed 'Circumstances for taking control', and states: "Control by the Superintendent under subsection (1) [(i.e., subsection 648(1) of the Bank Act (text to fns 284 and 285),)] may be taken in respect of a bank[,] where **(a)** the bank has failed to pay its liabilities or, in the opinion of the Superintendent, will not be able to pay its liabilities as they become due and payable; **(b)** [Repealed … ;] **(c)** the assets of the bank are not, in the opinion of the Superintendent, sufficient to give adequate protection to the bank's depositors and creditors; **(d)** any asset appearing on the books or records of the bank[,] or held under its administration[,] is not, in the opinion of the Superintendent, satisfactorily accounted for; **(e)** the regulatory capital of the bank has, in the opinion of the Superintendent, reached a level[,] or is eroding in a manner[,] that may detrimentally affect its depositors or creditors; **(f)** the bank has failed to comply with an order of the Superintendent under paragraph 485(3)(a) [of the Bank Act]; **(g)** the bank's deposit insurance has been terminated by the Canada Deposit Insurance Corporation; or **(h)** in the opinion of the Superintendent, any other state of affairs exists in respect of the bank that may be materially prejudicial to the interests of the bank's depositors or creditors[,] or the owners of any assets under the bank's administration, including where

assets and those under the latter's administration for a period of no more than sixteen days [403], or take control of these assets for a period of more than sixteen days, extend such control from an initial period not exceeding sixteen days, or take control of the bank, unless the Minister[285] informs the Superintendent that (s)he opines that it is not in the public interest to take one of these three latter steps [404]. When the Superintendent has control of the abovementioned assets, (s)he may do everything that is expedient or necessary to safeguard the rights and interests of the bank's depositors and creditors [405], and the bank is restricted its use of those assets[286].

Sanctions

Every person[287] who, without reasonable cause, breaches any provision of the Bank Act or the regulations, has committed an offence [406]. Each person who knowingly supplies false or misleading information concerning any issue under the Bank Act or the regulations, has perpetrated an offence [407]. Every director, employee or officer of a bank[288] or an authorized foreign bank[289] who wilfully gives, or concurs in giving, unfair, undue or fraudulent preference over other creditors to any creditor of the bank or authorized foreign bank, has carried out an offence [408]. The Bank Act provides for collaborative individuals of legal persons held to be offenders, to be guilty of an offence[290].

---

proceedings under a law relating to bankruptcy or insolvency have been commenced in Canada or elsewhere in respect of the holding body corporate of the bank." (Government of Canada (2022), "Bank Act, S.C. 1991, c. 46," adopted on December 13, 1991, entered into force on June 1, 1992, last amended on February 26, 2022, consolidated to May 2, 2022, s.648(1.1); emphasis original). The second sentence of fn 231 comprises subsection 485(3) of the Bank Act. Fn 155 defines the term '*Superintendent*'. The first sentence of fn 141 defines the term '*bank*'.

[285] The term '*Minister*' means the Minister of Finance (penultimate sentence of fn 142). Regarding these latter three possible actions of the Superintendent, i.e., those that the Minister of Finance may prohibit, "[t]he Superintendent must notify [the] bank of any action proposed to be taken in respect of it ... and of its right to make written representations to the Superintendent within the time specified in the notice, not exceeding ten days after it receives the notice" (Government of Canada (2022), "Bank Act, S.C. 1991, c. 46," adopted on December 13, 1991, entered into force on June 1, 1992, last amended on February 26, 2022, consolidated to May 2, 2022, s.648(1.2)). Fn 155 defines the term '*Superintendent*'. The first sentence of fn 141 defines the term '*bank*'.

[286] Subsection 648(3) of the Bank Act declares: "Where, pursuant to subsection (1) [(i.e., subsection 648(1) of the Bank Act (text to fns 284 and 285))], the Superintendent has control of the assets of a bank referred to in that subsection, **(a)** the bank shall not make, acquire or transfer any loan[,] or make any purchase, sale or exchange of securities[,] or any disbursement or transfer of cash of any kind[,] without the prior approval of the Superintendent or a representative designated by the Superintendent; and **(b)** no director, officer or employee of the bank shall have access to any cash or securities held by the bank[,] unless **(i)** a representative of the Superintendent accompanies the director, officer or employee, or **(ii)** the access is previously authorized by the Superintendent or the Superintendent's representative." (Government of Canada (2022), "Bank Act, S.C. 1991, c. 46," adopted on December 13, 1991, entered into force on June 1, 1992, last amended on February 26, 2022, consolidated to May 2, 2022, s.648(3)). Fn 155 defines the term '*Superintendent*'. The first sentence of fn 141 defines the term '*bank*'.

[287] The first sentence of fn 148 defines the term '*person*'.

[288] The first sentence of fn 141 defines the term '*bank*'.

[289] The first sentence of fn 142 defines the term '*authorized foreign bank*'.

[290] The applicable section of the Bank Act reads: "If an entity commits an offence under this Act, [then] any officer, director, agent or principal officer of the entity who directed, authorized, assented to, acquiesced in or participated in the commission of the offence is a party to[,] and guilty of[,] the offence[,] and liable on summary conviction or on conviction on indictment to the punishment provided under paragraph 985(1)(a) [of the Bank Act] for the offence, whether or not the entity has been prosecuted or convicted." (Government of Canada

Comment

The Bank Act is comprehensive. It includes a large number of provisions on bank holding companies[291] that this chapter does not address. Whilst different elements of the Act tend to fit together well, it contains singularities – for instance the definition of the word '*deposit*' within the Act cites an abridged version of the definition of this term in the Canada Deposit Insurance Corporation Act[292], and the definition of the word '*bank*' in the Bank Act is a reference to the institutions which Schedules I and II to the Act list. It may be helpful for the Government of Canada to revisit the Act, firstly in order to simplify it without losing the essence of its rules and, secondly, to renumber the sections in a way that is less convoluted and which does not include repealed subsections and paragraphs.

Canada Deposit Insurance Corporation Act

Constitution of the Canada Deposit Insurance Corporation

The Canada Deposit Insurance Corporation Act establishes the Canada Deposit Insurance Corporation [409], which, for the purposes of the Act, is "an agency of Her Majesty [the Queen (now His Majesty King Charles III)] in right in Canada" [410]. Its head office is in Ottawa [411].

(2022), "Bank Act, S.C. 1991, c. 46," adopted on December 13, 1991, entered into force on June 1, 1992, last amended on February 26, 2022, consolidated to May 2, 2022, s.986). The second sentence of fn 148 defines the term '*entity*'. The first sentence of fn 154 defines the term '*director*'. Subsection 985(1) of the Bank Act specifies: "Every person who is guilty of an offence under any of sections 980 to 984 [of the Bank Act] is **(a)** in the case of a natural person, liable **(i)** on summary conviction, to a fine of not more than $100,000 [(i.e., CAD 100,000)] or to imprisonment for a term of not more than twelve months, or to both, or **(ii)** on conviction on indictment, to a fine of not more than $1,000,000 [(i.e., CAD 1 million)] or to imprisonment for a term of not more than five years, or to both; and **(b)** in the case of an entity, liable **(i)** on summary conviction, to a fine of not more than $500,000 [(i.e., CAD 500,000)], or **(ii)** on conviction on indictment, to a fine of not more than $5,000,000 [(i.e., CAD 5 million)]." (Government of Canada (2022), "Bank Act, S.C. 1991, c. 46," adopted on December 13, 1991, entered into force on June 1, 1992, last amended on February 26, 2022, consolidated to May 2, 2022, s.985(1); emphasis original). The first sentence of fn 148 defines the term '*person*'. Section 985 of the Bank Act provides the following additional sanctions: "**(2)** If a person has been convicted of an offence under this Act, [then] the court may, in addition to any punishment [that] it may otherwise impose, order the person to comply with the provisions of this Act or the regulations in respect of which the person was convicted." … **(3)** If a person has been convicted of an offence under this Act, [then] the court may, if it is satisfied that[,] as a result of the commission of the offence[,] the convicted person acquired any monetary benefits[,] or that monetary benefits accrued to the convicted person or their spouse, common-law partner or other dependent, order the convicted person to pay, despite the maximum amount of any fine that may otherwise be imposed under this Act, an additional fine in an amount equal to three times the court's estimation of the amount of those monetary benefits." (Government of Canada (2022), "Bank Act, S.C. 1991, c. 46," adopted on December 13, 1991, entered into force on June 1, 1992, last amended on February 26, 2022, consolidated to May 2, 2022, s.985(2)-(3); emphasis original). Fn 282 defines the term '*court*'.

[291] Part XV of the Bank Act sets out these rules. It is entitled 'Bank Holding Companies' and comprises sections 662-964 of this Act.

[292] Fn 262 defines the term '*deposit*'.

Objects and Powers of the Canada Deposit Insurance Corporation

The Canada Deposit Insurance Corporation's objects are to supply insurance against the loss of all, or part, of deposits[293] [412], contribute to the stability of Canada's financial system [413],

---

[293] The word '*deposit*' is as defined in the Schedule to the Canada Deposit Insurance Corporation Act (Government of Canada (2022), "Canada Deposit Insurance Corporation Act, R.S.C. 1985, c. C-3," adopted on February 17, 1984, entered into force on February 17, 1984, last amended on April 30, 2022, consolidated to May 2, 2022, s.2). Section 2 of the Schedule to the Canada Deposit Insurance Corporation Act defines the word '*deposit*' "for the purposes of this Act and the by-laws of the Canada Deposit Insurance Corporation" (Government of Canada (2022), "Canada Deposit Insurance Corporation Act, R.S.C. 1985, c. C-3," adopted on February 17, 1984, entered into force on February 17, 1984, last amended on April 30, 2022, consolidated to May 2, 2022, Schedule, s.2(1)). Fn 262 lays down subsections 2(1), 2(1.1), 2(1.2), 2(3) and 2(7) of the Schedule to the Canada Deposit Insurance Corporation Act, and subsections 2(2.1), 2(2.2) and 2(4) of the Schedule to the Canada Deposit Insurance Corporation Act have been repealed. The remaining subsections of section 2 of the Schedule to the Canada Deposit Insurance Corporation Act are as follows: "**(2)** Moneys held by the institution that were received by it when it was not a federal institution, a provincial institution or a local cooperative credit society[,] are excluded from the moneys referred to in subsection (1) [(i.e., subsection 2(1) of the Schedule to the Canada Deposit Insurance Corporation Act (fn 262))]. … **(5)** Despite subsection (1) [(i.e., subsection 2(1) of the Schedule to the Canada Deposit Insurance Corporation Act (fn 262))], for the purposes of deposit insurance with the [Canada Deposit Insurance] Corporation, if moneys are[,] or were[,] received by a member institution on or after April 1, 1977[,] for which the institution has issued[,] or is obligated to issue[,] an instrument evidencing a deposit, other than a draft, certified draft or cheque, prepaid letter of credit or money order, [then] **(a)** the moneys do not constitute a deposit[,] unless the instrument and records of the institution specify the person entitled, at the date of issue of the instrument, to the repayment of the moneys evidenced thereby; **(b)** the person referred to in paragraph (a) shall be deemed to be the depositor in respect of the moneys[,] unless particulars of a transfer of the instrument are entered in the records of the institution, in which case the most recent transferee shown in the records shall be deemed to be the depositor; and **(c)** the entry of a transfer in the records of a member institution is ineffective for the purposes of paragraph (b), if the entry is made subsequent to the termination or cancellation of the policy of deposit insurance of the member institution. … **(6)** Despite subsection (1) [(i.e., subsection 2(1) of the Schedule to the Canada Deposit Insurance Corporation Act (fn 262))], moneys received by a member institution on or after January 1, 1977, for which the institution has issued[,] or is obligated to issue[,] an instrument of indebtedness, other than a draft, certified draft or cheque, prepaid letter of credit or money order, do not constitute a deposit where the instrument is payable outside Canada." (Government of Canada (2022), "Canada Deposit Insurance Corporation Act, R.S.C. 1985, c. C-3," adopted on February 17, 1984, entered into force on February 17, 1984, last amended on April 30, 2022, consolidated to May 2, 2022, Schedule, ss.2(2), 2(5) and 2(6); emphasis original). A '*federal institution*' is "a bank, company or association referred to in section 8 [of the Canada Deposit Insurance Corporation Act]" (Government of Canada (2022), "Canada Deposit Insurance Corporation Act, R.S.C. 1985, c. C-3," adopted on February 17, 1984, entered into force on February 17, 1984, last amended on April 30, 2022, consolidated to May 2, 2022, s.2). A '*bank*' is a bank that is listed in Schedule I or II of the Bank Act; fn 141 states the names of these banks. Section 8 of the Canada Deposit Insurance Corporation Act is titled 'Federal institutions', and declares: "For the purposes of this Act, the following are federal institutions: **(a)** a bank; **(b)** a company to which the *Trust and Loan Companies Act* applies; and **(c)** a retail association within the meaning of regulations made under the *Cooperative Credit Associations Act*." (Government of Canada (2022), "Canada Deposit Insurance Corporation Act, R.S.C. 1985, c. C-3," adopted on February 17, 1984, entered into force on February 17, 1984, last amended on April 30, 2022, consolidated to May 2, 2022, s.8; emphasis original). A '*provincial institution*' is "a company referred to in section 9 [of the Canada Deposit Insurance Corporation Act]" (Government of Canada (2022), "Canada Deposit Insurance Corporation Act, R.S.C. 1985, c. C-3," adopted on February 17, 1984, entered into force on February 17, 1984, last amended on April 30, 2022, consolidated to May 2, 2022, s.2). Section 9 of the Canada Deposit Insurance Corporation Act is entitled 'Provincial institutions', and reads: "For the purposes of this Act, an incorporated company that carries on, under an Act of the legislature of a province or a constating instrument under provincial jurisdiction, a business [that is] substantially similar to the business of a company to which the *Trust and Loan Companies Act* applies[,] and that is authorized by or under an Act of the legislature of a province to accept deposits from the public[,] is a provincial institution." (Government of Canada (2022), "Canada Deposit Insurance Corporation Act, R.S.C. 1985, c. C-3," adopted on February 17, 1984, entered into force on February 17, 1984, last amended on April 30, 2022, consolidated to May 2, 2022, s.9; emphasis original). The phrase '*local cooperative credit society*' "has the same meaning as in section 2 of the Bank Act" (Government of Canada (2022), "Canada Deposit Insurance Corporation Act, R.S.C. 1985, c. C-3," adopted on February 17, 1984, entered into force on February 17, 1984, last amended on April 30, 2022, consolidated to May 2, 2022,

work towards these two objects for the benefit of persons who have deposits with member institutions[294] in such a way as will minimize the Canada Deposit Insurance Corporation's exposure to loss [414], and act as the resolution authority for those members [415]. The Governor in Council may, by order, exempt the Canada Deposit Insurance Corporation from the requirement that it seeks to achieve its objects in a way that will minimize its exposure to loss, when it takes steps to attend to a situation which the order specifies[295] [416]. The Canada Deposit Insurance Corporation may do everything that is necessary for, or incidental to, its objects, and may perform specified acts[296] to advance these [417].

---

s.2). Section 2 of the Bank Act defines the phrase '*local cooperative credit society*' as: " a body corporate organized on cooperative principles[,] incorporated by or under an Act of the legislature of a province **(a)** whose members or shareholders consist substantially of natural persons, and **(b)** whose principal purpose is to receive deposits from[,] and make loans to[,] its members and shareholders" (Government of Canada (2022), "Canada Deposit Insurance Corporation Act, R.S.C. 1985, c. C-3," adopted on February 17, 1984, entered into force on February 17, 1984, last amended on April 30, 2022, consolidated to May 2, 2022, s.2; emphasis original). The final sentence of fn 154 defines the term '*body corporate*'. The phrase '*deposit insurance*' is "the insurance referred to in paragraph 7(a) [of the Canada Deposit Insurance Corporation Act]" (Government of Canada (2022), "Canada Deposit Insurance Corporation Act, R.S.C. 1985, c. C-3," adopted on February 17, 1984, entered into force on February 17, 1984, last amended on April 30, 2022, consolidated to May 2, 2022, s.2). The text to the current footnote (i.e., fn 293) comprises paragraph 7(a) of the Canada Deposit Insurance Corporation Act. The word '*depositor*' is as defined in the Schedule to the Canada Deposit Insurance Corporation Act (Government of Canada (2022), "Canada Deposit Insurance Corporation Act, R.S.C. 1985, c. C-3," adopted on February 17, 1984, entered into force on February 17, 1984, last amended on April 30, 2022, consolidated to May 2, 2022, s.2). The Schedule to the Canada Deposit Insurance Corporation Act defines the word '*depositor*' as: "a person whose account has been[,] or is to be[,] credited in respect of moneys constituting a deposit or part of a deposit[,] or a person to whom a member institution is liable in respect of an instrument issued for moneys constituting a deposit or part of a deposit" (Government of Canada (2022), "Canada Deposit Insurance Corporation Act, R.S.C. 1985, c. C-3," adopted on February 17, 1984, entered into force on February 17, 1984, last amended on April 30, 2022, consolidated to May 2, 2022, Schedule, s.1).

294 The phrase '*member institution*' "means a corporation that has deposit insurance under this Act [(i.e., the Canada Deposit Insurance Corporation Act)] (Government of Canada (2022), "Canada Deposit Insurance Corporation Act, R.S.C. 1985, c. C-3," adopted on February 17, 1984, entered into force on February 17, 1984, last amended on April 30, 2022, consolidated to May 2, 2022, s.2). The preantepenultimate and antepenultimate sentence of fn 293, and the text to that footnote, define the term '*deposit insurance*'.

295 The Governor in Council may only make this order, "if the Minister is of the opinion, after consultation with the Board, the Governor of the Bank of Canada and the Superintendent, that the requirement that the Corporation pursues its objects in a manner which will minimize its exposure to loss, in respect of a situation that will be specified in the order, might have an adverse effect on the stability of the financial system in Canada[,] or public confidence in that stability" (Government of Canada (2022), "Canada Deposit Insurance Corporation Act, R.S.C. 1985, c. C-3," adopted on February 17, 1984, entered into force on February 17, 1984, last amended on April 30, 2022, consolidated to May 2, 2022, s.7.1(2)). The word '*Minister*' "means the Minister of Finance" (Government of Canada (2022), "Canada Deposit Insurance Corporation Act, R.S.C. 1985, c. C-3," adopted on February 17, 1984, entered into force on February 17, 1984, last amended on April 30, 2022, consolidated to May 2, 2022, s.2). The word '*Superintendent*' "means the Superintendent of Financial Institutions appointed pursuant to subsection 5(1) of the *Office of the Superintendent of Financial Institutions Act*" Government of Canada (2022), "Canada Deposit Insurance Corporation Act, R.S.C. 1985, c. C-3," adopted on February 17, 1984, entered into force on February 17, 1984, last amended on April 30, 2022, consolidated to May 2, 2022, s.2; emphasis original). The third sentence of fn 155 sets out subsection 5(1) of the Office of the Superintendent of Financial Institutions Act. The word '*Corporation*' "means the Canada Deposit Insurance Corporation" (Government of Canada (2022), "Canada Deposit Insurance Corporation Act, R.S.C. 1985, c. C-3," adopted on February 17, 1984, entered into force on February 17, 1984, last amended on April 30, 2022, consolidated to May 2, 2022, s.2).

296 In furthering its objects, the Canada Deposit Insurance Corporation may "**(a)** acquire assets from a member institution; **(a.1)** make or guarantee loans or advances, with or without security, to a member institution; **(a.11)** make or guarantee a deposit with a member institution; **(a.12)** assume liabilities of a member institution; **(a.2)** enter into an agreement with the government of a province, or an agent of the government of a province, respecting any matter relating to the insurance of deposits with provincial institutions in that province; **(b)** make any investment[,] and enter into any transaction[, which is] necessary or desirable for the financial management of the [Canada Deposit Insurance] Corporation; **(c)** act as liquidator, receiver or inspector of a member institution

Deposit Insurance

The Canada Deposit Insurance Corporation must insure every deposit with a member institution[297], other than a deposit which is not payable in Canada, a deposit with regard to which "Her Majesty in right of Canada" is a prior claimant, and the part of any one deposit that exceeds CAD 100,000 [418]. The Canada Deposit Insurance Corporation shall – to the extent and in the way that the Canada Deposit Insurance Corporation Act and the by-laws provide – insure the deposits that are held by a federal institution[298] regarding which the Superintendent has made an order approving the initiation and continuation of business, subject to four exceptions[299] [419]. Every member institution is considered to have obtained a policy of deposit insurance[300] upon the day on which it became a member institution [420].

For every premium year[301], the Canada Deposit Insurance Corporation shall evaluate and collect from each member institution an annual premium equal to the smaller of the annual premium for the latter determined in accordance with the by-laws, and the maximum annual

---

or a subsidiary thereof, when duly appointed as such[,] and appoint qualified and competent persons, whether employees of the Corporation or not, to carry out any or all of the functions of the Corporation under the appointment of the Corporation; **(d)** assume the costs of a winding-up of a member institution when the Corporation is appointed to act as a liquidator in the winding-up, or assume the costs of the receiver when the Corporation is appointed to act as such; **(e)** guarantee the payment of the fees of, and the costs incurred by any person as, the liquidator or receiver of a member institution[,] when that person is appointed as such; **(f)** acquire assets and assume liabilities of a member institution from its liquidator or receiver; **(f.1)** acquire, by way of security or otherwise, shares and subordinated debt of a member institution[,] and ... hold and dispose of those shares and subordinated debt; **(g)** make an advance for the purpose of paying a claim, against a member institution for which the Corporation is acting as receiver or liquidator, in respect of any insured deposit[,] and [for the purpose] of becoming subrogated as an unsecured creditor for the amount of the advance; **(h)** make[,] or cause to be made[,] such inspections of a member institution as may be authorized under this Act or a policy of deposit insurance; **(i)** acquire, hold and alienate real and personal property; **(i.1)** settle or compromise any claim by or against the Corporation; and **(j)** do all such other things as may be necessary for the exercising of any power of the Corporation" (Government of Canada (2022), "Canada Deposit Insurance Corporation Act, R.S.C. 1985, c. C-3," adopted on February 17, 1984, entered into force on February 17, 1984, last amended on April 30, 2022, consolidated to May 2, 2022, s.10(1); emphasis original). The first sentence of fn 294 defines the term '*member institution*'. Fn 293 defines the terms '*deposit*' and '*provincial institution*'. The preantepenultimate and antepenultimate sentence of fn 293, and the text to that footnote, define the term '*deposit insurance*'.

297 The first sentence of fn 294 defines the term '*member institution*'.

298 Fn 293 defines the term '*federal institution*' – for which the word '*bank*' qualifies.

299 These exceptions are as follows: "**(a)** that order prohibits the [federal] institution from accepting deposits in Canada; **(b)** that order authorizes the institution to accept deposits in Canada solely in accordance with subsection 413(3) of the *Bank Act*, subsection 378.1(2) of the *Cooperative Credit Associations Act* or subsection 413(2) of the *Trust and Loan Companies Act*; **(c)** the institution has been authorized under section 26.03 [of the Cooperative Credit Associations Act] to accept deposits payable in Canada while no longer being a member institution; or **(d)** the institution's policy of deposit insurance has been terminated under section 31 [of the Cooperative Credit Associations Act] or cancelled under section 33 [of the Cooperative Credit Associations Act]" (Government of Canada (2022), "Canada Deposit Insurance Corporation Act, R.S.C. 1985, c. C-3," adopted on February 17, 1984, entered into force on February 17, 1984, last amended on April 30, 2022, consolidated to May 2, 2022, s.17(1); emphasis original). The final sentence of fn 187 lays down subsection 413(3) of the Bank Act. Fn 293 defines the terms '*federal institution*' and '*deposit*'. The first sentence of fn 294 defines the term '*member institution*'. The preantepenultimate and antepenultimate sentence of fn 293, and the text to that footnote, define the term '*deposit insurance*'.

300 The preantepenultimate and antepenultimate sentence of fn 293, and the text to that footnote, define the term '*deposit insurance*'.

301 The phrase '*premium year*' "means, in relation to the calculation and payment of premiums pursuant to this Act [(i.e., the Canada Deposit Insurance Corporation Act)], the period beginning on May 1 in one year and ending on April 30 in the next year" (Government of Canada (2022), "Canada Deposit Insurance Corporation Act, R.S.C. 1985, c. C-3," adopted on February 17, 1984, entered into force on February 17, 1984, last amended on April 30, 2022, consolidated to May 2, 2022, s.2).

premium[302] [421]. For the purposes of the present section, i.e., section 21 of the Canada Deposit Insurance Corporation Act, a member institution may use any method that the Canada Deposit Insurance Corporation approves for the premium year to determine or estimate the sum of its deposits that are deemed to be insured there [422].

Acts of Good Faith

"Her Majesty in right of Canada," any agent or servant of Her Majesty the Queen (now His Majesty King Charles III), the Canada Deposit Insurance Corporation, its directors, officers and employees, and any person who acts on behalf of the Canada Deposit Insurance Corporation, are not liable to any to any member institution or person for any compensation, contribution, damages, indemnity or payment that any such member institution or person may experience or claim because of anything done, or not done, in good faith, in the actual or purported carrying out, exercise or performance of any duties, powers and functions under the Canada Deposit Insurance Corporation Act [423]. This does not relieve the Canada Deposit Insurance Corporation from its obligation to make payment in respect of a deposit which is insured under the Canada Deposit Insurance Corporation Act or from that to pay compensation [424].

Comment

The Canada Deposit Insurance Corporation Act sets out clearly how deposit insurance works for depositors of funds in Canadian banks. The member institutions of the Canada Deposit Insurance Corporation pay the specified annual premium, the aggregate of which the Corporation uses to insure against the loss of deposits held at those member institutions, at federal institutions, and – subject to the Canada Deposit Insurance Corporation's approval and three other conditions – provincial institutions[303].

---

[302] In this section, i.e., section 21 of the Canada Deposit Insurance Corporation Act, the phrase '*maximum annual premium*' means the larger of CAD 5,000 and "one third of one percent, or such smaller proportion of one per cent as may be fixed in respect of the premium year by the Governor in Council, of an amount equal to the sum of so much of the deposits as are considered to be insured by the [Canada Deposit Insurance] Corporation and deposited with the member institution as of April 30 in the immediately preceding premium year" (Government of Canada (2022), "Canada Deposit Insurance Corporation Act, R.S.C. 1985, c. C-3," adopted on February 17, 1984, entered into force on February 17, 1984, last amended on April 30, 2022, consolidated to May 2, 2022, s.21(4)). Fn 301 defines the term '*premium year*'. Fn 293 defines the term '*deposit*'. The first sentence of fn 294 defines the term '*member institution*'.

[303] Section 17.1 of the Canada Deposit Insurance Corporation Act states: "On the application of a provincial institution, the [Canada Deposit Insurance] Corporation may insure the deposits [that are] held by the institution in the manner and to the extent provided in this Act and the by-laws, if **(a)** the Corporation approves the institution for deposit insurance; **(b)** the institution is authorized by the province of its incorporation to apply for deposit insurance; **(c)** the institution agrees, in carrying on its business, not to exercise powers [that are] substantially different from the powers exercisable by a company to which the *Trust and Loan Companies Act* applies, and **(d)** the Corporation is satisfied that[,] at all times[,] the Corporation will have adequate access to information regarding the institution." (Government of Canada (2022), "Canada Deposit Insurance Corporation Act, R.S.C. 1985, c. C-3," adopted on February 17, 1984, entered into force on February 17, 1984, last amended on April 30, 2022, consolidated to May 2, 2022, s.17.1; emphasis original). Fn 293 defines the terms '*provincial institution*' and '*deposit*'. The preantepenultimate and antepenultimate sentence of fn 293, and the text to that footnote, define the term '*deposit insurance*'.

Canadian Payments Act

Establishment of the Canadian Payments Association

The Canadian Payments Act establishes the Canadian Payments Association [425], which is not an agent of Her Majesty the Queen (now His Majesty King Charles III)[304] [426].

[304] The first sentence of fn 137 sets out subsection 4(1) of the Canadian Payments Act, which lists the members of the Canadian Payments Association. In addition, subsection 4(2) of the Canadian Payments Act specifies other persons who are entitled to apply for membership of the Canadian Payments Association, as follows: "Each of the following persons is entitled to be a member of the [Canadian Payments] Association[,] if they meet the requirements [which are] set out in the regulations and the by-laws: **(a)** a central [cooperative credit society], a trust company, a loan company and any other person, other than a local [cooperative credit society] that is a member of a central or a cooperative credit association, that accepts deposits transferable by order; **(b)** [Repealed …]; **(c)** Her Majesty [the Queen (now His Majesty King Charles III)] in right of a province[,] or an agent or mandatary of Her Majesty in right of a province, if Her Majesty in right of a province or the agent or mandatory accepts deposits transferable by order; **(d)** a life insurance company; **(e)** a securities dealer; **(f)** a cooperative credit association; **(g)** the trustee of a qualified trust; and **(h)** a qualified corporation, on behalf of its money market mutual fund." (Government of Canada (2022), "Canadian Payments Act, R.S.C., 1985, c. C-21," adopted on November 26, 1980, as "An Act to revise the Bank Act, to amend the Quebec Savings Bank Act and the Bank of Canada Act, to establish the Canadian Payments Association and to amend other Acts in consequence thereof: Part IV – An Act to establish the Canadian Payments Association," entered into force on December 1, 1980, last amended on April 2, 2021, consolidated to May 2, 2022, s.4(2)). The phrase '*central cooperative credit society*' and the word '*central*', "mean a cooperative credit society [that is] incorporated by[,] or under[,] an Act of the legislature of a province, one of whose principal purposes is to provide liquidity support to local cooperative credit societies, and **(a)** whose membership consists wholly or primarily of local cooperative credit societies, or **(b)** whose directors are wholly or primarily persons elected or appointed by local cooperative credit societies" (Government of Canada (2022), "Canada Deposit Insurance Corporation Act, R.S.C. 1985, c. C-3," adopted on February 17, 1984, entered into force on February 17, 1984, last amended on April 30, 2022, consolidated to May 2, 2022, s.2(1); emphasis original). The phrase '*local cooperative credit society*', and the word '*local*', "mean a cooperative credit society [that is] incorporated by[,] or under[,] an Act of the legislature of a province **(a)** whose members consists substantially of individuals, and **(b)** whose principal purpose is to receive deposits from, and make loans to, its members" (Government of Canada (2022), "Canada Deposit Insurance Corporation Act, R.S.C. 1985, c. C-3," adopted on February 17, 1984, entered into force on February 17, 1984, last amended on April 30, 2022, consolidated to May 2, 2022, s.2(1); emphasis original). A '*trust company*' is "a corporation that accepts deposits transferable by order[,] and that **(a)** is a company to which the *Trust and Loan Companies Act* applies[,] and that is a trust company pursuant to subsection 57(2) of that Act, or **(b)** carries on, under an Act of the legislature of a province or a constating instrument issued under provincial jurisdiction, a business [that is] substantially similar to the business of a company referred to in paragraph (a)" (Government of Canada (2022), "Canada Deposit Insurance Corporation Act, R.S.C. 1985, c. C-3," adopted on February 17, 1984, entered into force on February 17, 1984, last amended on April 30, 2022, consolidated to May 2, 2022, s.2(1); emphasis original). A '*loan company*' is "a corporation that accepts deposits [which are] transferable by order[,] and that **(a)** is a company to which the *Trust and Loan Companies Act* applies[,] and that is not a trust company pursuant to subsection 57(2) of that Act, or **(b)** carries on, under an Act of the legislature of a province or a constating instrument issued under provincial jurisdiction, a business [that is] substantially similar to the business of a company referred to in paragraph (a)" (Government of Canada (2022), "Canada Deposit Insurance Corporation Act, R.S.C. 1985, c. C-3," adopted on February 17, 1984, entered into force on February 17, 1984, last amended on April 30, 2022, consolidated to May 2, 2022, s.2(1); emphasis original). A '*cooperative credit association*' is "an association to which the Cooperative Credit Associations Act applies" (Government of Canada (2022), "Canada Deposit Insurance Corporation Act, R.S.C. 1985, c. C-3," adopted on February 17, 1984, entered into force on February 17, 1984, last amended on April 30, 2022, consolidated to May 2, 2022, s.2(1)). A '*life insurance company*' is "**(a)** a life company within the meaning of subsection 2(1) of the *Insurance Companies Act*, **(b)** a foreign life company within the meaning of subsection 571 of that Act, acting in respect of its insurance business in Canada, or **(c)** a body corporate that carries on[,] under a constating instrument issued under an Act of the legislature or a province[,] a business [which is] substantially similar to the business of a life company referred to in paragraph (a)" (Government of Canada (2022), "Canada Deposit Insurance Corporation Act, R.S.C. 1985, c. C-3," adopted on February 17, 1984, entered into force on February 17, 1984, last amended on April 30, 2022, consolidated to May 2, 2022, s.2(1); emphasis original). A '*securities dealer*' is "a body corporate that is registered or licensed under the laws of a province to trade in securities, as

Objects and Powers of the Canadian Payments Association

The Canadian Payments Association has the following objects: to found and operate national systems for the clearing and settlement of payments, as well as other facilities for the making and exchange of payments [427], to ease the interaction of its clearing and settlement systems and associated arrangements with other systems or arrangements concerning clearing, settlement or exchange of payments [428], and to faciliate the advancement of new payment methods and technologies [429]. In pursuing these objects, the Canadian Payments Association must further the safety, soundness and efficiency of its clearing and settlement systems, and consider users' interests [430].

In fulfilling its objects, the Canadian Payments Association may arrange the exchange of payment items within Canada [431], determine the amount of dues that are payable by members and require the remittance of these [432], employ such persons and hire such agents, advisers and consultants as it deems to be necessary for the right conduct of its business, and set the terms and conditions of their engagement and remuneration [433], and furnish – or procure the supply of – benefits for the Association's[305] officers and employees [434]. For the purposes of implementing its objects, the Canadian Payments Association has the capacity, powers, privileges and rights of a natural person [435].

---

agent or for its own behalf" (Government of Canada (2022), "Canada Deposit Insurance Corporation Act, R.S.C. 1985, c. C-3," adopted on February 17, 1984, entered into force on February 17, 1984, last amended on April 30, 2022, consolidated to May 2, 2022, s.2(1)). A '*trustee*', "in respect of a qualified trust, [is] a trustee that is a body corporate" (Government of Canada (2022), "Canada Deposit Insurance Corporation Act, R.S.C. 1985, c. C-3," adopted on February 17, 1984, entered into force on February 17, 1984, last amended on April 30, 2022, consolidated to May 2, 2022, s.2(1)). A '*qualified trust*' is "an *inter vivos* trust **(a)** in which the interest of its beneficiaries is described by reference to units of the trust that have been issued to the public under a prospectus, filed in accordance with the laws of the province in which the units were issued, having conditions attached to the units requiring the trustee to accept the surrender of any fully-paid units, or fractions or portions of the units, **(i)** at the demand of their holder, and **(ii)** at prices [that are] determined and payable in accordance with specified conditions, **(b)** whose units referred to in paragraph (a) have a fair market value, determined without regard to any voting rights attached to the units, that is not less than 95% of the fair market value of all of the issued units of the trust, and **(c)** whose assets constitute a money market mutual fund" (Government of Canada (2022), "Canada Deposit Insurance Corporation Act, R.S.C. 1985, c. C-3," adopted on February 17, 1984, entered into force on February 17, 1984, last amended on April 30, 2022, consolidated to May 2, 2022, s.2(1); emphasis original). A '*money market mutual fund*' is "a fund **(a)** the assets of which are fully or principally invested in short-term and highly liquid debt securities, and **(b)** that satisfies conditions prescribed by regulation" (Government of Canada (2022), "Canada Deposit Insurance Corporation Act, R.S.C. 1985, c. C-3," adopted on February 17, 1984, entered into force on February 17, 1984, last amended on April 30, 2022, consolidated to May 2, 2022, s.2(1); emphasis original). A '*qualified corporation*' is "a body corporate **(a)** that has issued shares to the public sector under a prospectus, filed in accordance with the laws of the province in which the shares were issued, having conditions attached to the shares requiring the body corporate to accept the surrender of any fully-paid shares, or fractions or portions of the shares, **(i)** at the demand of their holder, and **(ii)** at prices [that are] determined and payable in accordance with specified conditions, **(b)** whose shares referred to in paragraph (a) have a fair market value, determined without regard to any voting rights attached to the shares, that is not less than 95% of the fair market value of all of the issued shares of the capital stock of the body corporate, and **(c)** having assets that constitute a money market mutual fund" (Government of Canada (2022), "Canada Deposit Insurance Corporation Act, R.S.C. 1985, c. C-3," adopted on February 17, 1984, entered into force on February 17, 1984, last amended on April 30, 2022, consolidated to May 2, 2022, s.2(1); emphasis original).

305 The word '*Association*' means the Canadian Payments Association (Government of Canada (2022), "Canada Deposit Insurance Corporation Act, R.S.C. 1985, c. C-3," adopted on February 17, 1984, entered into force on February 17, 1984, last amended on April 30, 2022, consolidated to May 2, 2022, s.2(1)).

By-Laws, Rules, Standards, Statements of Principle and Directives

The Board[306] may make any by-laws that it deems to be advisable for the achievement of the Canadian Payments Association's objects[307] [436]. Subject to the by-laws, the Board may make any rules which it considers to be advisable for the accomplishment of the Association's objects [437].

Subject to the by-laws and rules, the Board may make any standards and statements of principle that it deems to be advisable for the attainment of the Association's objects [438]. If the Minister[308] opines that it is in the public interest, (s)he may issue a written directive to the Canadian Payment Association – which may comprise an instruction to make, amend or repeal a by-law, rule or standard [439].

Designated Payment Systems[309]

The Minister[310] may, if (s)he judges it to be in the public interest[311], designate a payment system that (s)he opines is national, or largely national, in its ambit, or plays a significant role in supporting transactions financial markets or the economy within Canada [440]. Before the Minister designates a payment system, (s)he *must* consult the payment system's manager and participants[312] – and *may* consult interested parties, regarding the effect of the designation [441]. The Minister may issue guidelines[313] regarding any matter concerning the administration or enforcement of Part 2 of the Canadian Payments Act [442], which is titled 'Designated Payment Systems' and which comprises sections 36 to 42 of the Canadian Payments Act.

---

306 The word '*Board*' means "Board of Directors of the Association" (Government of Canada (2022), "Canada Deposit Insurance Corporation Act, R.S.C. 1985, c. C-3," adopted on February 17, 1984, entered into force on February 17, 1984, last amended on April 30, 2022, consolidated to May 2, 2022, s.2(1)). Fn 305 defines the term '*Association*'.

307 The first sentence of the first paragraph of the subsection titled 'Objects and Powers of the Canadian Payments Association', above in the current section (i.e., that entitled 'Canadian Payments Act'), states the objects of the Canadian Payments Association.

308 The word '*Minister*' "means the Minister of Finance" (Government of Canada (2022), "Canada Deposit Insurance Corporation Act, R.S.C. 1985, c. C-3," adopted on February 17, 1984, entered into force on February 17, 1984, last amended on April 30, 2022, consolidated to May 2, 2022, s.2(1)).

309 Part 2 of the Canadian Payments Act, which is titled 'Designated Payment Systems' and consists of sections 36-42 of this Act, does not apply to the Canadian Payments Association (Government of Canada (2022), "Canada Deposit Insurance Corporation Act, R.S.C. 1985, c. C-3," adopted on February 17, 1984, entered into force on February 17, 1984, last amended on April 30, 2022, consolidated to May 2, 2022, s.36.1).

310 Fn 308 defines the term '*Minister*'.

311 The Minister must consider the following factors "in a determination of whether it is the public interest to designate a payment system: **(a)** the level of financial safety [that is] provided by the payment system to the participants and users; **(b)** the efficiency and competitiveness of payment systems in Canada; and **(c)** the best interests of the financial system in Canada" (Government of Canada (2022), "Canada Deposit Insurance Corporation Act, R.S.C. 1985, c. C-3," adopted on February 17, 1984, entered into force on February 17, 1984, last amended on April 30, 2022, consolidated to May 2, 2022, s.37(2); emphasis original).

312 Before the Minister designates a payment system, (s)he is to "notify the manager and the participants of a designated payment system in any manner that the Minister considers appropriate" (Government of Canada (2022), "Canada Deposit Insurance Corporation Act, R.S.C. 1985, c. C-3," adopted on February 17, 1984, entered into force on February 17, 1984, last amended on April 30, 2022, consolidated to May 2, 2022, s.37(4)).

313 The guidelines are to "be made available to the public"; the Minister may give notice of these in any way in which (s)he deems to be appropriate (Government of Canada (2022), "Canada Deposit Insurance Corporation Act, R.S.C. 1985, c. C-3," adopted on February 17, 1984, entered into force on February 17, 1984, last amended on April 30, 2022, consolidated to May 2, 2022, s.39(2)).

The Minister may issue a written directive to the manager of, or a participant in, a designated payment system, in respect of the conditions that a person must satisfy to become a participant in this system [443], the functioning of the designated payment system [444], the interaction of this system with other payment systems [445], or the relationship between the designated payment system and its users [446]. Before the Minister gives a directive, (s)he *must* consult the person to whom (s)he is to give it, and *may* consult any interested party, concerning its content and effect [447]. Within a directive, the Minister may specify that a manager of, or a participant in, a designated payment system shall – within the time which the Minister deems to be necessary – cease, or refrain from, carrying out an act or pursuing a course of conduct [448], discharge such acts as the Minister considers to be requisite in the public interest [449], or make, amend or repeal a rule [450]. A directive is binding upon the person to whom it is issued[314] [451].

Comment

The Canadian Payments Act is a clear, straightforward legislative instrument. Notwithstanding this, it is not wholly intelligible how the Canadian Payments Association relates to Designated Payment Systems – i.e., payment systems that are designated as such by the Minister of Finance under Part 2 of the Act. The first object[315] of the Canadian Payments Association is to establish and operate national systems for the clearing and settlement of payments and other structures for the making and exchange of payments – neither of which, it seems, are Designated Payment Systems. The second object of the Canadian Payment Association – to facilitate the interaction of its clearing and settlement systems and associated arrangements with other systems or arrangements concerning clearing, settlement or exchange of payments – may indicate the link between the Canadian Payments Association and Designated Payment Systems, as these may fall within the descriptor 'other systems or arrangements concerning clearing, settlement or exchange of payments'. If this is correct, then the Government of Canada should add to Canadian Payments Act a provision that lays down the deduced connection.

[314] This has the following consequence: "As soon as is practicable after implementing a directive and completing any actions [that are] required to be taken in connection with it, the person to whom it is given shall notify the Minister that the directive has been implemented and the action completed." (Government of Canada (2022), "Canada Deposit Insurance Corporation Act, R.S.C. 1985, c. C-3," adopted on February 17, 1984, entered into force on February 17, 1984, last amended on April 30, 2022, consolidated to May 2, 2022, s.40(4)). Fn 308 defines the term '*Minister*'.

[315] The first sentence of the first paragraph of the subsection titled 'Objects and Powers of the Canadian Payments Association', above in the current section (i.e., that entitled 'Canadian Payments Act'), sets out the objects of the Canadian Payments Association.

Retail Payment Activities Act

Subject to the exceptions that the Retail Payment Activities Act lays down[316], this Act applies to any retail payment activity[317] that a payment service provider[318] with a place of business in Canada undertakes [452], and which a payment service provider without a place of business in Canada performs for an end user[319] in Canada – this latter payment service provider directing retail payment activities at entities[320] or individuals within Canada [453].

The Retail Payment Activities Act does not apply to a payment service provider that carries out retail payment activities, if the payment service provider is a bank[321] or an authorized foreign bank[322] [454]. Therefore, the present monograph does not consider further the provisions of this Act.

Comments

The federal legislation in Canada is detailed as to the regulation of banks in that state. This is demonstrated by the presence in the Bank Act of separate Parts on the regulation of foreign banks and the regulation of authorized foreign banks. New consolidations of these laws are

---

[316] Sections 6-10 of the Retail Payments Activities Act contain these exceptions (Government of Canada (2022). "Retail Payment Activities Act, S.C. 2021, c. 23, s. 177," adopted on June 29, 2021, entered into force on June 29, 2021, consolidated to May 2, 2022, ss.4 and 5).

[317] A '*retail payment activity*' is "a payment function that is performed in relation to an electronic funds transfer that is made in the currency of Canada or another country[,] or using a unit that meets prescribed criteria (Government of Canada (2022). "Retail Payment Activities Act, S.C. 2021, c. 23, s. 177," adopted on June 29, 2021, entered into force on June 29, 2021, consolidated to May 2, 2022, s.2). The phrase '*payment function*' means "**(a)** the provision or maintenance of an account that, in relation to an electronic funds transfer, is held on behalf of one or more end users; **(b)** the holding of funds on behalf of an end user until they are withdrawn by the end user or transferred to another individual or entity; **(c)** the initiation of an electronic funds transfer at the request of an end user; **(d)** the authorization of an electronic funds transfer or the transmission, reception or facilitation of an instruction in relation to an electronic funds transfer; or **(e)** the provision of clearing or settlement services" (Government of Canada (2022). "Retail Payment Activities Act, S.C. 2021, c. 23, s. 177," adopted on June 29, 2021, entered into force on June 29, 2021, consolidated to May 2, 2022, s.2; emphasis original). An '*electronic funds transfer*' is "a placement, transfer or withdrawal of funds by electronic means that is initiated by[,] or on behalf of[,] an individual or entity" (Government of Canada (2022). "Retail Payment Activities Act, S.C. 2021, c. 23, s. 177," adopted on June 29, 2021, entered into force on June 29, 2021, consolidated to May 2, 2022, s.2). Fn 319 defines the term '*end user*'. Fn 320 defines the term '*entity*'.

[318] A '*payment service provider*' is "an individual or entity that performs payment functions as a service or business activity that is not incidental to another service or business activity" (Government of Canada (2022). "Retail Payment Activities Act, S.C. 2021, c. 23, s. 177," adopted on June 29, 2021, entered into force on June 29, 2021, consolidated to May 2, 2022, s.2). Fn 320 defines the term '*entity*'.

[319] An '*end user*' is "an individual or entity that uses a payment service as a payer or payee" (Government of Canada (2022). "Retail Payment Activities Act, S.C. 2021, c. 23, s. 177," adopted on June 29, 2021, entered into force on June 29, 2021, consolidated to May 2, 2022, s.2). Fn 320 defines the term '*entity*'.

[320] An '*entity*' is "a corporation, trust, partnership, fund, an unincorporated association or organization, the government of a foreign country or of a political subdivision of a foreign country, or an agency of a foreign country or of a subdivision of a foreign country" (Government of Canada (2022). "Retail Payment Activities Act, S.C. 2021, c. 23, s. 177," adopted on June 29, 2021, entered into force on June 29, 2021, consolidated to May 2, 2022, s.2).

[321] The first sentence of fn 141 defines the term '*bank*'.

[322] The first sentence of fn 142 defines the term '*authorized foreign bank*'.

regularly published. Furthermore, Canada's financial legislation continues to develop – as is the case with the Retail Payment Activities Act[323].

Conclusion

This chapter introduces the legal system of Canada. It sets out provisions from the Bank of Canada Act, the Bank Act, the Canada Deposit Insurance Corporation Act, the Canadian Payments Act and the Retail Payment Activities Act, focusing on elements of the Bank Act. Chapter 3 investigates the law of banking in New Zealand.

---

[323] On enquiry to the Bank of Canada about the date on which the Retail Payment Activities Act enters or entered into force, I received the following reply: "Thank you for your email regarding the Retail Payment Activities Act. The Act establishes the legal framework for the Bank [of Canada] to supervise retail payment providers, including its scope and powers. It was approved by Parliament on June 29, 2021[,] and is expected to come into force in stages over the next few years. The federal cabinet will decide how and when each provision of the Act will come into force." (Bank of Canada (2022), "RE: {External} When did specified legislation enter into force?," reply to the e-mail from Dr. Baber to the Bank of Canada, May 31, 2022).

Chapter 3

New Zealand

Abstract

In 1947, New Zealand passed the Statute of Westminster Adoption Act, thereby gaining formal, legal independence from the United Kingdom (UK) in the conduct of its foreign relations. The unicameral Parliament of New Zealand comprises a Head of State (currently His Majesty King Charles III) who is represented there by a Governor-General, and the House of Representatives. New Zealand has a common law system. Its final step towards full independence from the UK took place on 1st January 1987, when the Constitution Act 1986 entered into force. Subsection 15(2) of that Act held that no Act of the UK Parliament passed after the former Act's commencement was to constitute the law of New Zealand. The conversion of a bill to an Act of Parliament involves a first reading before the House of Representatives, referral to a select committee of the House, a second reading before the House, a debate before committee of the whole House in which any Member of Parliament may participate, its third reading before the House, and Royal Assent. New Zealand has no codified constitution – its law is developed from statutes and case law, where the former supersedes the latter. The judgments of the Supreme Court of New Zealand are binding on all inferior courts there. The Senior Courts, which comprise the Supreme Court, the Court of Appeal and the High Court, may inspect the judgments of the highest-level courts in other jurisdictions – especially those from Australia, Canada and the UK – for comparison or guidance. The legal system of New Zealand is connected, historically and contemporaneously, to that of Australia, Canada and the UK. Furthermore, there are similarities between Australia, Canada and New Zealand in their routes to independence from the UK. The purposes of the Reserve Bank of New Zealand Act 2021 are to provide for the Reserve Bank of New Zealand (RBNZ) to continue, advance the well-being and prosperity of New Zealanders, and contribute to a productive, sustainable economy. The financial stability objective of the RBNZ is to safeguard and further the stability of New Zealand's financial system. This Act's provision for the Council of Financial Regulators to modulate the regulation of this financial system is significant. The Banking (Prudential Supervision) Act 1989 has a similar purpose, which it addresses by providing for the RBNZ to be responsible for registering banks and undertaking their prudential supervison – amongst other things. The provisions within this Act tend to be drafted clearly and logically. The purpose of the Non-Bank Deposit Takers Act 2013 is to promote the maintenance of a sound, efficient financial system. This Act provides a comprehensive licensing and prudential supervision regime for non-bank deposit takers (NBDTs). The upcoming Deposit Takers Act will combine the regulatory regime regarding deposits for banks and NBDTs. To the extent that the legislative approach used in the Non-Bank Deposit Takers Act 2013 is followed in the forthcoming Deposit Takers Act, its quality indicates that the new regime is likely to benefit from an ordered start.

Keywords: bank, court, deposit, licence, offence, prudential, register, settlement

Introduction

The next section introduces the legal system of New Zealand. The succeeding section titled 'Banking Law is in Flux' presents the state of New Zealand's banking legislation at the time of writing. There follow sections on the Reserve Bank of New Zealand Act 2021, the Banking (Prudential Supervision) Act 1989 and the Non-Bank Deposit Takers Act 2013. The final section concludes.

An Introduction to the Legal System of New Zealand

Essentials

In 1947, New Zealand passed the Statute of Westminster Adoption Act – thereby gaining formal, legal independence from the UK in the conduct of its foreign relations [455, 456]. The unicameral Parliament of New Zealand comprises the Head of State – Her Majesty Queen Elizabeth II (now His Majesty King Charles III) who is represented there by a Governor-General, and the House of Representatives [457]. New Zealand has a common law legal system, in which statute is a superior source of law to case law and to customary law – which includes Māori customary law [458].

New Zealand's Road to Full Independence from the UK

Section 15 of the Constitution Act 1986 is entitled 'Power of Parliament to make laws', and states the following.

> (1) The Parliament of New Zealand continues to have full power to make laws. (2) No Act of the Parliament of the United Kingdom passed after the commencement of this Act[324] shall extend to New Zealand as part of its law [459].

This provision is the last piece in the establishment of full independence of New Zealand from the United Kingdom, which occurred thus.

> In 1852, twelve years after the signing of the Treaty of Waitangi[325], the United Kingdom Parliament passed the New Zealand Constitution Act (NZCA), which provided for six

[324] The Constitution Act 1986 entered into force on 1st January 1987 (Government of New Zealand (2005), "Constitution Act 1986, Public Act 1986 No 114," adopted on December 13, 1986, entered into force on January 1, 1987, last amended on May 16, 2005, s.1(2)).

[325] The Treaty of Waitangi is the document that signifies the establishment of British New Zealand, "tak[ing] its name from the place in the Bay of Islands where it was first signed, on 6 February 1840. … The Treaty is an agreement, in Māori and English, that was made between the British Crown and about 540 Māori rangatira (chiefs). Growing numbers of British migrants arrived in New Zealand in the late 1830s, and there were plans for extensive settlement. Around this time[,] there were large-scale land transactions with Māori, unruly behaviour by some settlers[,] and signs that the French were interested in annexing New Zealand. The British government was initially unwilling to act, but it eventually realised that annexing the country could protect Māori, regulate British subjects and secure commercial interests. Lieutenant-Governor William Hobson had the task of securing British sovereignty over New Zealand. … About 40 [Māori] chiefs … signed the Māori version of the Treaty on 6

elected provincial councils, a General Assembly consisting of a Governor (the monarch's representative), a Legislative Council, and a House of Representatives. ... The first step in achieving more than nominal independence from [Great] Britain was taken on 7 May 1856, when the first responsible ministry ... was formed following the dissolution of Parliament and fresh elections in 1855. Because both the first and second ministries lasted only a few weeks, confidence of the House [of Representatives] could not be demonstrated. Responsible government was thus not consolidated until 1857, the year in which a further degree of autonomy was achieved when the British Parliament passed the New Zealand Constitution Amendment Act. This gave the New Zealand Parliament authority to amend all but a few entrenched sections of the 1852 NZCA. It also enabled responsibility for native affairs to be gradually transferred from the British to the Colonial Government, which was essentially achieved by 1870. ... In the 19th century, New Zealand ... had little influence in ... defining or acquiring its own territory. Despite New Zealand passing the Confederation and Annexation Act 1883[,] giving it the power to annex any unappropriated Pacific Islands ... , permission was still needed from Britain before New Zealand could annex its first territory – the Kermadec Islands – in 1887. The Cook Islands were made a British protectorate in 1888, and transferred to New Zealand in 1901. Niue and Tokelau became New Zealand protectorates in 1905 and 1926[,] respectively. ... More independence was asserted in 1901[,] when the colony of New Zealand refused to join Australia as its seventh state. ... Following the 1907 Imperial Conference, the New Zealand House of Representatives passed a motion respectfully requesting that His Majesty the King "take such steps as he may consider necessary" to change the designation of New Zealand from the "Colony of New Zealand" to the "Dominion of New Zealand." This change in status took effect on 26 September, 1907[, and] provided for "internal self-government and a considerable measure of freedom in their foreign relations," but complete autonomy in New Zealand's foreign affairs was not obtained. ... The External Affairs Act 1919 established a department responsible for New Zealand's Pacific territories ... . New Zealand received recognition as a 'State' when it signed the Versailles Peace Treaty and joined the League of Nations in 1920. ... At the 1923 Imperial Conference[,] New Zealand finally acquired the right to conduct its own international trade negotiations

---

February [1840]. By September [1840], another 500 [Māori chiefs] had signed the copies of the document that were sent around the country. ... Almost all signed the Māori text. The Colonial Office in England later declared that the Treaty applied to Māori tribes whose chiefs had not signed. British sovereignty over the country was proclaimed on 21 May 1840. The Treaty is a broad statement of principles on which the British and Māori made a political compact to found a nation state and build a government in New Zealand. The document has three articles. In the English version, Māori cede the sovereignty of New Zealand to [Great] Britain; Māori give the Crown an exclusive right to buy lands [that] they wish to sell, and, in return, are guaranteed full rights of ownership of their lands, forests, fisheries and other possessions; and Māori are given the rights and privileges of British subjects. The Treaty in Māori was deemed to convey the meaning of the English version, but there are important differences. Most significantly, the word 'sovereignty' was translated as 'kawanatanga' (governance). Some Māori believed [that] they were giving up government over their lands[,] but retaining the right to manage their own affairs. The English version guaranteed 'undisturbed possession' of all their 'properties', but the Māori version guaranteed 'tino rangatiratanga' (full authority) over 'taonga' (treasures, which may be intangible). Māori understanding was at odds with the understanding of those negotiating the Treaty for the Crown, and[,] as Māori society valued the spoken word, explanations given at the time were probably as important as the wording of the document. ... The Treaty of Waitangi is not considered [to be] part of New Zealand domestic law, except where its principles are referred to in Acts of Parliament. The exclusive right to determine the meaning of the Treaty rests with the Waitangi Tribunal, a commission of inquiry created in 1975 to investigate alleged breaches of the Treaty by the Crown. More than 2[,]000 claims have been lodged with the tribunal, and a number of major settlements have been reached. (Government of New Zealand (2022), "NZ History: The Treaty in brief: Page 1 – Introduction," accessed August 4, 2022, <https://nzhistory.govt.nz/politics/treaty/the-treaty-in-brief>).

> independently of Britain. … In its Report to the Imperial Conference of 1926, the Inter-Imperial Relations Committee, chaired by Lord Balfour, declared that Great Britain and the self-governing Dominions were "autonomous Communities within the British Empire, equal in status, in no way subordinate one to another in any aspect of their domestic and external affairs"[.] … [T]he Balfour Declaration of New Zealand's sovereignty … did not "as a matter of law exist in respect of legislation." Indeed, it required the Statute of Westminster, passed in the British Parliament in December 1931, to give legal effect to the Balfour Declaration's recognition of the change in status of the Dominions. … New Zealand could not legislate extra-territorially, and was constrained by sections of two British acts, the Merchant Shipping Act 1894 and the Colonial Courts of Admiralty Act 1890. … Section 3 of the [Statute of Westminster] Act [1931] "declared and enacted" that Dominions had full power to make laws having extraterritorial effect. … New Zealand … did not enact the provisions of the Statute of Westminster – as the Statute of Westminster Adoption Act – until 1947. [R]easons … for the delay of 16 years … include concerns about New Zealand's relationship with Britain, a lack of practical difficulties until wartime emergencies presented them, and New Zealand's desire to abolish its upper house. … [T]o abolish the Legislative Council required New Zealand to pass both the Statute of Westminster Adoption Act 1947, and the New Zealand Constitution Amendment (Request and Consent) Act 1947. These received the Royal assent on 25 November 1947. … Full New Zealand sovereignty can therefore be dated to 1947 – both in terms of gaining formal legal control over the conduct of its foreign policy and the attainment of constitutional and plenary powers by its legislature. … The Constitution Act 1986 states that the New Zealand Constitution Act 1852 of the Parliament of the United Kingdom shall cease to have effect as part of the law of New Zealand. It also repealed the Statute of Westminster Adoption Act 1947, the New Zealand Constitution Amendment (Request and Consent) Act 1947, the New Zealand Constitution Amendment Act 1970, and the New Zealand Constitution Amendment Act 1973. In effect, the Constitution Act 1986 declares the power of the United Kingdom Parliament to legislate for New Zealand to be at an end. New Zealand, as of 1987, is a free-standing constitutional monarchy whose Parliament has unlimited sovereign power [455].

The Parliamentary Legislative Process

A bill is introduced to the House of Representatives, and is then debated there no earlier than the third sitting day after its introduction – which enables Members of Parliament to scrutinize it [460]. An affirmative vote at the end of the first reading of the bill sees it referred to a select committee; if the bill is defeated in the vote, then it is discontinued [460]. The select committee normally has six months to examine the bill – during which time it may invite public submissions and hold public hearings on the basis of those submissions, decide upon changes to the bill, and prepare a report for the House of Representatives – which includes a reprint of the bill with the committee's amendments to it, and a commentary that explains those alterations and the matters that the committee has considered [460].

The second reading of a bill must take place no sooner than the third sitting day after the select committee reports to the House of Representatives [460]. Changes that are not endorsed by every member of the select committee, are subject to a single vote at the end of the debate [460]. Whilst the bill is terminated if this vote is lost, an affirmative vote signifies that the second reading is agreed – in which case it proceeds for a debate by a committee of the whole House of Representatives [460]. Any Member of Parliament may participate therein, in which the Speaker is absent from the chair [460]. These debates provide an opportunity to inspect the bill in detail and, having no time limit, may last several days [460]. As soon as the bill's final form is agreed, it is reprinted and is ready for the third reading – which is a concluding debate [460].

If a bill is passed in the vote at the end of its third reading – as is usual, then it only becomes an Act of Parliament when signed by the Head of State – Her Majesty Queen Elizabeth II (now His Majesty King Charles III) – or her (his) representative in New Zealand the Governor General [460]. This is known as the Royal Assent [460].

Subordinate Legislation

Parliament may delegate law-making powers to other entities [458]. This subordinate legislation must be within the power that Parliament delegates, and may be reviewed by the courts [458]. Such delegation is usually in technical spheres or fields subject to material change, and includes, for instance, specific rules for immigration to New Zealand that the executive sets [458].

Sources of Law

New Zealand lacks a 'written'[326] constitution [461]. Its law is developed from statutes that its parliament enacts, and from case law [461]. The statute law supersedes any case law that addresses the same issue [461].

Courts

The judgments of the Supreme Court of New Zealand are binding on all inferior courts there [458]. Those of the Court of Appeal of New Zealand bind the High Court, the Employment Court and the District Court[327] of New Zealand, and those of the High Court bind the District Court [458] – which hears the majority of cases [461]. Whilst the judiciary is responsible for the work of the courts, the Secretary of Justice – through the Minister for Courts – is

[326] It is submitted that stating the statement 'a country does not have a written constitution' – or, put in another way, 'a country has an unwritten constitution' – does not necessarily mean that the relevant state has no rules of constitutional significance. The UK is said to lack a written constitution (or to have an unwritten constitution); but it does have constitutional rules as, for instance, its Parliament notes: "The United Kingdom constitution is composed of the laws and rules that create the institutions of the state, regulate the relationships between those institutions, or regulate the relationship between the state and the individual. These laws and rules are not codified in a single, written document. Constitutional laws and rules [in the UK] have no special legal status." (Political and Constitutional Reform Committee of the House of Commons of the United Kingdom (2015), Our Democratic Settlement (London: House of Commons), 5).

[327] The Environment Court, Youth Court and Family Court function as divisions of the District Court, and equate to the last-mentioned in New Zealand's hierarchy of Courts (Greville, M. (2019), "UPDATE: Access to New Zealand Law," accessed August 8, 2022, <https://www.nyulawglobal.org/globalex/New_Zealand1.html>).

accountable to the Parliament of New Zealand for the expenditure of those public funds that are required to administer justice within these courts [462].

The Supreme Court, the Court of Appeal and the High Court are referred to as the Senior Courts [458]. Although these courts have inherent jurisdiction and operate their own procedure, they also function within the limits that the Supreme Court Act 2016[328], the Supreme Court Rules 2004[329], the Court of Appeal (Civil) Rules 2005[330], the Court of Appeal (Criminal) Rules 2001[331] and the High Court Rules 2016[332] (as applicable) set out [458]. The Senior Courts may examine the judgments of the highest-level courts in other jurisdictions – especially those concluded in Australia, Canada and the UK – for comparison or guidance [458].

Tribunals

New Zealand's tribunals comprise a miscellany of decision-making entities with differing specialist functions[333] [458]. Whilst some of these have statutory rights of appeal to the District Court and higher, their decisions may also be judicially-reviewed [458].

Comment

The common law system of New Zealand is connected, historically and contemporaneously, to the common law system of the UK and – without the federalism – to the common law system of Australia and the bijural (though mainly common law) system of Canada. There are also similarities between Australia, Canada and New Zealand in their routes to independence from the UK – in particular, the last step to this of non-applicability of future UK legislation being achieved by constitutional acts passed in the 1980s (i.e., the Constitution Act 1982 (Canada), the Australia Act 1986 (Australia) and the Constitution Act 1986 (New Zealand)). Furthermore, the parliamentary legislative process in Australia, Canada, New Zealand and the UK is

---

328 The consolidated Senior Courts Act 2016 is available from the New Zealand Parliamentary Counsel Office, at https://www.legislation.govt.nz/act/public/2016/0048/latest/DLM5759262.html.

329 The updated Supreme Court Rules 2004 are available from the New Zealand Parliamentary Counsel Office, at https://www.legislation.govt.nz/regulation/public/2004/0199/latest/DLM270805.html.

330 The updated Court of Appeal (Civil) Rules 2005 are available from the New Zealand Parliamentary Counsel Office, at https://www.legislation.govt.nz/regulation/public/2005/0069/latest/DLM319746.html.

331 The updated Court of Appeal (Criminal) Rules 2001 are available from the New Zealand Parliamentary Counsel Office, at https://www.legislation.govt.nz/regulation/public/2001/0371/latest/DLM95709.html.

332 The updated High Court Rules 2016 are available from the New Zealand Parliamentary Counsel Office, at https://www.legislation.govt.nz/regulation/public/2016/0225/latest/DLM6959801.html.

333 The Ministry of Justice of New Zealand lists, and briefly describes, the following on its 'Tribunals' web page: the Disputes Tribunal, the Tenancy Tribunal, the Motor Vehicle Disputes Tribunal, the Human Rights Review Tribunal, the Abortion Supervisory Committee, the Canterbury Earthquakes Insurance Tribunal, the Customs Appeal Authority, the Land Valuation Tribunal, the Legal Aid Tribunal, the Student Allowance Appeal Authority, the Trans-Tasman Occupations Tribunal, the Waitangi Tribunal, COVID-19 commercial lease dispute services, licensing and certification authorities, the Alcohol Regulatory and Licensing Authority, the Real Estate Agents Tribunal, the Accident Compensation Appeals District Court Registry, the Accident Compensation Appeal Authority, the Copyright Tribunal, the Immigration and Protection Tribunal, the Immigration Advisers Complaints and Disciplinary Tribunal, the Legal Complaints Review Officer, the Lawyers and Conveyancers Disciplinary Tribunal, the Social Security Appeal Authority, the Taxation Review Authority, the Weathertight Homes Tribunal, and the Judicial Control Panel (Government of New Zealand (2022), "Ministry of Justice: Tribunals," accessed August 8, 2022, <https://www.justice.govt.nz/tribunals/>). The penultimate and final sentences of fn 325 provide information concerning the Waitangi Tribunal.

fundamentally the same but with jurisdictional differences – for instance, New Zealand has a unicameral parliament, the UK a bicameral parliament, and Australia and Canada each a bicameral federal parliament. Will this legislative process in Australia, Canada and New Zealand gradually diverge further from the original model, i.e., that of the UK, and from each other? Given that Australia, Canada and New Zealand each provide for needs of their indigenous populations – which differ to some extent from those of each other – and that Canada includes a civil-law based province (i.e., Quebec), individual features of legal procedure in the four states may expand at the expense of common aspects between them. However, for many years to come there is likely to be a collective bond.

Banking Law in New Zealand is in Flux

Reserve Bank of New Zealand Acts 1989 and 2021

The Reserve Bank of New Zealand Act 1989 was renamed the Banking (Prudential Supervision) Act 1989 on the completion of the passage of the Reserve Bank of New Zealand Act 2021 through the Parliament of New Zealand on 16th August 2021[334] [463]. The Reserve Bank of New Zealand Act 2021 addresses the functions of the Reserve Bank of New Zealand (RBNZ) as a central bank, and relevant rules from this Act are considered in the next section.

Financial Markets Infrastructures Act 2021

Provisions that relate to the regulation of financial markets and infrastructure have been moved from the Reserve Bank of New Zealand Act 1989 to the Financial Markets Infrastructures Act 2021 [463]. The Financial Markets Infrastructures Act 2021 appoints the RBNZ and the New Zealand Financial Markets Authority as co-regulators of systemically important financial markets infrastructure, and the latter co-regulator contributes to the regulation of banks in its capacity as administrator of this Act [463]. As the Financial Markets Infrastructure Act 2021 is integral to securities law in new Zealand, it is explored in the current monograph's sister book – which is titled '*An Overview of Corporate Securities Law in Six-English Language Jurisdictions*'.

---

[334] The Banking (Prudential Supervision Act 1989 declares: "Act name: amended, on *1 July 2022*, by section 298(2) of the Reserve Bank of New Zealand Act 2021 (2021 No 31)." (Government of New Zealand (2022), "Banking (Prudential Supervision) Act 1989, Public Act 1989 No 157," adopted on December 20, 1989, as "Reserve Bank of New Zealand Act 1989," entered into force on February 1, 1990, last amended on July 1, 2022, Preamble; emphasis added), which refers to the date upon which subsection 298(2) of the latter Act entered into force. The aforementioned subsection reads: "In section 1(1) [of the Reserve Bank of New Zealand Act 1989], replace "may be cited as the Reserve Bank of New Zealand" with "is the Banking (Prudential Supervision)"." (Government of New Zealand (2022), "Reserve Bank of New Zealand Act 2021, Public Act 2021 No 31," adopted on August 16, 2021, entered into force on July 1, 2022, consolidated to July 1, 2022, s.298(2)). Section 1(1) of the Banking (Prudential Supervision) Act 1989 – formerly the Reserve Bank of New Zealand Act 1989 – specifies: "This Act is the Banking (Prudential Supervision) Act 1989." (Government of New Zealand (2022), "Banking (Prudential Supervision) Act 1989, Public Act 1989 No 157," adopted on December 20, 1989, as "Reserve Bank of New Zealand Act 1989," entered into force on February 1, 1990, last amended on July 1, 2022, s.1(1)).

Banking (Prudential Supervision) Act 1989

The Banking (Prudential Supervision) Act 1989 sets out the powers of the RBNZ as the prudential – and main – regulator of banks in New Zealand [463]. The section immediately-following the next one considers this Act. The forthcoming Deposit Takers Act will combine the regulatory regime regarding deposits for banks and non-bank deposit takers, that for banks being present in the Reserve Bank of New Zealand Act 1989[335] until the repeal of the provisions concerning deposit-taking therein by subsections 92(1) and Schedule 2 of the Non-Bank Deposit Takers Act 2013[336], and that for non-bank deposit takers being currently located in the last-mentioned Act[337].

Non-Bank Deposit Takers Act 2013

The Non-Bank Deposit Takers Act 2013 requires the licensing of all Non-Bank Deposit Takers [464]. This Act is concisely reviewed in the section below with the same title.

---

[335] These provisions comprised sections 157A-157ZZ of the Reserve Bank of New Zealand Act 1989, which were the constituent provisions of Part 5D of that Act – entitled 'Deposit takers'. Part 5D of the Banking (Prudential Supervision) Act 1989 – formerly titled 'Reserve Bank of New Zealand Act 1989' – states: "Part 5D: repealed, on 1 May 2014, by section 92(1) of the Non-bank Deposit Takers Act 2013 (2013 No 104)." (Government of New Zealand (2022), "Banking (Prudential Supervision) Act 1989, Public Act 1989 No 157," adopted on December 20, 1989, as "Reserve Bank of New Zealand Act 1989," entered into force on February 1, 1990, last amended on July 1, 2022, Part 5D).

[336] Subsection 92(1) of the Non-Bank Deposit Takers Act 2013 declares: "The Reserve Bank of New Zealand Act 1989 is consequentially amended in the manner set out in Schedule 2 [of the Non-Bank Deposit Takers Act 2013]." (Government of New Zealand (2022), "Non-bank Deposit Takers Act 2013, Public Act 2013 No 104," adopted on December 3, 2013, entered into force on May 1, 2014, consolidated to July 1, 2022, s.92(1)). Schedule 2 of the Non-Bank Deposit Takers Act 2013 is entitled 'Consequential amendments to Reserve Bank of New Zealand Act 1989', and includes the following words: "**Part 5D** Repeal." (Government of New Zealand (2022), "Non-bank Deposit Takers Act 2013, Public Act 2013 No 104," adopted on December 3, 2013, entered into force on May 1, 2014, consolidated to July 1, 2022, Schedule 2; emphasis original).

[337] The website of the Reserve Bank of New Zealand reads: "The Deposit Takers Bill was introduced to Parliament on 22 September 2022. It is expected to come into force as law after receiving Royal Assent in mid-to-late 2023. ... After the [Deposit Takers] Act comes into force, there will be a transition period to allow both the Reserve Bank and regulated entities time to adapt to the new regime. A significant work programme over several years will be required to implement the new prudential framework for deposit takers. Further public consultation is expected on the funding framework, which includes industry levies, before the Depositor Compensation Scheme is implemented. ... While we anticipate [that] the Bill will pass into law in mid-to-late 2023, a substantial work programme is needed to implement the new prudential framework for deposit takers. It will take some years for the Reserve Bank to develop and consult on the secondary legislation that will implement the regulatory requirements for the new regime, and complete a licensing process for deposit takers to operate under the regime. The parts of the current Reserve Bank Act [(i.e., the Banking (Prudential Supervision) Act 1989 – which is the new name for the Reserve Bank of New Zealand Act 1989 (fn 334 and accompanying text),)] relating to the regulation and supervision of registered banks[,] and the Non-bank Deposit Takers Act 2013[,] will remain in force until the remaining parts of the DTA [(i.e., the Deposit Takers Act)] have been fully implemented. The Depositor Compensation Scheme is being prioritised ahead of the rest of the [Deposit Takers] Act coming into effect[,] and is expected to be up and running in late 2024." (Government of New Zealand (2023), "Reserve Bank of New Zealand: Proposed Deposit Takers Act," accessed April 22, 2023, <https://www.rbnz.govt.nz/about-us/responsibility-and-accountability/our-legislation/proposed-deposit-takers-act>).

Financial Service Providers (Registration and Dispute Resolution) Act 2008

The Financial Service Providers (Registration and Dispute Resolution) Act 2008 requires a bank to register as a financial service provider [465], as, by definition therein, a registered bank supplies a financial service [466].

Financial Markets Conduct Act 2013

In addition to be required to be registered as a bank under the Banking (Prudential Supervision) Act 1989 and as a financial service provider under the Financial Service Providers (Registration and Dispute Resolution) Act 2008, a bank is likely to require further licences under the Financial Markets Conduct Act 2013 – for instance, if it gives regulated financial advice to retail customers or issues derivatives [463]. The companion monograph '*An Overview of Corporate Securities Law in Six-English Language Jurisdictions*' covers the Financial Markets Conduct Act 2013.

Reserve Bank of New Zealand Act 2021

The Purposes of the Reserve Bank of New Zealand Act 2021

The purposes of the Reserve Bank of New Zealand Act 2021 are to provide for the RBNZ to continue [467], and to further the well-being and prosperity of New Zealanders and contribute to a productive, sustainable economy [468].

The Objectives and Functions of the RBNZ

The main objectives of the RBNZ comprise the economic objectives of accomplishing and maintaining stability in the general level of prices in the medium term [469] and upholding maximum sustainable employment[338] [470], the financial stability objective of safeguarding and furthering the stability of New Zealand's financial system [471], and the central bank objective of acting in other respects as the central bank of New Zealand in a manner that advances the purposes of the Reserve Bank of New Zealand Act 2021[339] [472]. If the RBNZ is performing a function or exercising a power which other legislation imposes or confers, then it also has the objective of acting in a way that furthers the aims or purposes of those laws [473].

---

[338] If an Order in Council is in effect under section 125 of the Reserve Bank of New Zealand Act 2021, then the economic objectives that apply are those which this Order specifies (Government of New Zealand (2022), "Reserve Bank of New Zealand Act 2021, Public Act 2021 No 31," adopted on August 16, 2021, entered into force on July 1, 2022, consolidated to July 1, 2022, s.9(2)).

[339] The subsection titled 'Purposes of the Reserve Bank of New Zealand Act 2021', above in the present section (i.e., that entitled 'Reserve Bank of New Zealand Act 2021'), sets out the purposes of the Reserve Bank of New Zealand Act 2021.

The functions of the RBNZ are to: (a) act as the central bank for New Zealand, including by preparing through the Monetary Policy Committee of the RBNZ[340] – and implementing – a monetary policy which is directed to the economic objectives[341], and performing the other acts that section 116 of the Reserve Bank of New Zealand Act 2021 describes[342] [474], (b) act as regulator and supervisor in accordance with prudential legislation, by undertaking prudential supervision, introducing prudential standards or other requirements, monitoring compliance with, inquiring into behaviour that constitutes or may constitute a breach of, and enforcing, this legislation, and taking suitable action with regard to persons who have infracted, are contravening, or are likely to infringe, this legislation or are otherwise in difficulty [475], (c) monitor the financial system [476], (d) surveil the needs of the public for bank notes and coins [477], (e) co-operate with foreign entities that discharge functions which correspond with, or are similar to, any of those that are conferred upon the RBNZ [478], (f) furnish, or facilitate the supply of, information to the public which pertains to the objectives of the RBNZ, and other information in association with the powers or functions that are conferred or imposed upon the

---

[340] The Monetary Policy Committee "is a committee of the Bank" (Government of New Zealand (2022), "Reserve Bank of New Zealand Act 2021, Public Act 2021 No 31," adopted on August 16, 2021, entered into force on July 1, 2022, consolidated to July 1, 2022, s.97(2)). Within the Reserve Bank of New Zealand Act 2021 – unless the context requires otherwise, the word '*Bank*' "means the Reserve Bank of New Zealand continued under this Act [(i.e., the Reserve Bank of New Zealand Act 2021)]" (Government of New Zealand (2022), "Reserve Bank of New Zealand Act 2021, Public Act 2021 No 31," adopted on August 16, 2021, entered into force on July 1, 2022, consolidated to July 1, 2022, s.5(1)). The Monetary Policy Committee "must – (a) perform the function of formulating monetary policy in accordance with this Act [(i.e., the Reserve Bank of New Zealand Act 2021)]; and (b) perform or exercise any other function, power, or duty conferred on it under this Act" (Government of New Zealand (2022), "Reserve Bank of New Zealand Act 2021, Public Act 2021 No 31," adopted on August 16, 2021, entered into force on July 1, 2022, consolidated to July 1, 2022, s.98). The RBNZ, acting by way of the Monetary Policy Committee, "has the function of formulating a monetary policy [that is] directed to the economic objectives [of the RBNZ,] of – (a) achieving and maintaining stability in the general level of prices over the medium term; and (b) supporting maximum sustainable employment" (Government of New Zealand (2022), "Reserve Bank of New Zealand Act 2021, Public Act 2021 No 31," adopted on August 16, 2021, entered into force on July 1, 2022, consolidated to July 1, 2022, s.117(1)). The text to fn 338 lays down the economic objectives of the RBNZ, subject to fn 338. In formulating monetary policy, the Monetary Policy Committee must take account of "the importance of protecting and promoting the stability of New Zealand's financial system" (Government of New Zealand (2022), "Reserve Bank of New Zealand Act 2021, Public Act 2021 No 31," adopted on August 16, 2021, entered into force on July 1, 2022, consolidated to July 1, 2022, s.119(1)(a)).

[341] The text to fn 338 lays down the economic objectives of the RBNZ, subject to fn 338.

[342] This section of the Reserve Bank of England Act 2021 lists the central bank functions of the RBNZ, as follows: "(a) formulating (through the MPC [(i.e., the Monetary Policy Committee of the RBNZ)]) and implementing a monetary policy [that is] directed to the economic objectives, while recognizing the Crown's right to determine economic policy … ; and (b) managing foreign reserves[,] and otherwise dealing in foreign exchange for the purpose of the Bank's [(i.e., the RBNZ's)] objectives … ; and (c) doing the following to ensure that bank notes and coins in New Zealand meet the needs of the public … : (i) issuing bank notes and coins: (ii) monitoring the distribution of bank notes and coins (and, if the Bank thinks fit, distributing bank notes and coins); (iii) managing the quality of bank notes and coins: (iv) monitoring the impact of technological innovation on the needs of the public for bank notes and coins; and (d) providing liquidity facilities to entities approved by the Bank (on the terms and conditions [that] the Bank thinks fit)[,] in order to do either or both of the following: (i) manage liquidity in the financial system: (ii) protect or promote the stability of the financial system; and (e) providing settlement accounts for persons approved by the Bank; and (f) operating[,] or otherwise participating in[,] payments and settlement systems; and (g) liaising and co-operating with other central banks and relevant international institutions; and (h) carrying out any other central banking activities that are consistent with the Bank's objectives and the purposes of this Act" (Government of New Zealand (2022), "Reserve Bank of New Zealand Act 2021, Public Act 2021 No 31," adopted on August 16, 2021, entered into force on July 1, 2022, consolidated to July 1, 2022, s.116). The text to fn 338 sets out the economic objectives of the RBNZ, subject to fn 338. The second sentence of fn 340 defines the term '*Bank*'. The text to fns 338 and 339 lays down the main objectives of the RBNZ. The subsection titled 'Purposes of the Reserve Bank of New Zealand Act 2021', above in the current section (i.e., that entitled 'Reserve Bank of New Zealand Act 2021'), sets out the purposes of the Reserve Bank of New Zealand Act 2021.

RBNZ by any primary or secondary legislation [479], (g) retain under review the law, policies and practices which are relevant to functions (a) to (f) and (h) to (j) [480], (h) fulfil any other function compatible with the objectives of the RBNZ that the Minister[343] may direct the RBNZ to realise [481], (i) exercise the powers, and perform the functions, which any primary or secondary legislation confers or imposes upon the RBNZ [482], and (j) effect any functions that are incidental and related to, or contingent upon, functions (a) to (i) [483]. In carrying out its functions, the RBNZ must act in accordance with its objectives[344] [484].

The Minister's Power to Direct the RBNZ as to its Level of Capital

The Minister[345] may direct the RBNZ to take all reasonable steps to maintain a minimum level of capital that the (s)he specifies [485], and/or take account of his or her expectations as to the financial risk management of the RBNZ [486]. This direction may define the word '*capital*' [487], specify other issues that relate to the computation of the minimum required capital [488], and lay down the above-mentioned expectations [489].

The Council of Financial Regulators

The function of the Council of Financial Regulators is to ease co-operation and co-ordination between its members, in order to further responsive, effective regulation of New Zealand's financial system [490]. The RBNZ and the New Zealand Financial Markets Authority are

---

343 Within the Reserve Bank of New Zealand Act 2021 – unless the context requires otherwise, the word '*Minister*' means "the Minister of the Crown who, under the authority of a warrant or with the authority of the Prime Minister, is responsible for the administration of this Act" (Government of New Zealand (2022), "Reserve Bank of New Zealand Act 2021, Public Act 2021 No 31," adopted on August 16, 2021, entered into force on July 1, 2022, consolidated to July 1, 2022, s.5(1)). The Minister has the following role: "[T]o oversee and manage the Crown's interests in, and relationship with, the Bank[,] and to exercise any statutory responsibilities given to the Minister, including functions and powers – ... (a) in relation to the appointment and removal of – (i) the members of the board ... ; and (ii) the Governor ... ; and (iii) members of the MPC [(i.e., the Monetary Policy Committee of the RBNZ)]) ... : ... (b) to issue a remit for the MPC ... : (c) to give advice relating to different economic objectives ... : ... (d) to issue a financial policy remit ... : (e) to give directions to the Bank relating to its minimum level of capital and financial risk management (*see* section 208 [of the Reserve Bank of New Zealand Act 2021 (text to fn 345 and the sentence which immediately follows that text)]) ... : (f) to give directions to the Bank to deal in foreign exchange within guidelines[,] and to agree with the Bank on a framework for the management and co-ordination of foreign reserves ... (g) under the prudential legislation ... : (h) to add functions[,] if requested by the Bank ... : ... (i) to enter into a funding agreement with the Bank and to determine the Bank's annual dividend ... : ... (j) to review the operations and performance of the Bank ... : (k) to request information from the Bank ... : (l) to participate in the process of setting the Bank's strategic direction and performance expectations[,] and monitoring the Bank's performance ... : (m) in relation to other matters in ... legislation." (Government of New Zealand (2022), "Reserve Bank of New Zealand Act 2021, Public Act 2021 No 31," adopted on August 16, 2021, entered into force on July 1, 2022, consolidated to July 1, 2022, s.22(1); emphasis original). The second sentence of fn 340 defines the term '*Bank*'. Within the Reserve Bank of New Zealand Act 2021 – unless the context requires otherwise, the word '*Governor*' "means a person who occupies the position of Governor of the Bank" (Government of New Zealand (2022), "Reserve Bank of New Zealand Act 2021, Public Act 2021 No 31," adopted on August 16, 2021, entered into force on July 1, 2022, consolidated to July 1, 2022, s.5(1)).

344 The text to fns 338 and 339 sets out the main objectives of the RBNZ.

345 The first sentence of fn 343 defines the term '*Minister*'.

chairpersons of the Council of Financial Regulators[346] [491]. The Council of Financial Regulators comprises the RBNZ, the New Zealand Financial Markets Authority, the Treasury, the department of the government that – with the Prime Minister's authority – is responsible for administering the Financial Markets Conduct Act 2013, and any other department, agency or entity[347] which joins the Council of Financial Regulators with the agreement of one of the chairpersons of the Council [492].

Comment

The Reserve Bank of New Zealand Act 2021 sets out clearly the objectives and functions of the RBNZ. This Act's provision for the Council of Financial Regulators to modulate the regulation of the financial system of New Zealand, is significant.

Banking (Prudential Supervision) Act 1989

The Purpose of the Banking (Prudential Supervision) Act 1989

The purpose of the Banking (Prudential Supervision) Act 1989 is to advance the well-being and prosperity of New Zealanders, and contribute to a productive, sustainable economy, by providing for the RBNZ – as New Zealand's central bank – to be responsible for registering banks and undertaking their prudential supervision [493], and for performing other functions, and exercising powers, that this Act specifies [494].

Limits on the Use of the Words 'Bank', 'Banker' and 'Banking'

A person may neither be incorporated, formed or registered using a title or name that includes a restricted word[348] [495], nor alter a person's name or title to one which includes a restricted word [496], nor conduct any activity in New Zealand utilising a name or title that includes a restricted word[349] [497]. These limits do not apply to the RBNZ [498], a registered bank [499],

[346] The RBNZ and the New Zealand Financial Markets Authority "may agree that one of them is to carry out the chairperson's functions in relation to a matter or class of matters" (Government of New Zealand (2022), "Reserve Bank of New Zealand Act 2021, Public Act 2021 No 31," adopted on August 16, 2021, entered into force on July 1, 2022, consolidated to July 1, 2022, s.287(2)).

[347] Such a department, agency or entity "may – (a) resign as a member of the council; or (b) by written notice, be removed for any reason as a member of the council[,] by a chairperson of the council; or (c) be a member of the council for a term [that is] specified by a chairperson of the council (subject to paragraphs (a) and (b))" (Government of New Zealand (2022), "Reserve Bank of New Zealand Act 2021, Public Act 2021 No 31," Adopted on August 16, 2021, Entered into force on July 1, 2022, Consolidated to July 1, 2022, s.288(2)).

[348] Within the Banking (Prudential Supervision) Act 1989 – unless the context requires otherwise, the phrase '*restricted word*' "(a) means the words "bank," "banker," and "banking," and (b) includes – (i) any of those words as part of any other word: (ii) a translation of those words into another language (whether or not the translation of those words is part of any other word)" (Government of New Zealand (2022), "Banking (Prudential Supervision) Act 1989, Public Act 1989 No 157," adopted on December 20, 1989, as "Reserve Bank of New Zealand Act 1989," entered into force on February 1, 1990, last amended on July 1, 2022, s.2(1)).

[349] These limits do not apply "to a person using a name or title that includes a restricted word[,] if – (a) the restricted word signifies a geographic place name or the name of a natural person; and (b) the name or title is not used in

any person whom the RBNZ authorises under section 65 of the Banking (Prudential Supervision) Act 1989[350] to use a name or title which includes a restricted word – but only to the extent that the person is acting within the ambit of this authorisation [500], or any person whom section 66 of the Banking (Prudential Supervision) Act 1989[351] exempts – but solely to the extent that the person is acting within the compass of this exemption [501].

A person who contravenes the abovementioned limits on the use of the words 'bank', 'banker' and 'banking', commits an offence [502]. An individual who commits this offence is liable, on conviction, to imprisonment for a term not exceeding one year or a fine of no more than NZD 100,000 [503]. A body corporate which commits this offence is liable, on conviction, to a fine not exceeding NZD 1 million [504].

Registration of Banks

In accordance with the present Part of the Banking (Prudential Supervision) Act 1989[352], the RBNZ is to register banks [505]. The RBNZ must maintain a public register of entities that are registered banks[353] [506]. The register shall include the name of each registered bank, the current credit rating of each registered bank (if any), and any other specified information [507]. The RBNZ must take all reasonable steps to make sure that the information which the public register contains is accessible to members of the public at all reasonable times [508].

Any person may apply to the RBNZ to be registered as a registered bank [509]. Applications to be so registered are to be made in a way that the RBNZ may specify [510], and be accompanied by payment as the RBNZ may determine periodically with the Minister's[354]

respect of a financial institution, or could not reasonably be mistaken for the name or title of a financial institution" (Government of New Zealand (2022), "Banking (Prudential Supervision) Act 1989, Public Act 1989 No 157," adopted on December 20, 1989, as "Reserve Bank of New Zealand Act 1989," entered into force on February 1, 1990, last amended on July 1, 2022, s.66).

350 Section 65 is titled 'Bank may authorise use of restricted words in name or title'; its first subsection states: "The Bank may authorise any of the following persons to use a name or title that includes a restricted word: (a) a person licensed or registered as a bank in a country other than New Zealand: (b) a class of persons licensed or registered as banks in a country other than New Zealand: (c) a person that is formed, incorporated, or registered to represent the interests of – (i) any registered bank; or (ii) any person connected with a registered bank: (d) an associated person of a registered bank: (e) a registered bank[,] or an associated person of a registered bank[,] that intends to use a name or title that includes a restricted word in respect of a managed investment scheme of which the registered bank or the associated person is a supervisor or a manager within the meaning of section 6(1) of the Financial Markets Conduct Act 2013: (f) a person that is not a financial institution." (Government of New Zealand (2022), "Banking (Prudential Supervision) Act 1989, Public Act 1989 No 157," adopted on December 20, 1989, as "Reserve Bank of New Zealand Act 1989," entered into force on February 1, 1990, last amended on July 1, 2022, s.65(1)). Within the Banking (Prudential Supervision) Act 1989 – unless the context requires otherwise, the word '*Bank*' "means the Reserve Bank of New Zealand continued under the Reserve Bank of New Zealand Act 2021" (Government of New Zealand (2022), "Banking (Prudential Supervision) Act 1989, Public Act 1989 No 157," adopted on December 20, 1989, as "Reserve Bank of New Zealand Act 1989," entered into force on February 1, 1990, last amended on July 1, 2022, s.2(1)).

351 Fn 349 lays down section 66 of the Banking (Prudential Supervision) Act 1989.

352 This is Part 5 of the Banking (Prudential Supervision) Act 1989, which is entitled 'Registration of banks and prudential supervision of registered banks' and comprises ss.67A-156AC of the Act.

353 The RBNZ must decide upon the form of this register, and may revise the form periodically as it deems necessary (Government of New Zealand (2022), "Banking (Prudential Supervision) Act 1989, Public Act 1989 No 157," adopted on December 20, 1989, as "Reserve Bank of New Zealand Act 1989," entered into force on February 1, 1990, last amended on July 1, 2022, s.69(2)).

354 Within the Banking (Prudential Supervision) Act 1989 – unless the context requires otherwise, the word '*Minister*' "means the Treasurer, or other Minister of the Crown who, under the authority of any warrant or with the

approval [511]. Every person who makes such an application shall supply to the RBNZ the information that the latter may require, in order to help it to decide upon the application [512].

If a person provides false or misleading information to the RBNZ for the purposes of an application, then (s)he commits an offence [513]. An individual who commits this offence is liable, on conviction, to imprisonment for a term of no more than 18 months or a fine not exceeding NZD 200,000 [514]. A body corporate that commits this offence is liable, on conviction, to a fine of no more than NZD 2 million [515]. These penalties also apply to a person who commits the offence of using any name, title, description, designation, style or trademark which represents or implies – incorrectly – that this person is a registered bank [516].

The RBNZ shall not register any applicant as a registered bank, unless it is satisfied that the business which the latter conducts or proposes to undertake consists of, comprises to a substantial degree, will consist of, or will comprise to a considerable extent, the lending and borrowing of money, or the supply of other financial services, or both [517]. In determining an application for registration as a bank, the RBNZ must take into account the applicant's incorporation and ownership structure [518], the nature and size of – or of any part of – the applicant's business or proposed business [519], the applicant's ability to carry on its business or proposed business in a prudent way [520], the applicant's standing in the financial markets [521], the suitability of the directors and senior managers of the applicant for their positions [522], the standing of the applicant's owner in the financial markets [523], and any other issues that regulations may prescribe[355] [524].

In deciding upon an application from an overseas person[356], the RBNZ must – in addition to the matters that subsection 73(2) of the Banking (Prudential Supervision) Act 1989[357] lays down, consider: (i) the nature and extent of the information which the applicant discloses to the public [525], and (ii) the legislative and regulatory requirements of the applicant's home jurisdiction[358] that concern the recognition and priorities of claims of creditors – or classes of

---

authority of the Prime Minister, is[,] for the time being[,] responsible for the administration of this Act or particular provisions of this Act" (Government of New Zealand (2022), "Banking (Prudential Supervision) Act 1989, Public Act 1989 No 157," adopted on December 20, 1989, as "Reserve Bank of New Zealand Act 1989," entered into force on February 1, 1990, last amended on July 1, 2022, s.2(1)).

[355] For the purposes of paragraph 73(2)(g) of the Banking (Prudential Supervision) Act 1989, i.e., the text to the present footnote (fn 355) from 'and any other' to the end of the sentence, "the Governor-General may, from time to time, by Order in Council, on the advice of the Minister given in accordance with a recommendation of the Bank, make regulations prescribing additional matters to which the Bank shall have regard in considering applications for registration" (Government of New Zealand (2022), "Banking (Prudential Supervision) Act 1989, Public Act 1989 No 157," adopted on December 20, 1989, as "Reserve Bank of New Zealand Act 1989," entered into force on February 1, 1990, last amended on July 1, 2022, s.73(3)). Fn 354 defines the term '*Minister*'. The final sentence of fn 350 defines the term '*Bank*'.

[356] Within the Banking (Prudential Supervision) Act 1989 – unless the context requires otherwise, the phrase '*overseas person*' "means – (a) a body corporate incorporated outside New Zealand; or (b) an unincorporated body that has its head office or principal place of business outside New Zealand" (Government of New Zealand (2022), "Banking (Prudential Supervision) Act 1989, Public Act 1989 No 157," adopted on December 20, 1989, as "Reserve Bank of New Zealand Act 1989," entered into force on February 1, 1990, last amended on July 1, 2022, s.2(1)).

[357] The immediately-preceding sentence, i.e., the text to fn 355, sets out subsection 73(2) of the Banking (Prudential Supervision) Act 1989.

[358] Within the Banking (Prudential Supervision) Act 1989 – unless the context requires otherwise, the phrase '*home jurisdiction*' "means, – (a) in the case of an overseas person that is a body corporate, the country in which that body is incorporated: (b) in the case of an overseas person that is an unincorporated body, the country in which that body has its head office or principal place of business" (Government of New Zealand (2022), "Banking (Prudential Supervision) Act 1989, Public Act 1989 No 157," adopted on December 20, 1989, as "Reserve Bank of New Zealand Act 1989," entered into force on February 1, 1990, last amended on July 1, 2022, s.2(1)). Fn 356 defines the term '*overseas person*'.

creditors – if the applicant becomes insolvent, the disclosure by the applicant of information which is of the kind that a registered bank must disclose, the accounting and auditing standards which apply to the applicant, the powers and duties of the applicant's directors, and the registration, licensing, authorisation and supervision of the applicant [526]. In determining an application from a subsidiary[359] of an overseas person, the RBNZ must consider all of the factors mentioned in the immediately-preceding sentence except for the legislative and regulatory requirements of the overseas person's home jurisdiction that relate to the recognition and priorities of claims of creditors or classes of creditors in the event of the overseas person's insolvency [527].

The RBNZ may register a bank unconditionally, or subject to any conditions that the former may impose [528]. By notice in writing to a registered bank, the RBNZ may introduce new or additional conditions of registration [529], or remove, add to, substitute or vary any such conditions[360] [530]. If the registered bank does not observe a condition of its registration, then it commits an offence [531]. An individual who commits this offence is liable, on conviction, to imprisonment for a term not exceeding one year or a fine of no more than NZD 100,000 [532]. A body corporate that commits this offence is liable, on conviction, to a fine not exceeding NZD 1 million [533].

By notice in writing to the RBNZ that is given in compliance with one of its recommendations, the Minister[361] may direct the RBNZ to discontinue the registration of a registered bank [534]. The RBNZ may not cancel the registration of a registered bank, unless a number of specified conditions are fulfilled[362].

---

[359] Within the Banking (Prudential Supervision) Act 1989 – unless the context requires otherwise, the word '*subsidiary*' means a company in which another company holds more than 50% of the former's issued ordinary shares (Government of New Zealand (2022), "Banking (Prudential Supervision) Act 1989, Public Act 1989 No 157," adopted on December 20, 1989, as "Reserve Bank of New Zealand Act 1989," entered into force on February 1, 1990, last amended on July 1, 2022, s.2(1); Government of New Zealand (2022), "Companies Act 1993, Public Act 1993 No 105," adopted on September 28, 1993, entered into force on July 1, 1994, consolidated to July 1, 2022, s.5(1)(a)(iii)).

[360] The RBNZ must not change the situation with respect to conditions of registration, "unless – (a) the Bank gives the registered bank not less than 7 days' notice in writing of the Bank's intention to do so; and (b) the notice contains, or is accompanied by, a statement of the Bank's reasons; and (c) the registered bank has a reasonable opportunity to make submissions to the Bank; and (d) the Bank has regard to those submissions" (Government of New Zealand (2022), "Banking (Prudential Supervision) Act 1989, Public Act 1989 No 157," adopted on December 20, 1989, as "Reserve Bank of New Zealand Act 1989," entered into force on February 1, 1990, last amended on July 1, 2022, s.74(3)). The last sentence of fn 350 defines the term '*Bank*'.

[361] Fn 354 defines the term '*Minister*'.

[362] Subsections 77(2) and 77(3) of the Banking (Prudential Supervision) Act 1989 set out these conditions, which are as follows: "(2) … (a) that the registered bank was registered on information that was false or misleading in a material particular; or (b) that, in relation to a registered bank, – (i) there has been a change in any of the matters to which the Bank must have regard under section 73 [of the Banking (Prudential Supervision) Act 1989] (including a change in any of the matters prescribed by regulations made under section 73(2)(g)) [(fn 355 and accompanying text)]; and (ii) the Bank considers the change to be materially adverse to the registered bank's standing or financial position; or (ba) that, in relation to a registered bank, – (i) there has been a transfer of direct or indirect control of the registered bank; and (ii) the Bank considers the transfer to be materially adverse to the registered bank's standing or financial position; or (bb) that, in relation to a registered bank, – (i) there has been a change in any of the matters to which the Bank must have regard under section 73A [of the Banking (Prudential Supervision) Act 1989 (text to fns 356-358)] or section 73B [of the Banking (Prudential Supervision) Act 1989 (text to fn 359)]; and (ii) the Bank considers the change to be materially adverse; or (c) if the registered bank is a body corporate – (i) that an order has been made for the winding up of that body corporate; or (ii) that a resolution has been passed for the voluntary winding up of that body corporate; or (iii) that a receiver has been appointed in respect of that body corporate; or (d) *[Repealed]* (e) that a condition of registration has not been complied with; or (f) that a registered bank has not carried on its business in a prudent manner; or (g) that the registered bank has failed to comply with an obligation imposed under this Act[,] or imposed by regulations

Prudential Supervision of Registered Banks

The Central Principle

In conformity with the current Part of the Banking (Prudential Supervision) Act 1989[363], the RBNZ is to carry out prudential supervision of registered banks [535].

Directions Given by the RBNZ to Registered Banks

The RBNZ may give a registered bank, or an associated person of a registered bank, a direction[364] – in writing – if it has reasonable grounds to suppose that the registered bank or associated person is insolvent or likely to become bankrupt [536], the registered bank or associated person is on the point of suspending payment or unable to pay its debts as and when these become due [537], the concerns of the registered bank or associated person are being discharged in a way that prejudices the soundness of the financial system [538], the circumstances of the registered bank or associated person are such as to prejudice this soundness [539], the registered bank's business has not been, or is not being, conducted prudently [540], the registered bank, a director of that bank, or the chief executive officer in New Zealand of a bank registered and incorporated elsewhere, has not observed any requirement which the Banking (Prudential Supervision) Act 1989, or a regulation made under that Act, has imposed [541], any of the abovementioned persons has been convicted of an offence against the Banking (Prudential Supervision) Act 1989 [542], or the registered bank has broken a condition of its registration[365] [543]. The direction must specify the grounds upon which it is given [544]. With the Minister's[366] agreement, the RBNZ may revise, replace or revoke a direction [545]. The direction may require a registered bank, or an associated person of a registered bank, to consult with the RBNZ about the circumstances of the registered bank

made under this Act. (3) [that] (a) the Bank gives the registered bank not less than 7 days' notice in writing of the Bank's intention to consider making the recommendation; and (b) the notice contains[,] or is accompanied by[,] a statement of the Bank's reasons; and (c) the registered bank has a reasonable opportunity to make submissions to the Bank; and (d) the Bank has regard to those submissions" (Government of New Zealand (2022), "Banking (Prudential Supervision) Act 1989, Public Act 1989 No 157," adopted on December 20, 1989, as "Reserve Bank of New Zealand Act 1989," entered into force on February 1, 1990, last amended on July 1, 2022, s.77(2)-(3); emphasis original). The last sentence of fn 350 defines the term '*Bank*'. Within the Banking (Prudential Supervision) Act 1989 – unless the context requires otherwise, the word '*Governor*' "means a person who occupies the position of Governor of the Bank" (Government of New Zealand (2022), "Banking (Prudential Supervision) Act 1989, Public Act 1989 No 157," adopted on December 20, 1989, as "Reserve Bank of New Zealand Act 1989," entered into force on February 1, 1990, last amended on July 1, 2022, s.2(1)).

363 This is Part 5 of the Banking (Prudential Supervision) Act 1989, which is titled 'Registration of banks and prudential supervision of registered banks' and consists of ss.67A-156AC of the Act.

364 The RBNZ must secure the Minister's consent, before giving such a direction (Government of New Zealand (2022), "Banking (Prudential Supervision) Act 1989, Public Act 1989 No 157," adopted on December 20, 1989, as "Reserve Bank of New Zealand Act 1989," entered into force on February 1, 1990, last amended on July 1, 2022, s.113(2)). Fn 354 defines the term '*Minister*'.

365 If the RBNZ has reasonable grounds to believe that any of these circumstances exist and that it is necessary to appoint, remove or replace a director of a registered bank or of an associated person of a registered bank, then the RBNZ may remove or replace, or appoint, any such person (Government of New Zealand (2022), "Banking (Prudential Supervision) Act 1989, Public Act 1989 No 157," adopted on December 20, 1989, as "Reserve Bank of New Zealand Act 1989," entered into force on February 1, 1990, last amended on July 1, 2022, s.113B(1)-(2)). The RBNZ must secure the Minister's consent, before removing, replacing, or appointing any person as, a director of a registered bank or of an associated person of a registered bank (Government of New Zealand (2022), "Banking (Prudential Supervision) Act 1989, Public Act 1989 No 157," adopted on December 20, 1989, as "Reserve Bank of New Zealand Act 1989," entered into force on February 1, 1990, last amended on July 1, 2022, s.113B(3)(a)). Fn 354 defines the term '*Minister*'.

366 Fn 354 defines the term '*Minister*'.

or associated person and the methods of settling any problems encountered [546], conduct its business, or any part of its business, in line with the direction [547], cease to administer its business, or any part of its business, in compliance with the direction [548], make sure that any officer or employee of the registered bank or associated person stops participating in the management or conduct of its business – except with the RBNZ's permission and as far as this consent extends [549], remove or replace any of an associated person's directors [550], remove or replace its auditor, or appoint an auditor of whom or which the RBNZ approves [551], take the action that the direction specifies to address an infraction of any condition of its registration [552], take the steps which the direction lays down to attend to any circumstances of financial difficulties [553], or take any other measures that the direction may set out [554]. If the registered bank or associated person does not – without licit justification or excuse – abide by a direction, then it commits an offence [555]. An officer or employee of a registered bank, or of an associated person of such a bank, who – without legitimate justification or excuse – prevents, hinders or obstructs this registered bank or associated person from implementing any direction, commits an offence [556]. An individual who commits one of these offences is liable, on conviction, to imprisonment for a term of no more than 18 months or a fine not exceeding NZD 200,000 [557]. A body corporate that commits an abovementioned offence is liable, on conviction, to a fine of no more than NZD 2 million [558].

Statutory Management of Registered Banks

The Governor-General may periodically, by Order in Council, on the Minister's advice given in agreement with a recommendation of the RBNZ, declare that any registered bank and/or any associated person of a registered bank is subject to statutory management [559], and appoint at least one person as statutory manager(s) of this registered bank or associated person for a stated period [560]. If such an Order in Council is made, then every subsidiary[367] of a registered bank which is proclaimed to be subject to statutory management, is subject to statutory management – other than any subsidiary that is announced to be one to which the Order does not apply[368], and the appointment of a statutory manager for the specified period with regard to this registered bank also applies to these subsidiaries[369] [561]. Each Order in Council must set down

---

[367] Fn 359 defines the term '*subsidiary*'.

[368] If a registered bank acquires a subsidiary after the Governor-General has declared it to be subject to statutory management, then this subsidiary is not subject to statutory management – unless (s)he makes a further Order in Council declaring the subsidiary to be so subject (Government of New Zealand (2022), "Banking (Prudential Supervision) Act 1989, Public Act 1989 No 157," adopted on December 20, 1989, as "Reserve Bank of New Zealand Act 1989," entered into force on February 1, 1990, last amended on July 1, 2022, s.117(2A)).

[369] Subsection 117(3) of the Banking (Prudential Supervision) Act 1989 states: "Where a registered bank or an associated person of a registered bank that is declared to be subject to statutory management[,] or a subsidiary of a registered bank that becomes subject to statutory management under subsection (2) [(i.e., subsection 117(2) of the Banking (Prudential Supervision) Act 1989 (text to fns 368 and 369)], is incorporated outside New Zealand or is an unincorporated body having its head office or principal place of business outside New Zealand, the provisions of this Part relating to statutory management shall apply to the property, rights, assets and liabilities relating to its New Zealand business." (Government of New Zealand (2022), "Banking (Prudential Supervision) Act 1989, Public Act 1989 No 157," adopted on December 20, 1989, as "Reserve Bank of New Zealand Act 1989," entered into force on February 1, 1990, last amended on July 1, 2022, s.117(3)). 'This Part' is Part 5 of the Banking (Prudential Supervision) Act 1989, which is entitled 'Registration of banks and prudential supervision of registered banks' and comprises sections 67A-156AC of this Act. It is submitted that the 'provisions of this Part relating to statutory management' are those under the heading 'Statutory management of registered banks' – i.e., sections 117-139 of the Banking (Prudential Supervision) Act 1989, and that under the heading 'Statutory management, etc, of issuer' – i.e., section 139J of the Banking (Prudential Supervision) Act 1989.

the date upon which, and the time at which, the Order in Council enters into force [562], which must be no earlier than the date upon which – and the time at which – the Order in Council is made [563]. The RBNZ must not make a recommendation under section 117 of the Banking (Prudential Supervision) Act 1989[370], unless it is satisfied upon reasonable grounds that at least one of the circumstances that paragraphs 113(1)(a) to (e) list exist[371] [564], or a registered bank or an associated person of such a bank has not observed a direction given under section 113 of the Banking (Prudential Supervision) Act 1989[372] [565]. As soon as practicable after the making of an Order in Council that declares a registered bank or associated person to be subject to statutory management, the RBNZ is to give written notice to the registered bank or associated person – which specifies the grounds upon which its recommendation was made [566]. Subject to section 142 of the Banking (Prudential Supervision) Act 1989[373], each statutory manager of a registered bank must follow any directions that the RBNZ gives in writing which concern the exercise of the powers of this statutory manager under Part 5 of the Banking (Prudential Supervision) Act 1989[374] [567]. In exercising the powers that Part 5 of the Banking (Prudential Supervision) Act 1989 confers, a statutory manager of a registered bank is to consider the need to retain public confidence in the soundness and workings of the financial system [568], the need to avoid material harm to that system [569], the need to settle as fast as possible the registered bank's difficulties – to the extent which is compatible with the first two needs [570], maintaining the position, and the ranking of claims, of creditors – to the degree that is consistent with the first three needs [571], and the advice of the RBNZ [572]. A statutory manager who has reason to believe that an action which (s)he proposes to take is one that is likely to detrimentally affect the stability of the financial system in Australia[375], must notify the RBNZ as soon as practicable and secure its written consent before taking this step[376] [573]. If a

---

370 This is 'a recommendation of the RBNZ' to which the first sentence of the current paragraph, i.e., that headed 'Statutory management of registered banks', refers.

371 In the text to fns 364 and 365, paragraphs 113(1)(a)-(e) of the Banking (Prudential Supervision) Act 1989 are the first five clauses of the sentence, i.e., from the beginning of the sentence ('The RBNZ may give') up to and including the word 'prudently'.

372 The text to fns 364-366 sets out subsections 113(1), 113(3) and 113(4) of the Banking (Prudential Supervision) Act 1989. The first sentence of fn 364 lays down subsection 113(2) of the Banking (Prudential Supervision) Act 1989.

373 This section of the Banking (Prudential Supervision) Act 1989 is titled 'Statutory manager may apply to apply to High Court for directions', and reads: "(1) A statutory manager of a registered bank may apply to the High Court for directions concerning the business or property of the registered bank[,] or the management or administration of that business or property, or the exercise of any powers under this Part. (2) On any application under subsection (1)[,] the High Court may give directions concerning the business or property of the registered bank, or the management or administration of that business or property, or the exercise of any powers of this Part[,] and every person shall be bound by any such directions." (Government of New Zealand (2022), "Banking (Prudential Supervision) Act 1989, Public Act 1989 No 157," adopted on December 20, 1989, as "Reserve Bank of New Zealand Act 1989," entered into force on February 1, 1990, last amended on July 1, 2022, s.142). 'This Part' is Part 5 of the Banking (Prudential Supervision) Act 1989, which is entitled 'Registration of banks and prudential supervision of registered banks' and consists of sections 67A-156AC of this Act.

374 This is Part 5 of the Banking (Prudential Supervision) Act 1989, which is titled 'Registration of banks and prudential supervision of registered banks' and comprises ss.67A-156AC of the Act.

375 The website of the RBNZ notes: "The New Zealand subsidiaries of the four large Australian-owned banks (ANZ [Bank New Zealand Limited], ASB [Bank Limited], BNZ [(i.e., Bank of New Zealand)] and Westpac [New Zealand Limited]) have total assets of between 11% and 17% of their parent group's total assets." (Government of New Zealand (2022), "Reserve Bank of New Zealand: The banking sector," accessed August 21, 2022, <https://www.rbnz.govt.nz/financial-stability/about-the-new-zealand-financial-system/the-banking-sector>).

376 The statutory manager is not required to so notify the RBNZ, if (s)he is satisfied that is not reasonably practicable to do this under the circumstances, taking account of "urgency or other similar constraint" (Government of New Zealand (2022), "Banking (Prudential Supervision) Act 1989, Public Act 1989 No 157," adopted on December

registered bank is proclaimed to be subject to statutory management, then no person may start or continue any proceedings[377] [574], enforce any judgment or order obtained regarding this registered bank [575], take any measures to place the registered bank into liquidation or non-compulsory administration [576], enter into possession of, appoint a receiver of, or sell, the property of the registered bank – or property in relation to which this bank has an equity of redemption [577], exercise or continue any rights or power under, or in pursuance of, any security over the registered bank's property [578], recover or claim any property in the registered bank's possession [579], retake or re-enter any premises, determine or forfeit any tenancy, or exercise or continue any rights or power under, or in pursuance of, any lease, against this registered bank [580], or exercise a right of set-off against the registered bank [581]. If a registered bank – which is either a branch of a body corporate that is incorporated outside New Zealand or any unincorporated entity with its head office or principal place of business outside New Zealand – is announced to be subject to statutory management, then the statutory manager may establish and register a body corporate [582], subscribe for or acquire as trustee for the foreign company or overseas unincorporated entity any or all of the shares of the newly-founded body corporate [583], and/or issue or allot any or all of these shares as fully or partly paid up to the value of any rights, property and assets which are vested in that body corporate, less the value of any liabilities which are vested therein[378] [584]. Except with the statutory manager's consent, no person is to remove or transfer from New Zealand any assets or property of a registered bank that is declared to be subject to statutory management[379] [585]. In spite of

---

20, 1989, as "Reserve Bank of New Zealand Act 1989," entered into force on February 1, 1990, last amended on July 1, 2022, s.121A(2)).

[377] Notwithstanding this, proceedings "may be commenced or continued against a registered bank for the purpose of determining whether any right or liability exists[,] if the leave of the statutory manager or the High Court is first obtained" (Government of New Zealand (2022), "Banking (Prudential Supervision) Act 1989, Public Act 1989 No 157," adopted on December 20, 1989, as "Reserve Bank of New Zealand Act 1989," entered into force on February 1, 1990, last amended on July 1, 2022, s.122(2)).

[378] Subsection 123(2) of the Banking (Prudential Supervision) Act 1989 states: "The Governor-General may, by Order in Council, on the advice of the Minister, given in accordance with a recommendation of the Bank, declare that the whole[,] or any part[,] of any property, rights, assets, and liabilities of any such branch relating to the business carried on by that branch[,] shall vest in that body corporate on a date specified in the order[,] and the property, rights, assets, and liabilities shall vest in that body corporate on the date specified." (Government of New Zealand (2022), "Banking (Prudential Supervision) Act 1989, Public Act 1989 No 157," adopted on December 20, 1989, as "Reserve Bank of New Zealand Act 1989," entered into force on February 1, 1990, last amended on July 1, 2022, s.123(2)). Fn 354 defines the term '*Minister*'. The final sentence of fn 350 defines the term '*Bank*'. Such an "order may be made under section 123 [of the Banking (Prudential Supervision) Act 1989] vesting any property, rights, and assets of a branch in a body corporate formed and registered pursuant to that section[,] notwithstanding the existence, or the terms and conditions, of any security over that property, or those rights or assets, in favour of any other person" (Government of New Zealand (2022), "Banking (Prudential Supervision) Act 1989, Public Act 1989 No 157," adopted on December 20, 1989, as "Reserve Bank of New Zealand Act 1989," entered into force on February 1, 1990, last amended on July 1, 2022, s.124(1)). The text to the present footnote (i.e., fn 378) sets out subsection 123(1) of the Banking (Prudential Supervision) Act 1989. The first sentence of the current footnote lays down subsection 123(2) of the Banking (Prudential Supervision) Act 1989.

[379] If a person removes or transfers these assets or property from New Zealand, then this person commits an offence (Government of New Zealand (2022), "Banking (Prudential Supervision) Act 1989, Public Act 1989 No 157," adopted on December 20, 1989, as "Reserve Bank of New Zealand Act 1989," entered into force on February 1, 1990, last amended on July 1, 2022, ss.126(2) and 156AC(2)(q)). An individual who commits this offence is liable, on conviction, to imprisonment for a term of no more than 18 months or a fine not exceeding NZD 200,000 (Government of New Zealand (2022), "Banking (Prudential Supervision) Act 1989, Public Act 1989 No 157," adopted on December 20, 1989, as "Reserve Bank of New Zealand Act 1989," entered into force on February 1, 1990, last amended on July 1, 2022, ss.126(2A) and 156AC(1)(a)). A body corporate that commits this offence is liable, on conviction, to a fine of no more than NZD 2 million (Government of New Zealand (2022), "Banking (Prudential Supervision) Act 1989, Public Act 1989 No 157," adopted on December 20, 1989,

the terms of any contract, the statutory manager of a registered bank may suspend, in whole or in part, the discharge of any obligation to any person [586], and cancel the obligation to supply funding to any person [587]. This suspension or cancellation does not amount to a breach or repudiation of any contract that the registered bank has entered into with any person [588]. Subject to Part 5 of the Banking (Prudential Supervision) Act 1989[380], if a registered bank is proclaimed to be subject to statutory management, then the management of this registered bank shall vest in the statutory manager from the date and time specified in the Order in Council [589]. A statutory manager is to have all rights, powers and authorities as may be required for the purposes of Part 5 of the Banking (Prudential Supervision) Act 1989[381] [590]. Given this, the statutory manager possesses – and may exercise – all the rights, powers and privileges of the registered bank [591], all the powers of the members in general meeting and the board of directors of a body corporate – if the registered bank is a body corporate [592], and all the

as "Reserve Bank of New Zealand Act 1989," entered into force on February 1, 1990, last amended on July 1, 2022, ss.126(2A) and 156AC(1)(b)).

380 Part 5 of the Banking (Prudential Supervision) Act 1989 is entitled 'Registration of banks and prudential supervision of registered banks', and consists of ss.67A-156AC of the Act.

381 Without restricting these rights, powers and authorities, "a statutory manager has, and may exercise, all of the powers conferred on a liquidator of a company by section 269 of the Companies Act 1993 in the same manner as if the statutory manager was the liquidator of a company in liquidation under that Act, and all the provisions of that section shall apply in respect of the disclaimer of any property of the registered bank as if that property was property of a company to which that section applied" Government of New Zealand (2022), "Banking (Prudential Supervision) Act 1989, Public Act 1989 No 157," Adopted on December 20, 1989, as "Reserve Bank of New Zealand Act 1989," Entered into force on February 1, 1990, Last amended on July 1, 2022, Consolidated to July 1, 2022, s.129(3)). Section 269 of the Companies Act 1993 is titled 'Power to disclaim onerous property', and states: "(1) Subject to section 270 [of the Companies Act 1993], a liquidator may disclaim onerous property[,] even though the liquidator has taken possession of it, tried to sell it, or otherwise exercised rights of ownership in relation to it. (2) For the purposes of this section, **onerous property** – (a) means – (i) an unprofitable contract; or (ii) property of the company that is unsaleable, or not readily saleable, or that may give rise to a liability to pay money or perform an onerous act; or (iii) a litigation right that, in the opinion of the liquidator, has no reasonable prospect of success or cannot reasonably be funded from the assets of the company; but (b) does not include – (i) a netting agreement to which sections 310A to 310O [of the Companies Act 1993] apply; or (ii) any contract of the company that constitutes a transaction under a netting agreement; or (iii) a settlement instruction or a settlement under the rules of a settlement system that is declared to be a designated settlement system under Part 5C of the Banking (Prudential Supervision) Act 1989. (3) A disclaimer under this section – (a) brings to an end[,] on and from the date of the disclaimer[,] the rights, interests, and liabilities of the company in relation to the property disclaimed: (b) does not, except so far as necessary to release the company from a liability, affect the rights or liabilities of any other person. (4) A liquidator who disclaims onerous property must, within 10 working days of the disclaimer, give notice in writing of the disclaimer to every person whose rights are, to the knowledge of the liquidator, affected by the disclaimer. (5) A person suffering loss or damage as a result of the disclaimer under this section[,] may – (a) claim as a creditor of the company for the amount of the loss or damage, taking account of the effect of an order made by the court under paragraph (b): (b) apply to the court for an order that the disclaimed property be delivered to[,] or vested in[,] that person. (6) The court may make an order under subsection (5)(b)[,] if it is satisfied that it is just that the property should be vested in the applicant." (Government of New Zealand (2022), "Companies Act 1993, Public Act 1993 No 105," adopted on September 28, 1993, entered into force on July 1, 1994, consolidated to July 1, 2022, s.269; emphasis original). Section 270 of the Companies Act 2003 is entitled 'Liquidator may be required to elect whether to disclaim onerous property', and reads: "If a person[,] whose rights would be affected by the disclaimer of onerous property[,] gives the liquidator notice in writing requiring the liquidator to elect, before the close of such date as is stated in the notice, not being a date that is less than 20 working days after the date on which the notice is received by the liquidator, whether to disclaim the onerous property, [then] the liquidator is not entitled to disclaim the onerous property[,] unless he or she does so before the close of that date." (Government of New Zealand (2022), "Companies Act 1993, Public Act 1993 No 105," adopted on September 28, 1993, entered into force on July 1, 1994, consolidated to July 1, 2022, s.270). Part 5C of the Banking (Prudential Supervision) Act 1989 is titled 'Designated settlement systems', and comprises ss.156K-156ZQ of the Act. The section below entitled 'Designated Payment Systems' specifies selected provisions from Part 5C of the Banking (Prudential Supervision) Act 1989.

powers that are exercisable by a partner or partners – if the registered bank is a partnership [593]. Subject to Part 5 of the Banking (Prudential Supervision) Act 1989[382], a statutory manager of a registered bank may engage in all, or any part, of this bank's business, and has, and may exercise, in connection with the registered bank, all such rights, powers and authorities as may be necessary to continue that business [594]. Subject to Part 5 of the Banking (Prudential Supervision) Act 1989, a statutory manager of a registered bank – for the purposes of carrying on this bank's business – shall have power to pay, in whole or in part, any of the bank's creditors or classes of creditors [595], make any arrangement or compromise with any of the bank's creditors – or persons claiming to be such creditors [596], and compromise all debts, calls and claims subsisting – or assumed to remain in effect – between the bank and any other person, and all questions concerning the bank's assets, and give a full or partial discharge [597]. Subject to Part 5 of the Banking (Prudential Supervision) Act 1989, the statutory manager of a registered bank may dispose of its entire business, or any part of it, to such person and upon such terms and conditions as the statutory manager considers to be appropriate[383] [598]. A statutory manager may dispose of any assets or property of a registered bank pursuant to subsection 132(1) of the Banking (Prudential Supervision) Act 1989[384], dispose of any assets or property of a registered bank to any body corporate that is established and registered pursuant to paragraph 132(2)(a) of the Banking (Prudential Supervision) Act 1989[385], or dispose of any shares, assets or property of a body corporate which is founded and registered pursuant to paragraph 132(2)(a) of the Banking (Prudential Supervision) Act 1989, despite the presence –

---

[382] Part 5 of the Banking (Prudential Supervision) Act 1989 is titled 'Registration of banks and prudential supervision of registered banks', and consists of ss.67A-156AC of the Act.

[383] Without restricting any of the statutory manager's other powers, "for the purposes of subsection (1) [(i.e., subsection 132(1) of the Banking (Prudential Supervision) Act 1989 (text to the present footnote (fn 383)))], the statutory manager shall have power to – (a) form and register a body corporate under the Companies Act 1993 or any other Act: (b) subscribe for[,] or acquire[,] all or any of the shares of that body corporate: (c) transfer to that body corporate the whole[,] or any part[,] of the business undertaking of the registered bank: (d) allot or issue all[,] or any[,] of the shares in that body corporate to any person, credited as fully or partly paid, as the case may be, up to the value of the business undertaking [that is] transferred to that body corporate: (e) sell all or any of the shares, or the whole or any part of the business undertaking, of that body corporate to such person and upon such terms and conditions as the statutory manager thinks fit" (Government of New Zealand (2022), "Banking (Prudential Supervision) Act 1989, Public Act 1989 No 157," adopted on December 20, 1989, as "Reserve Bank of New Zealand Act 1989," entered into force on February 1, 1990, last amended on July 1, 2022, s.132(2)). However, "[t]he statutory manager shall not sell[,] or otherwise dispose of[,] – (a) the whole[,] or any substantial part[,] of the business undertaking of a registered bank pursuant to subsection (1) [(i.e., subsection 132(1) of the Banking (Prudential Supervision) Act 1989 (text to the current footnote (fn 383)))]: (b) any of the shares of any body corporate formed and registered pursuant to subsection (2)(a) [(i.e., paragraph 132(2)(a) of the Banking (Prudential Supervision) Act 1989 (point (a) in first sentence of the present footnote (fn 383)))]: (c) the whole[,] or any substantial part[,] of the business undertaking of any body corporate formed and registered pursuant to subsection (2)(a), – unless the statutory manager has consulted with the Bank[,] and the Bank, with the consent of the Minister, has given approval in writing to the sale or other disposition and the terms and conditions of it" (Government of New Zealand (2022), "Banking (Prudential Supervision) Act 1989, Public Act 1989 No 157," adopted on December 20, 1989, as "Reserve Bank of New Zealand Act 1989," entered into force on February 1, 1990, last amended on July 1, 2022, s.132(3)). The last sentence of fn 350 defines the term '*Bank*'. Fn 354 defines the term '*Minister*'.

[384] The text to fn 383 sets out subsection 132(1) of the Banking (Prudential Supervision) Act 1989. Subject to one exception, "[i]f the statutory manager of a registered bank sells[,] or otherwise disposes of[,] any property or assets of that bank under section 132(1) [of the Banking (Prudential Supervision) Act 1989], being property or assets subject to a security interest ... , [then] the person entitled to the security interest must be paid out of the proceeds of sale or other disposition in priority to all other claims[,] other than the costs of the statutory manager in selling[,] or disposing of[,] the property or assets" (Government of New Zealand (2022), "Banking (Prudential Supervision) Act 1989, Public Act 1989 No 157," adopted on December 20, 1989, as "Reserve Bank of New Zealand Act 1989," entered into force on February 1, 1990, last amended on July 1, 2022, s.134(2)).

[385] Point (a) in the first sentence of fn 383 is paragraph 132(2)(a) of the Banking (Prudential Supervision) Act 1989.

or the terms and conditions – of any security over those assets or the property, to the advantage of any other person [599]. If all, or part, of any liability of a registered bank is included in the disposition of the business of that registered bank – or any part of this business, then, pursuant to section 132 of the Banking (Prudential Supervision) Act 1989[386], the registered bank, from the date of this disposition, is to be released from all its obligations regarding this liability, or part of it[387] [600], the person entitled to performance concerning the liability is to be authorised to enforce performance of it, or part of it, against the person to whom the business is transferred [601], and the inclusion of part of a liability shall not free the registered bank from any obligation relating to any portion of the liability that is excluded from the disposition [602]. Subject to Part 5 of the Banking (Prudential Supervision) Act 1989, a statutory manager of a registered bank may, with the prior approval of the RBNZ, apply to put a registered bank into liquidation under the Companies Act 1983 [603], petition under the Insolvency Act 1986 to have a registered bank which is an individual declared bankrupt [604], or, in the case of a registered bank that is established under any other Act, take the steps which that Act provides for the liquidation, dissolution or winding up of this registered bank[388] [605]. The Governor-General may, by Order in Council, upon the Minister's[389] advice given in conformity with a recommendation of the RBNZ, announce that any registered bank, or associated person or subsidiary[390] of such a bank, which is subject to statutory management, shall no longer be subject to statutory management[391] [606]. Any registered bank, or associated person or

386 The text to fn 383 comprises subsection 132(1) of the Banking (Prudential Supervision) Act 1989. The first sentence of fn 383 lays down subsection 132(2) of the Banking (Prudential Supervision) Act 1989. The second sentence of fn 383 sets out subsection 132(3) of the Banking (Prudential Supervision) Act 1989.

387 If "all[,] or any part[,] of any liability of a body corporate formed and registered under section 123(1) [of the Banking (Prudential Supervision) Act 1989 (text to fn 378)], or all[,] or any part[,] of any liability relating to the business carried on by a branch of any body corporate incorporated outside New Zealand[,] or, as the case may be, any unincorporated body having its head office or principal place of business outside New Zealand, is included in such a sale or other disposition, [then] nothing in subsection (1)(a) [of section 137 of the Banking (Prudential Supervision) Act 1989 (text to the current footnote (i.e., fn 387))] shall relieve any body corporate incorporated outside New Zealand or, as the case may be, any unincorporated body having its head office or principal place of business outside New Zealand[,] from any obligation in respect of that liability" (Government of New Zealand (2022), "Banking (Prudential Supervision) Act 1989, Public Act 1989 No 157," adopted on December 20, 1989, as "Reserve Bank of New Zealand Act 1989," entered into force on February 1, 1990, last amended on July 1, 2022, s.137(2)).

388 By means of an Order in Council, "[t]he Governor-General may … on the advice of the Minister given in accordance with a recommendation of a statutory manager of a registered bank, not being a registered bank referred to in subsection (1) [(i.e., subsection 136(1) of the Banking (Prudential Supervision) Act 1989 (text to the present footnote (i.e., fn 388)))], order that the registered bank to which the recommendation relates shall be wound up in such manner as may be specified in the order[,] and, in any such case, the registered bank shall be wound up in the manner specified" (Government of New Zealand (2022), "Banking (Prudential Supervision) Act 1989, Public Act 1989 No 157," adopted on December 20, 1989, as "Reserve Bank of New Zealand Act 1989," entered into force on February 1, 1990, last amended on July 1, 2022, s.136(2)). Fn 354 defines the term '*Minister*'. A statutory manager shall not make a recommendation under subsection 136(2) of the Banking (Prudential Supervision) Act 1989 without the prior approval of the RBNZ (Government of New Zealand (2022), "Banking (Prudential Supervision) Act 1989, Public Act 1989 No 157," adopted on December 20, 1989, as "Reserve Bank of New Zealand Act 1989," entered into force on February 1, 1990, last amended on July 1, 2022, s.136(3)). The first sentence of the current footnote (i.e., fn 388) lays down subsection 136(2) of the Banking (Prudential Supervision) Act 1989.

389 Fn 354 defines the term '*Minister*'.

390 Fn 359 defines the term '*subsidiary*'.

391 Any person whom an Order in Council made under section 117 of the Banking (Prudential Supervision) Act 1989 affects, may, at any time, request the RBNZ to make a recommendation under subsection 144(1) of the Banking (Prudential Supervision) Act 1989 (Government of New Zealand (2022), "Banking (Prudential Supervision) Act 1989, Public Act 1989 No 157," adopted on December 20, 1989, as "Reserve Bank of New Zealand Act 1989," entered into force on February 1, 1990, last amended on July 1, 2022, s.144(3)). The first three sentences of the

subsidiary of such a bank, shall stop being subject to statutory management, if this registered bank, associated person or subsidiary is put into liquidation, on application to do so by the statutory manager[392] [607]. Obligations that a statutory manager of a registered bank incurs in the course of his or her professional duties are met on behalf of this bank; the statutory manager does not suffer personal liability for them [608]. In the liquidation or winding up of a registered bank, or of an associated person or subsidiary of such a bank, all sums which are required to fulfil obligations that are incurred by the statutory manager on behalf of the registered bank, associated person or subsidiary, must be paid in priority to all other debts [609]. All charges, costs and expenses which are incurred by statutory manager or a member of an advisory committee in the exercise of the statutory manager's, or member's, powers and functions under Part 5 of the Banking (Prudential Supervision) Act 1989[393], are to be payable from the property

---

present paragraph in the text, which is headed 'Statutory management of registered banks', set out subsections 117(1), 117(2), 117(4) and 117(5) of the Banking (Prudential Supervision) Act 1989. Fn 368 comprises subsection 117(2A) of the Banking (Prudential Supervision) Act 1989. The first sentence of fn 369 specifies subsection 117(3) of the Banking (Prudential Supervision) Act 1989. The text to the current footnote (i.e., fn 391) states subsection 144(1) of the Banking (Prudential Supervision) Act 1989.

[392] If "an Order in Council is made under subsection (1) [(i.e., subsection 144(1) of the Banking (Prudential Supervision) Act 1989 (text to fns 389-391))] or, a registered bank, associated person, or subsidiary is put into liquidation[, then] – (a) that person shall cease to be subject to statutory management at the specified time; and (b) the appointment of any statutory manager [who is] appointed in respect of that person[,] shall terminate at the specified time; and (c) the appointment of any person as a member of an advisory committee under section 119 [of the Banking (Prudential Supervision) Act 1989] in relation to the statutory management of that person[,] shall terminate at the specified time" (Government of New Zealand (2022), "Banking (Prudential Supervision) Act 1989, Public Act 1989 No 157," adopted on December 20, 1989, as "Reserve Bank of New Zealand Act 1989," entered into force on February 1, 1990, last amended on July 1, 2022, s.144(4)). Section 119 of the Banking (Prudential Supervision) Act 1989 is titled "Advisory committee"; its first two subsections read: "(1) Where an Order in Council is made under section 117 [of the Banking (Prudential Supervision) Act 1989,] declaring a registered bank or an associated person to be subject to statutory management, the Minister may, by notice in writing to the statutory manager of that registered bank or associated person, on the recommendation of the Bank, appoint the persons specified in the recommendation as an advisory committee. (2) The functions of an advisory committee shall be – (a) to advise the statutory manager on the conduct of the statutory management, including the exercise of the powers conferred by this Part: (b) to do such other things as may be specified by the Minister, from time to time, by notice in the *Gazette*." (Government of New Zealand (2022), "Banking (Prudential Supervision) Act 1989, Public Act 1989 No 157," adopted on December 20, 1989, as "Reserve Bank of New Zealand Act 1989," entered into force on February 1, 1990, last amended on July 1, 2022, s.119(1)-(2); emphasis original). The first three sentences of the present paragraph in the text, which is headed 'Statutory management of registered banks', lay down subsections 117(1), 117(2), 117(4) and 117(5) of the Banking (Prudential Supervision) Act 1989. Fn 368 sets out subsection 117(2A) of the Banking (Prudential Supervision) Act 1989. The first sentence of fn 369 comprises subsection 117(3) of the Banking (Prudential Supervision) Act 1989. Fn 354 defines the term '*Minister*'. The final sentence of fn 350 defines the term '*Bank*'. 'This Part' is Part 5 of the Banking (Prudential Supervision) Act 1989, which is entitled 'Registration of banks and prudential supervision of registered banks' and consists of sections 67A-156AC of this Act. It is opined that the '*Gazette*' refers to the *New Zealand Gazette*, which is the official newspaper of the Government of New Zealand, and which contains government and commercial notifications that legislation to be published requires (Government of New Zealand (2022), "New Zealand Gazette: About Us," accessed August 24, 2022, <https://gazette.govt.nz/about-us/>). For the purposes of subsection 144(4) of the Banking (Prudential Supervision) Act 1989, the phrase '*specified time*' "means, – (a) in any case where an Order in Council is made under subsection (1) [(i.e., subsection 144(1) of the Banking (Prudential Supervision) Act 1989 (text to fns 389-391))], the date and time [that are] specified in the order: (b) in any case where a liquidator is appointed, the date and time of the liquidator's appointment" (Government of New Zealand (2022), "Banking (Prudential Supervision) Act 1989, Public Act 1989 No 157," adopted on December 20, 1989, as "Reserve Bank of New Zealand Act 1989," entered into force on February 1, 1990, last amended on July 1, 2022, s.144(5)). The first sentence of the current footnote (i.e., fn 392), states subsection 144(4) of the Banking (Prudential Supervision) Act 1989.

[393] Part 5 of the Banking (Prudential Supervision) Act 1989 is titled 'Registration of banks and prudential supervision of registered banks', and comprises ss.67A-156AC of the Act.

of the registered bank, associated person of this bank, or subsidiary[394] of the bank, in respect of which the manager or member is appointed, in priority to all other claims[395] [610]. The statutory manager shall appoint at least one person to be the auditor of the registered bank [611], who must be licensed auditors within the meaning of subsection 6(1) of the Auditor Regulation Act 2011[396] and approved by the RBNZ[397] [612]. Within three months of the end of each financial year – or such later date as the RBNZ may approve, the statutory manager of a registered bank shall prepare the following statements: (a) a statement of financial position of the registered bank at the end of its financial year, and a statement of this bank's financial performance during the financial year, and (b) a consolidated statement of assets and liabilities of the registered bank and its subsidiaries at the close of the financial year, and a consolidated statement of trading of the bank and its subsidiaries for that financial year[398] [613]. After the end of each financial year, the statutory manager of a registered bank shall prepare a report on how the management and affairs of the registered bank and its subsidiaries have been conducted [614]. This annual report, together with the yearly accounts and the auditor's report on these, are to be submitted to the Minister[399] and the RBNZ within one week of completion of the auditor's report[400] [615].

---

[394] Fn 359 defines the term '*subsidiary*'.

[395] With the RBNZ's approval, "[t]he statutory manager may … apportion the costs, charges, and expenses referred to in subsection (1) [(i.e., subsection 148(1) of the Banking (Prudential Supervision) Act 1989 (text to fns 393-395))] between the registered bank and any associated person or subsidiary of the registered bank that is also subject to statutory management[,] in the amounts that the statutory manager considers just and equitable" (Government of New Zealand (2022), "Banking (Prudential Supervision) Act 1989, Public Act 1989 No 157," adopted on December 20, 1989, as "Reserve Bank of New Zealand Act 1989," entered into force on February 1, 1990, last amended on July 1, 2022, s.148(2)). Section 148 of the Banking (Prudential Supervision) Act 1989 prevails over section 145 of this Act (Government of New Zealand (2022), "Banking (Prudential Supervision) Act 1989, Public Act 1989 No 157," adopted on December 20, 1989, as "Reserve Bank of New Zealand Act 1989," entered into force on February 1, 1990, last amended on July 1, 2022, s.148(3)). The text to fns 393-395 sets out subsection 148(1) of the Banking (Prudential Supervision) Act 1989. The present footnote (i.e., fn 395) lays down subsections 148(2) and 148(3) of the Banking (Prudential Supervision) Act 1989. The next two sentences after the text to fn 392, specify section 145 of the Banking (Prudential Supervision) Act 1989.

[396] In the Auditor Regulation Act 2011, unless the context requires otherwise, the phrase '*licensed auditor*' "means a person who holds, or is treated as holding, a licence" (Government of New Zealand (2022), "Auditor Regulation Act 2011, Public Act 2011 No 21," adopted on May 19, 2011, entered into force on July 1, 2012, consolidated to May 25, 2022, s.6(1)). The Auditor Regulation Act 2011 defines the meaning of the word '*licence*'.

[397] Every appointment as auditor of a registered bank is to be for a term of no more than two years, but any person appointed as auditor shall continue in office until a successor is in place (Government of New Zealand (2022), "Banking (Prudential Supervision) Act 1989, Public Act 1989 No 157," adopted on December 20, 1989, as "Reserve Bank of New Zealand Act 1989," entered into force on February 1, 1990, last amended on July 1, 2022, s.154(2)). A person appointed as auditor of a registered bank is eligible for reappointment to this position (Government of New Zealand (2022), "Banking (Prudential Supervision) Act 1989, Public Act 1989 No 157," adopted on December 20, 1989, as "Reserve Bank of New Zealand Act 1989," entered into force on February 1, 1990, last amended on July 1, 2022, s.154(3)).

[398] The statutory manager is to sign each of the statement of financial position of the registered bank, and the consolidated statement of assets and liabilities of the registered bank and its subsidiaries (Government of New Zealand (2022), "Banking (Prudential Supervision) Act 1989, Public Act 1989 No 157," adopted on December 20, 1989, as "Reserve Bank of New Zealand Act 1989," entered into force on February 1, 1990, last amended on July 1, 2022, s.155(2)). The auditor is to audit, and report upon, the aforementioned annual accounts (Government of New Zealand (2022), "Banking (Prudential Supervision) Act 1989, Public Act 1989 No 157," adopted on December 20, 1989, as "Reserve Bank of New Zealand Act 1989," entered into force on February 1, 1990, last amended on July 1, 2022, s.155(3)).

[399] Fn 354 defines the term '*Minister*'.

[400] Within two weeks of their submission to the Minister, the annual report, the yearly accounts, and the auditor's report on these, are to "be filed – (a) in the case of a registered bank which is a company, with the Registrar of Companies: (b) in the case of a registered bank which is a building society, with the Registrar of Building Societies: (c) in the case of any other body corporate, with the person exercising the functions corresponding

Designated Payment Systems

Exercise of Powers under Part 5C of the Banking (Prudential Supervision) Act 1989[401]

The powers that Part 5C of the Banking (Prudential Supervision) Act 1989 confers upon the Minister[402] and the RBNZ, must be exercised for the following purposes: (a) furthering the maintenance of a sound, efficient financial system, and (b) avoiding material damage to the financial system that may ensue from the failure of a participant in a settlement system[403] [616].

---

with those of the Registrar of Companies or the Registrar of Building Societies" (Government of New Zealand (2022), "Banking (Prudential Supervision) Act 1989, Public Act 1989 No 157," adopted on December 20, 1989, as "Reserve Bank of New Zealand Act 1989," entered into force on February 1, 1990, last amended on July 1, 2022, s.156(3)). Fn 354 defines the term '*Minister*'.

[401] Part 5C of the Banking (Prudential Supervision) Act 1989 is entitled 'Designated settlement systems', and consists of ss.156K-156ZQ of the Act.

[402] Fn 354 defines the term '*Minister*'.

[403] Within Part 5C of the Banking (Prudential Supervision) Act 1989 – unless the context requires otherwise, the phrase '*settlement system*' "(a) means a system or arrangement for effecting settlements or processing settlement instructions in accordance with rules; and (b) includes a payment system" (Government of New Zealand (2022), "Banking (Prudential Supervision) Act 1989, Public Act 1989 No 157," adopted on December 20, 1989, as "Reserve Bank of New Zealand Act 1989," entered into force on February 1, 1990, last amended on July 1, 2022, s.156M(1)). Within Part 5C of the Banking (Prudential Supervision) Act 1989 – unless the context requires otherwise, the word '*settlement*' "means – (a) the making of a payment[,] or the transfer of the title to, or an interest in, property – (i) that is done in accordance with, or to give effect to, a settlement instruction; and (ii) that is on a gross basis or that uses netting; and (iii) whether by way of book entry on the accounts of a central bank or an operator of a settlement system[,] or otherwise; or (b) any other act that discharges an obligation to make a payment[,] or transfer the title to, or an interest in, property[,] in accordance with the rules of a settlement system" (Government of New Zealand (2022), "Banking (Prudential Supervision) Act 1989, Public Act 1989 No 157," adopted on December 20, 1989, as "Reserve Bank of New Zealand Act 1989," entered into force on February 1, 1990, last amended on July 1, 2022, s.156M(1)). Within Part 5C of the Banking (Prudential Supervision) Act 1989 – unless the context requires otherwise, the phrase '*settlement instruction* "means an instruction by a participant in, or to an operator of, a settlement system – (a) that is made in accordance with the rules of that settlement system; and (b) that results, or is intended to result, in 1 or more settlements being effected" (Government of New Zealand (2022), "Banking (Prudential Supervision) Act 1989, Public Act 1989 No 157," adopted on December 20, 1989, as "Reserve Bank of New Zealand Act 1989," entered into force on February 1, 1990, last amended on July 1, 2022, s.156M(1)). Within Part 5C of the Banking (Prudential Supervision) Act 1989 – unless the context requires otherwise, the word '*property*' "means personal property" (Government of New Zealand (2022), "Banking (Prudential Supervision) Act 1989, Public Act 1989 No 157," adopted on December 20, 1989, as "Reserve Bank of New Zealand Act 1989," entered into force on February 1, 1990, last amended on July 1, 2022, s.156M(1)). Within Part 5C of the Banking (Prudential Supervision) Act 1989 – unless the context requires otherwise, the word '*netting*' "means the conversion into 1 net claim or obligation, or the set-off, of different claims or obligations between participants in a settlement system that results from the issue and receipt of settlement instructions involving 2 or more participants in the settlement system[,] or that is otherwise provided for under the rules of the settlement system, – (a) whether on a bilateral or multilateral basis; and (b) whether or not through the interposition of an operator of the settlement system (whether by novation or otherwise); and (c) whether or not the obligations or claims constitute mutual credits, mutual debts, or other mutual dealings; and (d) whether or not the obligations or claims are denominated in New Zealand currency" (Government of New Zealand (2022), "Banking (Prudential Supervision) Act 1989, Public Act 1989 No 157," adopted on December 20, 1989, as "Reserve Bank of New Zealand Act 1989," entered into force on February 1, 1990, last amended on July 1, 2022, s.156M(1)). Within Part 5C of the Banking (Prudential Supervision) Act 1989 – unless the context requires otherwise, the word '*rules*' "(a) in relation to a settlement system, means the rules of the settlement system (whether made under bylaws, agreements, procedures, contracts, or other documents) that are evidenced in writing[,] and that provide, among other things, for – (i) the basis on which settlement obligations are given or received; and (ii) the basis on which settlement obligations are determined and calculated (either on a gross basis or using netting); and (iii) the basis on which settlements are effected (either on a gross basis or using netting); and (iv) any action to be taken[,] if a participant in the settlement system is unable, or likely to become unable, to meet the participant's obligations to any[,] or all[,] of the following: (A) an operator of the settlement system: (B) another participant in the settlement system: (C) any other party to those rules; and (b) in relation to a designated settlement system, means the rules of that settlement system that are contained in documents [which are] specified in the designation under section 156N

The powers which Part 5C of the Banking (Prudential Supervision) Act 1989 grants to the Minister responsible for the Financial Markets Conduct Act 2013[404] and to the New Zealand Financial Markets Authority, must be exercised for these purposes: (a) advancing the effectiveness and integrity of settlement systems – and markets related to them – in New Zealand, and (b) increasing the confidence of market participants in settlement systems – and markets related to these – in New Zealand [617]. The Governor-General must exercise the powers that Part 5C of the Banking (Prudential Supervision) Act 1989 confers upon him or her, for the purposes which subsections 156K(1) and 156K(2) of the Banking (Prudential Supervision) Act 1989[405] set out [618].

Designation of a Settlement System

On the advice of both the Minister[406] and the Minister responsible for the Financial Markets Conduct Act 2013[407], given in line with a joint recommendation of the joint regulators[408], the Governor-General may – by means of an Order in Council – proclaim any settlement system[409] to be a designated settlement system[410] [619]. This Order in Council must identify the settlement system which is the subject of the designation, the documents that evidence the

---

[of the Banking (Prudential Supervision) Act 1989]; and includes any amendments to those rules that have – (i) been notified, not been disallowed, and come into effect in accordance with the processes and the time frames [which are] set out in sections 156ZB and 156ZC [of the Banking (Prudential Supervision) Act 1989]; or (ii) been made pursuant to a variation of designation under section 156ZD [of the Banking (Prudential Supervision) Act 1989]" (Government of New Zealand (2022), "Banking (Prudential Supervision) Act 1989, Public Act 1989 No 157," adopted on December 20, 1989, as "Reserve Bank of New Zealand Act 1989," entered into force on February 1, 1990, last amended on July 1, 2022, s.156M(1)). The first sentence of fn 410 defines the term '*designated settlement system*'. The text to fns 406-410 sets out subsection 156N(1) of the Banking (Prudential Supervision) Act 1989. The text to fns 411-413 lays down subsection 156N(2) of the Banking (Prudential Supervision) Act 1989. The first sentence of fn 413 states subsection 156N(3) of the Banking (Prudential Supervision) Act 1989.

404 Within Part 5C of the Banking (Prudential Supervision) Act 1989 – unless the context requires otherwise, the phrase '*Minister responsible for the Financial Markets Conduct Act 2013*' "means the Minister of the Crown who, under the authority of any warrant or with the authority of the Prime Minister, is[,] for the time being[,] responsible for the administration of the Financial Markets Conduct Act 2013" (Government of New Zealand (2022), "Banking (Prudential Supervision) Act 1989, Public Act 1989 No 157," adopted on December 20, 1989, as "Reserve Bank of New Zealand Act 1989," entered into force on February 1, 1990, last amended on July 1, 2022, s.156M(1)).

405 The text to fns 402 and 403 states subsection 156K(1) of the Banking (Prudential Supervision) Act 1989. The text to fn 404 lays down subsection 156K(2) of the Banking (Prudential Supervision) Act 1989.

406 Fn 354 defines the term '*Minister*'.

407 Fn 404 defines the term '*Minister responsible for the Financial Markets Conduct Act 2013*'.

408 Within Part 5C of the Banking (Prudential Supervision) Act 1989 – unless the context requires otherwise, the phrase '*joint regulators*' "means – (a) the Bank; and (b) the FMA [(i.e., the New Zealand Financial Markets Authority)]" (Government of New Zealand (2022), "Banking (Prudential Supervision) Act 1989, Public Act 1989 No 157," adopted on December 20, 1989, as "Reserve Bank of New Zealand Act 1989," entered into force on February 1, 1990, last amended on July 1, 2022, s.156M(1)). The last sentence of fn 350 defines the term '*Bank*'.

409 The first sentence of fn 403 defines the term '*settlement system*'.

410 Within Part 5C of the Banking (Prudential Supervision) Act 1989 – unless the context requires otherwise, the phrase '*designated settlement system* "means a settlement system that is declared to be a designated settlement system under section 156N [of the Banking (Prudential Supervision) Act 1989]" (Government of New Zealand (2022), "Banking (Prudential Supervision) Act 1989, Public Act 1989 No 157," adopted on December 20, 1989, as "Reserve Bank of New Zealand Act 1989," entered into force on February 1, 1990, last amended on July 1, 2022, s.156M(1)). The first sentence of fn 403 defines the term '*settlement system*'. The text to fns 406-410 specifies subsection 156N(1) of the Banking (Prudential Supervision) Act 1989. The text to fns 411-413 sets out subsection 156N(2) of the Banking (Prudential Supervision) Act 1989. The first sentence of fn 413 comprises subsection 156N(3) of the Banking (Prudential Supervision) Act 1989.

rules[411] of this settlement system, the specified operator[412] of the settlement system, and the title or name of the person to whom notices concerning the settlement system must be given[413] [620].

Settlements Must Not Be Recovered, Repaid, Reversed or Set Aside

A settlement[414] that is effected in compliance with the rules of a designated payment system[415] must not, either wholly or partly, be recovered, repaid, reversed or set aside, notwithstanding any statute or rule of law that states or implies the opposite[416] [621].

---

[411] The sixth sentence of fn 403 defines the term '*rules*'.

[412] Within Part 5C of the Banking (Prudential Supervision) Act 1989 – unless the context requires otherwise, the phrase '*specified operator*' "means the operator of a settlement system specified in an Order in Council in accordance with section 156N(2)(c) [of the Banking (Prudential Supervision) Act 1989]" (Government of New Zealand (2022), "Banking (Prudential Supervision) Act 1989, Public Act 1989 No 157," adopted on December 20, 1989, as "Reserve Bank of New Zealand Act 1989," entered into force on February 1, 1990, last amended on July 1, 2022, s.156M(1)). The first sentence of fn 403 defines the term '*settlement system*'. The text to the present footnote (fn 412) – i.e., 'This Order must identify … the specified operator of the settlement system' – lays down paragraph 156N(2)(c) of the Banking (Prudential Supervision) Act 1989.

[413] The Order in Council "may also specify all[,] or any[,] of the following: (a) conditions to which the designation is subject: (b) that a particular operator is a participant in the settlement system that is the subject of the designation: (c) that the operator specified in accordance with subsection (2)(c) [(i.e., paragraph 156N(2)(c) of the Banking (Prudential Supervision) Act 1989)] is an operator to whom section 103A of the Personal Property Securities Act 1999 applies: (d) that the settlement system that is the subject of the designation is a pure payment system" (Government of New Zealand (2022), "Banking (Prudential Supervision) Act 1989, Public Act 1989 No 157," adopted on December 20, 1989, as "Reserve Bank of New Zealand Act 1989," entered into force on February 1, 1990, last amended on July 1, 2022, s.156N(3)). The text to fn 412 – i.e., 'This Order must identify … the specified operator of the settlement system' – sets out paragraph 156N(2)(c) of the Banking (Prudential Supervision) Act 1989. Section 103A of the Personal Property Securities Act 1999 is titled 'Priority of interests of certain operators of designated settlement system'; its subsection (6) defines the word '*operator*' within this section, as "an operator of a designated settlement system who is ([,] and at the time in question remains[,]) specified under section 156N(3)(c) of the Banking (Prudential Supervision) Act 1989 as being an operator to whom this section applies" (Government of New Zealand (2022), "Personal Property Securities Act 1999, Public Act 1999 No 126, adopted on October 14, 1999, entered into force on May 1, 2002, consolidated to July 1, 2022, s.103A(6)). Point (c) in the first sentence of the current footnote (i.e., fn 413), lays down paragraph 156N(3)(c) of the Banking (Prudential Supervision) Act 1989. Within Part 5C of the Banking (Prudential Supervision) Act 1989 – unless the context requires otherwise, the phrase '*pure payment system*' "means a designated settlement system that is a payment system that is declared to be a pure payment system in accordance with section 156N(3)(d) [of the Banking (Prudential Supervision) Act 1989" (Government of New Zealand (2022), "Banking (Prudential Supervision) Act 1989, Public Act 1989 No 157," adopted on December 20, 1989, as "Reserve Bank of New Zealand Act 1989," entered into force on February 1, 1990, last amended on July 1, 2022, s.156M(1)). Point (d) in the first sentence of the present footnote (i.e., fn 413), specifies paragraph 156N(3)(d) of the Banking (Prudential Supervision) Act 1989. The first sentence of fn 403 defines the term '*settlement system*'. The first sentence of fn 412 defines the term '*specified operator*'. The first sentence of fn 410 defines the term '*designated settlement system*'.

[414] The second sentence of fn 403 defines the term '*settlement*'.

[415] The first sentence of fn 410 defines the term '*designated settlement system*'.

[416] This provision "extends to any application [that is] made to a New Zealand court by a foreign court, foreign representative, or foreign creditor[,] to reverse, repay, recover, or set aside a settlement (whether in whole or in part) that relates to an insolvency (in any form, whether personal or corporate) that is within jurisdiction of the relevant foreign court, foreign representative, or foreign creditor" (Government of New Zealand (2022), "Banking (Prudential Supervision) Act 1989, Public Act 1989 No 157," adopted on December 20, 1989, as "Reserve Bank of New Zealand Act 1989," entered into force on February 1, 1990, last amended on July 1, 2022, s.156R(2)). In the current section of the Banking (Prudential Supervision) Act 1989 – which is section 156R, the phrase '*foreign court*' "means a judicial or other authority competent to control or supervise a foreign proceeding," the expression '*foreign proceeding*' "means a collective judicial or administrative proceeding in a foreign jurisdiction, including an interim proceeding, under a law relating to insolvency (in any form, whether personal or corporate), in which proceeding the assets and affairs of the debtor are subject to control or supervision by a foreign court, for the purpose of reorganisation or liquidation," and the term '*foreign representative*' "means a person or body, including one appointed on an interim basis, authorised in a foreign

Netting Is Valid and Enforceable

If the rules of a designated settlement system[417] make provision for netting[418], then any netting which is in line with these rules is valid and enforceable, notwithstanding any statute or rule of law that states or implies the contrary [622].

Application for Designation of a Settlement System

A person who would like a settlement system[419] to be declared a designated settlement system[420], may apply to one of the joint regulators[421] [623]. As soon as practicable, a joint regulator must advise the other joint regulator of its receipt of such an application [624]. An application must be accompanied by a copy of the settlement system's rules [625], any information that both or either of the joint regulators require [626], and any application fee [627]. It must lay down the name or title, and the contact details, of the person who is proposed to be the settlement system's contact person [628]. Both joint regulators must consider an application for a settlement system to be declared a designated settlement system [629]. In doing this, each of the joint regulators *may* have regard to specified matters[422], and *must* look at whether the settlement system should be particularised as a pure payment system[423] [630]. After considering an application for designation of a settlement system, the joint regulators, together, must either make a joint recommendation to both the Minister[424] and the Minister responsible for the Financial Markets Conduct Act 2013[425] that the settlement system to which the application relates be proclaimed as a designated settlement system under section 156N of

---

proceeding to administer the reorganisation or the liquidation of the debtor's assets or affairs[,] or to act as a representative of the foreign proceeding" (Government of New Zealand (2022), "Banking (Prudential Supervision) Act 1989, Public Act 1989 No 157," adopted on December 20, 1989, as "Reserve Bank of New Zealand Act 1989," entered into force on February 1, 1990, last amended on July 1, 2022, s.156R(3)).

417 The first sentence of fn 410 defines the term '*designated settlement system*'.

418 The fifth sentence of fn 403 defines the term '*netting*'.

419 The first sentence of fn 403 defines the term '*settlement system*'.

420 The first sentence of fn 410 defines the term '*designated settlement system*'.

421 The first sentence of fn 408 defines the term '*joint regulators*'. Together, the joint regulators may create guidelines regarding the application procedure (Government of New Zealand (2022), "Banking (Prudential Supervision) Act 1989, Public Act 1989 No 157," adopted on December 20, 1989, as "Reserve Bank of New Zealand Act 1989," entered into force on February 1, 1990, last amended on July 1, 2022, s.156Y(4)).

422 These matters are: "(a) the purpose and scope of the settlement system: (b) the rules of the settlement system: (c) any laws or regulatory requirements relating to the operation of the settlement system[,] and the extent to which the settlement system complies with those laws or regulatory requirements: (d) relevant international standards concerning clearing and settlement systems, to the extent that they are relevant in the circumstances: (e) the capability and capacity of the operators of the settlement system: (f) the financial resources of the settlement system: (g) the importance of the settlement system to the financial system: (h) the impact on creditors of participants in the settlement system of specifying that an operator of the settlement system is an operator to whom section 103A of the Personal Property Securities Act 1999 applies: (i) any other matters that the regulator considers appropriate" (Government of New Zealand (2022), "Banking (Prudential Supervision) Act 1989, Public Act 1989 No 157," adopted on December 20, 1989, as "Reserve Bank of New Zealand Act 1989," entered into force on February 1, 1990, last amended on July 1, 2022, s.156Z(2)). The third sentence of fn 413 sets out the definition of the term '*operator*' in subsection 6 of section 103A of the Personal Property Securities Act 1999. Furthermore, "[i]n considering an application, each of the joint regulators may have regard, or refer, to, and may rely upon, any relevant information, work, or matter held, or produced, by the other joint regulator" (Government of New Zealand (2022), "Banking (Prudential Supervision) Act 1989, Public Act 1989 No 157," adopted on December 20, 1989, as "Reserve Bank of New Zealand Act 1989," entered into force on February 1, 1990, last amended on July 1, 2022, s.156Z(4)). The first sentence of fn 403 defines the term '*settlement system*'. The sixth sentence of fn 403 defines the term '*rules*'.

423 The fifth sentence of fn 413 defines the term '*pure payment system*'.

424 Fn 354 defines the term '*Minister*'.

425 Fn 404 defines the term '*Minister responsible for the Financial Markets Conduct Act 2013*'.

the Banking (Prudential Supervision) Act 1989[426] [631], or decline to make that recommendation [632]. In the latter case, the joint regulators, together, must give written notice to the applicant, which states that they refuse to make a recommendation that this settlement system be declared to be a designated settlement system under section 156N of the Banking (Prudential Supervision) Act 1989 [633], and which provides the reasons for their refusal to do so [634].

Comment

The subsections above furnish a selection of the provisions in the Banking (Prudential Supervision) Act 1989 that are in force at the time of writing. In particular, the registration of banks and the statutory management of registered banks are covered therein in some detail. The provisions within this Act tend to be drafted clearly and logically.

Non-Bank Deposit Takers Act 2013

The Purpose of the Non-Bank Deposit Takers Act 2013

The purpose of the Non-Bank Deposit Takers Act 2013 is to further the maintenance of a sound, efficient financial system [635], and to avoid significant harm to the financial system – which the failure of a non-bank deposit taker (NBDT) could occasion [636].

Non-Bank Deposit Taker (NBDT) and Related Party – Defined

In the Non-Bank Deposit Takers Act 2013, '*NBDT*'[427] means a person that: (a) makes an NBDT regulated offer[428] of debt securities, and conducts the business of lending and borrowing money, or supplying financial services, or both [637], (b) is declared – either specifically or as a member of a class of persons – by regulations passed under paragraph 73(1)(c) of the Non-Bank Deposit Takers Act 2013[429] to be an NBDT for the purposes of this Act [638], (c) is – or

[426] The text to fns 406-410 lays down subsection 156N(1) of the Banking (Prudential Supervision) Act 1989. The text to fns 411-413 sets out subsection 156N(2) of the Banking (Prudential Supervision) Act 1989. The first sentence of fn 413 specifies subsection 156N(3) of the Banking (Prudential Supervision) Act 1989.

[427] The abbreviation '*NBDT*' stands for the phrase '*non-bank deposit taker*' (Government of New Zealand (2022), "Non-bank Deposit Takers Act 2013, Public Act 2013 No 104," adopted on December 3, 2013, entered into force on May 1, 2014, consolidated to July 1, 2022, s.4(1)).

[428] The phrase '*NBDT regulated offer*' "(a) means a regulated offer within the meaning of section 41 of the Financial Markets Conduct Act 2013; and (b) includes an offer of debt securities that would be a regulated offer within the meaning of that section[,] if clause 3(2)(b) and [clause 3](3)(a) of Schedule 1 of that Act were not in force; and (c) includes an offer of debt securities to the public in New Zealand to which the Securities Act 1978 applied before its repeal[,] or to which that Act applies or applied under Schedule 4 of the Financial Markets Conduct Act 2013" (Government of New Zealand (2022), "Non-bank Deposit Takers Act 2013, Public Act 2013 No 104," adopted on December 3, 2013, entered into force on May 1, 2014, consolidated to July 1, 2022, s.4(1)).

[429] This paragraph states: "The Governor-General may, by Order in Council, on the advice of the Minister [that is] given in accordance with a recommendation of the Bank, make regulations for all[,] or any[,] of the following purposes: ... (c) declaring any person or class of persons (other than a person referred to in section 5(2)(a) to (c) [of the Non-Bank Deposit Takers Act 2013]) to be an NBDT for the purposes of this Act, or declaring that, in

has been at any time since this section[430] entered into force[431] – an NBDT, and has debt securities that remain unpaid and which were offered under an NBDT regulated offer[432] [639], or (d) was a deposit taker … on or after 3rd August 2011 but prior to this section becoming effective, and has debt securities that were issued to the public in New Zealand before this section entered into force and which remain unpaid [640]. Notwithstanding the above definition of 'NBDT', each of the following is not an NBDT: a bank that is a registered bank under the Banking (Prudential Supervision) Act 1989[433] [641], a local authority [642], the Crown [643], an entity which is in receivership [644] or liquidation [645], and a person – or a member of a class of persons – that regulations made under paragraph 73(1)(d) of the Non-Bank Deposit Takers Act 2013[434] proclaim not be an NBDT for the purposes of this Act [646].

certain specified circumstances, any person or class of persons is not an NBDT for the purposes of this Act: … ." (Government of New Zealand (2022), "Non-bank Deposit Takers Act 2013, Public Act 2013 No 104," adopted on December 3, 2013, entered into force on May 1, 2014, consolidated to July 1, 2022, s.73(1)(c)). Within the Non-Bank Deposit Takers Act 2013 – unless the context requires otherwise, the word '*Minister*' "means the Minister of the Crown who, under the authority of any warrant or with the authority of the Prime Minister, is[,] for the time being[,] responsible for the administration of this Act" (Government of New Zealand (2022), "Non-bank Deposit Takers Act 2013, Public Act 2013 No 104," adopted on December 3, 2013, entered into force on May 1, 2014, consolidated to July 1, 2022, s.4(1)). Within the Non-Bank Deposit Takers Act 2013 – unless the context requires otherwise, the word '*Bank*' "means the Reserve Bank of New Zealand continued under the Reserve Bank of New Zealand Act 2021" (Government of New Zealand (2022), "Non-bank Deposit Takers Act 2013, Public Act 2013 No 104," adopted on December 3, 2013, entered into force on May 1, 2014, consolidated to July 1, 2022, s.4(1)). The persons to which paragraphs 5(2)(a)-(c) of the Non-Bank Deposit Takers Act 2013 refer are a bank that is a registered bank under the Banking (Prudential Supervision) Act 1989, a local authority, and the Crown (first three clauses of the text to fns 433 and 434).

430 'This section' is section 5 of the Non-Bank Deposit Takers Act 2013.

431 Section 5 of the Non-Bank Deposit Takers Act 2013 entered into force on 1st May 2014 (Government of New Zealand (2014), "Non-bank Deposit Takers Act Commencement Order 2014, 2014/14, Order in Council made at Wellington on February 17, 2014, pursuant to section 2(1) of the Non-bank Deposit Takers Act 2013," s.2).

432 Fn 428 defines the term '*NBDT regulated offer*'.

433 The subsection entitled 'Registration of Banks', in the section above titled 'Banking (Prudential Supervision) Act 1989', provides information concerning the registration of banks under the Banking (Prudential Supervision) Act 1989.

434 This paragraph declares: "The Governor-General may, by Order in Council, on the advice of the Minister [that is] given in accordance with a recommendation of the Bank, make regulations for all[,] or any[,] of the following purposes: … (d) declaring any person or class of persons not to be an NBDT for the purposes of this Act [(i.e., the Non-Bank Deposit Takers Act 2013)], or declaring that, in certain specified circumstances, such a person or class of persons is not an NBDT for the purposes of this Act: … ." (Government of New Zealand (2022), "Non-bank Deposit Takers Act 2013, Public Act 2013 No 104," adopted on December 3, 2013, entered into force on May 1, 2014, consolidated to July 1, 2022, s.73(1)(d)). The second sentence of fn 429 defines the term '*Minister*'. The third sentence of fn 429 defines the term '*Bank*'.

A person is a *related party* of an NBDT, if this person is a director[435] or senior officer[436], a relative[437] of a director or senior officer, or a subsidiary[438], of the NBDT or of any of its

---

[435] Within the Non-Bank Deposit Takers Act 2013 – unless the context requires otherwise, the word '*director*' "means – (a) a person occupying a position of director by whatever name called; or (b) in the case of an entity that does not have directors as such, any trustee, manager, or other person who acts in relation to that entity in the same or similar fashion as a director would act[,] were that entity a company incorporated in New Zealand under the Companies Act 1993" (Government of New Zealand (2022), "Non-bank Deposit Takers Act 2013, Public Act 2013 No 104," adopted on December 3, 2013, entered into force on May 1, 2014, consolidated to July 1, 2022, s.4(1)).

[436] Within the Non-Bank Deposit Takers Act 2013 – unless the context requires otherwise, the phrase '*senior officer*', regarding an NBDT, "(a) means a person occupying a position that allows the person to exercise significant influence over the management or administration of the NBDT (for example, a chief executive or a chief financial officer); and (b) includes any class or classes of persons declared by regulations to be senior officers for the purposes of this Act; but (c) does not include any class or classes of persons declared by regulations not to be senior officers for the purposes of this Act" (Government of New Zealand (2022), "Non-bank Deposit Takers Act 2013, Public Act 2013 No 104," adopted on December 3, 2013, entered into force on May 1, 2014, consolidated to July 1, 2022, s.4(1)). Within the Non-Bank Deposit Takers Act 2013 – unless the context requires otherwise, the word '*regulations*' means regulations that are made under the Non-Bank Deposit Takers Act 2013 (Government of New Zealand (2022), "Non-bank Deposit Takers Act 2013, Public Act 2013 No 104," adopted on December 3, 2013, entered into force on May 1, 2014, consolidated to July 1, 2022, s.4(1)).

[437] Within the Non-Bank Deposit Takers Act 2013 – unless the context requires otherwise, the word '*relative*' "in relation to any person, means – (a) the person's spouse, civil union partner, or *de facto* partner; or (b) any parent, step-parent, brother, sister, child, or stepchild of the person; or (c) any parent, step-parent, brother, sister, child, or stepchild of the person's spouse, civil union partner, or *de facto* partner" (Government of New Zealand (2022), "Non-bank Deposit Takers Act 2013, Public Act 2013 No 104," adopted on December 3, 2013, entered into force on May 1, 2014, consolidated to July 1, 2022, s.4(1); emphasis added).

[438] Within the Non-Bank Deposit Takers Act 2013 – unless the context requires otherwise, the word '*subsidiary*' "means – (a) a subsidiary within the meaning of sections 5 to 8 of the Companies Act 1993; or (b) a company, or body corporate, or association of persons that is classified as a subsidiary in any applicable financial reporting standard (as that term is defined in section 5(1) of the Financial Reporting Act 2013)" (Government of New Zealand (2022), "Non-bank Deposit Takers Act 2013, Public Act 2013 No 104," adopted on December 3, 2013, entered into force on May 1, 2014, consolidated to July 1, 2022, s.4(1)). The relevant provisions of the Companies Act 1993 read as follows: "**5 Meaning of** ... **subsidiary** (1) For the purposes of this Act, a company is a **subsidiary** of another company[,] if, but only if, – (a) that other company – (i) controls the composition of the board of the company; or (ii) is in a position to exercise, or control the exercise of, more than one-half [of] the maximum number of votes that can be exercised at a meeting of the company; or (iii) holds more than one-half of the issued shares of the company, other than shares that carry no right to participate beyond a specified amount in a distribution of either profits or capital; or (iv) is entitled to receive more than one-half of every dividend [that is] paid on shares [which are] issued by the company, other than shares that carry no right to participate beyond a specified amount in a distribution of either profits or capital; or (b) the company is a subsidiary of a company that is that other company's subsidiary. ... **7 Control defined** For the purposes of section 5 [of the Companies Act 1993], without limiting the circumstances in which the composition of a company's board is to be taken to be controlled by another company, the composition of the board is to be taken to be so controlled[,] if the other company, by exercising a power [that is] exercisable (whether with or without the consent or concurrence of any other person) by it, can appoint or remove all the directors of the company, or such number of directors as together hold a majority of the voting rights at meetings of the board of the company, and[,] for this purpose, the other company is to be taken as having power to make such an appointment[,] if – (a) a person cannot be appointed as a director of a company without the exercise by the other company of such a power in the person's favour; or (b) a person's appointment as a director of the company follows necessarily from the person being a director or other officer of the other company. **8 Certain matters to be disregarded** In determining whether a company is a subsidiary of another company, – (a) shares [that are] held[,] or a power [which is] exercisable[,] by that other company in a fiduciary capacity[,] are not to be treated as held or exercisable by it: (b) subject to paragraphs (c) and (d), shares [that are] held or a power [which is] exercisable – (i) by a person as a nominee for that other company, except where that other company is concerned only in a fiduciary capacity; or (ii) by, or by a nominee for, a subsidiary of that other company, not being a subsidiary which is concerned only in a fiduciary capacity, – are to be treated as held or exercisable by that other company: (c) shares [that are] held[,] or a power [which is] exercisable[,] by a person under the provisions of debentures of the company[,] or of a trust deed for securing an issue of debentures[,] shall be disregarded: (d) shares [that are] held or a power [which is] exercisable by, or by a nominee for, that other company or its subsidiary (not being held or exercisable in the manner described in paragraph (c)[,]) are not to be treated as

guaranteeing subsidiaries[439] [647], has a substantial interest[440] in the NBDT or in any of its guaranteeing subsidiaries [648], is a person in which the NBDT – or any of its guaranteeing subsidiaries – has a substantial interest [649], or is a person – or a member of a class of persons – that regulations[441] declare to be a related party [650], or another person with a substantial interest in the NBDT or any of its guaranteeing subsidiaries has a substantial interest in the person [651], or at least 40% of the person's governing body are the same persons as 40% or more of the governing body of the NBDT or any of its guaranteeing subsidiaries, or of the governing body of another person with a substantial interest[442] in the NBDT or any of its guaranteeing subsidiaries [652].

The RBNZ's role under the Non-Bank Deposit Takers Act 2013

The role of the RBNZ under the Non-Bank Deposit Takers Act 2013 is to act as the licensing authority and the prudential regulator for NBDTs, and to discharge any other functions that are introduced by, or under, this Act[443] [653].

---

held or exercisable by that other company[,] if – (i) the ordinary business of that other company or its subsidiary, as the case may be, includes the lending of money; and (ii) the shares are held[,] or the power is exercisable[,] by way of security only for the purposes of a transaction entered into in the ordinary course of that business." (Government of New Zealand (2022), "Companies Act 1993, Public Act 1993 No 105," adopted on September 28, 1993, entered into force on July 1, 1994, consolidated to July 1, 2022, ss.5(1), 7 and 8; emphasis original). Regarding the definition of the term '*financial reporting standard*' within the Financial Reporting Act 2013, the following provisions of that Act are relevant: "**5 Interpretation** (1) In this Act, unless the context otherwise requires, – … **financial reporting standard** means a financial reporting standard [which is] issued by the Board under section 12 [of the Financial Reporting Act 2013]; and includes an amendment to a financial reporting standard that is issued by the Board … . … **12 Functions of Board** The Board has the following functions: (a) to prepare and, if it thinks fit, issue financial reporting standards for the purposes of any enactment that requires – (i) financial statements or group financial statements to comply, or be prepared in accordance, with generally accepted accounting practice or non-GAAP standards; or (ii) a statement, report, or other information[,] to comply, or be prepared in accordance, with financial reporting standards: … ." (Government of New Zealand (2022), "Financial Reporting Act 2013, Public Act 2013 No 101," adopted on December 3, 2013, entered into force on April 1, 2014, consolidated to January 1, 2022, ss.5(1) and 12(a); emphasis original).

439 Within the Non-Bank Deposit Takers Act 2013 – unless the context requires otherwise, the phrase '*guaranteeing subsidiary*' "in relation to an NBDT, means a subsidiary of the NBDT that – (a) is unconditionally liable (whether or not jointly or severally with the NBDT or any other person) to repay all the debt securities issued by the NBDT; or (b) is liable to repay all the debt securities issued by the NBDT[,] subject only to the condition that the NBDT or any other person has failed to do so" (Government of New Zealand (2022), "Non-bank Deposit Takers Act 2013, Public Act 2013 No 104," adopted on December 3, 2013, entered into force on May 1, 2014, consolidated to July 1, 2022, s.4(1)). The first paragraph of the present subsection (i.e., that titled 'Non-Bank Deposit Taker and Related Party – Defined'), defines the abbreviation '*NBDT*' – which stands for the term '*non-bank deposit taker*' (fn 427).

440 In section 6 of the Non-Bank Deposit Takers Act 2013 (the current footnote (i.e., fn 440) and the text to fns 435-442), "a person (**person B**) has a **substantial interest** in an entity[,] if – (a) person B has control, directly or indirectly, or a significant influence over 25% or more of the composition[,] of the governing body of the entity; or (b) where the entity is a company, – (i) person B owns, or in any way has the power to control, directly or indirectly, or has the right to acquire, 10% or more of the ordinary shares or the voting rights of the entity; or (ii) person B has, by any other means, 10% or more of the control of the entity; or (c) where the entity is not a company, – (i) person B is in a position to control, directly or indirectly, 10% or more of the voting rights in relation to the entity; or (ii) person B has, by any other means, 10% or more of the control of the entity" (Government of New Zealand (2022), "Non-bank Deposit Takers Act 2013, Public Act 2013 No 104," adopted on December 3, 2013, entered into force on May 1, 2014, consolidated to July 1, 2022, s.6(2); emphasis original).

441 The second sentence of fn 436 defines the term '*regulations*'.

442 Fn 440 defines the term '*substantial interest*'.

443 The RBNZ must take the following principles into account, whilst exercising its powers and performing its functions under the Non-Bank Deposit Takers Act 2013 – "(a) the desirability of consistency in the treatment of

Licensing of NBDTs

Each NBDT is to be licensed[444] [654]. Any person may apply to the RBNZ to be licensed as an NBDT [655]. Every application for an NBDT licence must be in a form that the RBNZ specifies [656], include any stipulated application fee [657], and be accompanied by a suitablity notice[445]

similar institutions, regardless of matters such as their corporate form: (b) the importance of recognising – (i) that it is not the purpose of this Act to eliminate all risk in relation to the performance of NBDTs or to limit diversity among NBDTs; and (ii) that depositors are responsible for assessing risk in relation to potential investments and for their own investment choices: (c) the desirability of providing to depositors adequate information to enable them to assess risk in relation to potential investments[,] and to distinguish between high-risk and low-risk NBDTs: (d) the desirability of sound governance of NBDTs: (e) the desirability of effective risk management by NBDTs: (f) the need to avoid unnecessary compliance costs: (g) the need to maintain competition within the NBDT sector" (Government of New Zealand (2022), "Non-bank Deposit Takers Act 2013, Public Act 2013 No 104," adopted on December 3, 2013, entered into force on May 1, 2014, consolidated to July 1, 2022, s.8). The first paragraph of the subsection entitled 'Non-Bank Deposit Taker and Related Party – Defined', above in the present section (i.e., that titled 'Non-Bank Deposit Takers Act 2013'), defines the abbreviation '*NBDT*' – which stands for the term '*non-bank deposit taker*' (fn 427).

[444] A person that is an NBDT but not a licensed NBDT commits an offence, and is liable to a level 4 penalty on conviction (Government of New Zealand (2022), "Non-bank Deposit Takers Act 2013, Public Act 2013 No 104," adopted on December 3, 2013, entered into force on May 1, 2014, consolidated to July 1, 2022, s.11(2)). A level 4 penalty is, for an individual – imprisonment for no more than 18 months, a fine not exceeding NZD 200,000, or both, and, in any other case – a fine of no more than NZD 2 million (Government of New Zealand (2022), "Non-bank Deposit Takers Act 2013, Public Act 2013 No 104," adopted on December 3, 2013, entered into force on May 1, 2014, consolidated to July 1, 2022, s.64(1)). A person that is not an NBDT must not claim to be NBDT, and a person that is not a licensed NBDT must not profess to be a licensed NBDT; both are offences attracting a level 4 penalty (Government of New Zealand (2022), "Non-bank Deposit Takers Act 2013, Public Act 2013 No 104," adopted on December 3, 2013, entered into force on May 1, 2014, consolidated to July 1, 2022, s.12). The first paragraph of the subsection entitled 'Non-Bank Deposit Taker and Related Party – Defined', above in the current section (i.e., that titled 'Non-Bank Deposit Takers Act 2013'), defines the abbreviation '*NBDT*' – which stands for the term '*non-bank deposit taker*' (fn 427).

[445] Within the Non-Bank Deposit Takers Act 2013 – unless the context requires otherwise, a '*suitability notice*' "is a notice, in relation to a director or senior officer, or proposed director or senior officer, of an NBDT or proposed NBDT, that is supplied to the Bank and meets the requirements of section 15 [of the Non-Bank Deposit Takers Act 2013" (Government of New Zealand (2022), "Non-bank Deposit Takers Act 2013, Public Act 2013 No 104," adopted on December 3, 2013, entered into force on May 1, 2014, consolidated to July 1, 2022, s.4(1)). Fn 435 defines the term '*director*'. The first sentence of fn 436 defines the term '*senior officer*'. The first paragraph of the subsection entitled 'Non-Bank Deposit Taker and Related Party – Defined', above in the present section (i.e., that titled 'Non-Bank Deposit Takers Act 2013'), defines the abbreviation '*NBDT*' – which stands for the term '*non-bank deposit taker*' (fn 427). The third sentence of fn 429 defines the term '*Bank*'. Subsections 15(1)-(3) of the Non-Bank Deposit Takers Act 2013 lay down the following requirements for a suitability notice: "(1) A **suitability notice** must certify that a named director or senior officer, or proposed director or senior officer, of an NBDT – (a) does not raise any suitability concerns; or (b) does raise 1 or more suitability concerns. (2) If a suitability notice states that the person named in it raises 1 or more suitability concerns, [then] then notice must also – (a) identify the relevant suitability concern or concerns; and (b) include any other information [that is] required by the Bank to be included in such notices. (3) Every suitability notice must be signed, – (a) if the person named is a director or proposed director of the NBDT, by the person himself or herself; and (b) if the person named is a senior officer or proposed senior officer of the NBDT, by 2 directors of the NBDT." (Government of New Zealand (2022), "Non-bank Deposit Takers Act 2013, Public Act 2013 No 104," adopted on December 3, 2013, entered into force on May 1, 2014, consolidated to July 1, 2022, s.15(1)-(3); emphasis original). The phrase '*suitability concerns*' "means the matters, circumstances, or conditions, [which are] identified in regulations, that must be drawn to the attention of the Bank[,] if any 1 or more of them apply to a director or senior officer, or proposed director or senior officer, of an NBDT or proposed NBDT" (Government of New Zealand (2022), "Non-bank Deposit Takers Act 2013, Public Act 2013 No 104," adopted on December 3, 2013, entered into force on May 1, 2014, consolidated to July 1, 2022, s.4(1)). The second sentence of fn 436 defines the term '*regulations*'.

for each director[446] and senior officer[447] – or proposed director or senior officer – of the applicant [658].

The RBNZ must not grant a licence to an applicant, unless it is satisfied that[448] the latter would be able to continuously abide by the Non-Bank Deposit Takers Act 2013, the regulations[449], and any proposed conditions of its licence [659], and the RBNZ has received a suitability notice[450] for each director and senior officer, or proposed director or senior officer, of the applicant – and has issued a notice of non-objection regarding any of these individuals who brings up suitability concerns[451] [660]. In deciding upon whether or not to award a licence to the applicant, the RBNZ must take into account the following matters: whether the applicant has suitable ownership and an appropriate structure, given the size and nature of its business or proposed business – or any part of either of these [661], whether the applicant will be able to continuously observe all pertinent requirements of the Financial Markets Conduct Act 2013, the Anti-Money Laundering and Countering Financing of Terrorism Act 2009, the Securities Act 1978, and any relevant regulations that are made under these Acts [662], whether any other businesses or activities which the applicant undertakes, or proposes to carry on, are consonant with its possible role as an NBDT [663], whether – if the applicant is an overseas person[452] – the law and regulatory requirements of its home jurisdiction are satisfactory concerning prudential supervision, the powers and duties of directors, the disclosure of information, and the registration, authorisation or licensing of the applicant [664], and any other issues that regulations[453] identify as matters which the RBNZ is to consider [665].

If the RBNZ grants a licence to an applicant, then it must give the latter written notice of its decision, and record the bestowal of the licence in the register of NBDTs – which is kept under section 85 of the Non-Bank Deposit Takers Act 2013[454] [666]. If the RBNZ refuses to

---

[446] Fn 435 defines the term '*director*'.

[447] The first sentence of fn 436 defines the term '*senior officer*'.

[448] The RBNZ may also refuse to grant a licence to the applicant on grounds other than these (Government of New Zealand (2022), "Non-bank Deposit Takers Act 2013, Public Act 2013 No 104," adopted on December 3, 2013, entered into force on May 1, 2014, consolidated to July 1, 2022, s.14(3)).

[449] The second sentence of fn 436 defines the term '*regulations*'.

[450] Fn 445 defines the term '*suitability notice*'.

[451] The penultimate sentence of fn 445 defines the term '*suitability concerns*'.

[452] Within the Non-Bank Deposit Takers Act 2013 – unless the context requires otherwise, the phrase '*overseas person*' "means – (a) a body corporate [which is] incorporated outside New Zealand; or (b) an unincorporated body that has its head office or principal place of business outside New Zealand" (Government of New Zealand (2022), "Non-bank Deposit Takers Act 2013, Public Act 2013 No 104," adopted on December 3, 2013, entered into force on May 1, 2014, consolidated to July 1, 2022, s.4(1)).

[453] The second sentence of fn 436 defines the term '*regulations*'.

[454] This section of the Non-Bank Deposit Takers Act 2013 is entitled 'Register of licensed NBDTs', and reads: "(1) The Bank must keep a public register of licensed NBDTs. (2) The Bank must determine the form of the register[,] and may amend the form from time to time as it considers necessary. (3) The register must include – (a) the name of each licensed NBDT; and (b) the current rate of creditworthiness of each licensed NBDT or its borrowing group under section 23 [of the Non-Bank Deposit Takers Act 2013] (unless the NBDT is not required to have such a rating); and (c) and other prescribed information. (4) The Bank must take all reasonable steps to ensure that the information contained in the public register is available to members of the public at all reasonable times." (Government of New Zealand (2022), "Non-bank Deposit Takers Act 2013, Public Act 2013 No 104," adopted on December 3, 2013, entered into force on May 1, 2014, consolidated to July 1, 2022, s.85). The third sentence of fn 429 defines the term '*Bank*'. The first paragraph of the subsection titled 'Non-Bank Deposit Taker and Related Party – Defined', above in the present section (i.e., that entitled 'Non-Bank Deposit Takers Act 2013'), defines the abbreviation '*NBDT*' – which stands for the term '*non-bank deposit taker*' (fn 427). The first sentence of fn 463 defines the term '*borrowing group*'. The text to fns 462-464 lays down subsection 23(1) of the Non-Bank Deposit Takers Act 2013. The first sentence of fn 464 comprises subsection 23(2) of the Non-Bank Deposit Takers Act 2013.

accord a licence, then it must provide written notice to the applicant, together with a statement of its reasons for this refusal [667].

The RBNZ may impose conditions on an NBDT licence at the time that it is granted, and may introduce, amend or delete NBDT licence conditions in concurrence with section 20 of the Non-Bank Deposit Takers Act 2013[455], at any moment after the licence is conferred upon the applicant [668]. Each licensed NBDT must act in accordance with the conditions of its licence[456] [669].

The RBNZ may cancel an NBDT licence, if it is satisfied that: (i) the licence was provided on the basis of information which was misleading or false in a material respect [670], (ii) the licensee has breached the Non-Bank Deposit Takers Act 2013, the regulations[457], pertinent provisions of the Financial Markets Conduct Act 2013, the Anti-Money Laundering and Countering Financing of Terrorism Act 2009, the Securities Act 1978, or regulations made under these Acts [671], (iii) the licensee has contravened at least one condition of its licence [672], (iv) the requirements of section 25 of the Non-Bank Deposit Takers Act 2013[458] are not being fulfilled [673], (v) the licensee is no longer an NBDT [674], (vi) the licensee has ceased

---

[455] This section of the Non-Bank Deposit Takers Act 2013 is titled 'Changing or removing conditions', and specifies: "The Bank may not impose new or additional conditions on, or amend or remove the existing conditions of, an NBDT's licence[,] unless – (a) the Bank gives the NBDT not less than 7 working days' notice in writing of the Bank's intention to do so; and (b) the notice contains, or is accompanied by, a statement of the Bank's reasons for its proposed action; and (c) the NBDT has a reasonable opportunity to make submissions to the Bank; and (d) the Bank has regard to those submissions." (Government of New Zealand (2022), "Non-bank Deposit Takers Act 2013, Public Act 2013 No 104," adopted on December 3, 2013, entered into force on May 1, 2014, consolidated to July 1, 2022, s.20). The third sentence of fn 429 defines the term '*Bank*'. The first paragraph of the subsection entitled 'Non-Bank Deposit Taker and Related Party – Defined', above in the current section (i.e., that titled 'Non-Bank Deposit Takers Act 2013'), defines the abbreviation '*NBDT*' – which stands for the term '*non-bank deposit taker*' (fn 427).

[456] If a licensed NBDT infracts a condition of its licence, then it commits an offence and is liable – on conviction for this transgression – to a level 3 penalty (Government of New Zealand (2022), "Non-bank Deposit Takers Act 2013, Public Act 2013 No 104," adopted on December 3, 2013, entered into force on May 1, 2014, consolidated to July 1, 2022, s.18(4)). The first paragraph of the subsection entitled 'Non-Bank Deposit Taker and Related Party – Defined', above in the present section (i.e., that titled 'Non-Bank Deposit Takers Act 2013'), defines the abbreviation '*NBDT*' – which stands for the term '*non-bank deposit taker*' (fn 427). For an individual, a level 3 penalty for conviction of an offence against the Non-Bank Deposit Takers Act 2013 is imprisonment for a term of no more than 12 months, a fine not exceeding NZD 100,000, or both (Government of New Zealand (2022), "Non-bank Deposit Takers Act 2013, Public Act 2013 No 104," adopted on December 3, 2013, entered into force on May 1, 2014, consolidated to July 1, 2022, s.64(2)(a)). In any other case, such a penalty is a fine of no more than NZD 1 million (Government of New Zealand (2022), "Non-bank Deposit Takers Act 2013, Public Act 2013 No 104," adopted on December 3, 2013, entered into force on May 1, 2014, consolidated to July 1, 2022, s.64(2)(b)).

[457] The second sentence of fn 436 defines the term '*regulations*'.

[458] This section of the Non-Bank Deposit Takers Act 2013 is entitled ' Requirements for independent directors', and states: "(1) If a licensed NBDT is a company, building society, or overseas company, – (a) the governing body of the NBDT must include at least 2 independent directors; and (b) the chairperson of the governing body of the NBDT must not be an employee of either the licensed NBDT or a related party. (2) In subsection (1), **independent director** means a director who – (a) is not an employee of either the NBDT or a related party; and (b) is not a director of a related party[,] other than a related party that is a guaranteeing subsidiary; and (c) does not, directly or indirectly, have a qualifying interest in more than 10% of the voting securities of the NBDT or a related party. (3) A licensed NBDT that breaches this section commits an offence[,] and is liable on conviction to a level 3 penalty." (Government of New Zealand (2022), "Non-bank Deposit Takers Act 2013, Public Act 2013 No 104," adopted on December 3, 2013, entered into force on May 1, 2014, consolidated to July 1, 2022, s.25; emphasis original). The first paragraph of the subsection entitled 'Non-Bank Deposit Taker and Related Party – Defined', above in the current section (i.e., that titled 'Non-Bank Deposit Takers Act 2013'), defines the abbreviation '*NBDT*' – which stands for the term '*non-bank deposit taker*' (fn 427). Fn 435 defines the term '*director*'. The text to fns 435-442 defines the term '*related party*'. The first sentence of fn 439 defines the term '*guaranteeing subsidiary*'. The penultimate and final sentences of fn 456 describe a level 3 penalty.

to exist [675], (vii) the licensee has infringed the terms of a trust deed concerning an issue or offer of debt securities[459] [676], (viii) the licensee has requested cancellation of the licence, and the RBNZ is satisfied that the licensee no longer needs an NBDT licence [677], or (ix) any other issue that regulations[460] prescribe as a ground upon which the NBDT may cancel a licence, applies [678]. Section 22 of the Non-Bank Deposit Takers Act 2013 sets out the procedure for cancelling an NBDT licence[461].

Prudential Regulation of NBDTs

A licensed NBDT must hold a present rating of its creditworthiness, or – if regulations made under section 24 of the Non-Bank Deposit Takers Act 2013[462] require – have a current rating

---

459 Within the Non-Bank Deposit Takers Act 2013 – unless the context requires otherwise, the phrase '*debt security*' "means – (a) a debt security within the meaning given in section 8 of the Financial Markets Conduct Act 2013; or (b) any other security declared by regulations to be a debt security for the purposes of this Act" (Government of New Zealand (2022), "Non-bank Deposit Takers Act 2013, Public Act 2013 No 104," adopted on December 3, 2013, entered into force on May 1, 2014, consolidated to July 1, 2022, s.4(1)). The meaning of the phrase '*debt security*' given in section 8 of the Financial Markets Conduct Act 2013, is "a right to be repaid money[,] or paid interest on money[,] that is, or is to be, deposited with, lent to, or otherwise owing by, any person" (Government of New Zealand (2022), "Financial Markets Conduct Act 2013, Public Act 2013 No 69," adopted on September 13, 2013, entered into force on April 1 and December 1, 2014, consolidated to July 1, 2022, s.8(1)(a)). The second sentence of fn 436 defines the term '*regulations*'.

460 The second sentence of fn 436 defines the term '*regulations*'.

461 This section of the Non-Bank Deposit Takers Act 2013 is titled 'Procedures for cancelling licence', and declares: "(1) Before cancelling a licence, the Bank must send notice to the licence holder and the trustee of its intention to cancel the licence, and the notice – (a) must explain the reasons for the proposed cancellation; and (b) must specify the date by which any objections by the licence holder to the cancellation must be received by the Bank (which must be not less than 10 working days after the date of the notice). (2) The Bank must have regard to any objections received. (3) If the Bank cancels a licence, [then] it must – (a) give written notice of the cancellation to the licence holder and the trustee; and (b) give public notice of the cancellation[,] by publishing notice of it – (i) in 1 or more daily newspapers circulating in each of the cities of Auckland, Hamilton, Wellington, Christchurch, and Dunedin; and (ii) on an Internet site maintained by[,] or on behalf of[,] the Bank." (Government of New Zealand (2022), "Non-bank Deposit Takers Act 2013, Public Act 2013 No 104," adopted on December 3, 2013, entered into force on May 1, 2014, consolidated to July 1, 2022, s.22). The third sentence of fn 429 defines the term '*Bank*'. Within the Non-Bank Deposit Takers Act 2013 – unless the context requires otherwise, the word '*trustee*' regarding an NBDT "means a licensed supervisor … who is designated or appointed … as the trustee for any debt security offered by[,] or on behalf of[,] the NBDT" (Government of New Zealand (2022), "Non-bank Deposit Takers Act 2013, Public Act 2013 No 104," adopted on December 3, 2013, entered into force on May 1, 2014, consolidated to July 1, 2022, s.4(1)). The first paragraph of the subsection entitled 'Non-Bank Deposit Taker and Related Party – Defined', above in the current section (i.e., that titled 'Non-Bank Deposit Takers Act 2013'), defines the abbreviation '*NBDT*' – which stands for the term '*non-bank deposit taker*' (fn 427). The first two sentences of fn 459 define the term '*debt security*'.

462 This section of the Non-Bank Deposit Takers Act 2013 is entitled 'Regulations relating to credit ratings', and reads: "(1) The Governor-General may, by Order in Council, on the advice of the Minister given in accordance with a recommendation of the Bank, make regulations for either or both of the following purposes: (a) providing for the following matters in relation to ratings of creditworthiness [that are] required to be held by licensed NBDTs: (i) the type of rating (for example, whether it is a short-term or a long-term rating): (ii) what the rating relates to (for example, whether it indicates the creditworthiness of an NBDT with respect to a specific financial obligation or applies to the NBDT's overall creditworthiness): (b) requiring a licensed NBDT to have a rating of creditworthiness of the borrowing group of which it is a part. (2) Regulations under this section are secondary legislation … ." (Government of New Zealand (2022), "Financial Markets Conduct Act 2013, Public Act 2013 No 69," adopted on September 13, 2013, entered into force on April 1 and December 1, 2014, consolidated to July 1, 2022, s.24). The second sentence of fn 429 defines the term '*Minister*'. The third sentence of fn 429 defines the term '*Bank*'. The first paragraph of the subsection titled 'Non-Bank Deposit Taker and Related Party – Defined', above in the present section (i.e., that entitled 'Non-Bank Deposit Takers Act 2013'), defines the

of the creditworthiness of its borrowing group[463], which observes the requirements that regulations made under section 24 of the Non-Bank Deposit Takers Act 2013 prescribe and is provided by an approved rating agency[464] [679]. Every licensed NBDT is to operate a risk management programme which abides by subsection 27(2) of the Non-Bank Deposit Takers Act 2013[465], and must take feasible steps to adhere to that programme [680].

---

abbreviation '*NBDT*' – which stands for the term '*non-bank deposit taker*' (fn 427). The first sentence of fn 463 defines the term '*borrowing group*'.

[463] Within the Non-Bank Deposit Takers Act 2013 – unless the context requires otherwise, the phrase '*borrowing group*' "in relation to an NBDT, means the NBDT and all its guaranteeing subsidiaries" (Government of New Zealand (2022), "Non-bank Deposit Takers Act 2013, Public Act 2013 No 104," adopted on December 3, 2013, entered into force on May 1, 2014, consolidated to July 1, 2022, s.4(1)). The first paragraph of the subsection titled 'Non-Bank Deposit Taker and Related Party – Defined', above in the current section (i.e., that entitled 'Non-Bank Deposit Takers Act 2013'), defines the abbreviation '*NBDT*' – which stands for the term '*non-bank deposit taker*' (fn 427). The first sentence of fn 439 defines the term '*guaranteeing subsidiary*'.

[464] A licensed NBDT that contravenes the present section (i.e., section 23) of the Non-Bank Deposit Takers Act 2013 commits an offence, and is liable – on conviction for this crime – to a level 4 penalty (Government of New Zealand (2022), "Non-bank Deposit Takers Act 2013, Public Act 2013 No 104," adopted on December 3, 2013, entered into force on May 1, 2014, consolidated to July 1, 2022, s.23(2)). The first paragraph of the subsection titled 'Non-Bank Deposit Taker and Related Party – Defined', above in the current section (i.e., that entitled 'Non-Bank Deposit Takers Act 2013'), defines the abbreviation '*NBDT*' – which stands for the term '*non-bank deposit taker*' (fn 427). The second sentence of fn 444 describes a level 4 penalty. Within the Non-Bank Deposit Takers Act 2013 – unless the context requires otherwise, the phrase '*approved rating agency*' "means a rating agency [that is] approved by the Bank under section 86 [of the Non-Bank Deposit Takers Act 2013]" (Government of New Zealand (2022), "Non-bank Deposit Takers Act 2013, Public Act 2013 No 104," adopted on December 3, 2013, entered into force on May 1, 2014, consolidated to July 1, 2022, s.4(1)). The third sentence of fn 429 defines the term '*Bank*'. Section 86 of the Non-Bank Deposit Takers Act 2013 is titled 'Rating agencies', and reads: "(1) The Bank may approve a person as a rating agency for the purposes of this Act. (2) In deciding whether to approve a person as a rating agency, the Bank must have regard to the following: (a) the independence of the rating agency: (b) the adequacy of resources available to the rating agency; (c) the credibility and objectivity of the rating agency's methodology: (d) the consistency and comparability of the rating agency's ratings when assessed against ratings industry practice: (e) the adequacy of the rating agency's disclosure of information, including information about its processes, experience, and ownership: (f) relevant international standards, codes, and recommended practices relating to the ratings industry. (3) The Bank may, at any time, review the approval of a person as a rating agency, and[,] in conducting the review[,] the Bank must have regard to matters in subsection (2). (4) If, after conducting the review, the Bank considers that the person should no longer be an approved rating agency, [then] it may revoke the approval. (5) On request by an approved rating agency, the Bank may revoke its approval, without the need for a prior review. (6) The Bank must publish[,] and keep up to date[,] a list of approved rating agencies on an Internet site, maintained by[,] or on behalf of[,] the Bank, that is publicly accessible at all reasonable times." (Government of New Zealand (2022), "Financial Markets Conduct Act 2013, Public Act 2013 No 69," adopted on September 13, 2013, entered into force on April 1 and December 1, 2014, consolidated to July 1, 2022, s.86).

[465] This subsection of the Non-Bank Deposit Takers Act 2013 specifies: "The risk management programme must – (a) be in writing; and (b) set out the procedures that the NBDT will use for effectively identifying and managing the following risks: (i) credit risk: (ii) liquidity risk: (iii) market risk: (iv) operational risk; and (c) set out appropriate documentation and record-keeping requirements; and (d) describe the steps that the NBDT will take to ensure that the programme remains current, which must include procedures for – (i) regular review of the programme to systematically identify deficiencies in the effectiveness of the programme; and (ii) obtaining trustee approval to amendments to the programme that are necessary to address such deficiencies; and (e) be appropriate to the operations of the NBDT, having regard to the factors [that are] relevant to the risks referred to in paragraph (b) (for example, the size of the NBDT, its funding structure, the market sector in which it operates, its business strategy, and its relationship with its borrowing group)." (Government of New Zealand (2022), "Non-bank Deposit Takers Act 2013, Public Act 2013 No 104," adopted on December 3, 2013, entered into force on May 1, 2014, consolidated to July 1, 2022, s.27(2)). The first paragraph of the subsection entitled 'Non-Bank Deposit Taker and Related Party – Defined', above in the present section (i.e., that titled 'Non-Bank Deposit Takers Act 2013'), defines the abbreviation '*NBDT*' – which stands for the term '*non-bank deposit taker*' (fn 427). The first sentence of fn 463 defines the term '*borrowing group*'. A licensed NBDT that violates section 27 of the Non-Bank Deposit Takers Act 2013 commits an offence, and is liable – on conviction for this transgression – to a level 3 penalty (Government of New Zealand (2022), "Non-bank Deposit Takers Act 2013, Public Act 2013 No 104," adopted on December 3, 2013, entered into force on May 1, 2014, consolidated to

By Order in Council, the Governor-General may – on the Minister's[466] advice given in conformity with a recommendation of the RBNZ – make regulations[467] for the purpose of introducing a requirement that licensed NBDTs and trustees[468] make sure that trust deeds specify the minimum capital which licensed NBDTs, borrowing groups[469], or both, are required to retain [681]. Regulations made under section 30 of the Non-Bank Deposit Takers Act 2013[470] may require trust deeds to lay down a minimum amount of capital that licensed NBDTs, borrowing groups, or both, are required to keep[471] [682]. Each licensed NBDT must maintain minimum capital of at least the amount, if any, which a trust deed prescribes in observance of regulations made under section 30 of the Non-Bank Deposit Takers Act 2013[472] [683].

By Order in Council, the Governor General may – on the Minister's[473] advice provided in adherence to a recommendation of the RBNZ – make regulations[474] in order to impose a requirement that licensed NBDTs and trustees[475] ensure that trust deeds stipulate a capital ratio which the NBDT must maintain[476] [684]. Every licensed NBDT must maintain a capital ratio

July 1, 2022, s.27(4)). The text to the current footnote (i.e., fn 465) sets out subsection 27(1) of the Non-Bank Deposit Takers Act 2013. The first sentence of the present footnote lays down subsection 27(2) of the Non-Bank Deposit Takers Act 2013. The penultimate and last sentences of fn 456 describe a level 3 penalty.

466 The second sentence of fn 429 defines the term '*Minister*'.

467 The second sentence of fn 436 defines the term '*regulations*'.

468 The antepenultimate sentence of fn 461 defines the term '*trustee*'.

469 The first sentence of fn 463 defines the term '*borrowing group*'.

470 The text to fns 466-469 sets out subsection 30(1) of the Non-Bank Deposit Takers Act 2013. The text to fns 470 and 471 comprises subsection 30(2) of the Non-Bank Deposit Takers Act 2013. Fn 471 states subsection 30(3) of the Non-Bank Deposit Takers Act 2013.

471 Regulations made under section 30 of the Non-Bank Deposit Takers Act 2013 may also: "(a) provide that the amount of minimum capital [which is] specified in trust deeds must be not less than an amount [that is] prescribed in the regulations: (b) require that trust deeds define capital for the purpose of calculating the minimum capital required: (c) specify a definition of capital for that purpose" (Government of New Zealand (2022), "Non-bank Deposit Takers Act 2013, Public Act 2013 No 104," adopted on December 3, 2013, entered into force on May 1, 2014, consolidated to July 1, 2022, s.30(3)).

472 A licensed NBDT that infracts this section (i.e., section 32 of the Non-Bank Deposit Takers Act 2013) commits an offence, and is liable – on conviction for this crime – to a level 3 penalty (Government of New Zealand (2022), "Non-bank Deposit Takers Act 2013, Public Act 2013 No 104," adopted on December 3, 2013, entered into force on May 1, 2014, consolidated to July 1, 2022, s.32(2)). The first paragraph of the subsection entitled 'Non-Bank Deposit Taker and Related Party – Defined', above in the current section (i.e., that titled 'Non-Bank Deposit Takers Act 2013'), defines the abbreviation '*NBDT*' – which stands for the term '*non-bank deposit taker*' (fn 427). The penultimate and last sentences of fn 456 describe a level 3 penalty.

473 The second sentence of fn 429 defines the term '*Minister*'.

474 The second sentence of fn 436 defines the term '*regulations*'.

475 The antepenultimate sentence of fn 461 defines the term '*trustee*'.

476 Regulations made under this section (i.e., section 33 of the Non-Bank Deposit Takers Act 2013) may: "(a) provide for the capital ratio to be calculated in respect of either or both of the following: (i) the licensed NBDT: (ii) any borrowing group of which a licensed NBDT is part: (b) provide for the capital ratio to be set at a specified minimum for particular licensed NBDTs or classes of licensed NBDTs: (c) prescribe the framework in accordance with which the capital ratio must be calculated: [and/or] (d) provide for variation (whether as to content or otherwise) of the framework to apply to particular licensed NBDTs or classes of licensed NBDTs" (Government of New Zealand (2022), "Non-bank Deposit Takers Act 2013, Public Act 2013 No 104," adopted on December 3, 2013, entered into force on May 1, 2014, consolidated to July 1, 2022, s.33(2)). The first paragraph of the subsection entitled 'Non-Bank Deposit Taker and Related Party – Defined', above in the present section (i.e., that titled 'Non-Bank Deposit Takers Act 2013'), defines the abbreviation '*NBDT*' – which stands for the term '*non-bank deposit taker*' (fn 427). The first sentence of fn 463 defines the term '*borrowing group*'. Within the Non-Bank Deposit Takers Act 2013 – unless the context requires otherwise, the phrase '*capital ratio*' "in relation to an NBDT or borrowing group, means the level of capital in relation to the credit exposures and other risks of the NBDT or borrowing group" (Government of New Zealand (2022), "Non-bank Deposit Takers Act 2013, Public Act 2013 No 104," adopted on December 3, 2013, entered into force on May 1, 2014, consolidated to July 1, 2022, s.4(1)).

that regulations which are made under section 33 of the Non-Bank Deposit Takers Act 2013[477] require to be included in trust deeds[478] [685].

By Order in Council, the Governor General may – on the Minister's[479] advice given in line with a recommendation of the RBNZ – make regulations[480] for the purpose of bringing in a requirement that licensed NBDTs and trustees[481] make certain that trust deeds specify a maximum limit on exposures to related parties[482] [686]. A licensed NBDT must stay within any maximum limit on exposures to related parties which regulations that are made under section 36 of the Non-Bank Deposit Takers Act 2013[483] require to be placed in the trust deed[484] [687].

By Order in Council, the Governor-General may – on the Minister's[485] advice given in compliance with a recommendation of the RBNZ – make regulations[486] in order to institute a requirement that licensed NBDTs and trustees[487] must make sure that trust deeds include liquidity requirements[488] [688]. Each licensed NBDT must abide by the liquidity requirements

---

477 The text to fns 473-476 lays down subsection 33(1) of the Non-Bank Deposit Takers Act 2013. The first sentence of fn 476 comprises subsection 33(2) of the Non-Bank Deposit Takers Act 2013.

478 A licensed NBDT that contravenes this section (i.e., section 35 of the Non-Bank Deposit Takers Act 2013) commits an offence, and is liable – on conviction for this transgression – to a level 3 penalty (Government of New Zealand (2022), "Non-bank Deposit Takers Act 2013, Public Act 2013 No 104," adopted on December 3, 2013, entered into force on May 1, 2014, consolidated to July 1, 2022, s.35(2)). The first paragraph of the subsection entitled 'Non-Bank Deposit Taker and Related Party – Defined', above in the current section (i.e., that titled 'Non-Bank Deposit Takers Act 2013'), defines the abbreviation '*NBDT*' – which stands for the term '*non-bank deposit taker*' (fn 427). The penultimate and last sentences of fn 456 describe a level 3 penalty.

479 The second sentence of fn 429 defines the term '*Minister*'.

480 The second sentence of fn 436 defines the term '*regulations*'.

481 The antepenultimate sentence of fn 461 defines the term '*trustee*'.

482 Regulations made under this section (i.e., section 36 of the Non-Bank Deposit Takers Act 2013) may: "(a) provide that the maximum limit on exposures to related parties is relative to – (i) the capital of an individual licensed NBDT; or (ii) the capital of the borrowing group of which a licensed NBDT is part: (b) provide that the maximum limit on exposures to related parties applies in respect of exposures of individual licensed NBDTs or any borrowing group of which a licensed NBDT is part: (c) require every licensed NBDT and trustee to ensure that trust deeds include a specified maximum limit on exposures to related parties: [and/or] (d) require every licensed NBDT and trustee to ensure that trust deeds include a maximum limit on exposures to related parties that is fixed by agreement between the licensed NBDT and trustee ..." (Government of New Zealand (2022), "Non-bank Deposit Takers Act 2013, Public Act 2013 No 104," adopted on December 3, 2013, entered into force on May 1, 2014, consolidated to July 1, 2022, s.36(2)). The first paragraph of the subsection entitled 'Non-Bank Deposit Taker and Related Party – Defined', above in the present section (i.e., that titled 'Non-Bank Deposit Takers Act 2013'), defines the abbreviation '*NBDT*' – which stands for the term '*non-bank deposit taker*' (fn 427). The text to fns 435-442 defines the term '*related party*'. The first sentence of fn 463 defines the term '*borrowing group*'. The antepenultimate sentence of fn 461 defines the term '*trustee*'.

483 The text to fns 479-482 sets out subsection 36(1) of the Non-Bank Deposit Takers Act 2013. The first sentence of fn 482 consists of subsection 36(2) of the Non-Bank Deposit Takers Act 2013.

484 A licensed NBDT that infringes this section (i.e., section 38 of the Non-Bank Deposit Takers Act 2013) commits an offence, and is liable – on conviction for this crime – to a level 3 penalty (Government of New Zealand (2022), "Non-bank Deposit Takers Act 2013, Public Act 2013 No 104," adopted on December 3, 2013, entered into force on May 1, 2014, consolidated to July 1, 2022, s.38(2)). The first paragraph of the subsection entitled 'Non-Bank Deposit Taker and Related Party – Defined', above in the current section (i.e., that titled 'Non-Bank Deposit Takers Act 2013'), defines the abbreviation '*NBDT*' – which stands for the term '*non-bank deposit taker*' (fn 427). The penultimate and final sentences of fn 456 describe a level 3 penalty.

485 The second sentence of fn 429 defines the term '*Minister*'.

486 The second sentence of fn 436 defines the term '*regulations*'.

487 The antepenultimate sentence of fn 461 defines the term '*trustee*'.

488 Regulations made under this section (i.e., section 39 of the Non-Bank Deposit Takers Act 2013) may – "in relation to the liquidity requirements to be included in trust deeds, prescribe 1 or more of the following: (a) assets that qualify as liquid assets for the purposes of the regulations: (b) minimum amounts of liquid assets relative to liabilities that must be maintained by licensed NBDTs: (c) requirements concerning matching maturity of assets and liabilities: (d) requirements in respect of a licensed NBDT that require the liquidity of the borrowing group of which it is a part to be taken into account: (e) other measures relating to liquidity management, including the

which regulations made under section 39 of the Non-Bank Deposit Takers Act 2013[489] call to be included in the trust deed[490] [689].

Monitoring and Enforcement

By written notice[491] to a licensed NBDT, the RBNZ may require the NBDT to furnish it with any data, information or forecasts concerning issues that relate to the management, business, or functioning of the NBDT or its guaranteeing subsidiaries[492] [690]. For the purpose of inquiring into whether a licensed NBDT is acting in accordance with the Non-Bank Deposit Takers Act 2013 or the regulations[493], the RBNZ may, by notice to the NBDT or any associated

management of stress situations" (Government of New Zealand (2022), "Non-bank Deposit Takers Act 2013, Public Act 2013 No 104," adopted on December 3, 2013, entered into force on May 1, 2014, consolidated to July 1, 2022, s.39(2)). The second sentence of fn 436 defines the term '*regulations*'. The first paragraph of the subsection entitled 'Non-Bank Deposit Taker and Related Party – Defined', above in the present section (i.e., that titled 'Non-Bank Deposit Takers Act 2013'), defines the abbreviation '*NBDT*' – which stands for the term '*non-bank deposit taker*' (fn 427). The first sentence of fn 463 defines the term '*borrowing group*'.

489 The text to fns 485-488 lays down subsection 39(1) of the Non-Bank Deposit Takers Act 2013. The first sentence of fn 488 comprises subsection 39(2) of the Non-Bank Deposit Takers Act 2013.

490 A licensed NBDT that breaches this section (i.e., section 41 of the Non-Bank Deposit Takers Act 2013) commits an offence, and is liable – on conviction for this transgression – to a level 3 penalty (Government of New Zealand (2022), "Non-bank Deposit Takers Act 2013, Public Act 2013 No 104," adopted on December 3, 2013, entered into force on May 1, 2014, consolidated to July 1, 2022, s.41(2)). The first paragraph of the subsection entitled 'Non-Bank Deposit Taker and Related Party – Defined', above in the current section (i.e., that titled 'Non-Bank Deposit Takers Act 2013'), defines the abbreviation '*NBDT*' – which stands for the term '*non-bank deposit taker*' (fn 427). The penultimate and final sentences of fn 456 describe a level 3 penalty.

491 This notice may require data, information or forecasts regarding any business that the NBDT or its guaranteeing subsidiaries conducts – whether in New Zealand or overseas (Government of New Zealand (2022), "Non-bank Deposit Takers Act 2013, Public Act 2013 No 104," adopted on December 3, 2013, entered into force on May 1, 2014, consolidated to July 1, 2022, s.47(2)). The notice may also require all or any of the data, information or forecasts to be consolidated, audited or reviewed by a person whom the RBNZ approves, related to specified periods, provided by a stated time or within a specified period, supplied in a stated form, and/or transmitted to a specified place (Government of New Zealand (2022), "Non-bank Deposit Takers Act 2013, Public Act 2013 No 104," adopted on December 3, 2013, entered into force on May 1, 2014, consolidated to July 1, 2022, s.47(3)). The first paragraph of the subsection entitled 'Non-Bank Deposit Taker and Related Party – Defined', above in the present section (i.e., that titled 'Non-Bank Deposit Takers Act 2013'), defines the abbreviation '*NBDT*' – which stands for the term '*non-bank deposit taker*' (fn 427). The first sentence of fn 439 defines the term '*guaranteeing subsidiary*'.

492 The first sentence of fn 439 defines the term '*guaranteeing subsidiary*'. A licensed NBDT that does not comply with a notice given under this section (i.e., section 47 of the Non-Bank Deposit Takers Act 2013) commits an offence, and is liable – on conviction for this crime – to a level 3 penalty (Government of New Zealand (2022), "Non-bank Deposit Takers Act 2013, Public Act 2013 No 104," adopted on December 3, 2013, entered into force on May 1, 2014, consolidated to July 1, 2022, s.47(4)). The text to fns 491 and 492 sets out subsection 47(1) of the Non-Bank Deposit Takers Act 2013. The first sentence of fn 491 states subsection 47(2) of the Non-Bank Deposit Takers Act 2013. The second sentence of fn 491 lays down subsection 47(3) of the Non-Bank Deposit Takers Act 2013. The requirements for data, information or requirements that section 47 of the Non-Bank Deposit Takers Act prescribes for a licensed NBDT also applies to an associated person of a licensed NBDT – as does the level 3 penalty for non-observance of a notice (Government of New Zealand (2022), "Non-bank Deposit Takers Act 2013, Public Act 2013 No 104," adopted on December 3, 2013, entered into force on May 1, 2014, consolidated to July 1, 2022, s.48). The first paragraph of the subsection entitled 'Non-Bank Deposit Taker and Related Party – Defined', above in the current section (i.e., that titled 'Non-Bank Deposit Takers Act 2013'), defines the abbreviation '*NBDT*' – which stands for the term '*non-bank deposit taker*' (fn 427). The penultimate and last sentences of fn 456 describe a level 3 penalty. The first sentence of fn 494 defines the term '*associated person*'.

493 The second sentence of fn 436 defines the term '*regulations*'.

person[494], require the NBDT or associated person to provide it (i.e., the RBNZ) with a report – or a series of reports – which an approved person[495] must prepare[496], on matters that concern the management, business or working of the NBDT or any associated person[497] [691].

The RBNZ may give a direction to a licensed NBDT of an associated person[498], if has reasonable grounds to believe that the NBDT or associated person is unable – or probably will be unable – to pay its due debts [692], the NBDT or associated person – or any director[499] or senior officer[500] of the NBDT or associated person – has not observed, is not respecting, or is likely not to follow, the Non-Bank Deposit Takers Act 2013 or the regulations[501], the Financial

---

[494] Within the Non-Bank Deposit Takers Act 2013 – unless the context requires otherwise, the phrase '*associated person*' "in relation to an NBDT, means – (a) a person that directly or indirectly controls the management of the NBDT; or (b) a person that has a direct or indirect qualifying interest in 20% of more of the voting securities issued by the NBDT; or (c) a person whose management is controlled, directly or indirectly, by the NBDT; or (d) a person in whose voting securities the NBDT has a direct or indirect qualifying interest of 20% or more" (Government of New Zealand (2022), "Non-bank Deposit Takers Act 2013, Public Act 2013 No 104," adopted on December 3, 2013, entered into force on May 1, 2014, consolidated to July 1, 2022, s.4(1)). Within the Non-Bank Deposit Takers Act 2013 – unless the context requires otherwise, the phrase '*qualifying interest*' "in relation to a security, means – (a) the legal or beneficial ownership of the security; or (b) the power to exercise, or control the exercise of, any voting rights attached to the security; or (c) the power to acquire [,] or dispose of[,] the security; or (d) the power to control the acquisition or disposition of the security by another person; or (e) the powers referred to in paragraphs (b) to (d) under, or by virtue of, any trust, agreement, arrangement, or understanding relating to the security" (Government of New Zealand (2022), "Non-bank Deposit Takers Act 2013, Public Act 2013 No 104," adopted on December 3, 2013, entered into force on May 1, 2014, consolidated to July 1, 2022, s.4(1)). The first paragraph of the subsection entitled 'Non-Bank Deposit Taker and Related Party – Defined', above in the present section (i.e., that titled 'Non-Bank Deposit Takers Act 2013'), defines the abbreviation '*NBDT*' – which stands for the term '*non-bank deposit taker*' (fn 427).

[495] In this section (i.e., section 49 of the Non-Bank Deposit Takers Act 2013), an '*approved person*' is "a person approved or appointed by the Bank for the purposes of this section" (Government of New Zealand (2022), "Non-bank Deposit Takers Act 2013, Public Act 2013 No 104," adopted on December 3, 2013, entered into force on May 1, 2014, consolidated to July 1, 2022, s.49(4)). The third sentence of fn 429 defines the term '*Bank*'.

[496] The NBDT or associated person must pay for the report(s) (Government of New Zealand (2022), "Non-bank Deposit Takers Act 2013, Public Act 2013 No 104," adopted on December 3, 2013, entered into force on May 1, 2014, consolidated to July 1, 2022, s.49(3)). The first paragraph of the subsection entitled 'Non-Bank Deposit Taker and Related Party – Defined', above in the current section (i.e., that titled 'Non-Bank Deposit Takers Act 2013'), defines the abbreviation '*NBDT*' – which stands for the term '*non-bank deposit taker*' (fn 427). The first sentence of fn 494 defines the term '*associated person*'.

[497] The NBDT or associated person is to furnish the approved person with access to its records, and must provide information regarding those records – if the approved person requests the NBDT or associated person to do this to aid the report (Government of New Zealand (2022), "Non-bank Deposit Takers Act 2013, Public Act 2013 No 104," adopted on December 3, 2013, entered into force on May 1, 2014, consolidated to July 1, 2022, s.49(2)). The first sentence of fn 495 defines the term '*approved person*'. The first paragraph of the subsection entitled 'Non-Bank Deposit Taker and Related Party – Defined', above in the present section (i.e., that titled 'Non-Bank Deposit Takers Act 2013'), defines the abbreviation '*NBDT*' – which stands for the term '*non-bank deposit taker*' (fn 427). The first sentence of fn 494 defines the term '*associated person*'. Failure to provide the abovementioned access and/or the aforementioned information, or to furnish the RBNZ with a report, is an offence: "A licensed NBDT or an associated person commits an offence, and is liable on conviction to a level 3 penalty, if it – (a) fails to supply a report to the Bank[,] if required to do so under this section; or (b) fails to provide access to its accounting and other records, or fails to provide information relating to those records, if requested to do so for the purposes of a report under this section." (Government of New Zealand (2022), "Non-bank Deposit Takers Act 2013, Public Act 2013 No 104," adopted on December 3, 2013, entered into force on May 1, 2014, consolidated to July 1, 2022, s.49(5)). The penultimate and final sentences of fn 456 describe a level 3 penalty. The third sentence of fn 429 defines the term '*Bank*'. 'This section' is section 49 of the Non-Bank Deposit Takers Act 2013, whose five subsections are spread between the text to fns 493-497, fn 495, fn 496, and the current footnote (i.e., fn 497).

[498] The first sentence of fn 494 defines the term '*associated person*'.

[499] Fn 435 defines the term '*director*'.

[500] The first sentence of fn 436 defines the term '*senior officer*'.

[501] The second sentence of fn 436 defines the term '*regulations*'.

Markets Conduct Act 2013 or regulations made under this Act, the Securities Act 1978 or regulations made under it, or any condition of the licence of the NBDT [693], and/or the circumstances of the NBDT or associated person are – or the way in which the affairs of the NBDT or the associated person are being managed is – detrimental to the solvency of the NBDT or its ability to abide by the abovementioned legislation, regulations and conditions [694]. A direction to an NBDT or associated person may require it to consult with the RBNZ about the former's circumstances or the methods of settling any difficulties facing it [695], take any specified action to attend to any of its problems [696], take – or refrain from taking – any stipulated measures to address its actual or potential failure to adhere to the abovementioned legislation, regulations and conditions [697], ensure that any of its employees ceases to participate in the management or conduct of its business – except with the RBNZ's permission and as far as this permission extends [698], suspend, or stop, operating any part of its business [699], conduct its business – or any part thereof – in conformity with the direction [700], and/or replace its auditor with one that the RBNZ appoints [701].

Every person to whom a direction is given must obey it [702]. A person commits an offence, and is liable – on conviction for this transgression – to a level 4 penalty[502], if that person does not follow a direction, or prevents, hinders or obstructs an NBDT, associated person[503] or trustee[504] from effecting it [703].

A licensed NBDT, associated person or trustee commits an offence, and is liable – on conviction for this crime – to a level 3 penalty[505], if this entity makes any application or statement, or furnishes any item, to the RBNZ, knowing that it is false or misleading in a significant respect [704] or, without reasonable justification, hinders or obstructs an authorised person in the exercise of any powers that the Non-Bank Deposit Takers Act 2013, or regulations[506], have conferred on that person [705]. Section 67 of the Non-Bank Deposit Takers Act 2013 supplies a defence to any of the offences that this Act specifies[507].

---

502 The second sentence of fn 444 describes a level 4 penalty. Section 57 of the Non-Bank Deposit Takers Act 2013 provides different rules – and subsection 59(3) of the Non-Bank Deposit Takers Act 2013 specifies a level 1 penalty for infraction of these – for trustees to whom the RBNZ gives a direction. A level 1 penalty for an offence against the Non-Bank Deposit Takers Act 2013 is a fine of no more than NZD 200,000 (Government of New Zealand (2022), "Non-bank Deposit Takers Act 2013, Public Act 2013 No 104," adopted on December 3, 2013, entered into force on May 1, 2014, consolidated to July 1, 2022, s.64(4)). The antepenultimate sentence of fn 461 defines the term '*trustee*'.

503 The first sentence of fn 494 defines the term '*associated person*'.

504 The antepenultimate sentence of fn 461 defines the term '*trustee*'.

505 The penultimate and last sentences of fn 456 describe a level 3 penalty.

506 The second sentence of fn 436 defines the term '*regulations*'.

507 This section of the Non-Bank Deposit Takers Act 2013 is titled 'Defence to charge under Act', and states: "(1) In any prosecution of a licensed NBDT, associated person, or trustee[,] or former licensed NBDT, associated person, or trustee (the **defendant**) for an offence under this Act, it is a defence[,] if the defendant proves that – (a) the contravention was due to the act or omission of another person, or some other cause beyond the defendant's control; and (b) the defendant took reasonable precautions and exercised due diligence to avoid the contravention. (2) For the purposes of subsection (1)(a), **another person** does not include a director, employee, or agent of the defendant. (3) A defendant is not, without the leave of the court, entitled as part of a defence [which is] provided by this section to rely on any of the matters [that are] specified in subsection (1)(a)[,] unless it has, not later than 7 working days before the date on which the hearing of the proceedings commences, served on the prosecution a notice in writing identifying the act, omission, or cause [that is being] relied on by the defendant." (Government of New Zealand (2022), "Non-bank Deposit Takers Act 2013, Public Act 2013 No 104," adopted on December 3, 2013, entered into force on May 1, 2014, consolidated to July 1, 2022, s.67; emphasis original). The first paragraph of the subsection titled 'Non-Bank Deposit Taker and Related Party – Defined', above in the present section (i.e., that entitled 'Non-Bank Deposit Takers Act 2013'), defines the abbreviation '*NBDT*' – which stands for the term '*non-bank deposit taker*' (fn 427). The first sentence of fn 494

If an NBDT or associated person[508] commits an offence under the Non-Bank Deposit Takers Act 2013, then each director[509] of the NBDT or associated person perpetrates the same transgression, and is liable to the penalty which applies to an individual for this crime – if it is proved that the act which constituted this offence occurred with the authority, permission or consent of the director [706], or that the director knew, or could reasonably be expected to have known, that the abovementioned transgression was to be or was being committed, and that (s)he did not take reasonable steps to prevent or halt it [707]. Such a director may be convicted of an offence as a result of the operation of this section of the Non-Bank Deposit Takers Act 2013[510], even though (s)he has not be charged with that crime [708].

Exemptions from the Non-Bank Deposit Takers Act 2013

The RBNZ may exempt any licensed NBDT, class of licensed NBDTs, or trustee[511] from being required to fulfil any provision(s) which it specifies, of the Non-Bank Deposit Takers Act 2013 or the regulations[512] [709]. The RBNZ may grant this exemption on any terms and conditions that it wishes [710], but subject to it being satisfied regarding three specified issues[513].

Comment

The Non-Deposit Takers Act 2013 provides a comprehensive licensing and prudential supervision regime for NBDTs, and is equipped with its own system of offences – which are set out therein, together with accompanying penalties. To the extent that this approach contributes to the forthcoming Deposit Takers Act[514], its quality signals that the new legislative regime is likely to benefit from an ordered start.

defines the term '*associated person*'. The antepenultimate sentence of fn 461 defines the term '*trustee*'. Fn 435 defines the term '*director*'.

[508] The first sentence of fn 494 defines the term '*associated person*'.

[509] Fn 435 defines the term '*director*'.

[510] 'This section of the Non-Bank Deposit Takers Act 2013 is section 68 of this Act, which is titled 'Liability of directors for offences of NBDTs and associated persons' and which the text to fns 508-510 sets out.

[511] The antepenultimate sentence of fn 461 defines the term '*trustee*'.

[512] The second sentence of fn 436 defines the term '*regulations*'.

[513] The RBNZ may only grant an exemption from one or more provisions of the Non-Bank Deposit Takers Act 2013 or the regulations, if "it is satisfied that – (a) the exemption will be consistent with the maintenance of a sound and efficient financial system; and (b) compliance with the relevant provision or provisions would, in the circumstances, require the licensed NBDT, class of licensed NBDTs, or trustee to comply with requirements that are unduly onerous or burdensome; and (c) the extent of the exemption is not broader than is reasonably necessary to address the matters that gave rise to the exemption." (Government of New Zealand (2022), "Non-bank Deposit Takers Act 2013, Public Act 2013 No 104," adopted on December 3, 2013, entered into force on May 1, 2014, consolidated to July 1, 2022, s.70(2)). The first paragraph of the subsection entitled 'Non-Bank Deposit Taker and Related Party – Defined', above in the current section (i.e., that titled 'Non-Bank Deposit Takers Act 2013'), defines the abbreviation '*NBDT*' – which stands for the term '*non-bank deposit taker*' (fn 427). The antepenultimate sentence of fn 461 defines the term '*trustee*'.

[514] The upcoming Deposit Takers Act is to combine the regulatory regime concerning deposits for banks and non-bank deposit takers (text to fn 335). Fn 337 furnishes information about the Deposit Takers Bill.

Conclusion

This chapter introduces the legal system of New Zealand. It presents relevant legislation, and then lays down pertinent provisions of three of these Acts, namely the Reserve Bank of New Zealand Act 2021, the Banking (Prudential Supervision) Act 1989 and the Non-Bank Deposit Takers Act 2013. The next chapter surveys the law of banking in the USA.

Chapter 4

United States of America

Abstract

The Constitution of the USA is the longest-surviving written charter of government in the world. It vests all legislative powers in a Congress – which comprises a Senate and a House of Representatives, executive power in a President, and judicial power in one Supreme Court and such inferior courts as the Congress may decree and establish. Whilst the USA is a common law jurisdiction, it includes statutes, codes and regulations at the federal, state and local levels. The Constitution, federal legislation, and treaties between the USA and foreign countries, comprise sources of federal law that overrule the legal effect of any contradictory provisions of state law. Lower courts are bound by the decisions that higher courts set. Once a federal district court has adjudicated a case, this may be appealed to the court of appeals for the federal circuit upon which the state in which the case was heard is allocated. The Supreme Court is at the top of the federal court system, and may hear appeals from the federal circuit courts of appeals, and from the highest state courts if the appeal involves the Constitution or federal law. Unlike appeals from a federal district court to a federal circuit court of appeals, the Supreme Court has a discretion as to whether or not to hear an appeal. The Supreme Court typically hears a case when there are conflicting decisions across the USA on a particular issue or when there is a glaring error in a case. In addition to its participation in the federal court system, each state of the USA has a hierarchy of state courts. The Office of the Comptroller of the Currency (OCC) charters and regulates national banks, federal savings associations, and federal branches and agencies of foreign banks. State bank regulatory agencies charter state banks, and state branches, agencies and representative offices of foreign banks. The Federal Reserve promotes the stability of the financial system and the safety and soundness of individual financial institutions, and monitors their impact on the financial system as a whole. The Federal Deposit Insurance Corporation (FDIC) is an independent agency that maintains public confidence in the financial system by insuring deposits, examining and overseeing financial institutions for consumer protection, safety and soundness, engaging with the resolution of large, complex financial institutions, and managing receiverships. The Securities and Exchange Commission (SEC) regulates banks as issuers of securities, and as participants in the securities industry. The Volcker Rule aims to safeguard customers of banks in the USA by preventing the latter from making certain kinds of speculative investments, and prohibits banks or insured depository institutions from securing or retaining ownership in private equity funds or hedge funds, unless a specified exemption applies. Title 12 (Banks and Banking) of the United States Code sets out rules that apply to Federal reserve banks and to national banks, which contribute to a comprehensive, stable framework for the operation of banks within the USA.

Keywords: bank, code, Comptroller, FDIC, federal, national, reserve, rule, state

Introduction

The first section below introduces the legal system of the USA. The second section is dedicated to the regulation of banks within the USA, covering therein the roles of the OCC, the Federal Reserve, the FDIC and the SEC. The third section considers the Volcker Rule. The penultimate section introduces elements of Title 12 of the United States Code, which is titled 'Banks and Banking'. The final section of the chapter concludes.

An Introduction to the Legal System of the USA

Essentials

The Constitution of the USA is the longest-surviving written charter of government in the world; it was written in 1787 and ratified in 1788, and has been in force since 1789 [711]. It vests all legislative powers in a Congress – which comprises a Senate and a House of Representatives [712], executive power in a President [713], and judical power in one Supreme Court and such inferior courts as the Congress may decree and establish [714]. Whilst the USA is a common law jurisdiction, it includes statutes, codes and regulations at the federal, state and local levels [715].

The Constitution of the USA[515]

Article 1 of the Constitution concerns the design of the legislative branch of the federal government of the USA, i.e., the Congress [716]. An abriged version is as follows.

> … The House of Representatives shall be composed of members chosen every second year by the people of the several states, and the electors in each state shall have the qualifications requisite for electors of the most numerous branch of the state legislature. No person shall be a Representative who shall not have attained to the age of twenty five years, and been seven years a citizen of the United States, and who shall not, when elected, be an inhabitant of that state in which he shall be chosen. *Representatives and direct Taxes shall be apportioned among the several States which may be included within this union, according to their respective Numbers* … . The House of Representatives shall choose their speaker and other officers; and shall have the sole power of impeachment. … The Senate of the United States shall be composed of two Senators from each state, *chosen by the legislature thereof*, for six years; and each Senator shall have one vote. … No person shall be a Senator who shall not have attained to the age of thirty years, and been nine years a citizen of the United States and who shall not, when elected, be an inhabitant of that state for which he

[515] The Federal Judicial Center of the USA encapsulates this country's constitutional arrangements, thus: "The U.S. Constitution establishes a federal system of government. The constitution gives specific powers to the federal (national) government. All power not delegated to the federal government remains with the states. Each of the 50 states has its own state constitution, governmental structure, legal codes, and judiciary." (Government of the United. States of America (2022), The U.S. Legal System: A Short Description (Washington, D.C.: Federal Judicial Center), 1).

> shall be chosen. The Vice President of the United States shall be President of the Senate, but shall have no vote, unless they be equally divided. ... The Senate shall have the sole power to try all impeachments. When sitting for that purpose, they shall be on oath or affirmation. When the President of the United States is tried, the Chief Justice shall preside: And no person shall be convicted without the concurrence of two thirds of the members present. Judgment in cases of impeachment shall not extend further than to removal from office, and disqualification to hold and enjoy any office of honor, trust or profit under the United States: but the party convicted shall nevertheless be liable and subject to indictment, trial, judgment and punishment, according to law. ... All bills for raising revenue shall originate in the House of Representatives; but the Senate may propose or concur with amendments[,] as on other [b]ills. Every bill which shall have passed the House of Representatives and the Senate, shall, before it become a law, be presented to the President of the United States; if he approve[, then] he shall sign it, but[,] if not[, then] he shall return it, with his objections[,] to that House in which it shall have originated, who shall enter the objections at large on their journal, and proceed to reconsider it. If after such reconsideration two thirds of that House shall agree to pass the bill, [then] it shall be sent, together with the objections, to the other House, by which it shall likewise be reconsidered, and if approved by two thirds of that House, [then] it shall be come a law. ... If any bill shall not be returned by the President within ten days (Sundays excepted) after it shall have been presented to him, [then] the same shall be a law, in like manner as if he had signed it, unless the Congress by their adjournment prevent its return, in which case it shall not be a law. Every order, resolution, or vote to which the concurrence of the Senate and House of Representatives may be necessary (except on a question of adjournment) shall be presented to the President of the United States; and before the same shall take effect, shall be approved by him, or being disapproved by him, shall be repassed by two thirds of the Senate and House of Representatives, according to the rules and limitations prescribed in the case of a bill. ... The Congress shall have power to lay and collect taxes, duties, imposts and excises, to pay the debts and provide for the common defense and general welfare of the United States; but all duties, imposts and excises shall be uniform throughout the United States; To borrow money on the credit of the United States; To regulate commerce with foreign nations ... ; To establish ... uniform laws on the subject of bankruptcies throughout the United States; To coin money, regulate the value thereof, and of foreign coin ... ; To provide for the punishment of counterfeiting the securities and current coin of the United States; ... To make all laws which shall be necessary and proper for carrying into execution the foregoing powers, and all other powers vested by this Constitution in the government of the United States, or in any department or officer thereof. ...[516] [717]

The above passage sets out the legislative procedure in the USA, and involves roles for the House of Representatives, the Senate and the President of the USA. It specifies some areas of financial activity over which the Congress has power to legislate. The resulting laws are federal legislation.

Article 2 of the Constitution addresses the scope of the executive branch of the federal government of the USA. In part, it reads thus.

---

[516] The italics for the clause '*Representatives and direct Taxes shall be apportioned among the several States which may be included within this union, according to their respective Numbers*', and for the phrase '*chosen by the legislature of*', are present in the original text.

> The executive power shall be vested in a President of the United States of America. He shall hold his office during the term of four years … . No person except a natural born citizen, or a citizen of the United States, at the time of the adoption of this Constitution, shall be eligible to the office of President; neither shall any person be eligible to that office who shall not have attained to the age of thirty five years, and been fourteen Years a resident within the United States. … The President shall be commander in chief of the Army and Navy of the United States, and of the militia of the several states, when called into the actual service of the United States; he may require the opinion, in writing, of the principal officer in each of the executive departments, upon any subject relating to the duties of their respective offices, and he shall have power to grant reprieves and pardons for offenses against the United States, except in cases of impeachment. He shall have power, by and with the advice and consent of the Senate, to make treaties, provided [that] two thirds of the Senators present concur; and he shall nominate, and[,] by and with the advice and consent of the Senate, shall appoint ambassadors, other public ministers and consuls, judges of the Supreme Court, and all other officers of the United States, whose appointments are not herein otherwise provided for, and which shall be established by law: but the Congress may by law vest the appointment of such inferior officers, as they think proper, in the President alone, in the courts of law, or in the heads of departments. … He shall[,] from time to time[,] give to the Congress information of the state of the union, and recommend to their consideration such measures as he shall judge necessary and expedient; he may, on extraordinary occasions, convene both Houses, or either of them, and[,] in case of disagreement between them, with respect to the time of adjournment, he may adjourn them to such time as he shall think proper; he shall receive ambassadors and other public ministers; he shall take care that the laws be faithfully executed, and shall commission all the officers of the United States. … [718]

Notable in the immediately-preceding passage is the President's power to make treaties with other countries, in co-operation with the Senate. And it is with advice and consent of the Senate that the President makes official appointments.

Article III of the Constitution regulates the judicial branch of the federal government of the USA. A condensed replication of this Article is as follows.

> The judicial power of the United States, shall be vested in one Supreme Court, and in such inferior courts as the Congress may from time to time ordain and establish. The judges, both of the supreme and inferior courts, shall hold their offices during good behaviour … . The judicial power shall extend to all cases, in law and equity, arising under this Constitution, the laws of the United States, and treaties made, or which shall be made, under their authority; – to all cases affecting ambassadors, other public ministers and consuls; – to all cases of admiralty and maritime jurisdiction; – to controversies to which the United States shall be a party; – to controversies between two or more states; – *between a state and citizens of another state*[517]; – between citizens of different states; – between citizens of the same state claiming lands under grants of different states, and between a state, or the citizens thereof, and foreign states, citizens or subjects. In all cases affecting ambassadors, other public ministers and consuls, and those in which a state shall be party, the Supreme Court shall have original jurisdiction. In all the other cases before mentioned, the Supreme Court shall have appellate jurisdiction, both as to law and fact, with such

[517] Emphasis original.

> exceptions, and under such regulations[,] as the Congress shall make. The trial of all crimes, except in the case of impeachment, shall be by jury; and such trial shall be held in the state where the said crimes shall have been committed; but[,] when not committed within any state, the trial shall be at such place or places as the Congress may[,] by law[,] have directed. ... Treason against the United States, shall consist only in levying war against them, or in adhering to their enemies, giving them aid and comfort. No person shall be convicted of treason[,] unless on the testimony of two witnesses to the same overt act, or on confession in open court. The Congress shall have power to declare the punishment of treason ... [719].

It is submitted that the account of the jurisdiction of the Supreme Court is remarkable for its detail in a constitutional document. It is opined that this attention to specifics demonstrates the remarkable foresight of the drafters of the Constitution. The first few Presidents of the USA, who were party to this document and to the American War of Independence which preceded it, were inspired thinkers – and their heritage has lasted.

Sources of Law

The second paragraph of Article VI of the Constitution of the USA states the following.

> This Constitution, and the laws of the United States which shall be made in pursuance thereof; and all treaties made, or which shall be made, under the authority of the United States, shall be the supreme law of the land; and the judges in every state shall be bound thereby, anything in the Constitution or laws of any State to the contrary notwithstanding [720].

These three sources of federal law overrule the legal effect of any contradictory provisions of state law – including any state rule or regulation and any county or city ordinance [721]. The following sources of law constitute the legal system of the USA: (i) the Constitution of the USA, (ii) federal legislation, (iii) treaties between the USA and foreign countries, (iv) federal judicial decisions interpreting federal law, state law, or – in some instances – international law, (v) the fifty state constitutions, (vi) state laws, (vii) state judicial decisions interpreting the Constitution of the USA, the laws of the fifty states or of the District of Columbia, or – in some cases – international law, and (viii) the common law of England – upon which the federal and state courts[518] must sometimes rely in order to ascertain whether certain rights that existed in England at the time at which the Constitution of the USA was adopted must also be recognized in the USA under federal law or state law [721].

---

518 Louisiana has a civil law system (Henegan, T., and Kimball, B. (2022), "Legal systems in the United States: overview," published October 1, 2022, accessed November 1, 2022, <https://uk.practicallaw.thomsonreuters.com/w-019-5918?transitionType=Default&contextData=(sc.Default)&firstPage=true>).

Courts

Lower courts are bound by the precedents that higher courts set [721]. In the federal court system of the USA, a district court is bound by the decision of the court of appeals from its circuit, and by the decisions of the Supreme Court of the USA [721].

There are 94 district courts throughout the USA – at least one district court is situated in each state [722]. These courts are the courts of first instance in the federal court system [722]. District judges sit individually to hear trials [722]. District court judges – of which there are more than 670 across the USA – are responsible for managing the court and overseeing its employees [723]. Federal magistrate judges undertake many duties under the general superintendence of district judges [722]. Federal magistrate judges may oversee some criminal cases, issue arrest warrants and search warrants, carry out initial hearings at criminal law, set bail, and determine certain motions – such as one to suppress evidence [723]. These judges may also manage a variety of matters in civil cases – for instance, pre-trial motions and discovery [723]. Each federal district has a bankruptcy court [723]. Furthermore, some courts have nationwide jurisdiction for issues such as taxation (i.e., the United States Tax Court), claims against the federal government of the USA (i.e., the United States Court of Federal Claims), and international trade (i.e., the United States Court of International Trade) [723].

Once a federal district court has adjudicated a case, this case may be appealed to the court of appeals for the federal circuit upon which the state in which the case was heard is allocated [723]. There are twelve federal circuits; the Fifth Circuit, for example, comprises the states of Louisiana, Mississippi and Texas [723]. Additionally, there is a Federal Circuit Court of Appeals, which has a nationwide jurisdiction over particular issues, such as patents [723]. Each circuit court has several judges – ranging from six on the First Circuit to twenty-nine on the Ninth Circuit [723]. Any case may be appealed to the relevant circuit court of appeals, as soon as the district court has finalized a decision[519] – and some matters may be appealed before this by making an interlocutory appeal [723]. An appeal to a circuit court is heard by a panel of three judges [723, 724]. Parties file 'briefs' to this court, arguing why the decision of the trial judge should be 'affirmed' or 'reversed' [723]. Then, the circuit court of appeals will schedule 'oral argument', in which the legal representatives of each party make that party's case and answer the questions of the circuit court judges [723]. These regional circuit courts also hear appeals from judgments of federal administrative agencies [724]. Beyond the federal circuit, a few courts have been founded in order to consider appeals on specific subjects, such as military matters (i.e., the United States Court of Appeals for the Armed Forces) and claims of veterans (i.e., the United States Court of Appeals for Veterans Claims) [723].

The Supreme Court of the USA is at the top of the federal court system [724]. It comprises nine justices, who sit together to adjudicate cases [724]. The Supreme Court may hear appeals from the federal circuit courts of appeals, and from the highest state courts if the appeal involves the Constitution of the USA or federal law [724]. As the following passage relates – and unlike appeals from a federal district court to a federal circuit court of appeals, the Supreme Court has a discretion as to whether or not to hear an appeal.

[519] However, the federal government of the USA has no right of appeal to a circuit court of appeals in a criminal case, if the verdict given in the district court is 'Not Guilty' (Government of the United. States of America (2022), The U.S. Legal System: A Short Description, 2).

> After the circuit court or state supreme court has ruled on a case, either party may choose to appeal to the Supreme Court. Unlike circuit court appeals, however, the Supreme Court is usually not required to hear the appeal. Parties may file a "writ of *certiorari*[520]" to the court, asking it to hear the case. If the writ is granted, [then] the Supreme Court will take briefs and conduct oral argument. If the writ is not granted, [then] the lower court's opinion stands. *Certiorari*[521] is not often granted; less than 1% of appeals to the high court are actually heard by it. The Court typically hears cases when there are conflicting decisions across the country on a particular issue or when there is an egregious error in a case [723].

In addition to its participation in the federal court system, each state of the USA has a hierarchy of state courts – which is described thus.

> Most states have courts of limited jurisdiction presided over by a single judge who hears minor civil and criminal cases. States also have general jurisdiction trial courts that are presided over by a single judge. These trial courts are usually called circuit courts or superior courts and hear major civil and criminal cases. Some states have specialized courts that hear only certain kinds of cases[,] such as traffic or family law cases. All states have a highest court, usually called a state supreme court, that serves as an appellate court. Many states also have an intermediate appellate court called a court of appeals that hears appeals from the trial court. A party in a case generally has one right of appeal [724].

Comment

The USA has a comprehensive legal system, which is able to manage its large system of fifty federated states. To a considerable extent, this is thanks to the quality of the Constitution of the USA – which sets out the framework for the operation of federal law there, and which has stood the test of time. The Constitution Act 1867 of Canada is more forthcoming than the Constitution of the USA about the desired contents of state legislation[522]. However, on the principle that state legislation of the USA may concern any subject which the Constitution has not exclusively reserved for federal lawmakers, there is little to choose between these two instruments over this area. Both are excellent bases upon which to manage a vast, federal state.

---

[520] Emphasis added. The word '*certiorari*' is from Law Latin, literally 'to be informed'; it means "a writ or order by which a higher court reviews a case tried in a lower court" (Pearsall, J. (editor) (1998), *The New Oxford Dictionary of English* (Oxford: Oxford University Press), 299). Dr. McFarlane's dictionary defines the term '*certiorari*' as "[an] order of the High Court to review proceedings where there is a suggestion of bias, excess of jurisdiction, or an error on the record" (McFarlane, G. (1984), *The Layman's Dictionary of English Law* (London: Waterlow Publishers Limited), 40). It is submitted that, whilst the latter definition applies in English law – so please read 'Supreme Court' for 'High Court', it accords with the idea that the Supreme Court will only admit appeals in exceptional circumstances.

[521] Emphasis added.

[522] The subsection titled 'Sources of Law', in the section entitled 'An Introduction to the Legal System of Canada' in Chapter 2, describes sections 91 and 92 of the Constitution Act 1867 of Canada – which lay down topics reserved exclusively for the federal legislature (i.e., the Parliament of Canada) and those allocated exclusively to provincial and territorial legislatures, respectively.

The Regulation of Banking in the USA

Office of the Comptroller of the Currency (OCC)

A bank can either be chartered by the relevant regulatory agency of its state, or by the federal government's regulatory agency – the OCC [725]. Whilst state bank regulatory agencies charter state banks and state branches, agencies and representative offices of foreign banks, the OCC charters – and regulates – national banks[523], federal savings associations, and federal branches and agencies of foreign banks [725].

Section 1 of the National Bank Act 1864 establishes the OCC[524], in these words.

> *Be it enacted by the Senate and House of Representatives of the United States of America in Congress assembled*[525], That there shall be established in the treasury department a separate bureau, which shall be charged with the execution of this and all other laws that may be passed by congress respecting the issue and regulation of a national currency secured by United States bonds. The chief officer of the said bureau shall be denominated the comptroller of the currency, and shall be under the general direction of the Secretary of the Treasury. ... [726]

Section 5 of the National Bank Act 1864 provides for a prospective bank to submit a copy of its articles of association to the Comptroller of the Currency, and Section 17 of this Act for the Comptroller of the Currency to determine whether this association is authorized to commence banking business.

> *And it be further enacted*[526], That associations for carrying on the business of banking may be formed by any number of persons, not less in any case than five, who shall enter into articles of association, which shall specify in general terms the object for which the association is formed, and may contain any other provisions, not inconsistent with the provisions of this act, which the association may see fit to adopt for the regulation of the business of the association and the conduct of its affairs, which said articles shall be signed

---

[523] In the USA, "a national bank is a commercial bank. The comptroller of the currency of the U.S. Treasury will charter a national bank. This institution will function as a member bank of the Federal Reserve and is an investing member of its district Federal Reserve Bank." (Kagan, J. (2020), "National Bank," updated October 31, 2020, accessed November 8, 2022, <https://www.investopedia.com/terms/n/national-bank.asp>).

[524] The OCC was established by the National Currency Act 1863, of which the National Bank Act 1864 was a major refashioning: "On February 25, 1863, President [Abraham] Lincoln signed the National Currency Act into law. The Act established the Office of the Comptroller of the Currency (OCC), charged with responsibility for organizing and administering a system of nationally chartered banks and a uniform national currency. In June 1864, the legislation underwent substantial amendment and became known as the National Bank Act." (Government of the United States of America (2022), "Office of the Comptroller of the Currency: Founding of the OCC & the National Banking System," accessed November 8, 2022, <https://www.occ.treas.gov/about/who-we-are/history/founding-occ-national-bank-system/index-founding-occ-national-banking-system.html>). The National Bank Act 1864 repealed the National Currency Act 1863: "*And it be further enacted*, That the act titled "An act to provide a national currency, secured by a pledge of United States stocks, and to provide for the circulation and redemption thereof," approved February twenty-fifth, eighteen hundred and sixty-three, is hereby repealed: ... ." (Government of the United States of America (1864), "An Act to provide a National Currency, secured by a Pledge of United States Bonds, and to provide for the Circulation and Redemption thereof (National Bank Act 1864)," adopted on June 3, 1864, s.62; emphasis original).

[525] Emphasis original.

[526] Emphasis original.

by the persons uniting to form the association, and a copy of them forwarded to the comptroller of the currency, to be filed and preserved in his office [727].

And it be further enacted[527], That whenever a certificate shall have been transmitted to the comptroller of the currency, as provided in this act, and the association transmitting the same shall notify the comptroller that at least fifty per centum of its capital stock has been paid as aforesaid, and that such association has complied with all the provisions of this act as required to be complied with before such association shall be authorized to commence the business of banking, the comptroller shall examine into the condition of such association, ascertain … whether such association has complied with all the requirements of this act to entitle it to engage in the business of banking; and shall cause to be made and attested by the oaths of a majority of the directors and by the president or cashier of such association, a statement of all the facts necessary to enable the comptroller to determine whether such association is lawfully entitled to commence the business of banking under this act [728].

In its own words, the OCC "Supervise[s] & Examine[s]"[528], "Regulate[s] & Enforce[s]"[529], "Charter[s] & License[s]"[530], and "Protect[s] Consumers & Communities"[531] [729].

Federal Reserve

The Federal Reserve Act 1913 created the Federal Reserve System as the central banking system of the USA [730], and to oversee the national banks – which were (and are) regulated

---

527 Emphasis original.

528 The OCC states: "• The OCC provides high-quality, fair, and balanced supervision to its chartered banks. • Our well-trained examiners conduct on-site reviews of banks and provide ongoing supervision of the banks' operations. • Examiners meet with bank management and the bank's board of directors throughout the supervisory cycle to obtain information or discuss issues." (Government of the United States of America (2022), "Office of the Comptroller of the Currency: What We Do," accessed November 8, 2022, <https://www.occ.treas.gov/about/what-we-do/index-what-we-do.html>).

529 The OCC declares: "• The OCC is the primary regulator of banks chartered under the National Bank Act and federal savings associations chartered under the Home Owners' Loan Act. • The OCC issues rules and regulations that govern the banks [which] it supervises. • The agency takes supervisory actions against banks that do not comply with these statutes or that otherwise engage in risky practices." (Government of the United States of America (2022), "Office of the Comptroller of the Currency: What We Do," accessed November 8, 2022, <https://www.occ.treas.gov/about/what-we-do/index-what-we-do.html>).

530 The OCC specifies: "• Financial institutions follow an in-depth application process to be chartered as an OCC-supervised bank. • Chartered banks apply to the OCC to make substantial changes to their activities or structure. • The OCC evaluates the applications to make sure [that] banks' corporate structures are established and maintained in accordance with the principles of a safe and sound banking system. • Our licensing department works closely with the agency's supervisory and legal divisions to render independent decisions regarding applications." (Government of the United States of America (2022), "Office of the Comptroller of the Currency: What We Do," accessed November 8, 2022, <https://www.occ.treas.gov/about/what-we-do/index-what-we-do.html>).

531 The OCC asserts: "• Ensuring fair access and equal treatment to bank customers is a fundamental part of the OCC's mission. • The OCC helps banks [to] be leaders in safe and sound community development financing and making financial services accessible to underserved communities and consumers. • OCC examiners make sure [that] banks comply with consumer banking laws." (Government of the United States of America (2022), "Office of the Comptroller of the Currency: What We Do," accessed November 8, 2022, <https://www.occ.treas.gov/about/what-we-do/index-what-we-do.html>).

by the OCC pursuant to the National Bank Act 1864 [731]. Elements of the original version of the Federal Reserve Act 1913 are as follows.

> As soon as practicable, the Secretary of the Treasury, the Secretary of Agriculture and the Comptroller of the Currency, acting as "The Reserve Bank Organization Committee," shall designate not less than eight nor more than twelve cities to be known as Federal reserve cities, and shall divide the continental United States, excluding Alaska, into districts, each district to contain only one of such Federal reserve cities[532]. ... The districts thus created may be readjusted and new districts may from time to time be created by the Federal Reserve Board, not to exceed twelve in all. Such districts shall be known as Federal reserve districts ... . The said committee shall supervise the organization in each of the cities designated of a Federal reserve bank, which shall include in its title the name of the city in which it is situated, as "Federal Reserve Bank of Chicago." ... [E]very national banking association[533] within that district shall be required within thirty days after notice from the organization committee, to subscribe to the capital stock of such Federal reserve bank ... . Stock not held by member banks[534] shall not be entitled to voting power. The Federal Reserve Board is hereby empowered to adopt and promulgate rules and regulations governing the transfers of said stock. ... [732]
>
> Any bank[535] incorporated by special law of any State, or organized under the general laws of any State or of the United States, may make application to the reserve bank organization committee, pending organization, and thereafter to the Federal Reserve Board[,] for the right to subscribe to the stock of the Federal reserve bank [that is] organized[,] or to be organized[,] within the Federal reserve district where the applicant is located. The organization committee or the Federal Reserve Board, under such rules and regulations as it may prescribe, subject to the provisions of this section [(i.e., section 9 of the Federal Reserve Act 1913)], may permit the applying bank to become a stockholder in the Federal reserve bank of the district in which the applying bank is located. ... [733]
>
> A Federal Reserve Board is hereby created which shall consist of seven members, including the Secretary of the Treasury and the Comptroller of the Currency, who shall be

---

532 The twelve Federal reserve cities are Atlanta, Boston, Chicago, Cleveland, Dallas, Kansas City, Minneapolis, New York, Philadelphia, Richmond, San Francisco, and St. Louis (Chen, J. (2022), "1913 Federal Reserve Act: Definition and Why It's Important," updated January 12, 2022, accessed November 8, 2022. <https://www.investopedia.com/terms/f/1913-federal-reserve-act.asp>).

533 The phrases '*national bank*' and '*national banking association*' that are used in the Federal Reserve Act 1913 "shall be held to be synonymous and interchangeable" (Government of the United States of America (1913), "An Act To provide for the establishment of Federal reserve banks, to furnish an elastic currency, to afford means of rediscounting commercial paper, to establish a more effective supervision of banking in the United States and for other purposes (Federal Reserve Act 1913)," adopted on December 23, 1913, s.1). Fn 523 defines the term '*national bank*'.

534 The expression '*member bank*' within the Federal Reserve Act 1913 "shall be held to mean any national bank, State bank, or bank or trust company which has become a member of one of the reserve banks created by this Act"; the word '*bank*' within the Federal Reserve Act 1913 "shall be held to include State bank, banking association, and trust company, except where national banks or Federal reserve banks are specifically referred to" (Government of the United States of America (1913), "An Act To provide for the establishment of Federal reserve banks, to furnish an elastic currency, to afford means of rediscounting commercial paper, to establish a more effective supervision of banking in the United States and for other purposes (Federal Reserve Act 1913)," adopted on December 23, 1913, s.1). Fn 523 defines the term '*national bank*'.

535 Fn 534 defines the term '*bank*', as used within the Federal Reserve Act 1913.

members *ex officio*[536], and five members[, who are] appointed by the President of the United States, by and with the advice and consent of the Senate. ... No member of the Federal Reserve Board shall be an officer or director of any bank[537], banking institution, trust company, or Federal reserve bank[,] nor hold stock in any bank, banking institution, or trust company ... . The Federal Reserve Board shall annually make a full report of its operations to the Speaker of the House of Representatives, who shall cause the same to be printed for the information of the Congress. ... [734]

The Federal Reserve Board shall be authorized and empowered: (a) To examine at its discretion the accounts, books and affairs of each Federal reserve bank and of each member bank[538][,] and to require such statements and reports as it may deem necessary. ... (b) To permit, or, on the affirmative vote of at least five members of the Reserve Board[,] to require Federal reserve banks to rediscount the discounted paper of other Federal reserve banks at rates of interest to be fixed by the Federal Reserve Board. (c) To suspend for a period not exceeding thirty days, and from time to time renew such suspension for periods not exceeding fifteen days, any reserve requirement [that is] specified in this Act ... . (d) To supervise and regulate[,] through the bureau under the charge of the Comptroller of the Currency[,] the issue and retirement of Federal reserve notes ... . (e) To add to the number of cities [that are] classified as reserve and central reserve cities under existing law in which national banking associations[539] are subject to the reserve requirements set forth in section twenty of this Act; or to reclassify existing reserve and central reserve cities[,] or to terminate their designation as such. (f) To suspend or remove any officer or director of any Federal reserve bank ... . (g) To require the writing off of doubtful or worthless assets upon the books and balance sheets of Federal reserve banks. (h) To suspend, for the violation of any of the provisions of this Act, the operations of any Federal reserve bank, to take possession thereof, administer the same during the period of suspension, and, when deemed advisable, to liquidate or reorganize such bank. (i) To require bonds of Federal reserve agents, [and] to make regulations for the safeguarding of all collateral, bonds, Federal reserve notes, money or property of any kind [that is] deposited in the hands of such agents ... . (j) To exercise general supervision over said Federal reserve banks. (k) To grant by special permit to national banks applying therefor, when not in contravention of State or local law, the right to act as trustee, executor, administrator, or registrar of stocks and bonds[,] under such rules and regulations as the said board[540] may prescribe. (l) To employ such ... employees as may be deemed necessary to conduct the business of the board. ... [735]

Any Federal reserve bank may receive from any of its member banks[541], and from the United States, deposits of current funds in lawful money, national-bank notes, Federal

[536] Emphasis added. The phrase '*ex officio*' is from Latin, from *ex* ('out of, from') plus *officium* ('duty'); it means "by virtue of one's position or status" (Pearsall, J. (editor) (1998), *The New Oxford Dictionary of English*, 645).

[537] Fn 534 defines the term '*bank*', as used within the Federal Reserve Act 1913.

[538] Fn 534 defines the term '*member bank*' as used within the Federal Reserve Act 1913.

[539] Within the Federal Reserve Act 1913, the term '*national banking association*' is synonymous with the expression '*national bank*' (fn 533). Fn 523 defines the term '*national bank*'.

[540] The word '*board*' within the Federal Reserve Act 1913 "shall be held to mean Federal Reserve Board" (Government of the United States of America (1913), "An Act To provide for the establishment of Federal reserve banks, to furnish an elastic currency, to afford means of rediscounting commercial paper, to establish a more effective supervision of banking in the United States and for other purposes (Federal Reserve Act 1913)," adopted on December 23, 1913, s.1).

[541] Fn 534 defines the term '*member bank*' as used within the Federal Reserve Act 1913.

reserve notes, or checks and drafts upon solvent member banks, payable upon presentation; or, solely for exchange purposes, may receive from other Federal reserve banks deposits of current funds in lawful money, national-bank notes, or checks and drafts upon solvent member [banks] or other Federal reserve banks, payable upon presentation. Upon the indorsement of any of its member banks, with a waiver of demand, notice and protest by such bank, any Federal reserve bank may discount notes, drafts, and bills of exchange arising out of actual commercial transactions; that is, notes, drafts, and bills of exchange issued or drawn for agricultural, industrial, or commercial purposes, or the proceeds of which have been used, or are to be used, for such purposes … . Nothing in this Act contained shall be construed to prohibit such notes, drafts, and bills of exchange, secured by staple agricultural products, or other goods, wares, or merchandise[,] from being eligible for such discount; but such definition shall not include notes, drafts, or bills covering merely investments[,] or issued or drawn for the purpose of carrying or trading in stocks, bonds, or other investment securities, except bonds and notes of the Government of the United States. Notes, drafts, and bills [that are] admitted to discount under the terms of this paragraph must have a maturity at the time of discount of not more than ninety days: … . Any Federal reserve bank may discount acceptances which are based on the importation or exportation of goods[,] and which have a maturity at time of discount of not more than three months, and [which are] indorsed by at least one member bank. The amount of acceptances so discounted shall at no time exceed one-half of the paid-up capital stock and surplus of the bank for which the rediscounts are made. … Any member bank may accept drafts or bills of exchange [that are] drawn upon it and [which are] growing out of transactions involving the importation or exportation of goods having not more than six months sight to run; but no bank shall accept such bills to an amount equal at any time in the aggregate to more than one-half [of] its paid-up capital stock and surplus. … [736]

Any Federal reserve bank may, under rules and regulations [that are] prescribed by the Federal Reserve Board, purchase and sell in the open market, at home or abroad, either from[,] or to[,] domestic or foreign banks, firms, corporations, or individuals, cable transfers and bankers' acceptances and bills of exchange of the kinds and maturities by this Act made eligible for rediscount, with or without the indorsement of a member bank[542]. Every Federal reserve bank shall have power: (a) To deal in gold coin and bullion at home or abroad … ; (b) To buy and sell, at home or abroad, bonds and notes of the United States, and bills, notes, revenue bonds, and warrants with a maturity from date of purchase of not exceeding six months, [which are] issued in anticipation of the collection of taxes or in anticipation of the receipt of assured revenues by any State, county, district[543], political subdivision, or municipality in the continental United States … ; (c) To purchase from member banks and to sell, with or without its indorsement, bills of exchange arising out of commercial transactions, as hereinbefore defined[544]; (d) To establish from time to time,

542 Fn 534 defines the term '*member bank*' as used within the Federal Reserve Act 1913.

543 The word '*district*' within the Federal Reserve Act 1913 "shall be held to mean Federal reserve district" (Government of the United States of America (1913), "An Act To provide for the establishment of Federal reserve banks, to furnish an elastic currency, to afford means of rediscounting commercial paper, to establish a more effective supervision of banking in the United States and for other purposes (Federal Reserve Act 1913)," adopted on December 23, 1913, s.1).

544 Section 13 of the Federal Reserve Act 1983 defines 'actual commercial transactions' as "notes, drafts, and bills of exchange issued or drawn for agricultural, industrial, or commercial purposes, or the proceeds of which have been used, or are to be used, for such purposes" (second clause of the second sentence of the immediately-preceding paragraph in the current passage of quoted text).

subject to review and determination of the Federal Reserve Board, rates of discount to be charged by the Federal reserve bank for each class of paper, which shall be fixed with a view of accommodating commerce and business; (e) To establish accounts with other Federal reserve banks for exchange purposes[,] and, with the consent of the Federal Reserve Board, to open and maintain banking accounts in foreign countries, appoint correspondents, and establish agencies in such countries wheresoever it may deem best for the purpose of purchasing, selling, and collecting bills of exchange … [737].

The moneys held in the general fund of the Treasury, except the five per centum fund for the redemption of outstanding national-bank notes and the funds [that are] provided in this Act for the redemption of Federal reserve notes[,] may, upon the direction of the Secretary of the Treasury, be deposited in Federal reserve banks, which banks, when required by the Secretary of the Treasury, shall act as fiscal agents of the United States; and the revenues of the Government or any part thereof may be deposited in such banks, and disbursements may be made by checks drawn against such deposits. … [738]

Federal reserve notes, to be issued at the discretion of the Federal Reserve Board for the purpose of making advances to Federal reserve banks through Federal reserve agents[,] as hereinafter set forth and for no other purpose, are hereby authorized. … [739]

Demand deposits within the meaning of this Act shall comprise all deposits payable within thirty days[;] time deposits shall comprise all deposits payable after thirty days, and all savings accounts and certificates of deposit which are subject to not less than thirty days' notice before payment. [E]very subscribing member bank[545] shall establish and maintain reserves[,] as follows: (a) A bank[546] [that is] not in a reserve or central reserve city … shall hold and maintain reserves equal to twelve per centum of the aggregate amount of its demand deposits and five per centum of its time deposits … . … (b) A bank [that is] in a reserve city … shall hold and maintain reserves equal to fifteen per centum of the aggregate amount of its demand deposits and five per centum of its time deposits … . … (c) A bank [that is] in a central reserve city … shall hold and maintain a reserve equal to eighteen per centum of the aggregate amount of its demand deposits and five per centum of its time deposits … . … In estimating the reserves [which are] required by this Act, the net balance of the amounts due to[,] and from[,] other banks shall be taken as the basis for ascertaining the deposits against which reserves shall be determined. Balances in reserve banks[547] due to member banks shall, to the extent herein provided, be counted as reserves. National banks[548] [that are] located in Alaska or outside the continental United States may remain nonmember banks, and shall[,] in that event[,] maintain reserves and comply with all the conditions [which are] now provided by law regulating them; or said banks … may, with the consent of the [Federal] Reserve Board, become member banks of any one of the [Federal] reserve districts, and shall, in that event, take stock, maintain reserves, and be subject to all the other provisions of this Act [740].

---

[545] Fn 534 defines the term '*member bank*' as used within the Federal Reserve Act 1913.

[546] Fn 534 defines the term '*bank*', as used within the Federal Reserve Act 1913.

[547] The phrase '*reserve bank*' within the Federal Reserve Act 1913 "shall be held to mean Federal reserve bank" (Government of the United States of America (1913), "An Act To provide for the establishment of Federal reserve banks, to furnish an elastic currency, to afford means of rediscounting commercial paper, to establish a more effective supervision of banking in the United States and for other purposes (Federal Reserve Act 1913)," adopted on December 23, 1913, s.1).

[548] Fn 523 defines the term '*national bank*'.

> The Comptroller of the Currency, with the approval of the Secretary of the Treasury, shall appoint examiners who shall examine every member bank[549] at least twice in each calendar year[,] and oftener if considered necessary: ... ... [E]very Federal reserve bank may, with the approval of the Federal reserve agent or the Federal Reserve Board, provide for special examination of member banks within its district[550]. ... The Federal Reserve Board shall, at least once each year, order an examination of each Federal reserve bank, and[,] upon joint application of ten member banks[,] the Federal Reserve Board shall order a special examination and report of the condition of any Federal reserve bank. ... [741]

In its own words, the Federal Reserve undertakes the following general functions.

> The Federal Reserve[: 1] conducts the nation's monetary policy to promote maximum employment, stable prices, and moderate long-term interest rates in the U.S. economy; [2] promotes the stability of the financial system[,] and seeks to minimize and contain systemic risks through active monitoring and engagement in the U.S. and abroad; [3] promotes the safety and soundness of individual financial institutions[,] and monitors their impact on the financial system as a whole; [4] fosters payment and settlement system safety and efficiency through services to the banking industry and the U.S. government that facilitate U.S.-dollar transactions and payments; and [5] promotes consumer protection and community development through consumer-focused supervision and examination, research and analysis of emerging consumer issues and trends, community economic development activities, and the administration of consumer laws and regulations [742].

Federal Deposit Insurance Corporation (FDIC)

The FDIC is an independent agency that the Congress created to maintain public confidence and stability in the financial system of the USA [743]. To achieve this, the FDIC: (i) insures deposits, (ii) examines and superintends financial institutions for consumer protection, safety and soundness, (iii) engages with the resolution of large, complex financial institutions, and (iv) manages receiverships [743].

The Banking Act 1933 – i.e., the Glass-Steagall Act – founded the FDIC as a temporary agency [730]. The Banking Act 1935 established this as a permanent agency of the government [730]. The Federal Deposit Insurance Act 1950 revised and consolidated previous legislation on the FDIC into one statute, and contains the fundamental authority for the functioning of this entity [730]. Elements the Federal Deposit Insurance Act 1950, as amended, are as follows.

---

549 Fn 534 defines the term '*member bank*' as used within the Federal Reserve Act 1913.

550 The word '*district*' within the Federal Reserve Act 1913 "shall be held to mean Federal reserve district" (Government of the United States of America (1913), "An Act To provide for the establishment of Federal reserve banks, to furnish an elastic currency, to afford means of rediscounting commercial paper, to establish a more effective supervision of banking in the United States and for other purposes (Federal Reserve Act 1913)," adopted on December 23, 1913, s.1).

There is hereby established a Federal Deposit Insurance Corporation (hereinafter referred to as the "Corporation") which shall insure, as hereinafter provided, the deposits[551] of all

[551] As used in the Federal Deposit Insurance Act 1950, the word '*deposit*' means "(1) the unpaid balance of money[,] or its equivalent[, which is] received or held by a bank or savings association in the usual course of business[,] and for which it has given[,] or is obligated to give[,] credit, either conditionally or unconditionally, to a commercial, checking, savings, time, or thrift account, or which is evidenced by its certificate of deposit, thrift certificate, investment certificate, certificate of indebtedness, or other similar name, or a check or draft [that is] drawn against a deposit account and certified by the bank or savings association, or a letter of credit or a traveler's check on which the bank or savings association is primarily liable: *Provided*, That, without limiting the generality of the term "money or its equivalent," any such account or instrument must be regarded as evidencing the receipt of the equivalent of money[,] when created or issued in exchange for checks or drafts or for a promissory note upon which the person obtaining any such credit or instrument is primarily or secondarily liable, or for a charge against a deposit account, or in settlement of checks, drafts, or other instruments [that are] forwarded to such bank or savings association for collection, (2) trust funds[,] as defined in this Act [(first sentence of fn 559), which are] received or held by such bank or savings association … , (3) money [that is] received or held by a bank or savings association, or the credit given for money or its equivalent [which is] received or held by a bank or savings association, in the usual course of business for a special or specific purpose, regardless of the legal relationship thereby established, including[,] without being limited to, escrow funds, funds [that are] held as security for an obligation [which is] due to the bank or savings association or others (including funds [that are] held as dealers reserves)[,] or for securities [which are] loaned by the bank or savings association, funds [that are] deposited by a debtor to meet maturing obligations, funds [which are] deposited as advance payment on subscriptions to United States Government securities, funds [that are] held for distribution or purchase of securities, funds [which are] held to meet its acceptances or letters of credit, and withheld taxes: *Provided*, That there shall not be included funds which are received by the bank or savings association for immediate application to the reduction of an indebtedness to the receiving bank or savings association, or under condition that the receipt thereof immediately reduces or extinguishes such an indebtedness, (4) outstanding draft (including advice or authorization to charge a bank's[,] or a savings association's[,] balance in another bank or savings association), cashier's check, money order, or other officer's check [that is] issued in the usual course of business for any purpose … and (5) such other obligations of a bank or savings association as the Board of Directors, after consultation with the Comptroller of the Currency, and the Board of Governors of the Federal Reserve System, shall find and prescribe by regulation to be deposit liabilities by general usage, except that the following shall not be a deposit for any of the purposes of this Act[,] or be included as part of the total deposits or of an insured deposit: (A) any obligation of a depository institution which is carried on the books and records of an office of such bank or savings association [that is] located outside of any State, unless – (i) such obligation would be a deposit[,] if it were carried on the books and records of the depository institution, and would be payable at, an office located in any State; and (ii) the contract evidencing the obligation provides by express terms, and not by implication, for payment at an office of the depository institution [which is] located in any State; (B) any international banking facility deposit … , (C) any liability of an insured depository institution that arises under an annuity contract, the income of which is tax deferred under section 72 of the Internal Revenue Code of 1986." (Government of the United States of America (2021), "Federal Deposit Insurance Act 1950," adopted on September 21, 1950, updated to August 31, 2021, s.3(l); emphasis original). The first sentence of fn 552 defines the term '*bank*'. The first sentence of fn 553 defines the term '*savings association*'. The first sentence of fn 559 defines the term '*trust funds*'. The first sentence of fn 563 defines the term '*insured deposit*'. The first sentence of fn 554 defines the term '*depository institution*'. The fourth sentence of fn 552 defines the term '*State*'. The penultimate sentence of fn 554 defines the term '*insured depository institution*'.

banks[552] and savings associations[553] which are entitled to the benefits of insurance under this Act, and which shall have the powers hereinafter granted [744].

Each bank which is an insured depository institution[554] on … the effective date of this amendment [(i.e., September 21, 1950)], shall be and continue to be, without application or approval, an insured depository institution[,] and shall be subject to the provisions of this Act[555] [745].

---

552 As used in the Federal Deposit Insurance Act 1950, the word '*bank*' "means any national bank and State bank, and any Federal branch and insured branch," and "includes any former savings association" (Government of the United States of America (2021), "Federal Deposit Insurance Act 1950," adopted on September 21, 1950, updated to August 31, 2021, s.3(a)(1)). Fn 523 defines the term '*national bank*'. As used in the Federal Deposit Insurance Act 1950, the phrase '*State bank*' "means any bank, banking association, trust company, savings bank, industrial bank … , or other banking institution[,] which – (A) is engaged in the business of receiving deposits, other than trust funds … ; and (B) is incorporated under the laws of any State or which is operating under the Code of Law for the District of Columbia, including any cooperative bank or other unincorporated bank the deposits of which were insured by the Corporation [(i.e., the FDIC)] on the day before August 9, 1989" (Government of the United States of America (2021), "Federal Deposit Insurance Act 1950," adopted on September 21, 1950, updated to August 31, 2021, s.3(a)(2)). As used in the Federal Deposit Insurance Act 1950, the word '*State*' "means any State of the United States, the District of Columbia, any territory of the United States, Puerto Rico, Guam, American Samoa, the Trust Territory of the Pacific Islands, the Virgin Islands, and the Northern Mariana Islands" (Government of the United States of America (2021), "Federal Deposit Insurance Act 1950," adopted on September 21, 1950, updated to August 31, 2021, s.3(a)(3)). The first sentence of fn 553 defines the term '*savings association*'. As used in the Federal Deposit Insurance Act 1950, the phrase '*savings bank*' "means a bank (including a mutual savings bank) which transacts its ordinary banking business strictly as a savings bank under State laws imposing special requirements on such banks governing the manner of investing their funds and of conducting their business" (Government of the United States of America (2021), "Federal Deposit Insurance Act 1950," adopted on September 21, 1950, updated to August 31, 2021, s.3(g)). As used in the Federal Deposit Insurance Act 1950, the phrase '*mutual savings bank*' "means a bank without capital stock transacting a savings bank business, the net earnings of which inure wholly to the benefit of its depositors[,] after payment of obligations for any advances by its organizers" (Government of the United States of America (2021), "Federal Deposit Insurance Act 1950," adopted on September 21, 1950, updated to August 31, 2021, s.3(f)). The first sentence of fn 559 defines the term '*trust funds*'.

553 As used in the Federal Deposit Insurance Act 1950, the phrase '*savings association*' "means – (A) any Federal savings association; (B) any State savings association; and (C) any corporation (other than a bank) that the Board of Directors and the Comptroller of the Currency jointly determine to be operating in substantially the same manner as a savings association" (Government of the United States of America (2021), "Federal Deposit Insurance Act 1950," adopted on September 21, 1950, updated to August 31, 2021, s.3(b)(1)). As used in the Federal Deposit Insurance Act 1950, the phrase '*Federal savings association*' "means any [chartered] Federal savings association or Federal savings bank" (Government of the United States of America (2021), "Federal Deposit Insurance Act 1950," adopted on September 21, 1950, updated to August 31, 2021, s.3(b)(2)). As used in the Federal Deposit Insurance Act 1950, the phrase '*State savings association*' "means – (A) any building and loan association, savings and loan association, or homestead association; or (B) any cooperative bank (other than a cooperative bank which is a State bank as defined in subsection [3(a)(2) of the Federal Deposit Insurance Act 1950 (third sentence of fn 552)], which is organized and operating according to the laws of the State (as defined in subsection [3(a)(3) of the Federal Deposit Insurance Act 1950 (fourth sentence of fn 552)] in which it is chartered or organized" (Government of the United States of America (2021), "Federal Deposit Insurance Act 1950," adopted on September 21, 1950, updated to August 31, 2021, s.3(b)(3)).

554 As used in the Federal Deposit Insurance Act 1950, the phrase '*depository institution*' "means any bank or savings association" (Government of the United States of America (2021), "Federal Deposit Insurance Act 1950," adopted on September 21, 1950, updated to August 31, 2021, s.3(c)(1)). The first sentence of fn 552 defines the term '*bank*'. The first sentence of fn 553 defines the term '*savings association*'. As used in the Federal Deposit Insurance Act 1950, the phrase '*insured depository institution*' "means any bank or savings association the deposits of which are insured by the Corporation [(i.e., the FDIC)] pursuant to this Act" (Government of the United States of America (2021), "Federal Deposit Insurance Act 1950," adopted on September 21, 1950, updated to August 31, 2021, s.3(b)(2)). The first sentence of fn 551 defines the term '*deposit*'.

555 This continuation of deposit insurance also applies to Savings Associations, the accounts of which the Federal Savings and Loans Insurance Corporation was insuring on 9th August 1989 (Government of the United States of America (2021), "Federal Deposit Insurance Act 1950," adopted on September 21, 1950, updated to August 31, 2021, s.4(a)(2)). Furthermore, the continuation of deposit insurance applies to insured banks that are admitted to membership of the Federal Reserve System, any depository institution which is converted from a state

Except as provided in paragraphs (2)[556] and (3)[557], any depository institution[558] which is engaged in the business of receiving deposits other than trust funds (as defined in [sub]section 3(p) [of the Federal Deposit Insurance Act 1950])[559], upon application to[,] and examination by[,] the Corporation and approval by the Board of Directors, may become an insured depository institution [746].

In reviewing any application [to the Federal Deposit Insurance Corporation for deposit insurance,] the Board of Directors shall consider the [following] factors[:] (1) The financial history and condition of the depository institution. (2) The adequacy of the depository institution's capital structure. (3) The future earnings prospects of the depository institution. (4) The general character and fitness of the management of the depository institution. (5) The risk presented by such depository institution to the Deposit Insurance Fund. (6) The convenience and needs of the community to be served by such depository institution. (7) Whether the depository institution's corporate powers are consistent with the purposes of this Act[560] [747].

---

depository institution to a federal depository institution or *vice versa* – subject to payment of any insurance fee and one other provision, and any depository institution that results from the merger or consolidation of depository institutions at least one of which is insured (Government of the United States of America (2021), "Federal Deposit Insurance Act 1950," adopted on September 21, 1950, updated to August 31, 2021, s.4(b)-(d)). As used in the Federal Deposit Insurance Act 1950, the phrase '*insured bank*' "means any bank (including a foreign bank having an insured branch)[,] the deposits of which are insured in accordance with the provisions of this Act; and the term "noninsured bank" means any bank the deposits of which are not so insured" (Government of the United States of America (2021), "Federal Deposit Insurance Act 1950," adopted on September 21, 1950, updated to August 31, 2021, s.3(h)). The first sentence of fn 554 defines the term '*depository institution*'. The first sentence of fn 551 defines the term '*deposit*'. As used in the Federal Deposit Insurance Act 1950, the phrase '*State depository institution*' "means any State bank, any State savings association, and any insured branch which is not a Federal branch" (Government of the United States of America (2021), "Federal Deposit Insurance Act 1950," adopted on September 21, 1950, updated to August 31, 2021, s.3(c)(5)). The third sentence of fn 552 defines the term '*State bank*'. The last sentence of fn 553 defines the term '*State savings association*'. As used in the Federal Deposit Insurance Act 1950, the phrase '*federal depository institution*' "means any national bank, any Federal savings association, and any Federal branch" (Government of the United States of America (2021), "Federal Deposit Insurance Act 1950," adopted on September 21, 1950, updated to August 31, 2021, s.3(c)(4)). Fn 523 defines the term '*national bank*'. The second sentence of fn 553 defines the term '*Federal savings association*'.

556 Regarding "any interim Federal depository institution that is chartered by the appropriate Federal banking agency and will not open for business, the depository institution shall be an insured depository institution upon the issuance of the institution's charter by the agency" (Government of the United States of America (2021), "Federal Deposit Insurance Act 1950," adopted on September 21, 1950, updated to August 31, 2021, s.5(a)(2)). The antepenultimate sentence of fn 555 defines the term '*Federal depository institution*'. The first sentence of fn 554 defines the term '*depository institution*'. The penultimate sentence of fn 554 defines the term '*insured depository institution*'.

557 This provision within the text (i.e., paragraph 5(a)(1) of the Federal Deposit Insurance Act 1950) "shall not apply in the case of any depository institution whose insured status is continued pursuant to section 4 [of the Federal Deposit Insurance Act 1950]" (Government of the United States of America (2021), "Federal Deposit Insurance Act 1950," adopted on September 21, 1950, updated to August 31, 2021, s.5(a)(3)). The first sentence of fn 554 defines the term '*depository institution*'. The text to fns 554 and 555, and the first two sentences of fn 555, lay down section 4 of the Federal Deposit Insurance Act 1950.

558 The first sentence of fn 554 defines the term '*depository institution*'.

559 As used in the Federal Deposit Insurance Act 1950, the phrase '*trust funds*' "means funds [that are] held by an insured depository institution in a fiduciary capacity[,] and includes, without being limited to, funds held as trustee, executor, administrator, guardian, or agent" (Government of the United States of America (2021), "Federal Deposit Insurance Act 1950," adopted on September 21, 1950, updated to August 31, 2021, s.3(p)). The penultimate sentence of fn 554 defines the term '*insured depository institution*'.

560 If the Board of Directors votes to reject the application, then it "shall promptly notify the appropriate Federal banking agency and, in the case of any State depository institution, the appropriate State banking supervisor[,] of the denial of such application, giving specific reasons in writing for the Board of Directors' determination with reference to the factors described in section 6 [of the Federal Deposit Insurance Act 1950 (text to present footnote, i.e., fn 560)]" (Government of the United States of America (2021), "Federal Deposit Insurance Act

Subject to the provisions of this Act and to such terms and conditions as the Board of Directors may impose, any branch of a foreign bank, upon application by the bank to the Corporation, and examination by the Corporation of the branch, and approval by the Board of Directors, may become an insured branch. Before approving any such application, the Board of Directors shall give consideration to – (1) the financial history and condition of the bank, (2) the adequacy of its capital structure, (3) its future earnings prospects, (4) the general character and fitness of its management, including[,] but not limited to[,] the management of the branch proposed to be insured, (5) the risk presented to the Deposit Insurance Fund[,] (6) the convenience and needs of the community to be served by the branch, (7) whether or not its corporate powers, insofar as they will be exercised through the proposed insured branch, are consistent with the purposes of this Act, and (8) the probable adequacy and reliability of information supplied[,] and to be supplied[,] by the bank to the Corporation to enable it carry out its functions under this Act [748].

Each insured State nonmember bank[561][,] and each foreign bank having an insured branch which is not a Federal branch[,] shall make to the Corporation reports of condition[,] which shall be in such form[,] and shall contain such information[,] as the Board of Directors may require. ... [749]

The Board of Directors may[,] from time to time[,] require any insured depository institution[562] to file such additional reports as the Corporation, after consultation with the Comptroller of the Currency and the Board of Governors of the Federal Reserve System, as appropriate, may deem advisable for insurance purposes [750].

In addition to[,] or in connection with[,] any other report [that is] required under this subsection [(i.e., subsection 7(a) of the Federal Deposit Insurance Act 1950)], the Corporation shall take such action as may be necessary to ensure that – (A) each insured depository institution maintains; and (B) the Corporation receives on a regular basis from

1950," adopted on September 21, 1950, updated to August 31, 2021, s.5(a)(5)). The sixth sentence of fn 555 defines the term '*State depository institution*'.

561 The fourth sentence of fn 572 defines the term '*State nonmember bank*'.

562 The penultimate sentence of fn 554 defines the term '*insured depository institution*'.

such institution, information on the total amount of all insured deposits[563], preferred deposits[564], and uninsured deposits[565] at the institution [751].

The Board of Directors shall, by regulation, establish a risk-based assessment system[566] for insured depository institutions [752].

The Board of Directors shall set assessments for insured depository institutions in such amounts as the Board of Directors may determine to be necessary or appropriate, subject to subparagraph (D)[567] [753].

In setting assessments under subparagraph (A)[568], the Board of Directors shall consider the following factors: (i) The estimated operating expenses of the Deposit Insurance Fund. (ii) The estimated case resolution expenses and income of the Deposit Fund. (iii) The projected effects of the payment of assessments on the capital and earnings of insured

---

563 As used in the Federal Deposit Insurance Act 1950, the phrase '*insured deposit*' "(1) … [s]ubject to paragraph (2), … means the net amount due to any depositor for deposits in an insured depository institution[,] as determined under [sub]sections 7(i) and 11(a) [of the Federal Deposit Insurance Act 1950]. (2) In the case of any deposit in a branch of a foreign bank, the term "insured deposit" means an insured deposit as defined in paragraph (1) of this subsection [(i.e., paragraph 3(m)(1) of the Federal Deposit Insurance Act 1950),] which – (A) is payable in the United States to – (i) an individual who is a citizen or resident of the United States, (ii) a partnership, corporation, trust, or other legally cognizable entity [that is] created under the laws of the United States or any State[,] and having its principal place of business within the United States or any State, or (iii) an individual, partnership, corporation, trust, or other legally cognizable entity[,] which is determined by the Board of Directors[,] in accordance with its regulations[,] to have such business or financial relationships in the United States as to make the insurance of such deposit consistent with the purposes of this Act; and (B) meets any other criteria prescribed [that are] by the Board of Directors by regulation[,] as necessary or appropriate[,] in its judgment[,] to carry out the purposes of this Act or to facilitate the administration thereof." (Government of the United States of America (2021), "Federal Deposit Insurance Act 1950," adopted on September 21, 1950, updated to August 31, 2021, s.3(m)(1)-(2)). The first sentence of fn 551 defines the term '*deposit*'. The penultimate sentence of fn 554 defines the term '*insured depository institution*'. The fourth sentence of fn 552 defines the term '*State*'.

564 As used in the Federal Deposit Insurance Act 1950, the phrase '*preferred deposits*' "means deposits of any public unit … at any insured depository institution which are secured or collateralized[,] as required under State law" (Government of the United States of America (2021), "Federal Deposit Insurance Act 1950," adopted on September 21, 1950, updated to August 31, 2021, s.3(m)(4)). The first sentence of fn 551 defines the term '*deposit*'. The penultimate sentence of fn 554 defines the term '*insured depository institution*'. The fourth sentence of fn 552 defines the term '*State*'.

565 As used in the Federal Deposit Insurance Act 1950, the phrase '*uninsured deposit*' "means the amount of any deposit of any depositor at any insured depository institution in excess of the amount of the insured deposits of such depositor (if any) at such depository institution" (Government of the United States of America (2021), "Federal Deposit Insurance Act 1950," adopted on September 21, 1950, updated to August 31, 2021, s.3(m)(3)). The first sentence of fn 551 defines the term '*deposit*'. The penultimate sentence of fn 554 defines the term '*insured depository institution*'.

566 For the purposes of paragraph 7(b)(1) of the Federal Deposit Insurance Act 1950, the phrase '*risk-based assessment system*' "means a system for calculating a depository institution's assessment[, which is] based on – (i) the probability that the Deposit Insurance Fund will incur a loss with respect to the institution, taking into consideration the risks attributable to – (I) different categories and concentrations of assets; (II) different categories and concentrations of liabilities, both insured and uninsured, contingent and noncontingent; and (III) any other factors [that] the Corporation [(i.e., the FDIC)] determines are relevant to assessing such probability; (ii) the likely amount of any such loss; and (iii) the revenue needs of the Deposit Insurance Fund" (Government of the United States of America (2021), "Federal Deposit Insurance Act 1950," adopted on September 21, 1950, updated to August 31, 2021, s.7(b)(1)(C)).

567 'Subparagraph (D)' is subparagraph 7(b)(2)(D) of the Federal Deposit Insurance Act 1950, which is headed 'Notice of Assessments' and which states: "The Corporation [(i.e., the FDIC)] shall notify each insured depository institution of that institution's assessment." (Government of the United States of America (2021), "Federal Deposit Insurance Act 1950," adopted on September 21, 1950, updated to August 31, 2021, s.7(b)(2)(D)).

568 'Subparagraph (A)' is subparagraph 7(b)(2)(A) of the Federal Deposit Insurance Act 1950, which is the text to fn 567.

depository institutions. (iv) The risk factors and other factors taken into account pursuant to paragraph (1) [(i.e., paragraph 7(b)(1) of the Federal Deposit Insurance Act 1950)] under the risk-based assessment system, including the requirement under such paragraph to maintain a risk-based system. (v) Any other factors [that] the Board of Directors may determine to be appropriate [754].

Before the beginning of each calendar year, the Board of Directors shall designate the reserve ratio [that is] applicable with respect to the Deposit Insurance Fund and publish the reserve ratio so designated[569] [755].

The reserve ratio [that is] designated by the Board of Directors for any year may not be less than 1.35 percent of estimated insured deposits[570], or the comparable percentage of the assessment base set forth in paragraph (2)(C)[571] [756].

In designating a reserve ratio for any year, the Board of Directors shall – (i) take into account the risk of losses to the Deposit Insurance Fund in such year and future years, including historic experience and potential and estimated losses from insured depository institutions; (ii) take into account economic conditions generally affecting insured depository institutions[,] so as to allow the designated reserve ratio to increase during more favorable economic conditions and to decrease during less favorable economic conditions, notwithstanding the increased risks of loss that may exist during such less favorable conditions, as determined to be appropriate by the Board of Directors; (iii) seek to prevent sharp swings in the assessment rates for insured depository institutions; and (iv) take into account such other factors as the Board of Directors may determine to be appropriate, consistent with the requirements of this subparagraph [757].

If, at the end of a calendar year, the reserve ratio of the Deposit Insurance Fund exceeds 1.5 percent of estimated insured deposits, [then] the Corporation shall declare the amount in the Fund in excess of the amount required to maintain the reserve ratio at 1.5 percent of estimated insured deposits, as dividends to be paid to insured depository institutions [758].

---

569 The Board of Directors shall make any alteration to the designated reserve ratio, following notice and time to comment (Government of the United States of America (2021), "Federal Deposit Insurance Act 1950," adopted on September 21, 1950, updated to August 31, 2021, s.7(b)(3)(A)(ii)).

570 The first sentence of fn 563 defines the term '*insured deposit*'.

571 It is submitted that 'paragraph (2)(C)' refers to subparagraph 7(b)(2)(C) of the Federal Deposit Insurance Act 1950, which is omitted from this Act (i.e., paragraph 7(b)(2) of the Federal Deposit Insurance Act 1950 comprises subparagraphs (A), (B), (D) and (E)). Fn 1 to paragraph 7(b)(2) of the Federal Deposit Insurance Act 1950 confirms this omission; it states "So in original. Paragraph (2) does not contain a paragraph (C)." (Government of the United States of America (2021), "Federal Deposit Insurance Act 1950," adopted on September 21, 1950, updated to August 31, 2021, s.7(b)(2), fn 1).

The appropriate Federal banking agency[572] shall, not less than once during each 12-month period[573], conduct a full-scope, on-site examination of each insured depository institution[574] [759].

For the purposes of this Act, the term "standard maximum deposit insurance amount" means $250,000 [(i.e., USD 250,000)], adjusted as provided under subparagraph (F) after March 31, 2010[575]. … [760]

---

572 As used in the Federal Deposit Insurance Act 1950, the phrase '*appropriate Federal banking agency*' "means – (1) the Office of the Comptroller, in the case of – (A) any national banking association; (B) any Federal branch or agency of a foreign bank; and (C) any Federal savings association; (2) the Federal Deposit Insurance Corporation, in the case of – (A) any State nonmember insured bank; (B) any foreign bank having an insured branch; and (C) any State savings association; (3) the Board of Governors of the Federal Reserve System[,] in the case of – (A) any State member bank; (B) any branch or agency of a foreign bank with respect to any provision of the Federal Reserve Act which is made applicable under the International Banking Act of 1978; (C) any foreign bank which does not operate an insured branch; (D) any agency or commercial lending company[,] other than a Federal agency; (E) supervisory or regulatory proceedings arising from the authority [that is] given to the Board of Governors under section 7(c)(1) of the International Banking Act of 1978, including such proceedings under the Financial Institution Supervisory Act of 1966; (F) any bank holding company[,] and any subsidiary (other than a depository institution) of a bank holding company; and (G) any savings and loan holding company[,] and any subsidiary (other than a depository institution) of a savings and loan holding company. Under the rule set forth in this subsection [(i.e., subsection 3(q) of the Federal Deposit Insurance Act 1950)], more than one agency may be an appropriate Federal banking agency with respect to any given institution." (Government of the United States of America (2021), "Federal Deposit Insurance Act 1950," adopted on September 21, 1950, updated to August 31, 2021, s.3(q)). Fn 533 holds the terms '*national bank*' and '*national banking association*' to be synonymous and interchangeable – within the Federal Reserve Act 1913; fn 523 defines the term '*national bank*'. The second sentence of fn 553 defines the term '*Federal savings association*'. The phrase '*State nonmember insured bank*' is a combination of the term '*State nonmember bank*' and the expression '*insured bank*'; as used in the Federal Deposit Insurance Act 1950, the phrase '*State nonmember bank*' "means any State bank which is not a member of the Federal Reserve System" (Government of the United States of America (2021), "Federal Deposit Insurance Act 1950," adopted on September 21, 1950, updated to August 31, 2021, s.3(e)(2)); the third sentence of fn 552 defines the term '*State bank*'; the third sentence of fn 555 defines the term '*insured bank*'. The final sentence of fn 553 defines the term '*State savings association*'. As used in the Federal Deposit Insurance Act 1950, the phrase '*State member bank*' "means any State bank which is a member of the Federal Reserve System" (Government of the United States of America (2021), "Federal Deposit Insurance Act 1950," adopted on September 21, 1950, updated to August 31, 2021, s.3(d)(2)).

573 Paragraph 10(d)(4) of the Federal Deposit Insurance Act 1950 permits the on-site examination to be carried out every 18 months (rather than every 12 months), if the insured depository institution satisfies five criteria stated therein to qualify as a 'small' institution (Government of the United States of America (2021), "Federal Deposit Insurance Act 1950," adopted on September 21, 1950, updated to August 31, 2021, s.10(d)(4)).

574 These examinations "may be conducted in alternate 12-month periods, as appropriate, if the appropriate Federal banking agency determines that an examination of the insured depository institution [which is] conducted by the State during the intervening 12-month period carries out the purpose of this subsection" (Government of the United States of America (2021), "Federal Deposit Insurance Act 1950," adopted on September 21, 1950, updated to August 31, 2021, s.10(d)(3)). The penultimate sentence of fn 554 defines the term '*insured depository institution*'. The fourth sentence of fn 552 defines the term '*State*'. 'This subsection' is subsection 10(d) of the Federal Deposit Insurance Act 1950.

575 Subparagraph 11(a)(1)(F) of the Federal Deposit Insurance Act 1950 is headed 'Inflation Adjustment'; its first clause is labelled 'In General', and reads thus: "By April 1 of 2010, and the 1st day of each subsequent 5-year period, the Board of Directors and the National Credit Union Administration Board shall jointly consider the factors set forth under clause (v), and, upon determining that an inflation adjustment is appropriate, shall jointly prescribe the amount by which the standard maximum deposit insurance amount and the standard maximum share insurance amount [that are] applicable to any depositor at an insured depository institution shall be increased[,] by calculating the product of – (I) $100,000 [(i.e., USD 100,000)]; and (II) the ratio of the published annual value of the Personal Consumption Expenditures Chain-Type Price Index (or any successor index thereto) published by the Department of Commerce, for the calendar year preceding the year in which the adjustment is calculated under this clause, to the published annual value of such index for the calendar year preceding [April 1, 2006], the date [that] this subparagraph takes effect under the Federal Deposit Insurance Reform Act of 2005. The values [that are] used in the calculation under subclause (II) shall be, as of the date of the calculation, the values [which are] most recently published by the Department of Commerce." (Government of the United States of America (2021), "Federal Deposit Insurance Act 1950," adopted on September 21, 1950,

There is established a separate fund to be designated as the FSLIC [(i.e., Federal Savings and Loans Insurance Corporation)] Resolution Fund[,] which shall be managed by the [Federal Deposit Insurance] Corporation and separately maintained and not commingled [761].

Assets and liabilities [that are] transferred to the FSLIC Resolution Fund shall be the assets and liabilities of the Fund and not of the [Federal Deposit Insurance] Corporation[,] and shall not be consolidated with the assets and liabilities of the Deposit Insurance Fund or the Corporation for accounting, reporting, or any other purpose[576] [762].

Funds held in the Deposit Insurance Fund or the FSLIC Resolution Fund, that are not otherwise employed[,] shall be invested in obligations of the United States or in obligations [which are] guaranteed as to principal and interest by the United States [763].

The Corporation is authorized, in its sole discretion and upon such terms and conditions as the Board of Directors may prescribe, to make loans to, to make deposits in, to purchase the assets or securities of, to assume the liabilities of, or to make contributions to, any insured depository institution – (A) if such action is taken to prevent the default of such insured depository institution; (B) if, with respect to an insured bank[577] in default, such action is taken to restore such insured bank to normal operation; or (C) if, when severe financial conditions exist which threaten the stability of a significant number of insured depository institutions or of insured depository institutions possessing significant financial resources, such action is taken in order to lessen the risk to the Corporation [that is] posed by such insured depository institution under such threat of instability [764].

Any conservator, receiver, or liquidator appointed for any insured depository institution in default, including the Corporation acting in such capacity, shall be entitled to offer the assets of such depository institutions for sale to the Corporation or as security for loans from the Corporation[578] [765].

All notes, debentures, bonds, or other such obligations [that are] issued by the Corporation shall be exempt, both as to principal and interest, from all taxation (except

updated to August 31, 2021, s.11(a)(1)(F)(i)). 'Clause (v)' is clause 11(a)(1)(F)(v) of the Federal Deposit Insurance Act 1950; it is labelled 'Inflation Adjustment Consideration', and states: "In making any determination under clause (i) to increase the standard maximum deposit insurance amount and the standard maximum share insurance amount, the Board of Directors and the National Credit Union Administration Board shall jointly consider – (I) the overall state of the Deposit Insurance Fund and the economic conditions affecting insured depository institutions; (II) potential problems affecting insured depository institutions; or (III) whether the increase will cause the reserve ratio of the fund to fall below 1.15 per cent of estimated insured deposits." (Government of the United States of America (2021), "Federal Deposit Insurance Act 1950," adopted on September 21, 1950, updated to August 31, 2021, s.11(a)(1)(F)(v)). 'Clause (i)' is clause 11(a)(1)(F)(i) of the Federal Deposit Insurance Act 1950; it is set out in the first sentence of the present footnote (i.e., fn 575). The penultimate sentence of fn 554 defines the term '*insured depository institution*'.

576 The FDIC "shall have all rights, powers, and duties to carry out [its] duties with respect to the assets and liabilities of the FSLIC Resolution Fund that the [FDIC] otherwise has under this Act" (Government of the United States of America (2021), "Federal Deposit Insurance Act 1950," adopted on September 21, 1950, updated to August 31, 2021, s.11A(a)(4)).

577 The third sentence of fn 555 defines the term '*insured bank*'.

578 The takings of every loan or sale of assets to the FDIC "shall be utilized for the same purposes and in the same manner as other funds [that are] realized from the liquidation of the assets of such depository institutions" (Government of the United States of America (2021), "Federal Deposit Insurance Act 1950," adopted on September 21, 1950, updated to August 31, 2021, s.13(d)(2)).

estate and inheritance taxes) [which is] now or hereafter imposed by the United States, by any Territory, dependency, or possession thereof, or by any State[579], county, municipality, or local taxing authority: *Provided*[580], That interest upon[,] or any income from[,] any such obligations[,] and gain from the sale or other disposition of such obligations[,] shall not have any exemption, as such, and loss from the sale or other disposition of shall not have any special treatment, as such, under the Internal Revenue Code, or laws amendatory or supplementary thereto. The Corporation, including its franchise, its capital, reserves, and surplus, and its income, shall be exempt from all taxation now or hereafter imposed by the United States, by any Territory, dependency, or possession thereof, or by any State, county, municipality, or local taxing authority, except that any real property of the Corporation shall be subject to State, Territorial, county, municipal or local taxation to the same extent[,] according to its value[,] as other real property is taxed [766].

[A]n insured State bank[581] may not engage as principal in any type of activity that is not permissible for a national bank[,] unless (A) the Corporation has determined that the activity would pose no significant risk to the Deposit Insurance Fund; and (B) the State bank is, and continues to be, in compliance with applicable capital standards [that are] prescribed by the appropriate Federal banking agency[582] [767].

An insured State bank may not, directly or indirectly, acquire or retain any equity investment of a type that is not permissible for a national bank[583] [768].

An insured State bank shall not acquire or retain, directly or indirectly, any equity investment of a type[,] or in an amount[,] that is not permissible for a national bank[,] or is not otherwise permitted under this section[584] [769].

[A] savings association[585] [which is] chartered under State law[586] may not engage as principal in any type of activity, or in any activity in an amount, that is not permissible for a Federal savings association[587][,] unless – (1) the Corporation has determined that the

---

[579] The fourth sentence of fn 552 defines the term '*State*'.

[580] Emphasis original.

[581] The third sentence of fn 555 defines the term '*insured bank*'. The third sentence of fn 552 defines the term '*State bank*'.

[582] A "subsidiary of an insured State bank may not engage as principal in any type of activity that is not permissible for a subsidiary of a national bank[,] unless – (A) the Corporation [(i.e., the FDIC)] has determined that the activity poses no significant risk to the Deposit Insurance Fund; and (B) the bank is, and continues to be, in compliance with applicable capital standards [that are] prescribed by the appropriate Federal banking agency" (Government of the United States of America (2021), "Federal Deposit Insurance Act 1950," adopted on September 21, 1950, updated to August 31, 2021, s.24(d)(1)). The third sentence of fn 555 defines the term '*insured bank*'. The third sentence of fn 552 defines the term '*State bank*'. The second sentence of fn 600 defines the term '*subsidiary*'. Fn 523 defines the term '*national bank*'.

[583] This rule "shall not prohibit an insured State bank from acquiring or retaining an equity investment in a subsidiary of which the insured State bank is a majority owner" (Government of the United States of America (2021), "Federal Deposit Insurance Act 1950," adopted on September 21, 1950, updated to August 31, 2021, s.24(c)(2)). The third sentence of fn 555 defines the term '*insured bank*'. The third sentence of fn 552 defines the term '*State bank*'. The second sentence of fn 600 defines the term '*subsidiary*'.

[584] 'It is submitted that 'this section' refers to subsection 24(f) of the Federal Deposit Insurance Act 1950, which is entitled 'Common and Preferred Stock Investment'. Paragraphs 24(f)(2) and 24(f)(3) of the Federal Deposit Insurance Act 1950 provide exceptions to the rule in paragraph 24(f)(1) of the Federal Deposit Insurance Act 1950, which the text to the current footnote (i.e., fn 584) lays down.

[585] The first sentence of fn 553 defines the term '*savings association*'.

[586] The last sentence of fn 553 defines the term '*State savings association*'.

[587] The second sentence of fn 553 defines the term '*Federal savings association*'.

activity would pose no significant risk to the Deposit Insurance Fund; and (2) the savings association is[,] and continues to be[,] in compliance with the fully phased-in capital standards [that are] prescribed under [sub]section 5(t) of the Home Owners' Loan Act[588] [770].

[A] savings association [which is] chartered under State law may not directly acquire or retain any equity investment of a type[,] or in an amount[,] that is not permissible for a Federal savings association[589] [771].

No savings association may, directly or through a subsidiary[590], acquire or retain any corporate debt security that does not meet standards of credit-worthiness[,] as established by the Corporation[591] [772].

An insured depository institution that is not well capitalized may not accept funds [that are] obtained, directly or indirectly, by or through any deposit broker for deposit into 1 or more deposit accounts[592] [773].

---

588 The first paragraph of subsection 5(t) of the Home Owners' Loan Act 1933 is labelled 'In General', and reads thus: "(A) … The appropriate Federal banking agency shall, by regulation, prescribe and maintain uniformly applicable capital standards for savings associations. Those standards shall include – (i) a leverage limit; (ii) a tangible capital requirement; and (iii) a risk-based capital requirement. (B) … A savings association is not in compliance with capital standards for purposes of this subsection[,] unless it complies with all capital standards [that are] prescribed under this paragraph. (C) … The standards [which are] prescribed under this paragraph shall be no less stringent than the capital standards [that are] applicable to national banks." (Government of the United States of America (2002), "Home Owners' Loan Act 1993," adopted on June 13, 1933, updated to November 17, 2022., s.5(t)(1)). The first sentence of fn 553 defines the term '*savings association*'. Fn 523 defines the term '*national bank*'.

589 Paragraph 28(c)(2) of the Federal Deposit Insurance Act 1950 furnishes an exception to the rule in paragraph 28(c)(1) of the Federal Deposit Insurance Act 1950, which the text to the present footnote (i.e., fn 589) sets out.

590 The second sentence of fn 600 defines the term '*subsidiary*'.

591 Paragraph 28(d)(2) of the Federal Deposit Insurance Act 1950 supplies an exception to the rule in paragraph 28(d)(1) of the Federal Deposit Insurance Act 1950, which the text to the current footnote (i.e., fn 591) specifies.

592 The FDIC "may, on a case-by-case basis[,] and upon application by an insured depository institution which is adequately capitalized (but not well capitalized), waive the applicability of subsection (a)[,] upon a finding that the acceptance of such deposits does not constitute an unsafe or unsound practice with respect to such institution" (Government of the United States of America (2021), "Federal Deposit Insurance Act 1950," adopted on September 21, 1950, updated to August 31, 2021, s.29(c)). 'Subsection (a)' is subsection 29(a) of the Federal Deposit Insurance Act 1950, which the text to the present footnote (i.e., fn 592) lays down. The penultimate sentence of fn 554 defines the term '*insured depository institution*'. The first sentence of fn 551 defines the term '*deposit*'. An insured depository institution is '*well capitalized*' "if it significantly exceeds the required minimum level for each relevant capital measure," '*adequately capitalized*' "if it meets the required minimum level for each relevant capital measure," '*undercapitalized*' "if it fails to meet the required minimum level for any relevant capital measure," '*significantly undercapitalized*' "if it is significantly below the required minimum level for any relevant capital measure," and '*critically undercapitalized*' "if it fails to meet any level [that is] specified under subsection (c)(3)(A)" (Government of the United States of America (2021), "Federal Deposit Insurance Act 1950," adopted on September 21, 1950, updated to August 31, 2021, s.38(b)(1)). 'Subsection (c)(3)(A)' is subparagraph 38(c)(3)(A) of the Federal Deposit Insurance Act 1950, which is headed 'Agency to Specify Level', and reads thus: "(i) … Each appropriate Federal banking agency shall, by regulation, in consultation with the Corporation [(i.e., the FDIC)], specify the ratio of tangible equity to total assets at which an insured depository institution is critically undercapitalized. (ii) … The agency may, by regulation, specify for 1 or more other relevant capital measures, the level at which an insured depository institution is critically undercapitalized." (Government of the United States of America (2021), "Federal Deposit Insurance Act 1950," adopted on September 21, 1950, updated to August 31, 2021, s.38(c)(3)(A)). The phrase '*required minimum level*' "means, with respect to each relevant capital measure, the minimum acceptable capital level [that is] specified by the appropriate Federal banking agency by regulation" (Government of the United States of America (2021), "Federal Deposit Insurance Act 1950," adopted on September 21, 1950, updated to August 31, 2021, s.38(b)(2)(G)). The phrase '*relevant capital measure*' "means the measures described in subsection (c)"

An insured depository institution may not enter into a written or oral contract with any person to provide goods, products, or services to[,] or for the benefit of[,] such depository institution[,] if the performance of such contract would adversely affect the safety or soundness of the institution[593] [774].

No insured depository institution may discharge or otherwise discriminate against any employee with respect to compensation, terms, conditions, or privileges of employment[,] because the employee (or any person acting pursuant to the request of the employee) provided information to any Federal banking agency or to the Attorney General[,] regarding – (A) a possible violation of any law or regulation; or (B) gross mismanagement, a gross waste of funds, an abuse of authority, or a substantial and specific danger to public health or safety; by the depository institution or any director, officer, or employee of the institution [775].

Any appropriate Federal banking agency shall notify the Securities and Exchange Commission of any concerns of the agency regarding significant financial or operational risks to any registered broker or dealer, or any registered municipal securities dealer, government securities broker, or government securities dealer for which the [Securities and Exchange] Commission is the appropriate regulatory agency (as defined in section 3 of the Securities Exchange Act of 1934[594]), resulting from the activities of any insured depository

(Government of the United States of America (2021), "Federal Deposit Insurance Act 1950," adopted on September 21, 1950, updated to August 31, 2021, s.38(b)(2)(F)). 'Subsection (c)' is subsection 38(c) of the Federal Deposit Insurance Act 1950, which is entitled 'Capital Standards'. The capital measures that subsection 38(c) of the Federal Deposit Insurance Act 1950 mentions include the ratio of tangible equity to total assets – the pertinent Federal banking agency must, in consultation with the FDIC, specify the level of this ratio below which an insured depository institution is critically undercapitalized; the Federal banking agency must set this level so as to require the insured depository institution to hold tangible equity of at least 2% of tangible assets (Government of the United States of America (2021), "Federal Deposit Insurance Act 1950," adopted on September 21, 1950, updated to August 31, 2021, ss.38(c)(3)(A)(i) and 38(c)(3)(B)(i)).

593 The FDIC "shall prescribe such regulations and issue such orders, including definitions consistent with this section, as may be necessary to administer and carry out the purposes of, and prevent evasions of, this section" (Government of the United States of America (2021), "Federal Deposit Insurance Act 1950," adopted on September 21, 1950, updated to August 31, 2021, s.30(b)). 'This section' is section 30 of the Federal Deposit Insurance Act 1950, which is titled 'Contracts between Depository Institutions and Persons providing Goods, Products, or Services'.

594 Unless the context requires otherwise, when used in the Securities Exchange Act of 1934, the phrase '*appropriate regulatory agency*' "means – (A) When used with respect to a municipal securities dealer: (i) the Comptroller of the Currency, in the case of a national bank, a subsidiary or a department or division of any such bank, a Federal savings association (as defined in section 3(b)(2) of the Federal Deposit Insurance Act [1950 (second sentence of fn 553)]), the deposits of which are insured by the Federal Deposit Insurance Corporation, or a subsidiary or department or division of any such Federal savings association; (ii) the Board of Governors of the Federal Reserve System, in the case of a State member bank of the Federal Reserve System, a subsidiary or a department or division thereof, a bank holding company, a subsidiary of a bank holding company which is a bank other than a bank [that is] specified in clause (i), (iii), or (iv) of this subparagraph, a subsidiary or a department or division of such subsidiary, or a savings and loan holding company; (iii) the Federal Deposit Insurance Corporation, in the case of a bank [that is] insured by the Federal Deposit Insurance Corporation (other than a member of the Federal Reserve System), a subsidiary or department or division of any such bank, a State savings association (as defined in section 3(b)(3) of the Federal Deposit Insurance Act [1950 (final sentence of fn 553)]), the deposits of which are insured by the Federal Deposit Insurance Corporation, or a subsidiary or a department or division of any such State savings association; and (iv) the [Securities and Exchange] Commission[,] in the case of all other municipal securities dealers. (B) When used with respect to a clearing agency or transfer agent: (i) the Comptroller of the Currency, in the case of a national bank, a subsidiary of any such bank, a Federal savings association (as defined in section 3(b)(2) of the Federal Deposit Insurance Act [1950 (second sentence of fn 553)]), the deposits of which are insured by the Federal Deposit Insurance Corporation, or a subsidiary of any such Federal savings association; (ii) the Board of Governors of the Federal

Reserve System, in the case of a State member bank of the Federal Reserve System, a subsidiary thereof, a bank holding company, a subsidiary of a bank holding company that is a bank other than a bank [that is] specified in clause (i) or (iii) or this subparagraph, or a savings and loan holding company; (iii) the Federal Deposit Insurance Corporation, in the case of a bank [that is] insured by the Federal Deposit Insurance Corporation (other than a member of the Federal Reserve System), a subsidiary of any such bank, a State savings association (as defined in section 3(b)(3) of the Federal Deposit Insurance Act [1950 (last sentence of fn 553)]), the deposits of which are insured by the Federal Deposit Insurance Corporation, or a subsidiary of any such State savings association; and (iv) the [Securities and Exchange] Commission[,] in the case of all other clearing agencies and transfer agents. (C) When used with respect to a participant or applicant to become a participant in a clearing agency[,] or a person requesting or having access to services [that are] offered by a clearing agency: (i) the Comptroller of the Currency, in the case of a national bank or a Federal savings association (as defined in section 3(b)(2) of the Federal Deposit Insurance Act [1950 (second sentence of fn 553)]), the deposits of which are insured by the Federal Deposit Insurance Corporation[,] when the appropriate regulatory agency for such clearing agency is not the [Securities and Exchange] Commission; (ii) the Board of Governors of the Federal Reserve System[,] in the case of a State member bank of the Federal Reserve System, a bank holding company, or a subsidiary of a bank holding company, a subsidiary of a bank holding company that is a bank other than a bank [that is] specified in clause (i) or (iii) of this subparagraph, or a savings and loan holding company[,] when the appropriate regulatory agency for such clearing agency is not the [Securities and Exchange] Commission; (iii) the Federal Deposit Insurance Corporation, in the case of a bank [that is] insured by the Federal Deposit Insurance Corporation (other than a member of the Federal Reserve System) or a State savings association (as defined in section 3(b)(3) of the Federal Deposit Insurance Act [1950 (final sentence of fn 553)]), the deposits of which are insured by the Federal Deposit Insurance Corporation; and when the appropriate regulatory agency for such clearing agency is not the [Securities and Exchange] Commission; (iv) the [Securities and Exchange] Commission[,] in all other cases. (D) When used with respect to an institutional investment manager[,] which is a bank the deposits of which are insured in accordance with the Federal Deposit Insurance Act [1950]: (i) the Comptroller of the Currency, in the case of a national bank or a Federal savings association (as defined in section 3(b)(2) of the Federal Deposit Insurance Act [1950 (second sentence of fn 553)]), the deposits of which are insured by the Federal Deposit Insurance Corporation; (ii) the Board of Governors of the Federal Reserve System, in the case of any other member bank of the Federal Reserve System; and (iii) the Federal Deposit Insurance Corporation, in the case of any other insured bank or a State savings association (as defined in section 3(b)(3) of the Federal Deposit Insurance Act [1950 (last sentence of fn 553)]), the deposits of which are insured by the Federal Deposit Insurance Corporation. (E) When used with respect to a national securities exchange or registered securities association, member thereof, person associated with a member thereof, applicant to become a member thereof or to become associated with a member thereof, or person requesting or having access to services [that are] offered by such exchange or association or member thereof, or the Municipal Securities Rulemaking Board, the [Securities and Exchange] Commission. (F) When used with respect to a person exercising investment discretion with respect to an account: (i) the Comptroller of the Currency, in the case of a national bank or a Federal savings association (as defined in section 3(b)(2) of the Federal Deposit Insurance Act [1950 (second sentence of fn 553)]), the deposits of which are insured by the Federal Deposit Insurance Corporation; (ii) the Board of Governors of the Federal Reserve System[,] in the case of any other member bank of the Federal Reserve System; and (iii) the Federal Deposit Insurance Corporation, in the case of any other bank the deposits of which are insured in accordance with the Federal Deposit Insurance Act [1950] or a State savings association (as defined in section 3(b)(3) of the Federal Deposit Insurance Act [1950 (final sentence of fn 553)]), the deposits of which are insured by the Federal Deposit Insurance Corporation; and (iv) the [Securities and Exchange] Commission[,] in the case of all other such persons. (G) When used with respect to a government securities broker or government securities dealer, or person associated with a government securities broker or government securities dealer: (i) the Comptroller of the Currency, in the case of a national bank, a Federal savings association (as defined in section 3(b)(2) of the Federal Deposit Insurance Act [1950 (second sentence of fn 553)]), the deposits of which are insured by the Federal Deposit Insurance Corporation, or a Federal branch or Federal agency of a foreign bank (as such terms are used in the International Banking Act of 1978); (ii) the Board of Governors of the Federal Reserve System, in the case of a State member bank of the Federal Reserve System, a foreign bank, an uninsured State branch or State agency of a foreign bank, a commercial lending company [that is] owned or controlled by a foreign bank (as such terms are used in the International Banking Act of 1978), or a corporation [which is] organized or having an agreement with the Board of Governors of the Federal Reserve System pursuant to section 25 or section 25A of the Federal Reserve Act; (iii) the Federal Deposit Insurance Corporation, in the case of a bank [that is] insured by the Federal Deposit Insurance Corporation (other than a member of the Federal Reserve System or a Federal savings bank), a State savings association (as defined in section 3(b)(3) of the Federal Deposit Insurance Act [1950 (last sentence of fn 553)]), the deposits of which are insured by the Federal Deposit Insurance Corporation, or an insured State branch of a foreign bank (as such terms are used in the International Banking Act of 1978); and (iv) the [Securities and Exchange] Commission, in the case of all other government securities brokers and government securities dealers.

institution, any depository institution holding company, or any affiliate of any such institution or company[,] if such broker, dealer, municipal securities dealer, government securities broker, or government securities dealer is an affiliate of any such institution, company, or affiliate [776].

(1) … Each insured depository institution shall submit an annual report to the Corporation, the appropriate Federal banking agency[595], and any appropriate State bank supervisor[596] (including any State bank supervisor of a host State). (2) … Any annual report [that is] required under paragraph (1) shall contain – (A) the information [which is] required to be provided by – (i) the institution's management under subsection (b) [(i.e., subsection 36(b) of the Federal Deposit Insurance Act 1950, which the next paragraph sets out)]; and (ii) an independent public accountant under subsections (c) and (d) [(i.e., subsections 36(c) and 36(d) of the Federal Deposit Insurance Act 1950, which the two paragraphs after the next paragraph respectively lay down)]; and (B) such other information as the Corporation and the appropriate Federal banking agency may determine to be necessary to assess the financial condition and management of the institution. (3) … [777].

Each insured depository institution shall prepare – (1) annual financial statements in accordance with general accepted accounting principles[,] and such other disclosure requirements as the Corporation and the appropriate Federal banking agency may prescribe; and (2) a report [that is] signed by the chief executive officer and the chief accounting or financial officer of the institution[,] which contains – (A) a statement of the management's responsibilities for – (i) preparing financial statements; (ii) establishing and maintaining an adequate internal control structure and procedures for financial reporting; and (iii) complying with the laws and regulations relating to safety and soundness[,] which are designated by the Corporation and the appropriate Federal banking agency; and (B) an assessment, as of the end of the institution's most recent fiscal year, of – (i) the effectiveness of such internal control structure and procedures; and (ii) the institution's compliance with the laws and regulations relating to safety and soundness[,] which are designated by the Corporation and the appropriate Federal banking agency [778].

(H) When used with respect to an institution [that is] described in subparagraph (D), (F), or (G) of section 2(c)(2), or held under section 4(f), of the Bank Holding Company Act of 1956 – (i) the Comptroller of the Currency, in the case of a national bank; (ii) the Board of Governors of the Federal Reserve System, in the case of a State member bank of the Federal Reserve System or any corporation [that is] chartered under section 25A of the Federal Reserve Act; (iii) the Federal Deposit Insurance Corporation, in the case of any other bank the deposits of which are insured in accordance with the Federal Deposit Insurance Act [1950]; or (iv) the [Securities and Exchange] Commission[,] in the case of all other such institutions. As used in this paragraph, the terms "*bank holding company*" and "*subsidiary of a bank holding company*" have the meanings given [to] them in section 2 of the Bank Holding Company Act of 1956. As used in this paragraph, the term "*savings and loan holding company*" has the same meaning as in section 10(a) of the Home Owners' Loan Act … ." (Government of the United States of America (2023), "Securities Exchange Act of 1934," adopted on June 6, 1934, updated to February 12, 2023, s.3(a)(34); emphasis added). Fn 523 defines the term '*national bank*'. The second sentence of fn 553 defines the term '*Federal savings association*'. The final sentence of fn 572 defines the term '*State member bank*'. The last sentence of fn 553 defines the term '*State savings association*'. The third sentence of fn 555 defines the term '*insured bank*'.

[595] The first sentence of fn 572 defines the term '*appropriate Federal banking agency*'.

[596] As used in the Federal Deposit Insurance Act 1950, the phrase '*State bank supervisor*' "means any officer, agency, or other entity of any State which has primary regulatory authority over State banks or State savings associations in such State" (Government of the United States of America (2021), "Federal Deposit Insurance Act 1950," adopted on September 21, 1950, updated to August 31, 2021, s.3(r)(1)). The third sentence of fn 552 defines the term '*State bank*'. The final sentence of fn 553 defines the term '*State savings association*'.

(1) … With respect to any internal control report [that is] required by subsection (b)(2) [(i.e., paragraph 36(b)(2) of the Federal Deposit Insurance Act 1950, which is point (2) of the immediately-preceding paragraph,)] of any institution, the institution's independent public accountant shall attest to, and report separately on, the assertions of the institution's management [that are] contained in such report. (2) … Any attestation pursuant to paragraph (1) shall be made in accordance with generally accepted standards for attestation engagements [779].

The Corporation, in consultation with the appropriate Federal banking agencies, shall prescribe regulations requiring that each insured depository institution shall have an annual independent audit made of the institution's financial statements by an independent public accountant[,] in accordance with generally accepted auditing standards and section 37 [of the Federal Deposit Insurance Act 1950[597]] (2) … In connection with any audit under this subsection, the independent public accountant shall determine and report whether the financial statements of the institution – (A) are presented fairly in accordance with generally accepted accounting principles; and (B) comply with such other disclosure requirements as the Corporation and the appropriate Federal banking agency may prescribe. (3) … [780].

Each appropriate Federal banking agency shall, for all insured depository institutions, prescribe – (1) standards relating to – (A) internal controls, information systems, and internal audit systems, in accordance with section 36 [of the Federal Deposit Insurance Act 1950[598]]; (B) loan documentation; (C) credit underwriting; (D) interest rate exposure; (E) asset growth; and (F) compensation, fees, and benefits, in accordance with subsection (c) [(i.e., subsection 39(c) of the Federal Deposit Insurance Act 1950, which the next paragraph but one lays down)]; and (2) such other operational and managerial standards as the agency determines to be appropriate [781].

---

597 Section 37 of the Federal Deposit Insurance Act 1950 is entitled 'Accounting Objectives, Standards, and Requirements'; the first two paragraphs of its subsection (a) read as follows: "(1) … Accounting principles [which are] applicable to reports or statements [that are] required to be filed with Federal banking agencies by insured depository institutions should – (A) result in financial statements and reports of condition that accurately reflect the capital of such institutions; (B) facilitate effective supervision of the institutions; and (C) facilitate prompt corrective action to resolve the institutions(,) at the least cost to the Deposit Insurance Fund. " (2) … (A) … Subject to the requirements of this Act and any other provision of Federal law, the accounting principles [which are] applicable to reports or statements [that are] required to be filed with Federal banking agencies by all insured depository institutions shall be uniform[,] and consistent with generally accepted accounting principles. (B) … If the appropriate Federal banking agency or the Corporation [(i.e., the FDIC)] determines that the application of any generally accepted accounting principle to any insured depository institution is inconsistent with the objectives described in paragraph (1), [then] the agency or the Corporation may, with respect to reports or statements [that are] required to be filed with such agency or Corporation, prescribe an accounting principle which is applicable to such institutions[,] which is no less stringent than generally accepted accounting principles." (Government of the United States of America (2021), "Federal Deposit Insurance Act 1950," adopted on September 21, 1950, updated to August 31, 2021, s.37(a)(1)-(2)). The penultimate sentence of fn 554 defines the term '*insured depository institution*'.

598 The four paragraphs of the text immediately preceding the current one respectively set out the first four subsections of section 36 of the Federal Deposit Insurance Act 1950.

Each appropriate Federal banking agency shall, prescribe standards, by regulation or guideline, for all insured depository institutions relating to asset quality, earnings, and stock valuation[,] that the agency determines to be appropriate [782].

Each appropriate Federal banking agency shall, for all insured depository institutions, prescribe – (1) standards prohibiting as an unsafe and unsound practice any employment contract, compensation or benefit agreement, fee arrangement, perquisite, stock option plan, postemployment benefit, or other contemporary arrangement[,] that – (A) would provide any executive officer, employee, director, or principal shareholder of the institution with excessive compensation, fees or benefits; or (B) could lead to material financial loss to the institution; (2) standards specifying when compensation, fees, or benefits [that are] referred to in paragraph (1) are excessive, which shall require the agency to determine whether the amounts are unreasonable or disproportionate to the services actually performed by the individual[,] by considering – (A) the combined value of all cash and noncash benefits [that are] provided to the individual; (B) the compensation history of the individual and other individuals with comparable expertise at the institution; (C) the financial condition of the institution; (D) comparable compensation practices at comparable institutions, based upon such factors as asset size, geographic location, and the complexity of the loan portfolio or other assets; (E) for postemployment benefits, the projected total cost and benefit to the institution; (F) any connection between the individual and any fraudulent act or omission, breach of trust or fiduciary duty, or insider abuse with regard to the institution; and (G) other factors that the agency determines to be relevant; and (3) such other standards relating to compensation, fees, and benefits[,] as the agency determines to be appropriate [783].

[T]he responsible agency may approve a merger transaction under [sub]section 18(c) [of the Federal Deposit Insurance Act 1950[599]] between insured banks with different home States, without regard to whether such transaction is prohibited under the law of any State [784].

[599] Paragraph 1 of subsection 18(c) of the Federal Deposit Insurance Act 1950 states: "Except with the prior written approval of the responsible agency, which shall[,] in every case [that is] referred to in this paragraph[,] be the Corporation [(i.e., the FDIC)], no insured depository institution shall – (A) merge or consolidate with any noninsured bank or institution; (B) assume liability to pay any deposits (including liabilities which would be "deposits" except for the proviso in section 3(l)(5) of this Act [(point (5) in the first sentence of fn 551)]) [that are] made in, or similar liabilities of, any noninsured bank or institution; or (C) transfer assets to any noninsured bank or institution[,] in consideration of the assumption of liabilities for any portion of the deposits [that are] made in such insured depository institution." (Government of the United States of America (2021), "Federal Deposit Insurance Act 1950," adopted on September 21, 1950, updated to August 31, 2021, s.18(c)(1)). The penultimate sentence of fn 554 defines the term '*insured depository institution*'. The third sentence of fn 555 defines the term '*insured bank*'. The first sentence of fn 551 defines the term '*deposit*'.

An insured State bank may control[,] or hold an interest in[,] a subsidiary[600] that engages in activities as principal that would only be permissible for a national bank to conduct through a financial subsidiary[601][,] if – (1) the State bank and each insured

[600] For the purposes of the current section, i.e., section 46 of the Federal Deposit Insurance Act 1950, which is titled 'Safety and Soundness Firewalls applicable to Financial Subsidiaries of Banks', the word '*subsidiary*' "means any company that is a subsidiary (as defined in section 3(w)(4) [(i.e., paragraph 3(w)(4) of the Federal Deposit Insurance Act 1950)]) of 1 or more insured banks" (Government of the United States of America (2021), "Federal Deposit Insurance Act 1950," adopted on September 21, 1950, updated to August 31, 2021, s.46(c)(1)). As used in the Federal Deposit Insurance Act 1950, the word '*subsidiary*' "(A) means any company which is owned or controlled[,] directly or indirectly[,] by another company; and (B) includes any service corporation [that is] owned[,] in whole or in part[,] by an insured depository institution or any subsidiary of such a service corporation" (Government of the United States of America (2021), "Federal Deposit Insurance Act 1950," adopted on September 21, 1950, updated to August 31, 2021, s.3(w)(4)). The third sentence of fn 555 defines the term '*insured bank*'. The penultimate sentence of fn 554 defines the term '*insured depository institution*'.

[601] For the purposes of the present section, i.e., section 46 of the Federal Deposit Insurance Act 1950, which is entitled 'Safety and Soundness Firewalls applicable to Financial Subsidiaries of Banks', the phrase '*financial subsidiary*' "has the meaning given [to] the term in section 5136A(g) of the Revised Statutes of the United States" (Government of the United States of America (2021), "Federal Deposit Insurance Act 1950," adopted on September 21, 1950, updated to August 31, 2021, s.46(c)(2)). Section 5136A of the Revised Statutes of the United States is classified to section 24a of Title 12 (Banks and Banking) of the United States Code (Government of the United States of America (2022), "Editorial notes to section 1306 of Title 18 – Crimes and Criminal Procedure – of the United States Code," last updated November 24, 2022, accessed November 25, 2022; <https://uscode.house.gov/view.xhtml?req=granuleid:USC-prelim-title18-section1306&num=0&edition =prelim>). Thus, subsection 5136A(g) of the Revised Statutes of the United States is now subsection 24a(g) of Title 12 of the United States Code, which is titled 'Definitions'. The definition of the phrase '*financial subsidiary*' is in paragraph (3) of subsection 24a(g) of Title 12 of the United States Code; a '*financial subsidiary*' is "any company that is controlled by 1 or more insured depository institutions[,] other than a subsidiary that – (A) engages solely in activities that national banks are permitted to engage in directly[,] and [which] are conducted subject to the same terms and conditions that govern the conduct of such activities by national banks; or (B) a national bank is specifically authorized by the express terms of a Federal statute (other than this section), and not by implication or interpretation, to control, such as by section 25 or 25A of the Federal Reserve Act … or the Bank Service Company Act …" (Government of the United States of America (2022), "United States Code, Updated," Title 12 – Banks and Banking, s.24a(g)(3)). 'This section' is section 24a of Title 12 (Banks and Banking) of the United States Code, which is entitled 'Financial subsidiaries of national banks'. Fn 523 defines the term '*national bank*'. The term '*insured depository institution*' has the meaning to which section 1813 of Title 12 (Banks and Banking) gives to it (Government of the United States of America (2022), "United States Code, Updated," Title 12 – Banks and Banking, s.24a(g)(2)). Accordingly, the phrase '*insured depository institution*' "means any bank or savings association the deposits of which are insured by the [Federal Deposit Insurance] Corporation[,] pursuant to this chapter" (Government of the United States of America (2022), "United States Code, Updated," Title 12 – Banks and Banking, s.1813(c)(2)). 'This chapter' is Chapter 16 of Title 12 (Banks and Banking) of the United States Code, which is titled 'Federal Deposit Insurance Corporation'. The terms '*company*', '*control*' and '*subsidiary*' have the meanings to which section 1841 of Title 12 (Banks and Banking) gives to them (Government of the United States of America (2022), "United States Code, Updated," Title 12 – Banks and Banking, s.24a(g)(1)). Accordingly, (i) the word '*company*' "means any corporation, partnership, business trust, association, or similar organization, or any other trust unless by its terms it must terminate within twenty-five years or not later than twenty-one years and ten months after the death of individuals living on the effective date of the trust[,] but shall not include any corporation the majority of the shares of which are owned by the United States or by any State, and shall not include a qualified family partnership" (Government of the United States of America (2022), "United States Code, Updated," Title 12 – Banks and Banking, s.1841(b)); (ii) "[a]ny company has *control* over a bank or over any company[,] if – (A) the company[,] directly or indirectly or acting through one or more other persons[,] owns, controls, or has power to vote 25 per centum or more of any class of voting securities of the bank or company; (B) the company controls in any manner the election of a majority of the directors or trustees of the bank or company; or (C) the Board determines, after notice and opportunity for hearing, that the company[,] directly or indirectly[,] exercises a controlling influence over the management or policies of the bank or company" (Government of the United States of America (2022), "United States Code, Updated," Title 12 – Banks and Banking, s.1841(a)(2); emphasis added); (iii) the word '*subsidiary*', "with respect to a specified bank holding company, means (1) any company 25 per centum or more of whose voting shares (excluding shares owned by the United States or by any company [that is] wholly owned by the United States) is[,] directly or indirectly[,] owned or controlled by such bank holding company, or is held by it with power to vote; (2) any company the election of a majority of whose

depository institution affiliate of the State bank are well capitalized[602] (after the capital deduction [that is] required by paragraph (2)); (2) the State bank complies with the capital deduction and financial statement disclosure requirements in section 5136A(c) of the Revised Statute of the United States[603]; (3) the State bank complies with the financial and operational safeguards [that are] required by section 5136A(d) of the Revised Statutes of the United States[604]; and (4) the State bank complies with the amendments to sections 23A and 23B of the Federal Reserve Act [which are] made by [sub]section 121(b) of the Gramm-Leach-Bliley Act[605] [785].

---

directors is controlled[,] in any manner[,] by such bank holding company; or (3) any company with respect to the management of policies of which such bank holding company has the power, directly or indirectly, to exercise a controlling influence, as determined by the Board, after notice and opportunity for hearing" (Government of the United States of America (2022), "United States Code, Updated," Title 12 – Banks and Banking, s.1841(d)).

[602] The fifth sentence of fn 592 defines the term '*well capitalized*'.

[603] Section 5136A of the Revised Statutes of the United States is classified to section 24a of Title 12 (Banks and Banking) of the United States Code (Government of the United States of America (2022), "Editorial notes to section 1306 of Title 18 – Crimes and Criminal Procedure – of the United States Code," last updated November 24, 2022, accessed November 25, 2022; <https://uscode.house.gov/view.xhtml?req=granuleid:USC-prelim-title18-section1306&num=0&edition=prelim>). Thus, subsection 5136A(c) of the Revised Statutes of the United States is now subsection 24a(c) of Title 12 of the United States 12, which is entitled 'Capital deduction', and which states: "**(1) Capital deduction required** In determining compliance with applicable capital standards – (A) the aggregate amount of the outstanding equity investment, including retained earnings, of a national bank in all financial subsidiaries shall be deducted from the assets and tangible equity of the national bank; and (B) the assets and liabilities of the financial subsidiaries shall not be consolidated with those of the national bank. **(2) Financial statement disclosure of capital deduction** Any published financial statement of a national bank that controls a financial subsidiary shall, in addition to providing information [that is] prepared in accordance with generally accepted accounting principles, separately present financial information for the bank in the manner [which is] provided in paragraph (1)." (Government of the United States of America (2022), "United States Code, Updated," Title 12 – Banks and Banking, s.24a(c); emphasis original). Fn 523 defines the term '*national bank*'.

[604] Section 5136A of the Revised Statutes of the United States is classified to section 24a of Title 12 (Banks and Banking) of the United States Code (Government of the United States of America (2022), "Editorial notes to section 1306 of Title 18 – Crimes and Criminal Procedure – of the United States Code," last updated November 24, 2022, accessed November 25, 2022; <https://uscode.house.gov/view.xhtml?req=granuleid:USC-prelim-title18-section1306&num=0&edition=prelim>). Thus, subsection 5136A(d) of the Revised Statutes of the United States is now subsection 24a(d) of Title 12 of the United States Code, which is titled 'Safeguards for the bank', and which reads: "A national bank that establishes or maintains a financial subsidiary shall assure that – (1) the procedures of the national bank for identifying and managing financial and operational risks within the national bank and the financial subsidiary adequately protect the national bank from such risks; (2) the national bank has, for the protection of the bank, reasonable policies and procedures to preserve the separate corporate identity and limited liability of the national bank and the financial subsidiaries of the national bank; and (3) the national bank is in compliance with this section." (Government of the United States of America (2022), "United States Code, Updated," Title 12 – Banks and Banking, s.24a(d)). 'This section' is section 24a of Title 12 (Banks and Banking) of the United States Code, which is entitled 'Financial subsidiaries of national banks'. Fn 523 defines the term '*national bank*'.

[605] Subsection 121(b) of the Gramm-Leach-Bliley Act reads as follows: "SECTIONS 23A AND 23B OF THE FEDERAL RESERVE ACT. – (1) LIMITING THE EXPOSURE OF A BANK TO A FINANCIAL SUBSIDIARY TO THE AMOUNT OF PERMISSIBLE EXPOSURE TO AN AFFILIATE. – Section 23A of the Federal Reserve Act … is amended – (A) by redesignating subsection (e) as subsection (f); and (B) by inserting after subsection (d), the following new subsection: "(e) RULES RELATING TO BANKS WITH FINANCIAL SUBSIDIARIES. – "(1) FINANCIAL SUBSIDIARY DEFINED. – For purposes of this section and section 23B [of the Federal Reserve Act], the term 'financial subsidiary' means any company that is a subsidiary of a bank that would be a financial subsidiary of a national bank under section 5136A of the Revised Statutes of the United States [, which is classified to section 24a of Title 12 (Banks and Banking) of the United States Code (second sentence of fn 601)]. … (2) FINANCIAL SUBSIDIARY TREATED AS AN AFFILIATE. For purposes of applying this section and section 23B [of the Federal Reserve Act], and notwithstanding subsection (b)(2) of this section or section 23B(d)(1) [of the Federal Reserve Act], a financial subsidiary of a bank – … (A) shall be deemed to be an affiliate of the bank; and (B) shall not be deemed to be a subsidiary of the bank. … (3) EXCEPTIONS FOR TRANSACTIONS WITH FINANCIAL

Notwithstanding clause (i) or (ii) of section 8(b)(6)(A) [of the Federal Deposit Insurance Act 1950][606] or section 38(e)(2)(E)(i) [of the Federal Deposit Insurance Act

---

SUBSIDIARIES. – … (A) EXCEPTION FROM LIMIT ON COVERED TRANSACTIONS WITH ANY INDIVIDUAL FINANCIAL SUBSIDIARY. – Notwithstanding paragraph (2), the restriction contained in subsection (a)(1)(A) shall not apply with respect to covered transactions between a bank and any individual financial subsidiary of the bank. … (B) EXCEPTION FOR EARNINGS RETAINED BY FINANCIAL SUBSIDIARIES. – Notwithstanding paragraph (2) or subsection (b)(7), a bank's investment in a financial subsidiary of the bank shall not include retained earnings of the financial subsidiary. … (4) ANTI-EVASION PROVISION. – For purposes of this section and section 23B [of the Federal Reserve Act] – … (A) any purchase of, or investment in, the securities of a financial subsidiary of a bank by an affiliate of the bank shall be considered to be a purchase of[,] or investment in[,] such securities by the bank; and … (B) any extension of credit by an affiliate of a bank to a financial subsidiary of the bank shall be considered to be an extension of credit by the bank to the financial subsidiary[,] if the Board determines that such treatment is necessary or appropriate to prevent evasions of this Act and the Gramm-Leach-Bliley Act." (2) REBUTTABLE PRESUMPTION OF CONTROL OF PORTFOLIO COMPANY. – Section 23A(b) of the Federal Reserve Act … is amended by adding at the end the following new paragraph – "(11) REBUTTABLE PRESUMPTION OF CONTROL OF PORTFOLIO COMPANIES. – In addition to paragraph (3), a company or shareholder shall be presumed to control any other company[,] if the company or shareholder, directly or indirectly, or acting through 1 or more other persons, owns or controls 15 percent or more of the equity capital of the other company pursuant to subparagraph (H) or (I) of section 4(k)(4) of the Bank Holding Company Act of 1956 or rules [that are] adopted under section 122 of the Gramm-Leach-Bliley Act, if any, unless the company or shareholder provides information [that is] acceptable to the Board to rebut this presumption of control." (3) RULEMAKING REQUIRED CONCERNING DERIVATIVE TRANSACTIONS AND INTRADAY CREDIT. – Section 23A(f) of the Federal Reserve Act …. (as so redesignated by paragraph (1)(A) of this subsection) is amended[,] by inserting at the end the following new paragraph: "(3) RULEMAKING REQUIRED CONCERNING DERIVATIVE TRANSACTIONS AND INTRADAY CREDIT. – … (A) IN GENERAL. – Not later than 18 months after the date of the enactment of the Gramm-Leach-Bliley Act, the Board shall adopt final rules under this section to address as covered transactions credit exposure arising out of derivative transactions between member banks and their affiliates[,] and intraday extensions of credit by member banks to their affiliates. … (B) EFFECTIVE DATE. – The effective date of any final rule [that is] adopted by the Board pursuant to subparagraph (A) shall be shall be delayed for such period as the Board deems necessary or appropriate to permit banks to conform their activities to the requirements of the final rule without undue hardship." (Government of the United States of America (1999), "Gramm-Leach-Bliley Act 1999," adopted on November 12, 1999, s.121(b); emphasis original).

606 Subparagraph 8(b)(6)(A) of the Federal Deposit Insurance Act 1950 states: "The authority to issue an order under this subsection and subsection (c) which requires an insured depository institution or any institution-affiliated party to take affirmative action to correct or remedy any conditions resulting from any violation or practice with respect to which such order is issued(,) includes the authority to require such depository institution or such party to – (A) make restitution or provide reimbursement, indemnification, or guarantee against loss[,] if – (i) such depository institution or such party was unjustly enriched in connection with such violation or practice; or (ii) the violation or practice involved a reckless disregard for the law or any applicable regulations or prior order of the appropriate Federal banking agency; (B) … ." (Government of the United States of America (2021), "Federal Deposit Insurance Act 1950," adopted on September 21, 1950, updated to August 31, 2021, s.8(b)(6)(A)). 'This subsection' is subsection 8(b) of the Federal Deposit Insurance Act 1950, which is titled 'Cease-and-Desist Proceedings'. 'Subsection (c)' is subsection 8(c) of the Federal Deposit Insurance Act 1950, which is entitled 'Temporary Cease-and-Desist Orders'. The penultimate sentence of fn 554 defines the term '*insured depository institution*'. The first sentence of fn 610 defines the term '*institution-affiliated party*'. The first sentence of fn 572 defines the term '*appropriate Federal banking agency*'.

1950][607], the appropriate Federal banking agency[608] for a depository institution may enforce, under section 8 [of the Federal Deposit Insurance Act 1950][609], the terms of – (1) any condition [that is] imposed in writing by the agency on the depository institution or an institution-affiliated party[610] in connection with any action on any application, notice, or

---

607 Clause 38(e)(2)(E)(i) of the Federal Deposit Insurance Act 1950 specifies: "The aggregate liability under subparagraph (C)(ii) of all companies having control of an insured depository institution shall be the lesser of – (I) an amount equal to 5 percent of the institution's total assets at the time [that] the institution became undercapitalized; or (II) the amount which is necessary (or would have been necessary) to bring the institution into compliance with all capital standards [that are] applicable with respect to such institution[,] as of the time [that] the institution fails to comply with a plan under this subsection." (Government of the United States of America (2021), "Federal Deposit Insurance Act 1950," adopted on September 21, 1950, updated to August 31, 2021, 38(e)(2)(E)(i)). 'This subsection' is subsection 38(e) of the Federal Deposit Insurance Act 1950, which is titled 'Provisions applicable to Undercapitalized Institutions'. 'Subparagraph (C)(ii)' is clause 38(e)(2)(C)(ii) of the Federal Deposit Insurance Act 1950, which reads as follows: "The appropriate Federal banking agency shall not accept a capital restoration plan[,] unless the agency determines that – ... (ii) if the insured depository institution is undercapitalized, each company having control of the institution has – (I) guaranteed that the institution will comply with the plan until the institution has been adequately capitalized on average during each of 4 consecutive calendar quarters; and (II) provided appropriate assurances of performance." (Government of the United States of America (2021), "Federal Deposit Insurance Act 1950," adopted on September 21, 1950, updated to August 31, 2021, 38(e)(2)(C)(ii)). The penultimate sentence of fn 554 defines the term '*insured depository institution*'. The fifth sentence of fn 592 defines the terms '*undercapitalized*' and '*adequately capitalized*'. The first sentence of fn 572 defines the term '*appropriate Federal banking agency*'.

608 The first sentence of fn 572 defines the term '*appropriate Federal banking agency*'.

609 Section 8 of the Federal Deposit Insurance Act 1950 is entitled 'Termination of Status as Insured Depository Institution'.

610 As used in the Federal Deposit Insurance Act 1950, the phrase '*institution-affiliated party*' "means – (1) any director, officer, employee, or controlling stockholder (other than a bank holding company or savings and loan holding company) of, or agent for, an insured depository institution; (2) any other person who has filed[,] or is required to file[,], a change-in-control notice with the appropriate Federal banking agency under [sub]section 7(j) [of the Federal Deposit Insurance Act 1950]; (3) any shareholder (other than a bank holding company or savings and loan holding company), consultant, joint venture partner, and any other person as determined by the appropriate Federal banking agency (by regulation or case-by-case) who participates in the conduct of the affairs of an insured depository institution; and (4) any independent contractor (including any attorney, appraiser, or accountant)[,] who knowingly or recklessly participates in – (A) any violation of any law or regulation; (B) any breach of fiduciary duty; or (C) any unsafe or unsound practice, which caused[,] or is likely to cause[,] more than a minimal financial loss to, or a significant adverse effect on, the insured depository institution" (Government of the United States of America (2021), "Federal Deposit Insurance Act 1950," adopted on September 21, 1950, updated to August 31, 2021, s.3(u)). The penultimate sentence of fn 554 defines the term '*insured depository institution*'. The first sentence of fn 572 defines the term '*appropriate Federal banking agency*'. Subsection 7(j) of the Federal Deposit Insurance Act 1950 is titled 'Change in Control of Insured Depository Institutions'; its first paragraph states: "No person, acting directly or indirectly or through or in concert with one or more persons, shall acquire control of any insured depository institution through a purchase, assignment, transfer, pledge, or other disposition of voting stock of such insured depository institution[,] unless the appropriate Federal banking agency has been given sixty days' prior written notice of such proposed acquisition and[,] within that time period[,] the agency has not issued a notice disapproving the proposed acquisition or, in the discretion of the agency, extending for an additional 30 days the period during which such a disapproval may issue. The period for disapproval under the preceding sentence may be extended not to exceed 2 additional times for not more than 45 days each time[,] if – (A) the agency determines that any acquiring party has not furnished all the information [that is] required under paragraph (6); (B) in the agency's judgment, any material information submitted is substantially inaccurate; (C) the agency has been unable to complete the investigation of an acquiring party under paragraph (2)(B) because of any delay caused by, or the inadequate cooperation of, such acquiring party; or (D) the agency determines that additional time is needed – (i) to investigate and determine that no acquiring party has a record of failing to comply with the requirements of subchapter II of chapter 53 of title 31, United States Code[;] (ii) to analyze the safety and soundness of any plans or proposals [that are] described in paragraph (6)(E) or the future prospects of the institution. An acquisition may be made prior to expiration of the disapproval period[,] if the agency issues written notice of its intent not to disapprove the action." (Government of the United States of America (2021), "Federal Deposit Insurance Act 1950," adopted on September 21, 1950, updated to August 31, 2021, s.7(j)(1)). 'Paragraph (6)' is paragraph 7(j)(6) of the Federal Deposit Insurance 1950, which reads thus: "Except as otherwise provided by regulation of the appropriate Federal banking agency, a notice filed pursuant to this subsection [(i.e., subsection 7(j) of the

other request concerning the depository institution; or (2) any written agreement [that is] entered into by the agency and the depository institution or an institution-affiliated party [786].

Securities and Exchange Commission (SEC)

The mission of the SEC is threefold – to protect investors, facilitate the formation of capital, and maintain fair, efficient and orderly markets [787]. As the following passage points out, banks come within the regulatory remit of the SEC to the extent that they issue securities, and to the degree that they participate within the securities industry. This monograph's sister publication, which is entitled '*An Overview of Corporate Securities Law in Four English-Language Jurisdictions*', provides further information concerning the SEC.

> The SEC supervises: • Banking organisations as issuers of securities: The SEC (and the relevant stock exchange) requires issuers [to] provide financial and other information about securities issuances [that are] offered for public sale with specific disclosures. Bank

Federal Deposit Insurance Act 1950 – which is entitled 'Change in Control of Insured Depository Institutions')] shall contain the following information: (A) The identity, personal history, business background and experience of each person by whom or on whose behalf the acquisition is to be made, including his material business activities and affiliations during the past five years, and a description of any material pending legal or administrative proceedings in which he is a party and any criminal indictment or conviction of such person by a State or Federal court. (B) A statement of the assets and liabilities of each person by whom[,] or on whose behalf[,] the acquisition is to be made, as of the end of the fiscal year for each of the five fiscal years immediately preceding the date of the notice, together with related statements of income[,] and source and application of funds[,] for each of the fiscal years then concluded, all prepared in accordance with generally accepted accounting principles [that are] consistently applied, and an interim statement of the assets and liabilities for each such person, together with related statements of income[,] and source and application of funds, as of a date not more than ninety days prior to the date of the filing of the notice. (C) The terms and conditions of the proposed acquisition and the manner in which the acquisition is to be made. (D) The identity, source and amount of the funds or other consideration used[,] or to be used[,] in making the acquisition, and[,] if any part of these funds or other consideration has been[,] or is[,] to be borrowed or otherwise obtained for the purpose of making the acquisition, a description of the transaction, the names of the parties, and any arrangements, agreements, or understandings with such persons. (E) Any plans or proposals which any acquiring party making the acquisition may have to liquidate the bank, to sell its assets or merge it with any company[,] or to make any other major change in its business or corporate structure or management. (F) The identification of any person employed, retained, or to be compensated[,] by the acquiring party, or by any person on his behalf, to make solicitations or recommendations to stockholders for the purpose of assisting in the acquisition, and a brief description of the terms of such employment, retainer, or arrangement for compensation. (G) Copies of all invitations or tenders or advertisements making a tender offer to stockholders for purchase of their stock to be used in connection with the proposed acquisition. (H) Any additional relevant information in such form as the appropriate Federal banking agency may require by regulation[,] or by specific request in connection with any particular notice." (Government of the United States of America (2021), "Federal Deposit Insurance Act 1950," adopted on September 21, 1950, updated to August 31, 2021, s.7(j)(6)). 'Paragraph (2)(B)' is subparagraph 7(j)(2)(B) of the Federal Deposit Insurance 1950, which is headed 'Investigation of Principles Required', and which declares: "Upon receiving any notice under this subsection [(i.e., subsection 7(j) of the Federal Deposit Insurance Act 1950 – which is titled 'Change in Control of Insured Depository Institutions')], the appropriate Federal banking agency shall – (i) conduct an investigation of the competence, experience, integrity, and financial ability of each person named in a notice of a proposed acquisition as a person by whom[,] or for whom[,] such acquisition is to be made; and (ii) make an independent determination of the accuracy and completeness of any information [that is] described in paragraph (6) [(i.e., paragraph 7(j)(6) of the Federal Deposit Insurance Act 1950 (above in the present footnote (fn 610)))] with respect to such person." (Government of the United States of America (2021), "Federal Deposit Insurance Act 1950," adopted on September 21, 1950, updated to August 31, 2021, s.7(j)(2)(B)). Subchapter II of Chapter 53 (Monetary Transactions) of Title 31 (Money and Finance) of the United States Code, is entitled 'Records and Reports on Monetary Instruments Transactions' and comprises sections 5311-5336 of this Title.

deposits are exempt from many of these requirements[,] and there are specific rules for bank debt securities. The SEC requires periodic reporting[,] and governs proxy solicitations. • Banking organisations as participants in the securities industry: The SEC's role depends on whether the activity is conducted by a chartered bank, where the bank regulator's rules would primarily govern, or a holding company affiliate (such as a broker-dealer, investment adviser, underwriter, or fund manager), where the SEC rules would primarily govern. The SEC's and the bank regulator's rules often overlap in practice [725].

Comment

This section introduces four federal agencies that regulate banks in the USA – the OCC, the Federal Reserve, the FDIC and the SEC. Between them, these bodies oversee much of the activity at these banks – especially at national banks.

The Volcker Rule

Background to the Volcker Rule

The Volcker Rule[611] aims to safeguard customers of banks in the USA, by preventing the latter from making certain kinds of speculative investments that contributed to the global financial crisis of 2007 to 2009 [788]. It also prohibits banks or insured depository institutions from securing or retaining ownership interests in private equity funds or hedge funds, unless one of the specified exemptions applies [788]. The Volcker Rule came into effect on 1st April 2014, with the full compliance of banks required by 21st July 2015 [788].

[611] The Volcker Rule is set out in section 619 of the Dodd-Frank Act Wall Street Reform and Consumer Protection Act 2010, and is also laid down in section 1851 of Title 12 (Banks and Banking) of the United States Code. The latter is quoted and referenced in the current section of the text, i.e., that titled 'The Volcker Rule'.

The General Rule for Banks

The general rule as applied to banks[612] – in contrast to nonbank financial companies[613], is as follows.

[612] In section 1851 of Title 12 (Banks and Banking) of the United States Code, the phrase '*banking entity*' means "any insured depository institution (as defined in section 1813 of this title [(i.e., paragraph 1813(c)(2) of Title 12 of the United States Code (eighth sentence of fn 601))]), any company that controls an insured depository institution, or that is treated as a bank holding company for the purposes of section 8 of the International Banking Act of 1978, and any affiliate or subsidiary of any such entity" (Government of the United States of America (2022), "United States Code, Updated," Title 12 – Banks and Banking, s.1851(h)(1)). The last sentence of fn 601 defines the terms '*company*', '*control*' and '*subsidiary*'. Except as paragraph 1841(a)(5) of Title 12 (Banks and Banking) of the United States Code provides, the phrase '*bank holding company*' "means any company which has control over any bank or over any company that is[,] or becomes[,] a bank holding company by virtue of this chapter [(i.e., Chapter 17 (which is entitled 'Bank Holding Companies') of Title 12 (Banks and Banking) of the United States Code, which comprises sections 1841-1852 of Title 12 of the United States Code)]" (Government of the United States of America (2022), "United States Code, Updated," Title 12 – Banks and Banking, s.1841(a)(1)). Paragraph 1841(a)(5) of Title 12 (Banks and Banking) of the United States Code states: "Notwithstanding any other provision of this subsection [(i.e., subsection 1841(a) of Title 12 (Banks and Banking) of the United States Code)] – (A) No bank[,] and no company owning or controlling voting shares of a bank[,] is a bank holding company by virtue of its ownership or control of shares in a fiduciary capacity, except as provided in paragraphs (2) and (3) of subsection (g) of this section [(i.e., paragraphs 1841(g)(2) and 1841(g)(3) of Title 12 (Banks and Banking) of the United States Code)]. For the purpose of the preceding sentence, bank shares shall not be deemed to have been acquired in a fiduciary capacity[,] if the acquiring bank or company has sole discretionary authority to exercise voting rights with respect thereto; … . (B) No company is a bank holding company by virtue of its ownership or control of shares acquired by it in connection with its underwriting of securities[,] if such shares are held only for such period of time as will permit the sale thereof on a reasonable basis. (C) No company formed for the sole purpose of participating in a proxy solicitation is a bank holding company by virtue of its control of voting rights of shares acquired in the course of such solicitation. (D) No company is a bank holding company by virtue of its ownership or control of shares acquired in securing or collecting a debt previously contracted in good faith, until two years after the date of acquisition. … (E) No company is a bank holding company by virtue of its ownership or control of any State-chartered bank or trust company which – (i) is wholly owned by 1 or more thrift institutions or savings banks; and (ii) is restricted to accepting – (I) deposits from thrift institutions or savings banks; (II) deposits arising out of the corporate business of the thrift institutions or savings banks that own the bank or trust company; or (III) deposits of public moneys. (F) … ." (Government of the United States of America (2022), "United States Code, Updated," Title 12 – Banks and Banking, s.1841(a)(5)). In the present version of the United States Code (i.e., that applying as of 30th November 2022), there is no paragraph 1841(g)(3) of Title 12 (Banks and Banking) of the United States Code. Subsection 1481(g) of Title 12 of the United States Code reads as follows: "For the purposes of this chapter [(i.e., Chapter 17 of Title 12 of the United States Code, which is titled 'Bank Holding Companies' and which consists of sections 1841-1852 of this Title)] – (1) shares [that are] owned or controlled by any subsidiary of a bank holding company shall be deemed to be indirectly owned or controlled by such bank holding company; and (2) shares [that are] held or controlled[,] directly or indirectly[,] by trustees for the benefit of (A) a company, (B) the shareholders or members of a company, or (C) the employees (whether exclusively or not) of a company, shall be deemed to be controlled by such company, unless the Board determines that such treatment is not appropriate in the light of the facts and circumstances of the case and the purposes of this chapter." (Government of the United States of America (2022), "United States Code, Updated," Title 12 – Banks and Banking, s.1841(g)). The word '*Board*' means the Board of Governors of the Federal Reserve System (Government of the United States of America (2022), "United States Code, Updated," Title 12 – Banks and Banking, s.1841(f)). For the purposes of Chapter 17 of Title 12 (Banks and Banking) of the United States Code, the word '*affiliate*' "means any company that controls, is controlled by, or is under common control with[,] another company" (Government of the United States of America (2022), "United States Code, Updated," Title 12 – Banks and Banking, s.1841(k)).

[613] The phrase '*nonbank financial company supervised by the Board*' "means a nonbank financial company [that is] supervised by the Board of Governors, as defined in section 5311 of this title" (Government of the United States of America (2022), "United States Code, Updated," Title 12 – Banks and Banking, s.1851(h)(3)). The phrase '*Board of Governors*' "means the Board of Governors of the Federal Reserve System" (Government of the United States of America (2022), "United States Code, Updated," Title 12 – Banks and Banking, ss.5311(a)(4)(D) and 5301(3)). The general rule that applies to nonbank financial companies reads thus: "Any nonbank financial company supervised by the Board that engages in proprietary trading or takes or retains any equity, partnership, or other ownership interest in[,] or sponsors[,] a hedge fund or a private equity fund[,] shall be subject, by rule, as provided in subsection (b)(2) [(i.e., paragraph 1851(b)(2) of Title 12 of the United States Code – which is replicated in fn 615)], to additional capital requirements for[,] and additional quantitative limits with regards to[,] such proprietary trading[,] and taking or retaining any equity, partnership, or other ownership interest in[,] or sponsorship of[,] a hedge fund or a private equity fund, except that permitted activities as described in subsection (d) shall not be subject to the additional capital[,] and additional qualitative[,] limits except as provided in subsection (d)(3), as if the nonbank financial company supervised by the Board were a banking entity." (Government of the United States of America (2022), "United States Code, Updated," Title 12 – Banks and Banking, s.1851(a)(2)). 'Subsection (d)' is subsection 1851(d) of the United States Code, of which 'subsection (d)(3)' is the third paragraph. The first sentence of fn 615 defines the term '*proprietary trading*'. The first sentence of fn 616 defines the verb to '*sponsor*'. The first sentence of fn 617 defines the term '*hedge fund*'. The penultimate sentence of fn 617 defines the term '*private equity fund*'.

Unless otherwise provided in this section, a banking entity[614] shall not – (A) engage in proprietary trading[615]; or (B) acquire or retain any equity, partnership, or other ownership interest in[,] or sponsor[616][,] a hedge fund[617] or a private equity fund[618] [789].

---

[614] The first sentence of fn 612 defines the term '*banking entity*'.

[615] When used with regard to a banking entity or nonbank financial company supervised by the Board, the phrase '*proprietary trading*' "means engaging as a principal for the trading account of the banking entity or nonbank financial company supervised by the Board in any transaction to purchase or sell, or otherwise acquire or dispose of, any security, any derivative, any contract of sale of a commodity for future delivery, any option on any such security, derivative, or contract, or any other security or financial instrument that the appropriate Federal banking agencies, the Securities and Exchange Commission, and the Commodity Futures Trading Commission may, by rule as provided in subsection (b)(2), determine" (Government of the United States of America (2022), "United States Code, Updated," Title 12 – Banks and Banking, s.1851(h)(4)). 'Subsection (b)(2)' is paragraph 1851(b)(2) of Title 12 (Banks and Banking) of the United States Code, which is headed 'Rulemaking' and which reads as follows: "**(A) In general** Unless otherwise provided in this section [(i.e., section 1851 of Title 12 (Banks and Banking) of the United States Code)], not later than 9 months after the completion of the study under paragraph (1), the appropriate Federal banking agencies, the Securities and Exchange Commission, and the Commodity Futures Trading Commission, shall consider the findings of the study under paragraph (1) and adopt rules to carry out this section, as provided in subparagraph (B). **(B) Coordinated rulemaking (i) Regulatory authority** The regulations [that are] issued under this paragraph shall be issued by – (I) the appropriate Federal banking agencies, jointly, with respect to insured depository institutions; (II) the Board, with respect to any company that controls an insured depository institution, or that is treated as a bank holding company for purposes of section 8 of the International Banking Act, any nonbank financial company supervised by the Board, and any subsidiary of any of the foregoing (other than a subsidiary for which an agency described in subclause (I), (III) or (IV) is the primary financial regulatory agency); (III) the Commodity Futures Trading Commission, with respect to any entity for which the Commodity Futures Trading Commission is the primary financial regulatory agency, as defined in section 5301 of this title [(i.e., Title 12 (Banks and Banking) of the United States Code)]; and (IV) the Securities and Exchange Commission, with respect to any entity for which the Securities and Exchange Commission is the primary financial regulatory agency, as defined in section 5301 of this title. **(ii) Coordination, consistency, and comparability** In developing and issuing regulations pursuant to this section, the appropriate Federal banking agencies, the Securities and Exchange Commission, and the Commodities Futures Trading Commission shall consult and coordinate with each other, as appropriate, for the purpose of assuring, to the extent possible, that such regulations are comparable and provide for consistent application and implementation of the applicable provisions of this section to avoid providing advantages or imposing disadvantages to the companies affected by this subsection[,] and to protect the safety and soundness of banking entities and nonbank financial companies supervised by the Board. **(iii) Council Role** The Chairperson of the Financial Stability Oversight Council shall be responsible for coordination of the regulations [that are] issued under this section." (Government of the United States of America (2022), "United States Code, Updated," Title 12 – Banks and Banking, s.1851(b)(2); emphasis original). 'Paragraph 1' is paragraph 1851(b)(1) of Title 12 (Banks and Banking) of the United States Code, which is headed 'Study' and which states: "Not later than 6 months after July 21, 2010, the Financial Stability Oversight Council shall study and make recommendations on implementing the provisions of this section[,] so as to – (A) promote and enhance the safety and soundness of banking entities; (B) protect taxpayers and consumers[,] and enhance financial stability[,] by minimizing the risk that insured depository institutions and the affiliates of insured depository institutions will engage in unsafe and unsound activities; (C) limit the inappropriate transfer of Federal subsidies from institutions that benefit from deposit insurance and liquidity facilities of the Federal Government to unregulated entities; (D) reduce conflicts of interest between the self-interest of banking entities and nonbank financial companies supervised by the Board, and the interests of the customers of such entities and companies; (E) limit activities that have caused undue risk or loss in banking entities and nonbank financial companies supervised by the Board, or that might reasonably be expected to create undue risk or loss in such banking entities and nonbank financial companies supervised by the Board; (F) appropriately accommodate the business of insurance within an insurance company, subject to regulation in accordance with the relevant insurance company investment laws, while protecting the safety and soundness of any banking entity with which such insurance company is affiliated and of the United States financial system; and (G) appropriately time the divestiture of illiquid assets that are affected by the implementation of the prohibitions under subsection (a)." (Government of the United States of America (2022), "United States Code, Updated," Title 12 – Banks and Banking, s.1851(b)(1)). 'Subsection (a)' is subsection 1851(a) of Title 12 (Banks and Banking) of the United States Code, whose first paragraph is the text to fns 614-618, and whose second paragraph is the third sentence of fn 613. The penultimate sentence of fn 612 defines the term '*Board*'. The first sentence of fn 612 defines the term '*banking entity*'. The first sentence of fn 613 defines the term '*nonbank financial company supervised by the Board*'. The last sentence of fn 601 defines

The legislation sets out permitted activities, notwithstanding the general rule. These are as follows.

> Notwithstanding the restrictions under subsection (a) [(i.e., subsection 1851(a) of Title 12 (Banks and Banking) of the United States Code[619])], to the extent [that is] permitted by any other provision of Federal or State law, and subject to the limitations under paragraph (2) [(i.e., paragraph 1851(d)(2) of Title 12 (Banks and Banking) of the United States Code[620],)] and any restrictions or limitations that the appropriate Federal banking agencies, the Securities and Exchange Commission, and the Commodity Futures Trading Commission, may determine, the following activities (in this section referred to as "permitted activities") are permitted: (A) The purchase, sale, acquisition, or disposition of obligations of the United States or any agency thereof, obligations, participations, or other instruments of[,] or issued by[,] the Government National Mortgage Association, the Federal National Mortgage Association, the Federal Home Loan Mortgage Corporation, a Federal Home

---

the terms '*company*', '*control*' and '*subsidiary*'. The eighth sentence of fn 601 defines the term '*insured depository institution*'. The final sentence of fn 612 defines the term '*affiliate*'.

[616] To '*sponsor*' "a fund means – (A) to serve as a general partner, managing member, or trustee of a fund; (B) in any manner to select or to control (or to have employees, officers, or directors, or agents who constitute) a majority of the directors, trustees, or management of a fund; or (C) to share with a fund, for corporate, marketing, promotional, or other purposes, the same name or a variation of the same name, except as permitted under subsection (d)(1)(G)(vi)" (Government of the United States of America (2022), "United States Code, Updated," Title 12 – Banks and Banking, s.1851(h)(5)). 'Subsection (d)(1)(G)(vi)' is clause 1851(d)(1)(G)(vi) of Title 12 (Banks and Banking) of the United States Code.

[617] For the purposes of paragraph 1851(h)(7) of Title 12 (Banks and Banking) of the United States Code, the phrase '*hedge fund*' means any fund that is identified under paragraph 1851(h)(2) of Title 12 of the United States Code – and excludes a private equity fund (Government of the United States of America (2022), "United States Code, Updated," Title 12 – Banks and Banking, s.1851(h)(7)(B)). Subparagraph (A) of paragraph 1851(h)(7) defines the expression '*illiquid fund*' as "a hedge fund or private equity fund that – (i) as of May 1, 2010, was principally invested in, or was invested and contractually committed to principally invest in, illiquid assets, such as portfolio companies, real estate investments, and venture capital investments; and (ii) makes all investments pursuant to, and consistent with, an investment strategy to principally invest in illiquid assets" (Government of the United States of America (2022), "United States Code, Updated," Title 12 – Banks and Banking, s.1851(h)(7)(A)). Paragraph 1851(h)(2) of Title 12 (Banks and Banking) of the United States Code declares: "The terms "hedge fund" and "private equity fund" mean an issuer that would be an investment company, as defined in the Investment Company Act of 1940 … , but for section 3(c)(1) or 3(c)(7) of that Act ... , or such similar funds as the appropriate Federal banking agencies, the Securities and Exchange Commission, and the Commodities Futures Trading Commission may, by rule, as provided in subsection (b)(2), determine." (Government of the United States of America (2022), "United States Code, Updated," Title 12 – Banks and Banking, s.1851(h)(2)). 'Subsection (b)(2)' is paragraph 1851(b)(2) of Title 12 of the United States Code, which is reproduced in fn 615.

[618] The penultimate sentence of fn 617 defines the term '*private equity fund*'.

[619] The first paragraph of subsection 1851(a) of Title 12 (Banks and Banking) of the United States Code (i.e., paragraph 1851(a)(1)) is the text to fns 614-618. The second paragraph of subsection 1851(a) of Title 12 (Banks and Banking) of the United States Code (i.e., paragraph 1851(a)(2)) is the third sentence of fn 613. Subsection 1851(a) of the Title 12 (Banks and Banking) of the United States Code comprises only these two paragraphs.

[620] This paragraph is headed 'Limitation on permitted activities', and states: "**(A) In general** No transaction, class of transactions, or activity[,] may be deemed a permitted activity under paragraph (1) [(i.e., paragraph 1851(d)(1) of Title 12 (Banks and Banking) of the United States Code (text to fns 619-636)), if the transaction, class of transactions, or activity – (i) would involve[,] or result in[,] a material conflict of interest … ; (ii) would result, directly or indirectly, in a material exposure by the banking entity to high-risk assets or high-risk trading strategies … ; (iii) would pose a threat to the safety and soundness of such banking entity; or (iv) would pose a threat to the financial stability of the United States. **(B) Rulemaking** The appropriate Federal banking agencies, the Securities and Exchange Commission, and the Commodities Futures Trading Commission shall issue regulations to implement subparagraph (A), as part of the regulations [that are] issued under subsection (b)(2)." (Government of the United States of America (2022), "United States Code, Updated," Title 12 – Banks and Banking, s.1851(d)(2); emphasis original). 'Subsection (b)(2)' is paragraph 1851(b)(2) of Title 12 (Banks and Banking) of the United States Code, which is replicated in fn 615.

Loan Bank, the Federal Agricultural Mortgage Corporation, or a Farm Credit System institution [that is] chartered under[,] and [which is] subject to[,] the provisions of the Farm Credit Act of 1971 … , and obligations of any State or of any political subdivision thereof. (B) The purchase, sale, acquisition or disposition of securities and other instruments [that are] described in subsection (h)(4)[621] in connection with underwriting or market-making-related activities, to the extent that any such activities [which are] permitted by this subparagraph are designed not to exceed the reasonably expected near term demands of clients, customers, or counterparties. (C) Risk-mitigating hedging activities in connection with[,] and related to[,] individual or aggregated positions, contracts, or other holdings of a banking entity[622] that are designed to reduce the specific risks to the banking entity in connection with[,] and related to[,] such positions, contracts, or other holdings. (D) The purchase, sale, acquisition, or disposition of securities and other instruments [which are] described in subsection (h)(4)[,] on behalf of customers. (E) Investments in one or more small business investment companies … , investments [that are] designed primarily to promote the public welfare, of the type [which is] permitted under paragraph (11) of section 24 of this title[623], or investments that are qualified rehabilitation expenditures with respect to a qualified rehabilitated building or certified historic structure, as such terms are defined in section 47 of title 26[624][,] or a similar State historic tax credit program. (F) The purchase, sale, acquisition, or disposition of securities and other instruments [that are] described in subsection (h)(4)[625] by a regulated insurance company [which is] directly engaged in the business of insurance for the general account of the company and by any affiliate[626] of such regulated insurance company, provided that such activities by any affiliate are solely for the general account of the regulated insurance company, if – (i) the purchase, sale, acquisition, or disposition is conducted in compliance with, and subject to, the insurance company investment laws, regulations, and written guidance of the State or jurisdiction in which such insurance company is domiciled; and (ii) the appropriate Federal banking agencies, after consultation with the Financial Stability Oversight Council and the relevant insurance commissioners of the States and territories of the United States, have not jointly determined, after notice and comment, that a particular law, regulation, or written guidance described in clause (i) is insufficient to protect the safety and soundness of the banking entity, or of the financial stability of the United States. (G) Organizing and offering a private equity or hedge fund, including serving as a general partner, managing member, or trustee of the fund and in any manner selecting or controlling (or having employees, officers, directors, or agents who constitute) a majority of the directors, trustees, or management of the fund, including any necessary expenses for the foregoing, only if – (i)

---

621 'Subsection (h)(4)' is paragraph 1851(h)(4) of Title 12 (Banks and Banking) of the United States Code, which is headed 'Proprietary trading', and which the first sentence of fn 615 lays down.

622 The first sentence of fn 612 defines the term '*banking entity*'.

623 The first sentence of paragraph 11 of section 24 of Title 12 (Banks and Banking) of the United States Code states: "To make investments directly or indirectly, each of which is designed primarily to promote the public welfare, including the welfare of low- and moderate-income communities or families (such as by providing housing, services, or jobs). ..." (Government of the United States of America (2022), "United States Code, Updated," Title 12 – Banks and Banking, s.24(11)).

624 Section 47 of Title 26 (Internal Revenue Code) of the United States Code is entitled 'Rehabilitation credit'; its subsection (c) comprises definitions, which include those of the terms '*qualified rehabilitated building*', '*qualified rehabilitation expenditure*' and '*certified historic structure*'.

625 'Subsection (h)(4)' is paragraph 1851(h)(4) of Title 12 (Banks and Banking) of the United States Code, which is headed 'Proprietary trading', and which the first sentence of fn 615 specifies.

626 The final sentence of fn 612 defines the term '*affiliate*'.

the banking entity provides *bona fide*[627] trust, fiduciary, or investment advisory services; (ii) the fund is organized and offered only in connection with the provision of *bona fide*[628] trust, fiduciary, or investment advisory services[,] and only to persons that are customers of such services of the banking entity; (iii) the banking entity does not acquire or retain an equity interest, partnership interest, or other ownership interest in the funds[,] except for a *de minimis*[629] investment subject to[,] and in compliance with[,] paragraph (4)[630]; (iv) the banking entity complies with the restrictions under paragraphs (1) and (2) of subparagraph (f)[631]; (v) the banking entity does not, directly or indirectly, guarantee, assume, or otherwise

---

[627] Emphasis added.

[628] Emphasis added.

[629] Emphasis added.

[630] 'Paragraph (4)' is paragraph 1851(d)(4) of Title 12 (Banks and Banking) of the United States Code, which is headed 'De minimis investment', and which specifies: "**(A) In general** A banking entity may make and retain an investment in a hedge fund or private equity fund that the banking entity organizes and offers, subject to the limitations and restrictions in subparagraph (B)[,] for the purposes of – (i) establishing the fund[,] and providing the fund with sufficient initial equity for investment to permit the fund to attract unaffiliated investors; or (ii) making a de minimis investment. **(B) Limitations and restrictions on investments (i) Requirement to seek other investors** A banking entity shall actively seek unaffiliated investors to reduce or dilute the investment of the banking entity to the amount permitted under clause (ii). **(ii) Limitation on size of investments** Notwithstanding any other provision of law, investments by a banking entity in a hedge fund or private equity fund shall – (I) not later than 1 year after the date of establishment of the fund, be reduced[,] through redemption, sale, or dilution[,] to an amount that is not more than 3 percent of the total ownership interests of the fund; (II) be immaterial to the banking entity, as defined, by rule, pursuant to subsection (b)(2), but in no case may the aggregate of all of the interests of the banking entity in all such funds exceed 3 per cent of the Tier 1 capital of the banking entity. **(iii) Capital** For purposes of determining compliance with applicable capital standards under paragraph (3), the aggregate amount of the outstanding investments by a banking entity under this paragraph, including retained earnings, shall be deducted from the assets and tangible equity of the banking entity, and the amount of the deduction shall increase commensurate with the leverage of the hedge fund or private equity fund. **(C) Extension** Upon an application by a banking entity, the Board may extend the period of time to meet the requirements under subparagraph (B)(ii)(I) for 2 additional years, if the Board finds that an extension would be consistent with safety and soundness and in the public interest." (Government of the United States of America (2022), "United States Code, Updated," Title 12 – Banks and Banking, s.1851(d)(4); emphasis original). 'Subsection (b)(2)' is paragraph 1851(b)(2) of Title 12 (Banks and Banking) of the United States Code, which is reproduced in fn 615. 'Subparagraph (B)(ii)(I)' is subclause 1851(d)(4)(B)(ii)(I) of Title 12 (Banks and Banking) of the United States Code, which is point **(B)(ii)**(I) above in the present footnote (i.e., fn 630). The first sentence of fn 617 defines the term '*hedge fund*'. The penultimate sentence of fn 617 defines the term '*private equity fund*'. The first sentence of fn 612 defines the term '*banking entity*'. The penultimate sentence of fn 612 defines the term '*Board*'. 'Paragraph (3)' is paragraph 1851(d)(3) of Title 12 (Banks and Banking) of the United States Code, which is headed 'Capital and quantitative limitations', and which states: "The appropriate Federal banking agencies, the Securities and Exchange Commission, and the Commodity Futures Trading Commission shall, as provided in subsection (b)(2), adopt rules imposing additional capital requirements and quantitative limitations, including diversification requirements, regarding the activities [that are] permitted under this section[,] if the appropriate Federal banking agencies, the Securities and Exchange Commission, and the Commodities Futures Trading Commission determine that additional capital and quantitative limitations are appropriate to protect the safety and soundness of banking entities [that are] engaged in such activities." (Government of the United States of America (2022), "United States Code, Updated," Title 12 – Banks and Banking, s.1851(d)(3)). 'This section' is section 1851(d) of Title 12 (Banks and Banking) of the United States Code, which comprises paragraph 1 (text to fns 619-636), paragraph 2 (fn 620), paragraph 3 (immediately-preceding sentence in the current footnote (i.e., fn 630)), and paragraph 4 (above in the present footnote (i.e., fn 630)).

[631] It is opined that 'subparagraph (f)' is subsection 1851(f) of Title 12 (Banks and Banking) of the United States Code, which is titled 'Limitations on relationships with hedge funds and private equity funds', and whose first two paragraphs specify: "**(1) In general** No banking entity that serves, directly or indirectly, as the investment manager, investment adviser, or sponsor to a hedge fund or private equity fund, or that organizes and offers a hedge fund or private equity fund pursuant to paragraph (d)(1)(G), and no affiliate of such entity, may enter into a transaction with the fund, or with any other hedge fund or private equity fund that is controlled by such fund, that would be a covered transaction, as defined in section 371c of this title [(i.e., Title 12 (Banks and Banking) of the United States Code)], with the hedge fund or private equity fund, as if such banking entity and the affiliate

insure the obligations or performance of the hedge fund or private equity fund[,] or of any hedge fund or private equity fund in which such hedge fund or private equity fund invests; (vi) the banking entity does not share with the hedge fund or private equity fund, for corporate, marketing, promotional, or other purposes, the same name or a variation of the same name, except that the hedge fund or private equity fund may share the same name or a variation of the same name as a banking entity that is an investment adviser to the hedge fund or private equity fund, if – (I) such investment adviser is not an insured depository institution[632], a company that controls an insured depository institution, or a company that is treated as a bank holding company for purposes of section 8 of the International Banking Act of 1978 ... ; (II) such investment adviser does not share the same name[,] or a variation of the same name[,] as an insured depository institution, or any company that is treated as a bank holding company for the purposes of section 8 of the International Banking Act of 1978 ... ; and (III) such name does not contain the word "bank"; (vii) no director or employee of the banking entity takes or retains an equity interest, partnership interest, or other ownership interest in the hedge fund or private equity fund, except for any director or employee of the banking entity who is directly engaged in providing investment advisory or other services to the hedge fund or private equity fund; and (viii) the banking entity discloses to prospective and actual investors in the fund, in writing, that any losses in such hedge fund or private equity fund are borne solely by investors in the fund and not by the banking entity, and otherwise complies with any additional rules of the appropriate Federal banking agencies, the Securities and Exchange Commission, or the Commodity Futures Trading Commission, as provided in subsection (b)(2)[633], [which are] designed to ensure that the losses in such hedge fund or private equity fund are borne solely by investors in the fund[,] and not by the banking entity. (H) Proprietary trading [that is] conducted by a banking entity pursuant to paragraph (9) or (13) of section 1843(c) of this title[634], provided

---

thereof were a member bank and the hedge fund or private equity fund were an affiliate thereof. **(2) Treatment as member bank** A banking entity that serves, directly or indirectly, as the investment manager, investment adviser, or sponsor to a hedge fund or private equity fund, or that organizes and offers a hedge fund or private equity fund pursuant to paragraph (d)(1)(G), shall be subject to section 371c-1 of this title, as if such banking entity were a member bank and such hedge fund or private equity fund were an affiliate thereof." (Government of the United States of America (2022), "United States Code, Updated," Title 12 – Banks and Banking, s.1851(f)(1)-(2); emphasis original). The first sentence of fn 617 defines the term '*hedge fund*'. The penultimate sentence of fn 617 defines the term '*private equity fund*'. The first sentence of fn 612 defines the term '*banking entity*'. 'Paragraph (d)(1)(G)' is subparagraph 1851(d)(1)(G) of Title 12 (Banks and Banking) of the United States Code, which is point (G) in the current quoted passage (i.e., that to fns 619-636). Section 371c-1 of Title 12 (Banks and Banking) of the United States Code is entitled 'Restrictions on transactions with affiliates'; its first subsection is titled 'In general', and consists of paragraphs (1) (first sentence of fn 713), (2) (fn 711), and (3) (first sentence of fn 712); its second subsection is entitled 'Prohibited transactions', and contains paragraphs (1) (text to fns 709 and 710), (2) (first sentence of fn 710), and (3) (second sentence of fn 710); its fourth subsection (second sentence of fn 709) introduces definitions that apply within the section (i.e., within section 371c-1 of Title 12 (Banks and Banking) of the United States Code).

632 The eighth sentence of fn 601 defines the term '*insured depository institution*'.

633 'Subsection (b)(2)' is paragraph 1851(b)(2) of Title 12 (Banks and Banking) of the United States Code, which is replicated in fn 615.

634 These paragraphs read as follows: "The prohibitions in this section [(i.e., section 1843 of Title 12 (Banks and Banking) of the United States Code)] ... shall not ... apply to – ... (9) shares [that are] held[,] or activities [which are] conducted[,] by any company [that is] organized under the laws of a foreign country the greater part of whose business is conducted outside the United States, if the Board[,] by regulation or order[,] determines that, under the circumstances and subject to the conditions [which are] set forth in the regulation or order, the exemption would not be substantially at variance with the purposes of this chapter and would be in the public interest; ... (13) shares of, or activities [that are] conducted by, any company which does no business in the United States except as an incident to its international or foreign business, if the Board[,] by regulation or order[,] determines that, under the circumstances and subject to the conditions [which are] set forth in the regulation or

that the trading occurs solely outside the United States and that the banking entity is not directly or indirectly controlled by a banking entity that is organized under the laws of the United States or one or more States. (I) The acquisition or retention of any equity, partnership, or other ownership interest in, or the sponsorship of, a hedge fund or a private equity fund by a banking entity pursuant to paragraph (9) or (13) of section 1843(c) of this title[635] solely outside of the United States, provided that no ownership interest in such hedge fund or private equity fund is offered for sale[,] or sold[,] to a resident of the United States[,] and that the banking entity is not directly or indirectly controlled by a banking entity that is organized under the laws of the United States or of one or more States. (J) Such other activity as the appropriate Federal banking agencies, the Securities and Exchange Commission, and the Commodities Futures Trading Commission determine, by rule, as provided in subsection (b)(2)[636], would promote and protect the safety and soundness of the banking entity and the financial stability of the United States [790].

Comment

The purpose of the Volcker Rule is to reduce the risk to customers of retail banks in the USA being unable to be promptly repaid their deposits (or be paid interest on those deposits), by prohibiting the use of the funds of such banks for speculative engagements. The list of permitted activities furnishes a loosening of this principle, in cases in which such risk is limited or the bank reasonably needs to be involved in market-related transactions – such as in the instance of hedging future cash flows relating to movements in interest rates or foreign exchange rates. The Rule also provides, in carefully specified circumstances, for the bank to be able supply *bona fide* trust, fiduciary, and/or investment advisory services.

Although the Volcker Rule, taken as a whole, is complex, it falls short of fully separating investment banking from retail banking. The Rule achieves a reasonable compromise between the interests of shareholders of the retail bank and those of its depositors.

Title 12 of the United States Code

Introduction

Title 12 of the United States Code comprises federal statutes on banks and banking. Table 4.1 lists the chapters in Title 12 (Banks and Banking) and the sections that are contained within each of these.

---

order, the exemption would not be substantially at variance with the purpose of this chapter and would be in the public interest; ... ." (Government of the United States of America (2022), "United States Code, Updated," Title 12 – Banks and Banking, ss.1843(c)(9) and 1843(c)(13)). 'This chapter' is Chapter 17 of Title 12 (Banks and Banking) of the United States Code, which is titled 'Bank Holding Companies'. The penultimate sentence of fn 612 defines the term '*Board*'.

[635] Fn 634 sets out paragraphs (9) and (13) of subsection 1843(c) of Title 12 (Banks and Banking) of the United States Code.

[636] 'Subsection (b)(2)' is paragraph 1851(b)(2) of Title 12 (Banks and Banking) of the United States Code, which is reproduced in fn 615.

Table 4.1. A list of the chapters in Title 12 (Banks and Banking) of the United States Code and the sections included within each of these chapters [791]

Chapter	Sections contained in the chapter
1 – The Comptroller of the Currency	1 – 16
2 – National Banks	21 – 216d
3 – Federal Reserve System	221 – 522
4 – Taxation	541 – 547
5 – Crimes and Offenses	581 – 588d
6 – Foreign Banking	601 – 633
6A – Export-Import Bank of the United States	635 – 635t
7 – Farm Credit Administration	636 – 1138f
7A – Agricultural Marketing	1141 – 1141j
7B – Regional Agricultural Credit Corporations	1148 – 1148d
8 – Adjustment and Cancellation of Farm Loans	1150 – 1150c
9 – National Agricultural Credit Corporations	1151 – 1322
10 – Local Agricultural-Credit Corporations, Livestock-Loan Companies and Like Organizations; Loans to Individuals to aid in Formation or to increase Capital Stock	1401 – 1404
11 – Federal Home Loan Banks	1421 – 1449
11A – Federal Home Loan Mortgage Corporation	1451 – 1459
12 – Savings Associations	1461 – 1470
13 – National Housing	1701 – 1750g
14 – Federal Credit Unions	1751 – 1795k
15 – Federal Loan Agency	1801 – 1805
16 – Federal Deposit Insurance Corporation	1811 – 1835a
17 – Bank Holding Companies	1841 – 1852
18 – Bank Service Companies	1861 – 1867
19 – Security Measures for Banks and Savings Associations	1881 – 1884
20 – Credit Control	1901 – 1910
21 – Financial Recordkeeping	1951 – 1960
22 – Tying Arrangements	1971 – 1978
23 – Farm Credit System	2001 – 2279bb-7
24 – Federal Financing Bank	2281 – 2296
25 – National Commission on Electronic Fund Transfers	2401 – 2408
26 – Disposition of Abandoned Money Orders and Travelers Checks	2501 – 2503
27 – Real Estate Settlement Procedures	2601 – 2617
28 – Emergency Mortgage Relief	2701 – 2712
29 – Home Mortgage Disclosure	2801 – 2811
30 – Community Reinvestment	2901 – 2908
31 – National Consumer Cooperative Bank	3001 – 3051
32 – Foreign Bank Participation in Domestic Markets	3101 – 3111
33 – Depository Institution Management Interlocks	3201 – 3208
34 – Federal Financial Institutions Examination Council	3301 – 3311
34A – Appraisal Subcommittee of Federal Financial Institutions Examination Council	3331 – 3356
35 –Right to Financial Privacy	3401 – 3423
36 – Depository Institutions Deregulation and Financial Regulation Simplification	3501 – 3524 (These sections have all been repealed.)
37 – Solar Energy and Energy Conservation Bank	3601 – 3620
38 – Multifamily Mortgage Foreclosure	3701 – 3717
38A – Single Family Mortgage Foreclosure	3751 – 3768
39 – Alternative Mortgage Transactions	3801 – 3806
40 – International Lending Supervision	3901 – 3912
41 – Expedited Funds Availability	4001 – 4010

Chapter	Sections contained in the chapter
42 – Low-Income Housing Preservation and Resident Homeownership	4101 – 4147
43 – Actions Against Persons Committing Bank Fraud Crimes	4201 – 4207
44 – Truth in Savings	4301 – 4313
45 – Payment System Risk Reduction	4401 – 4407
46 – Government Sponsored Enterprises	4501 – 4642
47 – Community Development Banking	4701 – 4750
48 – Financial Institutions Regulatory Improvement	4801 – 4809
49 – Homeowners Protection	4901 – 4910
50 – Check Truncation	5001 – 5018
51 – Secure and Fair Enforcement for Mortgage Licensing	5101 – 5117
52 – Emergency Economic Stabilization	5201 – 5253
53 – Wall Street Reform and Consumer Protection	5301 – 5628
54 – State Small Business Credit Initiative	5701 – 5710
55 – Adjustable Interest Rate (LIBOR)	5801 – 5807

A subtitle is devoted to each of the following chapters: 2 (National Banks), 3 (Federal Reserve System), and 5 (Crimes and Offenses). In the subsections that follow, elements of the legislation within these chapters are considered.

National Banks (Chapter 2)[637]

A national bank must be established by at least five persons, who shall enter into articles of association – which are to state the object for which the bank is formed[638] [792]. These persons are to draw up an organization certificate, which shall state the bank's name – which is to include the word 'national', the place where its operations are to be conducted, the amount of capital stock and the number of shares into which this stock is to be divided, the names and places of residence of the shareholders and the number of shares that each of them holds, and the fact that the organization certificate is made to enable these persons to benefit from Title 62 of the Revised Statutes of the United States[639] [793].

Upon making, and filing, articles of association and an organization certificate, a national bank shall become a body corporate, and shall – in the name that the organization certificate designates and from the date of implementation of this certificate – have power to: (i) adopt, and use, a corporate seal, (ii) have succession until such time as two-thirds of the national bank's shareholders vote to dissolve it, until it forfeits its franchise by contravention of law or has this franchise terminated by an Act of Congress, or until its affairs are placed in receivership, (iii) make contracts, (iv) be a litigant, (v) appoint or elect directors and, by its board of directors, appoint and dismiss officers, (vi) prescribe, through its board of directors,

637 The provisions of all Acts of Congress that relate to national banks apply in the states of the USA, the District of Columbia, the territories and possessions of the USA, and the Commonwealth of Puerto Rico (Government of the United States of America (2022), "United States Code, Updated," Title 12 – Banks and Banking, s.42).

638 The national bank's articles of association are to be signed by the persons who set it up, and a copy of these articles is to be forwarded to the Comptroller of the Currency (Government of the United States of America (2022), "United States Code, Updated," Title 12 – Banks and Banking, s.21).

639 First published in 1875, the Revised Statutes of the United States is the immediate predecessor to the United States Code – which was first published in 1926 (Wood, M. (2015), "The Revised Statutes of the United States: Predecessor to the U.S. Code," published July 2, 2015, accessed December 5, 2022, <https://blogs.loc.gov/law/2015/07/the-revised-statutes-of-the-united-states-predecessor-to-the-u-s-code/>).

by-laws that are compatible with the law, (vii) exercise, through its board of directors or duly-authorized officers or agents, all such incidental powers as are necessary to continue the business of banking, provided that these are used in accordance with the law, (viii) contribute to community funds or to payments that are conducive to public welfare – if the national bank is situated in a state the laws of which do not expressly prohibit banks from so contributing, (ix) issue and sell securities whose repayments of principal and payments of interest are guaranteed by the Government National Mortgage Association [794], (x) invest up to 10% of the national bank's assets in tangible personal property, and (xi) make investments each of which is mainly designed to further public welfare [795]. Subject to paragraph 24a(a)(2) of Chapter 12 (Banks and Banking) of the United States Code,[640] a national bank may control, or hold an interest in, a financial subsidiary [796].

---

[640] Paragraph 24a(a)(2) of Chapter 12 (Banks and Banking) of the United States Code is headed 'Conditions and requirements', and reads as follows: "A national bank may control a financial subsidiary, or hold an interest in a financial subsidiary, only if – (A) the financial subsidiary engages only in – (i) activities that are financial in nature or incidental to a financial activity pursuant to subsection (b); and (ii) activities that are permitted for national banks to engage in directly (subject to the same terms and conditions that govern the conduct of the activities by a national bank); (B) the activities [that are] engaged in by the financial subsidiary as a principal do not include – (i) insuring, guaranteeing, or indemnifying against loss, harm, damage, illness, disability, or death ... or providing or issuing annuities the income of which is subject to tax treatment under section 72 of title 26; (ii) real estate development or real estate investment activities, unless otherwise expressly authorized by law; or (iii) any activity [which is] permitted in subparagraph (H) or (I) of section 1843(k)(4) of this title, except [that] activities described in section 1843(k)(4)(H) of this title may be permitted in accordance with section 122 of the Gramm-Leach-Bliley Act; (C) the national bank and each depository institution affiliate of the national bank are well capitalized and well managed; (D) the aggregate consolidated total assets of all financial subsidiaries of the national bank do not exceed the lesser of – (i) 45 percent of the consolidated total assets of the parent bank; or (ii) $50,000,000,000 [(i.e., USD 50 billion)]; (E) except as provided in paragraph (4), the national bank meets standards of creditworthiness [that are] established by the Comptroller of the Currency or other requirement [which is] set forth in paragraph (3); and (F) the national bank has received the approval of the Comptroller of the Currency for the financial subsidiary to engage in such activities, which approval shall be based solely upon the factors [that are] set forth in this section." (Government of the United States of America (2022), "United States Code, Updated," Title 12 – Banks and Banking, s.24(a)(2)). 'This section' (as stated in the immediately-preceding sentence) is section 24a of Chapter 12 (Banks and Banking) of the United States Code, which is entitled 'Financial subsidiaries of national banks'. 'Paragraph (4)' is paragraph 24a(a)(4) of Title 12 (Banks and Banking) of the United States Code, which is headed 'Financial agency subsidiary', and which specifies: "The requirement in paragraph (2)(E) [(i.e., subparagraph 24a(a)(2)(E) of Title 12 (Banks and Banking) of the United States Code – which is point (E) in the immediately-preceding sentence,)] shall not apply with respect to the ownership or control of a financial subsidiary that engages in activities [which are] described in subsection (b)(1) solely as agent[,] and not directly or indirectly as principal." (Government of the United States of America (2022), "United States Code, Updated," Title 12 – Banks and Banking, s.24a(a)(4)). 'Paragraph (3)' is paragraph 24a(a)(3) of Title 12 (Banks and Banking) of the United States Code, which is headed 'Requirement', and which specifies: "**(A) In general** A national bank meets the requirements of this paragraph[,] if the bank is one of the 100 largest insured banks and has not fewer than 1 issue of outstanding debt that meets standards of credit-worthiness or other criteria as the Secretary of the Treasury and the Board of Governors of the Federal Reserve System may jointly establish. **(B) Consolidated total assets** For purposes of this paragraph, the size of an insured bank shall be determined on the basis of the consolidated total assets of the bank as of the end of each calendar year." (Government of the United States of America (2022), "United States Code, Updated," Title 12 – Banks and Banking, s.24(a)(3); emphasis original). 'Section 72 of title 26' is section 72 of Title 26 (Internal Revenue Code) of the United States Code, which is titled 'Annuities; certain proceeds of endowment and life insurance contracts'; its first subsection is entitled 'General rules for annuities', and states: "**(1) Income inclusion** Except as otherwise provided in this chapter [(i.e., Chapter 1 of Title 26 (Internal Revenue Code) of the United States Code, which is titled 'Normal Taxes and Surtaxes', and which comprises sections 1 to 1400Z-2 of Title 26 of the United States Code)], gross income includes any amount [that is] received as an annuity (whether for a period certain or during one or more lives) under an annuity, endowment, or life insurance contract. **(2) Partial annuitization** If any amount is received as an annuity for a period of 10 years or more[,] or during one or more lives[,] under any portion of an annuity, endowment, or life insurance contract[, then] – (A) such portion shall be treated as a separate contract for purposes of this section [(i.e., section 72 of Title 26 (Internal Revenue Code) of the United States Code)], (B) for purposes of applying subsections (b), (c), and (e),

Whenever an organization certificate is conveyed to the Comptroller of the Currency, and the national bank transmitting this certificate notifies the Comptroller that all its capital stock has been paid in and that it has complied with all the necessary requirements before it shall be authorized to start the business of banking, the Comptroller shall inquire into the national bank's condition – with the latter's president and the majority of its directors providing a statement on oath of all the facts which are necessary to enable the former to decide whether the national bank is lawfully entitled to begin the business of banking [797]. If, upon a careful examination of these facts – and of any other information that may come to the Comptroller's knowledge, it appears that the national bank is lawfully entitled to start the business of banking, then the Comptroller shall give a signed, sealed certificate to the national bank which proclaims that the latter is authorized to commence this business[641] [798]. A national bank which is

---

the investment in the contract shall be allocated pro rata between each portion of the contract from which amounts are received as an annuity and the portion of the contract from which amounts are not received as an annuity, and (C) a separate annuity starting date under subsection (c)(4) shall be determined with respect to each portion of the contract from which amounts are received as an annuity." (Government of the United States of America (2022), "United States Code, Updated," Title 26 – Internal Revenue Code, s.72(a); emphasis original). 'Subparagraph (H) or (I) of section 1843(k)(4) of this title' means subsections 1843(k)(4)(H)-(I) of Title 12 (Banks and Banking) of the United States Code, which declare: "For the purposes of this subsection [(i.e., subsection 1843(k) of Title 12 (Banks and Banking) of the United States Code)], the following activities shall be considered to be financial in nature: ... (H) Directly or indirectly acquiring or controlling, whether as principal, on behalf of 1 or more entities ... or otherwise, shares, assets, or ownership interests (including debt or equity securities, partnership interests, trust certificates, or other instruments representing ownership) of a company or other entity, whether or not constituting control of such company or entity, [that is] engaged in any activity [which is] not authorized pursuant to this section [(i.e., section 1843 of Chapter 12 (Banks and Banking) of the United States Code),] if – (i) the shares, assets, or ownership interests are not acquired or held by a depository institution or subsidiary of a depository institution; (ii) such shares, assets, or ownership interests are acquired and held by – (I) a securities affiliate or an affiliate thereof; or (II) an affiliate of an insurance company described in subparagraph (I)(ii) that provides investment advice to an insurance company and is registered pursuant to the Investment Advisers Act of 1940 ... , or an affiliate of such investment adviser; as part of a *bona fide* underwriting[,] or merchant or investment banking[,] activity, including investment activities engaged in for the purpose of appreciation[,] and ultimate resale or disposition[,] of the investment; (iii) such shares, assets, or ownership interests are held for a period of time[,] to enable the sale or disposition thereof on a reasonable basis [which is] consistent with the financial viability of the activities described in clause (ii); and (iv) during the period [that] such shares, assets, or ownership interests are held, the bank holding company does not routinely manage or operate such company or entity[,] except as may be necessary or required to obtain a reasonable return on investment upon resale or disposition. (I) Directly or indirectly acquiring or controlling, whether as principal, on behalf of 1 or more entities ... or otherwise, shares, assets, or ownership interests (including debt or equity securities, partnership interests, trust certificates or other instruments representing ownership) of a company or other entity, whether or not constituting control of such company or entity, [which is] engaged in any activity [that is] not authorized pursuant to this section[,] if – (i) the shares, assets, or ownership interests are not acquired or held by a depository institution or a subsidiary of a depository institution; (ii) such shares, assets, or ownership interests are acquired and held by an insurance company that is predominantly engaged in underwriting life, accident and health, or property and casualty insurance (other than credit-related insurance)[,] or providing and issuing annuities; (iii) such shares, assets, or ownership interests represent an investment [which is] made in the ordinary course of business of such insurance company[,] in accordance with relevant State law governing such investments; and (iv) during the period [that] such shares, assets, or ownership interests are held, the bank holding company does not routinely manage or operate such company[,] except as may be necessary or required to obtain a reasonable return on investment." (Government of the United States of America (2022), "United States Code, Updated," Title 12 – Banks and Banking, s.1843(k)(4)(H)-(I); emphasis added).

[641] Pursuant to the present section – i.e., section 27 of Title 12 (Banks and Banking) of the United States Code, "[t]he Comptroller of the Currency may also issue a certificate of authority to commence the business of banking ... to a national banking association which is owned exclusively (except to the extent [that] directors' qualifying shares are required by law) by other depository institutions or depository institution holding companies[,] and is organized to engage exclusively in providing services to[,] or for[,] other depository institutions, their holding companies, and the officers, directors and employees of such institutions and companies, and in providing correspondent banking services at the request of other depository institutions or their holding companies (also

chartered in this way shall be subject to such rules, regulations and orders as the Comptroller considers to be appropriate and – except as specified therein – shall be vested with, or subject to, the same rights, duties, privileges, restrictions, conditions, liabilities, limitations and penalties that would apply under the national banking laws to any national bank [799].

Any bank which is incorporated by special law of the USA or of any of its states, or that is organized under the general law of the USA or of any of its states, and which has available capital that is enough to entitle it to become a national bank under existing legal provisions, may be converted into a national bank – with a name that includes the word 'national', by the vote of shareholders owning at least 51% of the bank's capital stock and with the Comptroller of the Currency's approval[642] [800]. A national bank may, with the approval of the Comptroller of the Currency, found and operate new branches within the bounds of the city, town or village in which the bank is located, provided that this establishment and functioning are – at the time – expressly authorized to state banks by the law of the state in which the bank is situated, and subject to the restrictions as to location that the law of the state imposes on state banks [801].

A national bank may only acquire, found or operate a branch in any state other than its home state[643] or a state in which the bank already has a branch, if this is authorized under the present section – which is section 36 of Title 12 (Banks and Banking) of the United States

referred to as a "banker's bank") (Government of the United States of America (2022), "United States Code, Updated," Title 12 – Banks and Banking, s.27(b)(1)).

642 The conversion of a state bank to a national bank must be compatible with the law of the relevant state (Government of the United States of America (2022), "United States Code, Updated," Title 12 – Banks and Banking, s.35).

643 For the purposes of this section (i.e., section 36 of Title 12 (Banks and Banking) of the United States Code), the phrase '*home State*' "means the State in which the main office of a national bank is located" (Government of the United States of America (2022), "United States Code, Updated," Title 12 – Banks and Banking, s.36(g)(3)(B)).

Code, subsection 1823(f)[644] or 1823(k)[645] of aforementioned Title, or section 1831u[646] of that Title [802]. Under specified circumstances, the Comptroller of the Currency may approve an application by a national bank to found and operate a new branch in a state other than its home state[647].

---

644 Section 1823 of Title 12 (Banks and Banking) of the United States Code is entitled 'Corporation monies', which refers to the funds of the FDIC; its subsection (f) is titled 'Assisted emergency interstate acquisitions', and includes the following provision: "Any subsidiary [that is] created by operation of this subsection may retain and operate any existing branch or branches of the institution merged with or acquired under paragraph (2) or (3), but otherwise shall be subject to the conditions upon which a national bank may establish and operate branches in the State in which such insured institution is located." (Government of the United States of America (2022), "United States Code, Updated," Title 12 – Banks and Banking, s.1823(f)(4)(B)). 'Paragraph 2' is paragraph 1823(f)(2) of Title 12 (Banks and Banking) of the United States Code; its first subparagraph declares: "Whenever an insured bank with total assets of $500,000,000 [(i.e., USD 500 million)] or more (as determined from its most recent report of condition) is in default, the [Federal Deposit Insurance] Corporation, as receiver, may, in its discretion and upon such terms and conditions as the Corporation may determine, arrange the sale of assets of the bank in default and the assumption of the liabilities of the bank in default, including the sale of such assets to[,] and the assumption of such liabilities by[,] an insured depository institution [that is] located in the State where the bank in default was chartered but established by an out-of-State bank or holding company. Where otherwise lawfully required, a transaction under this subsection must be approved by the primary Federal or State supervisor of all parties thereto." (Government of the United States of America (2022), "United States Code, Updated," Title 12 – Banks and Banking, s.1823(f)(2)(A)).

645 Section 1823 of Title 12 (Banks and Banking) of the United States Code is entitled 'Corporation monies' (first sentence of fn 644); its subsection (k) is titled 'Emergency acquisitions', and contains the following provision: "If a merger, consolidation, transfer, or acquisition under this subsection involves a savings association [that is] eligible for assistance and a bank or bank holding company, [then] a savings association may retain and operate any existing branch or branches or any other existing facilities. If the savings association continues to exist as a separate entity, [then] it may establish and operate new branches to the same extent as any savings association that is not affiliated with a bank holding company and the home office of which is located in the same State." (Government of the United States of America (2022), "United States Code, Updated," Title 12 – Banks and Banking, s.1823(k)(4)(A)); subparagraph 1823(k)(4)(A) of Title 12 (Banks and Banking) of the United States Code is subject to one derogation, which is contained in clause 1823(k)(4)(B)(i) of Title 12 (Banks and Banking) of the United States Code.

646 Section 1831u of Title 12 (Banks and Banking) of the United States Code is entitled 'Interstate bank mergers'; its subsection (a), which is titled 'Approval of interstate merger transactions authorized', includes paragraph (4) – which is headed 'Interstate merger transactions involving acquisitions of branches' and which states: "**(A) In general** An interstate merger transaction may involve the acquisition of a branch of an insured bank without the acquisition of the bank[,] only if the law of the State in which the branch is located permits out-of-State banks to acquire a branch of a bank in such State without acquiring the bank. **(B) Treatment of branch for purposes of this section** In the case of an interstate merger transaction which involves the acquisition of a branch of an insured bank without the acquisition of the bank, the branch shall be treated, for purposes of this section, as an insured bank the home State of which is the State in which the branch is located." (Government of the United States of America (2022), "United States Code, Updated," Title 12 – Banks and Banking, s.1831u(a)(4); emphasis original); its subsection (d), which is entitled 'Operations of the resulting bank', comprises three paragraphs of which the first two read: "**(1) Continued operations** A resulting bank may, subject to the approval of the appropriate Federal banking agency, retain and operate, as a main office or a branch, any office that any bank involved in an interstate merger transaction was operating as a main office or a branch immediately before the merger transaction. **(2) Additional branches** Following the consummation of any interstate merger transaction, the resulting bank may establish, acquire, or operate additional branches at any location where any bank involved in the transaction could have established, acquired, or operated a branch under applicable Federal or State law[,] if such bank had not been a party to the merger transaction." (Government of the United States of America (2022), "United States Code, Updated," Title 12 – Banks and Banking, s.1831u(d)(1)-(2); emphasis original). For the purposes of this section (i.e., section 1831u of Title 12 (Banks and Banking) of the United States Code), the phrase '*home State*' "(A) means – (i) with respect to a national bank, the State in which the main office of the bank is located; and (ii) with respect to a State bank, the State by which the bank is chartered; and (B) with respect to a bank holding company, has the same meaning as in section 1841(o)(4) of this title [(i.e., paragraph 1841(o)(4) of Title 12 (Banks and Banking) of the United States Code)]" (Government of the United States of America (2022), "United States Code, Updated," Title 12 – Banks and Banking, s.1831u(g)(4)).

647 Subsection 36(g) of Title 12 (Banks and Banking) of the United States Code is titled 'State "opt-in" election to permit interstate branching through de novo branches'; its first two paragraphs read thus: "**(1) In general** Subject

to paragraph (2), the Comptroller of the Currency may approve an application by a national bank to establish and operate a de novo branch in a State (other than the bank's home State) in which the bank does not maintain a branch[,] if – (A) the law of the State in which the branch is located, or is to be located, would permit establishment of the branch, if the national bank were a State bank chartered by such State; and (B) the conditions established in, or made applicable to this paragraph by, paragraph (2)[,] are met. **(2) Conditions on establishment and operation of interstate branch (A) Establishment** An application by a national bank to establish and operate a de novo branch in a host State shall be subject to the same requirements and conditions to which an application for an interstate merger transaction is subject under paragraphs (1), (3), and (4) of [sub]section 1831u(b) of this title. **(B) Operation** Subsections (c) and (d)(2) of section 1831u of this title shall apply with respect to each branch of a national bank which is established and operated pursuant to an application [that is] approved under this subsection[,] in the same manner and to the same extent [that] such provisions of such section 1831u of this title apply to a branch of a national bank which resulted from an interstate merger transaction [that is] approved pursuant to section 1831u of this title." (Government of the United States of America (2022), "United States Code, Updated," Title 12 – Banks and Banking, s.36(g)(1)-(2); emphasis original). Subsection 1831u(c) of Title 12 (Banks and Banking) of the United States Code is entitled 'Applicability of certain laws to interstate banking operations', and specifies: **"(1) State taxation authority not affected (A) In general** No provision of this section [(i.e., section 1831u of Title 12 (Banks and Banking) of the United States Code (fn 646),)] shall be construed as affecting the authority of any State or political subdivision of any State to adopt, apply, or administer any tax or method of taxation to any bank, bank holding company, or foreign bank, or any affiliate of any bank, bank holding company, or foreign bank, to the extent [that] such tax or tax method is otherwise permissible by[,] or under[,] the Constitution of the United States or other Federal law. **(B) Imposition of shares tax by host States** In the case of a branch of an out-of-State bank which results from an interstate merger transaction, a proportionate amount of the value of the shares of the out-of-State bank may be subject to any bank shares tax [that is] levied or imposed by the host State, or any political subdivision of such host State that imposes such tax based upon a method [that is] adopted by the host State, which may include allocation and apportionment. **(2) Applicability of antitrust laws** No provision of this section shall be construed as affecting – (A) the applicability of the antitrust laws; or (B) the applicability, if any, of any State law which is similar to the antitrust laws. **(3) Reservation of certain rights to States** No provision of this section shall be construed as limiting in any way the right of a State to – (A) determine the authority of State banks [which are] chartered by that State to establish and maintain branches; or (B) supervise, regulate, and examine State banks [which are] chartered by that State. **(4) State-imposed notice requirements** A host State may impose any notification or reporting requirement on a branch of an out-of-State bank[,] if the requirement – (A) does not discriminate against out-of-State banks or bank holding companies; and (B) is not preempted by any Federal law regarding the same subject." (Government of the United States of America (2022), "United States Code, Updated," Title 12 – Banks and Banking, ss.1831u(c); emphasis original). Paragraph 1831u(d)(2) of Title 12 (Banks and Banking) of the United States Code is point **(2)**, which is headed 'Additional branches', in the penultimate sentence of fn 646. Paragraphs (1), (3) and (4) of subsection 1831u(b) of Title 12 (Banks and Banking) of the United States Code state: "**(1) Compliance with State filing requirements (A) In general** Any bank which files an application for an interstate merger transaction shall – (i) comply with the filing requirements of any host State of the bank which will result from such transaction[,] to the extent that the requirement – (I) does not have the effect of discriminating against out-of-State banks or out-of-State bank holding companies[,] or subsidiaries of such banks or bank holding companies; and (II) is similar in effect to any requirement [that is] imposed by the host State on a nonbanking corporation [which is] incorporated in another State that engages in business in the host State; and (ii) submit a copy of the application to the State bank supervisor of the host State. **(B) Penalty for failure to comply** The responsible agency may not approve an application for an interstate merger transaction[,] if the applicant materially fails to comply with subparagraph (A). ... **(3) Community reinvestment compliance** In determining whether to approve an application for an interstate merger transaction in which the resulting bank would have a branch or bank affiliate immediately following the transaction in any State in which the bank submitting the application (as the acquiring bank) had no branch or bank affiliate immediately before the transaction, the responsible agency shall – (A) comply with the responsibilities of the agency regarding such application under section 2903 of this title; (B) take into account the most recent written evaluation under section 2903 of this title of any bank which would be an affiliate of the resulting bank; and (C) take into account the record of compliance of any applicant bank with applicable State community reinvestment laws. **(4) Adequacy of capital and management skills** The responsible agency may approve an application for an interstate merger transaction pursuant to subsection (a) [(i.e., subsection 1831u(a) of Title 12 (Banks and Banking) of the United States Code, which is titled 'Approval of interstate merger transactions authorized',)] only if – (A) each bank [that is] involved in the transaction is adequately capitalized as of the date the application is filed; and (B) the responsible agency determines that the resulting bank will be well capitalized and well managed upon the consummation of the transaction." (Government of the United States of America (2022), "United States Code, Updated," Title 12 – Banks and Banking, ss.1831u(b)(1) and 1831u(b)(3)-(4); emphasis original). For the purposes of section 1831u of Title 12 (Banks and Banking) of the

The general business of each national bank is to be transacted in the place that its organization certificate specifies, and in the branch(es), if any, which it establishes or maintains in conformity with the provisions of section 36 of Title 12 (Banks and Banking) of the United States Code[648] [803]. The total 'loans and extensions of credit'[649] that a national bank provides to a person[650] which are outstanding at one time and *not* fully secured by collateral with a market value equal to or greater than the amount of the loan or extension or credit, shall be no more than 15% of the unimpaired capital and unimpaired surplus of the bank [804]. Such loans and extensions of credit that *are* wholly secured by readily-marketable collateral with a market value, may not exceed 10% of the unimpaired capital and unimpaired surplus of the bank – a restriction that is separate from, and additional to, the limit in the immediately-preceding sentence [805]. These restrictions are subject to specified exceptions[651]. The rate of interest on loans and debt instruments provided by national banks is also regulated[652].

United States Code – and also of section 36 of Title 12 (Banks and Banking) of the United States Code, the phrase '*host State*' "means, with respect to a bank, a State other than the home State of the bank, in which the bank maintains, or seeks to establish and maintain, a branch" (Government of the United States of America (2022), "United States Code, Updated," Title 12 – Banks and Banking, s.1831u(g)(5); Government of the United States of America (2022), "United States Code, Updated," Title 12 – Banks and Banking, s.36(g)(3)(C)). For the purposes of section 36 of Title 12 (Banks and Banking) of the United States Code, the phrase '*de novo branch*' "means a branch of a national bank[,] which – (i) is originally established by the national bank as a branch; and (ii) does not become a branch of such bank as a result of – (I) the acquisition by the bank of an insured depository institution or a branch of an insured depository institution; or (II) the conversion, merger, or consolidation of any such institution or branch" (Government of the United States of America (2022), "United States Code, Updated," Title 12 – Banks and Banking, s.36(g)(3)(A)).

648 The sentence immediately following the text to fn 642 lays down subsection 36(c) of Title 12 (Banks and Banking) of the United States Code. The text to fns 643-646 sets out paragraph 36(e)(1) of Title 12 (Banks and Banking) of the United States Code. Fn 643 comprises subparagraph 36(g)(3)(B) of Title 12 (Banks and Banking) of the United States Code. The start to fn 647 comprises paragraphs (1) and (2) of subsection 36(g) of Title 12 (Banks and Banking) of the United States Code. The last sentence of fn 647 lays down subparagraph 36(g)(3)(A) of Title 12 (Banks and Banking) of the United States Code. The penultimate sentence of fn 647 sets out subparagraph 36(g)(3)(C) of Title 12 (Banks and Banking) of the United States Code. Thus, this monograph specifies subsections (c) and (g), and paragraph (e)(1), of section 36 of Title 12 (Banks and Banking) of the United States Code.

649 For the purposes of the current section (i.e., section 84 of Title 12 (Banks and Banking) of the United States Code), the phrase '*loans and extensions of credit*' "shall include – (A) all direct or indirect advances of funds to a person [which are] made on the basis of any obligation of that person to repay the funds[,] or repayable from specific property [that is] pledged by[,] or on behalf of[,] the person; (B) to the extent specified by the Comptroller of the Currency, any liability of a national banking association to advance funds to[,] or on behalf of[,] a person[,] pursuant to a contractual commitment; and (C) any credit exposure to a person arising from a derivative transaction, repurchase agreement, reverse repurchase agreement, securities lending transaction, or securities borrowing transaction[,] between the national banking association and the person" (Government of the United States of America (2022), "United States Code, Updated," Title 12 – Banks and Banking, s.84(b)(1)). Fn 650 defines the term '*person*'. For the purposes of the present section (i.e., section 84 of Title 12 (Banks and Banking) of the United States Code), the expression '*derivative transaction*' "includes any transaction that is a contract, agreement, swap, warrant, note, or option that is based, in whole or in part, on the value of, any interest in, or any quantitative measure or the occurrence of any event relating to, one or more commodities, securities, currencies, interest or other rates, indices, or other assets" (Government of the United States of America (2022), "United States Code, Updated," Title 12 – Banks and Banking, s.84(b)(3)).

650 For the purpose of the current section (i.e., section 84 of Title 12 (Banks and Banking) of the United States Code), the word '*person*' "shall include an individual, sole proprietorship, partnership, joint venture, association, trust, estate, business trust, corporation, sovereign government or agency, instrumentality, or political subdivision thereof, or any similar entity or organization" (Government of the United States of America (2022), "United States Code, Updated," Title 12 – Banks and Banking, s.84(b)(2)).

651 Subsection 84(c) of Title 12 (Banks and Banking) of the United States Code lists these exceptions.

652 Any national bank "may take, receive, reserve, and charge on any loan or discount made, or upon any notes, bills of exchange, or other evidences of debt, interest at the rate [that is] allowed by the laws of the State, Territory, or District where the bank is located, or at a rate of 1 per centum in excess of the discount rate on ninety-day

Federal Reserve System (Chapter 3)

Chapter 3 (Federal Reserve System) of Title 12 (Banks and Banking) of the United States Code specifically defines the following terms: '*bank*'[653], '*State bank*'[654], '*national bank/national banking association*'[655], '*member bank*'[656],'*board*'[657], '*district*'[658], '*reserve bank*'[659], '*the continental United States*'[660], '*bonds and/or notes of the (Government of the) United States*'[661],

---

commercial paper [that is] in effect at the Federal reserve bank in the Federal reserve district where the bank is located, whichever may be the greater, and no more, except that[,] where by the laws of any State a different rate is limited for banks organized under State laws, the rate so limited shall be allowed for [national bank] associations [which are] organized or existing in any such State under title 62 of the Revised Statutes. When no rate is fixed by the laws of the State, or Territory, or District, the bank may take, receive, reserve, or charge a rate not exceeding 7 per centum, or 1 per centum in excess of the discount rate on ninety day commercial paper [that is] in effect at the Federal reserve bank in the Federal reserve district where the bank is located, whichever may be the greater, and such interest may be taken in advance, reckoning the days for which the note, bill or other evidence of debt has to run. The maximum amount of interest or discount to be charged at a branch of an association [which is] located outside of the States of the United States and the District of Columbia shall be at the rate [that is] allowed by the laws of the country, territory, dependency, province, dominion, insular possession, or other political subdivision where the branch is located. And the purchase, discount, or sale, of a *bona fide* bill or exchange, [which is] payable at another place than the place of such purchase, discount, or sale, at not more than the current rate of exchange for sight drafts in addition to the interest, shall not be considered as taking or receiving a greater rate of interest." (Government of the United States of America (2022), "United States Code, Updated," Title 12 – Banks and Banking, s.85; emphasis added).

653 When used in Chapter 3 (Federal Reserve System) of Title 12 (Banks and Banking) of the United States Code, the word '*bank*' "shall be held to include State bank, banking association, and trust company, except where national banks or Federal reserve banks are specifically referred to" (Government of the United States of America (2022), "United States Code, Updated," Title 12 – Banks and Banking, s.221).

654 For the purposes of Chapter 3 (Federal Reserve System) of Title 12 (Banks and Banking) of the United States Code, the phrase '*State bank*' "includes any bank which is operating under the Code of Law for the District of Columbia" (Government of the United States of America (2022), "United States Code, Updated," Title 12 – Banks and Banking, s.221). Fn 653 defines the term '*bank*'.

655 The phrases '*national bank*' and '*national banking association*', as used in Chapter 3 (Federal Reserve System) of Title 12 (Banks and Banking) of the United States Code, are "to be synonymous and interchangeable" (Government of the United States of America (2022), "United States Code, Updated," Title 12 – Banks and Banking, s.221).

656 The phrase '*member bank*' "shall be held to mean any national bank, State bank, or bank or trust company which has become a member of one of the Federal reserve banks" (Government of the United States of America (2022), "United States Code, Updated," Title 12 – Banks and Banking, s.221). Fn 653 defines the term '*bank*'.

657 The word '*board*' "shall be held to mean Board of Governors of the Federal Reserve System" (Government of the United States of America (2022), "United States Code, Updated," Title 12 – Banks and Banking, s.221).

658 The word '*district*' "shall be held to mean Federal reserve district" (Government of the United States of America (2022), "United States Code, Updated," Title 12 – Banks and Banking, s.221).

659 The phrase '*reserve bank*' "shall be held to mean Federal reserve bank" (Government of the United States of America (2022), "United States Code, Updated," Title 12 – Banks and Banking, s.221).

660 The phrase '*the continental United States*' "means the States of the United States and the District of Columbia" (Government of the United States of America (2022), "United States Code, Updated," Title 12 – Banks and Banking, s.221).

661 As used in Chapter 3 (Federal Reserve System) of Title 12 (Banks and Banking) of the United States Code, the phrases '*bond and notes of the United States*', '*bonds and notes of the Government of the United States*', and '*bonds or notes of the United States*' "shall be held to include certificates of indebtedness and Treasury bills issued under section 3104 of title 31" (Government of the United States of America (2022), "United States Code, Updated," Title 12 – Banks and Banking, s.221). Section 3104 of Title 31 (Money and Finance) of the United States Code is entitled 'Certificates of indebtedness and treasury bills; its first subsection states: "The Secretary of the Treasury may borrow on the credit of the United States Government amounts [that are] necessary for expenditures [which are] authorized by law[,] and may buy, redeem, and make refunds[,] under section 3111 of this title. For amounts borrowed, the Secretary may issue – (1) certificates of indebtedness of the Government; and (2) Treasury bills of the Government." (Government of the United States of America (2022), "United States Code, Updated," Title 31 – Money and Finance, s.3104(a)). Section 3111 of Title 31 (Money and Finance) of the United States Code is titled 'New issue used to buy, redeem, or refund outstanding obligations', and declares:

and '*affiliate*'[662]. The continental United States, excluding Alaska, is to be divided in to eight to twelve Federal reserve districts[663] [806]. Each Federal reserve district contains only one Federal reserve city[664] [807]. A Federal reserve bank includes in its title the name of the city in which it is located[665] [808]. Every national bank in any state must become a member bank of the Federal Reserve System, by subscribing and paying for stock in the Federal reserve bank of its district[666] [806].

The Board of Governors of the Federal Reserve System is composed of seven members – each from a different Federal reserve district – whom the President of the USA appoints after securing the approval of the Senate, for terms of fourteen years[667] [809]. Each member of the Board of Governors is to decidate all his or her professional time to the business of the Board [809].

Every year, the Board of Governors of the Federal Reserve System must make a full report of its activities to the Speaker of the House of Representatives, who is to ensure that this is printed for the Congress' information[668] [810]. The Vice Chairman for Supervision of the Board of Governers of the Federal Reserve System is required to appear before the Congress on

---

"An obligation may be issued under this chapter to buy, redeem or refund, at or before maturity, outstanding bonds, notes, certificates of indebtedness, Treasury bills, or savings certificates of the United States Government. Under regulations of the Secretary of the Treasury, money received from the sale of an obligation and other in the general fund of the Treasury may be used in making the purchases, redemptions, or refunds." (Government of the United States of America (2022), "United States Code, Updated," Title 31 – Money and Finance, s.3111). 'This chapter' is Chapter 31 of Title 31 (Money and Finance) of the United States Code, which is entitled 'Public Debt'.

662 As used in Chapter 3 (Federal Reserve System) of Title 12 (Banks and Banking) of the United States Code, the word '*affiliate*', except in instances in which it is specifically provided otherwise, "shall include any corporation, business trust, association, or other similar organization – (1) Of which a member bank, directly or indirectly, owns or controls either a majority of the voting shares or more than 50 per centum of the number of shares [that are] voted for the election of its directors, trustees, or other persons exercising similar functions at the preceding election, or controls in any manner the election of a majority of its directors, trustees, or other persons exercising similar functions; or (2) Of which control is held, directly or indirectly, through stock ownership or in any other manner, by the shareholders of a member bank who own or control either a majority of the shares of such bank or more than 50 per centum of the number of shares [that are] voted for the election of directors of such bank at the preceding election, or by trustees for the benefit of shareholders of any such bank; or (3) Of which a majority of its directors, trustees, or other persons exercising similar functions[,] are directors of any one member bank; or (4) Which owns or controls, directly or indirectly, either a majority of the shares of capital stock of a member bank or more than 50 per centum of the number of shares voted for the election of directors of a member bank at the preceding election, or controls in any manner the election of a majority of the directors of a member bank, or for the benefit of whose shareholders or members all[,] or substantially all[,] the capital stock of a member bank is held by trustees" (Government of the United States of America (2022), "United States Code, Updated," Title 12 – Banks and Banking, s.221a(b)). The first sentence of fn 656 defines the term '*member bank*'.

663 The text to fn 532, and the two sentences that immediately follow this text, specify this information.

664 Fn 663. Fn 532 lists the twelve Federal reserve cities.

665 The sentence which immediately precedes the text to fn 533 furnishes this information.

666 Each national bank must become a member bank of the Federal Reserve System upon starting business, or within ninety days of being admitted to the USA or the state in which it is situated (Government of the United States of America (2022), "United States Code, Updated," Title 12 – Banks and Banking, s.222). The text to fn 533 contains a different rule on this matter. Thus, the law here has changed. The first sentence of fn 656 defines the term '*member bank*'.

667 In choosing the members of the Board of Governors of the Federal Reserve System, the President of the USA "shall have due regard to a fair representation of the financial, agricultural, industrial, and commercial interests, and geographical divisions of the country, [and] shall appoint at least 1 member with demonstrated primary experience [of] working in[,] or supervising[,] community banks having less than $10,000,000,000 [(i.e., USD 10 billion)] in total assets" (Government of the United States of America (2022), "United States Code, Updated," Title 12 – Banks and Banking, s.241).

668 The sentence which immediately follows the text to fn 537 supplies this information.

specified occasions[669] [811]. The Board of Governors has a large number of functions, which include, for example, examining the accounts and affairs of each Federal reserve bank and of each of the latter's member banks [812], exercising supervision over Federal reserve banks [813], and appointing the FDIC as receiver or conservator for a State member bank[670] [814].

---

[669] The Vice Chairman for Supervision of the Board of Governers of the Federal Reserve System "shall appear before the Committee on Banking, Housing, and Urban Affairs of the Senate and the Committee on Financial Services of the House of Representatives[,] and at semi-annual hearings regarding the efforts, activities, objectives, and plans of the Board with respect to the conduct of supervision and regulation of depository institution holding companies and other financial firms supervised by the Board" (Government of the United States of America (2022), "United States Code, Updated," Title 12 – Banks and Banking, s.247b). Fn 657 defines the term '*board*'.

[670] Section 248 of Title 12 (Banks and Banking) of the United States Code is titled 'Enumerated powers', and may be abridged as follows: "The Board of Governors of the Federal Reserve System shall be authorized and empowered: **(a) Examination of accounts and affairs of banks; publication of weekly statements; reports of liabilities and assets of depository institutions; covered institutions** (1) To examine at its discretion the accounts, books, and affairs of each Federal reserve bank and of each member bank[,] and to require such statements and reports as it may deem necessary. The said board shall publish once each week a statement showing the condition of each Federal reserve bank and a consolidated statement for all Federal reserve banks. Such statements shall show in detail the assets and liabilities of the Federal reserve banks, single and combined, and shall furnish full information regarding the character of the money [that is] held as reserve and the amount, nature, and maturities of the paper and other investments [which are] owned or held by Federal reserve banks. (2) To require any depository institution [that is] specified in this paragraph to make, at such intervals as the Board may prescribe, such reports of its liabilities and assets as the Board may determine to be necessary or desirable to enable the Board to discharge its responsibility to monitor and control monetary and credit aggregates. ... The Board shall endeavor to avoid the imposition of unnecessary burdens on reporting institutions and the duplication of other reporting requirements. Except as otherwise required by law, any data [that are] provided to any department, agency, or instrumentality of the United States pursuant to other reporting requirements[,] shall be made available to the Board. The Board may classify depository institutions for the purposes of this paragraph[,] and may impose different requirements on each such class. **(b) Permitting or requiring rediscounting of paper at specified rate** To permit, or, on the affirmative vote of at least five members of the Board of Governors, to require[,] Federal reserve banks to rediscount the discounted paper of other Federal reserve banks at rates of interest to be fixed by the Board. **(c) Suspending reserve requirements** To suspend for a period not exceeding thirty days, and from time to time to renew such suspension for periods not exceeding fifteen days, any reserve requirments [that are] specified in this chapter {(i.e., Chapter 3 of Title 12 (Banks and Banking) of the United States Code, which is entitled 'Federal Reserve System')]. **(d) Supervising and regulating issue and retirement of notes** To supervise and regulate[,] through the Secretary of the Treasury[,] the issue and retirement of Federal Reserve notes, except for the cancellation and destruction, and accounting with respect to such cancellation and destruction, of notes [that are] unfit for circulation, and to prescribe rules and regulations under which such notes may be delivered by the Secretary of the Treasury to the Federal Reserve agents applying therefor. **(e) Adding to or reclassifying reserve cities** To add to the number of cities [which are] classified as reserve cities under existing law ... . or to reclassify existing reserve cities or to terminate their designation as such. **(f) Suspending or removing officers or directors of reserve banks** To suspend or remove any officer or director of any Federal reserve bank, the cause of such removal to be forthwith communicated in writing by the Board of Governors of the Federal Reserve System to the removed officer or director and to the said bank. **(g) Requiring writing off of doubtful or worthless assets of banks** To require the writing off of doubtful or worthless assets upon the books and balance sheets of Federal reserve banks. **(h) Suspending operations of or liquidating or reorganizing banks** To suspend, for the violation of any of the provisions of this chapter, the operations of any Federal reserve bank, to take possession thereof, administer the same during the period of suspension, and, when deemed advisable, to liquidate or reorganize such bank. **(i) Requiring bonds of agents; safeguarding proprety in hands of agents** To require bonds of Federal reserve agents, to make regulations for the safeguarding of all collateral, bonds, Federal reserve notes, money, or property of any kind [that is] deposited in the hands of such agents ... . **(j) Exercising supervision over reserve banks** To exercise general supervision over said Federal reserve banks. **(k) Delegation of certain functions; power to delegate; review of delegated activities** To delegate, by published order or rule[,] and subject to subchapter II [(Administrative Procedure)] of chapter 5 [(Administrative Procedure)], and chapter 7 [(Judicial Review)], of title 5 [(Government Organization and Employees) of the United States Code], any of its functions, other than those relating to rulemaking or pertaining principally to monetary and credit policies, to one or more administrative law judges, members or employees of the Board, or Federal Reserve banks. ... The Board of Governors may not delegate to a Federal reserve bank its functions for the establishment of policies for the supervision and regulation of depository institution holding companies and other financial firms supervised by

---

the Board of Governors. **(l) Employing attorneys, experts, assistants, and clerks; salaries and fees** To employ such attorneys, experts, assistants, clerks, or other employees as may be deemed necessary to conduct the business of the board. ... **(m) [Repealed] (n) Board's authority to examine depository institutions and affiliates** To examine, at the Board's discretion, any depository institution, and any affiliate of such depository institution, in connection with any advance to, any discount of any instrument for, or any request for[,] any such advance or discount by, such depository institution under this chapter [(i.e., Chapter 3 (Federal Reserve System) of Title 12 (Banks and Banking) of the United States Code)]. **(o) Authority to appoint conservator or receiver** The Board may appoint the Federal Deposit Insurance Corporation as conservator or receiver for a State member bank under section 1821(c)(9) of this title [(i.e., paragraph 1821(c)(9) of Title 12 (Banks and Banking) of the United States Code, which is headed 'Appropriate Federal banking agency may appoint [the Federal Deposit Insurance] Corporation as conservator or receiver for an insured State depository institution to carry out section 1831o' (of Title 12 (Banks and Banking) of the United States Code, which is titled 'Prompt corrective action'))]. **(p) Authority** The Board may act in its own name[,] and through its own attorneys[,] in enforcing any provision of this title [(i.e., Title 12 (Banks and Banking) of the United States Code)], regulations [that are] promulgated hereunder, or any other law or regulation, or in any action, suit, or proceeding to which the Board is a party[,] and which involves the Board's regulation or supervision of any bank, bank holding company ... or other entity, or the administration of its operations. **(q) Uniform protection authority for Federal reserve facilities** (1) Notwithstanding any other provision of law, to authorize personnel to act as law enforcement officers to protect and safeguard the premises, grounds, property, [and] personnel, including members of the Board, of the Board, or any Federal reserve bank, and operations conducted by[,] or on behalf of[,] the Board or a reserve bank. (2) The Board may, subject to the regulations [that are] prescribed under paragraph (5), delegate authority to a Federal reserve bank to authorize personnel to act as law enforcement officers to protect and safeguard the bank's premises, grounds, property, personnel, and operatios conducted by[,] or on behalf of[,] the bank. (3) Law enforcement officers [who are] designated or authorized by the Board or a reserve bank under paragraph (1) or (2) are authorized[,] while on duty[,] to carry firearms and make arrests without warrants for any offense against the United States [that is] committed in their presence, or for any felony [that is] cognizable under the laws of the United States[, and which is] committed[,] or being committed[,] within the buildings and grounds of the Board or a reserve bank[,] if they have reasonable grounds to believe that the person to be arrested has committed[,] or is committing[,] such a felony. Such officers shall have access to law enforcement information that may be necessary for the protection of the property or personnel of the Board or a reserve bank. (4) For the purposes of this subsection [(i.e., subsection 248(q) of Title 12 (Banks and Banking) of the United States Code)], the term "law enforcement officers" means personnel who have succcessfully completed law enforcement training and are authorized to carry firearms and make arrests pursuant to this subsection. (5) The law enforcement authorities [that are] provided for in this subsection may be exercised only pursuant to regulations [which are] prescribed by the Board and approved by the Attorney General. **(r) Voting documentation of determinations** (1) Any action that this chapter provides may be taken only upon the affirmative vote of 5 members of the Board[, and] may be taken upon the unanimous vote of all members then in office if there are fewer than 5 members in office at the time of the action. (2)(A) Any action that the Board is otherwise authorized to take under [sub]section 343(3) of this title [(i.e., Title 12 (Banks and Banking) of the United States Code, which is divided into paragraphs (A) to (E) – and whose section head (i.e., section 343) is entitled 'Discount of obligations arising out of actual commercial transactions'),] may be taken upon the unanimous vote of all available members then in office, if – (i) at least 2 members are available[,] and all available members participate in the action; (ii) the available members unanimously determine that – (I) unusual and exigent circumstances exist[,] and the borrower is unable to secure adequate credit accommodations from other sources; (II) action on the matter is necessary to prevent, correct, or mitigate serious harm to the economy or the stability of the financial system of the United States; (III) despite the use of all means available ... , the other members of the Board have not been able to be contacted on the matter; and (IV) action on the matter is required before the number of Board members [who are] otherwise required to vote on the matter can be contacted through any available means ... ; and (iii) any credit [that is] extended by a Federal reserve bank pursuant to such action is payable upon demand of the Board. (B) The available members of the Board shall document[,] in writing[,] the determinations [that are] required by subparagraph (A)(ii) [(i.e., clause 248(r)(2)(A)(ii) of Title 12 (Banks and Banking) of the United States Code – which is point (ii) in subparagraph (A) of the present subsection (subsection 248(r)))], and such written findings shall be included in the record of the action and in the official minutes of the Board, and copies of such record shall be provided[,] as soon as practicable[,] to the members of the Board who were not available to participate in the action[,] and to the Chairman on the Committee on Banking, Housing, and Urban Affairs of the Senate[,] and to the Chairman of the Committee of Financial Services of the House of Representatives. **(s)[1] Federal Reserve transparency and release of information (1) In general** In order to ensure the disclosure in a timely manner[, which is] consistent with the purpose of this chapter [(i.e., Chapter 3 (Federal Reserve System) of Title 12 (Banks and Banking) of the United States Code),] of information concerning the borrowers and counterparties participating in emergency credit facilities, discount window lending programs, and open market operations [that are] authorized or conducted by the Board or a Federal reserve bank, the Board of Governors

Federal financial regulatory agencies in the USA are not required to submit their recommendations and comments on legislation to officials for prior approval.

> No officer or agency of the United States shall have any authority to require the Securities and Exchange Commission, the Board of Governors of the Federal Reserve System, the Federal Deposit Insurance Corporation, the Comptroller of the Currency, the Director of the Office of Thrift Supervision, the Director of the Federal Housing Finance Agency, or the National Credit Union Administration[,] to submit legislative recommendations, or testimony, or comments on legislation, to any officer or agency of the United States for approval, comments or review, prior to the submission of such recommendations, testimony, or comments to the Congress[,] if such recommendations, testimony, or comments to the Congress include a statement indicating that the views expressed therein are those of the agency submitting them and do not necessarily represent the views of the President [of the USA] [815].

Every five years, the Board of Governors of the Federal Reserve System conducts a study, and submits a report, which details the extent to which creditors lend to small businesses[671] [816]. This study identifies, to a practicable degree, factors that furnish policymakers with insights into the credit market for small businesses[672] [817].

---

shall disclose ... – (A) the names and identifying details of each borrower, participant, or counterparty in any credit facility or covered transaction; (B) the amount [that is] borrowed by[,] or transferred by or to[,] a specific borrower, participant, or counterparty in any credit facility or covered transaction; (C) the interest rate or discount [which is] paid by each borrower, participant, or counterparty in any credit facility or covered transaction; and (D) information identifying the types and amounts of collateral [that is] pledged[,] or assets [which are] transferred[,] in connection with participation in any credit facility or covered transaction. ... **(5) Termination of credit facility by operation of law** A credit facility shall be deemed to have terminated as of the end of the 24-month period beginning on the date on which the credit facility ceases to make extensions of credit and loans, unless the credit facility is otherwise terminated by the Board before such date. ... **(s)[2] Assessments, fees, and other charges for certain companies (1) In general** The Board shall collect a total amount of assessments, fees, or other charges from the companies [which are] described in paragraph (2)[,] that is equal to the total expenses [which] the Board estimates are necessary or appropriate to carry out the supervisory and regulatory responsibilities of the Board with respect to such companies. **(2) Companies** The companies [that are] described in this paragraph are – (A) all bank holding companies having total consolidated assets of $100,000,000,000 [(i.e., USD 100 billion)] or more; (B) all savings and loan holding companies having total consolidated assets of $100,000,000,000 [(i.e., USD 100 billion)] or more; and (C) all nonbank financial companies supervised by the Board under section 5323 of this title [(i.e., section 5323 of Title 12 (Banks and Banking) of the United States Code, which is titled 'Authority to require supervision and regulation of certain nonbank financial companies')]. **(3) Tailoring assessments** In collecting assessments, fees, or other charges under paragraph (1)[,] from each company described in paragraph (2) with total consolidated assets of between $100,000,000,000 [(i.e., USD 100 billion)] and $250,000,000,000 [(i.e., USD 250 billion)], the Board shall adjust the amount [that is] charged to reflect any changes in supervisory and regulatory responsibilities resulting from the Economic Growth, Regulatory Relief, and Consumer Protection Act with respect to each such company." (Government of the United States of America (2022), "United States Code, Updated," Title 12 – Banks and Banking, s.248; emphasis original). Fn 657 defines the term '*board*'. Fn 659 defines the term '*reserve bank*'.

671 The Board of Governors of the Federal Reserve System must carry out this study, and compose the report on it, "in consultation with the Director of the Office of Thrift Supervision, the Comptroller of the Currency, the Board of Directors of the [Federal Deposit Insurance] Corporation, the Administrator of the National Credit Union Administration, the Administrator of the Small Business Administration, and the Secretary of Commerce" (Government of the United States of America (2022), "United States Code, Updated," Title 12 – Banks and Banking, s.252(1)).

672 These factors include: "(A) the demand for small business credit, including consideration of the impact of economic cycles on the levels of such demand; (B) the availability of credit to small businesses; (C) the range of credit options [that are] available to small businesses, such as those [which are] available from insured depository institutions and other providers of credit; (D) the types of credit products [that are] used to finance

Each Federal reserve bank annually selects from its Federal reserve district one member of the Federal Advisory Council – which comprises as many members as there are Federal reserve districts[673] [818]. The powers of the Federal Advisory Council are threefold, as follows.

> The Federal Advisory Council shall have power, by itself or through its officers, (1) to confer directly with the Board of Governors of the Federal Reserve System on general business conditions; (2) to make oral or written representations concerning matters within the jurisdiction of [the] said board; (3) to call for information[,] and to make recommendations in regard to discount rates, rediscount business, note issues, reserve conditions in the various districts, the purchase and sale of gold or securities by reserve banks, open-market operations by [the] said banks, and the general affairs of the reserve banking system [819].

The Federal Open Market Committee consists of the members of the Board of Governors of the Federal Reserve System, and five representatives of the Federal reserve banks – which must be presidents or first vice presidents of the latter [820]. A Federal reserve bank may participate, or refuse to engage, in open-market operations, except in line with the direction of, and regulations adopted by, the Federal Open Market Committee [821].

Any bank that is incorporated by special law of any state (i.e., a state bank) that would like to become a member of the Federal Reserve System, may apply to the Board of Governors of the Federal Reserve System for the right to subscribe to the stock of the Federal reserve bank[674] within the district in which the applicant bank is situated [822]. In acting upon an application to become a member of the Federal Reserve System from a state bank, the Board of Governors of the Federal Reserve System must consider the financial condition of the applicant bank, the quality of its management, and whether or not the corporate powers that it exercises are compatible with the purposes of Chapter 3 (Federal Reserve System) of Title 12 (Banks and Banking) of the United States Code [823]. All state banks which are admitted to membership of the Federal Reserve System must comply with the capital and reserve requirements of that chapter, observe those legal provisions which prohibit national banks from lending on, or buying, their own stock and that concern the withdrawal or impairment of their capital stock,

---

small business operations, including the use of traditional loans, leases, lines of credit, home equity loans, credit cards, and other sources of financing; (E) the credit needs of small businesses, including, if appropriate, the extent to which such needs differ, based upon product type, size of business, cash flow requirements, characteristics of ownership or investors, or other aspects of such business; (F) the types of risks to creditors in providing credit to small businesses," as well as "(G) such other factors as the Board deems appropriate" (Government of the United States of America (2022), "United States Code, Updated," Title 12 – Banks and Banking, s.252(2)). Fn 657 defines the term '*board*'.

[673] There are twelve Federal reserve cities (fn 532) – and, consequently (text to fn 532), there are twelve Federal reserve districts. Accordingly, the Federal Advisory Council should consist of twelve members. This is confirmed by the 'Federal Advisory Council' web page on the website of the Board of Governors of the Federal Reserve System, which states: "The Federal Advisory Council ... is composed of twelve representatives of the banking industry," and which lists these as one member from each of the twelve Federal reserve districts; this web page lists two additional members – i.e., fourteen members in total – who are the aforementioned twelve plus the Secretary and the Deputy Secretary of the Federal Advisory Council (Government of the United States of America (2022), "Board of Governors of the Federal Reserve System: Advisory Councils – Federal Advisory Council," accessed December 12, 2022, <https://www.federalreserve.gov/aboutthefed/fac.htm>).

[674] This application must be for the same quantity of stock that the state bank would be required to subscribe to, if it were instead a national bank (Government of the United States of America (2022), "United States Code, Updated," Title 12 – Banks and Banking, s.321).

and abide by the provisions of section 56[675] and subsection 60(b)[676] of Title 12 (Banks and Banking) of the United States Code regarding the payment of dividends[677] [824]. No state bank may be admitted to membership of the Federal Reserve System, unless it possesses capital stock and surplus that, in the opinion of the Board of Governors of the Federal Reserve System, are sufficient in relation to the condition and character of its assets and to its actual and prospective deposit liabilities and other corporate responsibilities[678] [825].

Section 341 of Title 12 (Banks and Banking) of the United States Code confers eight powers on each Federal reserve bank as a body corporate, upon the filing of its organization

---

675 This section is entitled 'Prohibition on withdrawal of capital; unearned dividends' and states: "No [national banking] association, or any member thereof, shall, during the time [that] it shall continue its banking operations, withdraw, or permit to be withdrawn, either in the form of dividends or otherwise, any portion of its capital. If losses have[,] at any time[,] been sustained by any such association, [which are] equal to or exceeding its undivided profits then on hand, [then] no dividend shall be made; and no dividend shall ever be made by any association, while it continues its banking operations, to an amount [that is] greater than its undivided profits, subject to otherwise applicable provisions of law. But nothing in this section shall prevent the reduction of the capital stock of the association under section 59 of this title." (Government of the United States of America (2022), "United States Code, Updated," Title 12 – Banks and Banking, s.56). 'This title' is Title 12 (Banks and Banking) of the United States Code. Section 59 of Title 12 (Banks and Banking) of the United States Code is titled 'Reduction in Capital', and reads as follows: "**(a) In general** Subject to the approval of the Comptroller of the Currency, a national banking association may, by a vote of shareholders owning, in the aggregate, two-thirds of its capital stock, reduce its capital. **(b) Shareholder distributions authorized** As part of its capital reduction plan [that is] approved in accordance with subsection (a), and with the affirmative vote of shareholders owning at least two thirds of the shares of each class of its stock outstanding (each voting as a class), a national banking association may distribute cash or other assets to its shareholders." (Government of the United States of America (2022), "United States Code, Updated," Title 12 – Banks and Banking, s.59; emphasis original).

676 Section 60 of Title 12 (Banks and Banking) of the United States Code is entitled 'National bank dividends', and declares: "**(a) In general** Subsection to subsection (b), the directors of any national bank may declare a dividend of so much of the undivided profits of the bank as the directors judge to be expedient. **(b) Approval required under certain circumstances** A national bank may not declare and pay dividends in any year in excess of an amount [that is] equal to the sum of the total of the net income of the bank for that year and the retained net income of the bank for the preceding 2 years, minus the sum of any transfers [which are] required by the Comptroller of the Currency and any transfers [that are] required to be made to a fund for the retirement of any preferred stock, unless the Comptroller of the Currency approves the declaration and payment of dividends in excess of such amount." (Government of the United States of America (2022), "United States Code, Updated," Title 12 – Banks and Banking, s.60; emphasis original).

677 The references to Comptroller of the Currency in section 56 (first sentence of fn 675) and subsection 60(b) (point **(b)** in fn 676) of Title 12 (Banks and Banking) of the United States Code to the Comptroller of the Currency are considered – for the purposes of the current text (i.e., the text to fns 675-677) – to be references to the Board of Governors of the Federal Reserve System (Government of the United States of America (2022), "United States Code, Updated," Title 12 – Banks and Banking, s.324). It is submitted that, as section 56 of Title 12 (Banks and Banking) of the United States Code does not include the phrase 'Comptroller of the Currency', and as section 59 of Title 12 (Banks and Banking) of the United States Code – to which section 56 of Title 12 (Banks and Banking) of the United States Code refers – *does* include the expression 'Comptroller of the Currency' (point **(a)** in the second sentence of fn 675), section 324 of Title 12 (Banks and Banking) of the United States Code requires this phrase within section 59 of Title 12 (Banks and Banking) of the United States Code to be replaced by the expression 'Board of Governors of the Federal Reserve System'.

678 No state bank that is "engaged in the business of receiving deposits other than trust funds, which does not possess capital stock and surplus in an amount [which is] equal to that which would be required for the establishment of a national banking association in the place in which it is located, shall be admitted to membership[,] unless it is, or has been, approved for deposit insurance under the Federal Deposit Insurance Act [1950]. The capital stock of a State member bank shall not be reduced[,] except with the prior consent of the Board." (Government of the United States of America (2022), "United States Code, Updated," Title 12 – Banks and Banking, s.329). The subsection titled 'Federal Deposit Insurance Corporation (FDIC), in the section above entitled 'The Regulation of Banking in the USA', specifies provisions from the Federal Deposit Insurance Act 1950'. The first sentence of fn 656 defines the term '*member bank*'. Fn 657 defines the term '*board*'.

certificate with the Comptroller of the Currency[679]; but the Federal reserve bank may not transact business other than that which "is incidental and necessarily preliminary to its organization" before the Comptroller has authorized it to start businesses under the provisions of Chapter 3 (Federal Reserve System) of Title 12 (Banks and Banking) of the United States Code [826]. Subject to two provisos[680], any Federal reserve bank may receive from the Government of the USA, or from any of the former's member banks or other depository institutions, deposits of present funds in legal tender, national-bank notes, Federal reserve notes, or checks and drafts, which are payable upon the presentation of other items – and also maturing bills and notes for collection; (subject to the abovementioned provisos) only for purposes of collection or exchange, any Federal reserve bank may receive from other Federal reserve banks, deposits of current funds in lawful tender, national-bank notes, checks upon other Federal reserve banks, checks and drafts that are payable upon presentation within its district, or maturing bills and notes which are payable within its district; (subject to the aforementioned provisos) solely for purposes of collection or exchange, any Federal reserve bank may receive from any nonmember bank, trust company or other depository institution, deposits of present funds in licit tender, national-bank notes, Federal reserve notes, checks and drafts that are payable upon presentation, or maturing notes and bills [827].

Upon the indorsement of any of its member banks, any Federal reserve bank may discount bills of exchange, notes and drafts that are issued or drawn for commercial, industrial or agricultural purposes, or the proceeds of which have been used – or will be used – for these

---

[679] These are the eight powers: "First. To adopt[,] and use[,] a corporate seal. Second, To have succession after February 25, 1927, until dissolved by Act of Congress or until forfeiture of franchise for violation of law. Third. To make contracts. Fourth. To sue and be sued, complain and defend, in any court of law or equity. Fifth. To appoint by its board of directors a president, vice presidents, and such officers and employees as are not otherwise provided for in this chapter, to define their duties, require bonds for them and fix the penalty thereof, and to dismiss at pleasure such officers or employees. The president shall be the chief executive officer of the bank ... . Sixth. To prescribe by its board of directors, bylaws [that are] not inconsistent with law, regulating the manner in which its general business may be conducted, and [in which] the privileges [that are] granted to it by law may be exercised and enjoyed. Seventh. To exercise by its board of directors, or duly authorized officers or agents, all powers [which are] specifically granted by the provisions of this chapter[,] and such incidental powers as shall be necessary to carry on the business of banking within the limitations [that are] prescribed by this chapter. Eighth. Upon deposit with the Treasurer of the United States of any bonds of the United States in the manner [that is] provided by existing law relating to national banks, to receive from the Secretary of the Treasury circulating notes in blank, [which are] registered and countersigned as provided by law, equal in amount to the par value of the bonds so deposited, such notes to be issued under the same conditions and provisions of law as relate to the issue of circulating notes of national banks [that are] secured by bonds of the United States bearing the circulating privilege, except that the issue of such notes shall not be limited to the capital stock of such Federal reserve bank." (Government of the United States of America (2022), "United States Code, Updated," Title 12 – Banks and Banking, s.341). 'This chapter' is Chapter 3 (Federal Reserve System) of Title 12 (Banks and Banking) of the United States Code. The first sentence of fn 661 defines the term '*bonds of the United States*'.

[680] These provisos are as follows: "*Provided*, Such nonmember bank or trust company or other depository institution maintains with the Federal Reserve bank of its district a balance in such amount as the Board [of Governors of the Federal Reserve System (fn 657)] determines[,] taking into account items in transit, services [that are] provided by the Federal Reserve bank, and other factors as the Board may deem appropriate: *Provided further*, That nothing in this or any other section of this chapter shall be construed as prohibiting a member or nonmember bank or other depository institution from making reasonable charges, to be determined and regulated by the Board of Governors of the Federal Reserve System, but in no case to exceed 10 cents per $100 [(i.e., USD 0.1 per USD 100)] or fraction thereof, based on the total of checks and drafts [that are] presented at any one time, for collection or payment of checks and drafts[,] and remission therefor by exchange or otherwise; but no such charges shall be made against the Federal reserve banks" (Government of the United States of America (2022), "United States Code, Updated," Title 12 – Banks and Banking, s.342; emphasis original). The first sentence of fn 656 defines the term '*member bank*'.

intentions [828]. Subject to two provisos[681], upon the indorsement of any of its member banks, and subject to regulations and restrictions that the Board of Governors of the Federal Reserve System is to prescribe, any Federal reserve bank may discount or purchase bills of exchange, which are payable at sight or on demand, that arise from the shipment of nonperishable, readily-marketable staples, and which are secured by shipping documents that convey title to these staples[682] [829].

Subject to one proviso[683], any Federal reserve bank may discount acceptances with a maturity at the time of discount of no more than ninety days' sight – excluding days of grace, and which at least one member bank indorses [830]. Any Federal reserve bank may make advances for periods of no more than fifteen days to its member banks on their promissory notes that are secured by the pledge or deposit of bonds, notes, certificates of indebtedness or Treasury bills of the Government of the USA, by the pledge or deposit of debentures or other similar obligations of Federal intermediate credit banks which are eligible for Federal reserve banks to purchase under section 350 of Title 12 (Banks and Banking) of the United States Code[684], or by the pledge or deposit of bonds that are issued under the provisions of subsection 1463(c) of Title 12 (Banks and Banking) of the United States Code[685]; any Federal reserve bank may make advances for periods of no more than ninety days to its member banks on their promissory notes – if these are secured by such bills of exchange, bankers' acceptances, notes or drafts as are eligible under the provisions of Chapter 3 (Federal Reserve System) of Title 12

---

681 These provisos are as follows: "*Provided*, That all such bills of exchange shall be forwarded promptly for collection, and demand for payment shall be made with reasonable promptness after the arrival of such staples at their destination: *Provided further*, That no such bill shall[,] in any event[,] be held by[,] or for the account of[,] a Federal reserve bank for a period in excess of ninety days" (Government of the United States of America (2022), "United States Code, Updated," Title 12 – Banks and Banking, s.344; emphasis original).

682 In discounting these bills of exchange, "Federal reserve banks may compute the interest to be deducted on the basis of the estimated life of each bill[,] and adjust the discount[,] after payment of such bills[,] to conform to the actual life thereof" (Government of the United States of America (2022), "United States Code, Updated," Title 12 – Banks and Banking, s.344).

683 This proviso is as follows: "*Provided*, That such acceptances[,] if drawn for an agricultural purpose and secured at the time of acceptance by warehouse receipts or other such documents conveying or securing title covering readily marketable staples[,] may discounted with a maturity at the time of discount of not more than six months' sight exclusive of days of grace" (Government of the United States of America (2022), "United States Code, Updated," Title 12 – Banks and Banking, s.344; emphasis original).

684 Section 350 of Title 12 (Banks and Banking) of the United States Code is titled 'Purchase and sale of debentures and like obligations of intermediate credit banks and agricultural credit corporations', and states: "Any Federal reserve bank may also buy and sell debentures and other such obligations [that are] issued by a Federal intermediate credit bank or by a national agricultural credit corporation, but only to the same extent as[,] and subject to[,] the same limitations as those upon which it may buy and sell bonds under title I of the Federal Farm Loan Act." (Government of the United States of America (2022), "United States Code, Updated," Title 12 – Banks and Banking, s.350).

685 Section 1463 of Title 12 (Banks and Banking) of the United States Code was repealed in 1966 (Government of the United States of America (2022), "United States Code, Updated," Title 12 – Banks and Banking, s.347, fn 1; Government of the United States of America (2022), "United States Code, Updated," Title 12 – Banks and Banking, s.355(1), fn 1). The present version of the United States Code (i.e., that updated to 13th December 2022,) contains subsection 1463 of Title 12 (Banks and Banking) of the United States Code, which is entitled 'Supervision of savings associations'; its subsection (c) is titled 'Stringency of standards', and declares: "The regulations of the Comptroller [of the Currency] and the policies of the Comptroller and the [Federal Deposit Insurance] Corporation governing the safe and sound operation of savings associations, including regulations and policies governing asset classification and appraisals, shall be no less stringent than those established by the Comptroller for national banks." (Government of the United States of America (2022), "United States Code, Updated," Title 12 – Banks and Banking, s.1463(c)). It is opined that the current content of subsection 1463(c) of Title 12 (Banks and Banking) of the United States Code is unrelated to the reference to that subsection in the text to the present footnote (i.e., fn 685), and is unconnected to the reference to that subsection in the text to fn 686.

(Banks and Banking) of the United States Code for Federal reserve banks to purchase or rediscount, or by those obligations that are eligible for purchase under section 355 of Title 12 (Banks and Banking) of the United States Code[686] [831].

Upon receiving the consent of at least five members of the Board of Governors of the Federal Reserve System, any Federal reserve bank may make advances[687] to groups of at least five member banks within its district – as long as the majority of the latter are independently owned and controlled – upon their demand or time promissory notes, subject to one proviso[688] [832]. Under rules and regulations that the Board of Governors of the Federal Reserve System prescribes, any Federal reserve bank may make advances to any member bank on its demand or time notes with maturities of four months or less – provided that these are secured to the satisfaction of this Federal reserve bank; under such rules and regulations, any Federal reserve bank may make advances[689] to any member bank on its time notes which have such maturities as the Board may prescribe – and which are secured by mortgage loans that cover a residence with less than five dwelling units[690] [833].

---

[686] Section 355 of Title 12 (Banks and Banking) of the United States Code is entitled 'Purchase and sale of obligations of National, State, and municipal governments; open market operations; purchases and sales from or to United States; maximum aggregate amount of obligations acquired directly from or loaned directly to United States', and specifies: "Every Federal Reserve bank shall have power: (1) To buy and sell, at home or abroad, bonds and notes of the United States, bonds [that are] issued under the provisions of subsection (c) of section 1463 of this title [(fn 685)], and having maturities from date of purchase of not exceeding six months, and bills, notes, revenue bonds, and warrants with a maturity from date of purchase of not exceeding six months, [which are] issued in anticipation of the collection of taxes or in anticipation of the receipt of assured revenues by any State, county, district, political subdivision, or municipality in the continental United states, including irrigation, drainage and reclamation districts, and obligations of, or fully guaranteed as to principal and interest by, a foreign government or agency thereof, such purchases to be made in accordance with rules and regulations prescribed by the Board of Governors of the Federal Reserve System. Notwithstanding any other provision of this chapter, any bonds, notes, or other obligations which are direct obligations of the United States or which are fully guaranteed by the United States as to principal and interest[,] may be bought and sold without regard to maturities but only in the open market. (2) To buy and sell in the open market, under the direction and regulations of the Federal Open Market Committee, any obligation which is a direct obligation of, or fully guaranteed as to principal and interest by, any agency of the United States." (Government of the United States of America (2022), "United States Code, Updated," Title 12 – Banks and Banking, s.355). 'This chapter' is Chapter 3 (Federal Reserve System) of Title 12 (Banks and Banking) of the United States Code. The paragraph immediately preceding the text to fn 674 contains provisions concerning the Federal Open Market Committee. The first sentence of fn 661 defines the term '*bonds and notes of the United States*'.

[687] However, "[n]o obligations of any foreign government, individual, partnership, association, or corporation [that is] organized under the laws thereof[,] shall be eligible as collateral security for advances under this section" (Government of the United States of America (2022), "United States Code, Updated," Title 12 – Banks and Banking, s.347a).

[688] The Federal reserve bank may make these advances "provided [that] the bank or banks which receive the proceeds of such advances as herein provided have no adequate amounts of eligible and acceptable assets available to enable such bank or banks to obtain sufficient credit accommodations from the Federal reserve bank through rediscounts or advances[,] other than as provided in section 347b of this title [(i.e., Title 12 (Banks and Banking) of the United States Code)]" (Government of the United States of America (2022), "United States Code, Updated," Title 12 – Banks and Banking, s.347a). The text to fns 689 and 690, and fn 689, lay down subsection 347b(a) of Title 12 (Banks and Banking) of the United States Code. Fn 690 sets out paragraph (1), (3) and (4), and subparagraphs (2)(A), (2)(D) and (5)(E), of subsection 347b(b) of Title 12 (Banks and Banking) of the United States Code.

[689] These "advances shall bear interest at rate equal to the lowest discount rate in effect at such Federal Reserve bank on the date of such note" (Government of the United States of America (2022), "United States Code, Updated," Title 12 – Banks and Banking, s.347b(a)).

[690] Subsection 347b(b) of Title 12 (Banks and Banking) of the United States Code provides a limitation on advances (paragraph 347b(b)(1) of Title 12 (Banks and Banking) of the United States Code), that is subject to a viability exception (paragraph 347b(b)(2) of Title 12 (Banks and Banking) of the United States Code). Paragraph 347b(b)(1) of Title 12 (Banks and Banking) of the United States Code is headed 'Limitations on extended periods', and states: "Except as provided in paragraph (2), no advances to any undercapitalized depository

Subject to such regulations, restrictions and limitations as the Board of Governors of the Federal Reserve System may prescribe, any Federal reserve bank may make advances to any individual, corporation or partnership, on the promissory notes of that individual, corporation or partnership which are secured by direct obligations of the Government of the USA or by any commitment that is a direct obligation of, or whose principal repayments and interest payments are fully guaranteed by, an agency of that government[691] [834]. Subject to such regulations,

institution by any Federal Reserve bank under this section may be outstanding for more than 60 days in any 120-day period." (Government of the United States of America (2022), "United States Code, Updated," Title 12 – Banks and Banking, s.347b(b)(1)). 'This section' is section 347b of Title 12 (Banks and Banking) of the United States Code. 'Paragraph (2)' is paragraph 347b(b)(2) of Title 12 (Banks and Banking) of the United States Code, which is headed 'Viability exception' and whose first and final subparagraphs read as follows: "**(A) In general** If – (i) the head of the appropriate Federal banking agency certifies in advance in writing to the Federal Reserve bank that any depository institution is viable; or (ii) the Board [of Governors of the Federal Reserve System (fn 657)] conducts an examination of any depository institution[,] and the Chairman of the Board certifies in writing to the Federal Reserve bank that the institution is viable, [then] the limitation contained in paragraph (1) [(i.e., paragraph 357b(b)(1) of Title 12 (Banks and Banking) of the United States Code (second sentence of the current footnote (fn 690)),)] shall not apply during the 60-day period beginning on the date [that] such certification is received. ... **(D) Extended advances subject to paragraph (3)** Notwithstanding paragraph (1), an undercapitalized depository institution which does not have a certificate of viability in effect under this paragraph may have advances outstanding for more than 60 days in any 120-day period[,] if the Board elects to treat – (i) such institution as critically undercapitalized under paragraph (3); and (ii) any such advance as an advance [that is] described in subparagraph (A)(i) of paragraph (3)." (Government of the United States of America (2022), "United States Code, Updated," Title 12 – Banks and Banking, ss.347b(b)(2)(A) and 347b(b)(2)(D); emphasis original). 'Paragraph 3' is paragraph 347b(b)(3) of Title 12 (Banks and Banking) of the United States Code, which is headed 'Advances to critically undercapitalized depository institutions', and which declares: "**(A) Liability for increased loss** Notwithstanding any other provision of this section [(i.e., section 347b(b) of Title 12 (Banks and Banking) of the United States Code)], if – (i) in the case of any critically undercapitalized depository institution – (I) any advance under this section to such institution is outstanding without payment having been demanded as of the end of the 5-day period beginning on the date [that] the institution becomes a critically undercapitalized institution; or (II) any new advance is made to such institution under this section[,] after the end of such period; and (ii) after the end of that 5-day period, the Deposit Insurance Fund of the Federal Deposit Insurance Corporation incurs a loss exceeding the loss that the Corporation would have incurred if it had liquidated that institution as of the end of that period, [then] the Board [of Governors of the Federal Reserve System (fn 657)] shall, subject to the limitations in subparagraph (B), be liable to the Federal Deposit Insurance Corporation for the excess loss, without regard to the terms of the advance or any collateral [which is] pledged to secure the advance. **(B) Limitation on excess loss** The liability of the Board under subparagraph (A) shall not exceed the lesser of the following: (i) The amount of the loss [that] the Board[,] or any Federal Reserve bank[,] would have incurred on the increases in the amount of advances [which are] made after the 5-day period [that is] referred to in subparagraph (A)[,] if those increased advances had been unsecured. (ii) The interest [which is] received on the increases in the amount of advances [that are] made after the 5-day period [which is] referred to in subparagraph (A). **(C) Federal Reserve to pay obligation** The Board shall pay the Federal Deposit Insurance Corporation the amount of any liability of the Board under subparagraph (A). **(D) Report** The Board shall report to the Congress on any excess loss liability [that] it incurs under subparagraph (A), as limited by paragraph (B)(i), and the reasons therefore, not later than 6 months after incurring the liability." (Government of the United States of America (2022), "United States Code, Updated," Title 12 – Banks and Banking, s.347b(b)(3); emphasis original). A Federal reserve bank has "no obligation to make, increase, renew, or extend any advance or discount under this chapter to any depository institution" (Government of the United States of America (2022), "United States Code, Updated," Title 12 – Banks and Banking, s.347b(b)(4)). 'This chapter' is Chapter 3 (Federal Reserve System) of Title 12 (Banks and Banking) of the United States Code. A depository institution is '*viable*', "if the Board [of Governors of the Federal Reserve System (fn 657)] or the appropriate Federal banking agency determines, giving due regard to the economic conditions and circumstances in the market in which the institution operates, that the institution – (i) is not critically undercapitalized; (ii) is not expected to become critically undercapitalized; and (iii) is not expected to be placed in conservatorship or receivership" (Government of the United States of America (2022), "United States Code, Updated," Title 12 – Banks and Banking, s.347b(b)(5)(E)).

691 These advances are to "be made for periods not exceeding 90 days[,] and shall bear interest at rates [that are] fixed from time to time by the Federal reserve bank, subject to the review and determination of the Board of Governors of the Federal Reserve System" (Government of the United States of America (2022), "United States Code, Updated," Title 12 – Banks and Banking, s.347c).

restrictions and limitations as the Board of Governors of the Federal Reserve System may impose, each Federal reserve bank may make advances to, or receive deposits from, or discount paper which is endorsed by, any branch or agency of a foreign bank, in the same way and to the same degree that it may exercise these powers regarding a member bank, as long as this branch or agency is maintaining reserves with the Federal reserve bank pursuant to section 3105 of Title 12 (Banks and Banking) of the United States Code[692] [835]. The Board of Governors of the Federal Reserve System is to exercise special superintendence over all transactions and relationships that any Federal reserve bank enters into with any foreign bank or banker, or with any group of foreign banks or bankers, and all these transactions and relationships are to be subject to such regulations, limitations and conditions as the Board may prescribe[693] [836].

The Board of Governors of the Federal Reserve System may regulate to limit, to a percentage of the assets of a Federal reserve bank, the amount of acceptances, bills, drafts or notes having a maturity of between three and six months – excluding days of grace – which may be discounted by such a bank, and the value of acceptances, bills, drafts or notes having a maturity or betwixt six and nine mounts that may be rediscounted by such a bank [837]. Any Federal reserve bank may, under rules and regulations that the Board of Governors of the Federal Reserve System prescribes, buy and sell in the open market bills of exchange, bankers' acceptances and cable transfers of the kind and maturities that Chapter 3 (Federal Reserve

---

692 In exercising these powers in respect of "such branch or agency, each Federal Reserve bank shall give due regard to account balances being maintained by such branch or agency with such Reserve bank and the proportion of assets of such branch or agency being held as reserves under section 3105 of this title"(Government of the United States of America (2022), "United States Code, Updated," Title 12 – Banks and Banking, s.347d). 'Section 3105 of this title' is section 3105 of Title 12 (Banks and Banking) of the United States Code, which is titled 'Authority of Federal Reserve System'; its first subsection is entitled 'Bank reserves', and concerns the imposition by the Board of Governors of the Federal Reserve System of reserve requirements on agencies and branches of foreign banks, which are situated in the USA. For the purposes of section 347d of Title 12 (Banks and Banking) of the United States Code, the terms '*branch*', '*agency*' and '*foreign bank*' take the meanings that section 3101 of Title 12 (Banks and Banking) of the United States Code gives to them (Government of the United States of America (2022), "United States Code, Updated," Title 12 – Banks and Banking, s.347d). These are as follows: "For the purposes of this chapter – (1) "*agency*" means any office[,] or any place of business[,] of a foreign bank [that is] located in any State of the United States[,] at which credit balances are maintained incidental to[,] or arising out of[,] the exercise of banking powers, checks are paid, or money is lent[,] but at which deposits may not be accepted from citizens or residents of the United States; ... (3) "*branch*" means any office[,] or any place of business[,] of a foreign bank [that is] located in any State of the United States[,] at which deposits are received; ... (7) "*foreign bank*" means any company [which is] organized under the laws of a foreign country, a territory of the United States, Puerto Rico, Guam, American Samoa, or the Virgin Islands, which engages in the business of banking, or any subsidiary or affiliate, organized under such laws, of any such company. For the purposes of this chapter[,] the term "*foreign bank*" 'includes, without limitation, foreign commercial banks, foreign merchant banks[,] and other foreign institutions that engage in banking activities [which are] usual in connection with the business of banking in the countries where such foreign institutions are organized or operating; ... ." (Banks and Banking) of the United States Code gives to them (Government of the United States of America (2022), "United States Code, Updated," Title 12 – Banks and Banking, ss.3101(1), 3101(3) and 3101(7); emphasis added). 'This chapter' is Chapter 32 (Foreign Bank Participation in Domestic Markets) of Title 12 (Banks and Banking) of the United States Code.

693 Furthermore, "[n]o officer or other representative of any Federal reserve bank shall conduct negotiations of any kind with the officers or representatives of any foreign bank or banker[,] without first obtaining the permission of the Board of Governors of the Federal Reserve System. The Board of Governors of the Federal Reserve System shall have the right, in its discretion, to be represented in any conference or negotiations by such representative or representatives as the Board may designate. A full report of all conferences or negotiations, and all understandings or agreements [which are] arrived at or transactions [that are] agreed upon, and all other material facts appertaining to such conferences or negotiations, shall be filed with the Board of Governors of the Federal Reserve System in writing by a duly authorized officer of each Federal reserve bank which shall have participated in such conferences or negotiations." (Government of the United States of America (2022), "United States Code, Updated," Title 12 – Banks and Banking, s.348a).

System) of Title 12 (Banks and Banking) of the United States Code makes eligible for rediscount – with, or without, a member bank's indorsement [838].

Every Federal reserve bank is empowered to deal in gold coin and bullion, make loans thereon, exchange Federal reserve notes for gold, gold coin or gold certificates, and contract for loans of gold coin or bullion [839]. Each Federal reserve bank is enabled to buy from member banks, and to sell – with or without the endorsement of the Federal reserve bank – bills of exchange that arise from commercial transactions [840]. Every Federal reserve bank is empowered to set periodically – subject to review by, and determination of, the Board of Governors of the Federal Reserve System – rates of discount for the Federal reserve bank to charge for each class of paper, which shall be chosen with the intention of accommodating business and commerce[694] [841].

Each Federal reserve bank is empowered to establish accounts with other Federal reserve banks for the purpose of exchange, and – subject to the approval of the Board of Governors of the Federal Reserve System[695] – open and maintain accounts in foreign states in order to buy, sell and collect bills of exchange[696] [842]. Every Federal reserve bank is to receive cheques (or checks)[697] on deposit at par from other Federal reserve banks and from depository institutions[698]

---

694 Each Federal reserve bank is to establish these rates of discount every fourteen days, or more frequently if the Board of Governors of the Reserve System deems this to be necessary (Government of the United States of America (2022), "United States Code, Updated," Title 12 – Banks and Banking, s.357).

695 The provision is detailed thus: "Every Federal reserve bank shall have power to establish accounts with their Federal reserve banks for exchange purposes[,] and, with the consent[,] or upon the order and direction[,] of the Board of Governors of the Federal Reserve System[,] and under regulations to be prescribed by the said Board, to open and maintain accounts in foreign countries, appoint correspondents, and establish agencies in such countries[,] wheresoever it may be deemed best for the purpose of purchasing, selling, and collecting bills of exchange, and to buy and sell, with or without its indorsement, through such correspondents or agencies, bills of exchange (or acceptances) arising out of actual commercial transactions which have not more than ninety days to run, exclusive of days of grace, and which bear the signature of two or more responsible parties, and, with the consent of the Board of Governors of the Federal Reserve System, to open and maintain banking accounts for such foreign correspondents or agencies, or for foreign banks or bankers, or for foreign states as defined in section 632 of this title [(i.e., Title 12 (Banks and Banking) of the United States Code)]. ..." (Government of the United States of America (2022), "United States Code, Updated," Title 12 – Banks and Banking, s.358). For the purposes of section 632 of Title 12 (Banks and Banking) of the United States Code, the phrase '*foreign state*' "includes any foreign government or any department, district, province, county, possession, or other similar governmental organization or subdivision of a foreign government, and any agency or instrumentality of any such foreign government or of any such organization or subdivision" (Government of the United States of America (2022), "United States Code, Updated," Title 12 – Banks and Banking, s.632(2); there are three instances of the symbol '(2)' in section 632 of Title 12 (Banks and Banking) of the United States Code – the third of which precedes the definition of the term '*foreign state*').

696 This section continues: "Whenever any such account has been opened[,] or agency or correspondent has been appointed[,] by a Federal reserve bank, with the consent of[,] or under the order and direction of[,] the Board of Governors of the Federal Reserve System, any other Federal reserve bank may, with the consent and approval of the Board of Governors of the Federal Reserve System, be permitted to carry on or conduct, through the Federal reserve bank opening such account or appointing such agency or correspondent, any transaction [that is] authorized by this section under rules and regulations to be prescribed by the board [(i.e., the Board of Governors of the Federal Reserve System (fn 657))]." (Government of the United States of America (2022), "United States Code, Updated," Title 12 – Banks and Banking, s.358).

697 The word '*cheque*' means "an order to a bank to pay a stated sum from the drawer's account, written on a specially printed form"; its meaning originated in the early eighteenth century – then it denoted a counterfoil, or a form with a counterfoil; the noun '*cheque*' is a variant of the verb '*to check*', in the sense of being a "'device for checking the amount of an item'" (Pearsall, J. (editor) (1998), *The New Oxford Dictionary of English*, 313). This connection between the terms '*cheque*' and '*to check*' explains the alternative spelling of the word '*cheque*', i.e., '*check*', which is used in the USA.

698 This section is titled 'Receiving checks and drafts on deposit at par; charges for collections, exchange, and clearances'; it reads thus: "Every Federal reserve bank shall receive on deposit at par from depository institutions or from Federal reserve banks[,] checks and other items, including negotiable orders of withdrawal and share

[843]. The discount and rediscount, and the purchase and sale, by any Federal reserve bank of bills receivable, bills of exchange and acceptances, which are authorized by Chapter 3 (Federal Reserve System) of Title 12 (Banks and Banking) of the United States Code, are to be subject to such regulations, restrictions and limitations as the Board of Governors of the Federal Reserve System may impose [844].

Any national bank may make[699], arrange, buy or sell loans or extensions of credit that are secured by liens on interests in real estate, subject to requirements and restrictions as the Comptroller of the Currency may prescribe by regulation or order – and to subsection 1828(o) of Title 12 (Banks and Banking) of the United States Code[700] [845]. Periodically, and after consulting the Board of Directors of the Federal Deposit Insurance Corporation and the Federal Home Loan Bank Board, the Board of Governors of the Federal Reserve System may prescribe rules that govern the advertisement of interest payable by member banks on time and savings

drafts and drafts [that are] drawn upon any of its depositors, and[,] when remitted by a Federal reserve bank, checks and other items, including negotiable orders of withdrawal and share drafts and drafts [that are] drawn by any depositor in any other Federal reserve bank or depository institution upon funds to the credit of said depositor in said reserve bank or depository institution. Nothing herein contained shall be construed as prohibiting a depository institution from charging its actual expense [which is] incurred in collecting and remitting funds, or for exchange [that is] sold to its patrons. The Board of Governors of the Federal Reserve System shall, by rule, fix the charges to be collected by the depository institution from its patrons whose checks and other items, including negotiable orders of withdrawal and share drafts[,] are cleared through the Federal reserve bank[,] and the charge which may be imposed for the service of clearing or collection [that is] rendered by the Federal reserve bank." (Government of the United States of America (2022), "United States Code, Updated," Title 12 – Banks and Banking, s.360).

699 Notes that represent "loans made under this section [(i.e., section 371 of Title 12 (Banks and Banking) of the United States Code)] to finance the construction of residential or farm buildings[,] and having maturities not to exceed nine months[,] shall be eligible for discount as commercial paper within the terms of the first paragraph of section 343 of this title [(i.e., Title 12 (Banks and Banking) – these terms are for discount as notes that are issued or drawn for commercial, industrial or agricultural purposes, or the proceeds of which have been used – or will be used – for these intentions (sentence immediately-preceding the text to fns 681 and 682)),] if accompanied by a valid and binding agreement to advance the full amount of the loan[,] upon the completion of the building[, which is] entered into by an individual, partnership, association, or corporation [that is] acceptable to the discounting bank" (Government of the United States of America (2022), "United States Code, Updated," Title 12 – Banks and Banking, s.371(b)).

700 Subsection 1828(o) of Title 12 (Banks and Banking) of the United States Code is entitled 'Real estate lending', and specifies: "**(1) Uniform regulations** Not more than 9 months after December 19, 1991, each appropriate Federal banking agency shall adopt uniform regulations prescribing standards for extensions of credit that are – (A) secured by liens of interests in real estate; or (B) made for the purpose of financing the construction of a building[,] or other improvements to real estate. **(2) Standards (A) Criteria** In prescribing standards under paragraph (1), the agencies shall consider – (i) the risk [that is] posed to the Deposit Insurance Fund by such extensions of credit; (ii) the need for safe and sound operation of insured depository institutions; and (iii) the availability of credit. **(B) Variations permitted** In prescribing standards under paragraph (1), the appropriate Federal banking agencies may differentiate among types of loans – (i) as may be required by Federal statute; (ii) as may be warranted, based on the risk to the Deposit Insurance Fund; or (iii) as may be warranted, based on the safety and soundness of the institutions. **(3) Loan evaluation standard** No appropriate Federal banking agency shall adversely evaluate an investment or a loan [that is] made by an insured depository institution, or consider such a loan to be nonperforming, solely because the loan is made to[,] or the investment is in[,] commercial, residential, or industrial property, unless such investment or loan may affect the institution's safety and soundness. **(4) Effective date** The regulations [which are] adopted under paragraph (1) shall become effective not later than 15 months after December 19, 1991. Such regulations shall continue in effect[,] except as uniformly amended by the appropriate Federal banking agencies, acting in concert." (Government of the United States of America (2022), "United States Code, Updated," Title 12 – Banks and Banking, s.1828(o); emphasis original).

deposits which are held at these banks [846]. In order to limit the risk that the failure of a large depository institution would present to insured depository institutions [847], the Board of Governors of the Federal Reserve System shall, by making regulations or presenting orders, lay down standards which restrict the risks that an insured depository institution's exposure to any other depository institution[701] would pose [848].

[701] For the purposes of this subsection [(i.e., subsection 371b-2(b) of Title 12 (Banks and Banking) of the United States Code)], "an insured depository institution's "exposure" to another depository institution means – (A) all extensions of credit to the other depository institution, regardless of name or description, including – (i) all deposits at the other depository institution; (ii) all purchases of securities or other assets from the other depository institution [that are] subject to an agreement to repurchase; and (iii) all guarantees, acceptances, or letters of credit (including endorsements or standby letters of credit) on behalf of the other depository institution; (B) all purchases of[,] or investments in[,] securities [which are] issued by the other depository institution; (C) all securities [which are] issued by the other depository institution [that are] accepted as collateral for an extension of credit to any person; and (D) all similar transactions that the Board [of Governors of the Federal Reserve System (fn 657),] by regulation[,] determines to be exposure for the purposes of this section" (Government of the United States of America (2022), "United States Code, Updated," Title 12 – Banks and Banking, s.371b-2(c)(1)). 'This section' is section 371b-2 of Title 12 (Banks and Banking) of the United States Code. For the purposes of 'this section', "any transaction by an insured depository institution with any person is a transaction with another depository institution to the extent that the proceeds of the transaction are used for the benefit of, or transferred to, that other depository institution" (Government of the United States of America (2022), "United States Code, Updated," Title 12 – Banks and Banking, s.371b-2(c)(3)), and the term '*insured depository institution*' "has the same meaning as in section 1813 of this title [(i.e., Title 12 (Banks and Banking) of the United States Code)]" (Government of the United States of America (2022), "United States Code, Updated," Title 12 – Banks and Banking, s.371b-2(d)). As used in Chapter 16 (Federal Deposit Insurance Corporation) of Title 12 (Banks and Banking) of the United States Code, the phrase '*insured depository institution*' "means any bank or savings association the deposits of which are insured by the [Federal Deposit Insurance] Corporation pursuant to this chapter" [(i.e., Chapter 16 of Title 12 of the United States Code)]" (Government of the United States of America (2022), "United States Code, Updated," Title 12 – Banks and Banking, s.1813(c)(2)). Fn 653 defines the term '*bank*'.

A member bank and its subsidiaries[702] may participate in a covered transaction[703] with an affiliate[704], only if: (A) regarding any affiliate, the aggregate amount of covered transactions[705]

---

[702] For the purposes of the present section (i.e., section 371c of Title 12 (Banks and Banking) of the United States Code), the word '*subsidiary*', "with respect to a specified company[,] means a company that is controlled by such specified company" (Government of the United States of America (2022), "United States Code, Updated," Title 12 – Banks and Banking, s.371c(b)(4)). The second sentence of fn 704 defines the term '*company*'. The last sentence of fn 704 defines the situations in which a company or a shareholder is considered to have '*control*' over another company.

[703] For the purposes of the current section (i.e., section 371c of Title 12 (Banks and Banking) of the United States Code), the phrase '*covered transaction*' "means[,] with respect to an affiliate of a member bank[,] – (A) a loan or extension of credit to the affiliate, including a purchase of assets subject to an agreement to repurchase; (B) a purchase of[,] or an investment in[,] securities issued by the affiliate; (C) a purchase of assets from the affiliate, except such purchase of real and personal property as may be specifically exempted by the Board [of Governors of the Federal Reserve System (fn 657),] by order or regulation; (D) the acceptance of securities or other debt obligations issued by the affiliate as collateral security for a loan or extension of credit to any person or company; (E) the issuance of a guarantee, acceptance, or letter of credit, including an endorsement or standby letter of credit, on behalf of the affiliate; or (F) a transaction with an affiliate that involves the borrowing or lending or securities, to the extent that the transaction causes a member bank or a subsidiary to have credit exposure to the affiliate; or (G) a derivative transaction, as defined in paragraph (3) of section 84(b) of this title [(i.e., Title 12 (Banks and Banking) of the United States Code)], with an affiliate, to the extent that the transaction causes a member bank or a subsidiary to have credit exposure to the affiliate" (Government of the United States of America (2022), "United States Code, Updated," Title 12 – Banks and Banking, s.371c(b)(7)). The first sentence of fn 704 defines the term '*affiliate*'. The first sentence of fn 656 defines the term '*member bank*'. The first sentence of fn 702 defines the term '*subsidiary*'

[704] For the purposes of the present section (i.e., section 371c of Title 12 (Banks and Banking) of the United States Code), "(1) the term "*affiliate*"[,] with respect to a member bank[,] means – (A) any company that controls the member bank[,] and any other company that is controlled by the company that controls the member bank; (B) a bank subsidiary of the member bank; (C) any company – (i) that is controlled directly or indirectly, by a trust or otherwise, by or for the benefit of shareholders who beneficially or otherwise control, directly or indirectly, by trust or otherwise, the member bank or any company that controls the member bank; or (ii) in which a majority of its directors or trustees constitute a majority of the persons holding any such office with the member bank or any company that controls the member bank; (D) any investment fund with respect to which a member bank or affiliate thereof is an investment adviser; and (E) any company that the Board [of Governors of the Federal Reserve System (fn 657)] determines[,] by regulation or order[,] to have a relationship with the member bank[,] or any subsidiary or affiliate of the member bank, such that covered transactions by the member bank or its subsidiary with that company may be affected by the relationship to the detriment of the member bank or its subsidiary; and (2) the following shall not be considered to be an affiliate: (A) any company, other than a bank, that is a subsidiary of a member bank, unless a determination is made under paragraph (1)(E) not to exclude such subsidiary company from the definition of affiliate; (B) any company [which is] engaged solely in holding the premises of the member bank; (C) any company [that is] engaged solely in conducting a safe deposit business; (D) any company [which is] engaged solely in holding obligations of the [Government of the] United States or its agencies[,] or obligations [that are] fully guaranteed by the United States or its agencies as to principal and interest; and (E) any company where control results from the exercise of rights arising out of a *bona fide* debt [that was] previously contracted, but only for the period of time [which is] specifically authorized under applicable State or Federal law or regulation or, in the absence of such law or regulation, for a period of two years from the date of the exercise of such rights or the effective date of this Act, whichever date is later, subject, upon application, to authorization by the Board for good cause shown of extensions of time for not more than one year at a time, but such extensions in the aggregate shall not exceed three years;" (Government of the United States of America (2022), "United States Code, Updated," Title 12 – Banks and Banking, s.371c(b)(1)-(2); emphasis added). For the purposes of the current section (i.e., section 371c of Title 12 (Banks and Banking) of the United States Code), the word '*company*' "means a corporation, partnership, business trust, association, or similar organization[,] and, unless specifically excluded, the term "company" includes a "member bank" and a "bank"" (Government of the United States of America (2022), "United States Code, Updated," Title 12 – Banks and Banking, s.371c(b)(6)). For the purposes of the present section (i.e., section 371c of Title 12 (Banks and Banking) of the United States Code), the word '*bank*' "includes a State bank, national bank, banking association, and trust company" (Government of the United States of America (2022), "United States Code, Updated," Title 12 – Banks and Banking, s.371c(b)(5)). For the purposes of the current section (i.e., section 371c of Title 12 (Banks and Banking) of the United States Code), "(A) a company or shareholder shall be deemed to have control over another company[,] if – (i) such company or shareholder, directly or indirectly, or acting through one or more other persons[,] owns, controls, or has the power to vote 25 per centum or more of

of the member bank and its subsidiaries will be no more than 10% of the member bank's capital stock and surplus [849], and with respect to all affiliates, the aggregate amount of covered transactions of the member banks and its subsidiaries will be no greater than 20% of the member bank's capital stock and surplus[706] [850]. Any covered transactions, and any transactions that are exempt under subsection 371c(d) of Title 12 (Banks and Banking) of the United States

any class of voting securities of[,] the other company; (ii) such company or shareholder controls[,] in any manner[,] the election of a majority of the directors or trustees of the other company; or (iii) the Board [of Governors of the Federal Reserve System (fn 657)] determines, after notice and opportunity for hearing, that such company or shareholder, directly or indirectly, exercises a controlling influence over the management or policies of the other company; and (B) notwithstanding any other provision of this section, no company shall be deemed to own or control another company by virtue of its ownership or control of shares in a fiduciary capacity, except as provided in [sub]paragraph (1)(C) of this subsection [(i.e., subparagraph 371c(b)(1)(C) of Title 12 (Banks and Banking) of the United States Code, which is set out as point (C) within the first sentence of the present footnote (fn 704) – which defines the term '*affiliate*'),] or [except] if the company owning or controlling such shares is a business trust" (Government of the United States of America (2022), "United States Code, Updated," Title 12 – Banks and Banking, s.371c(b)(3)).

705 For the purposes of the current section (i.e., section 371c of Title 12 (Banks and Banking) of the United States Code), the phrase '*aggregate amount of covered transactions*' "means the amount of the covered transactions [that are] about to be engaged in[,] added to the current amount of all outstanding covered transactions" (Government of the United States of America (2022), "United States Code, Updated," Title 12 – Banks and Banking, s.371c(b)(8)). The first sentence of fn 703 defines the term '*covered transaction*'.

706 For the purposes of the present section (i.e., section 371c of Title 12 (Banks and Banking) of the United States Code), "any transaction by a member bank with any person shall be deemed to be a transaction with an affiliate to the extent that the proceeds of the transaction are used for the benefit of, or transferred to, that affiliate" (Government of the United States of America (2022), "United States Code, Updated," Title 12 – Banks and Banking, s.371c(a)(2)). The first sentence of fn 704 defines the term '*affiliate*'. A member bank and its subsidiaries may not buy a low-quality asset from an affiliate, unless the bank or relevant subsidiary, following an independent evaluation of its credit status, committed itself to purchase this asset before the time that the affiliate acquired the asset (Government of the United States of America (2022), "United States Code, Updated," Title 12 – Banks and Banking, s.371c(a)(3)). For the purposes of the current section, the phrase '*low-quality asset*' "means an asset that falls in any one or more of the following categories: (A) an asset [which is] classified as "substandard," "doubtful," or "loss"[,] or treated as "other loans especially mentioned"[,] in the most recent report of examination or inspection of an affiliate[, that is] prepared by either a Federal or State supervisory agency; (B) an asset in a nonaccrual status; (C) an asset on which principal or interest payments are more than thirty days past due; or (D) an asset whose terms have been renegotiated or compromised due to the deteriorating financial condition of the obligor" (Government of the United States of America (2022), "United States Code, Updated," Title 12 – Banks and Banking, s.371c(a)(10)).

Code[707], which are between a bank[708] and an affiliate, must be on terms and conditions which are in line with safe, sound banking practices [851].

A member bank or its subsidiary may not, as fiduciary, buy any assets (including securities[709]) from an affiliate, unless the purchase is allowed: (i) under the instrument that

---

707 This subsection is titled 'Exemptions', and states: "The provisions of this section [(i.e., section 371c of Title 12 (Banks and Banking) of the United States Code)], except paragraph (a)(4) [(i.e., paragraph 371c(a)(4) of Title 12 (Banks and Banking) of the United States Code (text to present footnote (i.e., fn 707)))], shall not be applicable to – (1) any transaction, subject to the prohibition [that is] contained in subsection (a)(3) [(i.e., paragraph 371c(a)(3) of Title 12 (Banks and Banking) of the United States Code (third sentence of fn 706))], with a bank – (A) which controls 80 per centum or more of the voting shares of the member bank; (B) in which the member bank controls 80 per centum or more of the voting shares; or (C) in which 80 per centum or more of the voting shares are controlled by the company that controls 80 per centum or more of the voting shares of the member bank; (2) making deposits in an affiliated bank or affiliated foreign bank in the ordinary course of correspondent business, subject to any restrictions that the Board [of Governors of the Federal Reserve System (fn 657)] may prescribe by regulation or order; (3) giving immediate credit to an affiliate for uncollected items [that are] received in the ordinary course of business; (4) making a loan or extension of credit to, issuing a guarantee, acceptance, or letter of credit on behalf of, or having credit exposure resulting from a securities borrowing or lending transaction, or derivative transaction to, an affiliate[,] that is fully secured by – (A) obligations of the [Government of the] United States or its agencies; (B) obligations [that are] fully guaranteed by United States or its agencies as to principal and interest; or (C) a segregated, earmarked deposit account with the member bank; (5) purchasing securities [that are] issued by any company of the kinds described in section 1843(c)(1) of this title [(i.e., Title 12 (Banks and Banking) of the United States Code)]; (6) purchasing assets having a readily identifiable and publicly available market quotation and [which are] purchased at that market quotation[,] or, subject to the prohibition [that is] contained in subsection (a)(3) [(i.e., paragraph 371c(a)(3) of Title 12 (Banks and Banking) of the United States Code (third sentence of fn 706))], purchasing loans on a nonrecourse basis from affiliated banks; and (7) purchasing[,] from an affiliate[,] a loan or extension of credit that was originated by the member bank and sold to the affiliate[,] subject to a repurchase agreement or with recourse." (Government of the United States of America (2022), "United States Code, Updated," Title 12 – Banks and Banking, s.371c(d)(10)). 'Any company of the kinds described in section 1843(c)(1) of this title' equates to the following description: "any company [that is] engaged[,] or to be engaged[,] solely in one or more of the following activities: (A) holding or operating properties [which are] used wholly or substantially by any banking subsidiary of such bank holding company in the operations of such banking subsidiary[,] or acquired for such future use; or (B) conducting a safe deposit business; or (C) furnishing services to[,] or performing services for[,] such bank holding company or its banking subsidiaries; or (D) liquidating assets [that are] acquired from such bank holding company or its banking subsidiaries[,] or [which were] acquired from any other source prior to May 9, 1956, or the date on which such company became a bank holding company, whichever is later" (Government of the United States of America (2022), "United States Code, Updated," Title 12 – Banks and Banking, s.1843(c)(1)). The penultimate sentence of fn 704 defines the term '*bank*'. The first sentence of fn 656 defines the term '*member bank*'. The final sentence of fn 704 defines the situations in which a company or a shareholder is considered to have '*control*' over another company. The second sentence of fn 704 defines the term '*company*'. The first sentence of fn 704 defines the term '*affiliate*'.

708 The penultimate sentence of fn 704 defines the term '*bank*'.

709 The last sentence of fn 710 defines the term '*security*', which, in the text to fns 709 and 710 – i.e., in subsection 371c-1(b) of Title 12 (Banks and Banking) of the United States Code – has the meaning that paragraph 78c(a)(10) of Title 15 (Commerce and Trade) of the United States Code give to it (second sentence of fn 710). For the purpose of section 371c-1 of Title 12 (Banks and Banking) of the United States Code, the word '*affiliate*' has the meaning that section 371c of Title 12 (Banks and Banking) of the United States Code gives to it – but excludes any company that paragraph 371c(b)(2) describes and any bank, the phrase '*covered transaction*' has the meaning that section 371c of Title 12 (Banks and Banking) of the United States Code gives to it – but excludes any transaction that is exempt from this definition under subsection 371c(d) of Title 12 (Banks and Banking) of the United States Code, and the words '*bank*', '*person*', '*security*' and '*subsidiary*' have the meanings which section 371c of Title 12 (Banks and Banking) of the United States Code gives to them – other than the term '*security*' as used in subsection 371c-1(b) of Title 12 (Banks and Banking) of the United States Code (Government of the United States of America (2022), "United States Code, Updated," Title 12 – Banks and Banking, s.371c-1(d)). Paragraphs (1)-(2), (4), (5), (7) and (9) subsection 371c(b) of Title 12 (Banks and Banking) of the United States Code lays down the definition of the term '*affiliate*', '*subsidiary*', '*bank*', '*covered transaction*' and '*securities*', respectively; the first sentence of fn 704 sets out this definition of the term '*affiliate*'; the first sentence of fn 702 states this definition of the term '*subsidiary*'; the penultimate sentence of fn 704 specifies this definition of the term '*bank*'; the first sentence of fn 703 sets down this definition of the

creates the fiduciary relationship, (ii) by an order of the court, or (iii) according to the law of the jurisdiction which governs the fiduciary relationship[710] [852]; it must not, either as principal or as fiduciary, knowingly acquire any security throughout the time of any selling or underwriting syndicate, if a principal underwriter of this security is an affiliate of the abovementioned member bank [853]. Paragraph 371c-1(a)(2) of Title 12 (Banks and Banking) of the United States Code lists transactions[711] which, if entered into between a member bank –

term '*covered transaction*'. Paragraph 371c(b)(9) of Title 12 of the United States Code defines the word '*securities*' – rather than the term '*security*'. Subsection 371c(b) of Title 12 of the United States Code omits a definition of the word '*person*'; the meaning of the term '*person*' may be that which subparagraph 371c(a)(2) supplies, which is as follows: "For the purposes of this section [(i.e., section 371c of Title 12 (Banks and Banking) of the United States Code)], any transaction by a member bank with any person shall be deemed to be a transaction with an affiliate to the extent that the proceeds of the transaction are used for the benefit of, or transferred to, that affiliate." (Government of the United States of America (2022), "United States Code, Updated," Title 12 – Banks and Banking, s.371c(a)(2)).

710 This prohibition "shall not apply[,] if the purchase or acquisition of such securities has been approved, before such securities are initially offered for sale to the public, by a majority of the directors of the bank[,] based on a determination that the purchase is a sound investment for the bank irrespective of the fact that an affiliate of the bank is a principal underwriter of the securities" (Government of the United States of America (2022), "United States Code, Updated," Title 12 – Banks and Banking, s.371c-1(b)(2)). For the purposes of subsection 371c-1(b) of Title 12 (Banks and Banking) of the United States Code, "(A) the term "*security*" has the meaning given to such term in section 78c(a)(10) of title 15; and (B) the term "*principal underwriter*" means any underwriter who, in connection with a primary distribution of securities – (i) is in privity of contract with the issuer or an affiliated person of the issuer; (ii) acting alone or in concert with one or more other persons, initiates or directs the formation of an underwriting syndicate; or (iii) is allowed a rate of gross commission, spread, or other profit [that is] greater than the rate allowed [to] another underwriter participating in the distribution" (Government of the United States of America (2022), "United States Code, Updated," Title 12 – Banks and Banking, s.371c-1(b)(3); emphasis added). 'Section 78c(a)(10) of title 15' is paragraph 78c(a)(10) of Title 15 (Commerce and Trade) of the United States Code, which reads as follows: "When used in this chapter [(i.e., Chapter 2B (Securities Exchanges) or Title 15 (Commerce and Trade) of the United States Code)], unless the context otherwise requires – ... (10) The term "*security*" means any note, stock, treasury stock, security future, security-based swap, bond, debenture, certificate of interest or participation in any profit-sharing agreement[,] or in any oil, gas, or other mineral royalty or lease, any collateral-trust certificate, preorganization certificate or subscription, transferable share, investment contract, voting-trust certificate, certificate of deposit for a security, any put, call, straddle, option, or privilege on any security, certificate of deposit, or group or index of securities (including any interest therein or based on the value thereof), or any put, call, straddle, option, or privilege [which is] entered into on a national securities exchange relating to foreign currency, or[,] in general, any instrument [that is] commonly known as a "*security*"; or any certificate of interest or participation in, temporary or interim certificate for, receipt for, or warrant or right to subscribe to or purchase, any of the foregoing; but shall not include currency[,] or any note, draft, bill of exchange, or banker's acceptance which has a maturity at the time of issuance of not exceeding nine months, exclusive of days of grace, or any renewal thereof the maturity of which is likewise limited." (Government of the United States of America (2022), "United States Code, Updated," Title 15 – Commerce and Trade, s.78c(a)(10); emphasis added). Fn 709 specifies how the term '*affiliate*' is defined in section 371c-1 of Title 12 (Banks and Banking) of the United States Code.

711 Paragraph 371c-1(a)(2) of Title 12 (Banks and Banking) of the United States Code is headed 'Transactions covered', and states: "Paragraph (1) applies to the following: (A) Any covered transaction with an affiliate. (B) The sale of securities or other assets to an affiliate, including assets [that are] subject to an agreement to repurchase. (C) The payment of money or the furnishing of services to an affiliate under contract, lease, or otherwise. (D) Any transaction in which an affiliate acts as an agent or broker[,] or receives a fee for its services to the bank or to any other person. (E) Any transaction or series of transactions with a third party – (i) if an affiliate has a financial interest in the third party, or (ii) if an affiliate is a participant in such transaction or series of transactions." (Government of the United States of America (2022), "United States Code, Updated," Title 12 – Banks and Banking, s.371c-1(a)(2)). 'Paragraph (1)' is paragraph 371c-1(a)(1) of Title 12 (Banks and Banking) of the United States Code, which the first sentence of fn 713 sets out. Fn 709 specifies how the terms '*covered transaction*', '*affiliate*', '*security*', '*bank*' and '*person*' are defined in section 371c-1 of Title 12 (Banks and Banking) of the United States Code.

or a subsidiary of that bank – and one of its affiliates[712], paragraph 371c-1(a)(1) of Title 12 (Banks and Banking) of the United States Code requires to be on arm's length terms[713].

A national bank or a State member bank may only invest in bank premises, or in the stock, bonds, debentures or other capital of any corporation that holds these premises, or make loans to, or on the security of, such a corporation, if one of three conditions[714] is satisfied [854]. Any member bank, and any federal or state branch or agency of a foreign bank which is subject to reserve requirements under section 3105 of Title 12 (Banks and Banking) of the United States Code[715], may accept drafts or bills of exchange drawn upon it that have no more than six

---

[712] For the purpose of subsection 371c-1(a) of Title 12 (Banks and Banking) of the United States Code, "any transaction by a member bank or its subsidiary with any person shall be deemed to be a transaction with an affiliate of such bank[,] if any of the proceeds of the transaction are used for the benefit of, or transferred to, such affiliate" (Government of the United States of America (2022), "United States Code, Updated," Title 12 – Banks and Banking, s.371c-1(a)(3)). Subsection 371c-1(a) of Title 12 (Banks and Banking) of the United States Code comprises paragraphs (1) (first sentence of fn 713), (2) (fn 711), and (3) (first sentence of the current footnote (i.e., fn 712)). The first sentence of fn 656 defines the term '*member bank*'. Fn 709 specifies how the terms '*bank*', '*subsidiary*', '*person*' and '*affiliate*' are defined in section 371c-1 of Title 12 (Banks and Banking) of the United States Code.

[713] Paragraph 371c-1(a)(1) of Title 12 (Banks and Banking) of the United States Code is headed 'Terms', and declares: "A member bank and its subsidiaries may engage in any of the transactions [that are] described in paragraph (2)[,] only – (A) on terms and under circumstances, including credit standards, that are substantially the same, or at least as favourable to such bank or its subsidiary, as those prevailing at the time for comparable transactions with[,] or involving[,] other nonaffiliated companies, or (B) in the absence of comparable transactions, on terms and under circumstances, including credit standards, that in good faith would be offered to, or would apply to, nonaffiliated companies." (Government of the United States of America (2022), "United States Code, Updated," Title 12 – Banks and Banking, s.371c-1(a)(1)). 'Paragraph (2)' is paragraph 371c-1(a)(2) of Title 12 (Banks and Banking) of the United States Code, which fn 711 lays down. The first sentence of fn 656 defines the term '*member bank*'. Fn 709 specifies how the terms '*bank*' and '*subsidiary*' are defined in section 371c-1 of Title 12 (Banks and Banking) of the United States Code.

[714] These conditions are: (1) "the bank receives the prior approval of the Comptroller of the Currency (with respect to a national bank) or the Board [of Governors of the Federal Reserve System (fn 657)] (with respect to a State member bank)"; (2) "the aggregate of all such investments and loans, together with the amount of any indebtedness [which is] incurred by any such corporation that is an affiliate of the bank, is less than or equal to the amount of the capital stock of such bank"; (3) "(A) the aggregate of all such investments and loans, together with the amount of any indebtedness [which is] incurred by any such corporation that is an affiliate of the bank, is less than or equal to 150 percent of the capital and surplus of the bank; and (B) the bank – (i) has a CAMEL composite rating of 1 or 2 under the Uniform Financial Institutions Rating System (or an equivalent rating under a comparable rating system)[,] as of the most recent examination of such bank; (ii) is well capitalized[,] and will continue to be well capitalized after the investment or loan; and (iii) provides notification to the Comptroller of the Currency (with respect to an national bank) or to the Board (with respect to a State member bank)[,] not later than 30 days after making the investment or loan" (Government of the United States of America (2022), "United States Code, Updated," Title 12 – Banks and Banking, s.371d(a)). For the purposes of the present section (i.e., section 371d of Title 12 (Banks and Banking) of the United States Code), the term '*affiliate*' has the meaning that section 221a of Title 12 (Banks and Banking) of the United States Code provides (Government of the United States of America (2022), "United States Code, Updated," Title 12 – Banks and Banking, s.371d(b)(1)); the first sentence of fn 662 comprises subsection 221a(b) of Title 12 (Banks and Banking) of the United States Code), which lays down this meaning of the term '*affiliate*'. For the purposes of the current section i.e., section 371d of Title 12 (Banks and Banking) of the United States Code), the term '*well capitalized*' has the meaning that subsection 1831o(b) of Title 12 (Banks and Banking) of the United States Code supplies (Government of the United States of America (2022), "United States Code, Updated," Title 12 – Banks and Banking, s.371d(b)(2)); accordingly, the national bank or State member bank to which subsection 371d(a) of Title 12 (Banks and Banking) of the United States Code refers (text to the present footnote (i.e., fn 714) is '*well capitalized*', "if it significantly exceeds the minimum level for each relevant capital measure" (Government of the United States of America (2022), "United States Code, Updated," Title 12 – Banks and Banking, s.1831o(b)(1)(A)).

[715] Section 3105 of Title 12 (Banks and Banking) of the United States Code, is entitled 'Authority of Federal Reserve System'. Its first subsection is titled 'Bank reserves', and covers the imposition by the Board of Governors of the Federal Reserve System of reserve requirements on agencies and branches of foreign banks, which are located in the USA.

months' sight to run – excluding days of grace: (i) which arise from transactions that involve the importation or exportation of goods, (ii) which emerge from transactions that concern the domestic shipment of goods, or (iii) which are secured by a document that conveys or secures title to readily-marketable staples [855]. Subject to two provisos[716], any member bank may accept bills of exchange or drafts that are drawn upon it, which have no more than three months' sight to run, – excluding days of grace, and which are drawn by banks or bankers in foreign states or in dependencies or insular possessions of the USA with the intention of furnishing USD exchange, as required by trade usages in the respective countries, dependencies or insular possessions[717] [856].

No member bank may act as a medium or agent of a nonmember bank in applying for, or receiving, discounts from a Federal reserve bank under the provisions of Chapter 3 (Federal Reserve System) of Title 12 (Banks and Banking) of the United States Code [857]. No member bank may act as a medium or agent of any nonbanking association, corporation, partnership, individual or business trust, in making loans to dealers or brokers on the security of stocks, bonds and the like[718] [858].

[716] These provisos are as follows: "*Provided, however*, That no member bank shall accept such drafts or bills of exchange [that are] referred to [in] this paragraph[,] for any one bank[,] to an amount exceeding in the aggregate ten per centum of the paid-up and unimpaired capital and surplus of the accepting bank[,] unless the draft or bill of exchange is accompanied by documents conveying or securing title or by some other adequate security: *Provided further*, That no member bank shall accept such drafts or bills in an amount exceeding at any time the aggregate of one-half of its paid-up and unimpaired capital and surplus." (Government of the United States of America (2022), "United States Code, Updated," Title 12 – Banks and Banking, s.373; emphasis original). The first sentence of fn 656 defines the term '*member bank*'.

[717] Federal reserve banks may acquire these bills of exchange and drafts "in such amounts and subject to such regulations, restrictions and limitations as may be prescribed by the Board of Governors of the Federal Reserve System" (Government of the United States of America (2022), "United States Code, Updated," Title 12 – Banks and Banking, s.373).

[718] If a member bank contravenes this provision (i.e., section 374a of Title 12 (Banks and Banking) of the United States Code), then it is punishable by a fine of up to USD 100 per day – which is the maximum quotidian charge – whilst the infraction continues (Government of the United States of America (2022), "United States Code, Updated," Title 12 – Banks and Banking, s.374a). The first sentence of fn 656 defines the term '*member bank*'.

Except as authorized under the current section[719], i.e., section 375a of Title 12 (Banks and Banking) of the United States Code, no member bank may provide credit to any of its executive officers, and, conversely, no executive officer of a member bank may become indebted to the latter except by way of an extension of credit which this bank is authorized to make under the present section [859]. But that section does not ban any executive officer of a member bank – for its protection – from guaranteeing or endorsing any loan or other asset which it has already acquired in good faith, or from incurring any indebtedness to the bank in order to safeguard it against loss or assist it financially [860].

---

719 Subsections 375a(2), 375a(3) and 375a(4) of Title 12 (Banks and Banking) of the United States Code – plus subsection 375a(5) of Title 12 (Banks and Banking) of the United States Code, which limits the scope of the last-mentioned of these three provisions – read as follows: "**(2) Mortgage loans** A member bank may make a loan to any executive officer of the bank[,] if, at the time [that] the loan is made – (A) it is secured by a first lien on a dwelling[,] which is expected, after the making of the loan, to be owned by the officer and used by him as his residence, and (B) no other loan by the bank to the officer under authority of this paragraph is outstanding. **(3) Educational loans** A member bank may make extensions of credit to any executive officer of the bank[,] to finance the education of the children of the officer. **(4) General limitation on amount of credit** A member bank may make extensions of credit [that are] not otherwise specifically authorized under this section to any executive officer of the bank, in an amount [which is] prescribed in a regulation of the member bank's appropriate Federal banking agency. **(5) Partnership loans** Except to the extent [that is] permitted under paragraph (4), a member bank may not extend credit to a partnership in which one or more of its executive officers are partners having[,] either individually or together[,] a majority interest. For the purpose of paragraph (4), the full amount of any credit so extended shall be considered to have been extended to each officer of the bank who is a member of the partnership." (Government of the United States of America (2022), "United States Code, Updated," Title 12 – Banks and Banking, s.375a(2)-(5); emphasis original). The first sentence of fn 656 defines the term '*member bank*'.

No member bank[720] may extend credit[721] to any of its directors, executive officers[722] or principal shareholders[723], or to a related interest[724] of any of these persons, except to the extent

[720] For the purposes of the current section (i.e., section 375b of Title 12 (Banks and Banking) of the United States Code), the phrase '*member bank*' includes any subsidiary of a member bank (Government of the United States of America (2022), "United States Code, Updated," Title 12 – Banks and Banking, s.375b(9)(E)). The first sentence of fn 656 defines the term '*member bank*'.

[721] For the purposes of the present section (i.e., section 375b of Title 12 (Banks and Banking) of the United States Code), a member bank (fn 720) '*extends credit*' "to a person[,] by – (I) making or renewing any loan, granting a line of credit, or entering into any similar transaction as a result of which the person becomes obligated (directly or indirectly, or by any means whatsoever) to pay money or its equivalent to the bank; or (II) having credit exposure to the person arising from a derivative transaction (as defined in [sub]section 84(b) of this title [(i.e., Title 12 (Banks and Banking) of the United States Code (final sentence of fn 649))], repurchase agreement, reverse repurchase agreement, securities lending transaction, or securities borrowing transaction[,] between the member bank and the person" (Government of the United States of America (2022), "United States Code, Updated," Title 12 – Banks and Banking, s.375b(9)(D)(i)). The Board of Governors of the Federal Reserve System "may, by regulation, make exceptions to clause (i) [(i.e., clause 375b(9)(D)(i) of Title 12 (Banks and Banking) of the United States Code (first sentence of the current footnote (fn 721)),)] for transactions that the Board determines pose minimal risk" (Government of the United States of America (2022), "United States Code, Updated," Title 12 – Banks and Banking, s.375b(9)(D)(ii)).

[722] For the purposes of the current section (i.e., section 375b of Title 12 (Banks and Banking) of the United States Code), a person is an '*executive officer*' of a company, or of a bank, "if that person participates[,] or has authority to participate (other than as a director)[,] in major policymaking functions of the company or bank" (Government of the United States of America (2022), "United States Code, Updated," Title 12 – Banks and Banking, s.375b(9)(C)). Fn 653 defines the term '*bank*'. For the purposes of the present section (i.e., section 375b of Title 12 (Banks and Banking) of the United States Code), the word '*company*', "[e]xcept as provided in clause (ii), ... means any corporation, partnership, business or other trust, association, joint venture, pool syndicate, sole proprietorship, unincorporated association, or other business entity" (Government of the United States of America (2022), "United States Code, Updated," Title 12 – Banks and Banking, s.375b(9)(A)(i)). 'Clause (ii)' is clause 375b(9)(A)(ii) of Title 12 (Banks and Banking) of the United States Code, which is headed 'Exceptions', and which excludes from the definition of the term '*company*' in clause 375b(9)(A)(i) of Title 12 (Banks and Banking) of the United States Code (third sentence of the current footnote (i.e., fn 722)) the following entities: "(I) an insured depository institution (as defined in section 1813 of this title [(i.e., Title 12 (Banks and Banking) of the United States Code)]; [and] (II) a corporation the majority of the shares of which are owned by the [Government of the] United States or by any State" (Government of the United States of America (2022), "United States Code, Updated," Title 12 – Banks and Banking, s.375b(9)(A)(ii)). Paragraph 1813(c)(2) of Title 12 (Banks and Banking) of the United States Code comprises a definition of the term '*insured depository institution*', which the last sentence of fn 701 reproduces.

[723] For the purposes of the present section (i.e., section 375b of Title 12 (Banks and Banking) of the United States Code), the phrase '*principal shareholder*' "(i) means any person that[,] directly or indirectly, or acting through[,] or in concert with[,] one or more persons, owns, controls, or has the power to vote more than 10 percent of any class of voting securities of[,] a member bank [(fn 720)] or company; and (ii) does not include a company of which a member bank is a subsidiary" (Government of the United States of America (2022), "United States Code, Updated," Title 12 – Banks and Banking, s.375b(9)(E)). The third and fourth sentences of fn 722 defines the term '*company*'. For the purposes of the current section (i.e., section 375b of Title 12 (Banks and Banking) of the United States Code), the word '*subsidiary*' "has the same meaning as in section 1841 of this title [(i.e., Title 12 (Banks and Banking) of the United States Code)]" (Government of the United States of America (2022), "United States Code, Updated," Title 12 – Banks and Banking, s.375b(9)(H)). Subsection 1841(d) of Title 12 (Banks and Banking) of the United States Code consists of a definition of the term '*subsidiary*', which the final sentence of fn 601 replicates.

[724] For the purposes of the present section (i.e., section 375b of Title 12 (Banks and Banking) of the United States Code), a person's '*related interest*' "is – (i) any company [which is] controlled by that person; and (ii) any political or campaign committee that is controlled by that person[,] or the funds or services of which will benefit that person" (Government of the United States of America (2022), "United States Code, Updated," Title 12 – Banks and Banking, s.375b(9)(G)). The third and fourth sentences of fn 722 define the term '*company*'. A person '*controls*' a bank or a company, "if that person, directly or indirectly, or acting through[,] or in concert with[,] 1 or more persons – (i) owns, controls, or has the power to vote 25% or more of[,] any class of the company's voting securities; (ii) controls in any manner the election of a majority of the company's directors; or (iii) has the power to exercise a controlling influence over the company's management or policies" (Government of the United States of America (2022), "United States Code, Updated," Title 12 – Banks and Banking, s.375b(9)(B)). Fn 653 defines the term '*bank*'.

that subsections 375b(2)[725], 375b(3)[726], 375b(4)[727], 375b(5)[728] and 375b(6)[729] of Title 12 (Banks and Banking) of the United States Code permit [861]. No member bank shall pay to any

---

[725] This subsection is entitled 'Preferential terms prohibited', and states: "**(A) In general** A member bank [(fn 720)] may extend credit to its executive officers, directors, or principal shareholders, or to any related interest of such a person, only if the extension of credit – (i) is made on substantially the same terms, including interest rates and collateral, as those prevailing at the time for comparable transactions by the bank with persons who are not executive officers, directors, principal shareholders, or employees of the bank; (ii) does not involve more than the normal risk of repayment[,] [n]or present other unfavorable features; and (iii) the bank follows credit underwriting procedures that are not less stringent than those [which are] applicable to comparable transactions by the bank with persons who are not executive officers, directors, principal shareholders, or employees of the bank. **(B) Exception** Nothing in this paragraph shall prohibit any extension of credit [that is] made pursuant to a benefit or consumption program – (i) that is widely available to employees of the member bank; and (ii) that does not give preference to any officer, director, or principal shareholder of the member bank, or to any related interest of such person, over other employees of the member bank." (Government of the United States of America (2022), "United States Code, Updated," Title 12 – Banks and Banking, s.375b(2); emphasis original). The first sentence of fn 722 defines the term '*executive officer*'. The first sentence of fn 723 defines the term '*principal shareholder*'. The first sentence of fn 724 defines the term '*related interest*'.

[726] This subsection is titled 'Prior approval required', and declares: "A member bank [(fn 720)] may extend credit to a person described in paragraph (1) [(i.e., subsection 375b(1) of Title 12 (Banks and Banking) of the United States Code (text to fns 720-729),)] in an amount that, when aggregated with the amount of all other outstanding extensions of credit by that bank to each such person and that person's related interests, would exceed an amount [which is] prescribed by regulation of the appropriate Federal banking agency[,] only if – (A) the extension of credit has been approved in advance by a majority vote of that bank's entire board of directors; and (B) the interested party has abstained from participating, directly or indirectly, in the deliberations or voting on the extension of credit." (Government of the United States of America (2022), "United States Code, Updated," Title 12 – Banks and Banking, s.375b(3)). The first sentence of fn 724 defines the term '*related interest*'.

[727] This subsection is entitled 'Aggregate limit on extensions of credit to any executive officer, director, or principal shareholder', and reads: "A member bank [(fn 720)] may extend credit to any executive officer, director, or principal shareholder, or to any related interest of such a person, only if the extension of credit is in an amount that, when aggregated with the amount of all outstanding extensions of credit by that bank to that person and that person's interests, would not exceed the limits on loans to a single borrower [that is] established by section 84 of this title [(i.e., Title 12 (Banks and Banking) of the United States Code)]. For the purposes of this paragraph, section 84 of this title shall be deemed to apply to a State member bank as if the State member bank were a national banking association." (Government of the United States of America (2022), "United States Code, Updated," Title 12 – Banks and Banking, s.375b(4)). Subject to twelve exceptions that subsection 84(c) of Title 12 (Banks and Banking) of the United States Code sets out, subsection 84(a) of Title 12 (Banks and Banking) of the United States Code is titled 'Total loans and extensions of credit', and comprises the following two paragraphs: paragraph 84(a)(1) of Title 12 (Banks and Banking) of the United States Code – which the text to fns 649 and 650 lays down, and paragraph 84(a)(2) of Title 12 (Banks and Banking) of the United States Code – which the sentence immediately following the text to fns 649 and 650 contains. The first sentence of fn 722 defines the term '*executive officer*'. The first sentence of fn 723 defines the term '*principal shareholder*'. The first sentence of fn 724 defines the term '*related interest*'.

[728] This subsection is entitled 'Aggregate limit on extensions of credit to all executive officers, directors, and principal shareholders', and specifies: "**(A) In general** A member bank [(fn 720)] may extend credit to any executive officer, director, or principal shareholder, or to any related interest of such a person, if the extension of credit is in an amount that, when aggregated with the amount of all outstanding extensions of credit by that bank to its executive officers, directors, principal shareholders, and those persons' related interests[,] would not exceed the bank's unimpaired capital and unimpaired surplus. **(B) More stringent limit authorized** The Board [of Governors of the Federal Reserve System (fn 657)] may, by regulation, prescribe a limit that is more stringent than that contained in subparagraph (A). **(C) Board may make exceptions for certain banks** The Board may, by regulation, make exceptions to subparagraph (A) for member banks with less than $100,000,000 [(i.e., USD 100 million)] in deposits[,] if the Board determines that the exceptions are important to avoid constricting the availability of credit in small communities or to attract directors to such banks. In no case may the aggregate amount of all outstanding extensions of credit to a bank's executive officers, directors, principal shareholders, and those persons' related interests[,] be more than 2 times the bank's unimpaired capital and unimpaired surplus." (Government of the United States of America (2022), "United States Code, Updated," Title 12 – Banks and Banking, s.375b(5); emphasis original). The first sentence of fn 722 defines the term '*executive officer*'. The first sentence of fn 723 defines the term '*principal shareholder*'. The first sentence of fn 724 defines the term '*related interest*'.

director, officer, employee or attorney a greater rate of interest on the deposits of such an individual than that paid to other depositors on similar deposits with this member bank [862].

Subject to two provisos[730], it is unlawful for any person, association, corporation, firm, business trust, or other similar organization that is involved in the business of issuing, selling, underwriting or distributing stocks, bonds, notes, debentures or other securities, to simultaneously engage in the work of receiving deposits [863]. It is also illegal for any person, association, corporation, firm, business trust, or other similar organization to participate with others – bar his, her or its officers, employees or agents – in the business of receiving deposits, unless this enterprise: (A) has been incorporated under, and is authorized to undertake such business by, the laws of the USA or of any of its states, territories or districts, and is subjected by such laws to regulation and examination, (B) is permitted by the Government of the USA or the authorities of any such state, territory or district to engage in the business of receiving deposits, and is subjected by the laws of the USA or of any such state, territory or district to regulation and examination, or (C) submits to periodic examination by the banking authority of the state, territory or district of the USA in which the business of receiving deposits takes place, and publishes regular reports of its condition – showing in detail its resources and liabilities, such examination and reports to be made and published simultaneously, in an identical way, and under the same conditions, as the law of such state, territory or district requires of incorporated banking institutions that are engaged in the business of receiving deposits in the same locality[731] [864].

---

[729] This subsection is titled 'Overdrafts by executive officers and directors prohibited', and states: "**(A) In general** If any executive officer or director has an account at the member bank [(fn 720)], [then] the bank may not pay on behalf of that person an amount exceeding the funds on deposit in the account. **(B) Exceptions** Subparagraph (A) does not prohibit a member bank from paying funds in accordance with – (i) a written[,] preauthorized, interest-bearing extension of credit specifying a method of repayment; or (ii) a written[,] preauthorized transfer of funds from another account of the executive officer or director at that bank." (Government of the United States of America (2022), "United States Code, Updated," Title 12 – Banks and Banking, s.375b(6); emphasis original). The first sentence of fn 722 defines the term '*executive officer*'.

[730] These provisos are as follows: "*Provided*, That the provisions of this paragraph [(i.e., paragraph 378(a)(1) of Title 12 (Banks and Banking) of the United States Code)] shall not prohibit national banks or State banks or trust companies (whether or not members of the Federal Reserve System) or other financial institutions or private bankers from dealing in, underwriting, purchasing, and selling investment securities, or issuing securities, to the extent [that is] permitted to national banking associations by the provisions of section 24 of this title [(i.e., Title 12 (Banks and Banking) of the United States Code)]: *Provided further*, That nothing in this paragraph shall be construed as affecting in any way such right as any bank, banking association, savings bank, trust company, or other banking institution, may otherwise possess to sell, without recourse or agreement to repurchase, obligations evidencing loans on real estate;" (Government of the United States of America (2022), "United States Code, Updated," Title 12 – Banks and Banking, s.378(a)(1); emphasis original). The sentence immediately preceding the text to fn 640 sets out section 24 of Title 12 (Banks and Banking) of the United States Code). Fn 653 defines the term '*bank*'.

[731] Any person who wilfully contravenes this provision (i.e., text to the current footnote (fn 731)) or the immediately-preceding rule (i.e., text to fn 730) shall, upon conviction for this offence, be imprisoned for a maximum of five years and/or fined up to USD 5,000; furthermore, any director, officer, employee or agent of a person, association, corporation, firm, business trust, or other similar organization, who knowingly takes part in any such transgression, shall be punished in the same way (Government of the United States of America (2022), "United States Code, Updated," Title 12 – Banks and Banking, s.378(b)).

Crimes and Offenses (Chapter 5)

Chapter 5 (Crimes and Offenses) of Title 12 (Banks and Banking) of the United States Code comprises two subchapters: Subchapter I – which is titled 'In General', and Subchapter II – which is entitled 'Federal Reserve and Member Banks, Officers, Employees, and Examiners. All nine sections within Subchapter II of Chapter 5 (i.e., sections 591 to 599) have been repealed [865], as have all except one (i.e., section 582) of the twelve sections within Subchapter I of Chapter 5 (i.e., sections 581, 582, 583, 584, 585, 586, 587, 588, 588a, 588b, 588c and 588d[732]) [866]. Inspection of the notes concerning the repeal of these sections reveals that the substance of most of the offences that they concern has been incorporated into Title 18 (Crimes and Criminal Procedure) of the United States Code [865, 866].

For example, section 599 of Title 12 (Banks and Banking) of the United States Code is described as "related to fees, commissions, and bonuses in connection with loans," and reference is made to section 214 of Title 18 (Crimes and Criminal Procedure) of the United States Code [865]. The latter section is headed 'Offer for procurement of Federal Reserve bank loan and discount of commercial paper', and reads as follows.

> Whoever stipulates for or gives or receives, or consents or agrees to give or receive, any fee, commission, bonus, or thing of value for procuring or endeavoring to procure from any Federal Reserve bank any advance, loan, or extension of credit or discount or purchase of any obligation or commitment with respect thereto, either directly from such Federal Reserve bank or indirectly through any financing institution, unless such fee, commission, bonus, or thing of value and all material facts with respect to the arrangement or understanding therefor shall be disclosed in writing in the application or request for such advance, loan, extension of credit, discount, purchase, or commitment, shall be fined under this title or imprisoned not more than one year, or both [867].

The historical and revision notes that accompany section 214 of Title 18 (Crimes and Criminal Procedure) of the United States Code declare that this provision is based on the 1940 version of section 599 of Title 12 (Banks and Banking) of the United States Code, and describes modifications that were made to the substance and form of the latter provision when it was used as the basis for the adoption of the former on 25th June 1948[733] [868].

> Based on section 599 of title 12, U.S.C., 1940 ed., Banks and Banking (Dec. 23, 1913, ch. 6, §22(k), as added by act June 19, 1934, ch. 653, §3, 48 Stat. 1108). Final sentence of said section 599, imposing civil liability on violators, was omitted as unnecessary, being merely

---

[732] The repeal of all twenty of these sections (i.e., sections 581, 583, 584, 585, 586, 587, 588, 588a, 588b, 588c, 588d, 591, 592, 593, 594, 595, 596, 597, 598 and 599 of Title 12 (Banks and Banking) of the United States Code) took place on 25th June 1948 (fn 733).

[733] Section 599 of Title 12 (Banks and Banking) of the United States Code – and also sections 581, 583, 584, 585, 586, 587, 588, 588a, 588b, 588c, 588d, 591, 592, 593, 594, 595, 596, 597 and 598 of Title 12 (Banks and Banking) of the United States Code – were repealed on that date (i.e., 25th June 1948), with this repeal coming into force on 1st September 1948 (Government of the United States of America (2022), "12 USC 591 to 599: Repealed. June 25, 1948, ch. 645, §21, 62 Stat. 862, eff. Sept. 1, 1948," accessed December 21, 2022, <https://uscode.house.gov/view.xhtml?req=granuleid:USC-prelim-title12-section591&num=0&edition=prelim>; Government of the United States of America (2022), "12 USC Chapter 5, Subchapter I: In General," accessed December 21, 2022, <https://uscode.house.gov/view.xhtml?path=/prelim@title12/chapter5/subchapter1&edition=prelim>).

a declaration of that rule of common law which in the absence of statute fixes civil liability on the wrongdoer. Minor changes were made in phraseology [868].

The one provision in Chapter 5 (Crimes and Offenses) of Title 12 (Banks and Banking) of the United States Code that remains in force, i.e., section 582 of the abovementioned title, is headed 'Receipt of United States or bank notes as collateral', and declares the following.

> No national banking association shall hereafter offer or receive United States notes or national-bank notes as security or as collateral security for any loan of money, or for a consideration agree to withhold the same from use, or offer or receive the custody or promise of custody of such notes as security, or as collateral security, or consideration for any loan of money. Any association offending against the provisions of this section shall be deemed guilty of a misdemeanor and shall be fined not more than $1,000 [(i.e., USD 1,000)] and a further sum equal to one-third of the money so loaned. The officer or officers of any association who shall make any such loan shall be liable for a further sum equal to one-quarter of the money loaned; and any fine or penalty incurred by a violation of this section shall be recoverable for the benefit of the party bringing such suit [869].

When offences are specific to the content of a particular provision of banking law, legislators may choose to place them within the same section of Title 12 (Banks and Banking) as that rule. The use of this option, together with the presence in the United States Code of Title 18 (Crimes and Criminal Procedure) – and its utilization for offences that relate to banking law, provides an explanation as to why lawmakers have not added further offences to Chapter 5 (Crimes and Offenses) of Title 12 (Banks and Banking) of the United States Code. Two examples of legislators placing an offence for breach of a provision adjacent to the rule itself are: (1) section 374a of Title 12 (Banks and Banking) of the United States Code, which is titled 'Acting as agent for nonbanking borrower in making loans on securities to dealers in stocks, bonds, etc.; penalties'[734], and (2) section 378 of Title 12 (Banks and Banking) of the United States Code, which is entitled 'Dealers in securities engaging in banking business; individuals or associations engaging in banking business; examinations and reports; penalties'[735].

Comment

There is a complex legal structure for the regulation of banking in the USA, which is based on historical considerations. In particular, federal legislation specifies the powers and responsibilities of Federal reserve banks, national banks and the FDIC in detail. The codification of federal legislation in the USA is useful, although codification is more often

[734] The text to fn 718 lays down the prohibitive rule in section 374a of Title 12 (Banks and Banking) of the United States Code. Fn 718 specifies the offence which relates to that rule, which is also located in section 374a of Title 12 (Banks and Banking) of the United States Code.

[735] The text to fn 730 sets out the first of two prohibitive rules in section 378 of Title 12 (Banks and Banking) of the United States Code, which paragraph 378(a)(1) of Title 12 (Banks and Banking) of the United States Code contains. The text to fn 731 lays down the second of the aforementioned prohibitive rules, which paragraph 378(a)(2) of Title 12 (Banks and Banking) of the United States Code states. Fn 731 sets out the offence that relates to these two rules, which subsection 378(b) of Title 12 (Banks and Banking) of the United States Code comprises.

associated with the laws of civil law systems than those of common law jurisdictions – of which the USA is one. Care needs to be taken regarding definitions of terms within the United States Code, as it is possible for a term to be defined slightly or somewhat differently in one section of the code to another. The definition of a term may even differ between subsections within a particular section of the code[736]. Notwithstanding these remarks, the selective review of federal banking law within this chapter reveals a comprehensive, stable framework for the operation of banks within the USA.

Conclusion

This chapter introduces the legal system of the USA. It considers the roles of four federal regulators of banks: the OCC, the Federal Reserve, the FDIC and the SEC. The last-mentioned is covered only briefly due to its role the regulation of transactions in securities, which is an issue for the current book's sister publication – titled '*An Overview of Corporate Securities Law in Four English-Language Jurisdictions*'. The present chapter then reviews the Volcker Rule, and, finally, addresses three of the chapters within Title 12 (Banks and Banking) of the United States Code, namely Chapter 2 (National Banks), Chapter 3 (Federal Reserve System) and Chapter 5 (Crimes and Offenses).

The last chapter is titled 'Concluding Comments'. It explores themes that have arisen from the survey of banking law across the four English-language jurisdictions, which its preceding chapters comprise.

[736] Fn 709 provides an instance of an intrasectional difference in the definition of the term '*security*'.

Chapter 5

Concluding Comments

Abstract

At first appearance, there seems to be little similarity between the banking laws which are covered in the earlier chapters of this book, each taken as a whole. Therefore, identification of themes amongst the four jurisdictions whose banking law is considered therein needs to be taken from first principles. One of these is that, in the three jurisdictions which are a federation of internal states, the regulation of banking is a matter exclusively or primarily for federal law rather than for state law. Another is that all four legal systems are based on statute law and the case law of the national courts. A third is the contrast between the codification of banking law in the USA and its absence regarding banking law in Australia, Canada and New Zealand. Other themes include the development of deposit insurance for the customers of banks, and the on-line presentation of banking law and regulations in the four jurisdictions. This monograph provides a glimpse of the way in which four English-language common law jurisdictions have approached the regulation of their banking sectors. And it shows that there is more than one way to address this matter. The book may also be a concise ground for the formation of insights as to how banking law within any one of these countries might be modified from the current time. As it is the value-added of each monograph that I have created that is of interest to the market, I, as its author, am required to learn about the subject. The jurisdictions whose banking law is covered within the present book have furnished such learning.

Keywords: author, banking, financial, history, jurisdiction, law, regulation, theme

At first appearance, there seems to be little similarity between the banking laws that are covered in the earlier chapters of this book, each taken as a whole. Australia, Canada, New Zealand and the USA each seem to have gone its own way in developing its regulation of banks, with little cognizance of what the others were doing. This is, perhaps, surprising, given that all four were, at one time in their history, colonies of the UK, and that the road to independence from the UK has common features between Canada on the one hand, and Australia on the other, and, especially, between Australia on the one hand and New Zealand on the other. There would be little help in inspecting UK banking law in order to identify common themes, because, until the implementation of the decision for the UK to leave the European Union – which is only taking place at the current time, as it was the election of the Conservative Party to office in December 2019 with an absolute majority that make this course of action inevitable rather than the marginal vote in favour of leaving in June 2016 – the UK does not effectively have much banking law that is additional to the relevant European Union Regulations and Directives. In other words, at the time of writing UK banking law remains synonymous with EU banking law – a state of affairs that the Government of the UK is determined to change.

Therefore, identification of themes amongst the four jurisdictions whose banking law is considered above needs to be taken from first principles. One of these is that, in the three jurisdictions that are a federation of internal states (rather than 'independent states' – which is the main unit of international law), namely Australia, Canada and the USA, the regulation of banking is a matter exclusively or primarily for federal law rather than for state law. Another is that, all four legal systems are based on statute law and the case law of the national courts – which interprets the purpose and wording of the provisions of the statutes and applies them to the facts of each case, with accumulative development of the lacunae in the statutes by virtue of the operation of the doctrine of precedent; this is clear from the fact that all of them are common law jurisdictions (although with elemental civil law inputs in Canada and the USA, i.e., the laws of Quebec and Louisiana, respectively). A third theme is the contrast between the codification of banking law in the USA and its absence regarding banking law in Australia, Canada and New Zealand. Whilst the United States Code works well for connecting federal law within the USA, codification is usually associated with civil law systems – in which the doctrine of precedent is absent – rather than with common law systems. Furthermore, there is a danger that working with the United States Code obscures the separation of banking law in the USA into its various acts, and underplays the role of history in the development of such law into what it is today. For past events have, in the USA as well as in other jurisdictions, influenced the timing and content of statutes concerning banking law that have been introduced there – especially the Great Depression of the 1930s and the Global Financial Crisis of 2007 to 2009.

Other themes include the development of deposit insurance for the customers of banks – the law of which is highly-developed in the USA, well-developed in Canada, in place in Australia[737], and in the process of introduction in New Zealand, and the on-line presentation of banking law and regulations in these four jurisdictions, which is excellent in New Zealand – with frequent, accurate hyperlinks between texts, very good within the United States Code, and less well-ordered in Canada and Australia. Although a traditional subject, banking law is a rapidly-evolving area, and, therefore, one would not expect all jurisdictions to be at a similar stage of progress in all its major aspects. The long- term trend, however, is likely to be in the direction of uniformity between jurisdictions, due to good, computer-based communications between them and because of the presence of international banking standards – such as the Basel Accords[738].

---

[737] The website of the APRA describes Australia's Financial Claims Scheme thus: "The Financial Claims Scheme (FCS) is an Australian Government scheme that was established during the 2008 global financial crisis to provide financial protection for consumers[,] in the unlikely event of a failure of a bank, credit union, building society or general insurer. The FCS provides protection for depositors of banks, credit unions and building societies that are incorporated in Australia (also known as authorised deposit-taking institutions or ADIs), for deposits of up to $250,000 [(i.e., AUD 250,000)] per account holder per ADI. The scheme aims to return deposits to account holders within seven days of activation of the FCS. The FCS also covers claims of up to $5,000 [(i.e., AUD 5,000)] from policyholders and claimants against general insurers in Australia, as well as providing protection for eligible claimants for claims above that. The FCS can be activated by the Australian Government[,] in the unlikely event that an ADI or general insurer fails. Once activated, the FCS will be administered by APRA. The objectives of the FCS are to: • protect depositors of ADIs, and claimants of general insurers, from potential loss in the unlikely event of the failure of these institutions; • provide depositors with prompt access to their deposits that are protected under the FCS; and • support the stability of the Australian financial system." (Government of Australia (2022), "APRA: About the Financial Claims Scheme," accessed December 24, 2022, <https://www.apra.gov.au/about-financial-claims-scheme>).

[738] The author covers the Basel Accords in depth in Chapter 5 (The Basel Committee on Banking Supervision) of his monograph entitled '*International Financial Law: Quo Vadis?*' (*see* Baber, G. (2017), *International Financial Law: Quo Vadis?* (New York: Nova Science Publishers Inc.), 245-330).

So, what is added to scholarly, educational and/or financial literature by the contents of this book? It provides a glimpse of the way in which four English-language common law jurisdictions have approached the regulation of their banking sectors. And it shows that, notwithstanding the development of international financial standards, there is more than one way to address this matter. It may also be a concise basis for the formation of insights by policymakers, academics and practitioners within one of these countries as to how banking law there might be modified from the current time, for instance, with a view to increasing the scope and depth of harmonisation of the rules between those of that place and of one or more of the others. This, in turn, may be fertile ground for the development of new international financial standards – which may start as common ground between the laws of different jurisdictions.

Finally, what has the research for, and writing of, this book done for me, its author? As for the majority of the monographs that I have created, I have worked mainly with original materials – as it would not be right only to repeat with appropriate attribution the views of specialists and experts. It is the value-added of each book that is of interest to the market. To provide this, the author has to learn about the subject, too, even if (s)he has some prior knowledge of it. The four jurisdictions whose banking law is covered within this monograph, and whose securities law is considered within its sister book titled '*An Overview of Corporate Securities Law in Four English-Language Jurisdictions*' have furnished such learning.

References

[1] Ciro, T., Goldwasser, V., and Verma, R. (2019). *Law and Business*, 5th Edition (Melbourne: Oxford University Press), 30.

[2] Harris, J., and Croese, C. (2015). *Contract Law in Context* (Melbourne: Oxford University Press Australia), 4-5.

[3] Ciro, T., Goldwasser, V., and Verma, R. (2019). *Law and Business*, 34-35.

[4] Ciro, T., Goldwasser, V., and Verma, R. (2019). *Law and Business*, 35.

[5] Ciro, T., Goldwasser, V., and Verma, R. (2019). *Law and Business*, 39.

[6] Ciro, T., Goldwasser, V., and Verma, R. (2019). *Law and Business*, 43.

[7] Harris, J., and Croese, C. (2015). *Contract Law in Context*, 8.

[8] Ciro, T., Goldwasser, V., and Verma, R. (2019). *Law and Business*, 48.

[9] Ciro, T., Goldwasser, V., and Verma, R. (2019). *Law and Business*, 48-49.

[10] Ciro, T., Goldwasser, V., and Verma, R. (2019). *Law and Business*, 49.

[11] Ciro, T., Goldwasser, V., and Verma, R. (2019). *Law and Business*, 50.

[12] Harris, J., and Croese, C. (2015). *Contract Law in Context*, 10.

[13] Government of New South Wales (2022). "Full Court of the Federal Court." Accessed February 2, 2022. https://www.legalaid.nsw.gov.au/for-lawyers/policyonline/glossary/full-court-of-the-federal-court.

[14] Harris, J., and Croese, C. (2015). *Contract Law in Context*, 9-10.

[15] Harris, J., and Croese, C. (2015). *Contract Law in Context*, 9.

[16] Harris, J., and Croese, C. (2015). *Contract Law in Context*, 11.

[17] Government of Australia (2021). "Commonwealth of Australia Constitution Act 1900," Adopted on July 9, 1900, Entered into force on January 1, 1901, Compilation No. 6 of July 29, 1977, Registered on November 18, 2021, Preamble, Paragraph 1.

[18] Government of Australia (2021). "Commonwealth of Australia Constitution Act 1900," Adopted on July 9, 1900, Entered into force on January 1, 1901, Compilation No. 6 of July 29, 1977, Registered on November 18, 2021, Preamble, Paragraphs 3 and 4.

[19] Government of Australia (2021). "Commonwealth of Australia Constitution Act 1900," Adopted on July 9, 1900, Entered into force on January 1, 1901, Compilation No. 6 of July 29, 1977, Registered on November 18, 2021, Part I, Paragraph 1.

[20] Government of Australia (2021). "Commonwealth of Australia Constitution Act 1900," Adopted on July 9, 1900, Entered into force on January 1, 1901, Compilation No. 6 of July 29, 1977, Registered on November 18, 2021, Part I, Paragraph 2.

[21] Government of Australia (2021). "Commonwealth of Australia Constitution Act 1900," Adopted on July 9, 1900, Entered into force on January 1, 1901, Compilation No. 6 of July 29, 1977, Registered on November 18, 2021, Part V, Paragraph 51(xii).

[22] Government of Australia (2021). "Commonwealth of Australia Constitution Act 1900," Adopted on July 9, 1900, Entered into force on January 1, 1901, Compilation No. 6 of July 29, 1977, Registered on November 18, 2021, Part V, Paragraph 51(xiii).

[23] Government of Australia (2021). "Commonwealth of Australia Constitution Act 1900," Adopted on July 9, 1900, Entered into force on January 1, 1901, Compilation No. 6 of July 29, 1977, Registered on November 18, 2021, Part V, Paragraph 51(xiv).

[24] Government of Australia (2021). "Commonwealth of Australia Constitution Act 1900," Adopted on July 9, 1900, Entered into force on January 1, 1901, Compilation No. 6 of July 29, 1977, Registered on November 18, 2021, Part V, Paragraph 51(xvi).

[25] Government of Australia (2021). "Commonwealth of Australia Constitution Act 1900," Adopted on July 9, 1900, Entered into force on January 1, 1901, Compilation No. 6 of July 29, 1977, Registered on November 18, 2021, Part V, Paragraph 51(xvii).

[26] Government of Australia (2021). "Commonwealth of Australia Constitution Act 1900," Adopted on July 9, 1900, Entered into force on January 1, 1901, Compilation No. 6 of July 29, 1977, Registered on November 18, 2021, Part V, Paragraph 109.

[27] Government of the United Kingdom (1986). "Australia Act 1986," Adopted on February 17, 1986, Entered into force on March 3, 1986, s.1.

[28] Government of the United Kingdom (1986). "Australia Act 1986," Adopted on February 17, 1986, Entered into force on March 3, 1986, s.2(1).

[29] Government of Australia (1911). "Commonwealth Bank Act 1911," Adopted on December 22, 1911, Repealed on August 3, 1945, s.5.

[30] Government of Australia (2020). "Reserve Bank Act 1959," Adopted on April 23, 1959, Entered into force on January 14, 1960, Compilation No. 30 of October 1, 2020, Registered on October 21, 2020, s.7(a).

[31] Government of Australia (2020). "Reserve Bank Act 1959," Adopted on April 23, 1959, Entered into force on January 14, 1960, Compilation No. 30 of October 1, 2020, Registered on October 21, 2020, s.8.

[32] Australian Securities and Investments Commission (2022). "Our role." Accessed February 19, 2022. https://asic.gov.au/about-asic/what-we-do/our-role/.

[33] Government of Australia (2022). "Australian Securities and Investments Commission Act 2001," Adopted on June 28, 2001, Entered into force on July 15, 2001, Compilation No. 86 of January 1, 2022, Registered on February 3, 2022, s.1(2)(a).

[34] Government of Australia (2022). "Australian Securities and Investments Commission Act 2001," Adopted on June 28, 2001, Entered into force on July 15, 2001, Compilation No. 86 of January 1, 2022, Registered on February 3, 2022, s.1(2)(b).

[35] Government of Australia (2022). "Australian Securities and Investments Commission Act 2001," Adopted on June 28, 2001, Entered into force on July 15, 2001, Compilation No. 86 of January 1, 2022, Registered on February 3, 2022, s.1(2)(d).

[36] Government of Australia (2022). "Australian Securities and Investments Commission Act 2001," Adopted on June 28, 2001, Entered into force on July 15, 2001, Compilation No. 86 of January 1, 2022, Registered on February 3, 2022, s.1(2)(e).

[37] Government of Australia (2022). "Australian Securities and Investments Commission Act 2001," Adopted on June 28, 2001, Entered into force on July 15, 2001, Compilation No. 86 of January 1, 2022, Registered on February 3, 2022, s.1(2)(f).

[38] Government of Australia (2022). "Australian Securities and Investments Commission Act 2001," Adopted on June 28, 2001, Entered into force on July 15, 2001, Compilation No. 86 of January 1, 2022, Registered on February 3, 2022, s.1(2)(g).

[39] Government of Australia (2022). "Australian Securities and Investments Commission Act 2001," Adopted on June 28, 2001, Entered into force on July 15, 2001, Compilation No. 86 of January 1, 2022, Registered on February 3, 2022, s.1(2A).

[40] Government of Australia (2021). "Australian Prudential Regulation Authority Act 1998," Adopted on June 29, 1998, Entered into force on July 1, 1998, Compilation No. 46 of July 1, 2021, Registered on July 30, 2021, s.7(1).

[41] Government of Australia (2021). "Australian Prudential Regulation Authority Act 1998," Adopted on June 29, 1998, Entered into force on July 1, 1998, Compilation No. 46 of July 1, 2021, Registered on July 30, 2021, s.8(1)(a).

[42] Government of Australia (2021). "Australian Prudential Regulation Authority Act 1998," Adopted on June 29, 1998, Entered into force on July 1, 1998, Compilation No. 46 of July 1, 2021, Registered on July 30, 2021, s.8(1)(b).

[43] Government of Australia (2021). "Australian Prudential Regulation Authority Act 1998," Adopted on June 29, 1998, Entered into force on July 1, 1998, Compilation No. 46 of July 1, 2021, Registered on July 30, 2021, s.8(1)(c).

[44] Government of Australia (2021). "Australian Prudential Regulation Authority Act 1998," Adopted on June 29, 1998, Entered into force on July 1, 1998, Compilation No. 46 of July 1, 2021, Registered on July 30, 2021, s.8(2).

[45] Government of Australia (2021). "Banking Act 1959," Adopted on April 23, 1959, Entered into force on January 14, 1960, Compilation No. 60 of December 8, 2021, Registered on December 16, 2021, s.2A(2)(b).

[46] Government of Australia (2021). "Banking Act 1959," Adopted on April 23, 1959, Entered into force on January 14, 1960, Compilation No. 60 of December 8, 2021, Registered on December 16, 2021, s.2A(1)(a).

[47] Government of Australia (2021). "Banking Act 1959," Adopted on April 23, 1959, Entered into force on January 14, 1960, Compilation No. 60 of December 8, 2021, Registered on December 16, 2021, s.2A(1)(b).

[48] Government of Australia (2021). "Banking Act 1959," Adopted on April 23, 1959, Entered into force on January 14, 1960, Compilation No. 60 of December 8, 2021, Registered on December 16, 2021, ss.7(1)(a)-(b), 7(2), 8(1)(a)-(c) and 8(2).

[49] Government of Australia (2021). "Banking Act 1959," Adopted on April 23, 1959, Entered into force on January 14, 1960, Compilation No. 60 of December 8, 2021, Registered on December 16, 2021, s.9(2).

[50] Government of Australia (2021). "Banking Act 1959," Adopted on April 23, 1959, Entered into force on January 14, 1960, Compilation No. 60 of December 8, 2021, Registered on December 16, 2021, s.9(2A).

[51] Government of Australia (2021). "Banking Act 1959," Adopted on April 23, 1959, Entered into force on January 14, 1960, Compilation No. 60 of December 8, 2021, Registered on December 16, 2021, s.9(3).

[52] Government of Australia (2021). "Banking Act 1959," Adopted on April 23, 1959, Entered into force on January 14, 1960, Compilation No. 60 of December 8, 2021, Registered on December 16, 2021, s.9(3A).

[53] Government of Australia (2021). "Banking Act 1959," Adopted on April 23, 1959, Entered into force on January 14, 1960, Compilation No. 60 of December 8, 2021, Registered on December 16, 2021, s.9AA(3).

[54] Government of Australia (2021). "Banking Act 1959," Adopted on April 23, 1959, Entered into force on January 14, 1960, Compilation No. 60 of December 8, 2021, Registered on December 16, 2021, s.9AA(1)(a).

[55] Government of Australia (2021). "Banking Act 1959," Adopted on April 23, 1959, Entered into force on January 14, 1960, Compilation No. 60 of December 8, 2021, Registered on December 16, 2021, s.9AA(1)(b).

[56] Government of Australia (2021). "Banking Act 1959," Adopted on April 23, 1959, Entered into force on January 14, 1960, Compilation No. 60 of December 8, 2021, Registered on December 16, 2021, s.11AF(1).

[57] Government of Australia (2021). "Banking Act 1959," Adopted on April 23, 1959, Entered into force on January 14, 1960, Compilation No. 60 of December 8, 2021, Registered on December 16, 2021, s.11AF(3).

[58] Government of Australia (2021). "Banking Act 1959," Adopted on April 23, 1959, Entered into force on January 14, 1960, Compilation No. 60 of December 8, 2021, Registered on December 16, 2021, s.11AG.

[59] Government of Australia (2021). "Banking Act 1959," Adopted on April 23, 1959, Entered into force on January 14, 1960, Compilation No. 60 of December 8, 2021, Registered on December 16, 2021, s.11B(a).

[60] Government of Australia (2021). "Banking Act 1959," Adopted on April 23, 1959, Entered into force on January 14, 1960, Compilation No. 60 of December 8, 2021, Registered on December 16, 2021, s.11B(b).
[61] Government of Australia (2021). "Banking Act 1959," Adopted on April 23, 1959, Entered into force on January 14, 1960, Compilation No. 60 of December 8, 2021, Registered on December 16, 2021, s.11B(c).
[62] Government of Australia (2021). "Banking Act 1959," Adopted on April 23, 1959, Entered into force on January 14, 1960, Compilation No. 60 of December 8, 2021, Registered on December 16, 2021, s.12(1).
[63] Government of Australia (2021). "Banking Act 1959," Adopted on April 23, 1959, Entered into force on January 14, 1960, Compilation No. 60 of December 8, 2021, Registered on December 16, 2021, s.13(1).
[64] Government of Australia (2021). "Banking Act 1959," Adopted on April 23, 1959, Entered into force on January 14, 1960, Compilation No. 60 of December 8, 2021, Registered on December 16, 2021, s.13(3)-(3A).
[65] Government of Australia (2021). "Banking Act 1959," Adopted on April 23, 1959, Entered into force on January 14, 1960, Compilation No. 60 of December 8, 2021, Registered on December 16, 2021, s.13A(1).
[66] Government of Australia (2021). "Banking Act 1959," Adopted on April 23, 1959, Entered into force on January 14, 1960, Compilation No. 60 of December 8, 2021, Registered on December 16, 2021, s.13A(1)(a).
[67] Government of Australia (2021). "Banking Act 1959," Adopted on April 23, 1959, Entered into force on January 14, 1960, Compilation No. 60 of December 8, 2021, Registered on December 16, 2021, s.13A(1)(b).
[68] Government of Australia (2021). "Banking Act 1959," Adopted on April 23, 1959, Entered into force on January 14, 1960, Compilation No. 60 of December 8, 2021, Registered on December 16, 2021, s.13A(1)(c).
[69] Government of Australia (2021). "Banking Act 1959," Adopted on April 23, 1959, Entered into force on January 14, 1960, Compilation No. 60 of December 8, 2021, Registered on December 16, 2021, s.13A(1)(d).
[70] Government of Australia (2021). "Banking Act 1959," Adopted on April 23, 1959, Entered into force on January 14, 1960, Compilation No. 60 of December 8, 2021, Registered on December 16, 2021, s.13A(1)(e).
[71] Government of Australia (2021). "Banking Act 1959," Adopted on April 23, 1959, Entered into force on January 14, 1960, Compilation No. 60 of December 8, 2021, Registered on December 16, 2021, s.13A(1B)-(1C).
[72] Government of Australia (2021). "Banking Act 1959," Adopted on April 23, 1959, Entered into force on January 14, 1960, Compilation No. 60 of December 8, 2021, Registered on December 16, 2021, s.13A(1B)(a).
[73] Government of Australia (2021). "Banking Act 1959," Adopted on April 23, 1959, Entered into force on January 14, 1960, Compilation No. 60 of December 8, 2021, Registered on December 16, 2021, s.13A(1B)(b).
[74] Government of Australia (2021). "Banking Act 1959," Adopted on April 23, 1959, Entered into force on January 14, 1960, Compilation No. 60 of December 8, 2021, Registered on December 16, 2021, s.13A(1B)(c).
[75] Government of Australia (2021). "Banking Act 1959," Adopted on April 23, 1959, Entered into force on January 14, 1960, Compilation No. 60 of December 8, 2021, Registered on December 16, 2021, s.13A(1B)(d).
[76] Government of Australia (2021). "Banking Act 1959," Adopted on April 23, 1959, Entered into force on January 14, 1960, Compilation No. 60 of December 8, 2021, Registered on December 16, 2021, s.13A(3)(a).

[77] Government of Australia (2021). "Banking Act 1959," Adopted on April 23, 1959, Entered into force on January 14, 1960, Compilation No. 60 of December 8, 2021, Registered on December 16, 2021, s.13A(3)(b).

[78] Government of Australia (2021). "Banking Act 1959," Adopted on April 23, 1959, Entered into force on January 14, 1960, Compilation No. 60 of December 8, 2021, Registered on December 16, 2021, s.13A(3)(c).

[79] Government of Australia (2021). "Banking Act 1959," Adopted on April 23, 1959, Entered into force on January 14, 1960, Compilation No. 60 of December 8, 2021, Registered on December 16, 2021, s.13A(3)(d).

[80] Government of Australia (2021). "Banking Act 1959," Adopted on April 23, 1959, Entered into force on January 14, 1960, Compilation No. 60 of December 8, 2021, Registered on December 16, 2021, s.13A(3)(e).

[81] Government of Australia (2021). "Banking Act 1959," Adopted on April 23, 1959, Entered into force on January 14, 1960, Compilation No. 60 of December 8, 2021, Registered on December 16, 2021, s.13A(3)(f).

[82] Government of Australia (2021). "Banking Act 1959," Adopted on April 23, 1959, Entered into force on January 14, 1960, Compilation No. 60 of December 8, 2021, Registered on December 16, 2021, ss.13A(4) and 13A(5).

[83] Government of Australia (2021). "Banking Act 1959," Adopted on April 23, 1959, Entered into force on January 14, 1960, Compilation No. 60 of December 8, 2021, Registered on December 16, 2021, s.13B(1).

[84] Government of Australia (2021). "Banking Act 1959," Adopted on April 23, 1959, Entered into force on January 14, 1960, Compilation No. 60 of December 8, 2021, Registered on December 16, 2021, s.13B(1A).

[85] Government of Australia (2021). "Banking Act 1959," Adopted on April 23, 1959, Entered into force on January 14, 1960, Compilation No. 60 of December 8, 2021, Registered on December 16, 2021, s.13BA(1).

[86] Government of Australia (2021). "Banking Act 1959," Adopted on April 23, 1959, Entered into force on January 14, 1960, Compilation No. 60 of December 8, 2021, Registered on December 16, 2021, s.13C(1)(a).

[87] Government of Australia (2021). "Banking Act 1959," Adopted on April 23, 1959, Entered into force on January 14, 1960, Compilation No. 60 of December 8, 2021, Registered on December 16, 2021, s.13C(1)(b).

[88] Government of Australia (2021). "Banking Act 1959," Adopted on April 23, 1959, Entered into force on January 14, 1960, Compilation No. 60 of December 8, 2021, Registered on December 16, 2021, s.16AAA(1).

[89] Government of Australia (2021). "Banking Act 1959," Adopted on April 23, 1959, Entered into force on January 14, 1960, Compilation No. 60 of December 8, 2021, Registered on December 16, 2021, s.16AAA(5).

[90] Government of Australia (2021). "Banking Act 1959," Adopted on April 23, 1959, Entered into force on January 14, 1960, Compilation No. 60 of December 8, 2021, Registered on December 16, 2021, s.16AB(a).

[91] Government of Australia (2021). "Banking Act 1959," Adopted on April 23, 1959, Entered into force on January 14, 1960, Compilation No. 60 of December 8, 2021, Registered on December 16, 2021, s.16AB(b).

[92] Government of Australia (2021). "Banking Act 1959," Adopted on April 23, 1959, Entered into force on January 14, 1960, Compilation No. 60 of December 8, 2021, Registered on December 16, 2021, s.16AB(c).

[93] Government of Australia (2021). "Banking Act 1959," Adopted on April 23, 1959, Entered into force on January 14, 1960, Compilation No. 60 of December 8, 2021, Registered on December 16, 2021, s.16AB(d).

[94] Government of Australia (2021). "Banking Act 1959," Adopted on April 23, 1959, Entered into force on January 14, 1960, Compilation No. 60 of December 8, 2021, Registered on December 16, 2021, s.16AD(1).

[95] Government of Australia (2021). "Banking Act 1959," Adopted on April 23, 1959, Entered into force on January 14, 1960, Compilation No. 60 of December 8, 2021, Registered on December 16, 2021, ss.19(1)(a) and 19(2)(a).

[96] Government of Australia (2021). "Banking Act 1959," Adopted on April 23, 1959, Entered into force on January 14, 1960, Compilation No. 60 of December 8, 2021, Registered on December 16, 2021, ss.19(1)(b)(i) and 19(2)(b)(i).

[97] Government of Australia (2021). "Banking Act 1959," Adopted on April 23, 1959, Entered into force on January 14, 1960, Compilation No. 60 of December 8, 2021, Registered on December 16, 2021, ss.19(1)(b)(ii) and 19(2)(b)(ii).

[98] Government of Australia (2021). "Banking Act 1959," Adopted on April 23, 1959, Entered into force on January 14, 1960, Compilation No. 60 of December 8, 2021, Registered on December 16, 2021, ss.19(1)(b)(iii) and 19(2)(b)(iii).

[99] Government of Australia (2021). "Banking Act 1959," Adopted on April 23, 1959, Entered into force on January 14, 1960, Compilation No. 60 of December 8, 2021, Registered on December 16, 2021, ss.19(1)(b)(iv) and 19(2)(b)(iv).

[100] Government of Australia (2021). "Banking Act 1959," Adopted on April 23, 1959, Entered into force on January 14, 1960, Compilation No. 60 of December 8, 2021, Registered on December 16, 2021, ss.19(1)(c) and 19(2)(c).

[101] Government of Australia (2021). "Banking Act 1959," Adopted on April 23, 1959, Entered into force on January 14, 1960, Compilation No. 60 of December 8, 2021, Registered on December 16, 2021, ss.19(4)(a) and 19(5)(a).

[102] Government of Australia (2021). "Banking Act 1959," Adopted on April 23, 1959, Entered into force on January 14, 1960, Compilation No. 60 of December 8, 2021, Registered on December 16, 2021, ss.19(4)(b)(i) and 19(5)(b)(i).

[103] Government of Australia (2021). "Banking Act 1959," Adopted on April 23, 1959, Entered into force on January 14, 1960, Compilation No. 60 of December 8, 2021, Registered on December 16, 2021, ss.19(4)(b)(ii) and 19(5)(b)(ii).

[104] Government of Australia (2021). "Banking Act 1959," Adopted on April 23, 1959, Entered into force on January 14, 1960, Compilation No. 60 of December 8, 2021, Registered on December 16, 2021, ss.19(4)(b)(iii) and 19(5)(b)(iii).

[105] Government of Australia (2021). "Banking Act 1959," Adopted on April 23, 1959, Entered into force on January 14, 1960, Compilation No. 60 of December 8, 2021, Registered on December 16, 2021, ss.19(4)(b)(iv) and 19(5)(b)(iv).

[106] Government of Australia (2021). "Banking Act 1959," Adopted on April 23, 1959, Entered into force on January 14, 1960, Compilation No. 60 of December 8, 2021, Registered on December 16, 2021, ss.19(4)(c) and 19(5)(c).

[107] Government of Australia (2021). "Banking Act 1959," Adopted on April 23, 1959, Entered into force on January 14, 1960, Compilation No. 60 of December 8, 2021, Registered on December 16, 2021, ss.19(4)(d) and 19(5)(d).

[108] Government of Australia (2021). "Banking Act 1959," Adopted on April 23, 1959, Entered into force on January 14, 1960, Compilation No. 60 of December 8, 2021, Registered on December 16, 2021, s.23(1)-(2).

[109] Government of Australia (2021). "Banking Act 1959," Adopted on April 23, 1959, Entered into force on January 14, 1960, Compilation No. 60 of December 8, 2021, Registered on December 16, 2021, s.23(2)(b).

[110] Government of Australia (2021). "Banking Act 1959," Adopted on April 23, 1959, Entered into force on January 14, 1960, Compilation No. 60 of December 8, 2021, Registered on December 16, 2021, s.23(2)(a)(i).

[111] Government of Australia (2021). "Banking Act 1959," Adopted on April 23, 1959, Entered into force on January 14, 1960, Compilation No. 60 of December 8, 2021, Registered on December 16, 2021, s.23(2)(a)(ii).

[112] Government of Australia (2021). "Banking Act 1959," Adopted on April 23, 1959, Entered into force on January 14, 1960, Compilation No. 60 of December 8, 2021, Registered on December 16, 2021, s.26(1).

[113] Government of Australia (2021). "Banking Act 1959," Adopted on April 23, 1959, Entered into force on January 14, 1960, Compilation No. 60 of December 8, 2021, Registered on December 16, 2021, s.26(3).

[114] Government of Australia (2021). "Banking Act 1959," Adopted on April 23, 1959, Entered into force on January 14, 1960, Compilation No. 60 of December 8, 2021, Registered on December 16, 2021, s.28.

[115] Government of Australia (2021). "Banking Act 1959," Adopted on April 23, 1959, Entered into force on January 14, 1960, Compilation No. 60 of December 8, 2021, Registered on December 16, 2021, s.29(1)-(2).

[116] Government of Australia (2021). "Banking Act 1959," Adopted on April 23, 1959, Entered into force on January 14, 1960, Compilation No. 60 of December 8, 2021, Registered on December 16, 2021, s.30(1).

[117] Government of Australia (2021). "Banking Act 1959," Adopted on April 23, 1959, Entered into force on January 14, 1960, Compilation No. 60 of December 8, 2021, Registered on December 16, 2021, s.30(3)(a).

[118] Government of Australia (2021). "Banking Act 1959," Adopted on April 23, 1959, Entered into force on January 14, 1960, Compilation No. 60 of December 8, 2021, Registered on December 16, 2021, s.30(3)(b).

[119] Government of Australia (2021). "Banking Act 1959," Adopted on April 23, 1959, Entered into force on January 14, 1960, Compilation No. 60 of December 8, 2021, Registered on December 16, 2021, s.31F(1).

[120] Government of Australia (2021). "Banking Act 1959," Adopted on April 23, 1959, Entered into force on January 14, 1960, Compilation No. 60 of December 8, 2021, Registered on December 16, 2021, s.31F(2).

[121] Government of Australia (2021). "Banking Act 1959," Adopted on April 23, 1959, Entered into force on January 14, 1960, Compilation No. 60 of December 8, 2021, Registered on December 16, 2021, s.37(1).

[122] Government of Australia (2021). "Banking Act 1959," Adopted on April 23, 1959, Entered into force on January 14, 1960, Compilation No. 60 of December 8, 2021, Registered on December 16, 2021, s.37(2).

[123] Government of Australia (2021). "Banking Act 1959," Adopted on April 23, 1959, Entered into force on January 14, 1960, Compilation No. 60 of December 8, 2021, Registered on December 16, 2021, s.37C(a).

[124] Government of Australia (2021). "Banking Act 1959," Adopted on April 23, 1959, Entered into force on January 14, 1960, Compilation No. 60 of December 8, 2021, Registered on December 16, 2021, s.37C(b).

[125] Government of Australia (2021). "Banking Act 1959," Adopted on April 23, 1959, Entered into force on January 14, 1960, Compilation No. 60 of December 8, 2021, Registered on December 16, 2021, s.37C(c).

[126] Government of Australia (2021). "Banking Act 1959," Adopted on April 23, 1959, Entered into force on January 14, 1960, Compilation No. 60 of December 8, 2021, Registered on December 16, 2021, s.37C(d).

[127] Government of Australia (2021). "Banking Act 1959," Adopted on April 23, 1959, Entered into force on January 14, 1960, Compilation No. 60 of December 8, 2021, Registered on December 16, 2021, s.37C(e).

[128] Government of Australia (2021). "Banking Act 1959," Adopted on April 23, 1959, Entered into force on January 14, 1960, Compilation No. 60 of December 8, 2021, Registered on December 16, 2021, s.37D(1)(a)(i).
[129] Government of Australia (2021). "Banking Act 1959," Adopted on April 23, 1959, Entered into force on January 14, 1960, Compilation No. 60 of December 8, 2021, Registered on December 16, 2021, s.37D(1)(a)(ii).
[130] Government of Australia (2021). "Banking Act 1959," Adopted on April 23, 1959, Entered into force on January 14, 1960, Compilation No. 60 of December 8, 2021, Registered on December 16, 2021, s.37D(1)(b).
[131] Government of Australia (2021). "Banking Act 1959," Adopted on April 23, 1959, Entered into force on January 14, 1960, Compilation No. 60 of December 8, 2021, Registered on December 16, 2021, s.37D(1)(c).
[132] Government of Australia (2021). "Banking Act 1959," Adopted on April 23, 1959, Entered into force on January 14, 1960, Compilation No. 60 of December 8, 2021, Registered on December 16, 2021, s.37D(1)(d).
[133] Government of Australia (2021). "Banking Act 1959," Adopted on April 23, 1959, Entered into force on January 14, 1960, Compilation No. 60 of December 8, 2021, Registered on December 16, 2021, s.37E(1)(a).
[134] Government of Australia (2021). "Banking Act 1959," Adopted on April 23, 1959, Entered into force on January 14, 1960, Compilation No. 60 of December 8, 2021, Registered on December 16, 2021, s.37E(1)(b).
[135] Government of Australia (2021). "Banking Act 1959," Adopted on April 23, 1959, Entered into force on January 14, 1960, Compilation No. 60 of December 8, 2021, Registered on December 16, 2021, s.37E(1)(c).
[136] Government of Australia (2021). "Banking Act 1959," Adopted on April 23, 1959, Entered into force on January 14, 1960, Compilation No. 60 of December 8, 2021, Registered on December 16, 2021, s.37E(1)(d).
[137] Government of Australia (2021). "Banking Act 1959," Adopted on April 23, 1959, Entered into force on January 14, 1960, Compilation No. 60 of December 8, 2021, Registered on December 16, 2021, s.37F(1)(a).
[138] Government of Australia (2021). "Banking Act 1959," Adopted on April 23, 1959, Entered into force on January 14, 1960, Compilation No. 60 of December 8, 2021, Registered on December 16, 2021, s.37F(1)(b).
[139] Government of Australia (2021). "Banking Act 1959," Adopted on April 23, 1959, Entered into force on January 14, 1960, Compilation No. 60 of December 8, 2021, Registered on December 16, 2021, s.37F(1)(c).
[140] Government of Australia (2021). "Banking Act 1959," Adopted on April 23, 1959, Entered into force on January 14, 1960, Compilation No. 60 of December 8, 2021, Registered on December 16, 2021, s.37F(1)(d).
[141] Government of Australia (2021). "Banking Act 1959," Adopted on April 23, 1959, Entered into force on January 14, 1960, Compilation No. 60 of December 8, 2021, Registered on December 16, 2021, s.39(1)(a).
[142] Government of Australia (2021). "Banking Act 1959," Adopted on April 23, 1959, Entered into force on January 14, 1960, Compilation No. 60 of December 8, 2021, Registered on December 16, 2021, s.39(1)(b).
[143] Government of Australia (2021). "Banking Act 1959," Adopted on April 23, 1959, Entered into force on January 14, 1960, Compilation No. 60 of December 8, 2021, Registered on December 16, 2021, s.39(1)(c).
[144] Government of Australia (2021). "Banking Act 1959," Adopted on April 23, 1959, Entered into force on January 14, 1960, Compilation No. 60 of December 8, 2021, Registered on December 16, 2021, s.39(2)(a).

[145] Government of Australia (2021). "Banking Act 1959," Adopted on April 23, 1959, Entered into force on January 14, 1960, Compilation No. 60 of December 8, 2021, Registered on December 16, 2021, s.39A(1).

[146] Government of Australia (2021). "Banking Act 1959," Adopted on April 23, 1959, Entered into force on January 14, 1960, Compilation No. 60 of December 8, 2021, Registered on December 16, 2021, s.40.

[147] Government of Australia (2021). "Banking Act 1959," Adopted on April 23, 1959, Entered into force on January 14, 1960, Compilation No. 60 of December 8, 2021, Registered on December 16, 2021, s.41(1).

[148] Government of Australia (2021). "Banking Act 1959," Adopted on April 23, 1959, Entered into force on January 14, 1960, Compilation No. 60 of December 8, 2021, Registered on December 16, 2021, s.42(1).

[149] Government of Australia (2021). "Banking Act 1959," Adopted on April 23, 1959, Entered into force on January 14, 1960, Compilation No. 60 of December 8, 2021, Registered on December 16, 2021, s.45(1).

[150] Government of Australia (2021). "Banking Act 1959," Adopted on April 23, 1959, Entered into force on January 14, 1960, Compilation No. 60 of December 8, 2021, Registered on December 16, 2021, s.46(1).

[151] Government of Australia (2021). "Banking Act 1959," Adopted on April 23, 1959, Entered into force on January 14, 1960, Compilation No. 60 of December 8, 2021, Registered on December 16, 2021, s.47(1).

[152] Government of Australia (2021). "Banking Act 1959," Adopted on April 23, 1959, Entered into force on January 14, 1960, Compilation No. 60 of December 8, 2021, Registered on December 16, 2021, s.48.

[153] Government of Australia (2021). "Banking Act 1959," Adopted on April 23, 1959, Entered into force on January 14, 1960, Compilation No. 60 of December 8, 2021, Registered on December 16, 2021, s.50(1)(a).

[154] Government of Australia (2021). "Banking Act 1959," Adopted on April 23, 1959, Entered into force on January 14, 1960, Compilation No. 60 of December 8, 2021, Registered on December 16, 2021, s.50(1)(b).

[155] Government of Australia (2021). "Banking Act 1959," Adopted on April 23, 1959, Entered into force on January 14, 1960, Compilation No. 60 of December 8, 2021, Registered on December 16, 2021, s.50(1)(c).

[156] Government of Australia (2021). "Banking Act 1959," Adopted on April 23, 1959, Entered into force on January 14, 1960, Compilation No. 60 of December 8, 2021, Registered on December 16, 2021, s.61(1)(a).

[157] Government of Australia (2021). "Banking Act 1959," Adopted on April 23, 1959, Entered into force on January 14, 1960, Compilation No. 60 of December 8, 2021, Registered on December 16, 2021, s.61(2).

[158] Government of Australia (2021). "Banking Act 1959," Adopted on April 23, 1959, Entered into force on January 14, 1960, Compilation No. 60 of December 8, 2021, Registered on December 16, 2021, s.61A(1).

[159] Government of Australia (2021). "Banking Act 1959," Adopted on April 23, 1959, Entered into force on January 14, 1960, Compilation No. 60 of December 8, 2021, Registered on December 16, 2021, s.61C(a).

[160] Government of Australia (2021). "Banking Act 1959," Adopted on April 23, 1959, Entered into force on January 14, 1960, Compilation No. 60 of December 8, 2021, Registered on December 16, 2021, s.61C(b).

[161] Government of Australia (2021). "Banking Act 1959," Adopted on April 23, 1959, Entered into force on January 14, 1960, Compilation No. 60 of December 8, 2021, Registered on December 16, 2021, s.61D(1)-(2).

[162] Government of Australia (2021). "Banking Act 1959," Adopted on April 23, 1959, Entered into force on January 14, 1960, Compilation No. 60 of December 8, 2021, Registered on December 16, 2021, s.61D(3).
[163] Government of Australia (2021). "Banking Act 1959," Adopted on April 23, 1959, Entered into force on January 14, 1960, Compilation No. 60 of December 8, 2021, Registered on December 16, 2021, s.61D(4).
[164] Government of Australia (2021). "Banking Act 1959," Adopted on April 23, 1959, Entered into force on January 14, 1960, Compilation No. 60 of December 8, 2021, Registered on December 16, 2021, s.61F(1).
[165] Government of Australia (2021). "Banking Act 1959," Adopted on April 23, 1959, Entered into force on January 14, 1960, Compilation No. 60 of December 8, 2021, Registered on December 16, 2021, s.61F(3).
[166] Government of Australia (2021). "Banking Act 1959," Adopted on April 23, 1959, Entered into force on January 14, 1960, Compilation No. 60 of December 8, 2021, Registered on December 16, 2021, s.61F(4).
[167] Government of Australia (2021). "Banking Act 1959," Adopted on April 23, 1959, Entered into force on January 14, 1960, Compilation No. 60 of December 8, 2021, Registered on December 16, 2021, s.62(1)(a)-(c).
[168] Government of Australia (2021). "Banking Act 1959," Adopted on April 23, 1959, Entered into force on January 14, 1960, Compilation No. 60 of December 8, 2021, Registered on December 16, 2021, s.62(1)(d).
[169] Government of Australia (2021). "Banking Act 1959," Adopted on April 23, 1959, Entered into force on January 14, 1960, Compilation No. 60 of December 8, 2021, Registered on December 16, 2021, s.62(1).
[170] Government of Australia (2021). "Banking Act 1959," Adopted on April 23, 1959, Entered into force on January 14, 1960, Compilation No. 60 of December 8, 2021, Registered on December 16, 2021, s.62(2).
[171] Government of Australia (2021). "Banking Act 1959," Adopted on April 23, 1959, Entered into force on January 14, 1960, Compilation No. 60 of December 8, 2021, Registered on December 16, 2021, s.65(1).
[172] Government of Australia (2021). "Banking Act 1959," Adopted on April 23, 1959, Entered into force on January 14, 1960, Compilation No. 60 of December 8, 2021, Registered on December 16, 2021, s.65(2).
[173] Government of Australia (2021). "Banking Act 1959," Adopted on April 23, 1959, Entered into force on January 14, 1960, Compilation No. 60 of December 8, 2021, Registered on December 16, 2021, s.65(4).
[174] Government of Australia (2021). "Banking Act 1959," Adopted on April 23, 1959, Entered into force on January 14, 1960, Compilation No. 60 of December 8, 2021, Registered on December 16, 2021, s.65A(1)-(2).
[175] Government of Australia (2021). "Banking Act 1959," Adopted on April 23, 1959, Entered into force on January 14, 1960, Compilation No. 60 of December 8, 2021, Registered on December 16, 2021, s.65A(4).
[176] Government of Australia (2021). "Banking Act 1959," Adopted on April 23, 1959, Entered into force on January 14, 1960, Compilation No. 60 of December 8, 2021, Registered on December 16, 2021, s.65A(7).
[177] Government of Australia (2021). "Banking Act 1959," Adopted on April 23, 1959, Entered into force on January 14, 1960, Compilation No. 60 of December 8, 2021, Registered on December 16, 2021, s.65A(9).
[178] Government of Australia (2021). "Banking Act 1959," Adopted on April 23, 1959, Entered into force on January 14, 1960, Compilation No. 60 of December 8, 2021, Registered on December 16, 2021, s.65A(11).

[179] Government of Australia (2021). "Banking Act 1959," Adopted on April 23, 1959, Entered into force on January 14, 1960, Compilation No. 60 of December 8, 2021, Registered on December 16, 2021, s.67(1).

[180] Government of Australia (2021). "Banking Act 1959," Adopted on April 23, 1959, Entered into force on January 14, 1960, Compilation No. 60 of December 8, 2021, Registered on December 16, 2021, s.69C(3).

[181] Government of Australia (2021). "Banking Act 1959," Adopted on April 23, 1959, Entered into force on January 14, 1960, Compilation No. 60 of December 8, 2021, Registered on December 16, 2021, s.69C(4).

[182] Government of Australia (2021). "Banking Act 1959," Adopted on April 23, 1959, Entered into force on January 14, 1960, Compilation No. 60 of December 8, 2021, Registered on December 16, 2021, s.70A(1).

[183] Government of Australia (2021). "Banking Act 1959," Adopted on April 23, 1959, Entered into force on January 14, 1960, Compilation No. 60 of December 8, 2021, Registered on December 16, 2021, s.70B.

[184] Government of the United Kingdom of Great Britain and Northern Ireland (2021). "British North America Act 1867," Adopted on March 29, 1867, Entered into force on July 1, 1867, Consolidated to January 1, 2021, s.6.

[185] Government of the United Kingdom of Great Britain and Northern Ireland (2021). "British North America Act 1867," Adopted on March 29, 1867, Entered into force on July 1, 1867, Consolidated to January 1, 2021, ss.3 and 5.

[186] United Nations (2022). "Dag Hammarskjöld Library: UN Membership." Accessed May 17, 2022. https://research.un.org/en/unmembers/founders.

[187] United Nations (1945). "Charter of the United Nations," *United Nations Treaty Series* Registration Number N/A, Article 110(2).

[188] Government of the United Kingdom of Great Britain and Northern Ireland (2021). "Canada Act 1982," Adopted on March 29, 1982, Entered into force on April 17, 1982, Consolidated to January 1, 2021, s.1.

[189] Government of the United Kingdom of Great Britain and Northern Ireland (2021). "Canada Act 1982," Adopted on March 29, 1982, Entered into force on April 17, 1982, Consolidated to January 1, 2021, s.2.

[190] Government of Canada (2015). Department of Justice: Canada's System of Justice, Cat. No J2-32/2015E-PDF. Ottawa: Her Majesty the Queen in Right of Canada, 10.

[191] Government of Canada (2015). Department of Justice: Canada's System of Justice, Cat. No J2-32/2015E-PDF. Ottawa: Her Majesty the Queen in Right of Canada, 12.

[192] Somerville, C., and Sun, W. (2021). "Legal systems in Canada: overview." Published July 1, 2021. Accessed May 17 and 19, 2022. https://uk.practicallaw.thomsonreuters.com/w-013-0460?transitionType=Default&contextData=(sc.Default)&firstPage=true.

[193] Government of the United Kingdom of Great Britain and Northern Ireland (2021). "British North America Act 1867," Adopted on March 29, 1867, Entered into force on July 1, 1867, Consolidated to January 1, 2021, s.91.

[194] Government of the United Kingdom of Great Britain and Northern Ireland (2021). "British North America Act 1867," Adopted on March 29, 1867, Entered into force on July 1, 1867, Consolidated to January 1, 2021, s.91(2).

[195] Government of the United Kingdom of Great Britain and Northern Ireland (2021). "British North America Act 1867," Adopted on March 29, 1867, Entered into force on July 1, 1867, Consolidated to January 1, 2021, s.91(3).

[196] Government of the United Kingdom of Great Britain and Northern Ireland (2021). "British North America Act 1867," Adopted on March 29, 1867, Entered into force on July 1, 1867, Consolidated to January 1, 2021, s.91(4).

[197] Government of the United Kingdom of Great Britain and Northern Ireland (2021). "British North America Act 1867," Adopted on March 29, 1867, Entered into force on July 1, 1867, Consolidated to January 1, 2021, s.91(14).

[198] Government of the United Kingdom of Great Britain and Northern Ireland (2021). "British North America Act 1867," Adopted on March 29, 1867, Entered into force on July 1, 1867, Consolidated to January 1, 2021, s.91(15).

[199] Government of the United Kingdom of Great Britain and Northern Ireland (2021). "British North America Act 1867," Adopted on March 29, 1867, Entered into force on July 1, 1867, Consolidated to January 1, 2021, s.91(16).

[200] Government of the United Kingdom of Great Britain and Northern Ireland (2021). "British North America Act 1867," Adopted on March 29, 1867, Entered into force on July 1, 1867, Consolidated to January 1, 2021, s.91(18).

[201] Government of the United Kingdom of Great Britain and Northern Ireland (2021). "British North America Act 1867," Adopted on March 29, 1867, Entered into force on July 1, 1867, Consolidated to January 1, 2021, s.91(19).

[202] Government of the United Kingdom of Great Britain and Northern Ireland (2021). "British North America Act 1867," Adopted on March 29, 1867, Entered into force on July 1, 1867, Consolidated to January 1, 2021, s.91(20).

[203] Government of the United Kingdom of Great Britain and Northern Ireland (2021). "British North America Act 1867," Adopted on March 29, 1867, Entered into force on July 1, 1867, Consolidated to January 1, 2021, s.91(21).

[204] Government of the United Kingdom of Great Britain and Northern Ireland (2021). "British North America Act 1867," Adopted on March 29, 1867, Entered into force on July 1, 1867, Consolidated to January 1, 2021, s.91(27).

[205] Government of the United Kingdom of Great Britain and Northern Ireland (2021). "British North America Act 1867," Adopted on March 29, 1867, Entered into force on July 1, 1867, Consolidated to January 1, 2021, s.91(29).

[206] Government of the United Kingdom of Great Britain and Northern Ireland (2021). "British North America Act 1867," Adopted on March 29, 1867, Entered into force on July 1, 1867, Consolidated to January 1, 2021, s.92.

[207] Government of the United Kingdom of Great Britain and Northern Ireland (2021). "British North America Act 1867," Adopted on March 29, 1867, Entered into force on July 1, 1867, Consolidated to January 1, 2021, s.92(2).

[208] Government of the United Kingdom of Great Britain and Northern Ireland (2021). "British North America Act 1867," Adopted on March 29, 1867, Entered into force on July 1, 1867, Consolidated to January 1, 2021, s.92(3).

[209] Government of the United Kingdom of Great Britain and Northern Ireland (2021). "British North America Act 1867," Adopted on March 29, 1867, Entered into force on July 1, 1867, Consolidated to January 1, 2021, s.92(9).

[210] Government of the United Kingdom of Great Britain and Northern Ireland (2021). "British North America Act 1867," Adopted on March 29, 1867, Entered into force on July 1, 1867, Consolidated to January 1, 2021, s.92(11).

[211] Government of the United Kingdom of Great Britain and Northern Ireland (2021). "British North America Act 1867," Adopted on March 29, 1867, Entered into force on July 1, 1867, Consolidated to January 1, 2021, s.92(14).

[212] Government of the United Kingdom of Great Britain and Northern Ireland (2021). "British North America Act 1867," Adopted on March 29, 1867, Entered into force on July 1, 1867, Consolidated to January 1, 2021, s.92(16).

[213] Government of Canada (2015). Department of Justice: Canada's System of Justice, Cat. No J2-32/2015E-PDF. Ottawa: Her Majesty the Queen in Right of Canada, 21.

[214] Government of Canada (2015). Department of Justice: Canada's System of Justice, Cat. No J2-32/2015E-PDF. Ottawa: Her Majesty the Queen in Right of Canada, 22.

[215] Government of Canada (2015). Department of Justice: Canada's System of Justice, Cat. No J2-32/2015E-PDF. Ottawa: Her Majesty the Queen in Right of Canada, 21-22.

[216] Government of Canada (2015). Department of Justice: Canada's System of Justice, Cat. No J2-32/2015E-PDF. Ottawa: Her Majesty the Queen in Right of Canada, 23.

[217] Government of the United Kingdom of Great Britain and Northern Ireland/Government of Canada (2021). "Constitution Act 1982," Adopted on March 29, 1982, Entered into force on April 17, 1982, Consolidated to January 1, 2021, s.52(2)(a).

[218] Government of the United Kingdom of Great Britain and Northern Ireland/Government of Canada (2021). "Constitution Act 1982," Adopted on March 29, 1982, Entered into force on April 17, 1982, Consolidated to January 1, 2021, s.52(2)(b).

[219] Government of the United Kingdom of Great Britain and Northern Ireland/Government of Canada (2021). "Constitution Act 1982," Adopted on March 29, 1982, Entered into force on April 17, 1982, Consolidated to January 1, 2021, s.52(2)(c).

[220] Government of the United Kingdom of Great Britain and Northern Ireland/Government of Canada (2021). "Constitution Act 1982," Adopted on March 29, 1982, Entered into force on April 17, 1982, Consolidated to January 1, 2021, s.52(1).

[221] Government of the United Kingdom of Great Britain and Northern Ireland/Government of Canada (2021). "Constitution Act 1982," Adopted on March 29, 1982, Entered into force on April 17, 1982, Consolidated to January 1, 2021, s.34.

[222] Government of the United Kingdom of Great Britain and Northern Ireland/Government of Canada (2021). "Constitution Act 1982," Adopted on March 29, 1982, Entered into force on April 17, 1982, Consolidated to January 1, 2021, s.1.

[223] Government of the United Kingdom of Great Britain and Northern Ireland/Government of Canada (2021). "Constitution Act 1982," Adopted on March 29, 1982, Entered into force on April 17, 1982, Consolidated to January 1, 2021, s.32(1).

[224] Government of the United Kingdom of Great Britain and Northern Ireland/Government of Canada (2021). "Constitution Act 1982," Adopted on March 29, 1982, Entered into force on April 17, 1982, Consolidated to January 1, 2021, s.33(1).

[225] Government of the United Kingdom of Great Britain and Northern Ireland/Government of Canada (2021). "Constitution Act 1982," Adopted on March 29, 1982, Entered into force on April 17, 1982, Consolidated to January 1, 2021, s.33(3).

[226] Government of the United Kingdom of Great Britain and Northern Ireland/Government of Canada (2021). "Constitution Act 1982," Adopted on March 29, 1982, Entered into force on April 17, 1982, Consolidated to January 1, 2021, s.33(4).

[227] Government of the United Kingdom of Great Britain and Northern Ireland/Government of Canada (2021). "Constitution Act 1982," Adopted on March 29, 1982, Entered into force on April 17, 1982, Consolidated to January 1, 2021, s.33(5).

[228] Government of the United Kingdom of Great Britain and Northern Ireland (2021). "British North America Act 1867," Adopted on March 29, 1867, Entered into force on July 1, 1867, Consolidated to January 1, 2021, Recital 1.

[229] Government of Canada (2015). Department of Justice: Canada's System of Justice, Cat. No J2-32/2015E-PDF. Ottawa: Her Majesty the Queen in Right of Canada, 14.

[230] Government of Canada (2022). "Bank of Canada Act, S.C., 1934 (24 & 25 Geo V), c. 43; R.S.C., 1985, c. B-2," Adopted on July 3, 1934, Entered into force on March 11, 1935, Last amended on January 31, 2020, Consolidated to May 2, 2022, s.3(1).

[231] Government of Canada (2022). "Bank of Canada Act, S.C., 1934 (24 & 25 Geo V), c. 43; R.S.C., 1985, c. B-2," Adopted on July 3, 1934, Entered into force on March 11, 1935, Last amended on January 31, 2020, Consolidated to May 2, 2022, s.3(2).

[232] Government of Canada (2022). "Bank of Canada Act, S.C., 1934 (24 & 25 Geo V), c. 43; R.S.C., 1985, c. B-2," Adopted on July 3, 1934, Entered into force on March 11, 1935, Last amended on January 31, 2020, Consolidated to May 2, 2022, s.4(1).

[233] Government of Canada (2022). "Bank of Canada Act, S.C., 1934 (24 & 25 Geo V), c. 43; R.S.C., 1985, c. B-2," Adopted on July 3, 1934, Entered into force on March 11, 1935, Last amended on January 31, 2020, Consolidated to May 2, 2022, s.18(a).

[234] Government of Canada (2022). "Bank of Canada Act, S.C., 1934 (24 & 25 Geo V), c. 43; R.S.C., 1985, c. B-2," Adopted on July 3, 1934, Entered into force on March 11, 1935, Last amended on January 31, 2020, Consolidated to May 2, 2022, s.18(b).

[235] Government of Canada (2022). "Bank of Canada Act, S.C., 1934 (24 & 25 Geo V), c. 43; R.S.C., 1985, c. B-2," Adopted on July 3, 1934, Entered into force on March 11, 1935, Last amended on January 31, 2020, Consolidated to May 2, 2022, s.18(c).

[236] Government of Canada (2022). "Bank of Canada Act, S.C., 1934 (24 & 25 Geo V), c. 43; R.S.C., 1985, c. B-2," Adopted on July 3, 1934, Entered into force on March 11, 1935, Last amended on January 31, 2020, Consolidated to May 2, 2022, s.18(d).

[237] Government of Canada (2022). "Bank of Canada Act, S.C., 1934 (24 & 25 Geo V), c. 43; R.S.C., 1985, c. B-2," Adopted on July 3, 1934, Entered into force on March 11, 1935, Last amended on January 31, 2020, Consolidated to May 2, 2022, s.18(f).

[238] Government of Canada (2022). "Bank of Canada Act, S.C., 1934 (24 & 25 Geo V), c. 43; R.S.C., 1985, c. B-2," Adopted on July 3, 1934, Entered into force on March 11, 1935, Last amended on January 31, 2020, Consolidated to May 2, 2022, ss.18(g) and 18.1(1).

[239] Government of Canada (2022). "Bank of Canada Act, S.C., 1934 (24 & 25 Geo V), c. 43; R.S.C., 1985, c. B-2," Adopted on July 3, 1934, Entered into force on March 11, 1935, Last amended on January 31, 2020, Consolidated to May 2, 2022, s.18(h).

[240] Government of Canada (2022). "Bank of Canada Act, S.C., 1934 (24 & 25 Geo V), c. 43; R.S.C., 1985, c. B-2," Adopted on July 3, 1934, Entered into force on March 11, 1935, Last amended on January 31, 2020, Consolidated to May 2, 2022, s.18(i).

[241] Government of Canada (2022). "Bank of Canada Act, S.C., 1934 (24 & 25 Geo V), c. 43; R.S.C., 1985, c. B-2," Adopted on July 3, 1934, Entered into force on March 11, 1935, Last amended on January 31, 2020, Consolidated to May 2, 2022, s.18(j).

[242] Government of Canada (2022). "Bank of Canada Act, S.C., 1934 (24 & 25 Geo V), c. 43; R.S.C., 1985, c. B-2," Adopted on July 3, 1934, Entered into force on March 11, 1935, Last amended on January 31, 2020, Consolidated to May 2, 2022, s.18(l).

[243] Government of Canada (2022). "Bank of Canada Act, S.C., 1934 (24 & 25 Geo V), c. 43; R.S.C., 1985, c. B-2," Adopted on July 3, 1934, Entered into force on March 11, 1935, Last amended on January 31, 2020, Consolidated to May 2, 2022, s.18(l.1).

[244] Government of Canada (2022). "Bank of Canada Act, S.C., 1934 (24 & 25 Geo V), c. 43; R.S.C., 1985, c. B-2," Adopted on July 3, 1934, Entered into force on March 11, 1935, Last amended on January 31, 2020, Consolidated to May 2, 2022, s.18(l.2).

[245] Government of Canada (2022). "Bank of Canada Act, S.C., 1934 (24 & 25 Geo V), c. 43; R.S.C., 1985, c. B-2," Adopted on July 3, 1934, Entered into force on March 11, 1935, Last amended on January 31, 2020, Consolidated to May 2, 2022, s.18(l.3).

[246] Government of Canada (2022). "Bank of Canada Act, S.C., 1934 (24 & 25 Geo V), c. 43; R.S.C., 1985, c. B-2," Adopted on July 3, 1934, Entered into force on March 11, 1935, Last amended on January 31, 2020, Consolidated to May 2, 2022, s.18(m).

[247] Government of Canada (2022). "Bank of Canada Act, S.C., 1934 (24 & 25 Geo V), c. 43; R.S.C., 1985, c. B-2," Adopted on July 3, 1934, Entered into force on March 11, 1935, Last amended on January 31, 2020, Consolidated to May 2, 2022, s.18(m.1).

[248] Government of Canada (2022). "Bank of Canada Act, S.C., 1934 (24 & 25 Geo V), c. 43; R.S.C., 1985, c. B-2," Adopted on July 3, 1934, Entered into force on March 11, 1935, Last amended on January 31, 2020, Consolidated to May 2, 2022, s.18(n).

[249] Government of Canada (2022). "Bank of Canada Act, S.C., 1934 (24 & 25 Geo V), c. 43; R.S.C., 1985, c. B-2," Adopted on July 3, 1934, Entered into force on March 11, 1935, Last amended on January 31, 2020, Consolidated to May 2, 2022, s.18(o).

[250] Government of Canada (2022). "Bank of Canada Act, S.C., 1934 (24 & 25 Geo V), c. 43; R.S.C., 1985, c. B-2," Adopted on July 3, 1934, Entered into force on March 11, 1935, Last amended on January 31, 2020, Consolidated to May 2, 2022, s.18(p).

[251] Government of Canada (2022). "Bank of Canada Act, S.C., 1934 (24 & 25 Geo V), c. 43; R.S.C., 1985, c. B-2," Adopted on July 3, 1934, Entered into force on March 11, 1935, Last amended on January 31, 2020, Consolidated to May 2, 2022, s.20(a).

[252] Government of Canada (2022). "Bank of Canada Act, S.C., 1934 (24 & 25 Geo V), c. 43; R.S.C., 1985, c. B-2," Adopted on July 3, 1934, Entered into force on March 11, 1935, Last amended on January 31, 2020, Consolidated to May 2, 2022, s.20(b).
[253] Government of Canada (2022). "Bank Act, S.C. 1991, c. 46," Adopted on December 13, 1991, Entered into force on June 1, 1992, Last amended on February 26, 2022, Consolidated to May 2, 2022, s.15.
[254] Daniel, F. (2002). Recent Changes to Canada's Financial Sector Legislation. *Bank of Canada Review*, Winter 2002-2003, 3-16, 3.
[255] Canadian Underwriter (2021). "Federal budget contains 'unexpected positive development' for brokers re: Bank Act." Accessed June 2, 2022. https://www.canadianunderwriter.ca/associations/federal-budget-contains-unexpected-positive-development-for-brokers-re-bank-act-1004206880/.
[256] Government of Canada (2022). "Bank Act, S.C. 1991, c. 46," Adopted on December 13, 1991, Entered into force on June 1, 1992, Last amended on February 26, 2022, Consolidated to May 2, 2022, s.21(1).
[257] Government of Canada (2022). "Bank Act, S.C. 1991, c. 46," Adopted on December 13, 1991, Entered into force on June 1, 1992, Last amended on February 26, 2022, Consolidated to May 2, 2022, s.22(1).
[258] Government of Canada (2022). "Bank Act, S.C. 1991, c. 46," Adopted on December 13, 1991, Entered into force on June 1, 1992, Last amended on February 26, 2022, Consolidated to May 2, 2022, s.24.
[259] Government of Canada (2022). "Bank Act, S.C. 1991, c. 46," Adopted on December 13, 1991, Entered into force on June 1, 1992, Last amended on February 26, 2022, Consolidated to May 2, 2022, s.25(1).
[260] Government of Canada (2022). "Bank Act, S.C. 1991, c. 46," Adopted on December 13, 1991, Entered into force on June 1, 1992, Last amended on February 26, 2022, Consolidated to May 2, 2022, s.27.
[261] Government of Canada (2022). "Bank Act, S.C. 1991, c. 46," Adopted on December 13, 1991, Entered into force on June 1, 1992, Last amended on February 26, 2022, Consolidated to May 2, 2022, s.27(a).
[262] Government of Canada (2022). "Bank Act, S.C. 1991, c. 46," Adopted on December 13, 1991, Entered into force on June 1, 1992, Last amended on February 26, 2022, Consolidated to May 2, 2022, s.27(b).
[263] Government of Canada (2022). "Bank Act, S.C. 1991, c. 46," Adopted on December 13, 1991, Entered into force on June 1, 1992, Last amended on February 26, 2022, Consolidated to May 2, 2022, s.27(c).
[264] Government of Canada (2022). "Bank Act, S.C. 1991, c. 46," Adopted on December 13, 1991, Entered into force on June 1, 1992, Last amended on February 26, 2022, Consolidated to May 2, 2022, s.27(d).
[265] Government of Canada (2022). "Bank Act, S.C. 1991, c. 46," Adopted on December 13, 1991, Entered into force on June 1, 1992, Last amended on February 26, 2022, Consolidated to May 2, 2022, s.27(e).
[266] Government of Canada (2022). "Bank Act, S.C. 1991, c. 46," Adopted on December 13, 1991, Entered into force on June 1, 1992, Last amended on February 26, 2022, Consolidated to May 2, 2022, s.27(f).
[267] Government of Canada (2022). "Bank Act, S.C. 1991, c. 46," Adopted on December 13, 1991, Entered into force on June 1, 1992, Last amended on February 26, 2022, Consolidated to May 2, 2022, s.27(g).
[268] Government of Canada (2022). "Bank Act, S.C. 1991, c. 46," Adopted on December 13, 1991, Entered into force on June 1, 1992, Last amended on February 26, 2022, Consolidated to May 2, 2022, s.27(h).
[269] Government of Canada (2022). "Bank Act, S.C. 1991, c. 46," Adopted on December 13, 1991, Entered into force on June 1, 1992, Last amended on February 26, 2022, Consolidated to May 2, 2022, s.27(i).
[270] Government of Canada (2022). "Bank Act, S.C. 1991, c. 46," Adopted on December 13, 1991, Entered into force on June 1, 1992, Last amended on February 26, 2022, Consolidated to May 2, 2022, s.28(1).
[271] Government of Canada (2022). "Bank Act, S.C. 1991, c. 46," Adopted on December 13, 1991, Entered into force on June 1, 1992, Last amended on February 26, 2022, Consolidated to May 2, 2022, s.28(3).
[272] Government of Canada (2022). "Bank Act, S.C. 1991, c. 46," Adopted on December 13, 1991, Entered into force on June 1, 1992, Last amended on February 26, 2022, Consolidated to May 2, 2022, s.48(1).
[273] Government of Canada (2022). "Bank Act, S.C. 1991, c. 46," Adopted on December 13, 1991, Entered into force on June 1, 1992, Last amended on February 26, 2022, Consolidated to May 2, 2022, s.59(1).
[274] Government of Canada (2022). "Bank Act, S.C. 1991, c. 46," Adopted on December 13, 1991, Entered into force on June 1, 1992, Last amended on February 26, 2022, Consolidated to May 2, 2022, s.59(2).
[275] Government of Canada (2022). "Bank Act, S.C. 1991, c. 46," Adopted on December 13, 1991, Entered into force on June 1, 1992, Last amended on February 26, 2022, Consolidated to May 2, 2022, s.60(1).
[276] Government of Canada (2022). "Bank Act, S.C. 1991, c. 46," Adopted on December 13, 1991, Entered into force on June 1, 1992, Last amended on February 26, 2022, Consolidated to May 2, 2022, s.60(1)(a).

[277] Government of Canada (2022). "Bank Act, S.C. 1991, c. 46," Adopted on December 13, 1991, Entered into force on June 1, 1992, Last amended on February 26, 2022, Consolidated to May 2, 2022, s.60(1)(b).
[278] Government of Canada (2022). "Bank Act, S.C. 1991, c. 46," Adopted on December 13, 1991, Entered into force on June 1, 1992, Last amended on February 26, 2022, Consolidated to May 2, 2022, s.60(1)(c).
[279] Government of Canada (2022). "Bank Act, S.C. 1991, c. 46," Adopted on December 13, 1991, Entered into force on June 1, 1992, Last amended on February 26, 2022, Consolidated to May 2, 2022, s.61(1)(a).
[280] Government of Canada (2022). "Bank Act, S.C. 1991, c. 46," Adopted on December 13, 1991, Entered into force on June 1, 1992, Last amended on February 26, 2022, Consolidated to May 2, 2022, s.61(1)(b).
[281] Government of Canada (2022). "Bank Act, S.C. 1991, c. 46," Adopted on December 13, 1991, Entered into force on June 1, 1992, Last amended on February 26, 2022, Consolidated to May 2, 2022, s.158(2).
[282] Government of Canada (2022). "Bank Act, S.C. 1991, c. 46," Adopted on December 13, 1991, Entered into force on June 1, 1992, Last amended on February 26, 2022, Consolidated to May 2, 2022, s.158(1)(a).
[283] Government of Canada (2022). "Bank Act, S.C. 1991, c. 46," Adopted on December 13, 1991, Entered into force on June 1, 1992, Last amended on February 26, 2022, Consolidated to May 2, 2022, s.158(1)(b).
[284] Government of Canada (2022). "Bank Act, S.C. 1991, c. 46," Adopted on December 13, 1991, Entered into force on June 1, 1992, Last amended on February 26, 2022, Consolidated to May 2, 2022, s.159(1).
[285] Government of Canada (2022). "Bank Act, S.C. 1991, c. 46," Adopted on December 13, 1991, Entered into force on June 1, 1992, Last amended on February 26, 2022, Consolidated to May 2, 2022, s.159(2).
[286] Government of Canada (2022). "Bank Act, S.C. 1991, c. 46," Adopted on December 13, 1991, Entered into force on June 1, 1992, Last amended on February 26, 2022, Consolidated to May 2, 2022, s.161.
[287] Government of Canada (2022). "Bank Act, S.C. 1991, c. 46," Adopted on December 13, 1991, Entered into force on June 1, 1992, Last amended on February 26, 2022, Consolidated to May 2, 2022, s.173(1).
[288] Government of Canada (2022). "Bank Act, S.C. 1991, c. 46," Adopted on December 13, 1991, Entered into force on June 1, 1992, Last amended on February 26, 2022, Consolidated to May 2, 2022, s.188(1).
[289] Government of Canada (2022). "Bank Act, S.C. 1991, c. 46," Adopted on December 13, 1991, Entered into force on June 1, 1992, Last amended on February 26, 2022, Consolidated to May 2, 2022, s.188(2).
[290] Government of Canada (2022). "Bank Act, S.C. 1991, c. 46," Adopted on December 13, 1991, Entered into force on June 1, 1992, Last amended on February 26, 2022, Consolidated to May 2, 2022, s.189.
[291] Government of Canada (2022). "Bank Act, S.C. 1991, c. 46," Adopted on December 13, 1991, Entered into force on June 1, 1992, Last amended on February 26, 2022, Consolidated to May 2, 2022, s.215.
[292] Government of Canada (2022). "Bank Act, S.C. 1991, c. 46," Adopted on December 13, 1991, Entered into force on June 1, 1992, Last amended on February 26, 2022, Consolidated to May 2, 2022, s.216(1).
[293] Government of Canada (2022). "Bank Act, S.C. 1991, c. 46," Adopted on December 13, 1991, Entered into force on June 1, 1992, Last amended on February 26, 2022, Consolidated to May 2, 2022, s.217(1)(a).
[294] Government of Canada (2022). "Bank Act, S.C. 1991, c. 46," Adopted on December 13, 1991, Entered into force on June 1, 1992, Last amended on February 26, 2022, Consolidated to May 2, 2022, s.217(1)(b).
[295] Government of Canada (2022). "Bank Act, S.C. 1991, c. 46," Adopted on December 13, 1991, Entered into force on June 1, 1992, Last amended on February 26, 2022, Consolidated to May 2, 2022, s.217(1)(c).
[296] Government of Canada (2022). "Bank Act, S.C. 1991, c. 46," Adopted on December 13, 1991, Entered into force on June 1, 1992, Last amended on February 26, 2022, Consolidated to May 2, 2022, s.217(1)(d).
[297] Government of Canada (2022). "Bank Act, S.C. 1991, c. 46," Adopted on December 13, 1991, Entered into force on June 1, 1992, Last amended on February 26, 2022, Consolidated to May 2, 2022, s.217(1)(e).

[298] Government of Canada (2022). "Bank Act, S.C. 1991, c. 46," Adopted on December 13, 1991, Entered into force on June 1, 1992, Last amended on February 26, 2022, Consolidated to May 2, 2022, s.217(1)(f).

[299] Government of Canada (2022). "Bank Act, S.C. 1991, c. 46," Adopted on December 13, 1991, Entered into force on June 1, 1992, Last amended on February 26, 2022, Consolidated to May 2, 2022, s.217(1)(g).

[300] Government of Canada (2022). "Bank Act, S.C. 1991, c. 46," Adopted on December 13, 1991, Entered into force on June 1, 1992, Last amended on February 26, 2022, Consolidated to May 2, 2022, s.217(1)(h).

[301] Government of Canada (2022). "Bank Act, S.C. 1991, c. 46," Adopted on December 13, 1991, Entered into force on June 1, 1992, Last amended on February 26, 2022, Consolidated to May 2, 2022, s.217(1)(i).

[302] Government of Canada (2022). "Bank Act, S.C. 1991, c. 46," Adopted on December 13, 1991, Entered into force on June 1, 1992, Last amended on February 26, 2022, Consolidated to May 2, 2022, s.217(1)(i.1).

[303] Government of Canada (2022). "Bank Act, S.C. 1991, c. 46," Adopted on December 13, 1991, Entered into force on June 1, 1992, Last amended on February 26, 2022, Consolidated to May 2, 2022, s.217(1)(j).

[304] Government of Canada (2022). "Bank Act, S.C. 1991, c. 46," Adopted on December 13, 1991, Entered into force on June 1, 1992, Last amended on February 26, 2022, Consolidated to May 2, 2022, s.217(2).

[305] Government of Canada (2022). "Bank Act, S.C. 1991, c. 46," Adopted on December 13, 1991, Entered into force on June 1, 1992, Last amended on February 26, 2022, Consolidated to May 2, 2022, s.270(2).

[306] Government of Canada (2022). "Bank Act, S.C. 1991, c. 46," Adopted on December 13, 1991, Entered into force on June 1, 1992, Last amended on February 26, 2022, Consolidated to May 2, 2022, s.270(3).

[307] Government of Canada (2022). "Bank Act, S.C. 1991, c. 46," Adopted on December 13, 1991, Entered into force on June 1, 1992, Last amended on February 26, 2022, Consolidated to May 2, 2022, s.270(4).

[308] Government of Canada (2022). "Bank Act, S.C. 1991, c. 46," Adopted on December 13, 1991, Entered into force on June 1, 1992, Last amended on February 26, 2022, Consolidated to May 2, 2022, s.409(1).

[309] Government of Canada (2022). "Bank Act, S.C. 1991, c. 46," Adopted on December 13, 1991, Entered into force on June 1, 1992, Last amended on February 26, 2022, Consolidated to May 2, 2022, s.409(2)(a).

[310] Government of Canada (2022). "Bank Act, S.C. 1991, c. 46," Adopted on December 13, 1991, Entered into force on June 1, 1992, Last amended on February 26, 2022, Consolidated to May 2, 2022, s.409(2)(b).

[311] Government of Canada (2022). "Bank Act, S.C. 1991, c. 46," Adopted on December 13, 1991, Entered into force on June 1, 1992, Last amended on February 26, 2022, Consolidated to May 2, 2022, s.409(2)(c).

[312] Government of Canada (2022). "Bank Act, S.C. 1991, c. 46," Adopted on December 13, 1991, Entered into force on June 1, 1992, Last amended on February 26, 2022, Consolidated to May 2, 2022, s.409(2)(d).

[313] Government of Canada (2022). "Bank Act, S.C. 1991, c. 46," Adopted on December 13, 1991, Entered into force on June 1, 1992, Last amended on February 26, 2022, Consolidated to May 2, 2022, s.422.1.

[314] Government of Canada (2022). "Bank Act, S.C. 1991, c. 46," Adopted on December 13, 1991, Entered into force on June 1, 1992, Last amended on February 26, 2022, Consolidated to May 2, 2022, s.415.3(1).

[315] Government of Canada (2022). "Bank Act, S.C. 1991, c. 46," Adopted on December 13, 1991, Entered into force on June 1, 1992, Last amended on February 26, 2022, Consolidated to May 2, 2022, s.415.2(1).

[316] Government of Canada (2022). "Bank Act, S.C. 1991, c. 46," Adopted on December 13, 1991, Entered into force on June 1, 1992, Last amended on February 26, 2022, Consolidated to May 2, 2022, s.415.1(1).

[317] Government of Canada (2022). "Bank Act, S.C. 1991, c. 46," Adopted on December 13, 1991, Entered into force on June 1, 1992, Last amended on February 26, 2022, Consolidated to May 2, 2022, s.465.

[318] Government of Canada (2022). "Bank Act, S.C. 1991, c. 46," Adopted on December 13, 1991, Entered into force on June 1, 1992, Last amended on February 26, 2022, Consolidated to May 2, 2022, s.465.1(1).
[319] Government of Canada (2022). "Bank Act, S.C. 1991, c. 46," Adopted on December 13, 1991, Entered into force on June 1, 1992, Last amended on February 26, 2022, Consolidated to May 2, 2022, s.466(1).
[320] Government of Canada (2022). "Bank Act, S.C. 1991, c. 46," Adopted on December 13, 1991, Entered into force on June 1, 1992, Last amended on February 26, 2022, Consolidated to May 2, 2022, s.468(1)(a).
[321] Government of Canada (2022). "Bank Act, S.C. 1991, c. 46," Adopted on December 13, 1991, Entered into force on June 1, 1992, Last amended on February 26, 2022, Consolidated to May 2, 2022, s.468(1)(b).
[322] Government of Canada (2022). "Bank Act, S.C. 1991, c. 46," Adopted on December 13, 1991, Entered into force on June 1, 1992, Last amended on February 26, 2022, Consolidated to May 2, 2022, s.468(1)(c).
[323] Government of Canada (2022). "Bank Act, S.C. 1991, c. 46," Adopted on December 13, 1991, Entered into force on June 1, 1992, Last amended on February 26, 2022, Consolidated to May 2, 2022, s.468(1)(d).
[324] Government of Canada (2022). "Bank Act, S.C. 1991, c. 46," Adopted on December 13, 1991, Entered into force on June 1, 1992, Last amended on February 26, 2022, Consolidated to May 2, 2022, s.468(1)(e).
[325] Government of Canada (2022). "Bank Act, S.C. 1991, c. 46," Adopted on December 13, 1991, Entered into force on June 1, 1992, Last amended on February 26, 2022, Consolidated to May 2, 2022, s.468(1)(f).
[326] Government of Canada (2022). "Bank Act, S.C. 1991, c. 46," Adopted on December 13, 1991, Entered into force on June 1, 1992, Last amended on February 26, 2022, Consolidated to May 2, 2022, s.468(1)(g).
[327] Government of Canada (2022). "Bank Act, S.C. 1991, c. 46," Adopted on December 13, 1991, Entered into force on June 1, 1992, Last amended on February 26, 2022, Consolidated to May 2, 2022, s.468(1)(h).
[328] Government of Canada (2022). "Bank Act, S.C. 1991, c. 46," Adopted on December 13, 1991, Entered into force on June 1, 1992, Last amended on February 26, 2022, Consolidated to May 2, 2022, s.468(1)(i).
[329] Government of Canada (2022). "Bank Act, S.C. 1991, c. 46," Adopted on December 13, 1991, Entered into force on June 1, 1992, Last amended on February 26, 2022, Consolidated to May 2, 2022, s.468(1)(j).
[330] Government of Canada (2022). "Bank Act, S.C. 1991, c. 46," Adopted on December 13, 1991, Entered into force on June 1, 1992, Last amended on February 26, 2022, Consolidated to May 2, 2022, s.473(1).
[331] Government of Canada (2022). "Bank Act, S.C. 1991, c. 46," Adopted on December 13, 1991, Entered into force on June 1, 1992, Last amended on February 26, 2022, Consolidated to May 2, 2022, s.476.
[332] Government of Canada (2022). "Bank Act, S.C. 1991, c. 46," Adopted on December 13, 1991, Entered into force on June 1, 1992, Last amended on February 26, 2022, Consolidated to May 2, 2022, s.482(1).
[333] Government of Canada (2022). "Bank Act, S.C. 1991, c. 46," Adopted on December 13, 1991, Entered into force on June 1, 1992, Last amended on February 26, 2022, Consolidated to May 2, 2022, s.482(2)(e).
[334] Government of Canada (2022). "Bank Act, S.C. 1991, c. 46," Adopted on December 13, 1991, Entered into force on June 1, 1992, Last amended on February 26, 2022, Consolidated to May 2, 2022, s.484.1(1).
[335] Government of Canada (2022). "Bank Act, S.C. 1991, c. 46," Adopted on December 13, 1991, Entered into force on June 1, 1992, Last amended on February 26, 2022, Consolidated to May 2, 2022, s.484.1(2).
[336] Government of Canada (2022). "Bank Act, S.C. 1991, c. 46," Adopted on December 13, 1991, Entered into force on June 1, 1992, Last amended on February 26, 2022, Consolidated to May 2, 2022, s.484.1(3).

[337] Government of Canada (2022). "Bank Act, S.C. 1991, c. 46," Adopted on December 13, 1991, Entered into force on June 1, 1992, Last amended on February 26, 2022, Consolidated to May 2, 2022, s.485(1).
[338] Government of Canada (2022). "Bank Act, S.C. 1991, c. 46," Adopted on December 13, 1991, Entered into force on June 1, 1992, Last amended on February 26, 2022, Consolidated to May 2, 2022, s.485(1.1).
[339] Government of Canada (2022). "Bank Act, S.C. 1991, c. 46," Adopted on December 13, 1991, Entered into force on June 1, 1992, Last amended on February 26, 2022, Consolidated to May 2, 2022, s.485(2)-(3.1).
[340] Government of Canada (2022). "Bank Act, S.C. 1991, c. 46," Adopted on December 13, 1991, Entered into force on June 1, 1992, Last amended on February 26, 2022, Consolidated to May 2, 2022, s.485(4).
[341] Government of Canada (2022). "Bank Act, S.C. 1991, c. 46," Adopted on December 13, 1991, Entered into force on June 1, 1992, Last amended on February 26, 2022, Consolidated to May 2, 2022, s.489(1).
[342] Government of Canada (2022). "Bank Act, S.C. 1991, c. 46," Adopted on December 13, 1991, Entered into force on June 1, 1992, Last amended on February 26, 2022, Consolidated to May 2, 2022, s.492.
[343] Government of Canada (2022). "Bank Act, S.C. 1991, c. 46," Adopted on December 13, 1991, Entered into force on June 1, 1992, Last amended on February 26, 2022, Consolidated to May 2, 2022, s.493.
[344] Government of Canada (2022). "Bank Act, S.C. 1991, c. 46," Adopted on December 13, 1991, Entered into force on June 1, 1992, Last amended on February 26, 2022, Consolidated to May 2, 2022, s.520(1)(a).
[345] Government of Canada (2022). "Bank Act, S.C. 1991, c. 46," Adopted on December 13, 1991, Entered into force on June 1, 1992, Last amended on February 26, 2022, Consolidated to May 2, 2022, s.520(1)(b).
[346] Government of Canada (2022). "Bank Act, S.C. 1991, c. 46," Adopted on December 13, 1991, Entered into force on June 1, 1992, Last amended on February 26, 2022, Consolidated to May 2, 2022, s.520(1)(c).
[347] Government of Canada (2022). "Bank Act, S.C. 1991, c. 46," Adopted on December 13, 1991, Entered into force on June 1, 1992, Last amended on February 26, 2022, Consolidated to May 2, 2022, s.520(2)(a).
[348] Government of Canada (2022). "Bank Act, S.C. 1991, c. 46," Adopted on December 13, 1991, Entered into force on June 1, 1992, Last amended on February 26, 2022, Consolidated to May 2, 2022, s.520(2)(b).
[349] Government of Canada (2022). "Bank Act, S.C. 1991, c. 46," Adopted on December 13, 1991, Entered into force on June 1, 1992, Last amended on February 26, 2022, Consolidated to May 2, 2022, s.520.1(1)(a).
[350] Government of Canada (2022). "Bank Act, S.C. 1991, c. 46," Adopted on December 13, 1991, Entered into force on June 1, 1992, Last amended on February 26, 2022, Consolidated to May 2, 2022, s.520.1(1)(b).
[351] Government of Canada (2022). "Bank Act, S.C. 1991, c. 46," Adopted on December 13, 1991, Entered into force on June 1, 1992, Last amended on February 26, 2022, Consolidated to May 2, 2022, s.520.1(4)(a).
[352] Government of Canada (2022). "Bank Act, S.C. 1991, c. 46," Adopted on December 13, 1991, Entered into force on June 1, 1992, Last amended on February 26, 2022, Consolidated to May 2, 2022, s.520.1(4)(b).
[353] Government of Canada (2022). "Bank Act, S.C. 1991, c. 46," Adopted on December 13, 1991, Entered into force on June 1, 1992, Last amended on February 26, 2022, Consolidated to May 2, 2022, s.522.04.
[354] Government of Canada (2022). "Bank Act, S.C. 1991, c. 46," Adopted on December 13, 1991, Entered into force on June 1, 1992, Last amended on February 26, 2022, Consolidated to May 2, 2022, s.524(1).
[355] Government of Canada (2023). "Bank Act, S.C. 1991, c. 46," Adopted on December 13, 1991, Entered into force on June 1, 1992, Last amended on March 4, 2023, Consolidated to March 20, 2023, s.524(2).
[356] Government of Canada (2022). "Bank Act, S.C. 1991, c. 46," Adopted on December 13, 1991, Entered into force on June 1, 1992, Last amended on February 26, 2022, Consolidated to May 2, 2022, s.525(1).
[357] Government of Canada (2022). "Bank Act, S.C. 1991, c. 46," Adopted on December 13, 1991, Entered into force on June 1, 1992, Last amended on February 26, 2022, Consolidated to May 2, 2022, s.526.

[358] Government of Canada (2022). "Bank Act, S.C. 1991, c. 46," Adopted on December 13, 1991, Entered into force on June 1, 1992, Last amended on February 26, 2022, Consolidated to May 2, 2022, s.527(1)(a).
[359] Government of Canada (2022). "Bank Act, S.C. 1991, c. 46," Adopted on December 13, 1991, Entered into force on June 1, 1992, Last amended on February 26, 2022, Consolidated to May 2, 2022, s.527(1)(b).
[360] Government of Canada (2022). "Bank Act, S.C. 1991, c. 46," Adopted on December 13, 1991, Entered into force on June 1, 1992, Last amended on February 26, 2022, Consolidated to May 2, 2022, s.527(1)(c).
[361] Government of Canada (2022). "Bank Act, S.C. 1991, c. 46," Adopted on December 13, 1991, Entered into force on June 1, 1992, Last amended on February 26, 2022, Consolidated to May 2, 2022, s.527(1)(d).
[362] Government of Canada (2022). "Bank Act, S.C. 1991, c. 46," Adopted on December 13, 1991, Entered into force on June 1, 1992, Last amended on February 26, 2022, Consolidated to May 2, 2022, s.534(1).
[363] Government of Canada (2022). "Bank Act, S.C. 1991, c. 46," Adopted on December 13, 1991, Entered into force on June 1, 1992, Last amended on February 26, 2022, Consolidated to May 2, 2022, s.534(3)(b).
[364] Government of Canada (2022). "Bank Act, S.C. 1991, c. 46," Adopted on December 13, 1991, Entered into force on June 1, 1992, Last amended on February 26, 2022, Consolidated to May 2, 2022, s.308(4).
[365] Government of Canada (2022). "Bank Act, S.C. 1991, c. 46," Adopted on December 13, 1991, Entered into force on June 1, 1992, Last amended on February 26, 2022, Consolidated to May 2, 2022, s.534(3)(a).
[366] Government of Canada (2022). "Bank Act, S.C. 1991, c. 46," Adopted on December 13, 1991, Entered into force on June 1, 1992, Last amended on February 26, 2022, Consolidated to May 2, 2022, s.534(3)(c).
[367] Government of Canada (2022). "Bank Act, S.C. 1991, c. 46," Adopted on December 13, 1991, Entered into force on June 1, 1992, Last amended on February 26, 2022, Consolidated to May 2, 2022, s.538(1).
[368] Government of Canada (2022). "Bank Act, S.C. 1991, c. 46," Adopted on December 13, 1991, Entered into force on June 1, 1992, Last amended on February 26, 2022, Consolidated to May 2, 2022, s.538(2)(a).
[369] Government of Canada (2022). "Bank Act, S.C. 1991, c. 46," Adopted on December 13, 1991, Entered into force on June 1, 1992, Last amended on February 26, 2022, Consolidated to May 2, 2022, s.538(2)(b).
[370] Government of Canada (2022). "Bank Act, S.C. 1991, c. 46," Adopted on December 13, 1991, Entered into force on June 1, 1992, Last amended on February 26, 2022, Consolidated to May 2, 2022, s.538(2)(c).
[371] Government of Canada (2022). "Bank Act, S.C. 1991, c. 46," Adopted on December 13, 1991, Entered into force on June 1, 1992, Last amended on February 26, 2022, Consolidated to May 2, 2022, s.538(2)(d).
[372] Government of Canada (2022). "Bank Act, S.C. 1991, c. 46," Adopted on December 13, 1991, Entered into force on June 1, 1992, Last amended on February 26, 2022, Consolidated to May 2, 2022, s.539(2).
[373] Government of Canada (2022). "Bank Act, S.C. 1991, c. 46," Adopted on December 13, 1991, Entered into force on June 1, 1992, Last amended on February 26, 2022, Consolidated to May 2, 2022, s.546(1).
[374] Government of Canada (2022). "Bank Act, S.C. 1991, c. 46," Adopted on December 13, 1991, Entered into force on June 1, 1992, Last amended on February 26, 2022, Consolidated to May 2, 2022, s.548.
[375] Government of Canada (2022). "Bank Act, S.C. 1991, c. 46," Adopted on December 13, 1991, Entered into force on June 1, 1992, Last amended on February 26, 2022, Consolidated to May 2, 2022, s.549(1).
[376] Government of Canada (2022). "Bank Act, S.C. 1991, c. 46," Adopted on December 13, 1991, Entered into force on June 1, 1992, Last amended on February 26, 2022, Consolidated to May 2, 2022, s.549(2).
[377] Government of Canada (2022). "Bank Act, S.C. 1991, c. 46," Adopted on December 13, 1991, Entered into force on June 1, 1992, Last amended on February 26, 2022, Consolidated to May 2, 2022, s.550.
[378] Government of Canada (2022). "Bank Act, S.C. 1991, c. 46," Adopted on December 13, 1991, Entered into force on June 1, 1992, Last amended on February 26, 2022, Consolidated to May 2, 2022, s.551(1).

[379] Government of Canada (2022). "Bank Act, S.C. 1991, c. 46," Adopted on December 13, 1991, Entered into force on June 1, 1992, Last amended on February 26, 2022, Consolidated to May 2, 2022, s.553.1(1).

[380] Government of Canada (2022). "Bank Act, S.C. 1991, c. 46," Adopted on December 13, 1991, Entered into force on June 1, 1992, Last amended on February 26, 2022, Consolidated to May 2, 2022, s.554(2).

[381] Government of Canada (2022). "Bank Act, S.C. 1991, c. 46," Adopted on December 13, 1991, Entered into force on June 1, 1992, Last amended on February 26, 2022, Consolidated to May 2, 2022, s.556(1).

[382] Government of Canada (2022). "Bank Act, S.C. 1991, c. 46," Adopted on December 13, 1991, Entered into force on June 1, 1992, Last amended on February 26, 2022, Consolidated to May 2, 2022, s.582(1)(a).

[383] Government of Canada (2022). "Bank Act, S.C. 1991, c. 46," Adopted on December 13, 1991, Entered into force on June 1, 1992, Last amended on February 26, 2022, Consolidated to May 2, 2022, s.582(1)(b).

[384] Government of Canada (2022). "Bank Act, S.C. 1991, c. 46," Adopted on December 13, 1991, Entered into force on June 1, 1992, Last amended on February 26, 2022, Consolidated to May 2, 2022, s.582(2).

[385] Government of Canada (2022). "Bank Act, S.C. 1991, c. 46," Adopted on December 13, 1991, Entered into force on June 1, 1992, Last amended on February 26, 2022, Consolidated to May 2, 2022, s.628(1).

[386] Government of Canada (2022). "Bank Act, S.C. 1991, c. 46," Adopted on December 13, 1991, Entered into force on June 1, 1992, Last amended on February 26, 2022, Consolidated to May 2, 2022, s.632(1)(a).

[387] Government of Canada (2022). "Bank Act, S.C. 1991, c. 46," Adopted on December 13, 1991, Entered into force on June 1, 1992, Last amended on February 26, 2022, Consolidated to May 2, 2022, s.632(1)(b).

[388] Government of Canada (2022). "Bank Act, S.C. 1991, c. 46," Adopted on December 13, 1991, Entered into force on June 1, 1992, Last amended on February 26, 2022, Consolidated to May 2, 2022, s.632(1)(c).

[389] Government of Canada (2022). "Bank Act, S.C. 1991, c. 46," Adopted on December 13, 1991, Entered into force on June 1, 1992, Last amended on February 26, 2022, Consolidated to May 2, 2022, s.632(1)(d).

[390] Government of Canada (2022). "Bank Act, S.C. 1991, c. 46," Adopted on December 13, 1991, Entered into force on June 1, 1992, Last amended on February 26, 2022, Consolidated to May 2, 2022, s.632(1)(e).

[391] Government of Canada (2022). "Bank Act, S.C. 1991, c. 46," Adopted on December 13, 1991, Entered into force on June 1, 1992, Last amended on February 26, 2022, Consolidated to May 2, 2022, s.632(1)(f).

[392] Government of Canada (2022). "Bank Act, S.C. 1991, c. 46," Adopted on December 13, 1991, Entered into force on June 1, 1992, Last amended on February 26, 2022, Consolidated to May 2, 2022, s.632(1)(g).

[393] Government of Canada (2022). "Bank Act, S.C. 1991, c. 46," Adopted on December 13, 1991, Entered into force on June 1, 1992, Last amended on February 26, 2022, Consolidated to May 2, 2022, s.632(1)(h).

[394] Government of Canada (2022). "Bank Act, S.C. 1991, c. 46," Adopted on December 13, 1991, Entered into force on June 1, 1992, Last amended on February 26, 2022, Consolidated to May 2, 2022, s.645(1).

[395] Government of Canada (2022). "Bank Act, S.C. 1991, c. 46," Adopted on December 13, 1991, Entered into force on June 1, 1992, Last amended on February 26, 2022, Consolidated to May 2, 2022, s.645(2).

[396] Government of Canada (2022). "Bank Act, S.C. 1991, c. 46," Adopted on December 13, 1991, Entered into force on June 1, 1992, Last amended on February 26, 2022, Consolidated to May 2, 2022, s.647.1(1)(a).

[397] Government of Canada (2022). "Bank Act, S.C. 1991, c. 46," Adopted on December 13, 1991, Entered into force on June 1, 1992, Last amended on February 26, 2022, Consolidated to May 2, 2022, s.647.1(1)(b).

[398] Government of Canada (2022). "Bank Act, S.C. 1991, c. 46," Adopted on December 13, 1991, Entered into force on June 1, 1992, Last amended on February 26, 2022, Consolidated to May 2, 2022, s.647.1(2).

[399] Government of Canada (2022). "Bank Act, S.C. 1991, c. 46," Adopted on December 13, 1991, Entered into force on June 1, 1992, Last amended on February 26, 2022, Consolidated to May 2, 2022, s.647.1(3).

[400] Government of Canada (2022). "Bank Act, S.C. 1991, c. 46," Adopted on December 13, 1991, Entered into force on June 1, 1992, Last amended on February 26, 2022, Consolidated to May 2, 2022, s.647.1(6).

[401] Government of Canada (2022). "Bank Act, S.C. 1991, c. 46," Adopted on December 13, 1991, Entered into force on June 1, 1992, Last amended on February 26, 2022, Consolidated to May 2, 2022, s.647.1(7).

[402] Government of Canada (2022). "Bank Act, S.C. 1991, c. 46," Adopted on December 13, 1991, Entered into force on June 1, 1992, Last amended on February 26, 2022, Consolidated to May 2, 2022, s.647.1(8).

[403] Government of Canada (2022). "Bank Act, S.C. 1991, c. 46," Adopted on December 13, 1991, Entered into force on June 1, 1992, Last amended on February 26, 2022, Consolidated to May 2, 2022, s.648(1)(a).

[404] Government of Canada (2022). "Bank Act, S.C. 1991, c. 46," Adopted on December 13, 1991, Entered into force on June 1, 1992, Last amended on February 26, 2022, Consolidated to May 2, 2022, s.648(1)(b).

[405] Government of Canada (2022). "Bank Act, S.C. 1991, c. 46," Adopted on December 13, 1991, Entered into force on June 1, 1992, Last amended on February 26, 2022, Consolidated to May 2, 2022, s.648(2).

[406] Government of Canada (2022). "Bank Act, S.C. 1991, c. 46," Adopted on December 13, 1991, Entered into force on June 1, 1992, Last amended on February 26, 2022, Consolidated to May 2, 2022, s.980.

[407] Government of Canada (2022). "Bank Act, S.C. 1991, c. 46," Adopted on December 13, 1991, Entered into force on June 1, 1992, Last amended on February 26, 2022, Consolidated to May 2, 2022, s.980.1.

[408] Government of Canada (2022). "Bank Act, S.C. 1991, c. 46," Adopted on December 13, 1991, Entered into force on June 1, 1992, Last amended on February 26, 2022, Consolidated to May 2, 2022, s.981.

[409] Government of Canada (2022). "Canada Deposit Insurance Corporation Act, R.S.C. 1985, c. C-3," Adopted on February 17, 1984, Entered into force on February 17, 1984, Last amended on April 30, 2022, Consolidated to May 2, 2022, s.3(1).

[410] Government of Canada (2022). "Canada Deposit Insurance Corporation Act, R.S.C. 1985, c. C-3," Adopted on February 17, 1984, Entered into force on February 17, 1984, Last amended on April 30, 2022, Consolidated to May 2, 2022, s.3(2).

[411] Government of Canada (2022). "Canada Deposit Insurance Corporation Act, R.S.C. 1985, c. C-3," Adopted on February 17, 1984, Entered into force on February 17, 1984, Last amended on April 30, 2022, Consolidated to May 2, 2022, s.4(1).

[412] Government of Canada (2022). "Canada Deposit Insurance Corporation Act, R.S.C. 1985, c. C-3," Adopted on February 17, 1984, Entered into force on February 17, 1984, Last amended on April 30, 2022, Consolidated to May 2, 2022, s.7(a).

[413] Government of Canada (2022). "Canada Deposit Insurance Corporation Act, R.S.C. 1985, c. C-3," Adopted on February 17, 1984, Entered into force on February 17, 1984, Last amended on April 30, 2022, Consolidated to May 2, 2022, s.7(b).

[414] Government of Canada (2022). "Canada Deposit Insurance Corporation Act, R.S.C. 1985, c. C-3," Adopted on February 17, 1984, Entered into force on February 17, 1984, Last amended on April 30, 2022, Consolidated to May 2, 2022, s.7(c).

[415] Government of Canada (2022). "Canada Deposit Insurance Corporation Act, R.S.C. 1985, c. C-3," Adopted on February 17, 1984, Entered into force on February 17, 1984, Last amended on April 30, 2022, Consolidated to May 2, 2022, s.7(d).

[416] Government of Canada (2022). "Canada Deposit Insurance Corporation Act, R.S.C. 1985, c. C-3," Adopted on February 17, 1984, Entered into force on February 17, 1984, Last amended on April 30, 2022, Consolidated to May 2, 2022, s.7.1(1).

[417] Government of Canada (2022). "Canada Deposit Insurance Corporation Act, R.S.C. 1985, c. C-3," Adopted on February 17, 1984, Entered into force on February 17, 1984, Last amended on April 30, 2022, Consolidated to May 2, 2022, s.10(1).

[418] Government of Canada (2022). "Canada Deposit Insurance Corporation Act, R.S.C. 1985, c. C-3," Adopted on February 17, 1984, Entered into force on February 17, 1984, Last amended on April 30, 2022, Consolidated to May 2, 2022, s.12.

[419] Government of Canada (2022). "Canada Deposit Insurance Corporation Act, R.S.C. 1985, c. C-3," Adopted on February 17, 1984, Entered into force on February 17, 1984, Last amended on April 30, 2022, Consolidated to May 2, 2022, s.17(1).

[420] Government of Canada (2022). "Canada Deposit Insurance Corporation Act, R.S.C. 1985, c. C-3," Adopted on February 17, 1984, Entered into force on February 17, 1984, Last amended on April 30, 2022, Consolidated to May 2, 2022, s.17.2.

[421] Government of Canada (2022). "Canada Deposit Insurance Corporation Act, R.S.C. 1985, c. C-3," Adopted on February 17, 1984, Entered into force on February 17, 1984, Last amended on April 30, 2022, Consolidated to May 2, 2022, s.21.1.

[422] Government of Canada (2022). "Canada Deposit Insurance Corporation Act, R.S.C. 1985, c. C-3," Adopted on February 17, 1984, Entered into force on February 17, 1984, Last amended on April 30, 2022, Consolidated to May 2, 2022, s.21.5.

[423] Government of Canada (2022). "Canada Deposit Insurance Corporation Act, R.S.C. 1985, c. C-3," Adopted on February 17, 1984, Entered into force on February 17, 1984, Last amended on April 30, 2022, Consolidated to May 2, 2022, s.45.1(1).

[424] Government of Canada (2022). "Canada Deposit Insurance Corporation Act, R.S.C. 1985, c. C-3," Adopted on February 17, 1984, Entered into force on February 17, 1984, Last amended on April 30, 2022, Consolidated to May 2, 2022, s.45.1(2).

[425] Government of Canada (2022). "Canadian Payments Act, R.S.C., 1985, c. C-21," Adopted on November 26, 1980, as "An Act to revise the Bank Act, to amend the Quebec Savings Bank Act and the Bank of Canada Act, to establish the Canadian Payments Association and to amend other Acts in consequence thereof: Part IV – An Act to establish the Canadian Payments Association," Entered into force on December 1, 1980, Last amended on April 2, 2021, Consolidated to May 2, 2022, s.3(1).

[426] Government of Canada (2022). "Canadian Payments Act, R.S.C., 1985, c. C-21," Adopted on November 26, 1980, as "An Act to revise the Bank Act, to amend the Quebec Savings Bank Act and the Bank of Canada Act, to establish the Canadian Payments Association and to amend other Acts in consequence thereof: Part IV – An Act to establish the Canadian Payments Association," Entered into force on December 1, 1980, Last amended on April 2, 2021, Consolidated to May 2, 2022, s.3(2).

[427] Government of Canada (2022). "Canadian Payments Act, R.S.C., 1985, c. C-21," Adopted on November 26, 1980, as "An Act to revise the Bank Act, to amend the Quebec Savings Bank Act and the Bank of Canada Act, to establish the Canadian Payments Association and to amend other Acts in consequence thereof: Part IV – An Act to establish the Canadian Payments Association," Entered into force on December 1, 1980, Last amended on April 2, 2021, Consolidated to May 2, 2022, s.5(1)(a).

[428] Government of Canada (2022). "Canadian Payments Act, R.S.C., 1985, c. C-21," Adopted on November 26, 1980, as "An Act to revise the Bank Act, to amend the Quebec Savings Bank Act and the Bank of Canada Act, to establish the Canadian Payments Association and to amend other Acts in consequence thereof: Part IV – An Act to establish the Canadian Payments Association," Entered into force on December 1, 1980, Last amended on April 2, 2021, Consolidated to May 2, 2022, s.5(1)(b).

[429] Government of Canada (2022). "Canadian Payments Act, R.S.C., 1985, c. C-21," Adopted on November 26, 1980, as "An Act to revise the Bank Act, to amend the Quebec Savings Bank Act and the Bank of Canada Act, to establish the Canadian Payments Association and to amend other Acts in consequence thereof: Part IV – An Act to establish the Canadian Payments Association," Entered into force on December 1, 1980, Last amended on April 2, 2021, Consolidated to May 2, 2022, s.5(1)(c).

[430] Government of Canada (2022). "Canadian Payments Act, R.S.C., 1985, c. C-21," Adopted on November 26, 1980, as "An Act to revise the Bank Act, to amend the Quebec Savings Bank Act and the Bank of Canada Act, to establish the Canadian Payments Association and to amend other Acts in

consequence thereof: Part IV – An Act to establish the Canadian Payments Association," Entered into force on December 1, 1980, Last amended on April 2, 2021, Consolidated to May 2, 2022, s.5(2).

[431] Government of Canada (2022). "Canadian Payments Act, R.S.C., 1985, c. C-21," Adopted on November 26, 1980, as "An Act to revise the Bank Act, to amend the Quebec Savings Bank Act and the Bank of Canada Act, to establish the Canadian Payments Association and to amend other Acts in consequence thereof: Part IV – An Act to establish the Canadian Payments Association," Entered into force on December 1, 1980, Last amended on April 2, 2021, Consolidated to May 2, 2022, s.6(1)(a).

[432] Government of Canada (2022). "Canadian Payments Act, R.S.C., 1985, c. C-21," Adopted on November 26, 1980, as "An Act to revise the Bank Act, to amend the Quebec Savings Bank Act and the Bank of Canada Act, to establish the Canadian Payments Association and to amend other Acts in consequence thereof: Part IV – An Act to establish the Canadian Payments Association," Entered into force on December 1, 1980, Last amended on April 2, 2021, Consolidated to May 2, 2022, s.6(1)(b).

[433] Government of Canada (2022). "Canadian Payments Act, R.S.C., 1985, c. C-21," Adopted on November 26, 1980, as "An Act to revise the Bank Act, to amend the Quebec Savings Bank Act and the Bank of Canada Act, to establish the Canadian Payments Association and to amend other Acts in consequence thereof: Part IV – An Act to establish the Canadian Payments Association," Entered into force on December 1, 1980, Last amended on April 2, 2021, Consolidated to May 2, 2022, s.6(1)(c).

[434] Government of Canada (2022). "Canadian Payments Act, R.S.C., 1985, c. C-21," Adopted on November 26, 1980, as "An Act to revise the Bank Act, to amend the Quebec Savings Bank Act and the Bank of Canada Act, to establish the Canadian Payments Association and to amend other Acts in consequence thereof: Part IV – An Act to establish the Canadian Payments Association," Entered into force on December 1, 1980, Last amended on April 2, 2021, Consolidated to May 2, 2022, s.6(1)(d).

[435] Government of Canada (2022). "Canadian Payments Act, R.S.C., 1985, c. C-21," Adopted on November 26, 1980, as "An Act to revise the Bank Act, to amend the Quebec Savings Bank Act and the Bank of Canada Act, to establish the Canadian Payments Association and to amend other Acts in consequence thereof: Part IV – An Act to establish the Canadian Payments Association," Entered into force on December 1, 1980, Last amended on April 2, 2021, Consolidated to May 2, 2022, s.6(2).

[436] Government of Canada (2022). "Canadian Payments Act, R.S.C., 1985, c. C-21," Adopted on November 26, 1980, as "An Act to revise the Bank Act, to amend the Quebec Savings Bank Act and the Bank of Canada Act, to establish the Canadian Payments Association and to amend other Acts in consequence thereof: Part IV – An Act to establish the Canadian Payments Association," Entered into force on December 1, 1980, Last amended on April 2, 2021, Consolidated to May 2, 2022, s.18(1).

[437] Government of Canada (2022). "Canadian Payments Act, R.S.C., 1985, c. C-21," Adopted on November 26, 1980, as "An Act to revise the Bank Act, to amend the Quebec Savings Bank Act and the Bank of Canada Act, to establish the Canadian Payments Association and to amend other Acts in consequence thereof: Part IV – An Act to establish the Canadian Payments Association," Entered into force on December 1, 1980, Last amended on April 2, 2021, Consolidated to May 2, 2022, s.19(1).

[438] Government of Canada (2022). "Canadian Payments Act, R.S.C., 1985, c. C-21," Adopted on November 26, 1980, as "An Act to revise the Bank Act, to amend the Quebec Savings Bank Act and the Bank of Canada Act, to establish the Canadian Payments Association and to amend other Acts in consequence thereof: Part IV – An Act to establish the Canadian Payments Association," Entered into force on December 1, 1980, Last amended on April 2, 2021, Consolidated to May 2, 2022, s.19.1.

[439] Government of Canada (2022). "Canadian Payments Act, R.S.C., 1985, c. C-21," Adopted on November 26, 1980, as "An Act to revise the Bank Act, to amend the Quebec Savings Bank Act and the Bank of Canada Act, to establish the Canadian Payments Association and to amend other Acts in consequence thereof: Part IV – An Act to establish the Canadian Payments Association," Entered into force on December 1, 1980, Last amended on April 2, 2021, Consolidated to May 2, 2022, s.19.3(1).

[440] Government of Canada (2022). "Canadian Payments Act, R.S.C., 1985, c. C-21," Adopted on November 26, 1980, as "An Act to revise the Bank Act, to amend the Quebec Savings Bank Act and the Bank of Canada Act, to establish the Canadian Payments Association and to amend other Acts in consequence thereof: Part IV – An Act to establish the Canadian Payments Association," Entered into force on December 1, 1980, Last amended on April 2, 2021, Consolidated to May 2, 2022, s.37(1).

[441] Government of Canada (2022). "Canadian Payments Act, R.S.C., 1985, c. C-21," Adopted on November 26, 1980, as "An Act to revise the Bank Act, to amend the Quebec Savings Bank Act and the Bank of Canada Act, to establish the Canadian Payments Association and to amend other Acts in consequence thereof: Part IV – An Act to establish the Canadian Payments Association," Entered into force on December 1, 1980, Last amended on April 2, 2021, Consolidated to May 2, 2022, s.37(3).

[442] Government of Canada (2022). "Canadian Payments Act, R.S.C., 1985, c. C-21," Adopted on November 26, 1980, as "An Act to revise the Bank Act, to amend the Quebec Savings Bank Act and the Bank of Canada Act, to establish the Canadian Payments Association and to amend other Acts in consequence thereof: Part IV – An Act to establish the Canadian Payments Association," Entered into force on December 1, 1980, Last amended on April 2, 2021, Consolidated to May 2, 2022, s.39(1).

[443] Government of Canada (2022). "Canadian Payments Act, R.S.C., 1985, c. C-21," Adopted on November 26, 1980, as "An Act to revise the Bank Act, to amend the Quebec Savings Bank Act and the Bank of Canada Act, to establish the Canadian Payments Association and to amend other Acts in consequence thereof: Part IV – An Act to establish the Canadian Payments Association," Entered into force on December 1, 1980, Last amended on April 2, 2021, Consolidated to May 2, 2022, s.40(1)(a).

[444] Government of Canada (2022). "Canadian Payments Act, R.S.C., 1985, c. C-21," Adopted on November 26, 1980, as "An Act to revise the Bank Act, to amend the Quebec Savings Bank Act and the Bank of Canada Act, to establish the Canadian Payments Association and to amend other Acts in consequence thereof: Part IV – An Act to establish the Canadian Payments Association," Entered into force on December 1, 1980, Last amended on April 2, 2021, Consolidated to May 2, 2022, s.40(1)(b).

[445] Government of Canada (2022). "Canadian Payments Act, R.S.C., 1985, c. C-21," Adopted on November 26, 1980, as "An Act to revise the Bank Act, to amend the Quebec Savings Bank Act and the Bank of Canada Act, to establish the Canadian Payments Association and to amend other Acts in consequence thereof: Part IV – An Act to establish the Canadian Payments Association," Entered into force on December 1, 1980, Last amended on April 2, 2021, Consolidated to May 2, 2022, s.40(1)(c).

[446] Government of Canada (2022). "Canadian Payments Act, R.S.C., 1985, c. C-21," Adopted on November 26, 1980, as "An Act to revise the Bank Act, to amend the Quebec Savings Bank Act and the Bank of Canada Act, to establish the Canadian Payments Association and to amend other Acts in consequence thereof: Part IV – An Act to establish the Canadian Payments Association," Entered into force on December 1, 1980, Last amended on April 2, 2021, Consolidated to May 2, 2022, s.40(1)(d).

[447] Government of Canada (2022). "Canadian Payments Act, R.S.C., 1985, c. C-21," Adopted on November 26, 1980, as "An Act to revise the Bank Act, to amend the Quebec Savings Bank Act and the Bank of Canada Act, to establish the Canadian Payments Association and to amend other Acts in consequence thereof: Part IV – An Act to establish the Canadian Payments Association," Entered into force on December 1, 1980, Last amended on April 2, 2021, Consolidated to May 2, 2022, s.40(2).

[448] Government of Canada (2022). "Canadian Payments Act, R.S.C., 1985, c. C-21," Adopted on November 26, 1980, as "An Act to revise the Bank Act, to amend the Quebec Savings Bank Act and the Bank of Canada Act, to establish the Canadian Payments Association and to amend other Acts in consequence thereof: Part IV – An Act to establish the Canadian Payments Association," Entered into force on December 1, 1980, Last amended on April 2, 2021, Consolidated to May 2, 2022, s.40(3)(a).

[449] Government of Canada (2022). "Canadian Payments Act, R.S.C., 1985, c. C-21," Adopted on November 26, 1980, as "An Act to revise the Bank Act, to amend the Quebec Savings Bank Act and the Bank of Canada Act, to establish the Canadian Payments Association and to amend other Acts in consequence thereof: Part IV – An Act to establish the Canadian Payments Association," Entered into force on December 1, 1980, Last amended on April 2, 2021, Consolidated to May 2, 2022, s.40(3)(b).

[450] Government of Canada (2022). "Canadian Payments Act, R.S.C., 1985, c. C-21," Adopted on November 26, 1980, as "An Act to revise the Bank Act, to amend the Quebec Savings Bank Act and the Bank of Canada Act, to establish the Canadian Payments Association and to amend other Acts in consequence thereof: Part IV – An Act to establish the Canadian Payments Association," Entered into force on December 1, 1980, Last amended on April 2, 2021, Consolidated to May 2, 2022, s.40(3)(c).

[451] Government of Canada (2022). "Canadian Payments Act, R.S.C., 1985, c. C-21," Adopted on November 26, 1980, as "An Act to revise the Bank Act, to amend the Quebec Savings Bank Act and the Bank of Canada Act, to establish the Canadian Payments Association and to amend other Acts in

consequence thereof: Part IV – An Act to establish the Canadian Payments Association," Entered into force on December 1, 1980, Last amended on April 2, 2021, Consolidated to May 2, 2022, s.40(6).

[452] Government of Canada (2022). "Retail Payment Activities Act, S.C. 2021, c. 23, s. 177," Adopted on June 29, 2021, Entered into force on June 29, 2021, Consolidated to May 2, 2022, s.4.

[453] Government of Canada (2022). "Retail Payment Activities Act, S.C. 2021, c. 23, s. 177," Adopted on June 29, 2021, Entered into force on June 29, 2021, Consolidated to May 2, 2022, s.5.

[454] Government of Canada (2022). "Retail Payment Activities Act, S.C. 2021, c. 23, s. 177," Adopted on June 29, 2021, Entered into force on June 29, 2021, Consolidated to May 2, 2022, s.9(a)-(b).

[455] Wilson, J. (2006). "New Zealand Sovereignty: 1857, 1907, 1947, or 1987?" Published August 28, 2007. Accessed August 3 and 4, 2022. https://www.parliament.nz/en/pb/research-papers/document/00PLLawRP07041/new-zealand-sovereignty-1857-1907-1947-or-1987.

[456] Government of New Zealand (2023). "NZ History: Statute of Westminster enacted: 11 December 1931." Accessed April 9, 2023. https://nzhistory.govt.nz/statute-of-westminster-passed-confirming-nz-autonomy.

[457] Parliament of New Zealand (2016). "Our system of government." Published January 20, 2016. Accessed August 4, 2022. https://www.parliament.nz/en/visit-and-learn/how-parliament-works/our-system-of-government/.

[458] Greville, M. (2019). "UPDATE: Access to New Zealand Law." Accessed August 4 and 8, 2022. https://www.nyulawglobal.org/globalex/New_Zealand1.html.

[459] Government of New Zealand (2005). "Constitution Act 1986, Public Act 1986 No 114," Adopted on December 13, 1986, Entered into force on January 1, 1987, Last amended on May 16, 2005, s.15.

[460] Parliament of New Zealand (2016). "How a bill becomes law." Published 22 January 2016. Accessed August 5, 2022. https://www.parliament.nz/en/visit-and-learn/how-parliament-works/how-laws-are-made/how-a-bill-becomes-law/.

[461] Menguy, G. (2022). "The Legal System in New Zealand." Accessed August 8, 2022. https://gm-avocats.com/the-legal-system-in-new-zealand/.

[462] Government of New Zealand (2018). "Courts of New Zealand: The Statement of Principles – Principles observed by Judiciary and Ministry of Justice in the Administration of the Courts." Published November 29, 2018. Accessed August 8, 2022. https://www.courtsofnz.govt.nz/about-the-judiciary/the-statement-of-principles.

[463] Jenson, S., Etwell, J., and Findlay, B. (2021). "Banking Regulation in New Zealand: Overview." Accessed August 11, 2022. https://uk.practicallaw.thomsonreuters.com/w-007-8664?transitionType=Default&contextData=(sc.Default)&firstPage=true.

[464] Government of New Zealand (2022). "Non-bank Deposit Takers Act 2013, Public Act 2013 No 104," Adopted on December 3, 2013, Entered into force on May 1, 2014, Consolidated to July 1, 2022, s.11(1).

[465] Government of New Zealand (2022). "Financial Service Providers (Registration and Dispute Resolution) Act 2008, Public Act 2008 No 97," Adopted on September 28, 2008, Entered into force on September 28, 2008, Consolidated to July 1, 2022, ss.11(1)(a), 4 and 6.

[466] Government of New Zealand (2022). "Financial Service Providers (Registration and Dispute Resolution) Act 2008, Public Act 2008 No 97," Adopted on September 28, 2008, Entered into force on September 28, 2008, Consolidated to July 1, 2022, s.5(1)(c).

[467] Government of New Zealand (2022). "Reserve Bank of New Zealand Act 2021, Public Act 2021 No 31," Adopted on August 16, 2021, Entered into force on July 1, 2022, Consolidated to July 1, 2022, s.3(a).

[468] Government of New Zealand (2022). "Reserve Bank of New Zealand Act 2021, Public Act 2021 No 31," Adopted on August 16, 2021, Entered into force on July 1, 2022, Consolidated to July 1, 2022, s.3(b).

[469] Government of New Zealand (2022). "Reserve Bank of New Zealand Act 2021, Public Act 2021 No 31," Adopted on August 16, 2021, Entered into force on July 1, 2022, Consolidated to July 1, 2022, s.9(1)(a)(i).

[470] Government of New Zealand (2022). "Reserve Bank of New Zealand Act 2021, Public Act 2021 No 31," Adopted on August 16, 2021, Entered into force on July 1, 2022, Consolidated to July 1, 2022, s.9(1)(a)(ii).

[471] Government of New Zealand (2022). "Reserve Bank of New Zealand Act 2021, Public Act 2021 No 31," Adopted on August 16, 2021, Entered into force on July 1, 2022, Consolidated to July 1, 2022, s.9(1)(b).

[472] Government of New Zealand (2022). "Reserve Bank of New Zealand Act 2021, Public Act 2021 No 31," Adopted on August 16, 2021, Entered into force on July 1, 2022, Consolidated to July 1, 2022, s.9(1)(c).

[473] Government of New Zealand (2022). "Reserve Bank of New Zealand Act 2021, Public Act 2021 No 31," Adopted on August 16, 2021, Entered into force on July 1, 2022, Consolidated to July 1, 2022, s.9(3).

[474] Government of New Zealand (2022). "Reserve Bank of New Zealand Act 2021, Public Act 2021 No 31," Adopted on August 16, 2021, Entered into force on July 1, 2022, Consolidated to July 1, 2022, s.10(1)(a).

[475] Government of New Zealand (2022). "Reserve Bank of New Zealand Act 2021, Public Act 2021 No 31," Adopted on August 16, 2021, Entered into force on July 1, 2022, Consolidated to July 1, 2022, s.10(1)(b).

[476] Government of New Zealand (2022). "Reserve Bank of New Zealand Act 2021, Public Act 2021 No 31," Adopted on August 16, 2021, Entered into force on July 1, 2022, Consolidated to July 1, 2022, s.10(1)(c).

[477] Government of New Zealand (2022). "Reserve Bank of New Zealand Act 2021, Public Act 2021 No 31," Adopted on August 16, 2021, Entered into force on July 1, 2022, Consolidated to July 1, 2022, s.10(1)(d).

[478] Government of New Zealand (2022). "Reserve Bank of New Zealand Act 2021, Public Act 2021 No 31," Adopted on August 16, 2021, Entered into force on July 1, 2022, Consolidated to July 1, 2022, s.10(1)(e).

[479] Government of New Zealand (2022). "Reserve Bank of New Zealand Act 2021, Public Act 2021 No 31," Adopted on August 16, 2021, Entered into force on July 1, 2022, Consolidated to July 1, 2022, s.10(1)(f).

[480] Government of New Zealand (2022). "Reserve Bank of New Zealand Act 2021, Public Act 2021 No 31," Adopted on August 16, 2021, Entered into force on July 1, 2022, Consolidated to July 1, 2022, s.10(1)(g).

[481] Government of New Zealand (2022). "Reserve Bank of New Zealand Act 2021, Public Act 2021 No 31," Adopted on August 16, 2021, Entered into force on July 1, 2022, Consolidated to July 1, 2022, ss.10(1)(h) and 11(1).

[482] Government of New Zealand (2022). "Reserve Bank of New Zealand Act 2021, Public Act 2021 No 31," Adopted on August 16, 2021, Entered into force on July 1, 2022, Consolidated to July 1, 2022, s.10(1)(i).

[483] Government of New Zealand (2022). "Reserve Bank of New Zealand Act 2021, Public Act 2021 No 31," Adopted on August 16, 2021, Entered into force on July 1, 2022, Consolidated to July 1, 2022, s.10(1)(j).

[484] Government of New Zealand (2022). "Reserve Bank of New Zealand Act 2021, Public Act 2021 No 31," Adopted on August 16, 2021, Entered into force on July 1, 2022, Consolidated to July 1, 2022, s.10(2).

[485] Government of New Zealand (2022). "Reserve Bank of New Zealand Act 2021, Public Act 2021 No 31," Adopted on August 16, 2021, Entered into force on July 1, 2022, Consolidated to July 1, 2022, s.208(1)(a).

[486] Government of New Zealand (2022). "Reserve Bank of New Zealand Act 2021, Public Act 2021 No 31," Adopted on August 16, 2021, Entered into force on July 1, 2022, Consolidated to July 1, 2022, s.208(1)(b).

[487] Government of New Zealand (2022). "Reserve Bank of New Zealand Act 2021, Public Act 2021 No 31," Adopted on August 16, 2021, Entered into force on July 1, 2022, Consolidated to July 1, 2022, s.208(2)(a).

[488] Government of New Zealand (2022). "Reserve Bank of New Zealand Act 2021, Public Act 2021 No 31," Adopted on August 16, 2021, Entered into force on July 1, 2022, Consolidated to July 1, 2022, s.208(2)(b).

[489] Government of New Zealand (2022). "Reserve Bank of New Zealand Act 2021, Public Act 2021 No 31," Adopted on August 16, 2021, Entered into force on July 1, 2022, Consolidated to July 1, 2022, s.208(2)(c).

[490] Government of New Zealand (2022). "Reserve Bank of New Zealand Act 2021, Public Act 2021 No 31," Adopted on August 16, 2021, Entered into force on July 1, 2022, Consolidated to July 1, 2022, s.286.

[491] Government of New Zealand (2022). "Reserve Bank of New Zealand Act 2021, Public Act 2021 No 31," Adopted on August 16, 2021, Entered into force on July 1, 2022, Consolidated to July 1, 2022, s.287(1).

[492] Government of New Zealand (2022). "Reserve Bank of New Zealand Act 2021, Public Act 2021 No 31," Adopted on August 16, 2021, Entered into force on July 1, 2022, Consolidated to July 1, 2022, s.288(1).

[493] Government of New Zealand (2022). "Banking (Prudential Supervision) Act 1989, Public Act 1989 No 157," Adopted on December 20, 1989, as "Reserve Bank of New Zealand Act 1989," Entered into force on February 1, 1990, Last amended on July 1, 2022, Consolidated to July 1, 2022, s.1A(a).

[494] Government of New Zealand (2022). "Banking (Prudential Supervision) Act 1989, Public Act 1989 No 157," Adopted on December 20, 1989, as "Reserve Bank of New Zealand Act 1989," Entered into force on February 1, 1990, Last amended on July 1, 2022, Consolidated to July 1, 2022, s.1A(b).

[495] Government of New Zealand (2022). "Banking (Prudential Supervision) Act 1989, Public Act 1989 No 157," Adopted on December 20, 1989, as "Reserve Bank of New Zealand Act 1989," Entered into force on February 1, 1990, Last amended on July 1, 2022, Consolidated to July 1, 2022, s.64(1)(a).

[496] Government of New Zealand (2022). "Banking (Prudential Supervision) Act 1989, Public Act 1989 No 157," Adopted on December 20, 1989, as "Reserve Bank of New Zealand Act 1989," Entered into force on February 1, 1990, Last amended on July 1, 2022, Consolidated to July 1, 2022, s.64(1)(b).

[497] Government of New Zealand (2022). "Banking (Prudential Supervision) Act 1989, Public Act 1989 No 157," Adopted on December 20, 1989, as "Reserve Bank of New Zealand Act 1989," Entered into force on February 1, 1990, Last amended on July 1, 2022, Consolidated to July 1, 2022, s.64(1)(c).

[498] Government of New Zealand (2022). "Banking (Prudential Supervision) Act 1989, Public Act 1989 No 157," Adopted on December 20, 1989, as "Reserve Bank of New Zealand Act 1989," Entered into force on February 1, 1990, Last amended on July 1, 2022, Consolidated to July 1, 2022, s.64(2)(a).

[499] Government of New Zealand (2022). "Banking (Prudential Supervision) Act 1989, Public Act 1989 No 157," Adopted on December 20, 1989, as "Reserve Bank of New Zealand Act 1989," Entered into force on February 1, 1990, Last amended on July 1, 2022, Consolidated to July 1, 2022, s.64(2)(b).

[500] Government of New Zealand (2022). "Banking (Prudential Supervision) Act 1989, Public Act 1989 No 157," Adopted on December 20, 1989, as "Reserve Bank of New Zealand Act 1989," Entered into force on February 1, 1990, Last amended on July 1, 2022, Consolidated to July 1, 2022, s.64(2)(c).

[501] Government of New Zealand (2022). "Banking (Prudential Supervision) Act 1989, Public Act 1989 No 157," Adopted on December 20, 1989, as "Reserve Bank of New Zealand Act 1989," Entered into force on February 1, 1990, Last amended on July 1, 2022, Consolidated to July 1, 2022, s.64(2)(d).

[502] Government of New Zealand (2022). "Banking (Prudential Supervision) Act 1989, Public Act 1989 No 157," Adopted on December 20, 1989, as "Reserve Bank of New Zealand Act 1989," Entered into force on February 1, 1990, Last amended on July 1, 2022, Consolidated to July 1, 2022, ss.64(5) and 66M(2)(a).

[503] Government of New Zealand (2022). "Banking (Prudential Supervision) Act 1989, Public Act 1989 No 157," Adopted on December 20, 1989, as "Reserve Bank of New Zealand Act 1989," Entered into force on February 1, 1990, Last amended on July 1, 2022, Consolidated to July 1, 2022, ss.64(6) and 66M(1)(a).

[504] Government of New Zealand (2022). "Banking (Prudential Supervision) Act 1989, Public Act 1989 No 157," Adopted on December 20, 1989, as "Reserve Bank of New Zealand Act 1989," Entered into force on February 1, 1990, Last amended on July 1, 2022, Consolidated to July 1, 2022, ss.64(6) and 66M(1)(b).

[505] Government of New Zealand (2022). "Banking (Prudential Supervision) Act 1989, Public Act 1989 No 157," Adopted on December 20, 1989, as "Reserve Bank of New Zealand Act 1989," Entered into force on February 1, 1990, Last amended on July 1, 2022, Consolidated to July 1, 2022, s.67(a).

[506] Government of New Zealand (2022). "Banking (Prudential Supervision) Act 1989, Public Act 1989 No 157," Adopted on December 20, 1989, as "Reserve Bank of New Zealand Act 1989," Entered into force on February 1, 1990, Last amended on July 1, 2022, Consolidated to July 1, 2022, s.69(1).

[507] Government of New Zealand (2022). "Banking (Prudential Supervision) Act 1989, Public Act 1989 No 157," Adopted on December 20, 1989, as "Reserve Bank of New Zealand Act 1989," Entered into force on February 1, 1990, Last amended on July 1, 2022, Consolidated to July 1, 2022, s.69(2A).

[508] Government of New Zealand (2022). "Banking (Prudential Supervision) Act 1989, Public Act 1989 No 157," Adopted on December 20, 1989, as "Reserve Bank of New Zealand Act 1989," Entered into force on February 1, 1990, Last amended on July 1, 2022, Consolidated to July 1, 2022, s.69(3).

[509] Government of New Zealand (2022). "Banking (Prudential Supervision) Act 1989, Public Act 1989 No 157," Adopted on December 20, 1989, as "Reserve Bank of New Zealand Act 1989," Entered into force on February 1, 1990, Last amended on July 1, 2022, Consolidated to July 1, 2022, s.70(1).

[510] Government of New Zealand (2022). "Banking (Prudential Supervision) Act 1989, Public Act 1989 No 157," Adopted on December 20, 1989, as "Reserve Bank of New Zealand Act 1989," Entered into force on February 1, 1990, Last amended on July 1, 2022, Consolidated to July 1, 2022, s.70(2)(a).

[511] Government of New Zealand (2022). "Banking (Prudential Supervision) Act 1989, Public Act 1989 No 157," Adopted on December 20, 1989, as "Reserve Bank of New Zealand Act 1989," Entered into force on February 1, 1990, Last amended on July 1, 2022, Consolidated to July 1, 2022, s.70(2)(b).

[512] Government of New Zealand (2022). "Banking (Prudential Supervision) Act 1989, Public Act 1989 No 157," Adopted on December 20, 1989, as "Reserve Bank of New Zealand Act 1989," Entered into force on February 1, 1990, Last amended on July 1, 2022, Consolidated to July 1, 2022, s.70(3).

[513] Government of New Zealand (2022). "Banking (Prudential Supervision) Act 1989, Public Act 1989 No 157," Adopted on December 20, 1989, as "Reserve Bank of New Zealand Act 1989," Entered into force on February 1, 1990, Last amended on July 1, 2022, Consolidated to July 1, 2022, ss.70(4) and 156AC(2)(a).

[514] Government of New Zealand (2022). "Banking (Prudential Supervision) Act 1989, Public Act 1989 No 157," Adopted on December 20, 1989, as "Reserve Bank of New Zealand Act 1989," Entered into force on February 1, 1990, Last amended on July 1, 2022, Consolidated to July 1, 2022, ss.70(5) and 156AC(1)(a).

[515] Government of New Zealand (2022). "Banking (Prudential Supervision) Act 1989, Public Act 1989 No 157," Adopted on December 20, 1989, as "Reserve Bank of New Zealand Act 1989," Entered into force on February 1, 1990, Last amended on July 1, 2022, Consolidated to July 1, 2022, s.70(5) and 156AC(1)(b).

[516] Government of New Zealand (2022). "Banking (Prudential Supervision) Act 1989, Public Act 1989 No 157," Adopted on December 20, 1989, as "Reserve Bank of New Zealand Act 1989," Entered into force on February 1, 1990, Last amended on July 1, 2022, Consolidated to July 1, 2022, ss.72, 156AC(1) and 156AC(2)(b).

[517] Government of New Zealand (2022). "Banking (Prudential Supervision) Act 1989, Public Act 1989 No 157," Adopted on December 20, 1989, as "Reserve Bank of New Zealand Act 1989," Entered into force on February 1, 1990, Last amended on July 1, 2022, Consolidated to July 1, 2022, s.73(1).

[518] Government of New Zealand (2022). "Banking (Prudential Supervision) Act 1989, Public Act 1989 No 157," Adopted on December 20, 1989, as "Reserve Bank of New Zealand Act 1989," Entered into force on February 1, 1990, Last amended on July 1, 2022, Consolidated to July 1, 2022, s.73(2)(a).

[519] Government of New Zealand (2022). "Banking (Prudential Supervision) Act 1989, Public Act 1989 No 157," Adopted on December 20, 1989, as "Reserve Bank of New Zealand Act 1989," Entered into force on February 1, 1990, Last amended on July 1, 2022, Consolidated to July 1, 2022, s.73(2)(b).

[520] Government of New Zealand (2022). "Banking (Prudential Supervision) Act 1989, Public Act 1989 No 157," Adopted on December 20, 1989, as "Reserve Bank of New Zealand Act 1989," Entered into force on February 1, 1990, Last amended on July 1, 2022, Consolidated to July 1, 2022, s.73(2)(c).
[521] Government of New Zealand (2022). "Banking (Prudential Supervision) Act 1989, Public Act 1989 No 157," Adopted on December 20, 1989, as "Reserve Bank of New Zealand Act 1989," Entered into force on February 1, 1990, Last amended on July 1, 2022, Consolidated to July 1, 2022, s.73(2)(d).
[522] Government of New Zealand (2022). "Banking (Prudential Supervision) Act 1989, Public Act 1989 No 157," Adopted on December 20, 1989, as "Reserve Bank of New Zealand Act 1989," Entered into force on February 1, 1990, Last amended on July 1, 2022, Consolidated to July 1, 2022, s.73(2)(e).
[523] Government of New Zealand (2022). "Banking (Prudential Supervision) Act 1989, Public Act 1989 No 157," Adopted on December 20, 1989, as "Reserve Bank of New Zealand Act 1989," Entered into force on February 1, 1990, Last amended on July 1, 2022, Consolidated to July 1, 2022, s.73(2)(f).
[524] Government of New Zealand (2022). "Banking (Prudential Supervision) Act 1989, Public Act 1989 No 157," Adopted on December 20, 1989, as "Reserve Bank of New Zealand Act 1989," Entered into force on February 1, 1990, Last amended on July 1, 2022, Consolidated to July 1, 2022, s.73(2)(g).
[525] Government of New Zealand (2022). "Banking (Prudential Supervision) Act 1989, Public Act 1989 No 157," Adopted on December 20, 1989, as "Reserve Bank of New Zealand Act 1989," Entered into force on February 1, 1990, Last amended on July 1, 2022, Consolidated to July 1, 2022, s.73A(b).
[526] Government of New Zealand (2022). "Banking (Prudential Supervision) Act 1989, Public Act 1989 No 157," Adopted on December 20, 1989, as "Reserve Bank of New Zealand Act 1989," Entered into force on February 1, 1990, Last amended on July 1, 2022, Consolidated to July 1, 2022, s.73A(a).
[527] Government of New Zealand (2022). "Banking (Prudential Supervision) Act 1989, Public Act 1989 No 157," Adopted on December 20, 1989, as "Reserve Bank of New Zealand Act 1989," Entered into force on February 1, 1990, Last amended on July 1, 2022, Consolidated to July 1, 2022, s.73B.
[528] Government of New Zealand (2022). "Banking (Prudential Supervision) Act 1989, Public Act 1989 No 157," Adopted on December 20, 1989, as "Reserve Bank of New Zealand Act 1989," Entered into force on February 1, 1990, Last amended on July 1, 2022, Consolidated to July 1, 2022, s.74(1).
[529] Government of New Zealand (2022). "Banking (Prudential Supervision) Act 1989, Public Act 1989 No 157," Adopted on December 20, 1989, as "Reserve Bank of New Zealand Act 1989," Entered into force on February 1, 1990, Last amended on July 1, 2022, Consolidated to July 1, 2022, s.74(2)(a).
[530] Government of New Zealand (2022). "Banking (Prudential Supervision) Act 1989, Public Act 1989 No 157," Adopted on December 20, 1989, as "Reserve Bank of New Zealand Act 1989," Entered into force on February 1, 1990, Last amended on July 1, 2022, Consolidated to July 1, 2022, s.74(2)(b).
[531] Government of New Zealand (2022). "Banking (Prudential Supervision) Act 1989, Public Act 1989 No 157," Adopted on December 20, 1989, as "Reserve Bank of New Zealand Act 1989," Entered into force on February 1, 1990, Last amended on July 1, 2022, Consolidated to July 1, 2022, ss.74(5) and 156AB(2)(a).
[532] Government of New Zealand (2022). "Banking (Prudential Supervision) Act 1989, Public Act 1989 No 157," Adopted on December 20, 1989, as "Reserve Bank of New Zealand Act 1989," Entered into force on February 1, 1990, Last amended on July 1, 2022, Consolidated to July 1, 2022, ss.74(6) and 156AB(1)(a).
[533] Government of New Zealand (2022). "Banking (Prudential Supervision) Act 1989, Public Act 1989 No 157," Adopted on December 20, 1989, as "Reserve Bank of New Zealand Act 1989," Entered into force on February 1, 1990, Last amended on July 1, 2022, Consolidated to July 1, 2022, ss.74(6) and 156AB(1)(b).
[534] Government of New Zealand (2022). "Banking (Prudential Supervision) Act 1989, Public Act 1989 No 157," Adopted on December 20, 1989, as "Reserve Bank of New Zealand Act 1989," Entered into force on February 1, 1990, Last amended on July 1, 2022, Consolidated to July 1, 2022, s.77(1).
[535] Government of New Zealand (2022). "Banking (Prudential Supervision) Act 1989, Public Act 1989 No 157," Adopted on December 20, 1989, as "Reserve Bank of New Zealand Act 1989," Entered into force on February 1, 1990, Last amended on July 1, 2022, Consolidated to July 1, 2022, s.67(b).

[536] Government of New Zealand (2022). "Banking (Prudential Supervision) Act 1989, Public Act 1989 No 157," Adopted on December 20, 1989, as "Reserve Bank of New Zealand Act 1989," Entered into force on February 1, 1990, Last amended on July 1, 2022, Consolidated to July 1, 2022, s.113(1)(a).
[537] Government of New Zealand (2022). "Banking (Prudential Supervision) Act 1989, Public Act 1989 No 157," Adopted on December 20, 1989, as "Reserve Bank of New Zealand Act 1989," Entered into force on February 1, 1990, Last amended on July 1, 2022, Consolidated to July 1, 2022, s.113(1)(b).
[538] Government of New Zealand (2022). "Banking (Prudential Supervision) Act 1989, Public Act 1989 No 157," Adopted on December 20, 1989, as "Reserve Bank of New Zealand Act 1989," Entered into force on February 1, 1990, Last amended on July 1, 2022, Consolidated to July 1, 2022, s.113(1)(c).
[539] Government of New Zealand (2022). "Banking (Prudential Supervision) Act 1989, Public Act 1989 No 157," Adopted on December 20, 1989, as "Reserve Bank of New Zealand Act 1989," Entered into force on February 1, 1990, Last amended on July 1, 2022, Consolidated to July 1, 2022, s.113(1)(d).
[540] Government of New Zealand (2022). "Banking (Prudential Supervision) Act 1989, Public Act 1989 No 157," Adopted on December 20, 1989, as "Reserve Bank of New Zealand Act 1989," Entered into force on February 1, 1990, Last amended on July 1, 2022, Consolidated to July 1, 2022, s.113(1)(e).
[541] Government of New Zealand (2022). "Banking (Prudential Supervision) Act 1989, Public Act 1989 No 157," Adopted on December 20, 1989, as "Reserve Bank of New Zealand Act 1989," Entered into force on February 1, 1990, Last amended on July 1, 2022, Consolidated to July 1, 2022, s.113(1)(f).
[542] Government of New Zealand (2022). "Banking (Prudential Supervision) Act 1989, Public Act 1989 No 157," Adopted on December 20, 1989, as "Reserve Bank of New Zealand Act 1989," Entered into force on February 1, 1990, Last amended on July 1, 2022, Consolidated to July 1, 2022, s.113(1)(g).
[543] Government of New Zealand (2022). "Banking (Prudential Supervision) Act 1989, Public Act 1989 No 157," Adopted on December 20, 1989, as "Reserve Bank of New Zealand Act 1989," Entered into force on February 1, 1990, Last amended on July 1, 2022, Consolidated to July 1, 2022, s.113(1)(h).
[544] Government of New Zealand (2022). "Banking (Prudential Supervision) Act 1989, Public Act 1989 No 157," Adopted on December 20, 1989, as "Reserve Bank of New Zealand Act 1989," Entered into force on February 1, 1990, Last amended on July 1, 2022, Consolidated to July 1, 2022, s.113(3).
[545] Government of New Zealand (2022). "Banking (Prudential Supervision) Act 1989, Public Act 1989 No 157," Adopted on December 20, 1989, as "Reserve Bank of New Zealand Act 1989," Entered into force on February 1, 1990, Last amended on July 1, 2022, Consolidated to July 1, 2022, s.113(4).
[546] Government of New Zealand (2022). "Banking (Prudential Supervision) Act 1989, Public Act 1989 No 157," Adopted on December 20, 1989, as "Reserve Bank of New Zealand Act 1989," Entered into force on February 1, 1990, Last amended on July 1, 2022, Consolidated to July 1, 2022, s.113A(a).
[547] Government of New Zealand (2022). "Banking (Prudential Supervision) Act 1989, Public Act 1989 No 157," Adopted on December 20, 1989, as "Reserve Bank of New Zealand Act 1989," Entered into force on February 1, 1990, Last amended on July 1, 2022, Consolidated to July 1, 2022, s.113A(b).
[548] Government of New Zealand (2022). "Banking (Prudential Supervision) Act 1989, Public Act 1989 No 157," Adopted on December 20, 1989, as "Reserve Bank of New Zealand Act 1989," Entered into force on February 1, 1990, Last amended on July 1, 2022, Consolidated to July 1, 2022, s.113A(c).
[549] Government of New Zealand (2022). "Banking (Prudential Supervision) Act 1989, Public Act 1989 No 157," Adopted on December 20, 1989, as "Reserve Bank of New Zealand Act 1989," Entered into force on February 1, 1990, Last amended on July 1, 2022, Consolidated to July 1, 2022, s.113A(d).
[550] Government of New Zealand (2022). "Banking (Prudential Supervision) Act 1989, Public Act 1989 No 157," Adopted on December 20, 1989, as "Reserve Bank of New Zealand Act 1989," Entered into force on February 1, 1990, Last amended on July 1, 2022, Consolidated to July 1, 2022, s.113A(e).
[551] Government of New Zealand (2022). "Banking (Prudential Supervision) Act 1989, Public Act 1989 No 157," Adopted on December 20, 1989, as "Reserve Bank of New Zealand Act 1989," Entered into force on February 1, 1990, Last amended on July 1, 2022, Consolidated to July 1, 2022, s.113A(f).
[552] Government of New Zealand (2022). "Banking (Prudential Supervision) Act 1989, Public Act 1989 No 157," Adopted on December 20, 1989, as "Reserve Bank of New Zealand Act 1989," Entered into force on February 1, 1990, Last amended on July 1, 2022, Consolidated to July 1, 2022, s.113A(g).

[553] Government of New Zealand (2022). "Banking (Prudential Supervision) Act 1989, Public Act 1989 No 157," Adopted on December 20, 1989, as "Reserve Bank of New Zealand Act 1989," Entered into force on February 1, 1990, Last amended on July 1, 2022, Consolidated to July 1, 2022, s.113A(h).

[554] Government of New Zealand (2022). "Banking (Prudential Supervision) Act 1989, Public Act 1989 No 157," Adopted on December 20, 1989, as "Reserve Bank of New Zealand Act 1989," Entered into force on February 1, 1990, Last amended on July 1, 2022, Consolidated to July 1, 2022, s.113A(i).

[555] Government of New Zealand (2022). "Banking (Prudential Supervision) Act 1989, Public Act 1989 No 157," Adopted on December 20, 1989, as "Reserve Bank of New Zealand Act 1989," Entered into force on February 1, 1990, Last amended on July 1, 2022, Consolidated to July 1, 2022, ss.114(1) and 156AC(2)(o).

[556] Government of New Zealand (2022). "Banking (Prudential Supervision) Act 1989, Public Act 1989 No 157," Adopted on December 20, 1989, as "Reserve Bank of New Zealand Act 1989," Entered into force on February 1, 1990, Last amended on July 1, 2022, Consolidated to July 1, 2022, ss.114(2) and 156AC(2)(p).

[557] Government of New Zealand (2022). "Banking (Prudential Supervision) Act 1989, Public Act 1989 No 157," Adopted on December 20, 1989, as "Reserve Bank of New Zealand Act 1989," Entered into force on February 1, 1990, Last amended on July 1, 2022, Consolidated to July 1, 2022, ss.114(3) and 156AC(1)(a).

[558] Government of New Zealand (2022). "Banking (Prudential Supervision) Act 1989, Public Act 1989 No 157," Adopted on December 20, 1989, as "Reserve Bank of New Zealand Act 1989," Entered into force on February 1, 1990, Last amended on July 1, 2022, Consolidated to July 1, 2022, ss.114(3) and 156AC(1)(b).

[559] Government of New Zealand (2022). "Banking (Prudential Supervision) Act 1989, Public Act 1989 No 157," Adopted on December 20, 1989, as "Reserve Bank of New Zealand Act 1989," Entered into force on February 1, 1990, Last amended on July 1, 2022, Consolidated to July 1, 2022, s.117(1)(a).

[560] Government of New Zealand (2022). "Banking (Prudential Supervision) Act 1989, Public Act 1989 No 157," Adopted on December 20, 1989, as "Reserve Bank of New Zealand Act 1989," Entered into force on February 1, 1990, Last amended on July 1, 2022, Consolidated to July 1, 2022, s.117(1)(b).

[561] Government of New Zealand (2022). "Banking (Prudential Supervision) Act 1989, Public Act 1989 No 157," Adopted on December 20, 1989, as "Reserve Bank of New Zealand Act 1989," Entered into force on February 1, 1990, Last amended on July 1, 2022, Consolidated to July 1, 2022, s.117(2).

[562] Government of New Zealand (2022). "Banking (Prudential Supervision) Act 1989, Public Act 1989 No 157," Adopted on December 20, 1989, as "Reserve Bank of New Zealand Act 1989," Entered into force on February 1, 1990, Last amended on July 1, 2022, Consolidated to July 1, 2022, s.117(4).

[563] Government of New Zealand (2022). "Banking (Prudential Supervision) Act 1989, Public Act 1989 No 157," Adopted on December 20, 1989, as "Reserve Bank of New Zealand Act 1989," Entered into force on February 1, 1990, Last amended on July 1, 2022, Consolidated to July 1, 2022, s.117(5).

[564] Government of New Zealand (2022). "Banking (Prudential Supervision) Act 1989, Public Act 1989 No 157," Adopted on December 20, 1989, as "Reserve Bank of New Zealand Act 1989," Entered into force on February 1, 1990, Last amended on July 1, 2022, Consolidated to July 1, 2022, s.118(1)(a).

[565] Government of New Zealand (2022). "Banking (Prudential Supervision) Act 1989, Public Act 1989 No 157," Adopted on December 20, 1989, as "Reserve Bank of New Zealand Act 1989," Entered into force on February 1, 1990, Last amended on July 1, 2022, Consolidated to July 1, 2022, s.118(1)(b).

[566] Government of New Zealand (2022). "Banking (Prudential Supervision) Act 1989, Public Act 1989 No 157," Adopted on December 20, 1989, as "Reserve Bank of New Zealand Act 1989," Entered into force on February 1, 1990, Last amended on July 1, 2022, Consolidated to July 1, 2022, s.118(2).

[567] Government of New Zealand (2022). "Banking (Prudential Supervision) Act 1989, Public Act 1989 No 157," Adopted on December 20, 1989, as "Reserve Bank of New Zealand Act 1989," Entered into force on February 1, 1990, Last amended on July 1, 2022, Consolidated to July 1, 2022, s.120.

[568] Government of New Zealand (2022). "Banking (Prudential Supervision) Act 1989, Public Act 1989 No 157," Adopted on December 20, 1989, as "Reserve Bank of New Zealand Act 1989," Entered into force on February 1, 1990, Last amended on July 1, 2022, Consolidated to July 1, 2022, s.121(1)(a).

[569] Government of New Zealand (2022). "Banking (Prudential Supervision) Act 1989, Public Act 1989 No 157," Adopted on December 20, 1989, as "Reserve Bank of New Zealand Act 1989," Entered into force on February 1, 1990, Last amended on July 1, 2022, Consolidated to July 1, 2022, s.121(1)(b).
[570] Government of New Zealand (2022). "Banking (Prudential Supervision) Act 1989, Public Act 1989 No 157," Adopted on December 20, 1989, as "Reserve Bank of New Zealand Act 1989," Entered into force on February 1, 1990, Last amended on July 1, 2022, Consolidated to July 1, 2022, s.121(1)(c).
[571] Government of New Zealand (2022). "Banking (Prudential Supervision) Act 1989, Public Act 1989 No 157," Adopted on December 20, 1989, as "Reserve Bank of New Zealand Act 1989," Entered into force on February 1, 1990, Last amended on July 1, 2022, Consolidated to July 1, 2022, s.121(1)(d).
[572] Government of New Zealand (2022). "Banking (Prudential Supervision) Act 1989, Public Act 1989 No 157," Adopted on December 20, 1989, as "Reserve Bank of New Zealand Act 1989," Entered into force on February 1, 1990, Last amended on July 1, 2022, Consolidated to July 1, 2022, s.121(1)(e).
[573] Government of New Zealand (2022). "Banking (Prudential Supervision) Act 1989, Public Act 1989 No 157," Adopted on December 20, 1989, as "Reserve Bank of New Zealand Act 1989," Entered into force on February 1, 1990, Last amended on July 1, 2022, Consolidated to July 1, 2022, s.121A(1).
[574] Government of New Zealand (2022). "Banking (Prudential Supervision) Act 1989, Public Act 1989 No 157," Adopted on December 20, 1989, as "Reserve Bank of New Zealand Act 1989," Entered into force on February 1, 1990, Last amended on July 1, 2022, Consolidated to July 1, 2022, s.122(1)(a).
[575] Government of New Zealand (2022). "Banking (Prudential Supervision) Act 1989, Public Act 1989 No 157," Adopted on December 20, 1989, as "Reserve Bank of New Zealand Act 1989," Entered into force on February 1, 1990, Last amended on July 1, 2022, Consolidated to July 1, 2022, s.122(1)(b).
[576] Government of New Zealand (2022). "Banking (Prudential Supervision) Act 1989, Public Act 1989 No 157," Adopted on December 20, 1989, as "Reserve Bank of New Zealand Act 1989," Entered into force on February 1, 1990, Last amended on July 1, 2022, Consolidated to July 1, 2022, s.122(1)(c).
[577] Government of New Zealand (2022). "Banking (Prudential Supervision) Act 1989, Public Act 1989 No 157," Adopted on December 20, 1989, as "Reserve Bank of New Zealand Act 1989," Entered into force on February 1, 1990, Last amended on July 1, 2022, Consolidated to July 1, 2022, s.122(1)(d).
[578] Government of New Zealand (2022). "Banking (Prudential Supervision) Act 1989, Public Act 1989 No 157," Adopted on December 20, 1989, as "Reserve Bank of New Zealand Act 1989," Entered into force on February 1, 1990, Last amended on July 1, 2022, Consolidated to July 1, 2022, s.122(1)(e).
[579] Government of New Zealand (2022). "Banking (Prudential Supervision) Act 1989, Public Act 1989 No 157," Adopted on December 20, 1989, as "Reserve Bank of New Zealand Act 1989," Entered into force on February 1, 1990, Last amended on July 1, 2022, Consolidated to July 1, 2022, s.122(1)(f).
[580] Government of New Zealand (2022). "Banking (Prudential Supervision) Act 1989, Public Act 1989 No 157," Adopted on December 20, 1989, as "Reserve Bank of New Zealand Act 1989," Entered into force on February 1, 1990, Last amended on July 1, 2022, Consolidated to July 1, 2022, s.122(1)(g).
[581] Government of New Zealand (2022). "Banking (Prudential Supervision) Act 1989, Public Act 1989 No 157," Adopted on December 20, 1989, as "Reserve Bank of New Zealand Act 1989," Entered into force on February 1, 1990, Last amended on July 1, 2022, Consolidated to July 1, 2022, s.122(1)(h).
[582] Government of New Zealand (2022). "Banking (Prudential Supervision) Act 1989, Public Act 1989 No 157," Adopted on December 20, 1989, as "Reserve Bank of New Zealand Act 1989," Entered into force on February 1, 1990, Last amended on July 1, 2022, Consolidated to July 1, 2022, s.123(1)(a).
[583] Government of New Zealand (2022). "Banking (Prudential Supervision) Act 1989, Public Act 1989 No 157," Adopted on December 20, 1989, as "Reserve Bank of New Zealand Act 1989," Entered into force on February 1, 1990, Last amended on July 1, 2022, Consolidated to July 1, 2022, s.123(1)(b).
[584] Government of New Zealand (2022). "Banking (Prudential Supervision) Act 1989, Public Act 1989 No 157," Adopted on December 20, 1989, as "Reserve Bank of New Zealand Act 1989," Entered into force on February 1, 1990, Last amended on July 1, 2022, Consolidated to July 1, 2022, s.123(1)(c).
[585] Government of New Zealand (2022). "Banking (Prudential Supervision) Act 1989, Public Act 1989 No 157," Adopted on December 20, 1989, as "Reserve Bank of New Zealand Act 1989," Entered into force on February 1, 1990, Last amended on July 1, 2022, Consolidated to July 1, 2022, s.126(1).

[586] Government of New Zealand (2022). "Banking (Prudential Supervision) Act 1989, Public Act 1989 No 157," Adopted on December 20, 1989, as "Reserve Bank of New Zealand Act 1989," Entered into force on February 1, 1990, Last amended on July 1, 2022, Consolidated to July 1, 2022, s.127(1)(a).
[587] Government of New Zealand (2022). "Banking (Prudential Supervision) Act 1989, Public Act 1989 No 157," Adopted on December 20, 1989, as "Reserve Bank of New Zealand Act 1989," Entered into force on February 1, 1990, Last amended on July 1, 2022, Consolidated to July 1, 2022, s.127(1)(b).
[588] Government of New Zealand (2022). "Banking (Prudential Supervision) Act 1989, Public Act 1989 No 157," Adopted on December 20, 1989, as "Reserve Bank of New Zealand Act 1989," Entered into force on February 1, 1990, Last amended on July 1, 2022, Consolidated to July 1, 2022, s.127(2).
[589] Government of New Zealand (2022). "Banking (Prudential Supervision) Act 1989, Public Act 1989 No 157," Adopted on December 20, 1989, as "Reserve Bank of New Zealand Act 1989," Entered into force on February 1, 1990, Last amended on July 1, 2022, Consolidated to July 1, 2022, s.128(1).
[590] Government of New Zealand (2022). "Banking (Prudential Supervision) Act 1989, Public Act 1989 No 157," Adopted on December 20, 1989, as "Reserve Bank of New Zealand Act 1989," Entered into force on February 1, 1990, Last amended on July 1, 2022, Consolidated to July 1, 2022, s.129(1).
[591] Government of New Zealand (2022). "Banking (Prudential Supervision) Act 1989, Public Act 1989 No 157," Adopted on December 20, 1989, as "Reserve Bank of New Zealand Act 1989," Entered into force on February 1, 1990, Last amended on July 1, 2022, Consolidated to July 1, 2022, s.129(2)(a).
[592] Government of New Zealand (2022). "Banking (Prudential Supervision) Act 1989, Public Act 1989 No 157," Adopted on December 20, 1989, as "Reserve Bank of New Zealand Act 1989," Entered into force on February 1, 1990, Last amended on July 1, 2022, Consolidated to July 1, 2022, s.129(2)(b).
[593] Government of New Zealand (2022). "Banking (Prudential Supervision) Act 1989, Public Act 1989 No 157," Adopted on December 20, 1989, as "Reserve Bank of New Zealand Act 1989," Entered into force on February 1, 1990, Last amended on July 1, 2022, Consolidated to July 1, 2022, s.129(2)(c).
[594] Government of New Zealand (2022). "Banking (Prudential Supervision) Act 1989, Public Act 1989 No 157," Adopted on December 20, 1989, as "Reserve Bank of New Zealand Act 1989," Entered into force on February 1, 1990, Last amended on July 1, 2022, Consolidated to July 1, 2022, s.130.
[595] Government of New Zealand (2022). "Banking (Prudential Supervision) Act 1989, Public Act 1989 No 157," Adopted on December 20, 1989, as "Reserve Bank of New Zealand Act 1989," Entered into force on February 1, 1990, Last amended on July 1, 2022, Consolidated to July 1, 2022, s.131(a).
[596] Government of New Zealand (2022). "Banking (Prudential Supervision) Act 1989, Public Act 1989 No 157," Adopted on December 20, 1989, as "Reserve Bank of New Zealand Act 1989," Entered into force on February 1, 1990, Last amended on July 1, 2022, Consolidated to July 1, 2022, s.131(b).
[597] Government of New Zealand (2022). "Banking (Prudential Supervision) Act 1989, Public Act 1989 No 157," Adopted on December 20, 1989, as "Reserve Bank of New Zealand Act 1989," Entered into force on February 1, 1990, Last amended on July 1, 2022, Consolidated to July 1, 2022, s.131(c).
[598] Government of New Zealand (2022). "Banking (Prudential Supervision) Act 1989, Public Act 1989 No 157," Adopted on December 20, 1989, as "Reserve Bank of New Zealand Act 1989," Entered into force on February 1, 1990, Last amended on July 1, 2022, Consolidated to July 1, 2022, s.132(1).
[599] Government of New Zealand (2022). "Banking (Prudential Supervision) Act 1989, Public Act 1989 No 157," Adopted on December 20, 1989, as "Reserve Bank of New Zealand Act 1989," Entered into force on February 1, 1990, Last amended on July 1, 2022, Consolidated to July 1, 2022, s.134(1).
[600] Government of New Zealand (2022). "Banking (Prudential Supervision) Act 1989, Public Act 1989 No 157," Adopted on December 20, 1989, as "Reserve Bank of New Zealand Act 1989," Entered into force on February 1, 1990, Last amended on July 1, 2022, Consolidated to July 1, 2022, s.137(1)(a).
[601] Government of New Zealand (2022). "Banking (Prudential Supervision) Act 1989, Public Act 1989 No 157," Adopted on December 20, 1989, as "Reserve Bank of New Zealand Act 1989," Entered into force on February 1, 1990, Last amended on July 1, 2022, Consolidated to July 1, 2022, s. 137(1)(b).
[602] Government of New Zealand (2022). "Banking (Prudential Supervision) Act 1989, Public Act 1989 No 157," Adopted on December 20, 1989, as "Reserve Bank of New Zealand Act 1989," Entered into force on February 1, 1990, Last amended on July 1, 2022, Consolidated to July 1, 2022, s. 137(1)(c).

[603] Government of New Zealand (2022). "Banking (Prudential Supervision) Act 1989, Public Act 1989 No 157," Adopted on December 20, 1989, as "Reserve Bank of New Zealand Act 1989," Entered into force on February 1, 1990, Last amended on July 1, 2022, Consolidated to July 1, 2022, s.136(1)(a).

[604] Government of New Zealand (2022). "Banking (Prudential Supervision) Act 1989, Public Act 1989 No 157," Adopted on December 20, 1989, as "Reserve Bank of New Zealand Act 1989," Entered into force on February 1, 1990, Last amended on July 1, 2022, Consolidated to July 1, 2022, s.136(1)(b).

[605] Government of New Zealand (2022). "Banking (Prudential Supervision) Act 1989, Public Act 1989 No 157," Adopted on December 20, 1989, as "Reserve Bank of New Zealand Act 1989," Entered into force on February 1, 1990, Last amended on July 1, 2022, Consolidated to July 1, 2022, s.136(1)(c).

[606] Government of New Zealand (2022). "Banking (Prudential Supervision) Act 1989, Public Act 1989 No 157," Adopted on December 20, 1989, as "Reserve Bank of New Zealand Act 1989," Entered into force on February 1, 1990, Last amended on July 1, 2022, Consolidated to July 1, 2022, s.144(1).

[607] Government of New Zealand (2022). "Banking (Prudential Supervision) Act 1989, Public Act 1989 No 157," Adopted on December 20, 1989, as "Reserve Bank of New Zealand Act 1989," Entered into force on February 1, 1990, Last amended on July 1, 2022, Consolidated to July 1, 2022, s.144(2).

[608] Government of New Zealand (2022). "Banking (Prudential Supervision) Act 1989, Public Act 1989 No 157," Adopted on December 20, 1989, as "Reserve Bank of New Zealand Act 1989," Entered into force on February 1, 1990, Last amended on July 1, 2022, Consolidated to July 1, 2022, s.145(1).

[609] Government of New Zealand (2022). "Banking (Prudential Supervision) Act 1989, Public Act 1989 No 157," Adopted on December 20, 1989, as "Reserve Bank of New Zealand Act 1989," Entered into force on February 1, 1990, Last amended on July 1, 2022, Consolidated to July 1, 2022, s.145(2).

[610] Government of New Zealand (2022). "Banking (Prudential Supervision) Act 1989, Public Act 1989 No 157," Adopted on December 20, 1989, as "Reserve Bank of New Zealand Act 1989," Entered into force on February 1, 1990, Last amended on July 1, 2022, Consolidated to July 1, 2022, s.148(1).

[611] Government of New Zealand (2022). "Banking (Prudential Supervision) Act 1989, Public Act 1989 No 157," Adopted on December 20, 1989, as "Reserve Bank of New Zealand Act 1989," Entered into force on February 1, 1990, Last amended on July 1, 2022, Consolidated to July 1, 2022, s.154(1).

[612] Government of New Zealand (2022). "Banking (Prudential Supervision) Act 1989, Public Act 1989 No 157," Adopted on December 20, 1989, as "Reserve Bank of New Zealand Act 1989," Entered into force on February 1, 1990, Last amended on July 1, 2022, Consolidated to July 1, 2022, s.154(1A).

[613] Government of New Zealand (2022). "Banking (Prudential Supervision) Act 1989, Public Act 1989 No 157," Adopted on December 20, 1989, as "Reserve Bank of New Zealand Act 1989," Entered into force on February 1, 1990, Last amended on July 1, 2022, Consolidated to July 1, 2022, s.155(1).

[614] Government of New Zealand (2022). "Banking (Prudential Supervision) Act 1989, Public Act 1989 No 157," Adopted on December 20, 1989, as "Reserve Bank of New Zealand Act 1989," Entered into force on February 1, 1990, Last amended on July 1, 2022, Consolidated to July 1, 2022, s.156(1).

[615] Government of New Zealand (2022). "Banking (Prudential Supervision) Act 1989, Public Act 1989 No 157," Adopted on December 20, 1989, as "Reserve Bank of New Zealand Act 1989," Entered into force on February 1, 1990, Last amended on July 1, 2022, Consolidated to July 1, 2022, s.156(2).

[616] Government of New Zealand (2022). "Banking (Prudential Supervision) Act 1989, Public Act 1989 No 157," Adopted on December 20, 1989, as "Reserve Bank of New Zealand Act 1989," Entered into force on February 1, 1990, Last amended on July 1, 2022, Consolidated to July 1, 2022, s.156K(1).

[617] Government of New Zealand (2022). "Banking (Prudential Supervision) Act 1989, Public Act 1989 No 157," Adopted on December 20, 1989, as "Reserve Bank of New Zealand Act 1989," Entered into force on February 1, 1990, Last amended on July 1, 2022, Consolidated to July 1, 2022, s.156K(2).

[618] Government of New Zealand (2022). "Banking (Prudential Supervision) Act 1989, Public Act 1989 No 157," Adopted on December 20, 1989, as "Reserve Bank of New Zealand Act 1989," Entered into force on February 1, 1990, Last amended on July 1, 2022, Consolidated to July 1, 2022, s.156K(3).

[619] Government of New Zealand (2022). "Banking (Prudential Supervision) Act 1989, Public Act 1989 No 157," Adopted on December 20, 1989, as "Reserve Bank of New Zealand Act 1989," Entered into force on February 1, 1990, Last amended on July 1, 2022, Consolidated to July 1, 2022, s.156N(1).

[620] Government of New Zealand (2022). "Banking (Prudential Supervision) Act 1989, Public Act 1989 No 157," Adopted on December 20, 1989, as "Reserve Bank of New Zealand Act 1989," Entered into force on February 1, 1990, Last amended on July 1, 2022, Consolidated to July 1, 2022, s.156N(2).
[621] Government of New Zealand (2022). "Banking (Prudential Supervision) Act 1989, Public Act 1989 No 157," Adopted on December 20, 1989, as "Reserve Bank of New Zealand Act 1989," Entered into force on February 1, 1990, Last amended on July 1, 2022, Consolidated to July 1, 2022, s.156R(1).
[622] Government of New Zealand (2022). "Banking (Prudential Supervision) Act 1989, Public Act 1989 No 157," Adopted on December 20, 1989, as "Reserve Bank of New Zealand Act 1989," Entered into force on February 1, 1990, Last amended on July 1, 2022, Consolidated to July 1, 2022, s.156T.
[623] Government of New Zealand (2022). "Banking (Prudential Supervision) Act 1989, Public Act 1989 No 157," Adopted on December 20, 1989, as "Reserve Bank of New Zealand Act 1989," Entered into force on February 1, 1990, Last amended on July 1, 2022, Consolidated to July 1, 2022, s.156Y(1).
[624] Government of New Zealand (2022). "Banking (Prudential Supervision) Act 1989, Public Act 1989 No 157," Adopted on December 20, 1989, as "Reserve Bank of New Zealand Act 1989," Entered into force on February 1, 1990, Last amended on July 1, 2022, Consolidated to July 1, 2022, s.156Y(2).
[625] Government of New Zealand (2022). "Banking (Prudential Supervision) Act 1989, Public Act 1989 No 157," Adopted on December 20, 1989, as "Reserve Bank of New Zealand Act 1989," Entered into force on February 1, 1990, Last amended on July 1, 2022, Consolidated to July 1, 2022, s.156Y(3)(a).
[626] Government of New Zealand (2022). "Banking (Prudential Supervision) Act 1989, Public Act 1989 No 157," Adopted on December 20, 1989, as "Reserve Bank of New Zealand Act 1989," Entered into force on February 1, 1990, Last amended on July 1, 2022, Consolidated to July 1, 2022, s.156Y(3)(b).
[627] Government of New Zealand (2022). "Banking (Prudential Supervision) Act 1989, Public Act 1989 No 157," Adopted on December 20, 1989, as "Reserve Bank of New Zealand Act 1989," Entered into force on February 1, 1990, Last amended on July 1, 2022, Consolidated to July 1, 2022, s.156Y(3)(d).
[628] Government of New Zealand (2022). "Banking (Prudential Supervision) Act 1989, Public Act 1989 No 157," Adopted on December 20, 1989, as "Reserve Bank of New Zealand Act 1989," Entered into force on February 1, 1990, Last amended on July 1, 2022, Consolidated to July 1, 2022, s.156Y(3)(c).
[629] Government of New Zealand (2022). "Banking (Prudential Supervision) Act 1989, Public Act 1989 No 157," Adopted on December 20, 1989, as "Reserve Bank of New Zealand Act 1989," Entered into force on February 1, 1990, Last amended on July 1, 2022, Consolidated to July 1, 2022, s.156Z(1).
[630] Government of New Zealand (2022). "Banking (Prudential Supervision) Act 1989, Public Act 1989 No 157," Adopted on December 20, 1989, as "Reserve Bank of New Zealand Act 1989," Entered into force on February 1, 1990, Last amended on July 1, 2022, Consolidated to July 1, 2022, s.156Z(3).
[631] Government of New Zealand (2022). "Banking (Prudential Supervision) Act 1989, Public Act 1989 No 157," Adopted on December 20, 1989, as "Reserve Bank of New Zealand Act 1989," Entered into force on February 1, 1990, Last amended on July 1, 2022, Consolidated to July 1, 2022, s.156ZA(1)(a).
[632] Government of New Zealand (2022). "Banking (Prudential Supervision) Act 1989, Public Act 1989 No 157," Adopted on December 20, 1989, as "Reserve Bank of New Zealand Act 1989," Entered into force on February 1, 1990, Last amended on July 1, 2022, Consolidated to July 1, 2022, s.156ZA(1)(b).
[633] Government of New Zealand (2022). "Banking (Prudential Supervision) Act 1989, Public Act 1989 No 157," Adopted on December 20, 1989, as "Reserve Bank of New Zealand Act 1989," Entered into force on February 1, 1990, Last amended on July 1, 2022, Consolidated to July 1, 2022, s.156ZA(2)(a).
[634] Government of New Zealand (2022). "Banking (Prudential Supervision) Act 1989, Public Act 1989 No 157," Adopted on December 20, 1989, as "Reserve Bank of New Zealand Act 1989," Entered into force on February 1, 1990, Last amended on July 1, 2022, Consolidated to July 1, 2022, s.156ZA(2)(b).
[635] Government of New Zealand (2022). "Non-bank Deposit Takers Act 2013, Public Act 2013 No 104," Adopted on December 3, 2013, Entered into force on May 1, 2014, Consolidated to July 1, 2022, s.3(a).
[636] Government of New Zealand (2022). "Non-bank Deposit Takers Act 2013, Public Act 2013 No 104," Adopted on December 3, 2013, Entered into force on May 1, 2014, Consolidated to July 1, 2022, s.3(b).
[637] Government of New Zealand (2022). "Non-bank Deposit Takers Act 2013, Public Act 2013 No 104," Adopted on December 3, 2013, Entered into force on May 1, 2014, Consolidated to July 1, 2022, s.5(1)(a).

[638] Government of New Zealand (2022). "Non-bank Deposit Takers Act 2013, Public Act 2013 No 104," Adopted on December 3, 2013, Entered into force on May 1, 2014, Consolidated to July 1, 2022, s.5(1)(b).

[639] Government of New Zealand (2022). "Non-bank Deposit Takers Act 2013, Public Act 2013 No 104," Adopted on December 3, 2013, Entered into force on May 1, 2014, Consolidated to July 1, 2022, s.5(1)(c).

[640] Government of New Zealand (2022). "Non-bank Deposit Takers Act 2013, Public Act 2013 No 104," Adopted on December 3, 2013, Entered into force on May 1, 2014, Consolidated to July 1, 2022, s.5(1)(d).

[641] Government of New Zealand (2022). "Non-bank Deposit Takers Act 2013, Public Act 2013 No 104," Adopted on December 3, 2013, Entered into force on May 1, 2014, Consolidated to July 1, 2022, s.5(2)(a).

[642] Government of New Zealand (2022). "Non-bank Deposit Takers Act 2013, Public Act 2013 No 104," Adopted on December 3, 2013, Entered into force on May 1, 2014, Consolidated to July 1, 2022, s.5(2)(b).

[643] Government of New Zealand (2022). "Non-bank Deposit Takers Act 2013, Public Act 2013 No 104," Adopted on December 3, 2013, Entered into force on May 1, 2014, Consolidated to July 1, 2022, s.5(2)(c).

[644] Government of New Zealand (2022). "Non-bank Deposit Takers Act 2013, Public Act 2013 No 104," Adopted on December 3, 2013, Entered into force on May 1, 2014, Consolidated to July 1, 2022, s.5(2)(d).

[645] Government of New Zealand (2022). "Non-bank Deposit Takers Act 2013, Public Act 2013 No 104," Adopted on December 3, 2013, Entered into force on May 1, 2014, Consolidated to July 1, 2022, s.5(2)(e).

[646] Government of New Zealand (2022). "Non-bank Deposit Takers Act 2013, Public Act 2013 No 104," Adopted on December 3, 2013, Entered into force on May 1, 2014, Consolidated to July 1, 2022, s.5(2)(f).

[647] Government of New Zealand (2022). "Non-bank Deposit Takers Act 2013, Public Act 2013 No 104," Adopted on December 3, 2013, Entered into force on May 1, 2014, Consolidated to July 1, 2022, s.6(1)(a)-(c).

[648] Government of New Zealand (2022). "Non-bank Deposit Takers Act 2013, Public Act 2013 No 104," Adopted on December 3, 2013, Entered into force on May 1, 2014, Consolidated to July 1, 2022, s.6(1)(d).

[649] Government of New Zealand (2022). "Non-bank Deposit Takers Act 2013, Public Act 2013 No 104," Adopted on December 3, 2013, Entered into force on May 1, 2014, Consolidated to July 1, 2022, s.6(1)(e).

[650] Government of New Zealand (2022). "Non-bank Deposit Takers Act 2013, Public Act 2013 No 104," Adopted on December 3, 2013, Entered into force on May 1, 2014, Consolidated to July 1, 2022, s.6(1)(h).

[651] Government of New Zealand (2022). "Non-bank Deposit Takers Act 2013, Public Act 2013 No 104," Adopted on December 3, 2013, Entered into force on May 1, 2014, Consolidated to July 1, 2022, s.6(1)(f).

[652] Government of New Zealand (2022). "Non-bank Deposit Takers Act 2013, Public Act 2013 No 104," Adopted on December 3, 2013, Entered into force on May 1, 2014, Consolidated to July 1, 2022, s.6(1)(g).

[653] Government of New Zealand (2022). "Non-bank Deposit Takers Act 2013, Public Act 2013 No 104," Adopted on December 3, 2013, Entered into force on May 1, 2014, Consolidated to July 1, 2022, s.7.

[654] Government of New Zealand (2022). "Non-bank Deposit Takers Act 2013, Public Act 2013 No 104," Adopted on December 3, 2013, Entered into force on May 1, 2014, Consolidated to July 1, 2022, s.11(1).

[655] Government of New Zealand (2022). "Non-bank Deposit Takers Act 2013, Public Act 2013 No 104," Adopted on December 3, 2013, Entered into force on May 1, 2014, Consolidated to July 1, 2022, s.13(1).

[656] Government of New Zealand (2022). "Non-bank Deposit Takers Act 2013, Public Act 2013 No 104," Adopted on December 3, 2013, Entered into force on May 1, 2014, Consolidated to July 1, 2022, s.13(2)(a).
[657] Government of New Zealand (2022). "Non-bank Deposit Takers Act 2013, Public Act 2013 No 104," Adopted on December 3, 2013, Entered into force on May 1, 2014, Consolidated to July 1, 2022, s.13(2)(b).
[658] Government of New Zealand (2022). "Non-bank Deposit Takers Act 2013, Public Act 2013 No 104," Adopted on December 3, 2013, Entered into force on May 1, 2014, Consolidated to July 1, 2022, s.13(2)(c).
[659] Government of New Zealand (2022). "Non-bank Deposit Takers Act 2013, Public Act 2013 No 104," Adopted on December 3, 2013, Entered into force on May 1, 2014, Consolidated to July 1, 2022, 14(1)(a).
[660] Government of New Zealand (2022). "Non-bank Deposit Takers Act 2013, Public Act 2013 No 104," Adopted on December 3, 2013, Entered into force on May 1, 2014, Consolidated to July 1, 2022, 14(1)(b).
[661] Government of New Zealand (2022). "Non-bank Deposit Takers Act 2013, Public Act 2013 No 104," Adopted on December 3, 2013, Entered into force on May 1, 2014, Consolidated to July 1, 2022, 14(2)(a).
[662] Government of New Zealand (2022). "Non-bank Deposit Takers Act 2013, Public Act 2013 No 104," Adopted on December 3, 2013, Entered into force on May 1, 2014, Consolidated to July 1, 2022, 14(2)(b).
[663] Government of New Zealand (2022). "Non-bank Deposit Takers Act 2013, Public Act 2013 No 104," Adopted on December 3, 2013, Entered into force on May 1, 2014, Consolidated to July 1, 2022, 14(2)(c).
[664] Government of New Zealand (2022). "Non-bank Deposit Takers Act 2013, Public Act 2013 No 104," Adopted on December 3, 2013, Entered into force on May 1, 2014, Consolidated to July 1, 2022, 14(2)(d).
[665] Government of New Zealand (2022). "Non-bank Deposit Takers Act 2013, Public Act 2013 No 104," Adopted on December 3, 2013, Entered into force on May 1, 2014, Consolidated to July 1, 2022, 14(2)(e).
[666] Government of New Zealand (2022). "Non-bank Deposit Takers Act 2013, Public Act 2013 No 104," Adopted on December 3, 2013, Entered into force on May 1, 2014, Consolidated to July 1, 2022, s.17(1).
[667] Government of New Zealand (2022). "Non-bank Deposit Takers Act 2013, Public Act 2013 No 104," Adopted on December 3, 2013, Entered into force on May 1, 2014, Consolidated to July 1, 2022, s.17(2).
[668] Government of New Zealand (2022). "Non-bank Deposit Takers Act 2013, Public Act 2013 No 104," Adopted on December 3, 2013, Entered into force on May 1, 2014, Consolidated to July 1, 2022, s.18(2).
[669] Government of New Zealand (2022). "Non-bank Deposit Takers Act 2013, Public Act 2013 No 104," Adopted on December 3, 2013, Entered into force on May 1, 2014, Consolidated to July 1, 2022, s.18(3).
[670] Government of New Zealand (2022). "Non-bank Deposit Takers Act 2013, Public Act 2013 No 104," Adopted on December 3, 2013, Entered into force on May 1, 2014, Consolidated to July 1, 2022, s.21(a).
[671] Government of New Zealand (2022). "Non-bank Deposit Takers Act 2013, Public Act 2013 No 104," Adopted on December 3, 2013, Entered into force on May 1, 2014, Consolidated to July 1, 2022, s.21(b).
[672] Government of New Zealand (2022). "Non-bank Deposit Takers Act 2013, Public Act 2013 No 104," Adopted on December 3, 2013, Entered into force on May 1, 2014, Consolidated to July 1, 2022, s.21(c).

[673] Government of New Zealand (2022). "Non-bank Deposit Takers Act 2013, Public Act 2013 No 104," Adopted on December 3, 2013, Entered into force on May 1, 2014, Consolidated to July 1, 2022, s.21(d).

[674] Government of New Zealand (2022). "Non-bank Deposit Takers Act 2013, Public Act 2013 No 104," Adopted on December 3, 2013, Entered into force on May 1, 2014, Consolidated to July 1, 2022, s.21(e).

[675] Government of New Zealand (2022). "Non-bank Deposit Takers Act 2013, Public Act 2013 No 104," Adopted on December 3, 2013, Entered into force on May 1, 2014, Consolidated to July 1, 2022, s.21(f).

[676] Government of New Zealand (2022). "Non-bank Deposit Takers Act 2013, Public Act 2013 No 104," Adopted on December 3, 2013, Entered into force on May 1, 2014, Consolidated to July 1, 2022, s.21(g).

[677] Government of New Zealand (2022). "Non-bank Deposit Takers Act 2013, Public Act 2013 No 104," Adopted on December 3, 2013, Entered into force on May 1, 2014, Consolidated to July 1, 2022, s.21(h).

[678] Government of New Zealand (2022). "Non-bank Deposit Takers Act 2013, Public Act 2013 No 104," Adopted on December 3, 2013, Entered into force on May 1, 2014, Consolidated to July 1, 2022, s.21(i).

[679] Government of New Zealand (2022). "Non-bank Deposit Takers Act 2013, Public Act 2013 No 104," Adopted on December 3, 2013, Entered into force on May 1, 2014, Consolidated to July 1, 2022, s.23(1).

[680] Government of New Zealand (2022). "Non-bank Deposit Takers Act 2013, Public Act 2013 No 104," Adopted on December 3, 2013, Entered into force on May 1, 2014, Consolidated to July 1, 2022, s.27(1).

[681] Government of New Zealand (2022). "Non-bank Deposit Takers Act 2013, Public Act 2013 No 104," Adopted on December 3, 2013, Entered into force on May 1, 2014, Consolidated to July 1, 2022, s.30(1).

[682] Government of New Zealand (2022). "Non-bank Deposit Takers Act 2013, Public Act 2013 No 104," Adopted on December 3, 2013, Entered into force on May 1, 2014, Consolidated to July 1, 2022, s.30(2).

[683] Government of New Zealand (2022). "Non-bank Deposit Takers Act 2013, Public Act 2013 No 104," Adopted on December 3, 2013, Entered into force on May 1, 2014, Consolidated to July 1, 2022, s.32(1).

[684] Government of New Zealand (2022). "Non-bank Deposit Takers Act 2013, Public Act 2013 No 104," Adopted on December 3, 2013, Entered into force on May 1, 2014, Consolidated to July 1, 2022, s.33(1).

[685] Government of New Zealand (2022). "Non-bank Deposit Takers Act 2013, Public Act 2013 No 104," Adopted on December 3, 2013, Entered into force on May 1, 2014, Consolidated to July 1, 2022, s.35(1).

[686] Government of New Zealand (2022). "Non-bank Deposit Takers Act 2013, Public Act 2013 No 104," Adopted on December 3, 2013, Entered into force on May 1, 2014, Consolidated to July 1, 2022, s.36(1).

[687] Government of New Zealand (2022). "Non-bank Deposit Takers Act 2013, Public Act 2013 No 104," Adopted on December 3, 2013, Entered into force on May 1, 2014, Consolidated to July 1, 2022, s.38(1).

[688] Government of New Zealand (2022). "Non-bank Deposit Takers Act 2013, Public Act 2013 No 104," Adopted on December 3, 2013, Entered into force on May 1, 2014, Consolidated to July 1, 2022, s.39(1).

[689] Government of New Zealand (2022). "Non-bank Deposit Takers Act 2013, Public Act 2013 No 104," Adopted on December 3, 2013, Entered into force on May 1, 2014, Consolidated to July 1, 2022, s.40(1).

[690] Government of New Zealand (2022). "Non-bank Deposit Takers Act 2013, Public Act 2013 No 104," Adopted on December 3, 2013, Entered into force on May 1, 2014, Consolidated to July 1, 2022, s.47(1).
[691] Government of New Zealand (2022). "Non-bank Deposit Takers Act 2013, Public Act 2013 No 104," Adopted on December 3, 2013, Entered into force on May 1, 2014, Consolidated to July 1, 2022, s.49(1).
[692] Government of New Zealand (2022). "Non-bank Deposit Takers Act 2013, Public Act 2013 No 104," Adopted on December 3, 2013, Entered into force on May 1, 2014, Consolidated to July 1, 2022, s.56(1)(a).
[693] Government of New Zealand (2022). "Non-bank Deposit Takers Act 2013, Public Act 2013 No 104," Adopted on December 3, 2013, Entered into force on May 1, 2014, Consolidated to July 1, 2022, s.56(1)(b).
[694] Government of New Zealand (2022). "Non-bank Deposit Takers Act 2013, Public Act 2013 No 104," Adopted on December 3, 2013, Entered into force on May 1, 2014, Consolidated to July 1, 2022, s.56(1)(c).
[695] Government of New Zealand (2022). "Non-bank Deposit Takers Act 2013, Public Act 2013 No 104," Adopted on December 3, 2013, Entered into force on May 1, 2014, Consolidated to July 1, 2022, ss.56(2)(a) and 56(3)(a).
[696] Government of New Zealand (2022). "Non-bank Deposit Takers Act 2013, Public Act 2013 No 104," Adopted on December 3, 2013, Entered into force on May 1, 2014, Consolidated to July 1, 2022, ss.56(2)(b) and 56(3)(b).
[697] Government of New Zealand (2022). "Non-bank Deposit Takers Act 2013, Public Act 2013 No 104," Adopted on December 3, 2013, Entered into force on May 1, 2014, Consolidated to July 1, 2022, ss.56(2)(c) and 56(3)(c).
[698] Government of New Zealand (2022). "Non-bank Deposit Takers Act 2013, Public Act 2013 No 104," Adopted on December 3, 2013, Entered into force on May 1, 2014, Consolidated to July 1, 2022, ss.56(2)(d) and 56(3)(d).
[699] Government of New Zealand (2022). "Non-bank Deposit Takers Act 2013, Public Act 2013 No 104," Adopted on December 3, 2013, Entered into force on May 1, 2014, Consolidated to July 1, 2022, ss.56(2)(e) and 56(3)(e).
[700] Government of New Zealand (2022). "Non-bank Deposit Takers Act 2013, Public Act 2013 No 104," Adopted on December 3, 2013, Entered into force on May 1, 2014, Consolidated to July 1, 2022, ss.56(2)(f) and 56(3)(f).
[701] Government of New Zealand (2022). "Non-bank Deposit Takers Act 2013, Public Act 2013 No 104," Adopted on December 3, 2013, Entered into force on May 1, 2014, Consolidated to July 1, 2022, ss.56(2)(g) and 56(3)(g).
[702] Government of New Zealand (2022). "Non-bank Deposit Takers Act 2013, Public Act 2013 No 104," Adopted on December 3, 2013, Entered into force on May 1, 2014, Consolidated to July 1, 2022, s.59(1).
[703] Government of New Zealand (2022). "Non-bank Deposit Takers Act 2013, Public Act 2013 No 104," Adopted on December 3, 2013, Entered into force on May 1, 2014, Consolidated to July 1, 2022, s.59(2).
[704] Government of New Zealand (2022). "Non-bank Deposit Takers Act 2013, Public Act 2013 No 104," Adopted on December 3, 2013, Entered into force on May 1, 2014, Consolidated to July 1, 2022, s.65(a).
[705] Government of New Zealand (2022). "Non-bank Deposit Takers Act 2013, Public Act 2013 No 104," Adopted on December 3, 2013, Entered into force on May 1, 2014, Consolidated to July 1, 2022, s.65(b).
[706] Government of New Zealand (2022). "Non-bank Deposit Takers Act 2013, Public Act 2013 No 104," Adopted on December 3, 2013, Entered into force on May 1, 2014, Consolidated to July 1, 2022, s.68(1)(a).

[707] Government of New Zealand (2022). "Non-bank Deposit Takers Act 2013, Public Act 2013 No 104," Adopted on December 3, 2013, Entered into force on May 1, 2014, Consolidated to July 1, 2022, s.68(1)(b).

[708] Government of New Zealand (2022). "Non-bank Deposit Takers Act 2013, Public Act 2013 No 104," Adopted on December 3, 2013, Entered into force on May 1, 2014, Consolidated to July 1, 2022, s.68(2).

[709] Government of New Zealand (2022). "Non-bank Deposit Takers Act 2013, Public Act 2013 No 104," Adopted on December 3, 2013, Entered into force on May 1, 2014, Consolidated to July 1, 2022, s.70(1).

[710] Government of New Zealand (2022). "Non-bank Deposit Takers Act 2013, Public Act 2013 No 104," Adopted on December 3, 2013, Entered into force on May 1, 2014, Consolidated to July 1, 2022, s.70(3).

[711] Government of the United States of America (2022). "Constitution of the United States." Accessed October 28, 2022. https://www.senate.gov/civics/constitution_item/constitution.htm.

[712] Government of the United States of America (1992). Constitution of the United States of America, as amended (Washington, D.C.: Government of the United States of America), Article I, s.1.

[713] Government of the United States of America (1992). Constitution of the United States of America, as amended, Article II, s.1.

[714] Government of the United States of America (1992). Constitution of the United States of America, as amended, Article III, s.1.

[715] Washington University in St. Louis (2014). "School of Law: Major Differences between the Mexican and U.S. Legal Systems." Published July 15, 2014. Accessed October 29, 2022. https://onlinelaw.wustl.edu/blog/major-differences-mexican-u-s-legal-systems/.

[716] Cornell University (2022). "Cornell Law School: Legal Information Institute – U.S. Constitution: Article 1." Accessed October 29, 2022. https://www.law.cornell.edu/constitution/articlei.

[717] Government of the United States of America (1992). Constitution of the United States of America, as amended, Article I, ss.2-3 and 7-8.

[718] Government of the United States of America (1992). Constitution of the United States of America, as amended, Article II, ss.1-3.

[719] Government of the United States of America (1992). Constitution of the United States of America, as amended, Article III.

[720] Government of the United States of America (1992). Constitution of the United States of America, as amended, Article VI.

[721] Henegan, T., and Kimball, B. (2022). "Legal systems in the United States: overview." Published October 1, 2022. Accessed November 1 and 2, 2022. https://uk.practicallaw.thomsonreuters.com/w-019-5918?transitionType=Default&contextData=(sc.Default)&firstPage=true.

[722] Government of the United. States of America (2022). The U.S. Legal System: A Short Description (Washington, D.C.: Federal Judicial Center), 1.

[723] Government of the United States of America (2022). "United States Department of Justice: Offices of the United States Attorneys – Justice 101: Introduction to the Federal Court System." Accessed November 2 and 3, 2022. https://www.justice.gov/usao/justice-101/federal-courts.

[724] Government of the United. States of America (2022). The U.S. Legal System: A Short Description, 2.

[725] Lustgarten, I. (2017). "Banking regulation in the United States: overview." Published March 30, 2017. Accessed November 7 and 29, 2022. https://content.next.westlaw.com/practical-law/document/Ib519c5822a5911e798dc8b09b4f043e0/Banking-regulation-in-the-United-States-overview?viewType=FullText&transitionType=Default&contextData=(sc.Default)&firstPage=true.

[726] Government of the United States of America (1864). "An Act to provide a National Currency, secured by a Pledge of United States Bonds, and to provide for the Circulation and Redemption thereof (National Bank Act 1864)," Adopted on June 3, 1864, s.1.

[727] Government of the United States of America (1864). "An Act to provide a National Currency, secured by a Pledge of United States Bonds, and to provide for the Circulation and Redemption thereof (National Bank Act 1864)," Adopted on June 3, 1864, s.5.

[728] Government of the United States of America (1864). "An Act to provide a National Currency, secured by a Pledge of United States Bonds, and to provide for the Circulation and Redemption thereof (National Bank Act 1864)," Adopted on June 3, 1864, s.17.
[729] Government of the United States of America (2022). "Office of the Comptroller of the Currency: What We Do." Accessed November 8, 2022. https://www.occ.treas.gov/about/what-we-do/index-what-we-do.html.
[730] Government of the United States of America (2021). "Federal Deposit Insurance Corporation: Laws & Regulations – Important Banking Laws." Last updated September 14, 2021. Accessed November 8 and 9, 2022. https://www.fdic.gov/resources/regulations/important-banking-laws/index.html.
[731] Martins, I. (2022). "Guide to U.S. Banking Laws." Updated May 31, 2022. Accessed November 8, 2022. https://www.investopedia.com/important-u-s-banking-laws-5217476.
[732] Government of the United States of America (1913). "An Act To provide for the establishment of Federal reserve banks, to furnish an elastic currency, to afford means of rediscounting commercial paper, to establish a more effective supervision of banking in the United States and for other purposes (Federal Reserve Act 1913)," Adopted on December 23, 1913, s.2.
[733] Government of the United States of America (1913). "An Act To provide for the establishment of Federal reserve banks, to furnish an elastic currency, to afford means of rediscounting commercial paper, to establish a more effective supervision of banking in the United States and for other purposes (Federal Reserve Act 1913)," Adopted on December 23, 1913, s.9.
[734] Government of the United States of America (1913). "An Act To provide for the establishment of Federal reserve banks, to furnish an elastic currency, to afford means of rediscounting commercial paper, to establish a more effective supervision of banking in the United States and for other purposes (Federal Reserve Act 1913)," Adopted on December 23, 1913, s.10.
[735] Government of the United States of America (1913). "An Act To provide for the establishment of Federal reserve banks, to furnish an elastic currency, to afford means of rediscounting commercial paper, to establish a more effective supervision of banking in the United States and for other purposes (Federal Reserve Act 1913)," Adopted on December 23, 1913, s.11.
[736] Government of the United States of America (1913). "An Act To provide for the establishment of Federal reserve banks, to furnish an elastic currency, to afford means of rediscounting commercial paper, to establish a more effective supervision of banking in the United States and for other purposes (Federal Reserve Act 1913)," Adopted on December 23, 1913, s.13.
[737] Government of the United States of America (1913). "An Act To provide for the establishment of Federal reserve banks, to furnish an elastic currency, to afford means of rediscounting commercial paper, to establish a more effective supervision of banking in the United States and for other purposes (Federal Reserve Act 1913)," Adopted on December 23, 1913, s.14.
[738] Government of the United States of America (1913). "An Act To provide for the establishment of Federal reserve banks, to furnish an elastic currency, to afford means of rediscounting commercial paper, to establish a more effective supervision of banking in the United States and for other purposes (Federal Reserve Act 1913)," Adopted on December 23, 1913, s.15.
[739] Government of the United States of America (1913). "An Act To provide for the establishment of Federal reserve banks, to furnish an elastic currency, to afford means of rediscounting commercial paper, to establish a more effective supervision of banking in the United States and for other purposes (Federal Reserve Act 1913)," Adopted on December 23, 1913, s.16.
[740] Government of the United States of America (1913). "An Act To provide for the establishment of Federal reserve banks, to furnish an elastic currency, to afford means of rediscounting commercial paper, to establish a more effective supervision of banking in the United States and for other purposes (Federal Reserve Act 1913)," Adopted on December 23, 1913, s.19.
[741] Government of the United States of America (1913). "An Act To provide for the establishment of Federal reserve banks, to furnish an elastic currency, to afford means of rediscounting commercial paper, to establish a more effective supervision of banking in the United States and for other purposes (Federal Reserve Act 1913)," Adopted on December 23, 1913, s.21.

[742] Government of the United States of America (2022). "Board of Governors of the Federal Reserve System: About the Fed." Accessed November 9, 2022. https://www.federalreserve.gov/aboutthefed.htm.

[743] Government of the United States of America (2022). "Federal Deposit Insurance Corporation: About." Accessed November 9, 2022. https://www.fdic.gov/about/.

[744] Government of the United States of America (2021). "Federal Deposit Insurance Act 1950," Adopted on September 21, 1950, Updated to August 31, 2021, s.1(a).

[745] Government of the United States of America (2021). "Federal Deposit Insurance Act 1950," Adopted on September 21, 1950, Updated to August 31, 2021, s.4(a)(1).

[746] Government of the United States of America (2021). "Federal Deposit Insurance Act 1950," Adopted on September 21, 1950, Updated to August 31, 2021, s.5(a)(1).

[747] Government of the United States of America (2021). "Federal Deposit Insurance Act 1950," Adopted on September 21, 1950, Updated to August 31, 2021, ss.5(a)(4) and 6.

[748] Government of the United States of America (2021). "Federal Deposit Insurance Act 1950," Adopted on September 21, 1950, Updated to August 31, 2021, s.5(b).

[749] Government of the United States of America (2021). "Federal Deposit Insurance Act 1950," Adopted on September 21, 1950, Updated to August 31, 2021, s.7(a)(1).

[750] Government of the United States of America (2021). "Federal Deposit Insurance Act 1950," Adopted on September 21, 1950, Updated to August 31, 2021, s.7(a)(2)(B).

[751] Government of the United States of America (2021). "Federal Deposit Insurance Act 1950," Adopted on September 21, 1950, Updated to August 31, 2021, s.7(a)(9).

[752] Government of the United States of America (2021). "Federal Deposit Insurance Act 1950," Adopted on September 21, 1950, Updated to August 31, 2021, s.7(b)(1)(A).

[753] Government of the United States of America (2021). "Federal Deposit Insurance Act 1950," Adopted on September 21, 1950, Updated to August 31, 2021, s.7(b)(2)(A).

[754] Government of the United States of America (2021). "Federal Deposit Insurance Act 1950," Adopted on September 21, 1950, Updated to August 31, 2021, s.7(b)(2)(B).

[755] Government of the United States of America (2021). "Federal Deposit Insurance Act 1950," Adopted on September 21, 1950, Updated to August 31, 2021, s.7(b)(3)(A)(i).

[756] Government of the United States of America (2021). "Federal Deposit Insurance Act 1950," Adopted on September 21, 1950, Updated to August 31, 2021, s.7(b)(3)(B).

[757] Government of the United States of America (2021). "Federal Deposit Insurance Act 1950," Adopted on September 21, 1950, Updated to August 31, 2021, s.7(b)(3)(C).

[758] Government of the United States of America (2021). "Federal Deposit Insurance Act 1950," Adopted on September 21, 1950, Updated to August 31, 2021, s.7(e)(2)(A).

[759] Government of the United States of America (2021). "Federal Deposit Insurance Act 1950," Adopted on September 21, 1950, Updated to August 31, 2021, s.10(d)(1).

[760] Government of the United States of America (2021). "Federal Deposit Insurance Act 1950," Adopted on September 21, 1950, Updated to August 31, 2021, s.11(a)(1)(E).

[761] Government of the United States of America (2021). "Federal Deposit Insurance Act 1950," Adopted on September 21, 1950, Updated to August 31, 2021, s.11A(a)(1).

[762] Government of the United States of America (2021). "Federal Deposit Insurance Act 1950," Adopted on September 21, 1950, Updated to August 31, 2021, s.11A(a)(3).

[763] Government of the United States of America (2021). "Federal Deposit Insurance Act 1950," Adopted on September 21, 1950, Updated to August 31, 2021, s.13(a)(1).

[764] Government of the United States of America (2021). "Federal Deposit Insurance Act 1950," Adopted on September 21, 1950, Updated to August 31, 2021, s.13(c)(1).

[765] Government of the United States of America (2021). "Federal Deposit Insurance Act 1950," Adopted on September 21, 1950, Updated to August 31, 2021, s.13(d)(1).

[766] Government of the United States of America (2021). "Federal Deposit Insurance Act 1950," Adopted on September 21, 1950, Updated to August 31, 2021, s.15(a).

[767] Government of the United States of America (2021). "Federal Deposit Insurance Act 1950," Adopted on September 21, 1950, Updated to August 31, 2021, s.24(a)(1).

[768] Government of the United States of America (2021). "Federal Deposit Insurance Act 1950," Adopted on September 21, 1950, Updated to August 31, 2021, s.24(c)(1).
[769] Government of the United States of America (2021). "Federal Deposit Insurance Act 1950," Adopted on September 21, 1950, Updated to August 31, 2021, s.24(f)(1).
[770] Government of the United States of America (2021). "Federal Deposit Insurance Act 1950," Adopted on September 21, 1950, Updated to August 31, 2021, s.28(a).
[771] Government of the United States of America (2021). "Federal Deposit Insurance Act 1950," Adopted on September 21, 1950, Updated to August 31, 2021, s.28(c)(1).
[772] Government of the United States of America (2021). "Federal Deposit Insurance Act 1950," Adopted on September 21, 1950, Updated to August 31, 2021, s.28(d)(i).
[773] Government of the United States of America (2021). "Federal Deposit Insurance Act 1950," Adopted on September 21, 1950, Updated to August 31, 2021, s.29(a).
[774] Government of the United States of America (2021). "Federal Deposit Insurance Act 1950," Adopted on September 21, 1950, Updated to August 31, 2021, s.30(a).
[775] Government of the United States of America (2021). "Federal Deposit Insurance Act 1950," Adopted on September 21, 1950, Updated to August 31, 2021, s.33(a)(1).
[776] Government of the United States of America (2021). "Federal Deposit Insurance Act 1950," Adopted on September 21, 1950, Updated to August 31, 2021, s.35.
[777] Government of the United States of America (2021). "Federal Deposit Insurance Act 1950," Adopted on September 21, 1950, Updated to August 31, 2021, s.36(a).
[778] Government of the United States of America (2021). "Federal Deposit Insurance Act 1950," Adopted on September 21, 1950, Updated to August 31, 2021, s.36(b).
[779] Government of the United States of America (2021). "Federal Deposit Insurance Act 1950," Adopted on September 21, 1950, Updated to August 31, 2021, s.36(c).
[780] Government of the United States of America (2021). "Federal Deposit Insurance Act 1950," Adopted on September 21, 1950, Updated to August 31, 2021, s.36(d).
[781] Government of the United States of America (2021). "Federal Deposit Insurance Act 1950," Adopted on September 21, 1950, Updated to August 31, 2021, s.39(a).
[782] Government of the United States of America (2021). "Federal Deposit Insurance Act 1950," Adopted on September 21, 1950, Updated to August 31, 2021, s.39(b).
[783] Government of the United States of America (2021). "Federal Deposit Insurance Act 1950," Adopted on September 21, 1950, Updated to August 31, 2021, s.39(c).
[784] Government of the United States of America (2021). "Federal Deposit Insurance Act 1950," Adopted on September 21, 1950, Updated to August 31, 2021, s.44(a)(1).
[785] Government of the United States of America (2021). "Federal Deposit Insurance Act 1950," Adopted on September 21, 1950, Updated to August 31, 2021, s.46(a).
[786] Government of the United States of America (2021). "Federal Deposit Insurance Act 1950," Adopted on September 21, 1950, Updated to August 31, 2021, s.50(a).
[787] Government of the United States of America (2022). "U.S. Securities and Exchange Commission: What We Do." Accessed November 29, 2022. https://www.sec.gov/about/what-we-do.
[788] Chen, J (2022). "Volcker Rule: Definition, Purpose, How It Works, and Criticism." Updated May 31, 2022. Accessed November 30, 2022. https://www.investopedia.com/terms/v/volcker-rule.asp.
[789] Government of the United States of America (2022). "United States Code, Updated," Title 12 – Banks and Banking, s.1851(a)(1).
[790] Government of the United States of America (2022). "United States Code, Updated," Title 12 – Banks and Banking, s.1851(d)(1).
[791] Government of the United States of America (2022). "U.S. House of Representatives: Office of the Law Revision Counsel – United States Code." Accessed December 5, 2022. https://uscode.house.gov/browse/prelim@title12&edition=prelim.
[792] Government of the United States of America (2022). "United States Code, Updated," Title 12 – Banks and Banking, s.21.
[793] Government of the United States of America (2022). "United States Code, Updated," Title 12 – Banks and Banking, s.22.

[794] Government of the United States of America (2022). "United States Code, Updated," Title 12 – Banks and Banking, s.1721(g)(1).
[795] Government of the United States of America (2022). "United States Code, Updated," Title 12 – Banks and Banking, s.24.
[796] Government of the United States of America (2022). "United States Code, Updated," Title 12 – Banks and Banking, s.24a(a)(1).
[797] Government of the United States of America (2022). "United States Code, Updated," Title 12 – Banks and Banking, s.26.
[798] Government of the United States of America (2022). "United States Code, Updated," Title 12 – Banks and Banking, s.27(a).
[799] Government of the United States of America (2022). "United States Code, Updated," Title 12 – Banks and Banking, s.27(b)(2).
[800] Government of the United States of America (2022). "United States Code, Updated," Title 12 – Banks and Banking, s.35.
[801] Government of the United States of America (2022). "United States Code, Updated," Title 12 – Banks and Banking, s.36(c).
[802] Government of the United States of America (2022). "United States Code, Updated," Title 12 – Banks and Banking, s.36(e)(1).
[803] Government of the United States of America (2022). "United States Code, Updated," Title 12 – Banks and Banking, s.81.
[804] Government of the United States of America (2022). "United States Code, Updated," Title 12 – Banks and Banking, s.84(a)(1).
[805] Government of the United States of America (2022). "United States Code, Updated," Title 12 – Banks and Banking, s.84(a)(2).
[806] Government of the United States of America (2022). "United States Code, Updated," Title 12 – Banks and Banking, s.222.
[807] Government of the United States of America (2022). "United States Code, Updated," Title 12 – Banks and Banking, s.223.
[808] Government of the United States of America (2022). "United States Code, Updated," Title 12 – Banks and Banking, s.225.
[809] Government of the United States of America (2022). "United States Code, Updated," Title 12 – Banks and Banking, s.241.
[810] Government of the United States of America (2022). "United States Code, Updated," Title 12 – Banks and Banking, s.247.
[811] Government of the United States of America (2022). "United States Code, Updated," Title 12 – Banks and Banking, s.247b.
[812] Government of the United States of America (2022). "United States Code, Updated," Title 12 – Banks and Banking, s.248(a).
[813] Government of the United States of America (2022). "United States Code, Updated," Title 12 – Banks and Banking, s.248(j).
[814] Government of the United States of America (2022). "United States Code, Updated," Title 12 – Banks and Banking, s.248(o).
[815] Government of the United States of America (2022). "United States Code, Updated," Title 12 – Banks and Banking, s.250.
[816] Government of the United States of America (2022). "United States Code, Updated," Title 12 – Banks and Banking, s.252(a)(1).
[817] Government of the United States of America (2022). "United States Code, Updated," Title 12 – Banks and Banking, s.252(a)(2).
[818] Government of the United States of America (2022). "United States Code, Updated," Title 12 – Banks and Banking, s.261.
[819] Government of the United States of America (2022). "United States Code, Updated," Title 12 – Banks and Banking, s.262.

[820] Government of the United States of America (2022). "United States Code, Updated," Title 12 – Banks and Banking, s.263(a).
[821] Government of the United States of America (2022). "United States Code, Updated," Title 12 – Banks and Banking, s.263(b).
[822] Government of the United States of America (2022). "United States Code, Updated," Title 12 – Banks and Banking, s.321.
[823] Government of the United States of America (2022). "United States Code, Updated," Title 12 – Banks and Banking, s.322.
[824] Government of the United States of America (2022). "United States Code, Updated," Title 12 – Banks and Banking, s.324.
[825] Government of the United States of America (2022). "United States Code, Updated," Title 12 – Banks and Banking, s.329.
[826] Government of the United States of America (2022). "United States Code, Updated," Title 12 – Banks and Banking, s.341.
[827] Government of the United States of America (2022). "United States Code, Updated," Title 12 – Banks and Banking, s.342.
[828] Government of the United States of America (2022). "United States Code, Updated," Title 12 – Banks and Banking, s.343.
[829] Government of the United States of America (2022). "United States Code, Updated," Title 12 – Banks and Banking, s.344.
[830] Government of the United States of America (2022). "United States Code, Updated," Title 12 – Banks and Banking, s.346.
[831] Government of the United States of America (2022). "United States Code, Updated," Title 12 – Banks and Banking, s.347.
[832] Government of the United States of America (2022). "United States Code, Updated," Title 12 – Banks and Banking, s.347a.
[833] Government of the United States of America (2022). "United States Code, Updated," Title 12 – Banks and Banking, s.347b(a).
[834] Government of the United States of America (2022). "United States Code, Updated," Title 12 – Banks and Banking, s.347c.
[835] Government of the United States of America (2022). "United States Code, Updated," Title 12 – Banks and Banking, s.347d.
[836] Government of the United States of America (2022). "United States Code, Updated," Title 12 – Banks and Banking, s.348a.
[837] Government of the United States of America (2022). "United States Code, Updated," Title 12 – Banks and Banking, s.352.
[838] Government of the United States of America (2022). "United States Code, Updated," Title 12 – Banks and Banking, s.353.
[839] Government of the United States of America (2022). "United States Code, Updated," Title 12 – Banks and Banking, s.354.
[840] Government of the United States of America (2022). "United States Code, Updated," Title 12 – Banks and Banking, s.356.
[841] Government of the United States of America (2022). "United States Code, Updated," Title 12 – Banks and Banking, s.357.
[842] Government of the United States of America (2022). "United States Code, Updated," Title 12 – Banks and Banking, s.358.
[843] Government of the United States of America (2022). "United States Code, Updated," Title 12 – Banks and Banking, s.360.
[844] Government of the United States of America (2022). "United States Code, Updated," Title 12 – Banks and Banking, s.361.
[845] Government of the United States of America (2022). "United States Code, Updated," Title 12 – Banks and Banking, s.371(a).

[846] Government of the United States of America (2022). "United States Code, Updated," Title 12 – Banks and Banking, s.371b.
[847] Government of the United States of America (2022). "United States Code, Updated," Title 12 – Banks and Banking, s.371b-2(a).
[848] Government of the United States of America (2022). "United States Code, Updated," Title 12 – Banks and Banking, s.371b-2(b).
[849] Government of the United States of America (2022). "United States Code, Updated," Title 12 – Banks and Banking, s.371c(a)(1)(A).
[850] Government of the United States of America (2022). "United States Code, Updated," Title 12 – Banks and Banking, s.371c(a)(1)(B).
[851] Government of the United States of America (2022). "United States Code, Updated," Title 12 – Banks and Banking, s.371c(a)(4).
[852] Government of the United States of America (2022). "United States Code, Updated," Title 12 – Banks and Banking, s.371c-1(b)(1)(A).
[853] Government of the United States of America (2022). "United States Code, Updated," Title 12 – Banks and Banking, s.371c-1(b)(1)(B).
[854] Government of the United States of America (2022). "United States Code, Updated," Title 12 – Banks and Banking, s.371d(a).
[855] Government of the United States of America (2022). "United States Code, Updated," Title 12 – Banks and Banking, s.372(a).
[856] Government of the United States of America (2022). "United States Code, Updated," Title 12 – Banks and Banking, s.373.
[857] Government of the United States of America (2022). "United States Code, Updated," Title 12 – Banks and Banking, s.374.
[858] Government of the United States of America (2022). "United States Code, Updated," Title 12 – Banks and Banking, s.374a.
[859] Government of the United States of America (2022). "United States Code, Updated," Title 12 – Banks and Banking, s.375a(1).
[860] Government of the United States of America (2022). "United States Code, Updated," Title 12 – Banks and Banking, s.375a(6).
[861] Government of the United States of America (2022). "United States Code, Updated," Title 12 – Banks and Banking, s.375b(1).
[862] Government of the United States of America (2022). "United States Code, Updated," Title 12 – Banks and Banking, s.376.
[863] Government of the United States of America (2022). "United States Code, Updated," Title 12 – Banks and Banking, s.378(a)(1).
[864] Government of the United States of America (2022). "United States Code, Updated," Title 12 – Banks and Banking, s.378(a)(2).
[865] Government of the United States of America (2022). "12 USC 591 to 599: Repealed. June 25, 1948, ch. 645, §21, 62 Stat. 862, eff. Sept. 1, 1948." Accessed December 21, 2022. https://uscode.house.gov/view.xhtml?req=granuleid:USC-prelim-title12-section591&num=0&edition=prelim.
[866] Government of the United States of America (2022). "12 USC Chapter 5, Subchapter I: In General." Accessed December 21, 2022. https://uscode.house.gov/view.xhtml?path=/prelim@title12/chapter5/subchapter1&edition=prelim.
[867] Government of the United States of America (2022). "United States Code, Updated," Title 18 – Crimes and Criminal Procedure, s.214.
[868] Government of the United States of America (2022). "18 USC 214: Offer for procurement of Federal Reserve bank loan and discount of commercial paper." Accessed December 21, 2022. https://uscode.house.gov/view.xhtml?req=(title:18 section:214 edition:prelim) OR (granuleid:USC-prelim-title18-section214)&f=treesort&num=0&edition=prelim.
[869] Government of the United States of America (2022). "United States Code, Updated," Title 12 – Banks and Banking, s.582.

Bibliography

Australian Prudential Regulation Authority (2021). APRA: Guidelines – Licensing: locally-incorporated ADIs – August 2021. Sydney: Australian Prudential Regulation Authority.

Australian Securities and Investments Commission (2022). "*Our role.*" Accessed February 19, 2022. https://asic.gov.au/about-asic/what-we-do/our-role/.

Bank of Canada (2022). "RE: {External} When did specified legislation enter into force?," reply to the e-mail from Dr. Baber to the Bank of Canada, May 31, 2022.

Canadian Underwriter (2021). "*Federal budget contains 'unexpected positive development' for brokers re: Bank Act.*" Accessed June 2, 2022. https://www.canadianunderwriter.ca/associations/federal-budget-contains-unexpected-positive-development-for-brokers-re-bank-act-1004206880/.

Chen, J. (2022a). "*1913 Federal Reserve Act: Definition and Why It's Important.*" Updated January 12, 2022. Accessed November 8, 2022. https://www.investopedia.com/terms/f/1913-federal-reserve-act.asp.

Chen, J (2022b). "*Volcker Rule: Definition, Purpose, How It Works, and Criticism.*" Updated May 31, 2022. Accessed November 30, 2022. https://www.investopedia.com/terms/v/volcker-rule.asp.

Ciro, T., Goldwasser, V., and Verma, R. (2019). *Law and Business.* 5th Edition. Melbourne: Oxford University Press.

Cornell University (2022). "*Cornell Law School: Legal Information Institute – U.S. Constitution: Article 1.*" Accessed October 29, 2022. https://www.law.cornell.edu/constitution/articlei.

Daniel, F. (2002). Recent Changes to Canada's Financial Sector Legislation. *Bank of Canada Review*, Winter 2002-2003, 3-16.

Encyclopedia Britannica (2022). "*British North America Act: United Kingdom [1867].*" Accessed May 18, 2022. https://www.britannica.com/event/British-North-America-Act.

Financial Stability Board (2021). 2021 List of Global Systemically Important Banks (G-SIBs): 23 November 2021. Basel: Financial Stability Board.

Government of Australia (1911). "Commonwealth Bank Act 1911," Adopted on December 22, 1911, Repealed on August 3, 1945.

Government of Australia (2019). "Legislation Act 2003," Adopted (as Legislative Instruments Act 2003) on December 17, 2003, Entered into force (as Legislative Instruments Act 2003) on January 1 2005, Compilation No. 39 of February 24, 2019, Registered on February 25, 2019.

Government of Australia (2020). "Reserve Bank Act 1959," Adopted on April 23, 1959, Entered into force on January 14, 1960, Compilation No. 30 of October 1, 2020, Registered on October 21, 2020.

Government of Australia (2021a). "Australian Prudential Regulation Authority Act 1998," Adopted on June 29, 1998, Entered into force on July 1, 1998, Compilation No. 46 of July 1, 2021, Registered on July 30, 2021.

Government of Australia (2021b). "Banking Act 1959," Adopted on April 23, 1959, Entered into force on January 14, 1960, Compilation No. 60 of December 8, 2021, Registered on December 16, 2021.

Government of Australia (2021c). "Commonwealth of Australia Constitution Act 1900," Adopted on July 9, 1900, Entered into force on January 1, 1901, Compilation No. 6 of July 29, 1977, Registered on November 18, 2021.

Government of Australia (2022a). "*APRA: About the Financial Claims Scheme.*" Accessed December 24, 2022. https://www.apra.gov.au/about-financial-claims-scheme.

Government of Australia (2022b). "*Infosheet 13 – The Constitution.*" Accessed February 2, 2022. https://www.aph.gov.au/About_Parliament/House_of_Representatives/Powers_practice_and_procedure/00_-_Infosheets/Infosheet_13_-_The_Constitution.

Government of Australia (2022c). "*National Library of Australia – Government Gazettes: Commonwealth.*" Accessed August 24, 2022. https://www.nla.gov.au/research-guides/finding-government-gazettes/finding-government-gazettes-commonwealth.

Government of Australia (2022d). "*Reserve Bank of Australia: About the RBA.*" Accessed February 16, 2022. https://www.rba.gov.au/about-rba/.

Government of Canada (2015). Department of Justice: Canada's System of Justice, Cat. No J2-32/2015E-PDF. Ottawa: Her Majesty the Queen in Right of Canada.

Government of Canada (2022a). "Bank Act, S.C. 1991, c. 46," Adopted on December 13, 1991, Entered into force on June 1, 1992, Last amended on February 26, 2022, Consolidated to May 2, 2022.

Government of Canada (2022b). "Bank of Canada Act, S.C., 1934 (24 & 25 Geo V), c. 43; R.S.C., 1985, c. B-2," Adopted on July 3, 1934, Entered into force on March 11, 1935, Last amended on January 31, 2020, Consolidated to May 2, 2022.

Government of Canada (2022c). "Canada Deposit Insurance Corporation Act, R.S.C. 1985, c. C-3," Adopted on February 17, 1984, Entered into force on February 17, 1984, Last amended on April 30, 2022, Consolidated to May 2, 2022.

Government of Canada (2022d). "Canadian Payments Act, R.S.C., 1985, c. C-21," Adopted on November 26, 1980, as "An Act to revise the Bank Act, to amend the Quebec Savings Bank Act and the Bank of Canada Act, to establish the Canadian Payments Association and to amend other Acts in consequence thereof: Part IV – An Act to establish the Canadian Payments Association," Entered into force on December 1, 1980, Last amended on April 2, 2021, Consolidated to May 2, 2022.

Government of Canada (2022e). "*Library and Archives Canada: Proclamation of the Constitution Act, 1982.*" Accessed May 17, 2022. https://www.bac-lac.gc.ca/eng/discover/politics-government/proclamation-constitution-act-1982/Pages/proclamation-constitution-act-1982.aspx.

Government of Canada (2022f). "Office of the Superintendent of Financial Institutions Act, R. S. C. 1985, c. 18 (3rd Supp.), Part I," Entered into force on July 2, 1987, Last amended on December 13, 2018, Consolidated to May 16, 2022.

Government of Canada (2022g). "Retail Payment Activities Act, S.C. 2021, c. 23, s. 177," Adopted on June 29, 2021, Entered into force on June 29, 2021, Consolidated to May 2, 2022.

Government of Canada (2023). "Bank Act, S.C. 1991, c. 46," Adopted on December 13, 1991, Entered into force on June 1, 1992, Last amended on March 4, 2023, Consolidated to March 20, 2023.

Government of New South Wales (2022). "*Full Court of the Federal Court.*" Accessed February 2, 2022. https://www.legalaid.nsw.gov.au/for-lawyers/policyonline/glossary/full-court-of-the-federal-court.

Government of New Zealand (2005). "Constitution Act 1986, Public Act 1986 No 114," Adopted on December 13, 1986, Entered into force on January 1, 1987, Last amended on May 16, 2005.

Government of New Zealand (2014). "Non-bank Deposit Takers Act Commencement Order 2014, 2014/14, Order in Council made at Wellington on February 17, 2014, pursuant to section 2(1) of the Non-bank Deposit Takers Act 2013."

Government of New Zealand (2022a). "Auditor Regulation Act 2011, Public Act 2011 No 21," Adopted on May 19, 2011, Entered into force on July 1, 2012, Consolidated to May 25, 2022.

Government of New Zealand (2022b). "Banking (Prudential Supervision) Act 1989, Public Act 1989 No 157," Adopted on December 20, 1989, as "Reserve Bank of New Zealand Act 1989," Entered into force on February 1, 1990, Last amended on July 1, 2022, Consolidated to July 1, 2022.

Government of New Zealand (2022c). "Companies Act 1993, Public Act 1993 No 105," Adopted on September 28, 1993, Entered into force on July 1, 1994, Consolidated to July 1, 2022.

Government of New Zealand (2022d). "Financial Markets Conduct Act 2013, Public Act 2013 No 69," Adopted on September 13, 2013, Entered into force on April 1 and December 1, 2014, Consolidated to July 1, 2022.

Government of New Zealand (2022e). "Financial Reporting Act 2013, Public Act 2013 No 101," Adopted on December 3, 2013, Entered into force on April 1, 2014, Consolidated to January 1, 2022.

Government of New Zealand (2022f). "Financial Service Providers (Registration and Dispute Resolution) Act 2008, Public Act 2008 No 97," Adopted on September 28, 2008, Entered into force on September 28, 2008, Consolidated to July 1, 2022.

Government of New Zealand (2022g). "*Ministry of Justice: Tribunals.*" Accessed August 8, 2022. https://www.justice.govt.nz/tribunals/.

Government of New Zealand (2022h). "*New Zealand Gazette: About Us.*" Accessed August 24, 2022. https://gazette.govt.nz/about-us/.

Government of New Zealand (2022i). "Non-bank Deposit Takers Act 2013, Public Act 2013 No 104," Adopted on December 3, 2013, Entered into force on May 1, 2014, Consolidated to July 1, 2022.

Government of New Zealand (2022j). "*NZ History: The Treaty in brief: Page 1 – Introduction.*" Accessed August 4, 2022. https://nzhistory.govt.nz/politics/treaty/the-treaty-in-brief.

Government of New Zealand (2022k). "Personal Property Securities Act 1999, Public Act 1999 No 126," Adopted on October 14, 1999, Entered into force on May 1, 2002, Consolidated to July 1, 2022.

Government of New Zealand (2022l). "Reserve Bank of New Zealand Act 2021, Public Act 2021 No 31," Adopted on August 16, 2021, Entered into force on July 1, 2022, Consolidated to July 1, 2022.

Government of New Zealand (2022m). "*Reserve Bank of New Zealand: The banking sector.*" Accessed August 21, 2022, https://www.rbnz.govt.nz/financial-stability/about-the-new-zealand-financial-system/the-banking-sector.

Government of New Zealand (2023a). "*NZ History: Statute of Westminster enacted: 11 December 1931.*" Accessed April 9, 2023. https://nzhistory.govt.nz/statute-of-westminster-passed-confirming-nz-autonomy.

Government of New Zealand (2023b). "*Reserve Bank of New Zealand: Proposed Deposit Takers Act.*" Accessed April 22, 2023. https://www.rbnz.govt.nz/about-us/responsibility-and-accountability/our-legislation/proposed-deposit-takers-act.

Government of the United Kingdom of Great Britain and Northern Ireland (1986). "Australia Act 1986," Adopted on February 17, 1986, Entered into force on March 3, 1986.

Government of the United Kingdom of Great Britain and Northern Ireland (2021a). "British North America Act 1867," Adopted on March 29, 1867, Entered into force on July 1, 1867, Consolidated to January 1, 2021.

Government of the United Kingdom of Great Britain and Northern Ireland (2021b). "Canada Act 1982," Adopted on March 29, 1982, Entered into force on April 17, 1982, Consolidated to January 1, 2021.

Government of the United Kingdom of Great Britain and Northern Ireland/Government of Canada (2021). "Constitution Act 1982," Adopted on March 29, 1982, Entered into force on April 17, 1982, Consolidated to January 1, 2021.

Government of the United States of America (1864). "An Act to provide a National Currency, secured by a Pledge of United States Bonds, and to provide for the Circulation and Redemption thereof (National Bank Act 1864)," Adopted on June 3, 1864.

Government of the United States of America (1913). "An Act To provide for the establishment of Federal reserve banks, to furnish an elastic currency, to afford means of rediscounting commercial paper, to establish a more effective supervision of banking in the United States and for other purposes (Federal Reserve Act 1913)," Adopted on December 23, 1913.

Government of the United States of America (1992). Constitution of the United States of America, as amended. Washington, D.C.: Government of the United States of America.

Government of the United States of America (1999). "Gramm-Leach-Bliley Act 1999," Adopted on November 12, 1999.

Government of the United States of America (2021a). "Federal Deposit Insurance Act 1950," Adopted on September 21, 1950, Updated to August 31, 2021.

Government of the United States of America (2021b). "*Federal Deposit Insurance Corporation: Laws & Regulations – Important Banking Laws.*" Last updated September 14, 2021. Accessed November 8 and 9, 2022. https://www.fdic.gov/resources/regulations/important-banking-laws/index.html.

Government of the United States of America (2022a). "*12 USC 591 to 599: Repealed. June 25, 1948, ch. 645, §21, 62 Stat. 862, eff. Sept. 1, 1948.*" Accessed December 21, 2022. https://uscode.house.gov/view.xhtml?req=granuleid:USC-prelim-title12-section591&num=0&edition=prelim.

Government of the United States of America (2022b). "*12 USC Chapter 5, Subchapter I: In General.*" Accessed December 21, 2022. https://uscode.house.gov/view.xhtml?path=/prelim@title12/chapter5/subchapter1&edition=prelim.

Government of the United States of America (2022c). "*18 USC 214: Offer for procurement of Federal Reserve bank loan and discount of commercial paper.*" Accessed December 21, 2022. https://uscode.house.gov/view.xhtml?req=(title:18 section:214 edition:prelim) OR (granuleid:USC-prelim-title18-section214)&f=treesort&num=0&edition=prelim.

Government of the United States of America (2022d). "*Board of Governors of the Federal Reserve System: About the Fed.*" Accessed November 9, 2022. https://www.federalreserve.gov/aboutthefed.htm.

Government of the United States of America (2022e). "*Board of Governors of the Federal Reserve System: Advisory Councils – Federal Advisory Council.*" Accessed December 12, 2022. https://www.federal reserve.gov/aboutthefed/fac.htm.

Government of the United States of America (2022f). "*Constitution of the United States.*" Accessed October 28, 2022. https://www.senate.gov/civics/constitution_item/constitution.htm.

Government of the United States of America (2022g). "*Editorial notes to section 1306 of Title 18 – Crimes and Criminal Procedure – of the United States Code.*" Last updated November 24, 2022. Accessed November 25, 2022. https://uscode.house.gov/view.xhtml?req=granuleid:USC-prelim-title18-section1306&num=0&edition=prelim.

Government of the United States of America (2022h). "*Federal Deposit Insurance Corporation: About.*" Accessed November 9, 2022. https://www.fdic.gov/about/.

Government of the United States of America (2002i). "Home Owners' Loan Act 1993," Adopted on June 13, 1933, Updated to November 17, 2022.

Government of the United States of America (2022j). "*Office of the Comptroller of the Currency: Founding of the OCC & the National Banking System.*" Accessed November 8, 2022. https://www.occ.treas.gov/about/who-we-are/history/founding-occ-national-bank-system/index-founding-occ-national-banking-system.html.

Government of the United States of America (2022k). "*Office of the Comptroller of the Currency: What We Do.*" Accessed November 8, 2022. https://www.occ.treas.gov/about/what-we-do/index-what-we-do.html.

Government of the United. States of America (2022l). The U.S. Legal System: A Short Description. Washington, D.C.: Federal Judicial Center.

Government of the United States of America (2022m). "United States Code, Updated."

Government of the United States of America (2022n). "*United States Department of Justice: Offices of the United States Attorneys – Justice 101: Introduction to the Federal Court System.*" Accessed November 2 and 3, 2022. https://www.justice.gov/usao/justice-101/federal-courts.

Government of the United States of America (2022o). "*U.S. House of Representatives: Office of the Law Revision Counsel – United States Code.*" Accessed December 5, 2022. https://uscode.house.gov/browse/prelim@title12&edition=prelim.

Government of the United States of America (2022p). "*U.S. Securities and Exchange Commission: What We Do.*" Accessed November 29, 2022. https://www.sec.gov/about/what-we-do.

Government of the United States of America (2023). "Securities Exchange Act of 1934," Adopted on June 6, 1934, Updated to February 12, 2023.

Greville, M. (2019). "*UPDATE: Access to New Zealand Law.*" Accessed August 4, 2022. https://www.nyulawglobal.org/globalex/New_Zealand1.html.

Harris, J., and Croese, C. (2015). *Contract Law in Context*. Melbourne: Oxford University Press Australia.

Henegan, T., and Kimball, B. (2022). "*Legal systems in the United States: overview.*" Published October 1, 2022. Accessed November 1 and 2, 2022. https://uk.practicallaw.thomsonreuters.com/w-019-5918?transitionType=Default&contextData=(sc.Default)&firstPage=true.

Jenson, S., Etwell, J., and Findlay, B. (2021). "*Banking Regulation in New Zealand: Overview.*" Accessed August 11, 2022. https://uk.practicallaw.thomsonreuters.com/w-007-8664?transitionType=Default&contextData=(sc.Default)&firstPage=true.

Kagan, J. (2020). "*National Bank.*" Updated October 31, 2020. Accessed November 8, 2022. https://www.investopedia.com/terms/n/national-bank.asp.

Lustgarten, I. (2017). "*Banking regulation in the United States: overview.*" Published March 30, 2017. Accessed November 7, 2022. https://content.next.westlaw.com/practical-law/document/Ib519c5822a5911e798dc8b09b4f043e0/Banking-regulation-in-the-United-States-overview?viewType=FullText&transitionType=Default&contextData=(sc.Default)&firstPage=true.

Martins, I. (2022). "*Guide to U.S. Banking Laws.*" Updated May 31, 2022. Accessed November 8, 2022. https://www.investopedia.com/important-u-s-banking-laws-5217476.

McFarlane, G. (1984). *The Layman's Dictionary of English Law*. London: Waterlow Publishers Limited.

Menguy, G. (2022). "*The Legal System in New Zealand.*" Accessed August 8, 2022. https://gm-avocats.com/the-legal-system-in-new-zealand/.

Office of the Superintendent of Financial Institutions – Canada (2021). "*Industry Letter: June 17, 2021 – OFSI sets the Domestic Stability Buffer level to 2.50% effective October 31, 2021.*" Accessed June 10, 2022. https://www.osfi-bsif.gc.ca/Eng/fi-if/in-ai/Pages/dsb20210617-let.aspx.

Parliament of New Zealand (2016a). "*How a bill becomes law.*" Published January 22, 2016. Accessed August 5, 2022. https://www.parliament.nz/en/visit-and-learn/how-parliament-works/how-laws-are-made/how-a-bill-becomes-law/.

Parliament of New Zealand (2016b). "*Our system of government.*" Published January 20, 2016. Accessed August 4, 2022. https://www.parliament.nz/en/visit-and-learn/how-parliament-works/our-system-of-government/.

Pearsall, J. (editor) (1998). *The New Oxford Dictionary of English*. Oxford: Oxford University Press.

Political and Constitutional Reform Committee of the House of Commons of the United Kingdom (2015). Our Democratic Settlement. London: House of Commons.

Somerville, C., and Sun, W. (2021). "*Legal systems in Canada: overview.*" Published July 1, 2021. Accessed May 17 and 19, 2022. https://uk.practicallaw.thomsonreuters.com/w-013-0460?transitionType=Default&contextData=(sc.Default)&firstPage=true.

United Nations (1945). "Charter of the United Nations," *United Nations Treaty Series* Registration Number N/A.

United Nations (2022). "*Dag Hammarskjöld Library: UN Membership.*" Accessed May 17, 2022. https://research.un.org/en/unmembers/founders.

Washington University in St. Louis (2014). "*School of Law: Major Differences between the Mexican and U.S. Legal Systems.*" Published July 15, 2014. Accessed October 29, 2022. https://onlinelaw.wustl.edu/blog/major-differences-mexican-u-s-legal-systems/.

Wilson, J. (2006). "*New Zealand Sovereignty: 1857, 1907, 1947, or 1987?*" Published August 28, 2007. Accessed August 3 and 4, 2022. https://www.parliament.nz/en/pb/research-papers/document/00PLLawRP07041/new-zealand-sovereignty-1857-1907-1947-or-1987.

Wood, M. (2015). "*The Revised Statutes of the United States: Predecessor to the U.S. Code.*" Published July 2, 2015. Accessed December 5, 2022. https://blogs.loc.gov/law/2015/07/the-revised-statutes-of-the-united-states-predecessor-to-the-u-s-code/.

Index

A

B

C

D

E

F

G

H

I

J

K

L

M

N

O

P

Q

R

S

T

U

V

About the Author

Graeme Baber, PhD, is a jurist and a legal researcher, specializing in financial law and international law. His previous monographs are *The Impact of Legislation and Regulation on the Freedom of Movement of Capital in Estonia, Poland and Latvia* (2010), *The Free Movement of Capital and Financial Services: An Exposition?* (2014), *The European Union and the Global Financial Crisis: A View from 2016* (2016), *Essays on International Law* (2017), *International Financial Law: Quo Vadis?* (2017), *Preferential Trade Agreements and International Law* (2018), *The United Nations System: A Synopsis* (2019), *The Global Law of the Sea: Baselines and Boundary Delimitation* (2020), *Achieving the Sustainable Development Goals Punctually: An Impossible Remit?* (2020), *The British Judges of the International Court of Justice: An Explication? Overview, McNair and Lauterpacht* (2021), and *The British Judges of the International Court of Justice: An Explication? The Later Jurists* (2022). Graeme has published many papers. He is also an experienced teacher of university students.

Since 2014, Graeme has written five monographs, four papers, and a book chapter, which Nova has published. The first of the books is *The European Union and the Global Financial Crisis: A View from 2016*, which compares – in places in which this is possible – the securities and banking legislation after the financial crisis with that preceding it. The second is *International Financial Law: Quo Vadis?*, which describes worldwide instruments set by the Financial Stability Board, the Bank for International Settlements, the Basel Committee on Banking Supervision, the International Organization of Securities Commissions, and the International Monetary Fund – giving views as to the structure and workings of the global financial architecture and as to the progression of this topic in the near and medium-term. The third is *The Global Law of the Sea: Baselines and Boundary Delimitation*. The fourth and fifth, which are Graeme's tenth and eleven monographs, respectively, are *The British Judges of the International Court of Justice: An Explication? Overview, McNair and Lauterpacht* and *The British Judges of the International Court of Justice: An Explication? The Later Jurists.* Pursuant to his earlier research contributing to *The Global Law of the Sea: Baselines and Boundary Delimitation* and a subsequent summary article concerning the life, scholarship and judgments of the eminent Swiss jurist Max Huber, in these two books, he investigates the academic and judicial output of the seven people who served as British members of the International Court of Justice between 1946 and 2018.